Autodesk Inventor 2026 Basics Tutorial

Tutorial Books

Download Resource Files from:

Online.books999@gmail.com

Contents

Introduction

Autodesk Inventor as a topic of learning is vast and has a broad scope. It is a package of many modules delivering exceptional value to enterprises. It offers a set of tools, which are easy-to-use to design, document, and simulate 3D models. Using this software, you can speed up the design process and reduce product development costs.

This book provides a step-by-step approach for users to learn Autodesk Inventor. It is aimed at those with no previous experience with Inventor. However, users of previous versions of Inventor may also find this book useful for them to learn the new enhancements. The user will be guided by starting an Autodesk Inventor 2026 session to creating parts, assemblies, and drawings. Each chapter has components explained with the help of real-world models.

Scope of this book

This book is written for students and engineers who are interested to learn Autodesk Inventor 2026 for designing mechanical components and assemblies, and then create drawings.

This book provides a step-by-step approach for learning Autodesk Inventor 2026. The topics include Getting Started with Autodesk Inventor 2026, Basic Part Modeling, Creating Assemblies, Creating Drawings, Additional Modeling Tools, Sheet Metal Modeling, Assembly Tools, Dimensions and Annotations, Model-Based Dimensioning, and Frame Generator.

Chapter 1 introduces Autodesk Inventor. The user interface and terminology are discussed in this chapter.

Chapter 2 takes you through the creation of your first Inventor model. You create simple parts.

Chapter 3 teaches you to create assemblies. It explains the Top-down and Bottom-up approaches for designing an assembly. You create an assembly using the Bottom-up approach.

Chapter 4 teaches you to create drawings of the models created in the earlier chapters. You will also learn to place exploded views and part list of an assembly.

Chapter 5: In this chapter, you will learn the sketching tools.

Chapter 6: In this chapter, you will learn additional modeling tools to create complex models.

Chapter 7 introduces you to Sheet Metal modeling. You will create a sheet metal part using the tools available in the Sheet Metal environment.

Chapter 8 teaches you to create Top-down assemblies. It also introduces you to create mechanisms by applying joints between the parts.

Chapter 9: teaches you to apply dimensions and annotations to a 2D drawing.

Chapter 10: teaches you to add 3D annotations and tolerances to a 3D model.

Chapter 11: teaches you to create structural elements using Frame Generator.

Chapter 1: Getting Started with Autodesk Inventor 2026

This tutorial book brings in the most commonly used features of the Autodesk Inventor.

In this chapter, you will:

- Understand the Inventor terminology
- Start a new file
- Understand the User Interface
- Understand different environments in Inventor

In this chapter, you will learn some common features of Autodesk Inventor. You will also learn about the user interface.

In Autodesk Inventor, you create 3D parts. You can use these parts to make 2D drawings and 3D assemblies.

Inventor is Feature Based. Features are shapes you combine to build a part. You can change these shapes one by one.

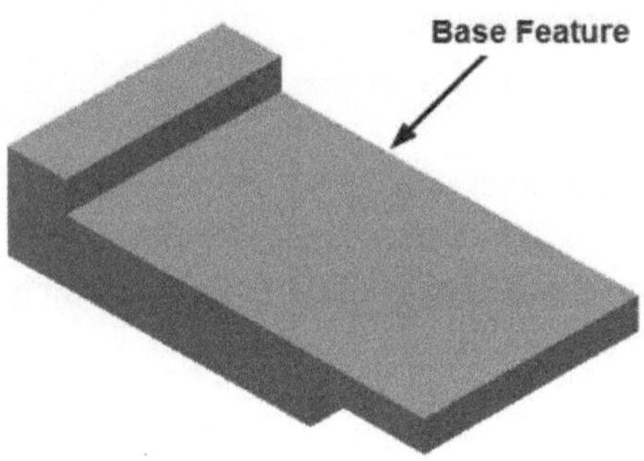

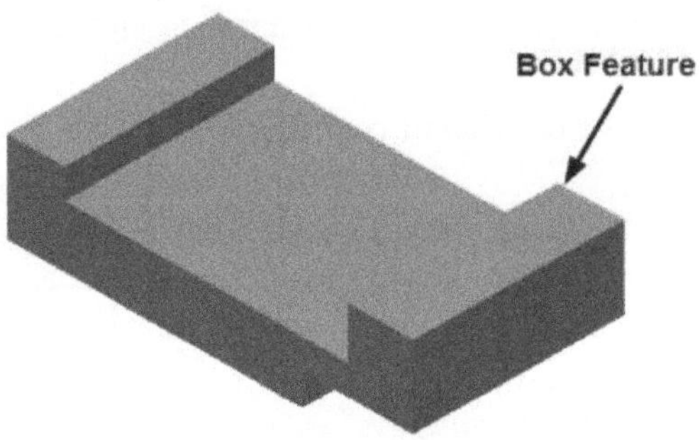

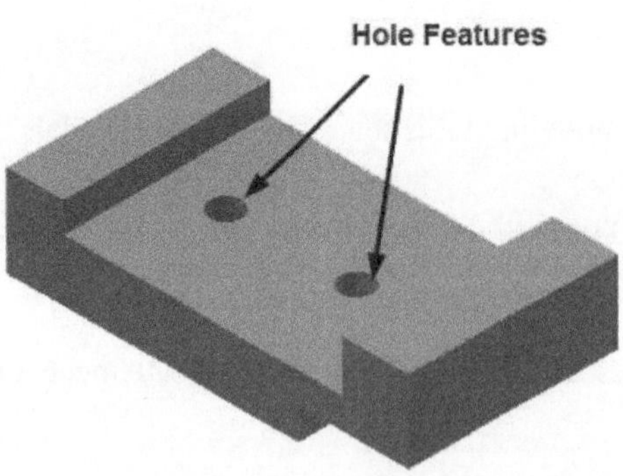

Most features start with a sketch. A sketch is a 2D drawing. You can make it into a 3D shape by extruding, revolving, or sweeping.

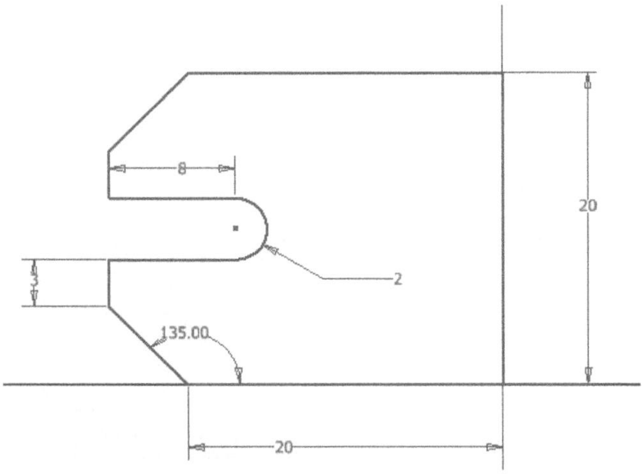

Inventor is parametric. This means you can set rules for how parts relate to each other. Changing these rules changes the part's size and shape. For example, look at the body of a flange before and after changing its rules.

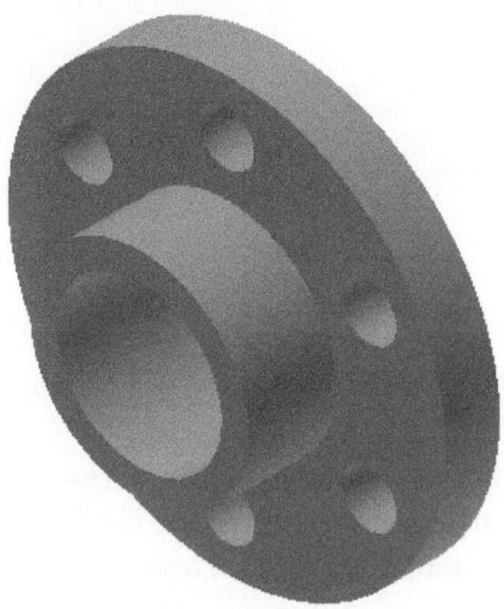

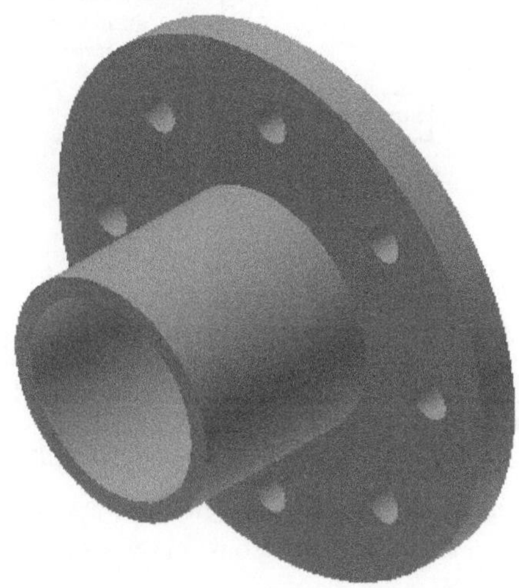

Autodesk Inventor also has tools for simulation. These tools help you test how parts will work in real life. You can check if parts will fit together and if they can handle stress.

Inventor supports collaboration. Multiple people can work on the same project. This is useful for big projects with many team members.

Starting Autodesk Inventor

- Click the Windows icon on the taskbar.
- Click **A** > **Autodesk Inventor 2026 > Autodesk Inventor 2026**.
- Select the **New** option from the **New** drop-down on the left side of the **Start** screen. You can also choose a template from the **New** drop-down to start a part, assembly, drawing, or presentation file.
- In the **Part – Create 2D and 3D objects** section, click the **Standard.ipt** icon.
- Click **Create** to start a new part file.

Notice these essential features of the Inventor window.

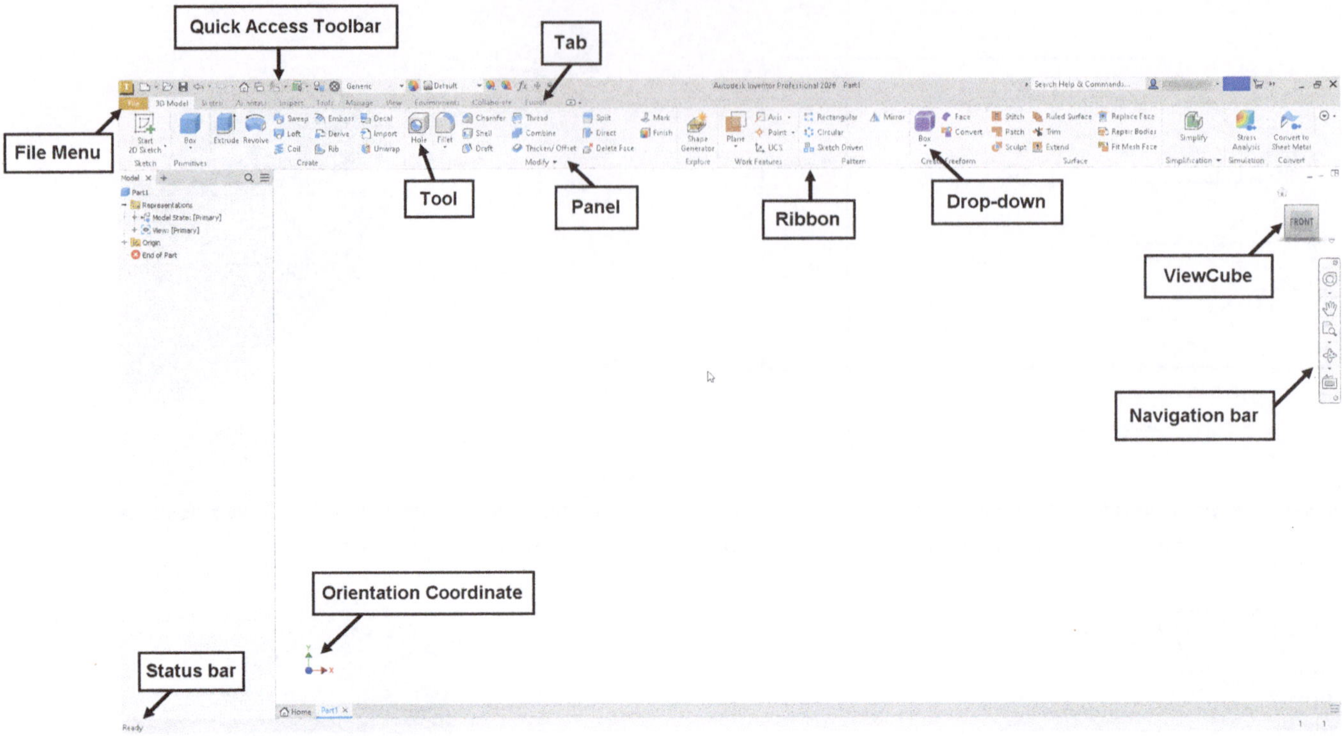

User Interface

Various components of the user interface are discussed next.

Ribbon

The ribbon at the top of the window contains multiple tabs. Clicking a tab reveals a set of tools organized in panels. The highlighted tab displays relevant commands, with frequently used ones represented by larger icons on the left and less common ones by smaller icons on the right. Some commands are accessible through drop-down lists or panel names.

The ribbon located at the top of the window has tabs. Click a tab to see tools grouped in panels. The active tab shows important commands with large icons on the left and less common commands with smaller icons on the right. Some commands can be accessed through drop-down lists or by clicking panel names.

You can customize the ribbon by right-clicking on a panel. A menu is displayed with some options. These options are explained next.

- **Ribbon Appearance**: It allows you to change how the ribbon looks, turn off text, and adjust command sizes.
- **Show Panels**: You can add or remove panels.
- **Customize User Commands:** This lets you add commands to your own user panel.
- **Undock Ribbon**: It enables you to move the ribbon freely.
- **Docking Positions**: You can change where the ribbon is located on your screen.

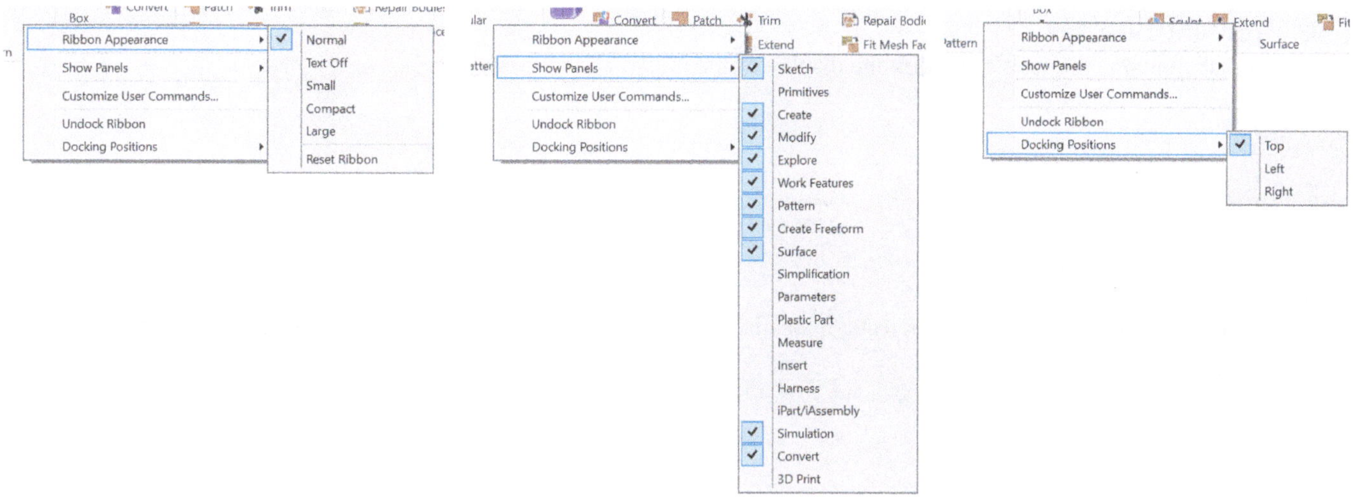

You can also click the down arrow to the right of the panel to turn panels on or off, as shown. Remember, you cannot make changes to panels in the sketch environment.

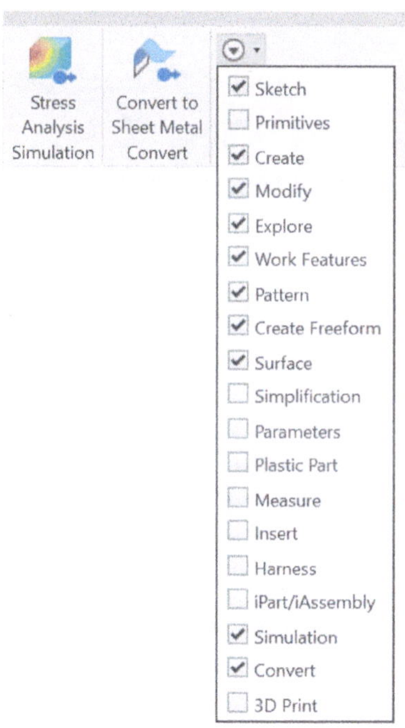

The following sections explain the various tabs of the ribbon available in Autodesk Inventor.

The 3D Model ribbon tab

This ribbon tab contains the tools to create 3D features, planes, and surfaces.

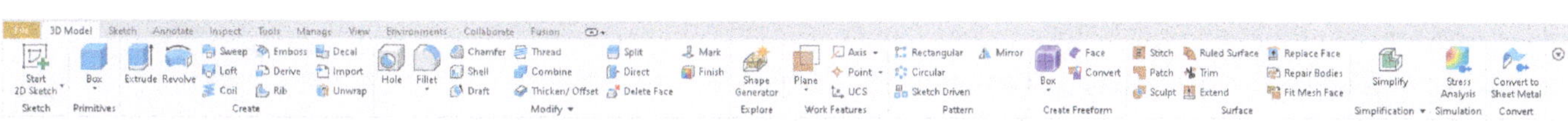

The View ribbon tab

This ribbon tab contains the tools to modify the display of the model and user interface.

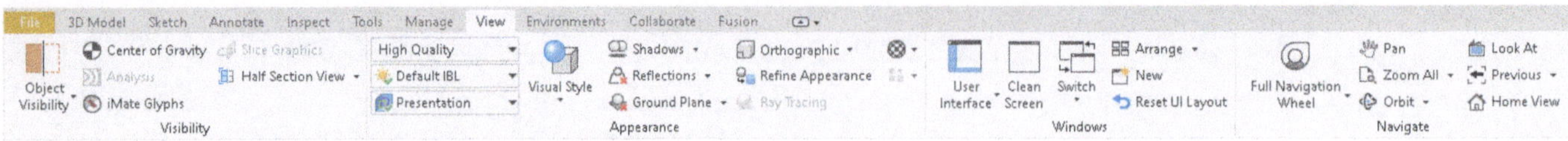

The Inspect ribbon tab

This ribbon tab has tools to measure the objects. It also has analysis tools to analyze the draft, curvature, and surface.

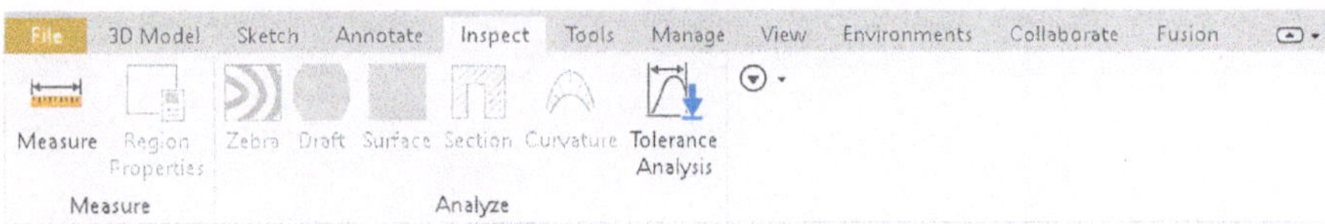

Sketch ribbon tab

This ribbon tab contains all the sketch tools.

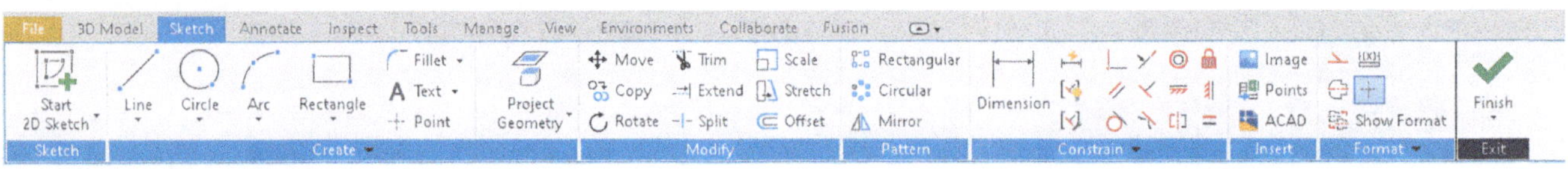

Assemble ribbon tab

This ribbon tab contains the tools to create an assembly. It is available in an assembly file.

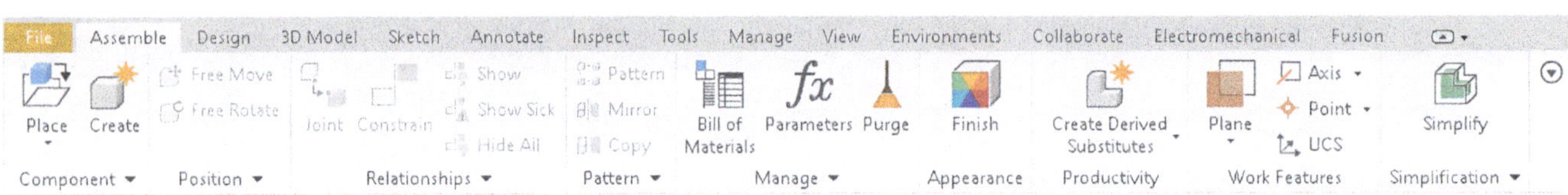

Presentation ribbon tab

This tab contains the tools to create the exploded views of an assembly. It also has the tools to create presentations, assembly instructions, and animation of an assembly.

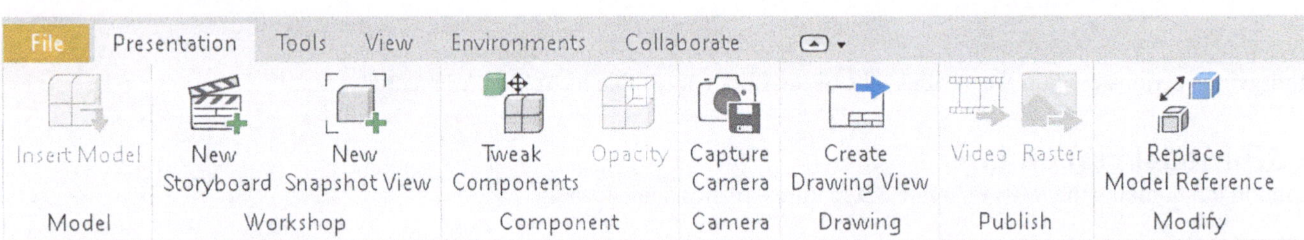

Drawing Environment ribbon tabs

In the Drawing Environment, you can create print-ready drawings of a 3D model. The ribbon tabs in this environment contain tools to create 2D drawings.

The Place Views ribbon tab

This ribbon tab has commands and options to create and modify drawing views on the drawing sheet.

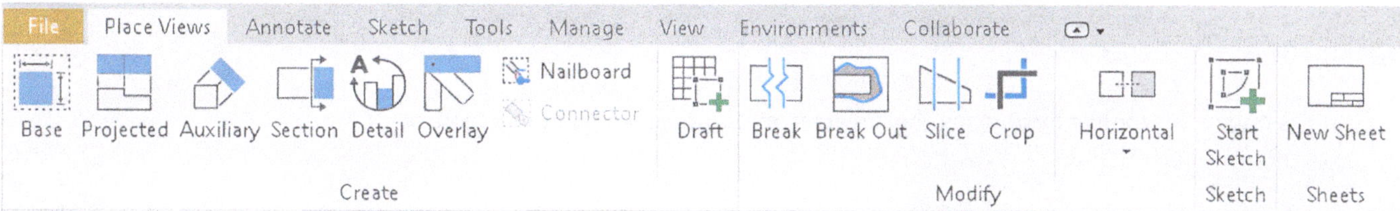

The Annotate ribbon tab

This ribbon tab has commands and options to add dimensions and annotations to the drawing views.

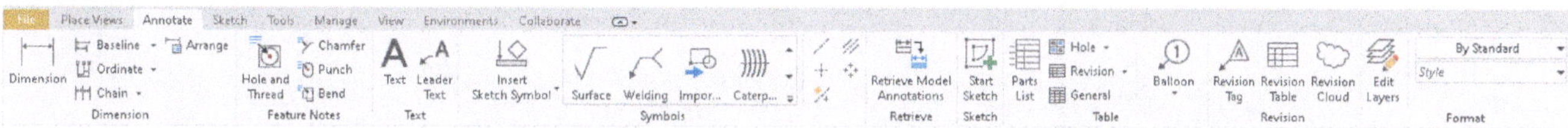

The Sheet Metal ribbon tab

The tools in this tab are used to create sheet metal components.

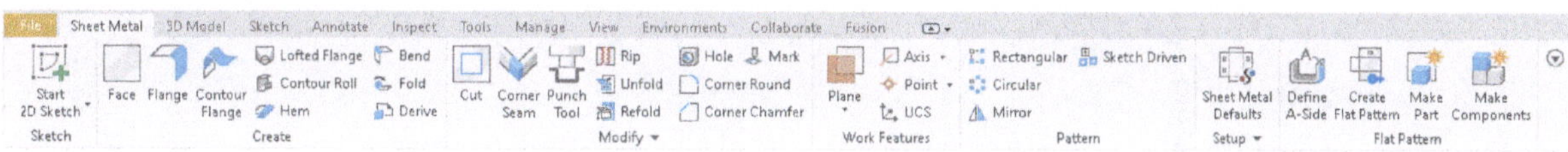

File Menu

The File Menu appears when you click on the **File** tab located at the top left corner. This menu contains the options to open, print, export, manage, save, and close a file.

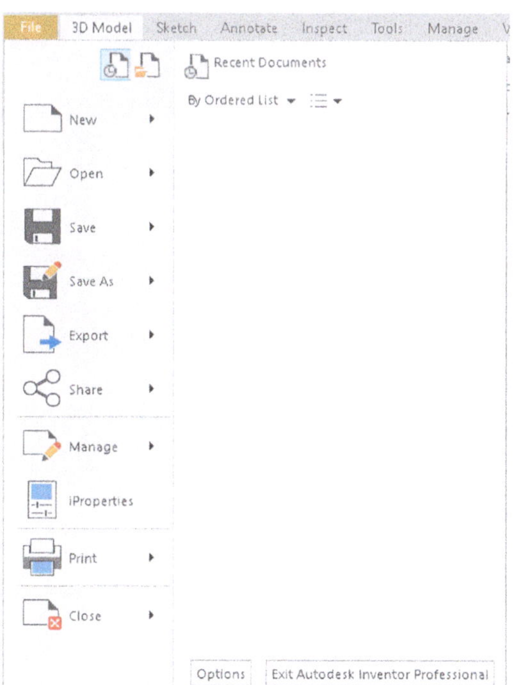

Quick Access Toolbar

The Quick Access Toolbar is available at the top left of the window. It contains tools such as **New**, **Save**, and **Open**.

You can customize this toolbar by clicking the down arrow at the right side of this toolbar.

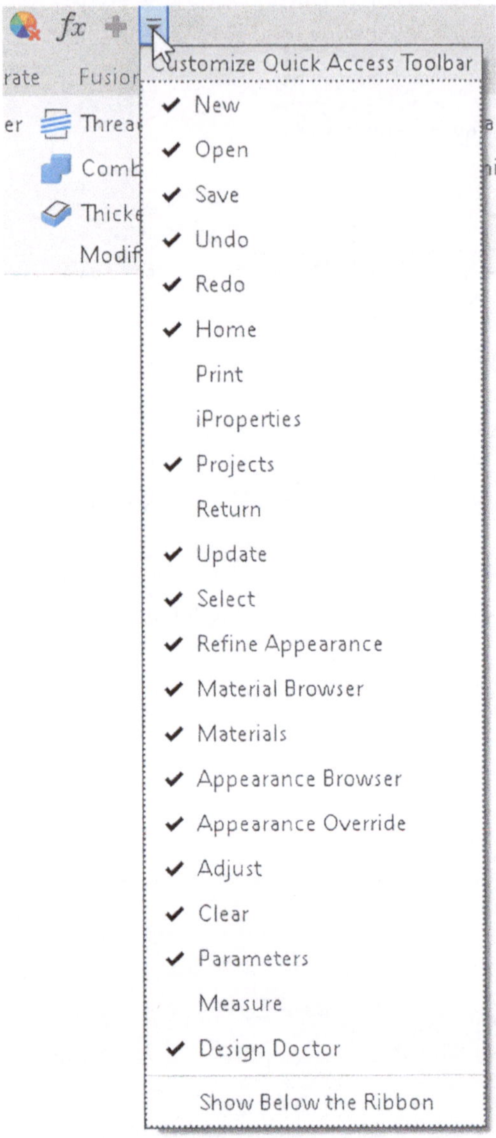

You can also customize the Quick Access Toolbar in two more ways:

1. To add a tool:
   - Place your mouse on the tool you want to add to the Quick Access Toolbar.
   - Click the right mouse button.
   - Choose "Add to Quick Access Toolbar".
2. To remove a tool:
   - Place your mouse on the tool in the Quick Access Toolbar.
   - Click the right mouse button.

- Choose "Remove from Quick Access Toolbar".

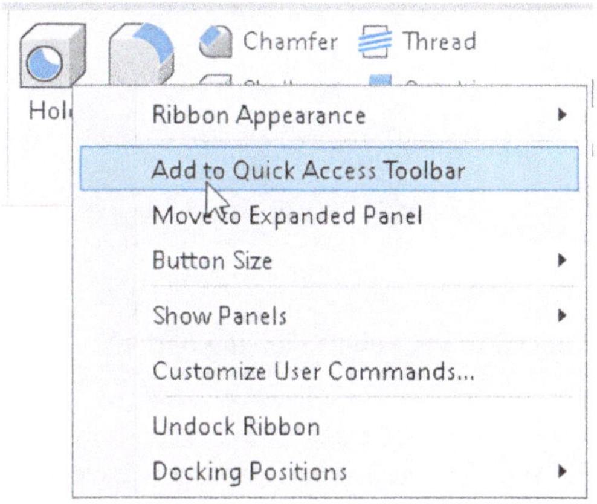

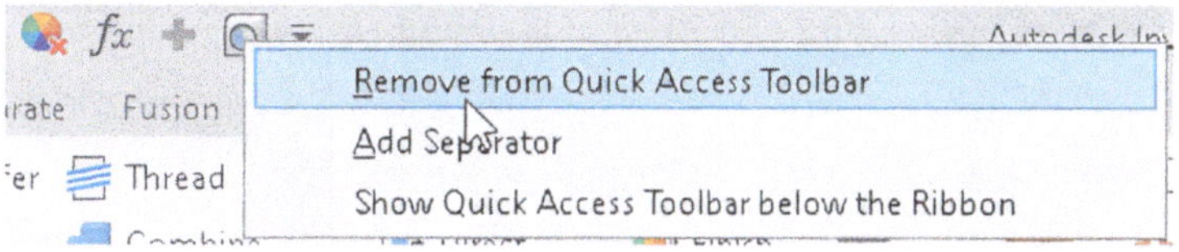

Making these changes helps you work faster by putting the tools you use most where you can easily find them.

Browser window

The Browser window is located on the left side of the window. It contains the list of operations carried in an Autodesk Inventor file.

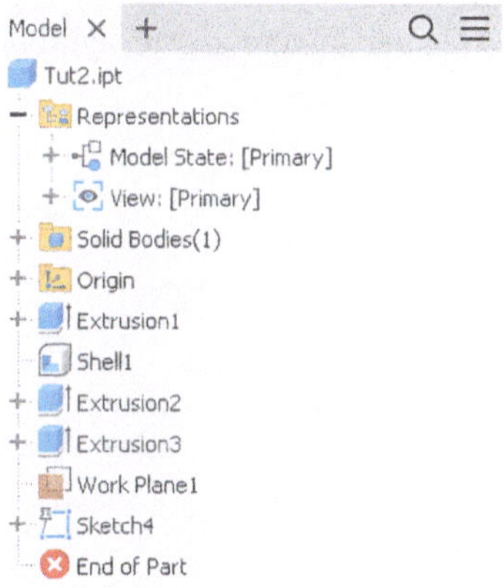

Status bar

The Status bar is available below the Browser window. It displays the prompts and the actions taken while using the tools.

Navigation Bar

The Navigation Bar is located on the right side of the window. It contains the tools to zoom, rotate, pan, or look at the face of the model.

You can move the Navigation bar to a different spot if you want. Below the main tools, you'll see more commands. If you pick one of these, it will become the main command you're using.

Navigation Controls
Access the Navigation Wheel by clicking its icon. This activates a steering wheel interface with eight viewing options.

View Manipulation

- Pan: Shift your view by using the Pan command or pressing F2. Drag with your left mouse button or mouse wheel to move the view.
- Zoom: Adjust magnification using the Zoom command or F3 key. Drag your mouse or use the wheel to change zoom level.
- Zoom All: View all parts in your current file at maximum size.
- Zoom Window: Magnify a specific area you define with two points.
- Zoom Selected: Fill your screen with face(s) or parts you select.

Rotation Functions

- Free Orbit: Rotate your viewpoint dynamically. Activate with the command or F4 key. Use the on-screen orbit symbol to control rotation.
- Constrained Orbit: Rotate your model around horizontal screen axes.

View Orientation

- Look At: Align your view perpendicular to a plane or parallel to an edge you choose.

Toolbar Customization
You can modify your Navigation bar. Click the arrow at the bottom to add or remove commands and adjust the toolbar's position as needed.

View Cube

The **ViewCube** is a navigation tool permanently located in the top-right corner of the graphics window. Its primary function is to control the view orientation of the displayed model.

Interaction Methods
The following interaction methods are available when the ViewCube is active:

1. **Isometric View:** Select any corner of the cube.
2. **Orthographic View:** Select any face to orient the view directly perpendicular to that principal plane.
3. **Incremental Rotation:** When viewing a face, select an adjacent arrow or triangle to rotate the view 90 degrees about the axis perpendicular to the current view.
4. **Edge View:** Select an edge to orient the view aligned with that edge.
5. **Free Rotation:** Click and drag the ViewCube to dynamically rotate the model.

View Management

- **Reset to Default:** Select the home icon to return to the default isometric view orientation.

Supplementary Navigation Tools
Alternative methods for view rotation include:

1. **Press-and-Hold Rotation:** Press and hold the F4 key while moving the cursor to rotate the view; release the key to stop rotation.
2. **Mouse-Based Rotation:** Press and hold the Shift key combined with the middle mouse button, then move the mouse to rotate the view about the model's center point; release the mouse button to stop rotation.

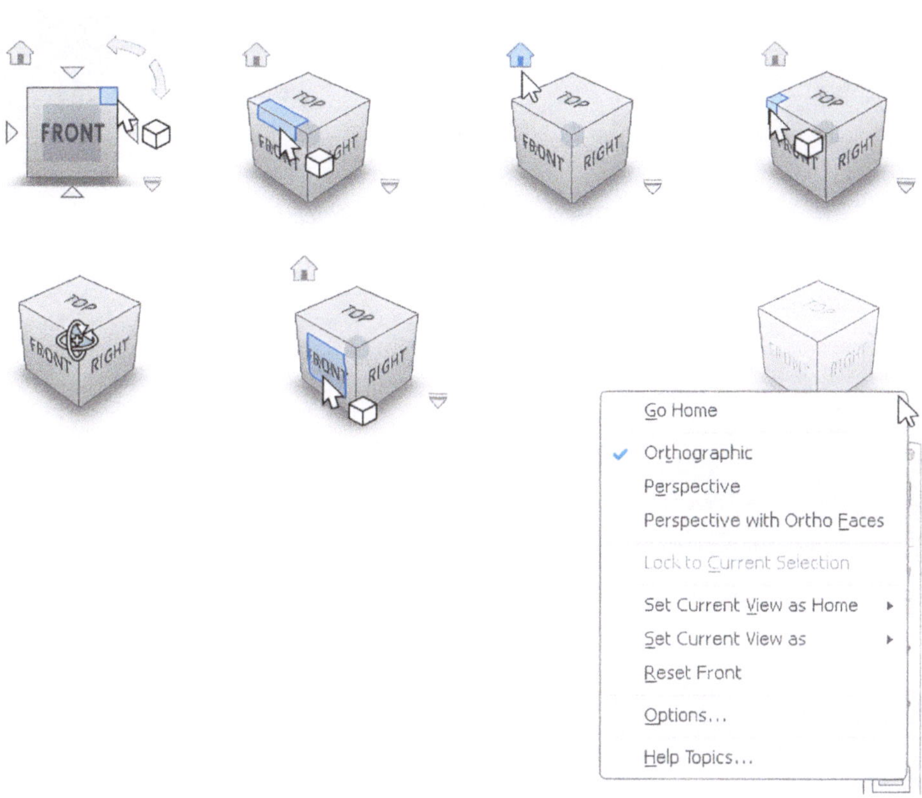

Understanding the Origin 3D Indicator in Autodesk Inventor

In the graphics window, you'll find an XYZ axis indicator in the lower left corner. This indicator represents the world coordinate system and helps you understand the orientation of your model. This helps you to know the orientation of the model.

1. **Axis Colors:**
   - Red arrow: X-axis
   - Green arrow: Y-axis
   - Blue arrow: Z-axis
2. **Turning On/Off the Axis Indicator:**
   - To toggle the axis indicator and labels, go to the Application Options dialog box > Display tab.
   - You can enable or disable the axis indicator as needed.
3. **Autoprojecting the Origin Point:**
   - When creating a new sketch in a part file, Inventor automatically projects the origin point (0,0).
   - The origin point serves as a reference for constraining sketches.
   - If desired, you can disable this feature:
     - Click the **Tools** tab > **Application Options**.
     - Alternatively, go to the **File** tab, click **Options > Sketch** tab, and uncheck **Autoproject part origin on sketch create**.

Shortcut Menus and Marking Menus

When you click the right mouse button, a shortcut menu along with a marking menu appears. A shortcut menu contains a list of some relevant options. Whereas, the marking menu contains essential tools. It allows you to access the tools quickly. You can customize the marking menu (add or remove tools).

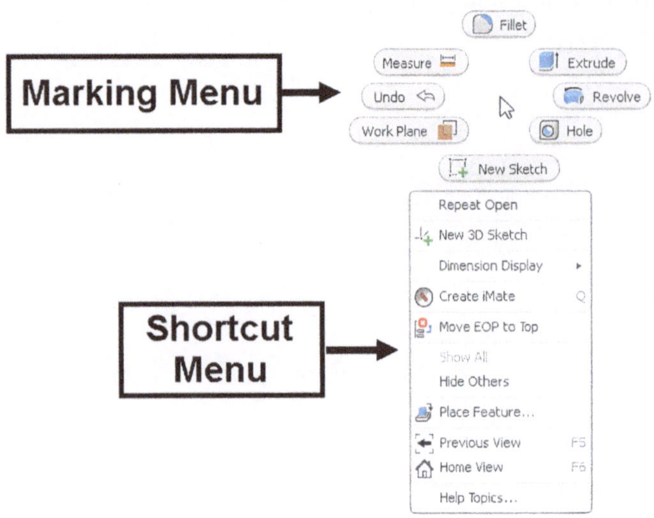

Dialogs

When you activate any tool in Autodesk Inventor, the dialog related to it appears. It consists of various options, which help you to complete the operation. The following figure shows the components of the dialog.

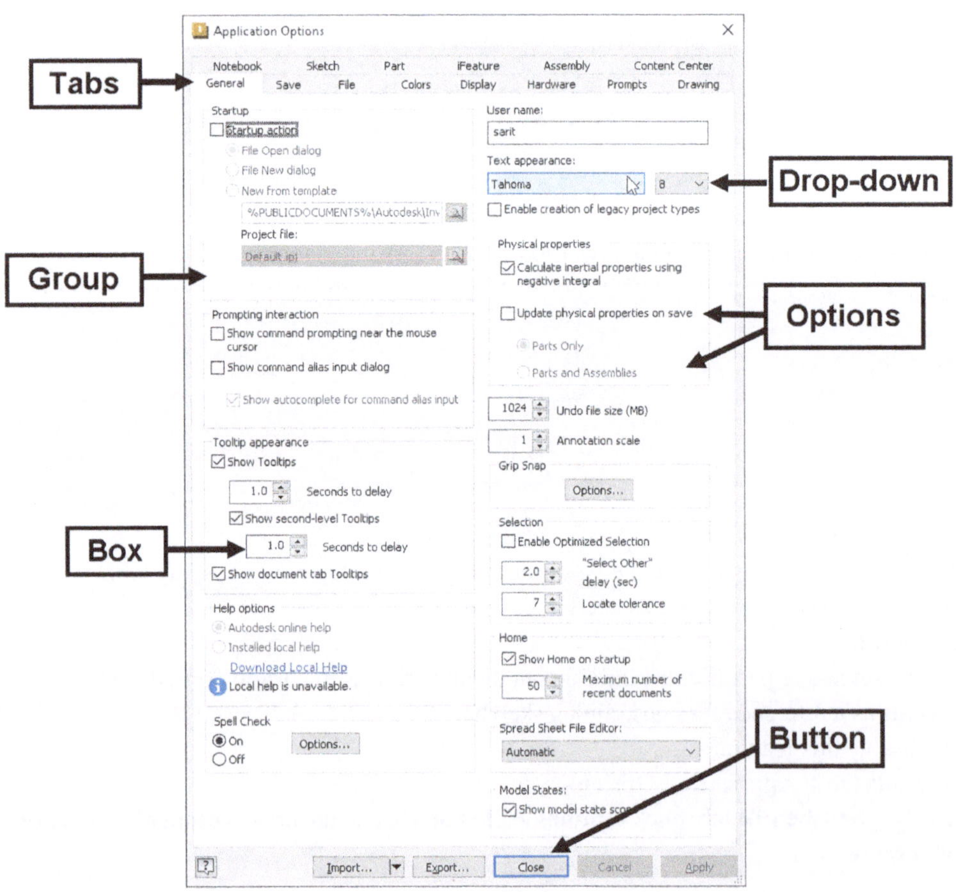

Customizing the Ribbon, Shortcut Keys, and Marking Menus

To customize the ribbon, shortcut keys, or marking menu, click **Tools > Options > Customize** on the ribbon. On the **Customize** dialog, use the tabs to customize the ribbon or marking menu or shortcut keys.

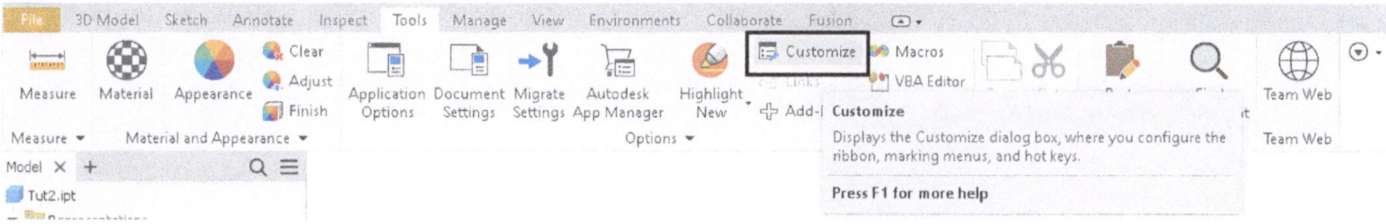

For example, to add a command to the ribbon, select the command from the list on the left side of the dialog and click the **Add** >> button. If you want to remove a command from the ribbon, then select it from the right-side list and click the **Remove** << button. Click **OK** to make the changes to effect.

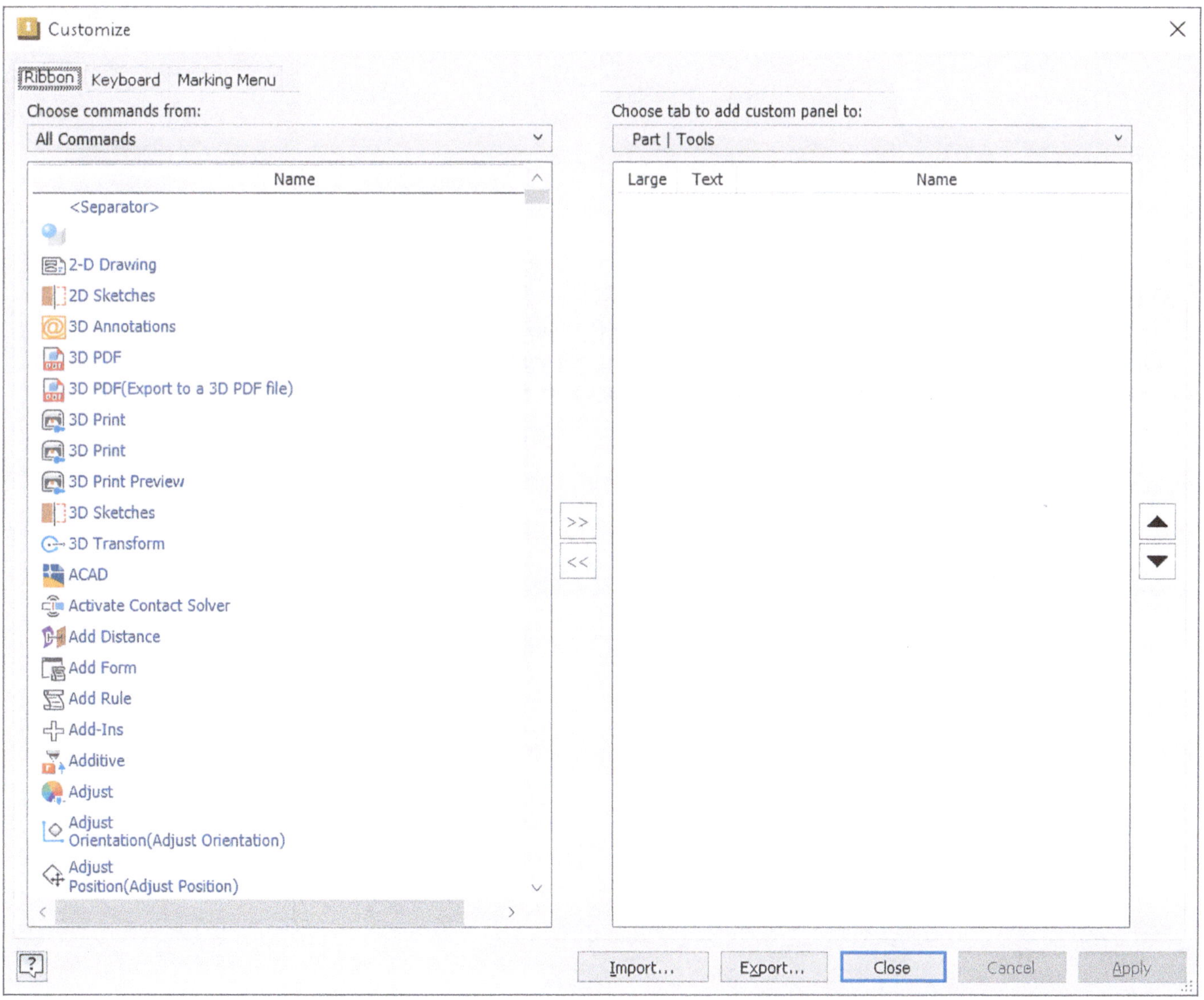

To add or remove panels from the ribbon, click the **Show Panels** icon located at the right side of the ribbon and check/uncheck the options on the flyout.

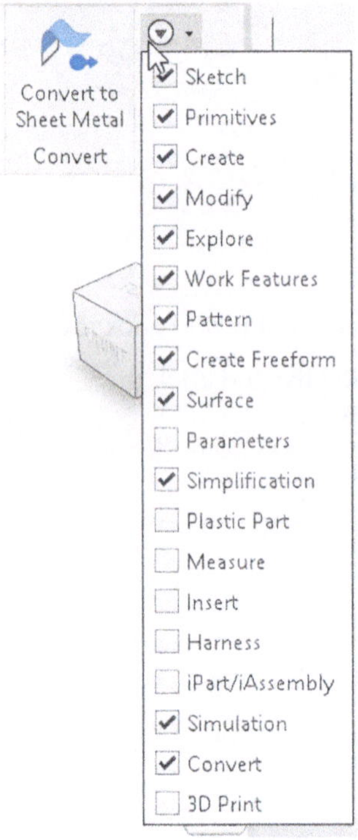

Color Settings

To change the background color of the window, click **Tools > Options > Application Options** on the ribbon. On the **Application Options** dialog, click the **Colors** tab on the dialog. Set the **Background** value to **1 Color** to change the background to plain. Select the required color scheme from the **Color Scheme** group. Click **OK**.

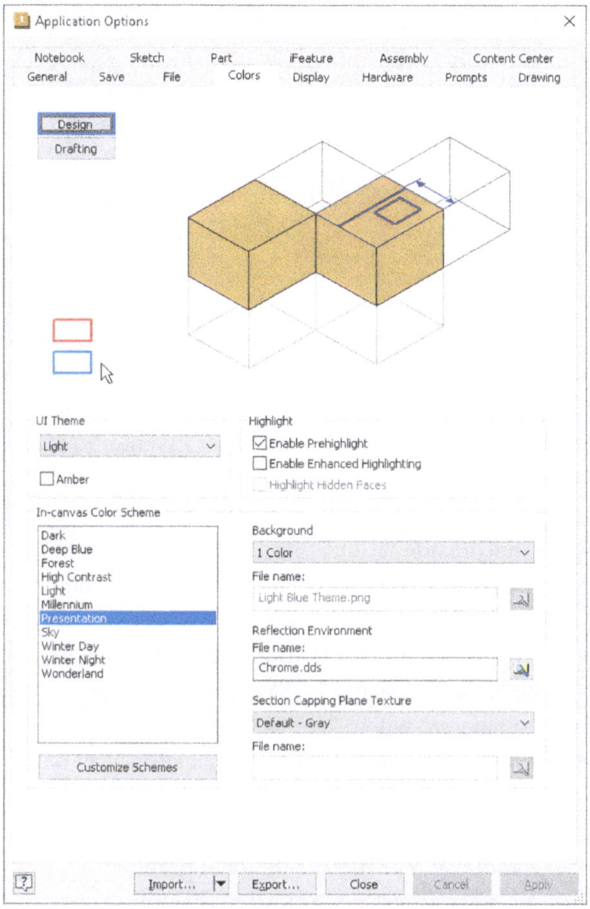

If you want to customize a scheme, click the **Customize Schemes** button; the **Color Scheme Editor** dialog appears. On this dialog, select the scheme to customize from the **Color Schemes** list. Next, expand the **Graphical Elements** tree and then click on the color swatch located next to the element of which the color is to be changed. Select a color from the **Color** dialog and click **OK**. On the **Color Scheme Editor** dialog, drag the **Translucency** dragger to change the intensity of the color. Next, click **OK** on the **Color Scheme Editor** and **Application Options** dialogs.

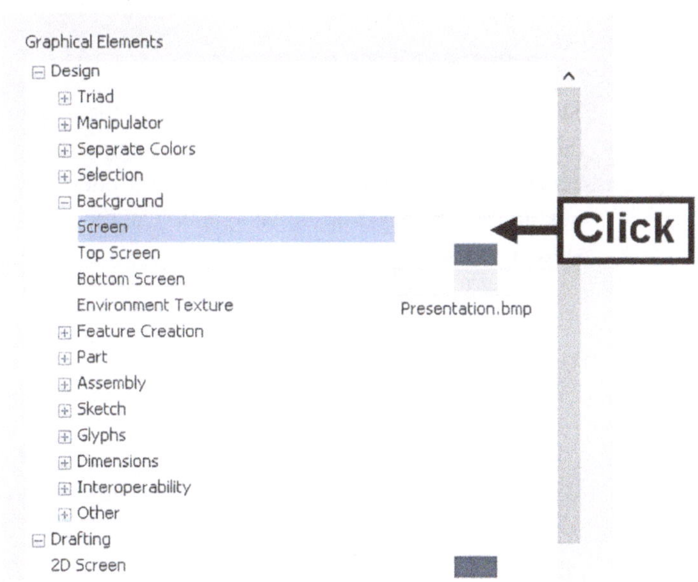

Chapter 2: Part Modeling Basics

This chapter takes you through the creation of your first Inventor model. You create simple parts:

In this chapter, you will:

- Create Sketches
- Create a base feature
- Add another feature to it
- Create revolved features
- Create cylindrical features
- Create box features
- Apply draft

Tutorial 1

This tutorial takes you through the creation of your first Inventor model. You will create the Disc of an Oldham coupling:

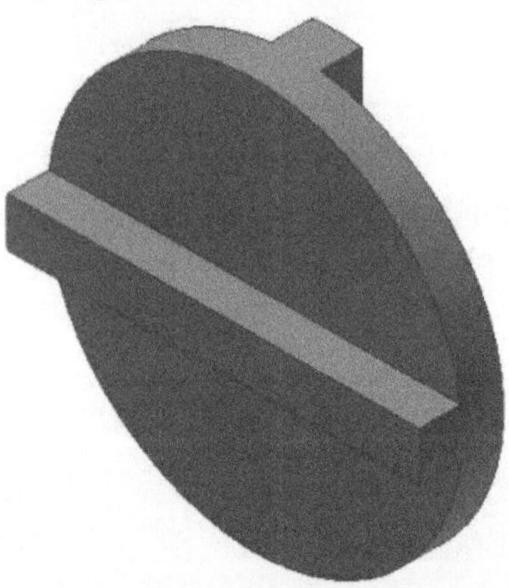

Creating a New Project

Autodesk Inventor design projects typically consist of multiple files with different extensions. These files are the components of a design and often work together to form a complete project.

File Types in an Inventor Project

Inventor projects may include:

- **Parts (.ipt)**: Individual components of a design
- **Assemblies (.iam)**: Collections of parts that form a complete assembly
- **Presentations (.ipn)**: Files that showcase a design in an interactive and dynamic way
- **Drawings (.idw)**: 2D representations of a design, used for documentation and communication

These files may reference each other, with assemblies including multiple parts, and drawings referencing assemblies.

Project File Functionality

Inventor uses a project file to manage the relationships between files and ensure they work together correctly. The project file serves as a reference point for Inventor to locate and connect relevant files in a design.

Project File Considerations

- **Single active project**: Only one project can be active at a time.
- **Multiple project creation**: Multiple projects can be created to work on different designs or collaborate with different teams.
- **File location flexibility**: File locations can be configured to suit design needs, whether working alone or as part of a team.
- **Autodesk Vault**: This optional program provides access control for multi-user teams, ensuring secure collaboration.

Default Project

Inventor includes a "Default" project, which may be sufficient for simple designs with files organized in a single folder or subfolder structure. This provides a starting point for new projects and can be customized as needed.

1. Start **Autodesk Inventor 2026** by double-clicking the **Autodesk Inventor 2026** icon on your desktop.
2. To create a new project, click the **Settings** button next to the **Project** drop-down available at the left side of the **Start** screen.

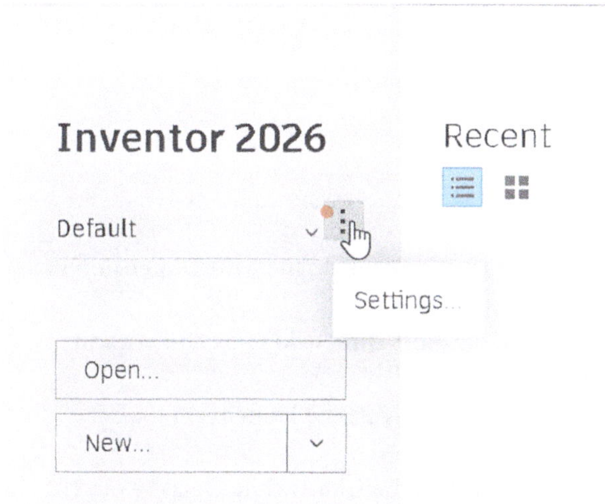

3. Click the **New** button on the **Projects** dialog.
4. On the **Inventor project wizard** dialog, select **New Single User Project** and click the **Next** button.
5. Enter **Oldham Coupling** in the **Name** field.
6. Enter **C:\Users\Username\Documents\Inventor\Oldham Coupling** in the **Project (Workspace) Folder** box and click **Next**.
7. Click **Finish**.
8. Click **OK** on the **Inventor Project Editor** dialog.
9. Click **Done**.

Starting a New Part File

1. To start a new part file, select the **New** option from the **New** drop-down available on the left of the **Start** screen.
2. On the **Create New File** dialog, click the **Templates** > **en-US** folder located in the top right corner.
3. Click the **Standard.ipt** icon located under the **Part – Create 2D and 3D Objects** section.
4. Click the **Create** button on the **Create New File** dialog.

A new model window appears.

Starting a Sketch

To create a sketch in Autodesk Inventor, you must first select a plane to draw on, which can be one of the three default planes (XY, YZ, and XZ) or a custom plane.

1. To start a new sketch, click **3D Model > Sketch > Start 2D Sketch** on the ribbon.

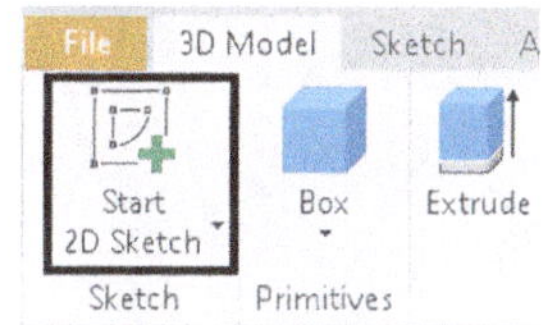

2. Click on the **XY Plane**. The sketch starts.

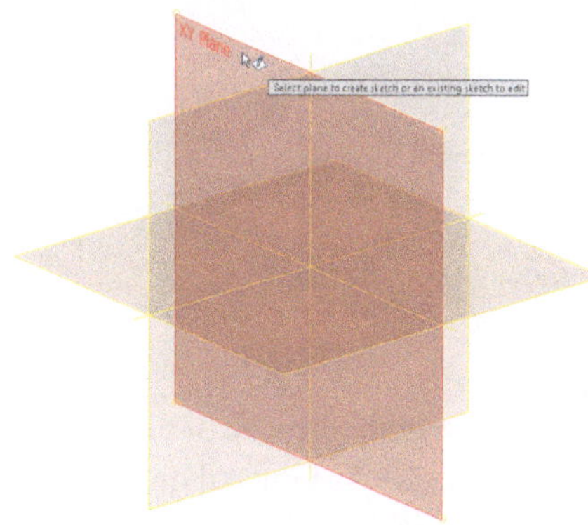

The first feature is an extruded feature from a sketched circular profile. You will begin by sketching the circle.

3. On the ribbon click **Sketch > Create > Circle > Circle Center Point**.

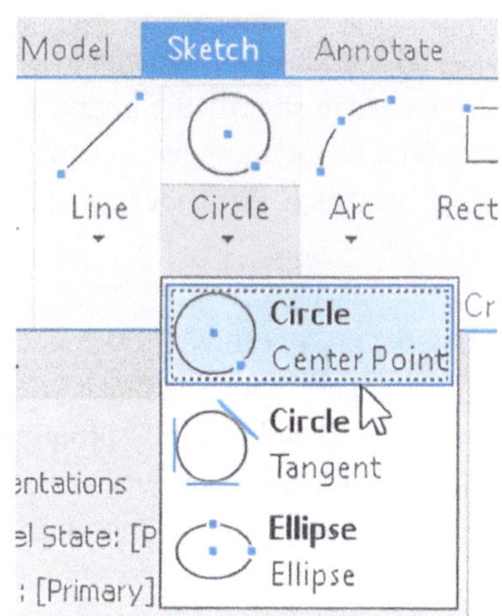

4. Move the cursor to the sketch origin located at the center of the graphics window, and then click on it.
5. Drag the cursor up to a random location, and then click to create a circle.

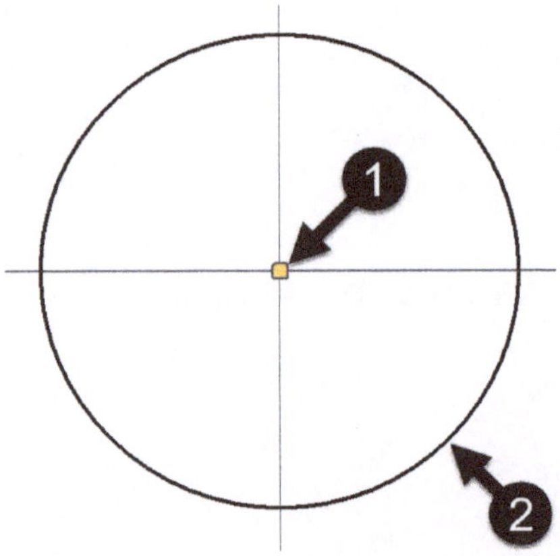

6. Press **ESC** to deactivate the tool.

Adding Dimensions

In this section, you will specify the size of the sketched circle by adding dimensions. As you add dimensions, the sketch can attain any one of the following states:

Fully Constrained sketch: In a fully constrained sketch, the positions of all the entities are fully described by dimensions, constraints, or both. In a fully constrained sketch, all the entities are a dark blue color.

Under Constrained sketch: Additional dimensions, constraints, or both are needed to specify the geometry completely. In this state, you can drag under constrained sketch entities to modify the sketch. An under constrained sketch entity is in black.

If you add any more dimensions to a fully constrained sketch, a message box will appear, showing that dimension over constraints the sketch. Also, it prompts you to convert the dimension into a driven dimension. Click **Accept** to convert the unwanted dimension into a driven dimension.

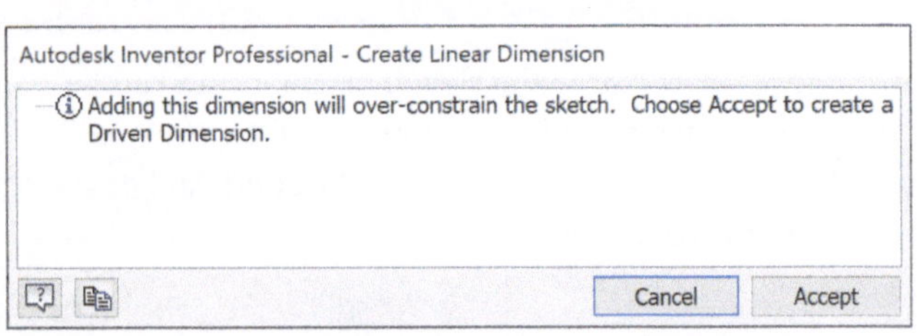

1. On the ribbon, click **Sketch > Constrain > Dimension**.

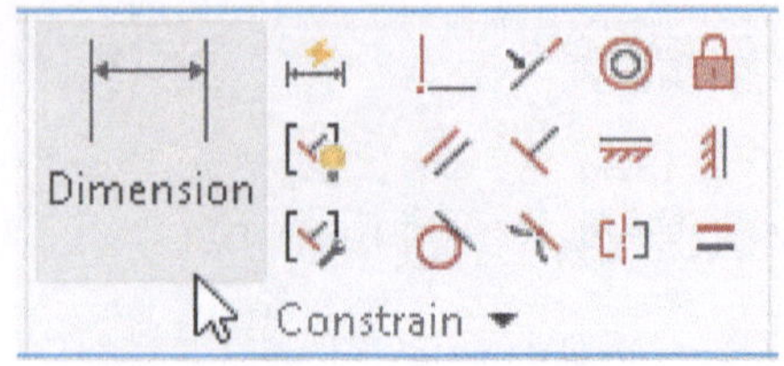

2. Select the circle and click; the **Edit Dimension** box appears.
3. Enter **4** in the **Edit Dimension** box and click the green check.
4. Press **Esc** to deactivate the **Dimension** tool.

You can also create dimensions while creating sketch objects. To do this, enter the dimension values in the boxes displayed while sketching.

5. To display the entire circle at full size and to center it in the graphics area, use one of the following methods:

   - Click **Zoom All** on the **Navigate Bar**.
   - Click **View > Navigate > Zoom All** on the ribbon.

6. Click **Finish** on the **Exit** panel.

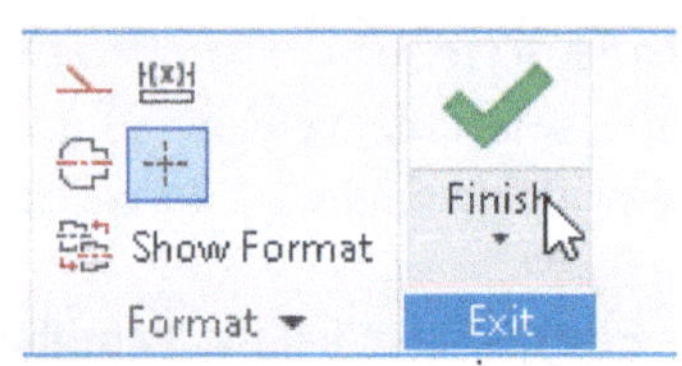

7. Again, click **Zoom All** on the **Navigate Bar**.

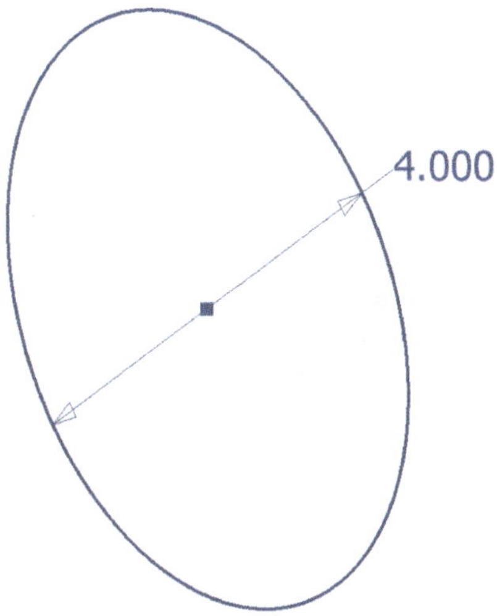

Creating the Base Feature

The first feature in any part is called a base feature. You now create this feature by extruding the sketched circle.

1. On the ribbon, click **3D Model > Create > Extrude.**

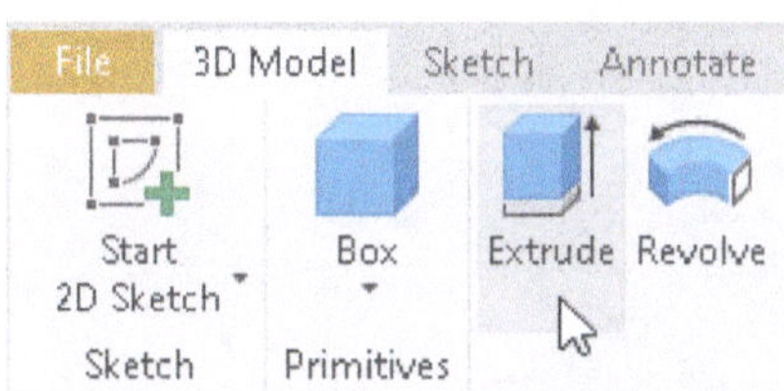

2. Type-in **0.4** in the **Distance A** box available on the **Extrude** Properties panel.
3. Click the **Direction > Default**  icon under the **Behavior** section on the **Extrude** Properties panel.
4. Click **OK** on the **Extrude** Properties panel to create the extrusion.

Notice the new feature, **Extrusion 1**, in the **Browser window**.

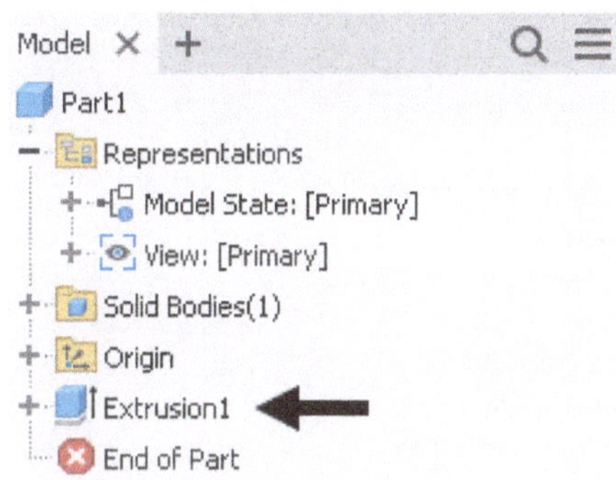

To magnify a model in the graphics area, you can use the zoom tools available on the **Zoom** drop-down in the **Navigate** panel of the **View** tab.

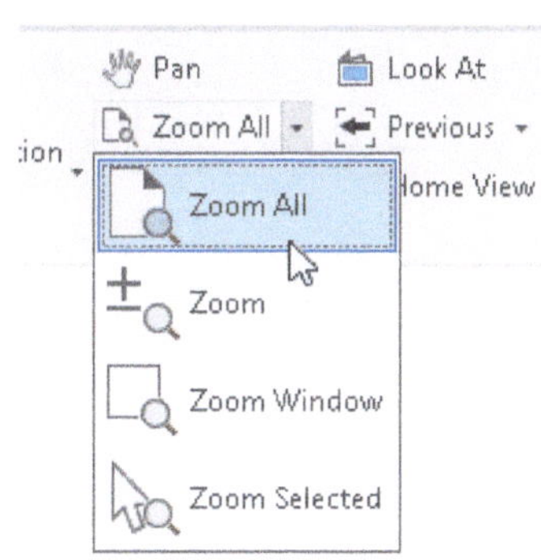

Click **Zoom All** to display the full part size in the current window.

Click **Zoom Window**, and then drag the pointer to create a rectangle; the area in the rectangle zooms to fill the window.

Click **Zoom**, and then drag the pointer. Dragging up zooms out, dragging down zooms in.

Click on a vertex, an edge, or a feature, and then click **Zoom Selected**; the selected item zooms to fill the window.

To display the part in different rendering modes, select the options in the **Visual Style** drop-down on the **Appearance** panel of the **View** tab.

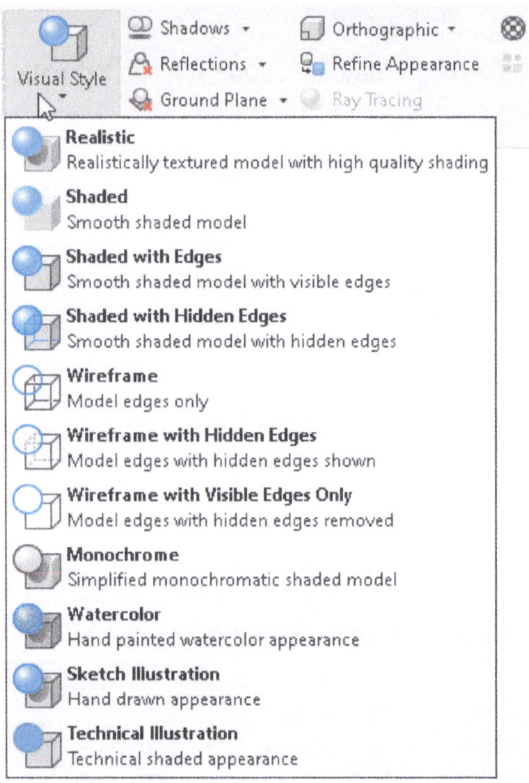

Realistic

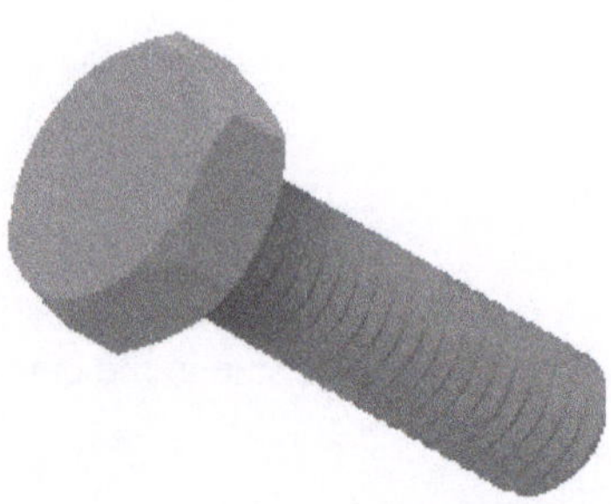

Shaded

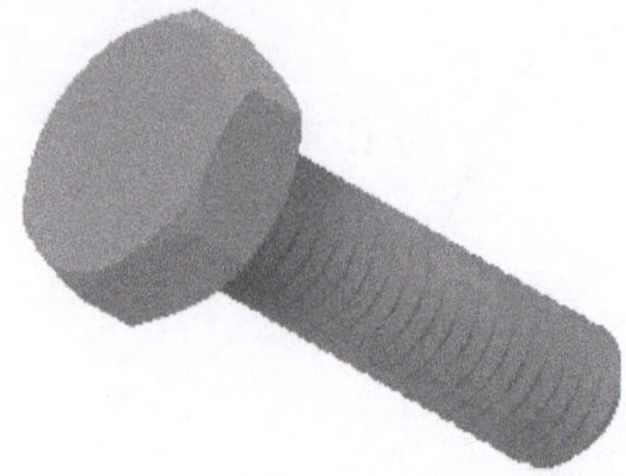

Shaded with Edges

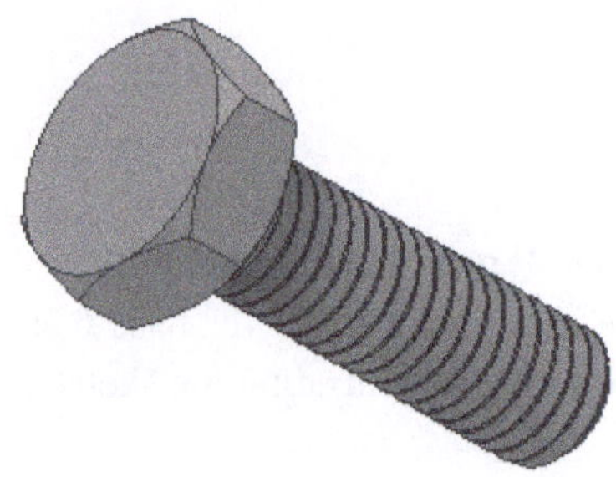

Shaded with Hidden Edges

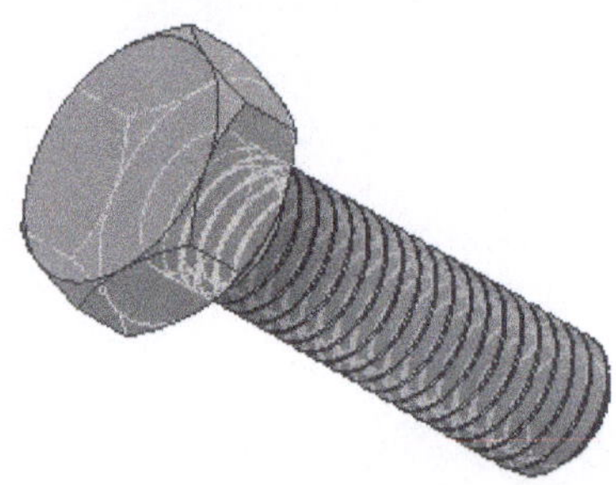

Wireframe

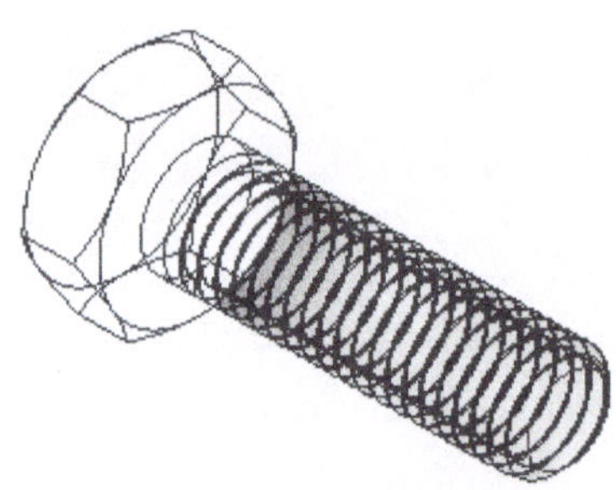

Wireframe with Hidden Edges

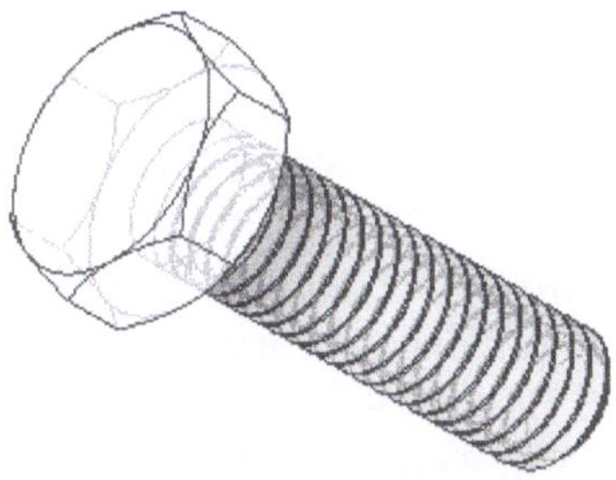

Wireframe with Visible Edges Only

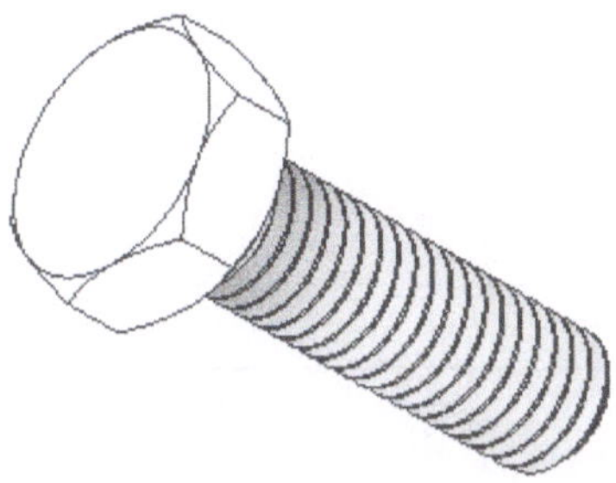

Monochrome

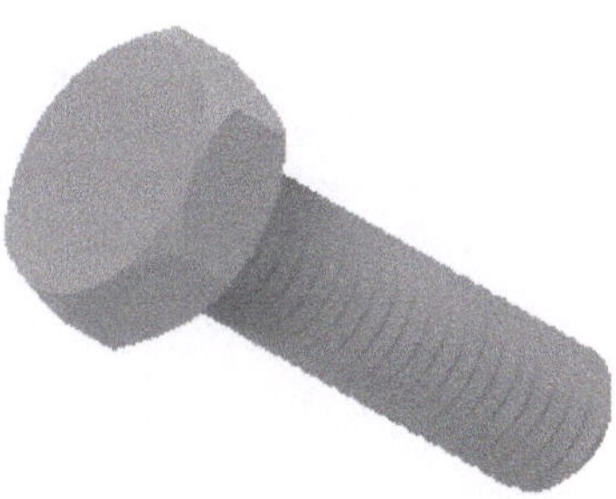

Watercolor

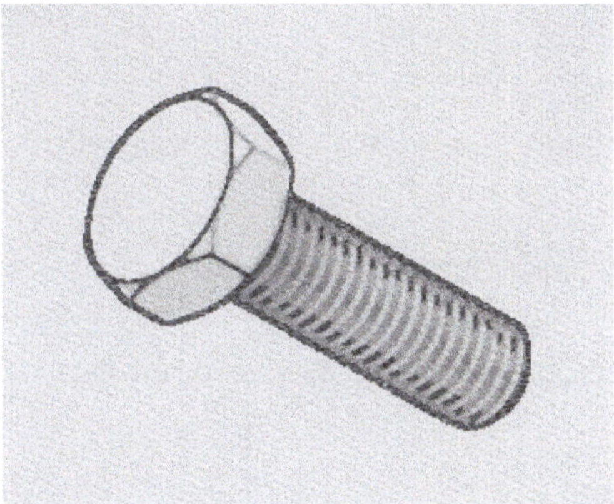

Sketch Illustration

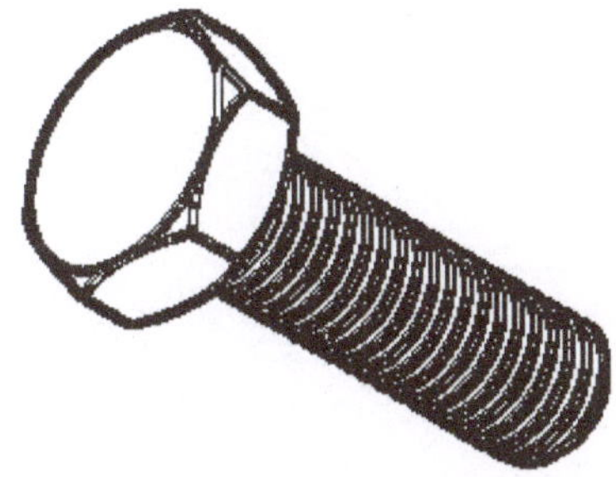

Technical Illustration

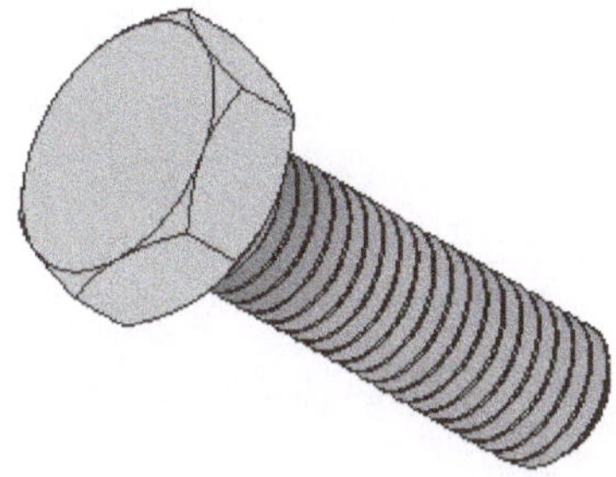

The default display mode for parts and assemblies is **Shaded with Edges**. You may change the display mode whenever you want.

Adding an Extruded Feature

To create additional features on the part, you need to draw sketches on the model faces or planes, and then extrude them.

1. On the ribbon, click **View > Appearance > Visual Style > Wireframe**.
2. On the ribbon, click **3D Model > Sketch > Start 2D Sketch**.
3. Click on the front face of the part.
4. Click **Line** on the **Create** panel.

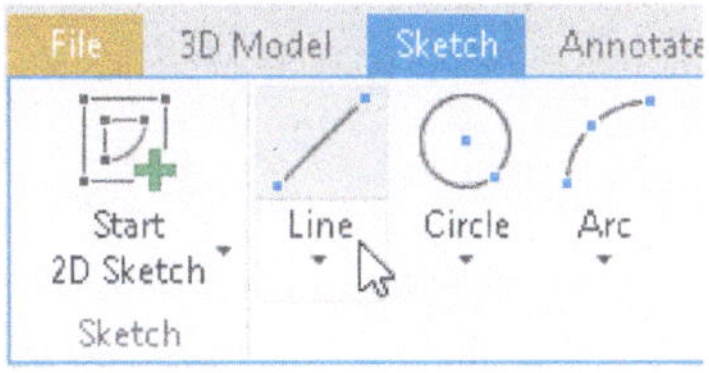

5. Click on the circular edge to specify the first point of the line.

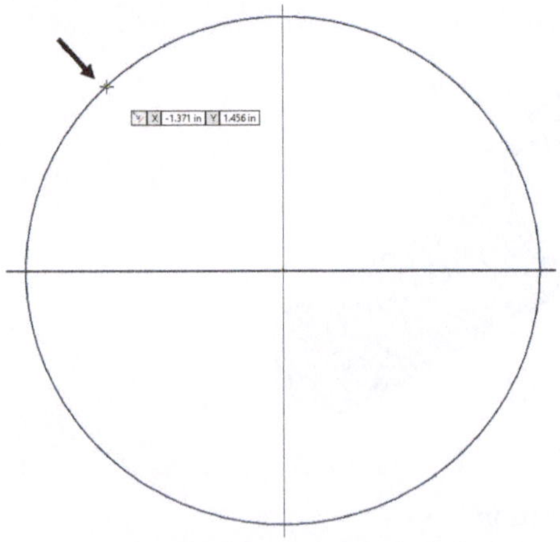

6. Move the cursor towards the right.
7. Click on the other side of the circular edge; a line is drawn.

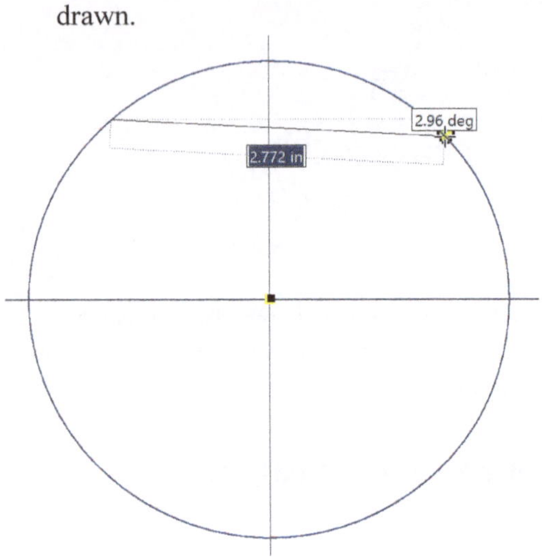

8. Draw another line below the previous line.

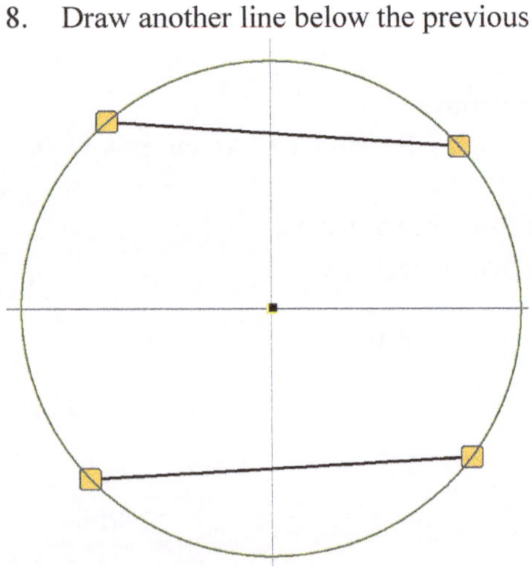

9. On the ribbon, click **Sketch > Constrain > Horizontal Constraint** .
10. Select the two lines to make them horizontal.
11. On the ribbon, click **Sketch > Constrain > Equal** .
12. Select the two horizontal lines to make them equal.
13. Click **Dimension** on the **Constrain** panel of the **Sketch** ribbon tab.
14. Select the two horizontal lines.
15. Move the cursor toward the right and click to locate the dimension; the **Edit Dimension** box appears.
16. Enter **0.472** in the **Edit Dimension** box and click the green check.

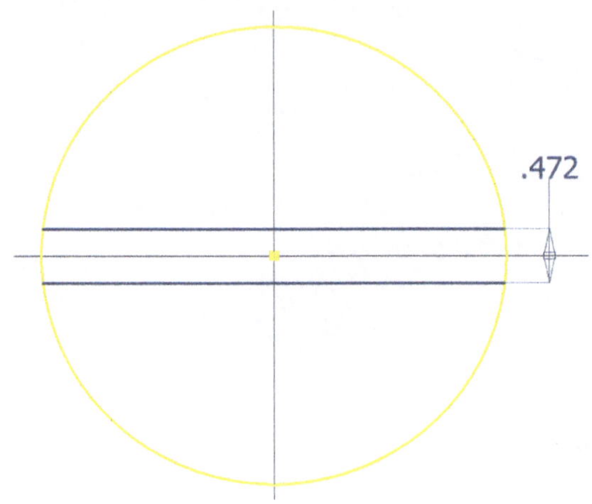

17. Click **Finish** on the **Exit** panel.
18. Click on the sketch, and then click **Create Extrude** on the **Mini Toolbar**; the **Extrude** Properties panel appears.

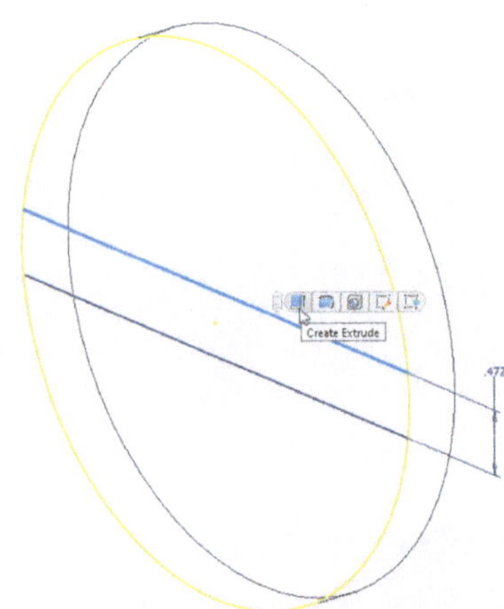

19. Click on the region bounded by the two horizontal lines.

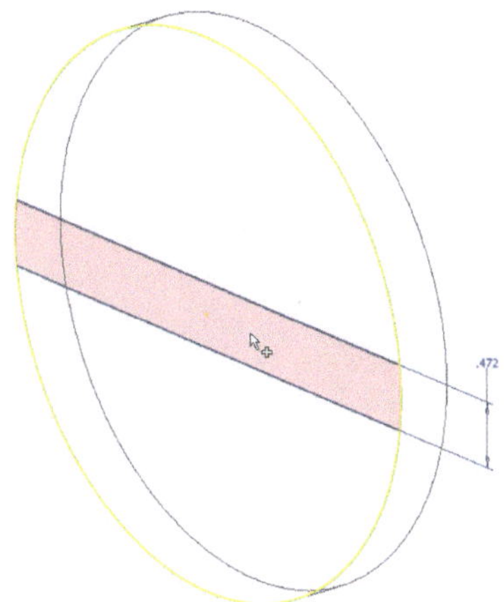

20. Enter **0.4** in the **Distance A** box on the **Extrude** Properties panel.
21. On the **Extrude** Properties panel, click the **Default** icon, and then **OK** to create the extrusion.

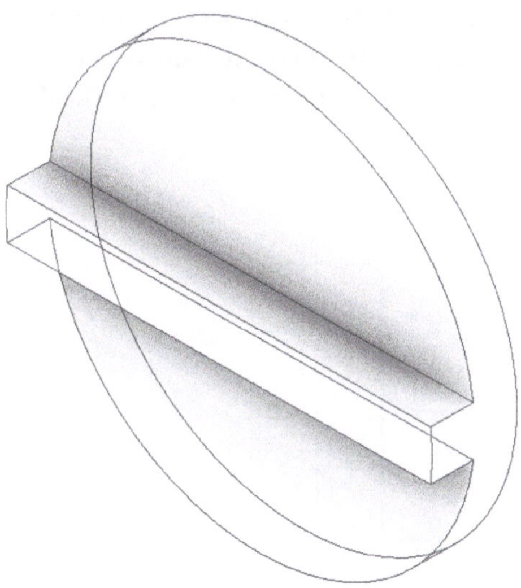

By default, the ambient shadows are displayed on the model. However, you can turn off the ambient shadows by clicking **View** tab > **Appearance** panel > **Shadows** drop-down, and then unchecking the **Ambient Shadows** option. The **Shadows** drop-down has two more options, which you use based on your requirement.

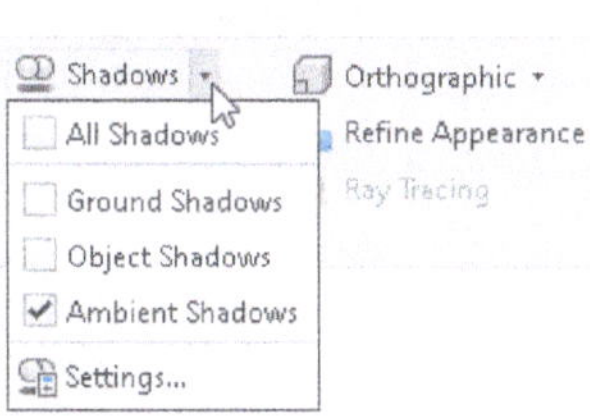

*You can reuse the sketch of an already existing feature. To do this, expand the feature in the Browser Window, right click on the sketch, and select **Share Sketch** from the shortcut menu. You will notice that the sketch is visible in the graphics window. You can also unshare the sketch by right-clicking on it and selecting **Unshare**.*

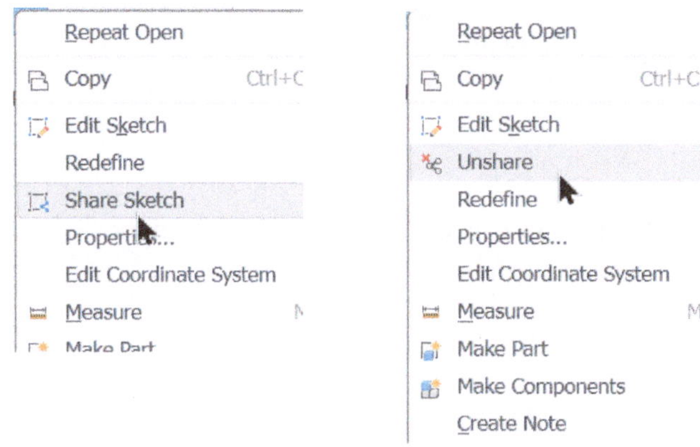

Adding another Extruded Feature

1. Click **Start 2D Sketch** on the **Sketch** panel of the **3D Model** ribbon tab.
2. Use the **Free Orbit** button from the **Navigate Bar** to rotate the model such that the back face of the part is visible.
3. Right click and select **OK**.
4. Click on the back face of the part.
5. Click **Line** on the **Create** panel.
6. Draw two lines, as shown below (refer to the **Adding an Extruded Feature** section to know how to draw lines). Make sure that the endpoints of the lines are coincident with the circular edge. Follow the next two steps, if they are not coincident.

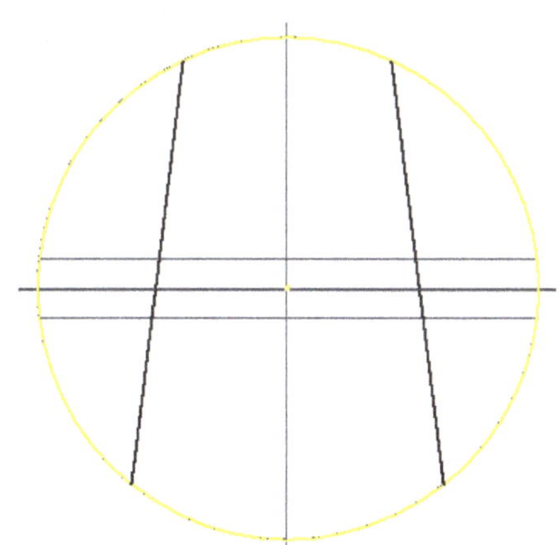

7. On the ribbon, click **Sketch > Constrain > Coincident Constraint** . Next, select the endpoint of the line and the circular edge.

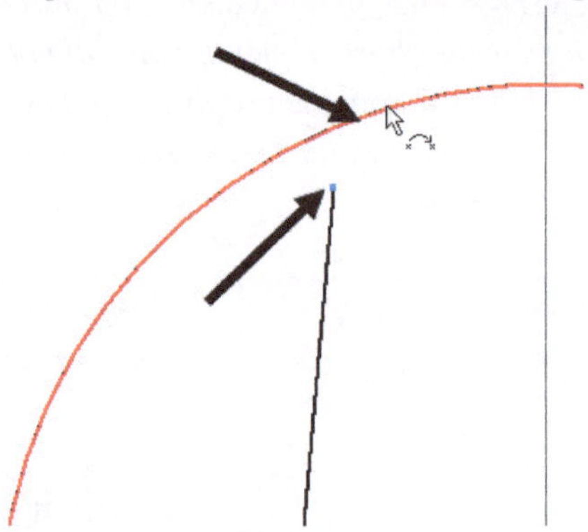

8. Likewise, make the other endpoints of the lines coincident with the circular edge.

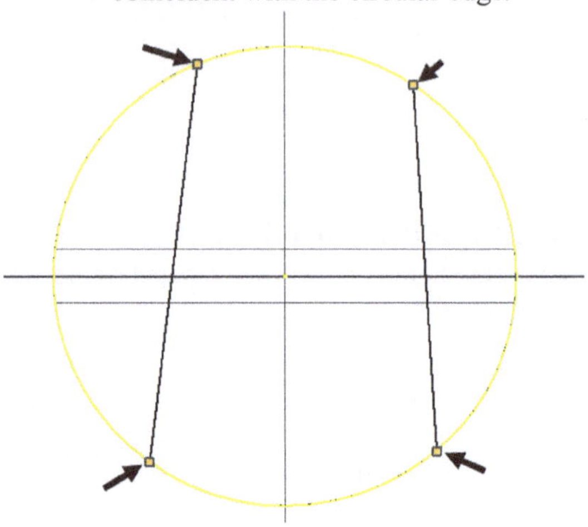

Skip the above two steps if the endpoints of the lines are coincident with the circular edge.

*You can specify a point using various point snap options. To do this, activate a sketching tool, right click, and select **Point Snaps**; a list of point snaps appears. Now, you can select only the specified point snap.*

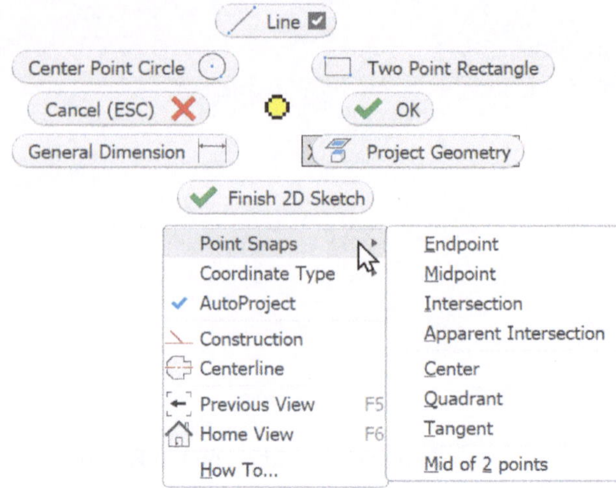

9. On the ribbon, click **Sketch > Constrain > Vertical Constraint** .
10. Select the two lines to make them vertical.
11. On the ribbon, click **Sketch > Constrain > Equal** = .
12. Select the two vertical lines to make them equal.
13. Create a dimension of **0.472in** between the vertical lines.

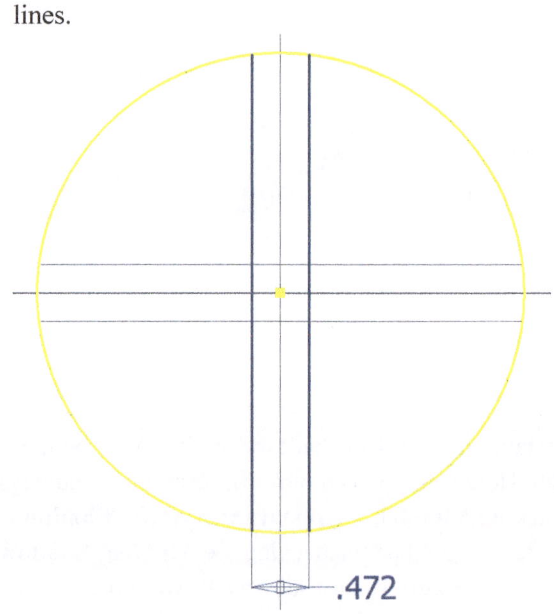

14. Click **Finish**.
15. On the ribbon, click **3D Model > Create > Extrude**.
16. Click inside the region enclosed by two lines, if they are not already selected.
17. Type **0.4** in the **Distance A** box on the **Extrude** Properties panel and click **OK**.

To move the part view, click **Pan** on **Navigate Bar**, and then drag the part to move it in the graphics area.

18. On the ribbon, click **View > Appearance > Visual Style > Shaded with Edges**.
19. On the ribbon, click **View > Navigate > Home View**.

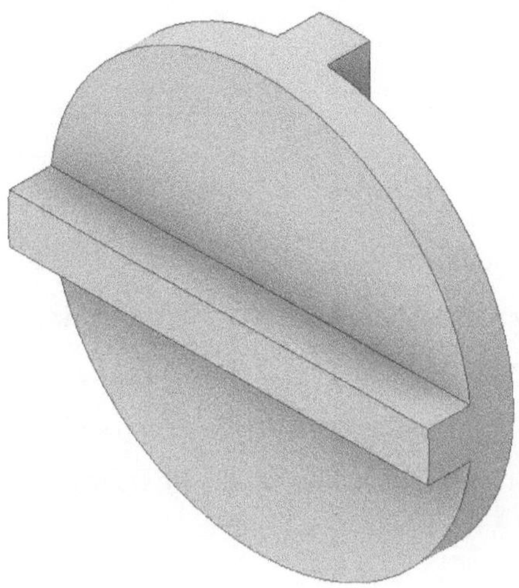

Saving the Part

1. Click **Save** on the **Quick Access Toolbar**.
2. On the **Save As** dialog, type-in **Disc** in the **File name** box.
3. Click **Save** to save the file.
4. Click **File Menu > Close**.

Note:
*.ipt is the file extension for all the files that you create in the Part environment of Autodesk Inventor.

Tutorial 2

In this tutorial, you create a flange by performing the following:

- Creating a revolved feature
- Creating cut features
- Adding fillets

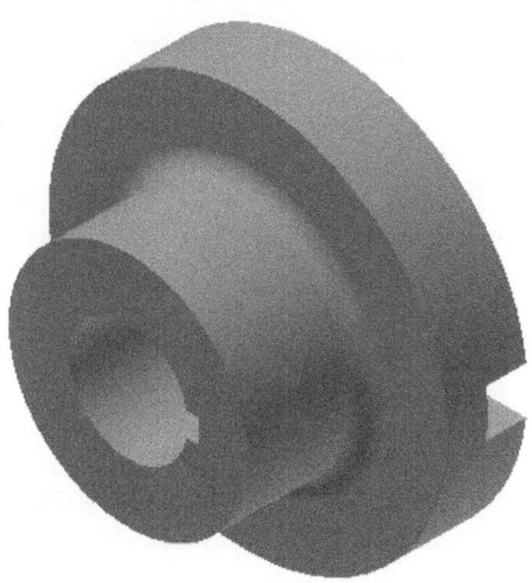

Starting a New Part File

1. To start a new part file, select the **Part (.ipt)** template from the **New** drop-down on the **Start** screen.

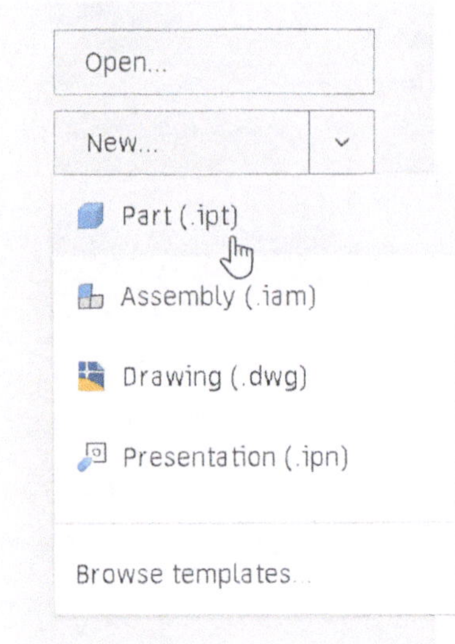

Sketching a Revolve Profile

You create the base feature of the flange by revolving a profile around a centerline.

1. Click **3D Model > Sketch > Start 2D Sketch** on the ribbon.
2. Select the YZ plane.

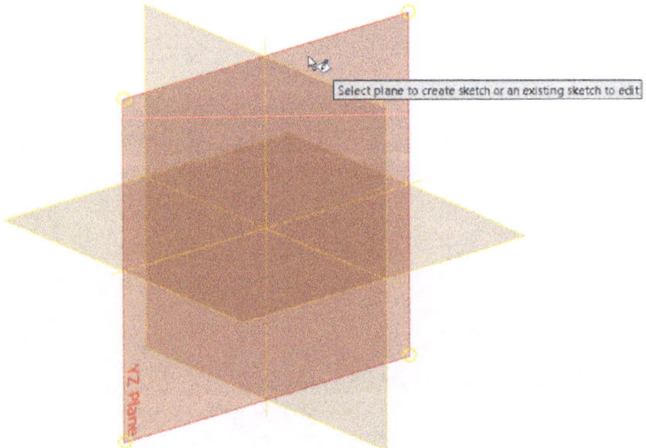

3. Click **Line** on the **Create** panel.
4. Create a sketch similar to that shown in the figure.

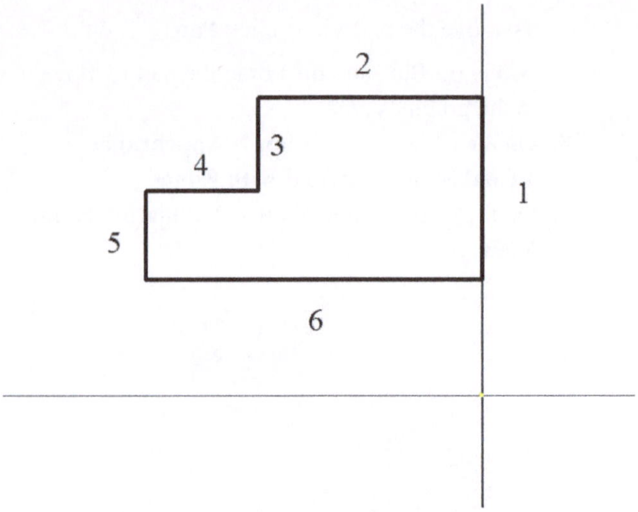

5. On the ribbon, click **Sketch > Format > Centerline** .
6. Click **Line** on the **Create** panel.
7. Create a centerline, as shown below.

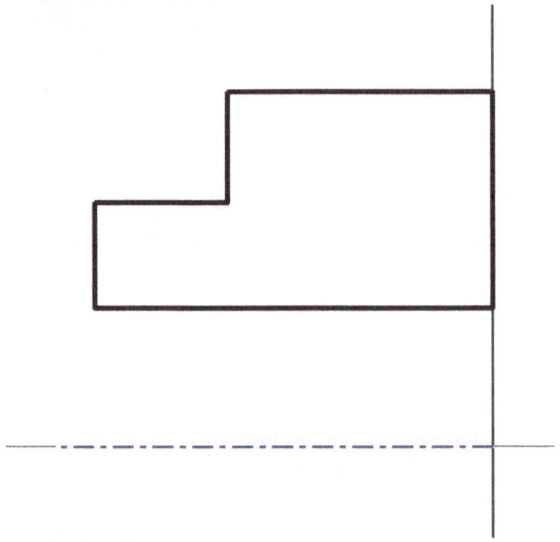

8. Click **Fix** on the **Constrain** panel.
9. Select Line 1.
10. Click **Dimension** on the **Constrain** panel.
11. Select the centerline and Line 2; a dimension appears.
12. Move the pointer horizontally toward the right and click to place the dimension.
13. Place the dimension and enter **4** in the **Edit Dimension** box.
14. Click the green check on the **Edit Dimension** dialog.
15. Select the centerline and Line 4; a dimension appears.
16. Move the pointer horizontally toward the left and click to place the dimension.

17. Enter **2.4** in the **Edit Dimension** box.
18. Click the green check on the **Edit Dimension** dialog.
19. Select the centerline and Line 6; a dimension appears.
20. Move the pointer horizontally toward the left and click to place the dimension.
21. Enter **1.2** in the **Edit Dimension** box.
22. Click the green check on the **Edit Dimension** dialog.
23. Create a dimension between Line 1 and Line 3.
24. Set the dimension value to **0.8** inches.
25. Create a dimension between Line 1 and Line 5.
26. Set the dimension value to **2** inches.

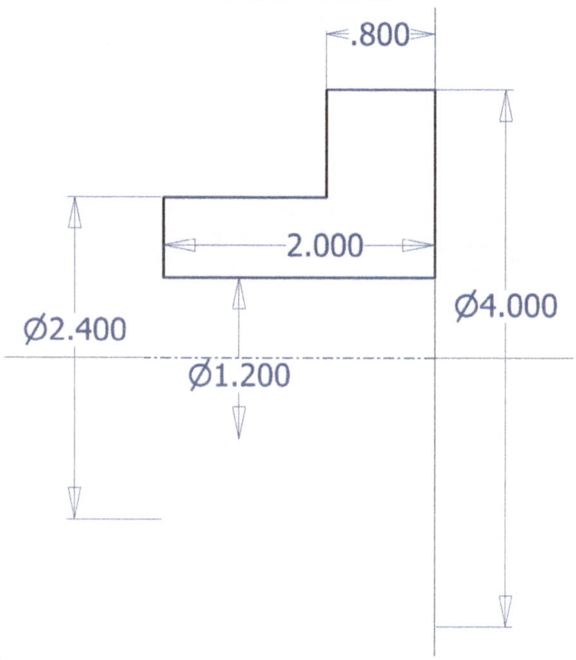

*You can display all the constraints by right-clicking and selecting **Show All Constraints** option. You can hide all the constraints by right-clicking and selecting the **Hide All Constraints** option.*

27. Right-click and select **Finish 2D Sketch**.

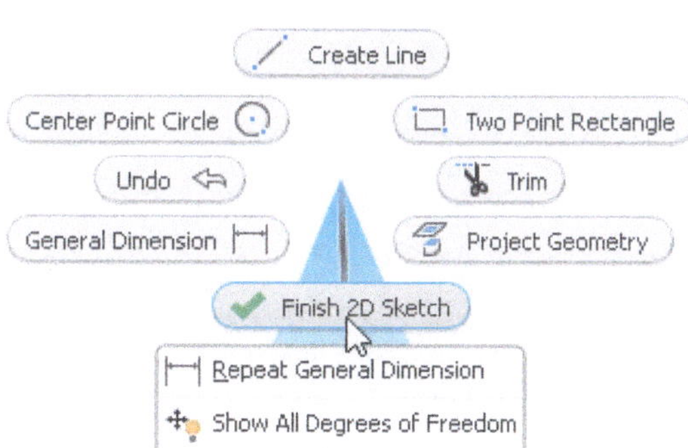

Creating the Revolved Feature

1. On the ribbon, click **3D Model > Create > Revolve** (or) right-click and select **Revolve** from the Marking Menu.

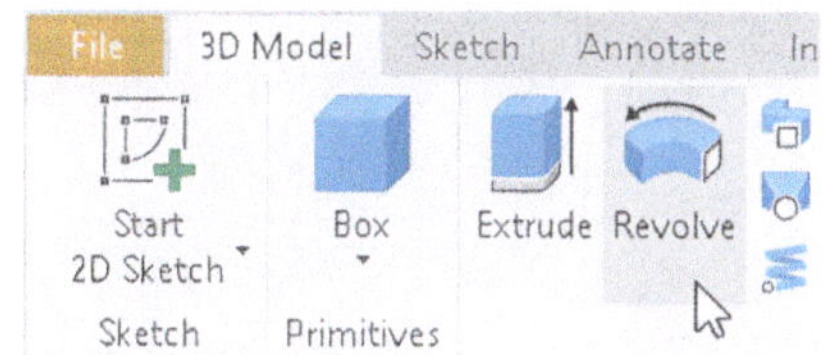

2. Click the **Full** button under the **Behavior** section on the **Revolve** Properties panel.

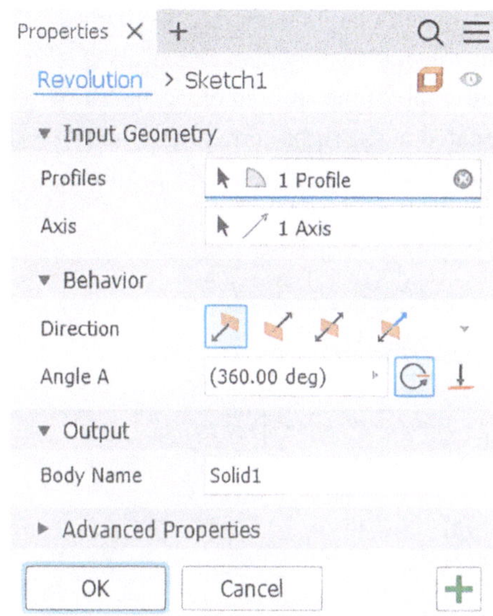

3. Click **OK** to create the revolved feature.

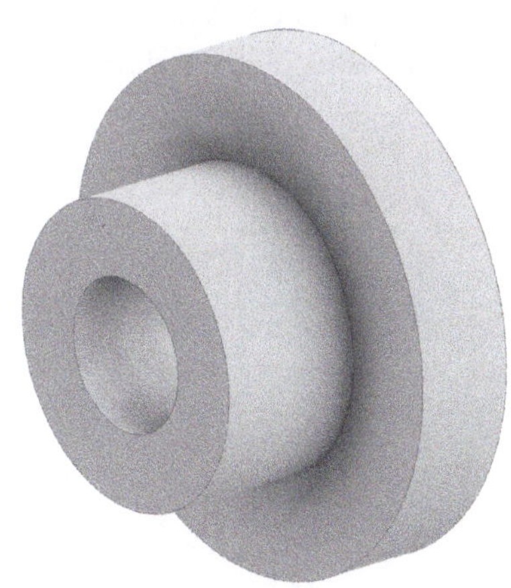

Creating the Cut feature

1. On the **Navigation** pane, click the **Orbit** icon.

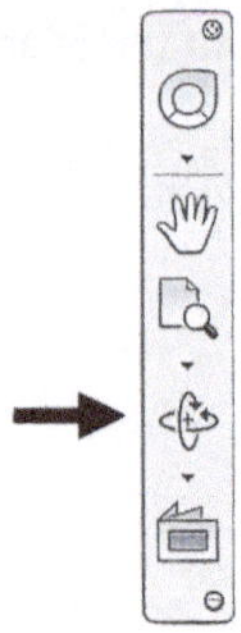

2. Press and hold the left mouse button and drag the mouse; the model is rotated.
3. Rotate the model such that its back face is visible.
4. Right click and select **OK**.
5. On the **3D Model** tab of the ribbon, click the **Show Panels** icon located at the right corner, and then check the **Primitives** option from the drop-down.

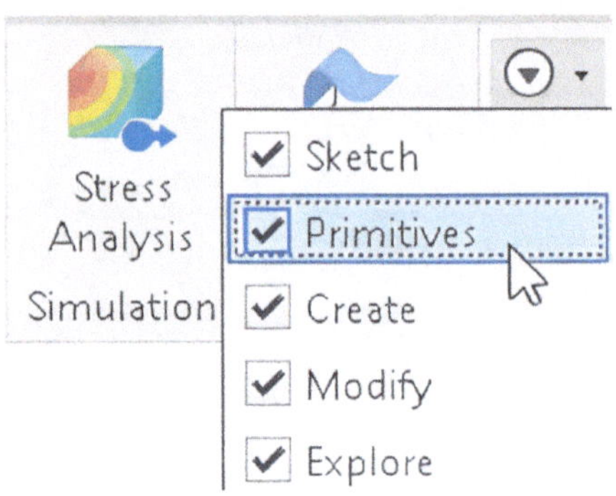

The **Primitives** panel is added to the ribbon. Skip the fifth step if the **Primitives** panel is already added.

6. On the ribbon, click **3D Model > Primitives > Primitive drop-down > Box** on the **Primitives** panel.

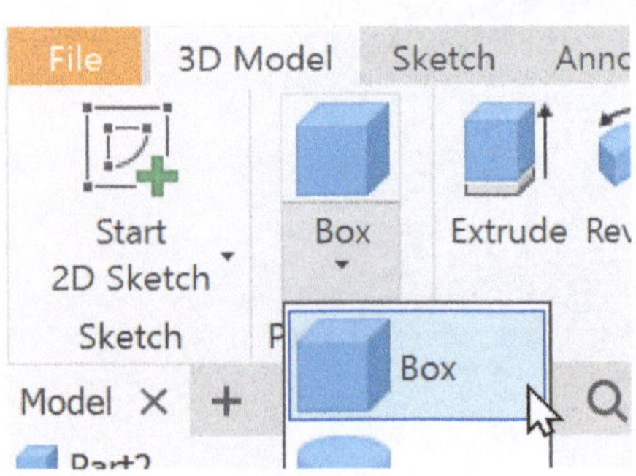

7. Click the back face of the part; the sketch starts.

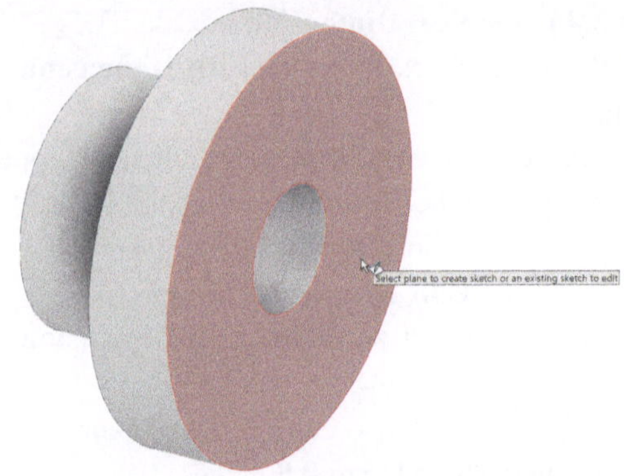

8. Select the origin to define the center point.
9. Move the cursor diagonally toward the right.
10. Enter **4.1** in the horizontal dimension box.
11. Press Tab key and enter **0.472** in the vertical dimension box.

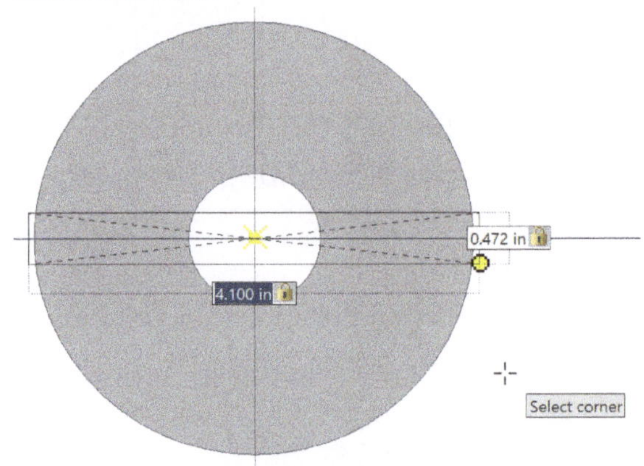

12. Press the Enter key; the **Extrude** Properties panel appears.
13. Expand the **Output** section on the **Extrude** Properties panel by clicking the **Output**.
14. Click the **Cut** icon under the **Output** section on the **Extrude** Properties panel.
15. Enter **0.4** in the **Distance A** box.
16. Click the **Direction** > **Flipped** icon under the **Behavior** section to reverse the direction.
17. Click **OK** to create the cut feature.

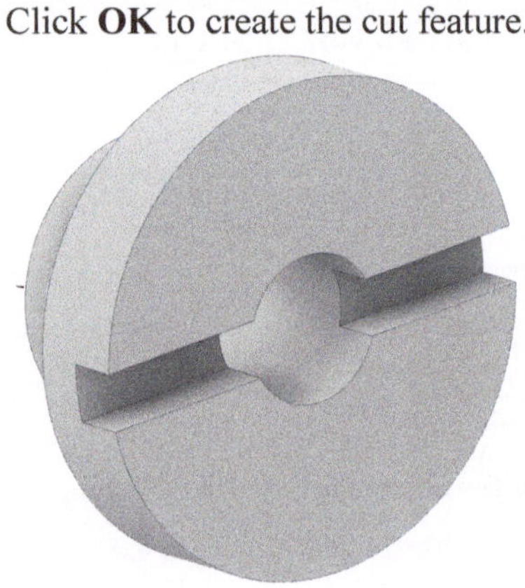

Creating another Cut feature

1. Click the **Home** icon located at the top left corner of the **ViewCube**.

2. Create a sketch on the front face of the base feature.

- On the ribbon, click **3D Model > Sketch > Start 2D Sketch**.
- Select the front face of the model.

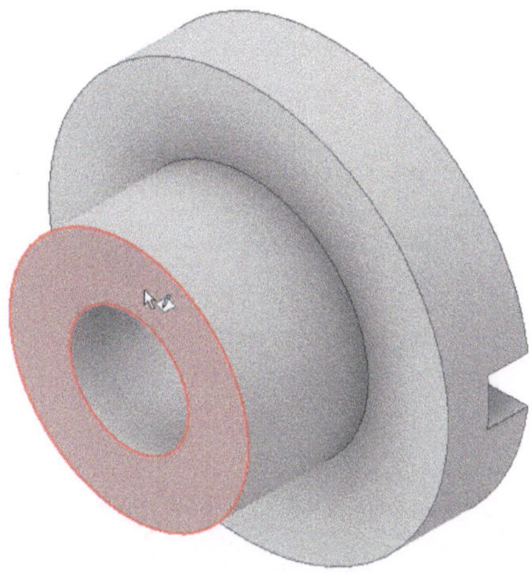

- Draw three lines and the circle, as shown in the figure.

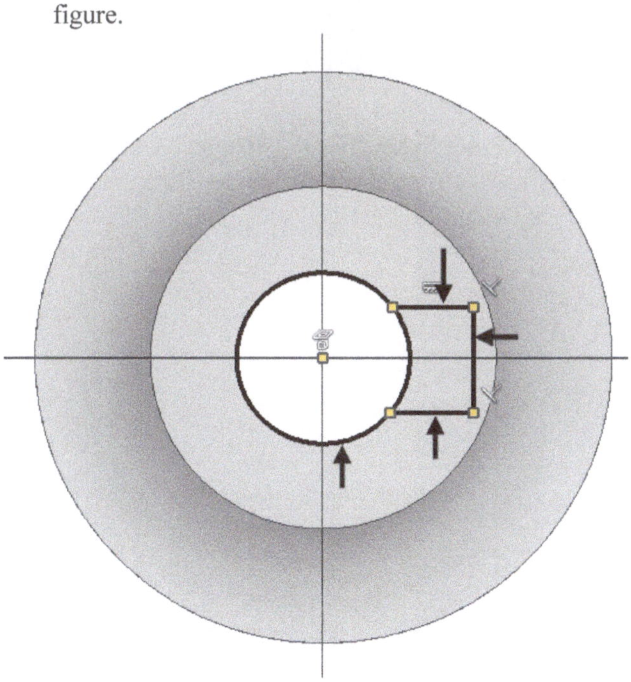

- Apply the **Horizontal** constraint to the horizontal lines, if not applied already.
- Apply the **Equal** constraint between the horizontal lines.
- Ensure that the endpoints of the horizontal line coincide with the circle.
- Apply dimension of **0.236** to the vertical line.
- Apply dimension of **0.118** to the horizontal line.
- Apply the dimension of the **1.2**-inch diameter to the circle.

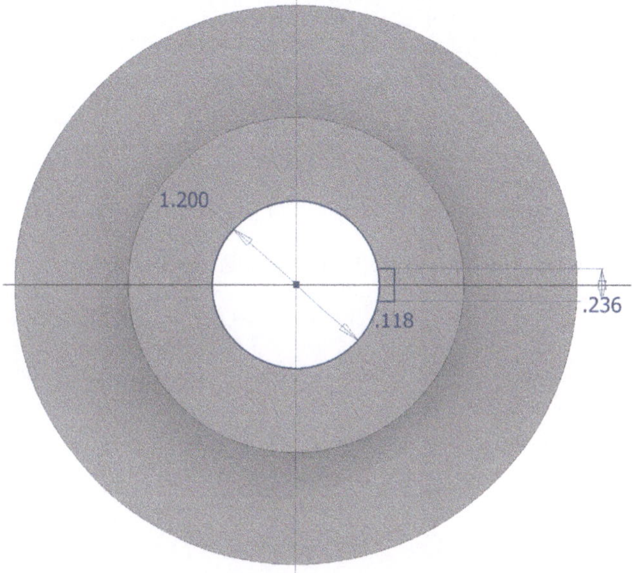

- Select the 1.2-inch diameter dimension and press DELETE
- On the ribbon, click **Sketch > Modify > Trim** .
- Click on the circle to trim it.

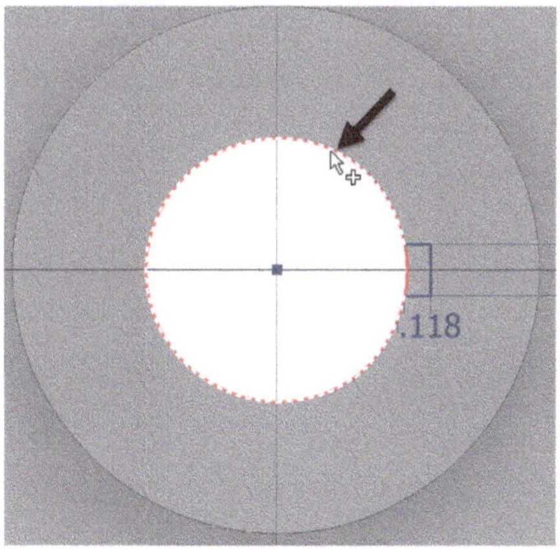

3. Finish the sketch.

4. Click **Extrude** on the **Create** panel of the **3D Model**.
5. Click on the region enclosed by the three lines and the arc.

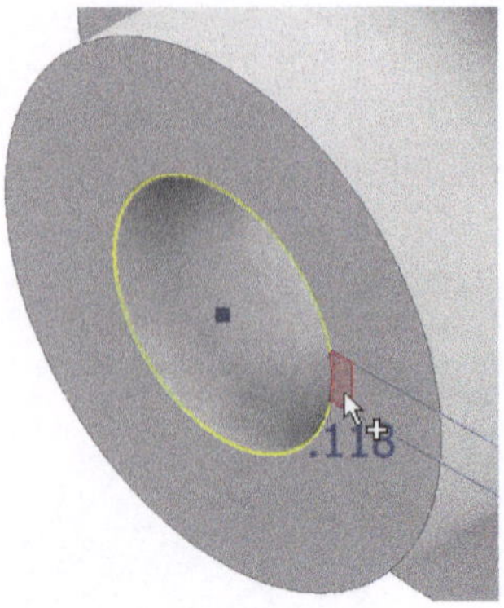

6. Click the **Through All** icon under the **Behavior** section.

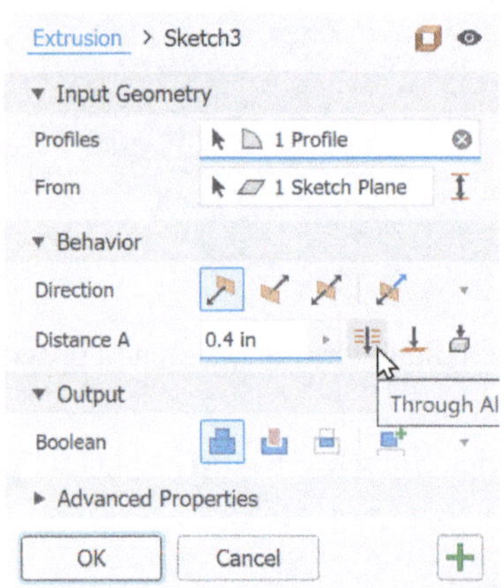

7. Click the **Cut** icon under the **Output** section on the **Extrude** Properties panel.
8. Click **OK** to create the cut feature.

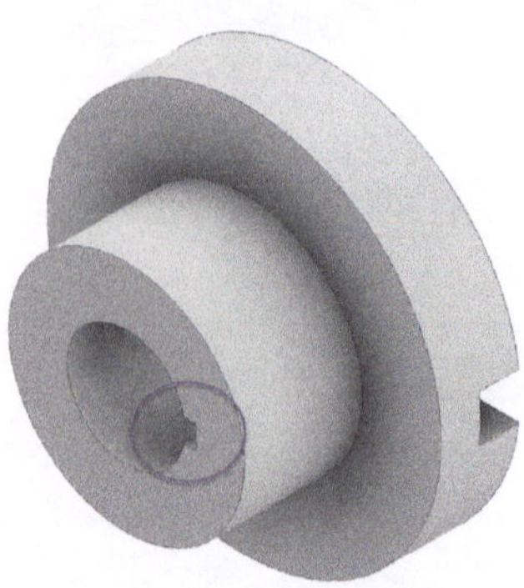

Adding a Fillet

1. On the ribbon, click **3D Model > Modify > Fillet** (or) right-click and select **Fillet** from the Marking Menu.

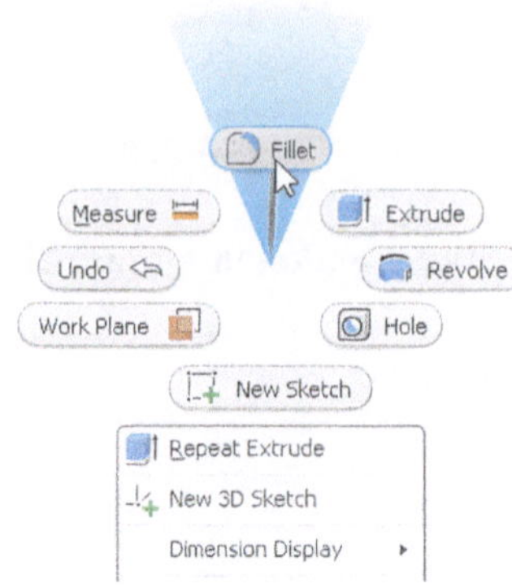

2. Click on the inner circular edge.

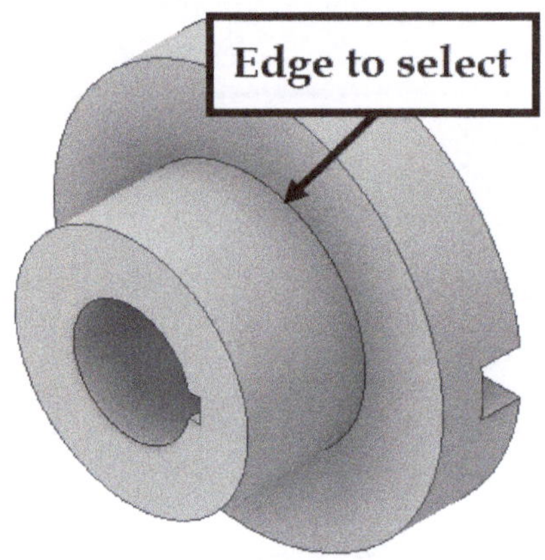

3. On the **Fillet Properties panel**, type **0.2** in the **Radius** box under the **Selection Sets** section.
4. Click **OK** to add the fillet.

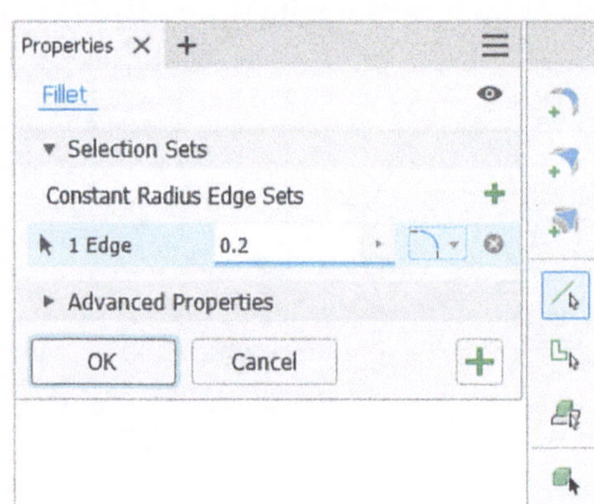

Saving the Part

1. Click **Save** on the **Quick Access Toolbar**.
2. On the **Save As** dialog, type-in **Flange** in the **File name** box.
3. Click **Save** to save the file.
4. Click **File Menu > Close**.

Tutorial 3

In this tutorial, you create the Shaft by performing the following:

- Creating a cylindrical feature
- Creating a cut feature

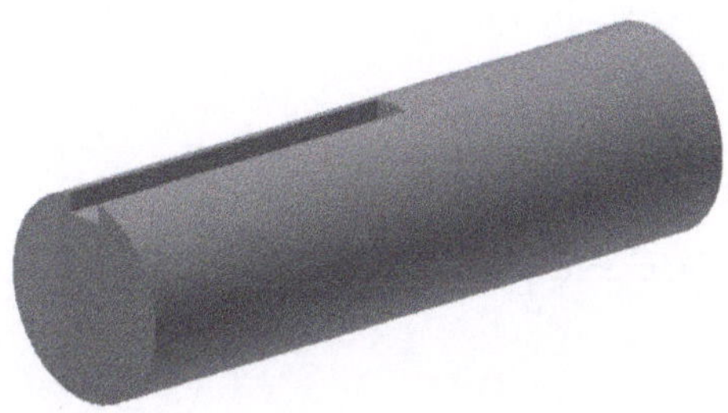

Starting a New Part File

1. On the Quick Access Toolbar, click **New**.
2. On the **Create New File** dialog, select **Standard.ipt**.

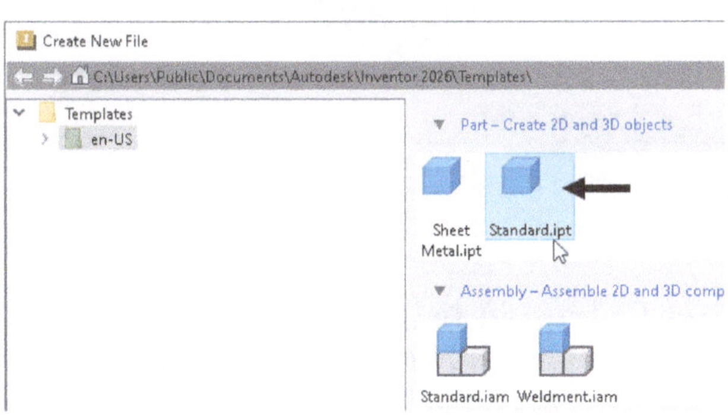

3. Click **Create**.

Creating the Cylindrical Feature

1. On the ribbon, click **Primitives > Primitive** drop-down > **Cylinder**.

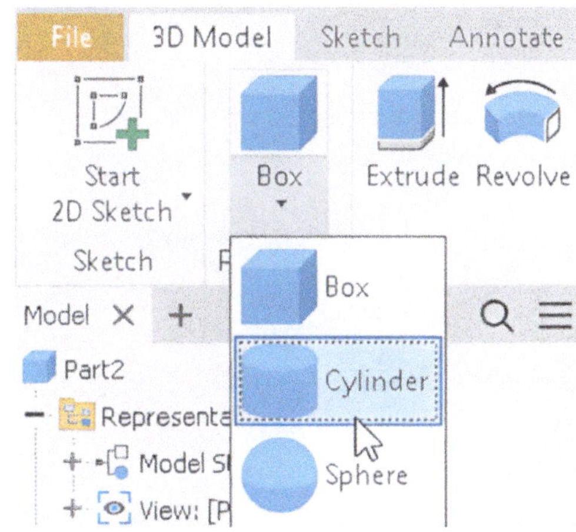

2. Click on the **XY** plane to select it; the sketch starts.
3. Click at the origin and move the cursor outward.
4. Enter **1.2** in the box attached to the circle.

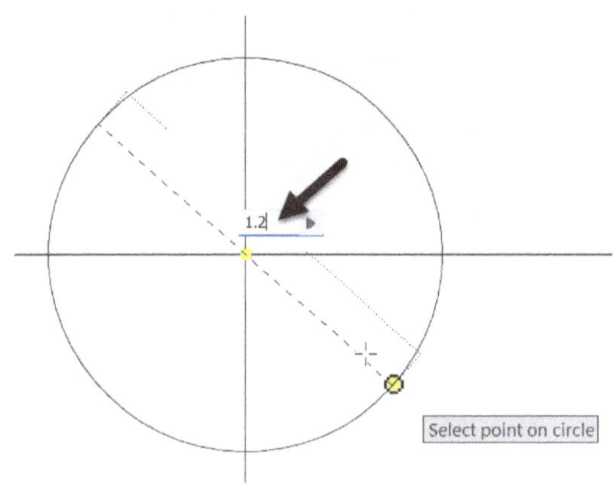

5. Press Enter key; the **Extrude** Properties panel appears.
6. Enter **4** in the **Distance A** box.

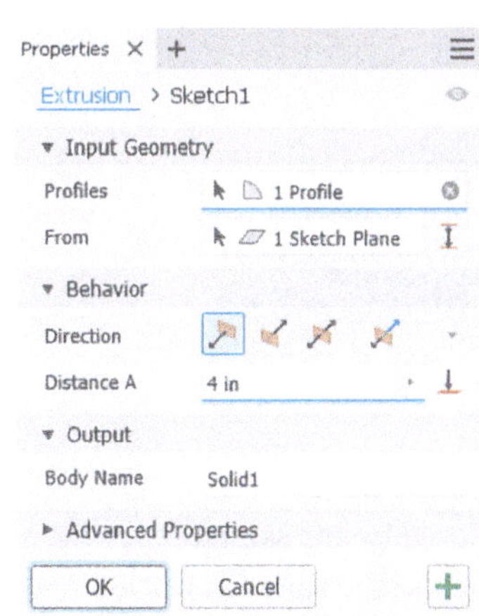

7. Click **OK** to create the cylinder.

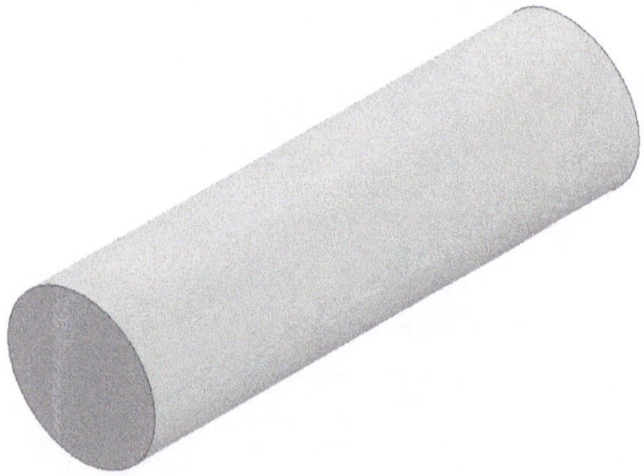

Creating Cut feature

1. Create a sketch on the front face of the base feature.
   - On the ribbon, click **3D Model > Sketch > Start 2D Sketch**.
   - Select the front face of the cylinder.
   - On the ribbon, click **Sketch > Create > Line**.
   - Draw three lines, as shown.

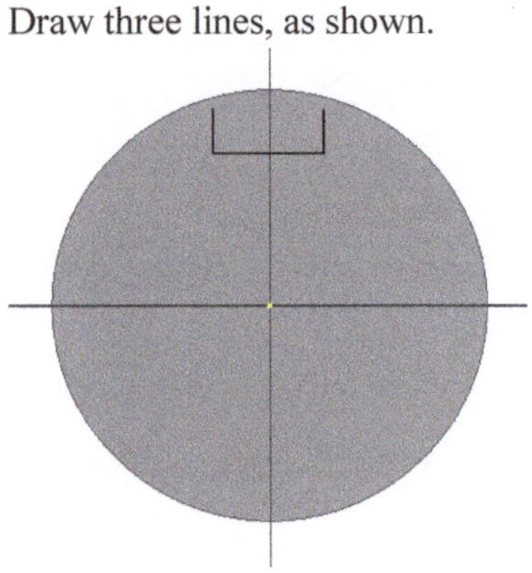

   - Apply the **Coincident** constraint between the endpoints of the vertical lines and the circular edge.
   - Add dimensions to the sketch.

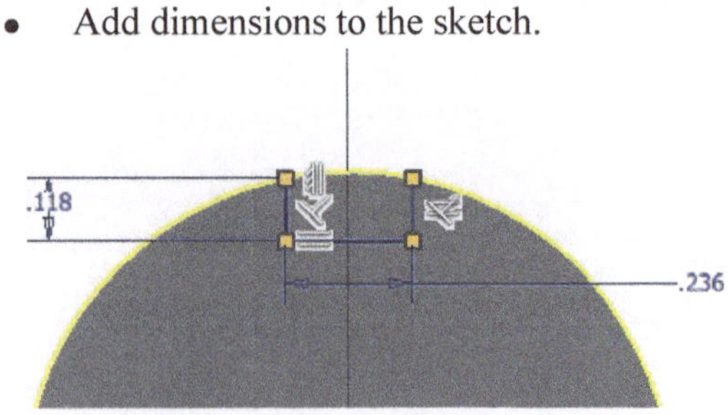

2. Finish the sketch.
3. Click **Extrude** on the **Create** panel.
4. Click on the region enclosed by the sketch.
5. Click the **Cut** icon on the **Extrude** Properties panel.
6. Set **Distance A** to **2.165**.
7. Click **OK** to create the cut feature.

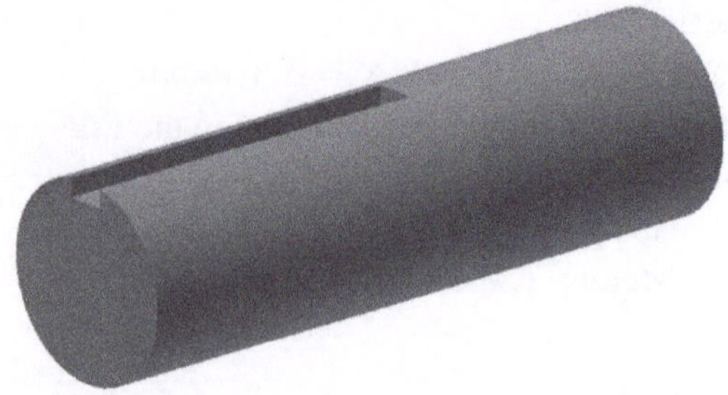

Saving the Part

1. Click **Save** on the **Quick Access Toolbar**; the **Save As** dialog appears.
2. Type-in **Shaft** in the **File name** box.
3. Click **Save** to save the file.
4. Click **File Menu > Close**.

Tutorial 4

In this tutorial, you create a Key by performing the following:

- Creating an Extruded feature
- Applying draft

Start Extruded feature

1. Start a new part file using the **Standard.ipt** template.
2. On the ribbon, **Primitives > Primitive** drop-down > **Box**.
3. Select the XY plane.
4. Create the sketch, as shown in the figure.

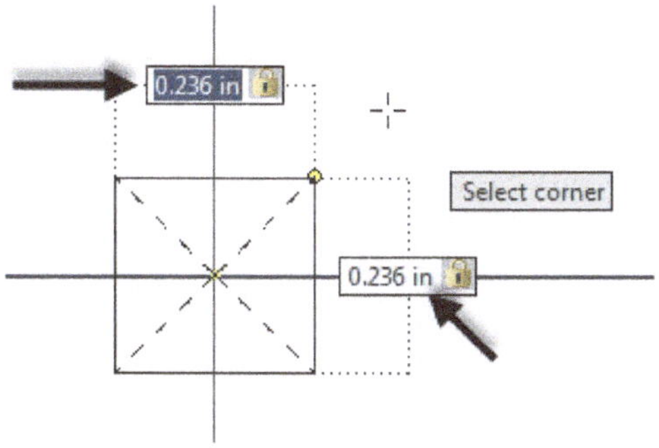

5. Press ENTER.
6. Enter **2** in the **Distance A** box.
7. Click **OK** to create the extrusion.

Applying Draft

1. On the ribbon, click **3D Model > Modify > Draft**.

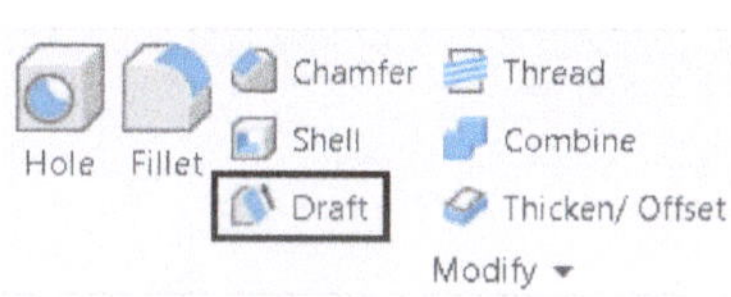

2. Select the **Fixed Plane** option.

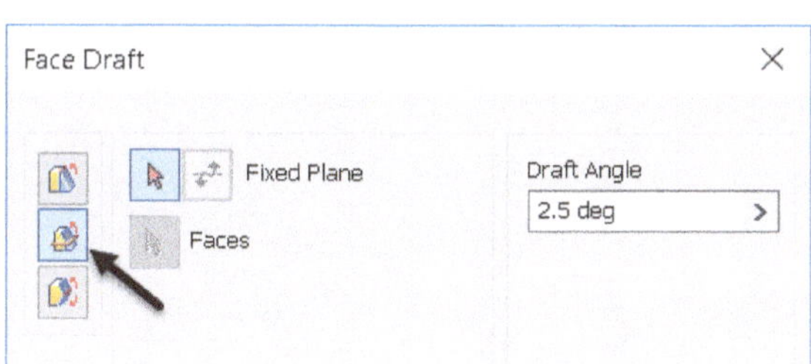

3. Select the front face as the fixed face.

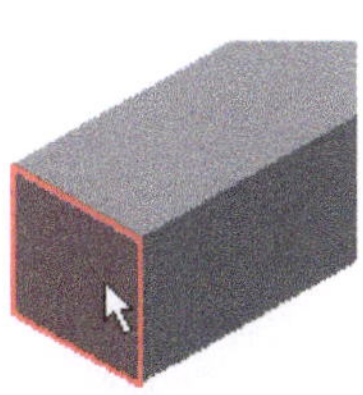

4. Select the top face as the face to be draft.

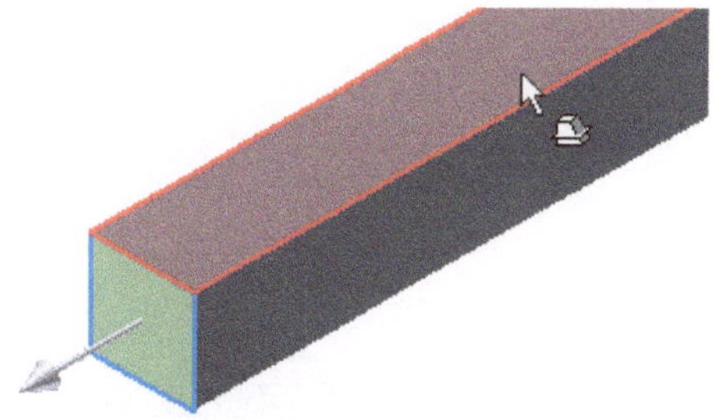

5. Set **Draft Angle** to **1**.
6. Click the **Flip pull direction** button on the **Face Draft** dialog.

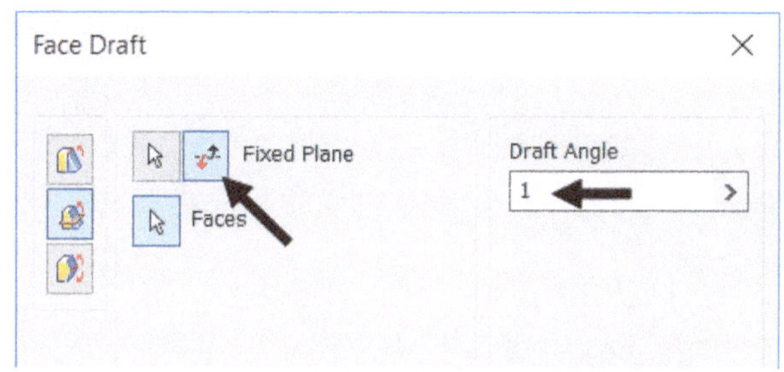

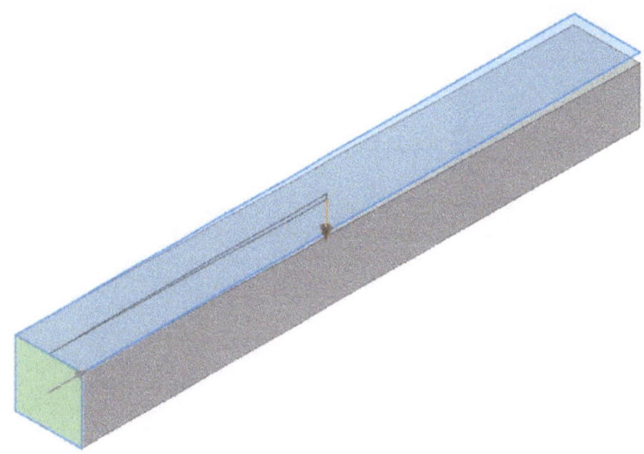

7. Click **OK** to create the draft.

Saving the Part

1. Click **Save** on the **Quick Access Toolbar**; the **Save As** dialog appears.
2. Type-in **Key** in the **File name** box.
3. Click **Save** to save the file.
4. Click **File Menu > Close**.

Chapter 3: Assembly Basics

In this chapter, you will:

- Add Components to assembly
- Apply constraints between components
- Check Degrees of Freedom
- Check Interference
- Create an exploded view of the assembly

Tutorial 1

This tutorial takes you through the creation of your first assembly. You create the Oldham coupling assembly:

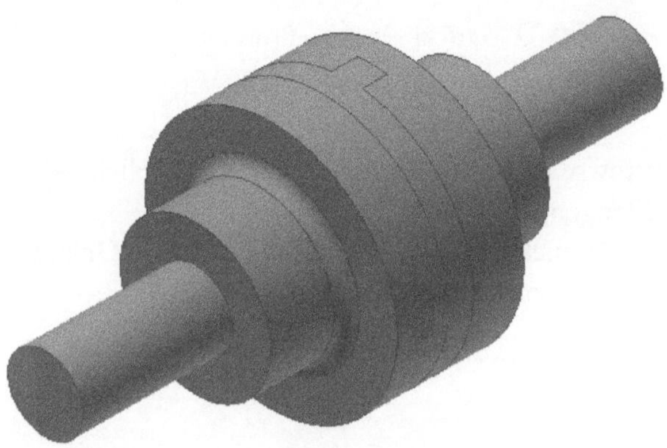

PARTS LIST		
ITEM	PART NUMBER	QTY
1	Disc	1
2	Flange	2
3	Shaft	2
4	Key	2

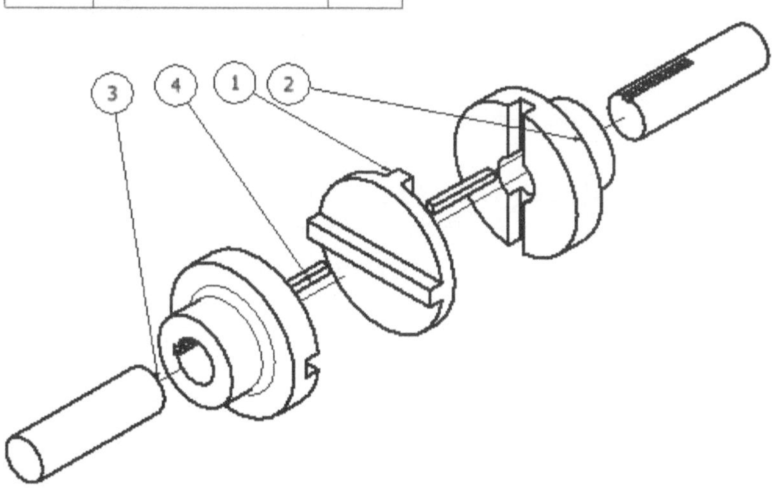

There are two ways of creating an assembly model.

- Top-Down Approach
- Bottom-Up Approach

Top-Down Approach

The assembly file is created first, and components are created in that file.

Bottom-Up Approach

The components are created first and then added to the assembly file. In this tutorial, you will create the assembly using this approach.

Starting a New Assembly File

1. To start a new assembly file, click the **New** drop-down and select **Assembly (.iam)** from the **Home** screen.

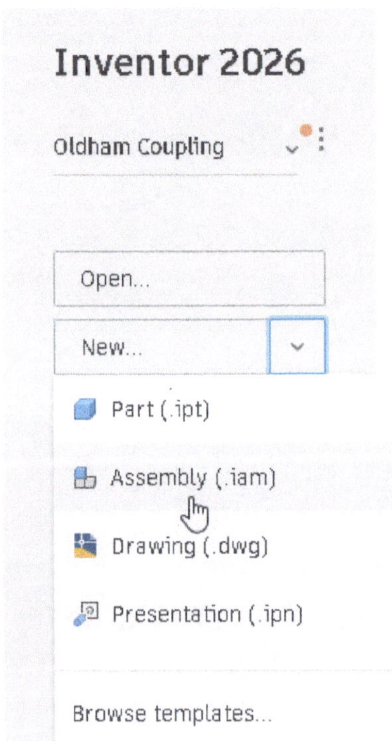

Inserting the Base Component

1. To insert the base component, click **Assemble > Component > Place from Content Center > Place** on the ribbon.

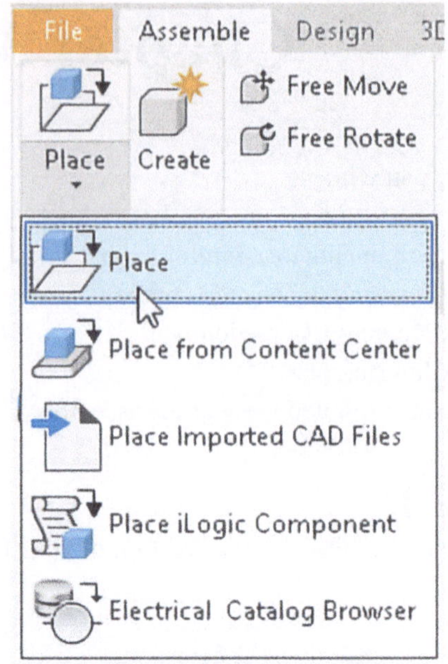

2. Browse to the project folder and double-click on **Flange.ipt**.
3. Right-click and select **Place Grounded at Origin**; the component is placed at the origin.

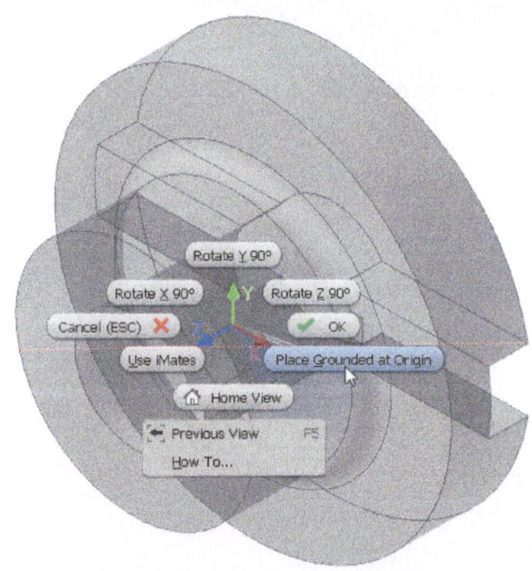

4. Right-click and select **OK**.

Adding the second component

1. To insert the second component, right-click and select **Place Component**; the **Place Component** dialog appears.

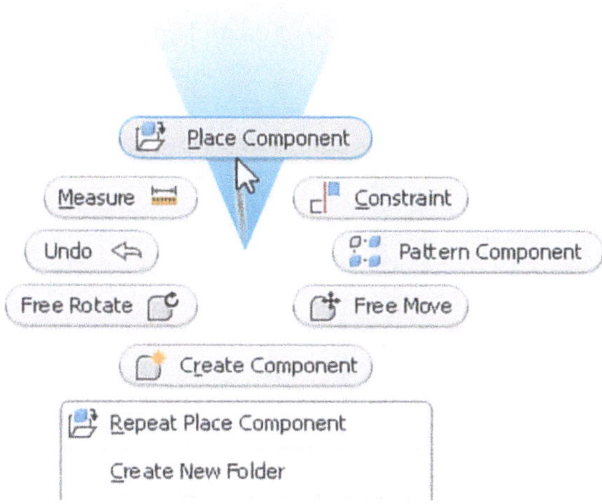

2. Browse to the project folder and double-click on **Shaft.ipt**.
3. Click in the window to place the component.

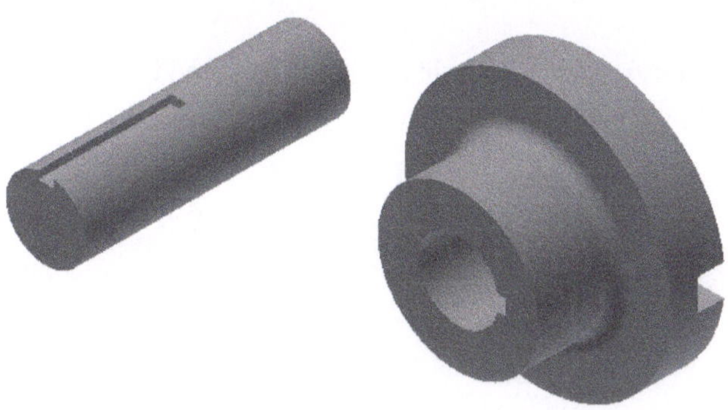

4. Right-click and select **OK**.

Applying Constraints

After adding the components to the assembly environment, you need to apply constraints between them. By applying constraints, you establish relationships between components.

1. To apply constraints, click **Assemble > Relationships > Constrain** on the ribbon.

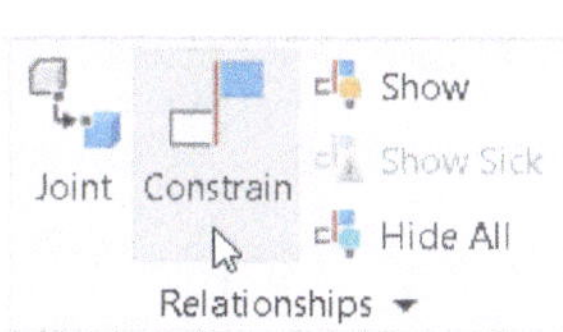

The **Place Constraint** dialog appears on the screen.

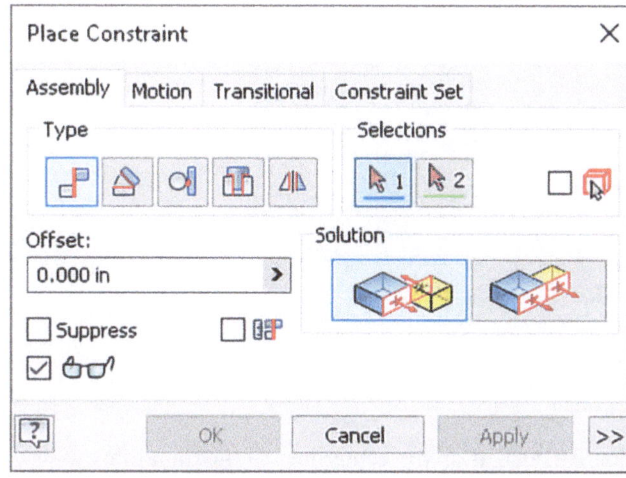

Different assembly constraints that can be applied using this dialog are given next.

Mate: Using this constraint, you can make two planar faces coplanar to each other.

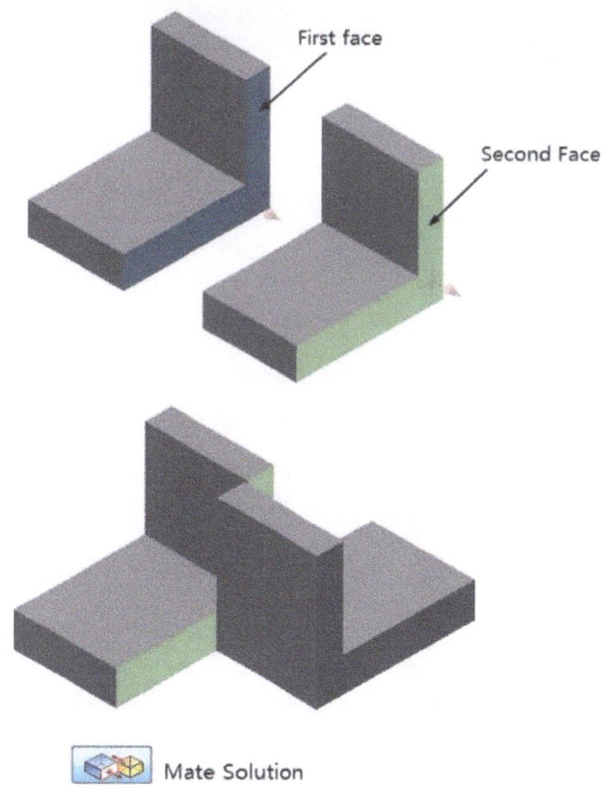

Note that if you set the **Solution** to **Flush**, the faces will point in the same direction.

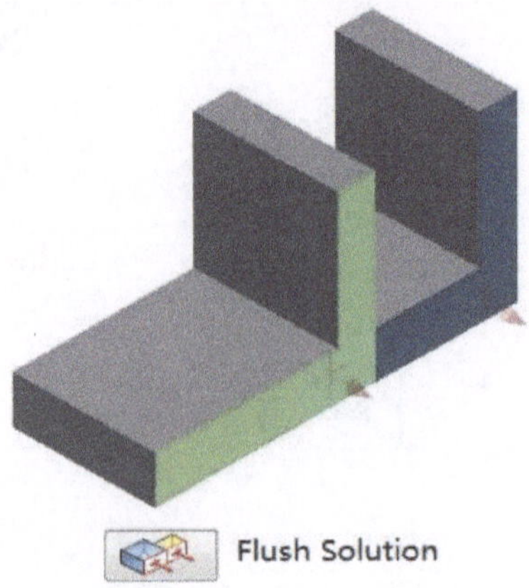

You can also align the centerlines of the round faces. Select the two cylindrical faces to be aligned.

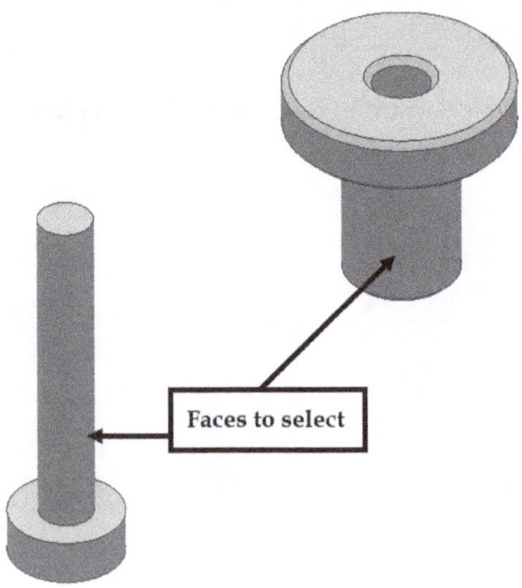

Select **Solution > Opposed**; the axes of the selected round faces will be positioned in the direction opposite to each other.

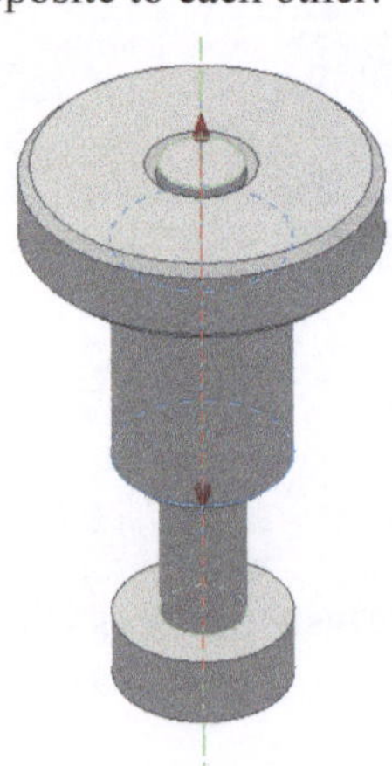

Select **Solution > Aligned**; the axes of the selected round faces will be positioned in the same direction.

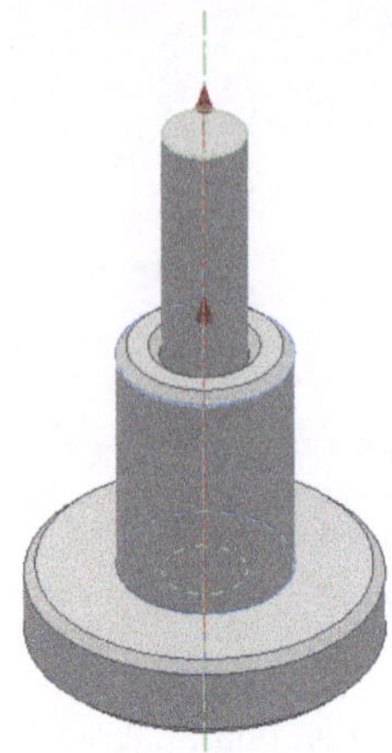

Select **Solution > Undirected** to the position component without specifying the axis direction.

Angle: Applies the angle constraint between two components.

Directed Angle

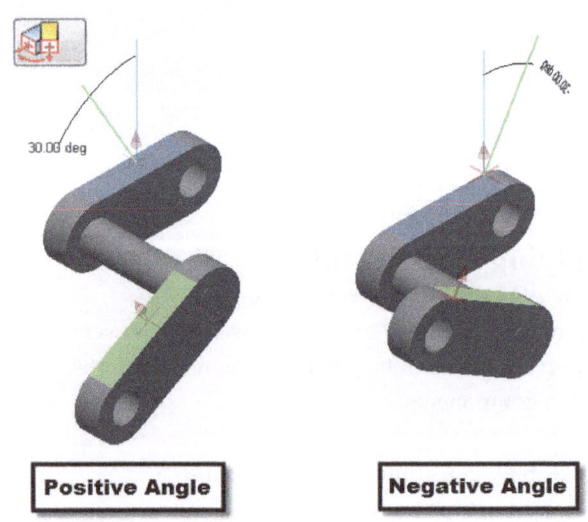

Undirected Angle

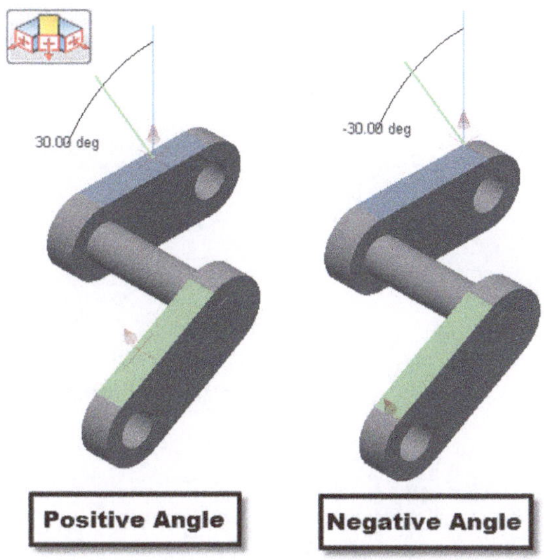

Explicit Reference Vector

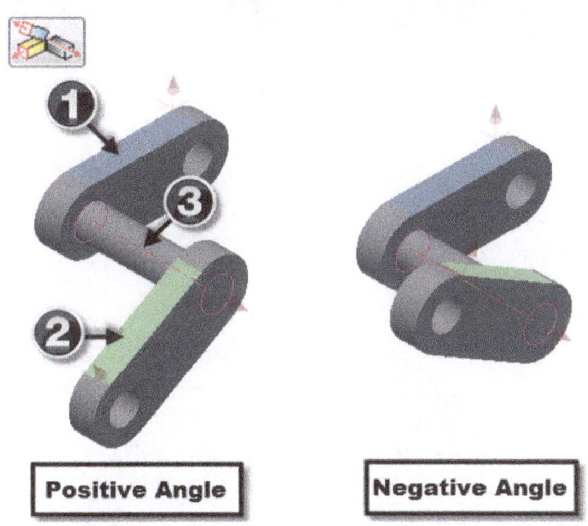

Tangent: This constraint is used to apply a tangent relation between two faces.

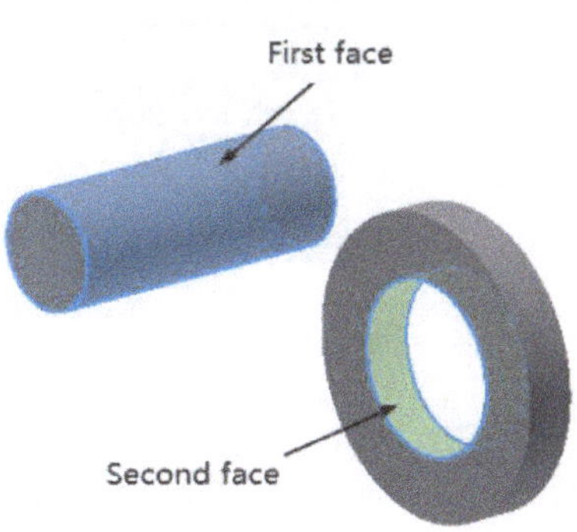

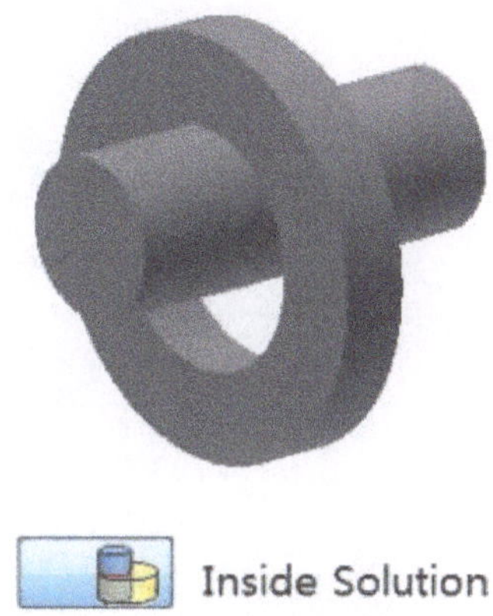

Insert: This constraint is used to make two round faces coaxial. Also, the planar faces of the cylindrical components will be on the same plane. Check the **Lock Rotation** option, if you want to lock the rotation of the component.

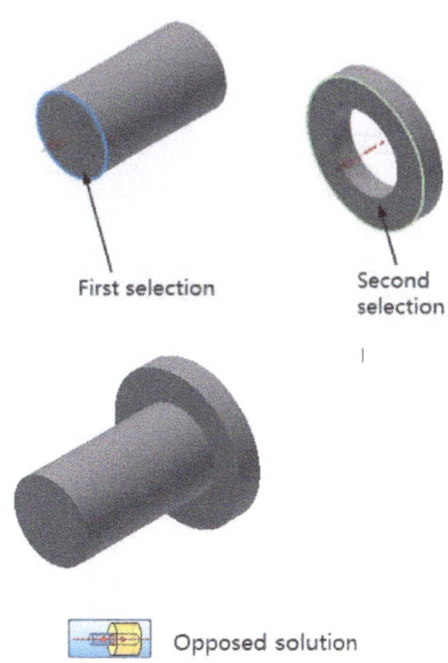

Symmetry: This constraint is used to position the two components symmetrically about a plane.

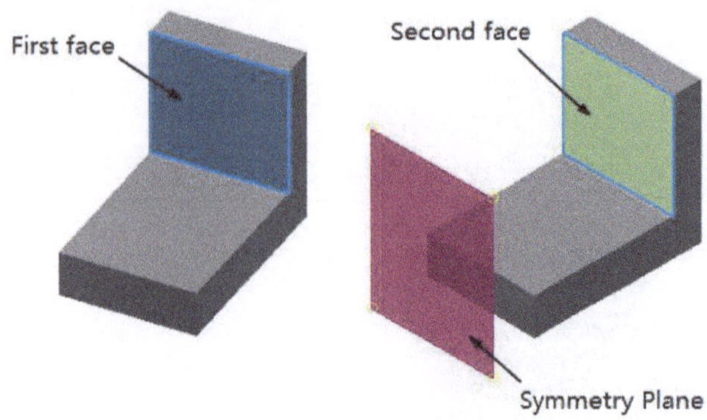

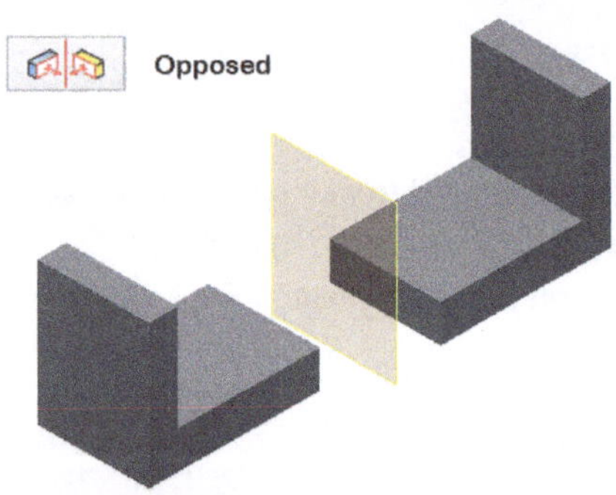

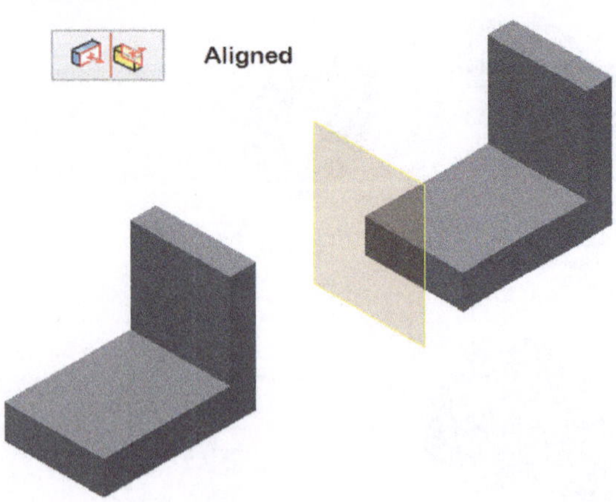

2. On the **Place Constraint** dialog, under the **Type** group, click the **Mate** icon.
3. Click on the round face of the Shaft.

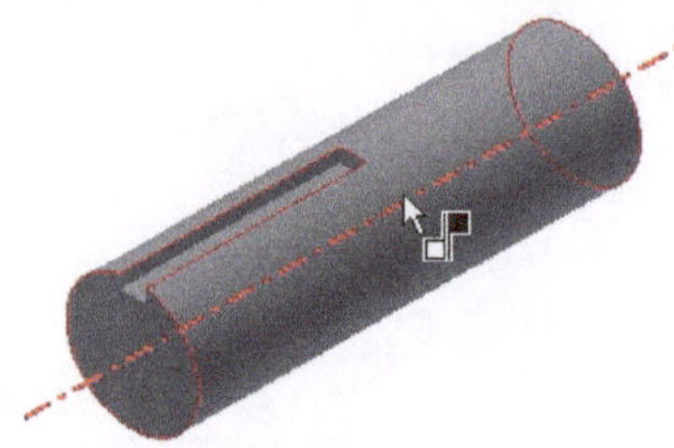

4. Click on the inner cylindrical face of the **Flange**.

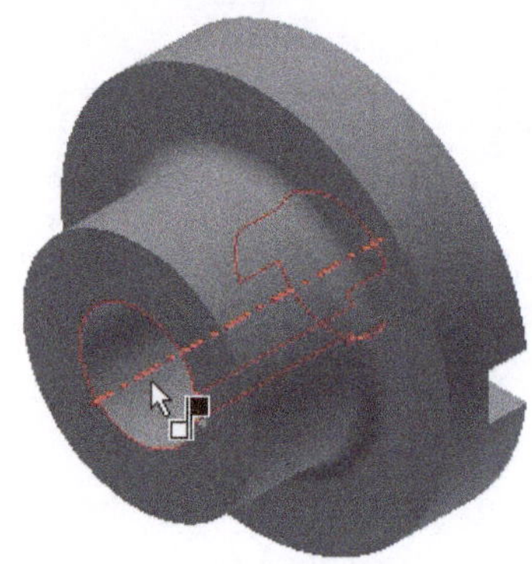

5. Click the **Aligned** icon on the **Place Constraint** dialog.

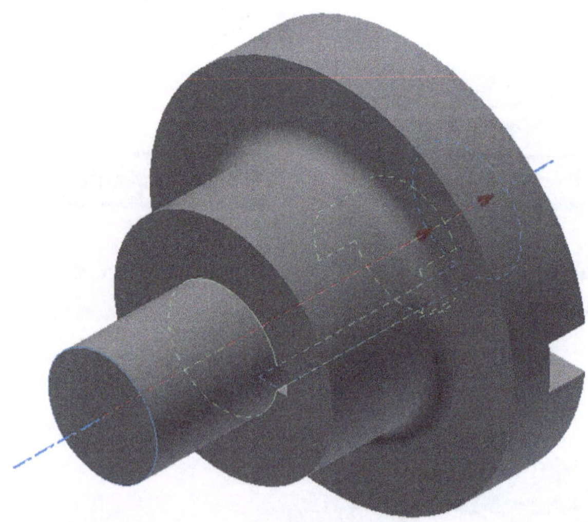

6. Click the **Apply** button.
7. Ensure that the **Mate** icon is selected in the **Type** group.

8. Click the **Free Orbit** icon on the Navigation Bar.

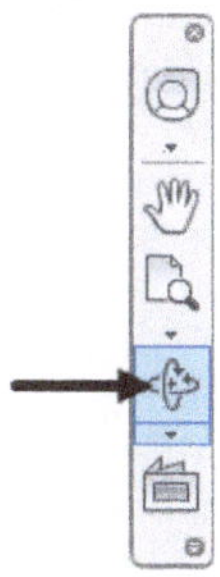

9. Move the pointer and place it on the model.
10. Click and drag the left mouse button toward left; the model is rotated such that the backside is displayed.
11. Right click and select **OK**.
12. Click the **Flush** button on the **Place Constraint** dialog.

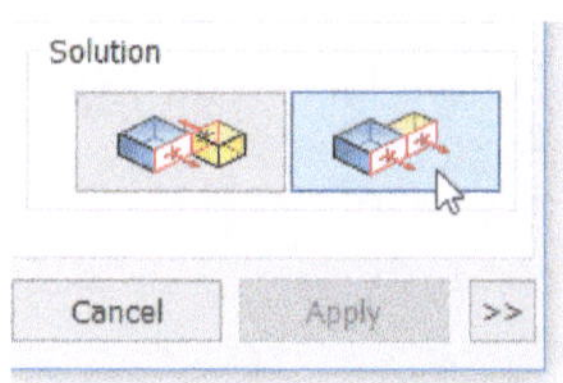

13. Click on the front face of the shaft.
14. Click on the slot face of the flange, as shown in the figure.

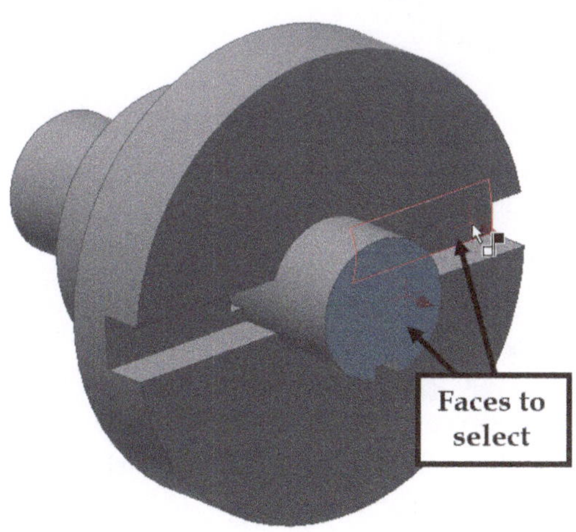

15. Click **Apply**. The front face of the Shaft and the slot face of the Flange are aligned.
16. Right click in the graphics window and select **Home View**.

17. Ensure that the **Mate** button is selected in the **Type** group.
18. Expand **Flange: 1** in the Browser window.
19. Select the **XZ Plane** of the Flange.

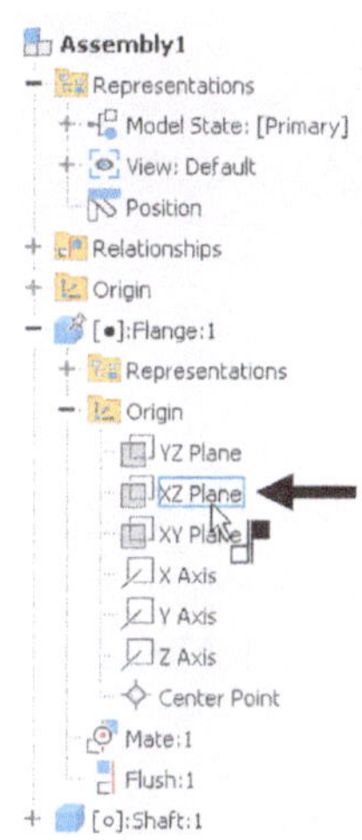

20. Expand **Shaft: 1** and select the **YZ Plane** of the Shaft.

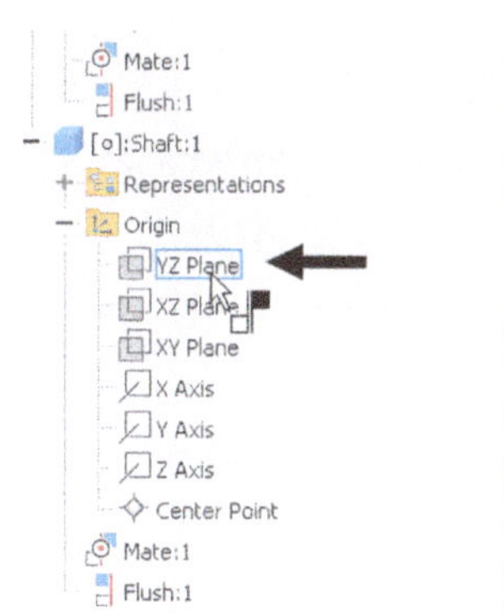

21. Click the **Flush** button on the **Place Constraint** dialog.

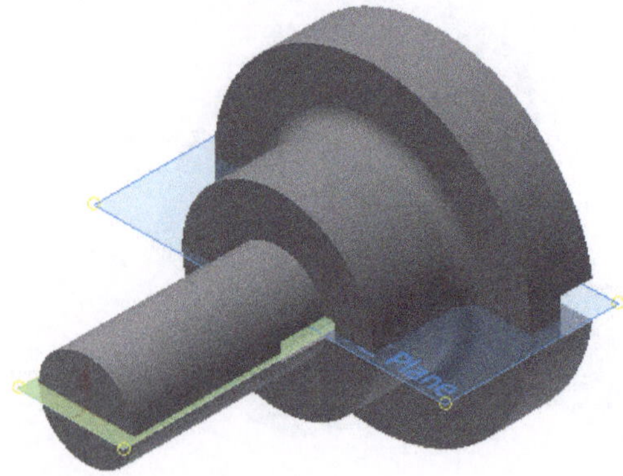

22. Click **OK** to assemble the components.

Adding the Third Component

1. To insert the third component, click **Assemble > Component** > **Place** on the ribbon.
2. Go to the project folder and double-click on **Key.ipt**.
3. Click in the graphics window to place the key.
4. Right-click and click **OK**.
5. Right-click on **Flange: 1** in the Browser window.
6. Click **Visibility** on the shortcut menu; the Flange is hidden.
7. Click **Constrain** on the **Relationships** panel.
8. Click **Mate** on the **Place Constraint** dialog.
9. Select **Mate** from the **Solution** group.

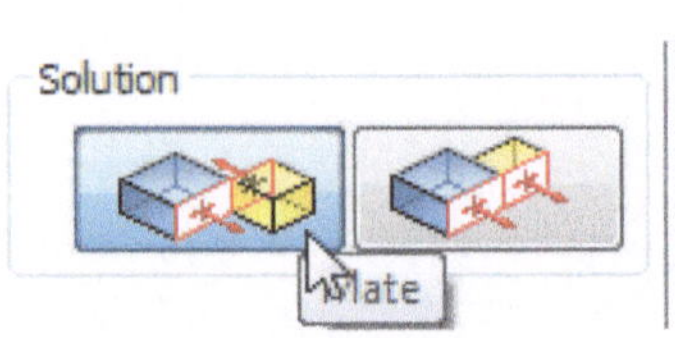

10. Click the right mouse button on the side face of the key and click **Select Other** on the shortcut menu.
11. Select the bottom face of the Key from the flyout.

12. Select the flat face of the slot.

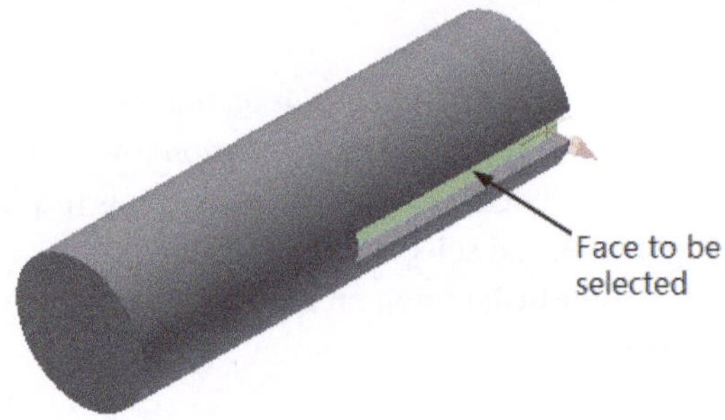

13. Click the **Apply** button. The bottom face of the key is aligned with the flat face of the slot.

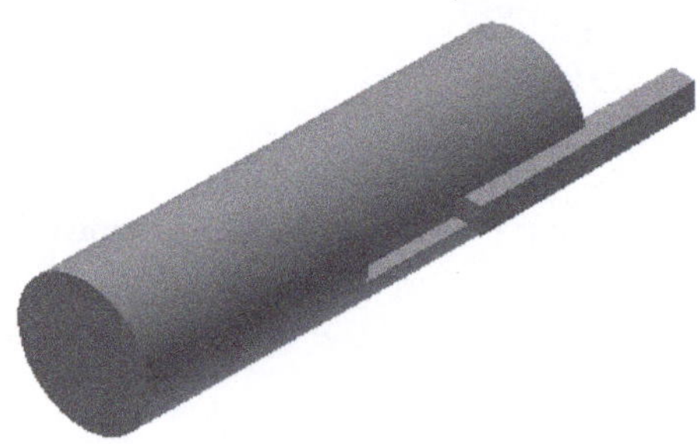

14. Click the **Mate** icon on the **Place Constraint** dialog.
15. Select **Flush** from the **Solution** group.

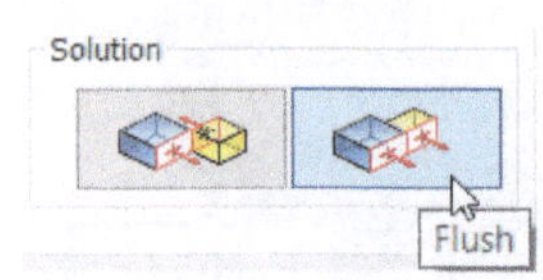

16. Select the front face of the Key and back face of the Shaft, as shown.

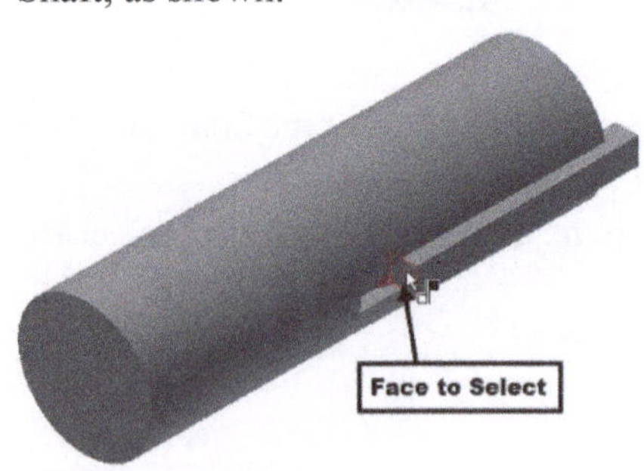

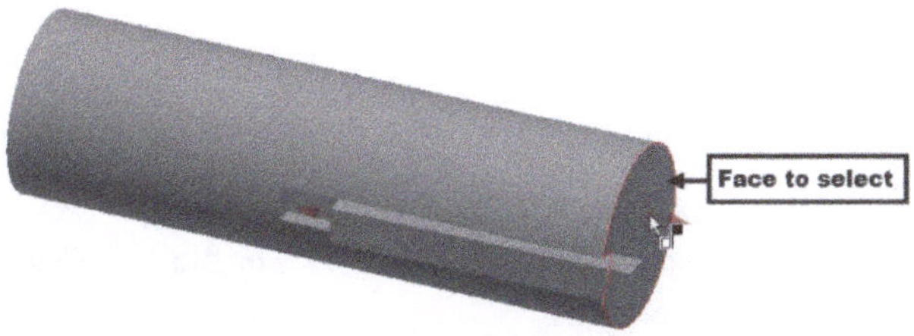

17. Click **Apply** on the dialog; the mate is applied.
18. Close the dialog.

Now, you need to check whether the parts are fully constrained or not.

19. Click **View > Visibility > Degrees of Freedom** on the ribbon.

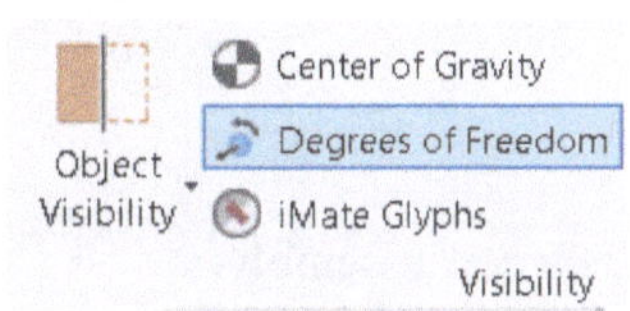

You will notice that an arrow appears pointing in the upward (or downward) direction. This means that the Key is not constrained in the Z-direction.

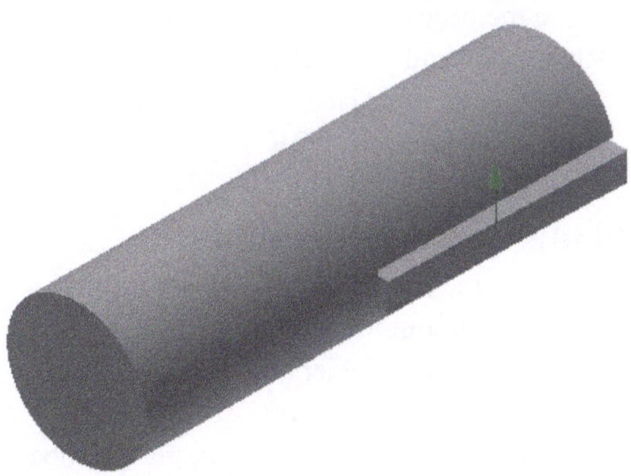

You must apply one more constraint to constrain the key.

20. Click **Constrain**  on the **Relationships** panel of the **Assemble** ribbon tab.
21. Click the **Mate** 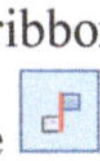 icon on the dialog.
22. Select **Flush** from the **Solution** group.
23. Expand the **Origin** node of the **Assembly** in the **Browser window** and select **XZ Plane**.

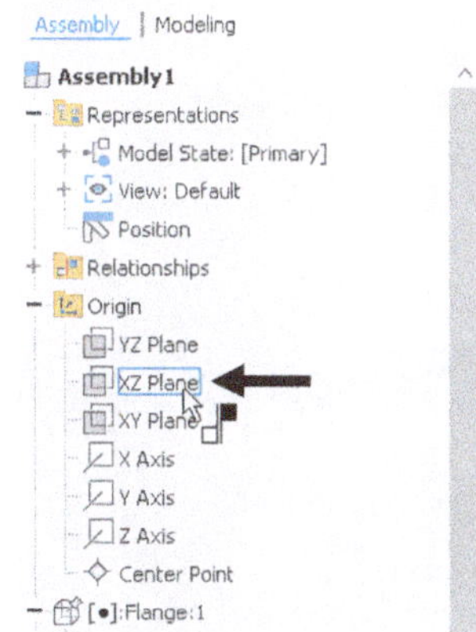

24. Expand the **Key: 1** node in the **Browser window** and select **YZ Plane**.

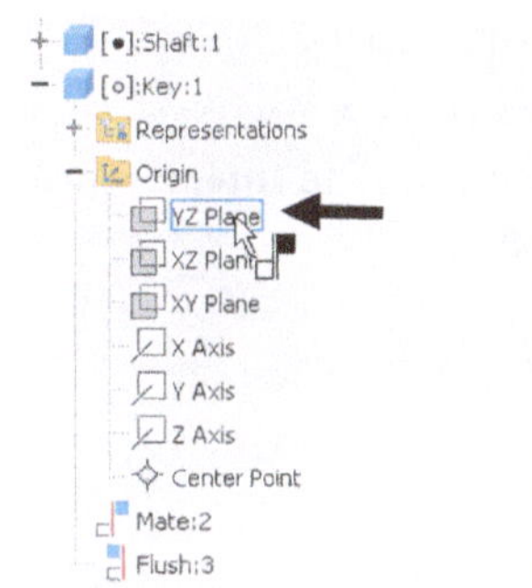

25. Click **OK**. The mate is applied between the two planes.

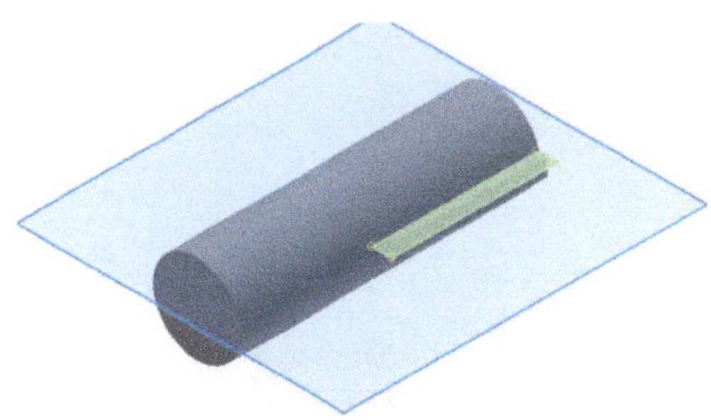

Now, you need to turn on the display of the Flange.

26. Right-click on the **Flange** in the **Browser window** and select **Visibility**; the **Flange** appears.

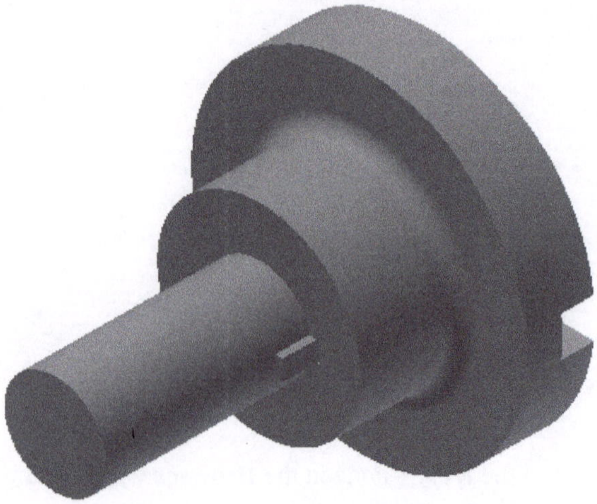

Checking the Interference

1. Click **Inspect > Interference > Analyze Interference** on the Ribbon. The **Interference Analysis** dialog appears.

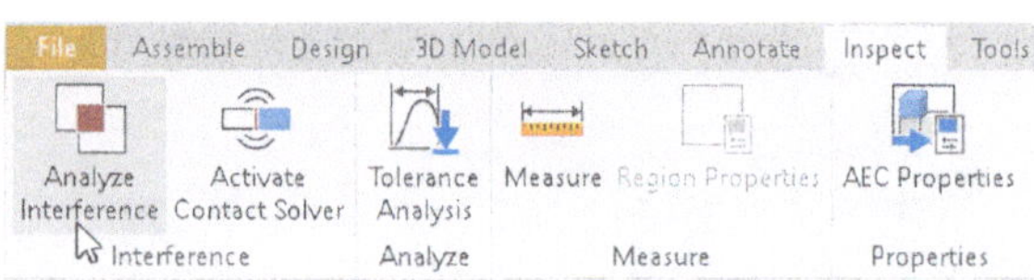

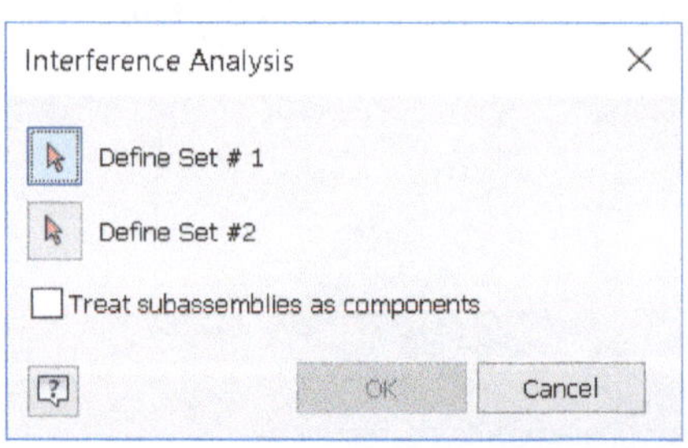

2. Select the Flange and Shaft as **Set #1**.
3. Click the **Define Set #2** button.
4. Select the Key as **Set # 2**.

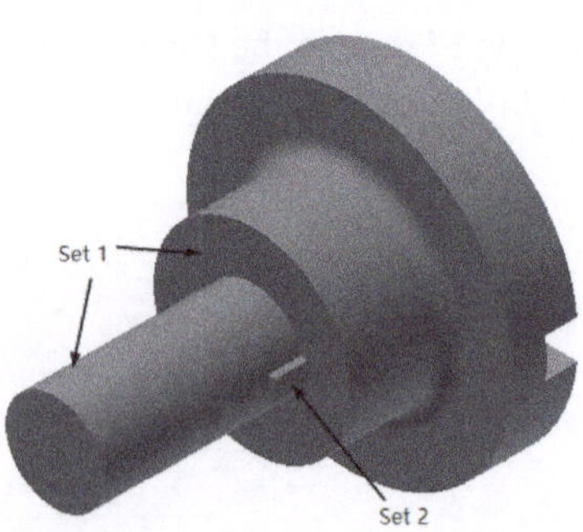

5. Click **OK**; the message box appears showing that there are no interferences.
6. Click **OK**.

Saving the Assembly

1. Click **Save** on the **Quick Access Toolbar**; the **Save As** dialog appears.
2. Type-in **Flange_subassembly** in the **File name box.**
3. Go to the project folder.
4. Click **Save** to save the file.
5. Click **File Menu > Close**.

Starting the Main assembly

1. On the ribbon, click **Get Started > Launch > New**.
2. On the **Create New File** dialog, click the **Standard.iam** icon.

3. Click **Create** to start a new assembly.

Adding Disc to the Assembly

1. Click **Assemble > Component > Place** 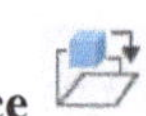 on the ribbon.
2. Go to the project folder and double-click on **Disc.ipt**.
3. Right-click and select **Place Grounded at Origin**; the component is placed at the origin.
4. Right-click and select **OK**.

Placing the Sub-assembly

1. To insert the sub-assembly, click the **Place**  button on the **Component** panel of the ribbon.
2. Go to the project folder and double-click on **Flange_subassembly.iam**.
3. Click in the window to place the flange subassembly.
4. Right-click and click **OK**.

Adding Constraints

1. Click **Constrain** 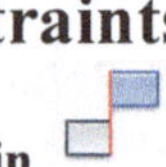 on the **Relationships** panel of the **Assemble** ribbon.
2. Click the **Insert** button on the **Place Constraint** dialog.

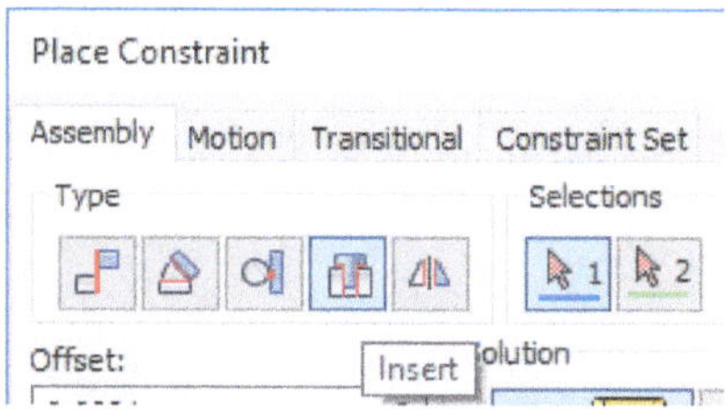

3. Select **Opposed** from the **Solution** group.

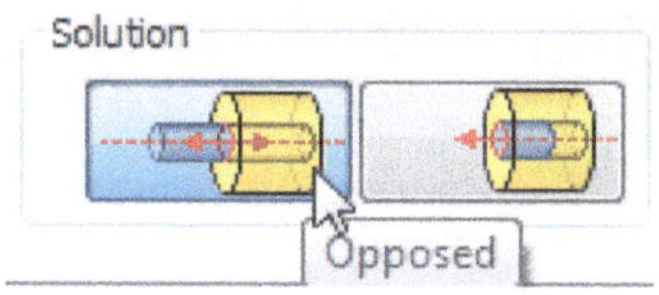

4. Click on the circular edge of the Flange.

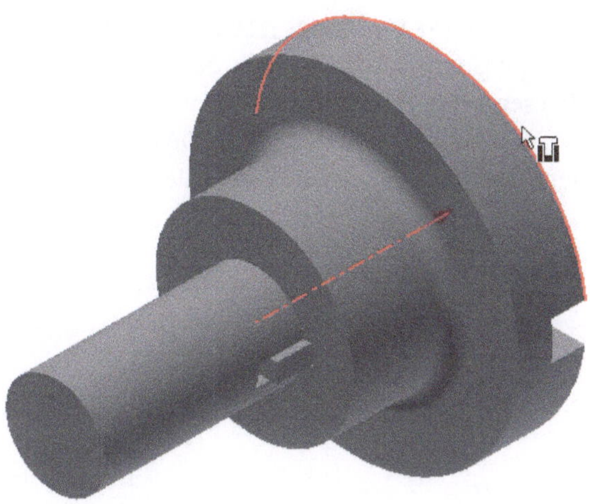

5. Click on the circular edge of the Disc.

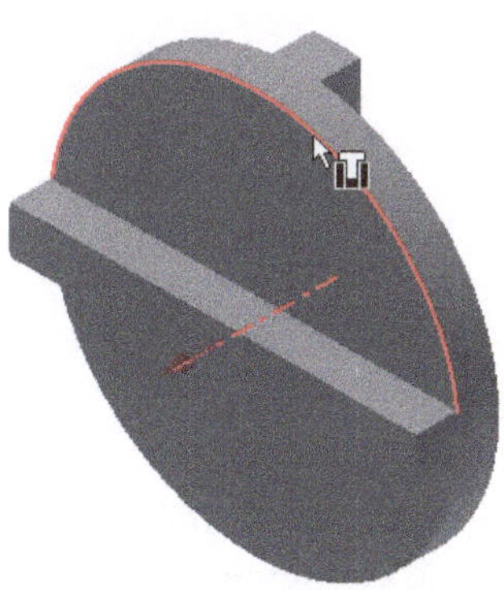

6. Click **OK** on the dialog.

Next, you have to move the subassembly away from the Disc to apply other constraints.

7. Click **Free Move** on the **Position** panel.

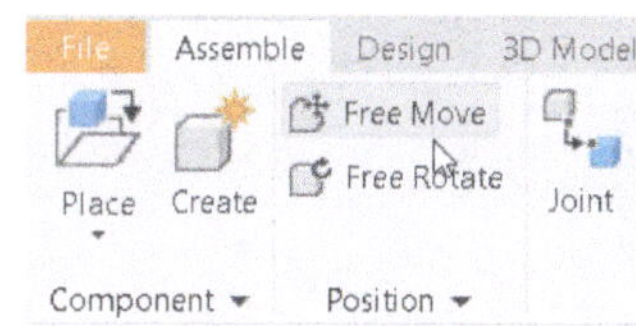

8. Select the flange subassembly and move it.

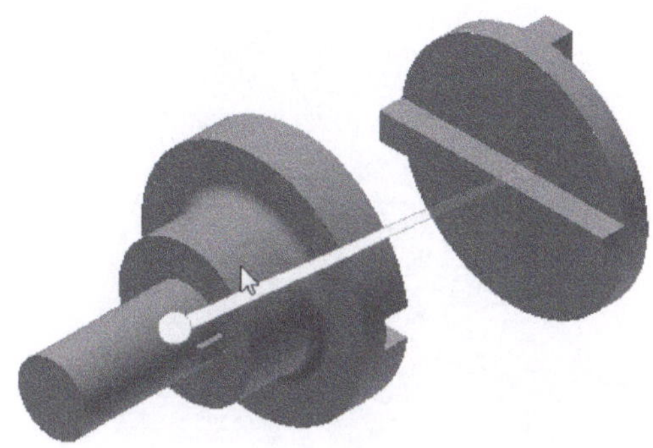

9. Click the **Constrain** button on the **Relationships** panel.
10. Click **Mate** on the **Place Constraints** dialog.
11. Select **Mate** from the **Solution** group.
12. Click the **View > Navigate > Orbit** on the ribbon.
13. Press and hold the left mouse button and drag the cursor toward left.
14. Release the mouse button, right click, and select **OK**.
15. Click on the face on the Flange, as shown in the figure.

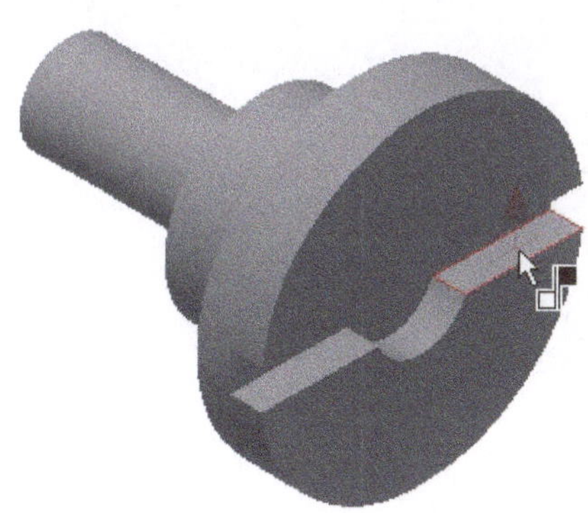

16. Click on the face on the Disc, as shown in the figure.

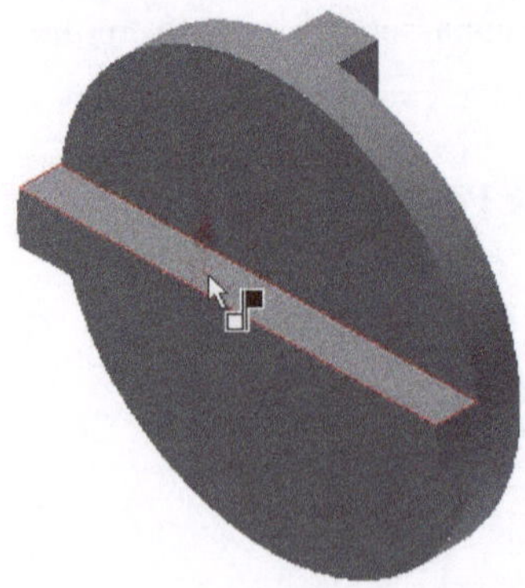

17. Click **OK** on the dialog.

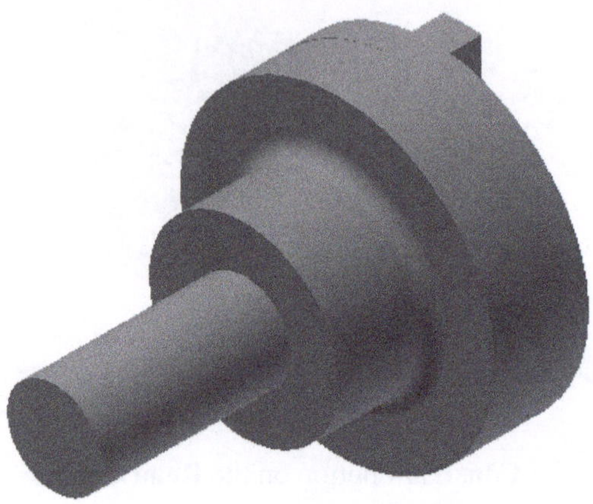

Placing the second instance of the Sub-assembly

1. Insert another instance of the Flange subassembly.
2. Apply the **Insert** and **Mate** constraints.

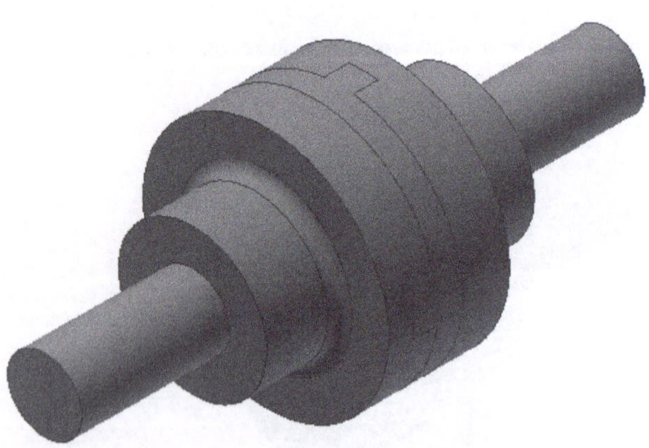

Saving the Assembly

1. Click **Save** on the **Quick Access Toolbar**; the **Save As** dialog appears.
2. Type-in **Oldham coupling** in the **File name box.**
3. Click **Save** to save the file.
4. Click **File Menu > Close**.

Tutorial 2

In this tutorial, you create the exploded view of the assembly:

Starting a New Presentation File

1. On the Home screen, click the **New** drop-down > **Presentation (ipn)** (or) click **New** on the Quick Access Toolbar, and then select the Standard.ipn template from the **Create New File** dialog.

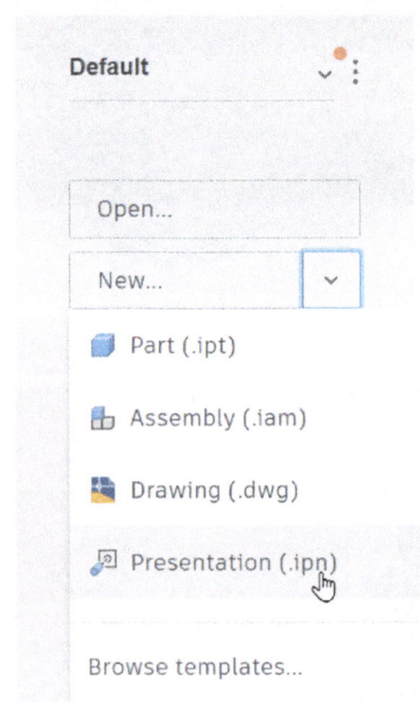

The Insert dialog appears.

2. On the **Insert** dialog, go to the project folder and double-click on the **Oldham Coupling.iam** file.

The Presentation Environment appears, as shown.

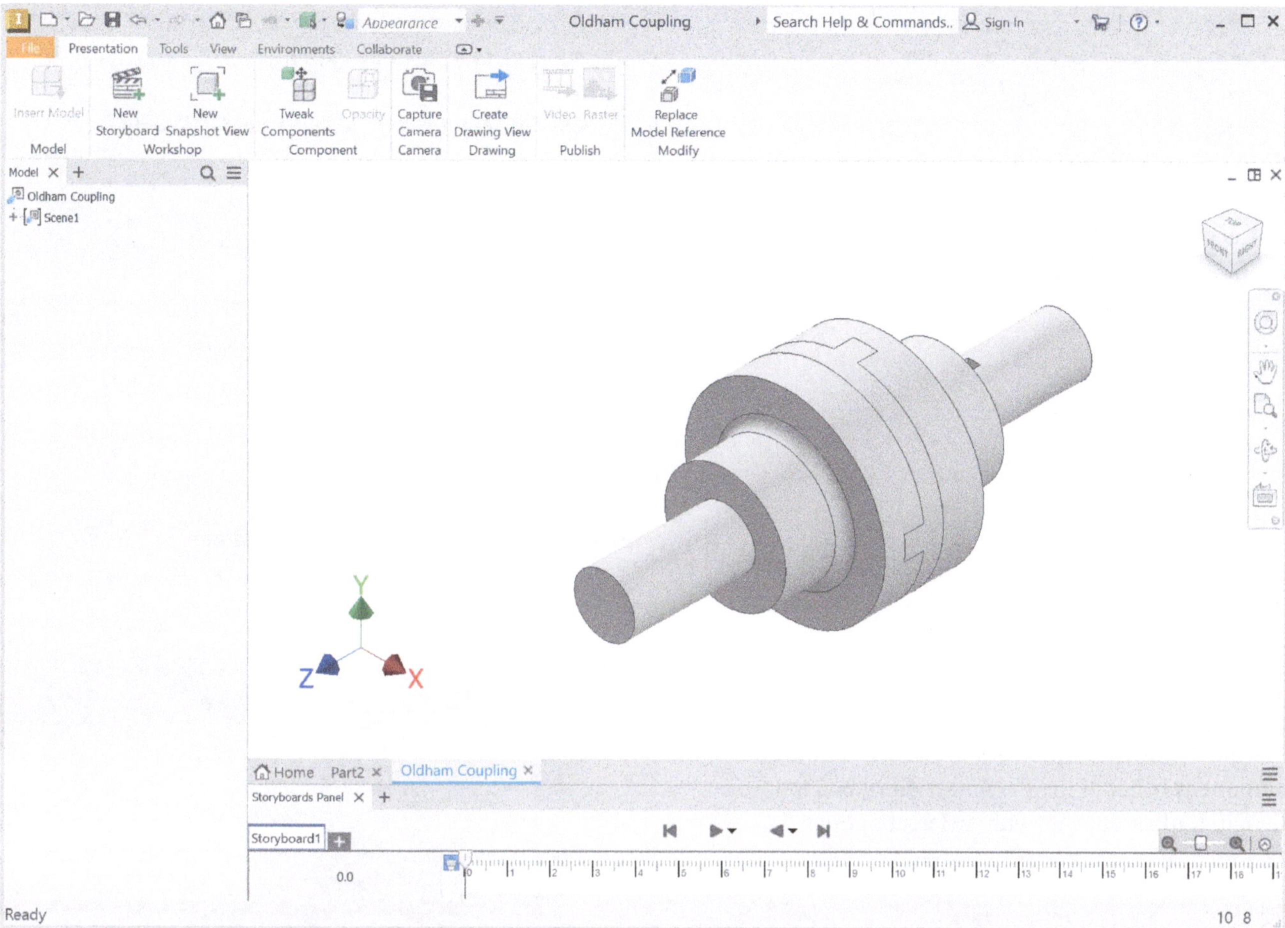

Creating a Storyboard Animation

1. In the **Model** tree, double-click on **Scene1** and type **Explosion**.

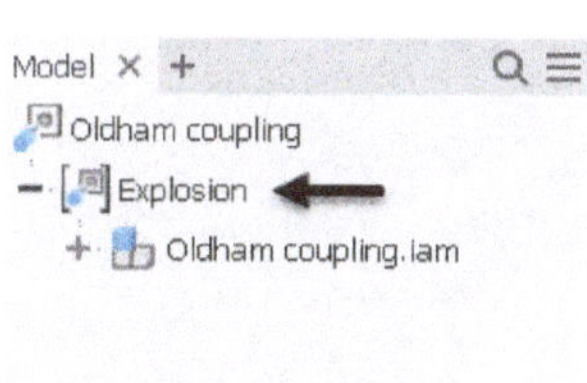

Before creating an exploded view, you need to take a look at the **Storyboard** displayed at the bottom of the window. The **Storyboard** has the **Scratch Zone** located on the left side of the timeline. Also, notice that the play marker is displayed at 0 seconds in the timeline.

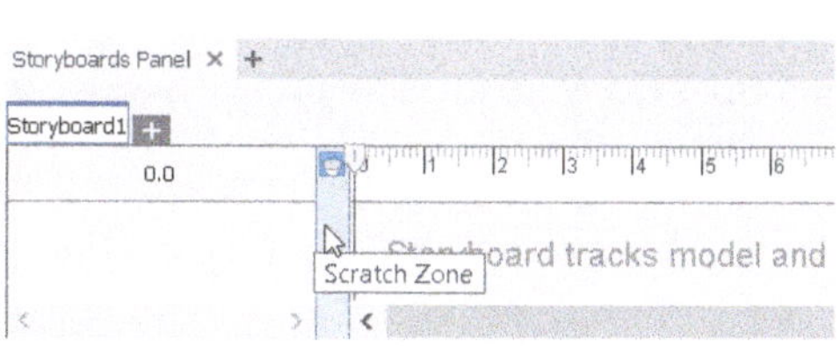

2. Click in the **Scratch Zone** area and notice that the play marker is displayed inside it.

   Now, the changes made to the assembly in the Scratch Zone will be the starting point of the exploded animation. You can change the orientation of the assembly, hide a component, or change the opacity of the component. Use the **Capture Camera**  tool on the **Camera** panel to set the camera position for the animation.

3. On the ribbon, click **View** tab > **Windows** panel > **User Interface** drop-down, and then check the **Mini toolbar** option. The Mini toolbar appears whenever you activate a tool.

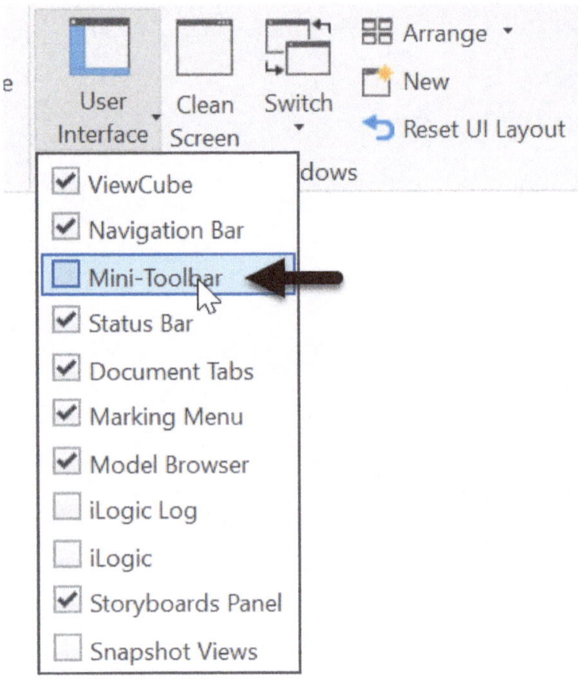

4. Click the **Tweak Components**  button on the **Component** panel of the **Presentation** ribbon tab. The mini toolbar appears with different options, as shown.

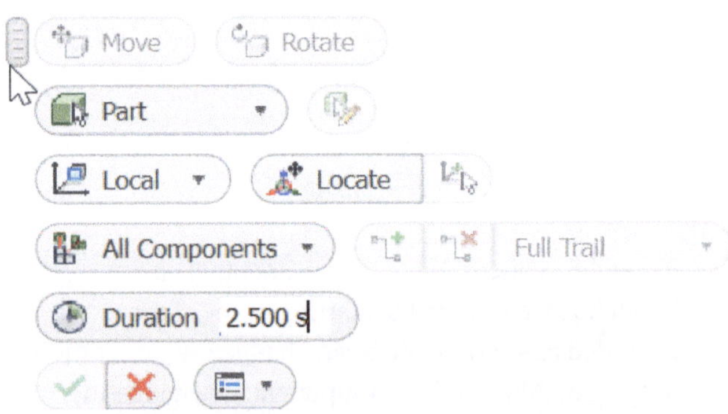

Notice that the default duration for a tweak is 2.500 s. You can type a new value in the **Duration** box available on the Mini toolbar.

5. Select **Component** from the **Selection Filter** drop-down of the Mini toolbar.
6. Select the **All Components** from the Tracelines drop-down. This will create trace lines of all exploded components.
7. Select the Flange subassembly from the graphics window. The manipulator appears on the assembly.

Now, you must specify the direction along which the sub-assembly will be exploded.

8. On the Mini toolbar, select **Local > World**.

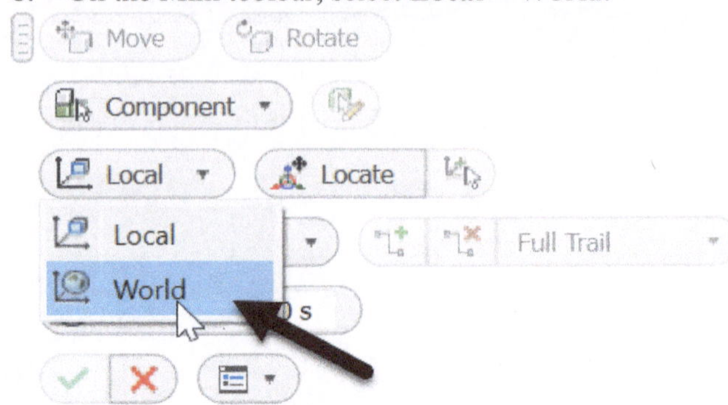

9. Click the **Z axis** of the manipulator.

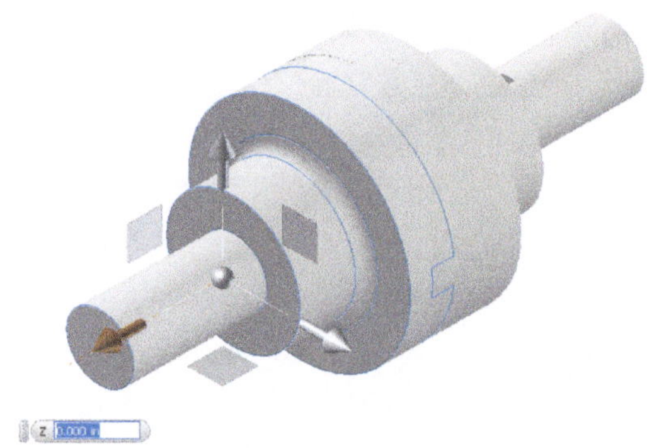

10. Type **4 inches** in the Z box attached to the manipulator.

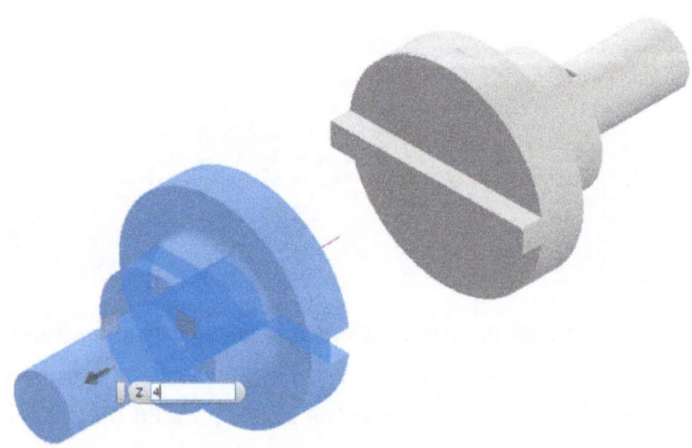

11. Click **OK**  on the Mini toolbar.
12. Right click in the graphics window and select **Tweak Components** from the Marking Menu.

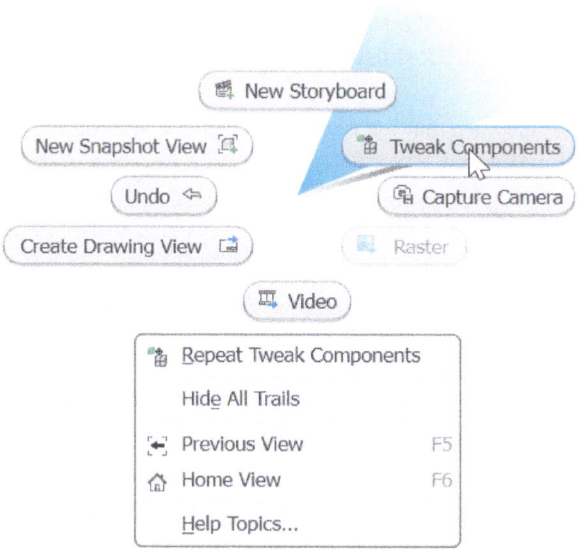

13. Select **Component** from the Selection filter drop-down on the Mini toolbar.
14. Select the other flange sub-assembly.
15. Click on the Z axis of the manipulator.
16. Type **-4 inches** in the Z box attached to the manipulator and click **OK** .

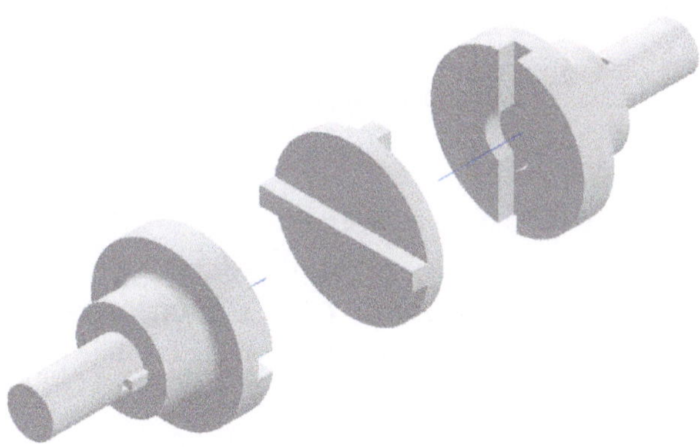

17. Click the **Tweak Components**  button on the **Component** panel of the **Presentation** ribbon tab.
18. On the Mini Toolbar, select **Part** from the drop-down, as shown.

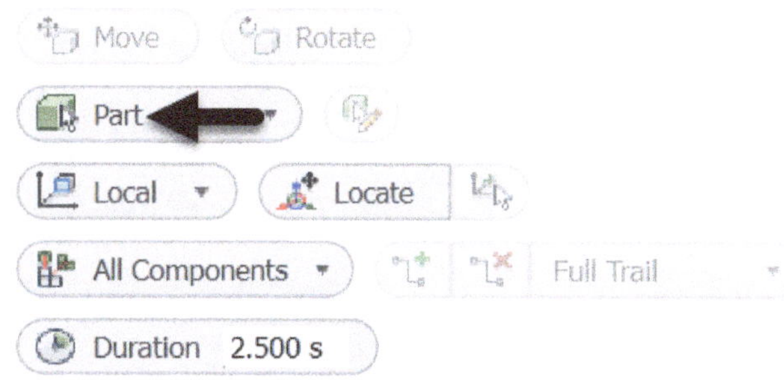

19. Select the front cylinder.
20. On the Mini toolbar, select **Local > World**.

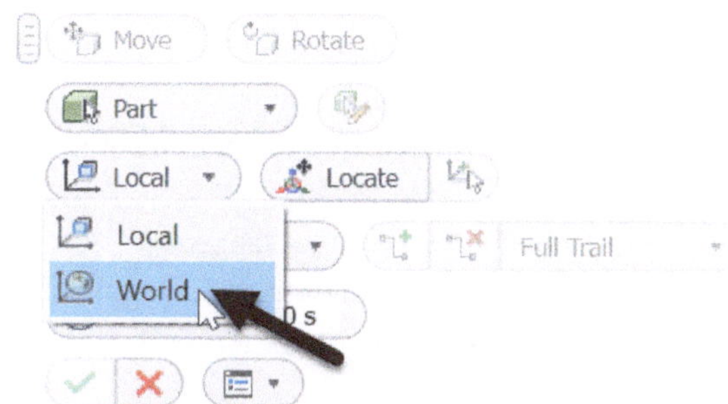

21. Click on the Z axis of the manipulator.

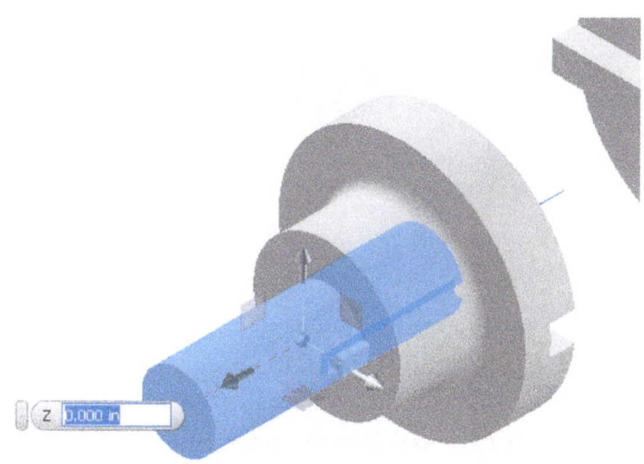

22. Type **4** in the box attached to the manipulator, and then press **Enter**.
23. Click **OK** on the Mini Toolbar.
24. Activate the **Tweak Components**  command.
25. Zoom into the flange and click on the key, as shown.

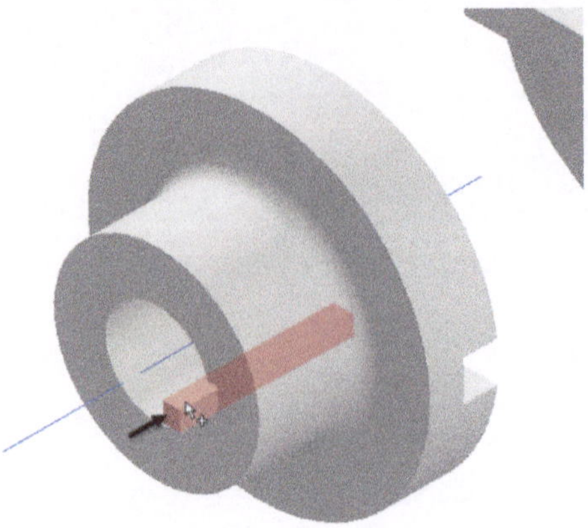

26. Select **Local > World** on the mini toolbar.
27. Click on the Z axis of the manipulator.
28. Type **-3.15** in the box attached to the manipulator and press **Enter**.
18. Likewise, explode the parts of the flange subassembly in the opposite direction. The explosion distances are the same.

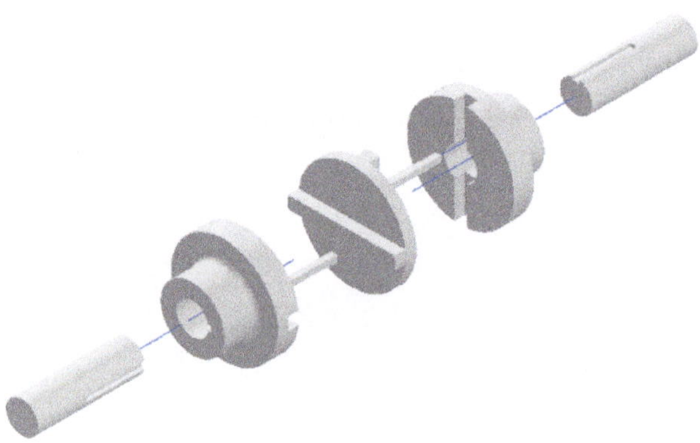

Animating the Explosion

1. To play the animation of the explosion, click the **Play Current Storyboard** button on the Storyboard.

2. Click the **Reverse Play Current Storyboard** button on the Storyboard.

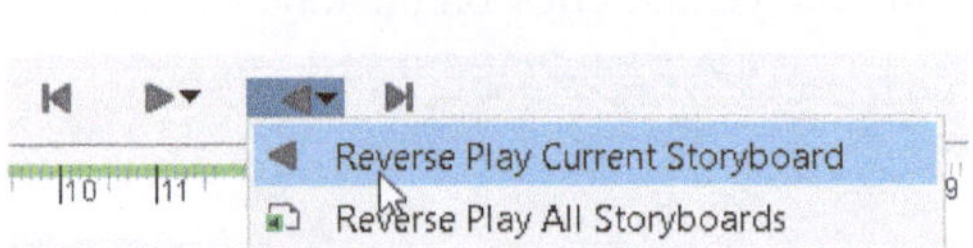

You can publish the animation video using the **Video** tool available on the **Publish** panel.

3. Make sure that the play marker is at 0 secs on the timeline.

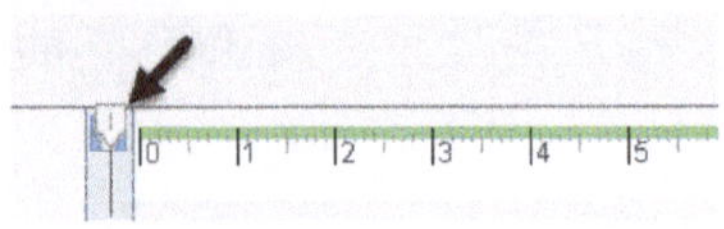

4. On the ribbon, click **Presentation** tab > **Publish** panel > **Video**  .
5. On the **Publish to Video** dialog, select **Current Storyboard** option from the **Publish Scope** section.

   You can also select **Current Storyboard Range** and specify the start and end position of the storyboard.

6. On the **Publish to Video** dialog, click the folder  icon and specify **the project folder as the File Location.**
7. Set the **File Format** to **WMV File (*.wmv)**.
8. Check the **Reverse** option to reverse the animation.
9. Leave the other default settings and click **OK; the Publish Video Progress dialog appears.**

   A message box appears that the video has been published.

10. Click **OK** on the message box.

Taking the Snapshot of the Explosion

1. Click and drag the play marker on the timeline to 15 seconds.

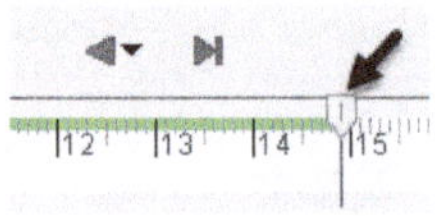

   You can capture the snapshot of the current position of the assembly using the **New Snapshot View** tool.
2. On the ribbon, click **Presentation** tab > **Workshop** panel > **New Snapshot View**  .

The snapshot appears in the Snapshot Views window. Notice that playmarker on the snapshot. It indicates that the snapshot is dependent on the storyboard.

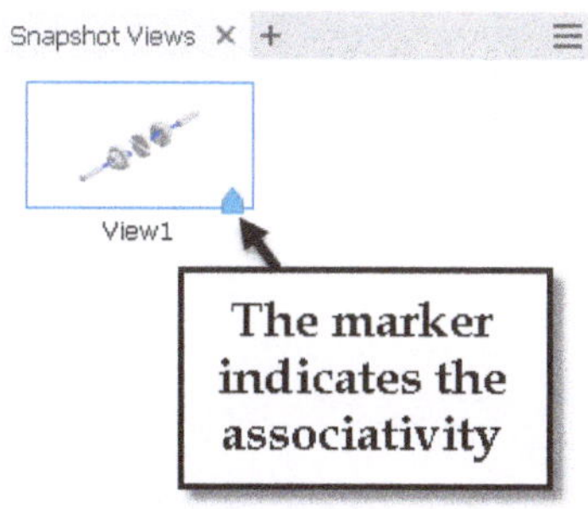

For example, if you make changes to the assembly at the position of the playmarker where the snapshot was taken, the Update View symbol appears on the snapshot view. You need to click on the Update View symbol to update the snapshot.

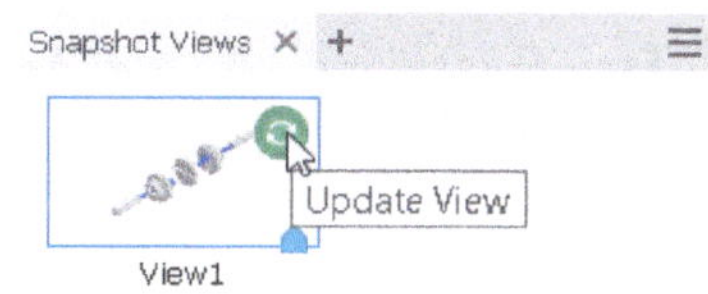

3. Click **Save** on the **Quick Access Toolbar**; the **Save As** dialog appears.
4. Type-in **Oldham_coupling** in the **File name box.**
5. Go to the project folder.
6. Click **Save** to save the file.
7. Click **OK**.
8. Click **File Menu > Close**.

Chapter 4: Creating Drawings

In this chapter, you will generate 2D drawings of the parts and assemblies.

In this chapter, you will:

- Insert standard views of a part model
- Create centerlines and centermarks
- Retrieve model dimensions
- Add additional dimensions and annotations
- Create Custom Sheet Formats and Templates
- Insert exploded view of the assembly
- Insert a bill of materials of the assembly
- Apply balloons to the assembly

TUTORIAL 1

In this tutorial, you will create the drawing of the Flange.ipt file created in the second chapter.

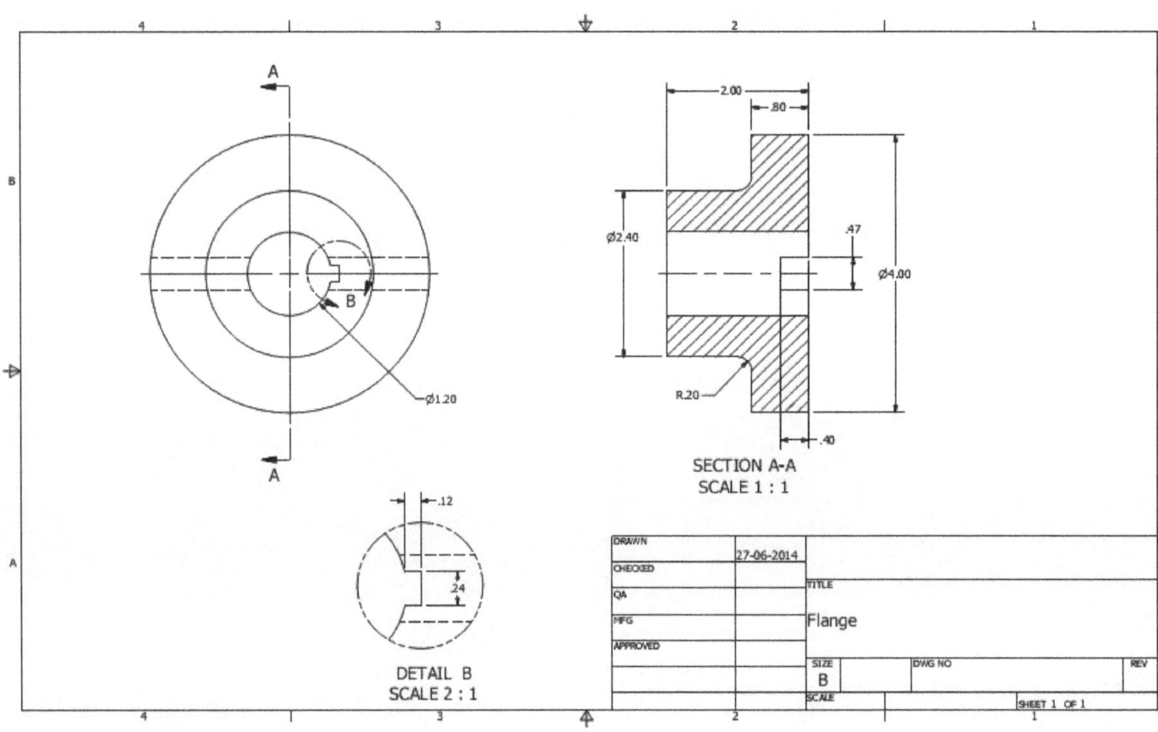

Starting a New Drawing File

1. To start a new drawing, click the **New** drop-down > **Drawing (.dwg)** on the **Home** screen.

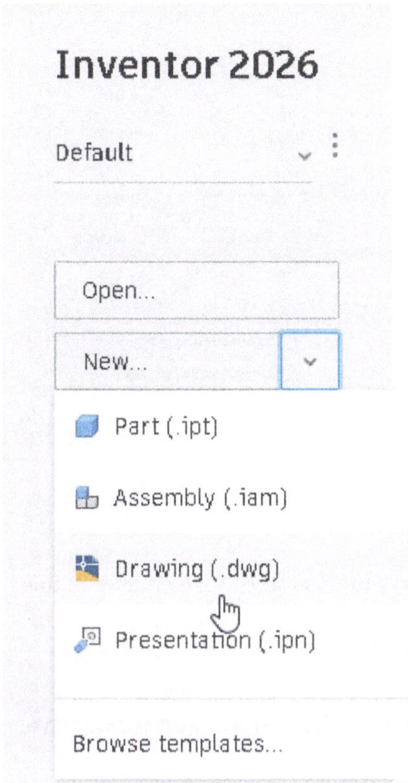
Inventor 2026
Default
Open...
New...
Part (.ipt)
Assembly (.iam)
Drawing (.dwg)
Presentation (.ipn)
Browse templates...

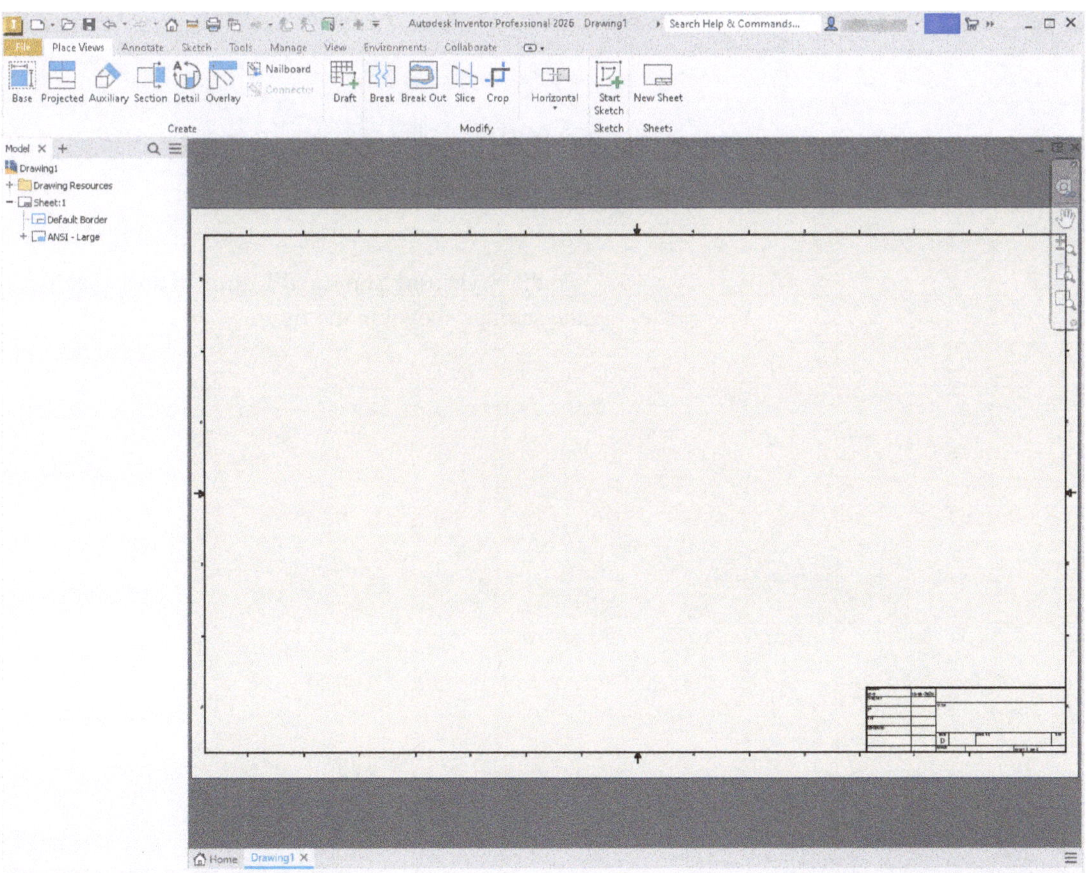

Editing the Drawing Sheet

1. To edit the drawing sheet, right-click on **Sheet:1** in the **Browser window** and select **Edit Sheet** from the shortcut menu.

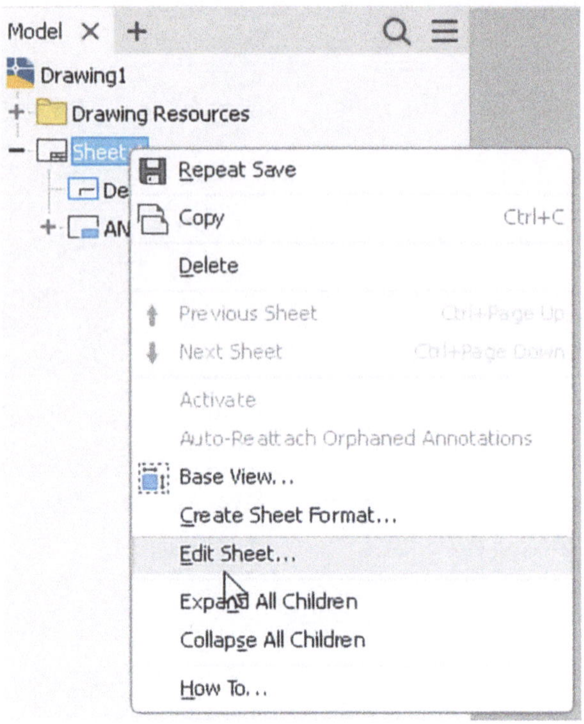

2. On the **Edit Sheet** dialog, set **Size** to **B**.

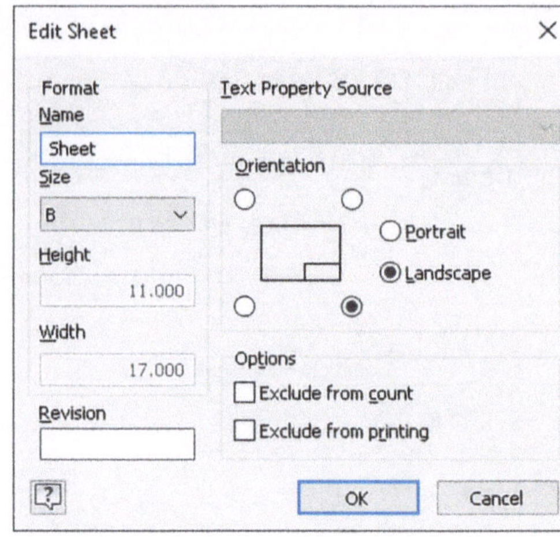

3. Click **OK**.

The drawing views in this tutorial are created in the Third Angle Projection. If you want to change the type of projection, then following the steps given next:

4. Click **Manage > Styles and Standards > Style Editor** on the ribbon.

5. On the **Style and Standard Editor** dialog, specify the settings shown in the figure.

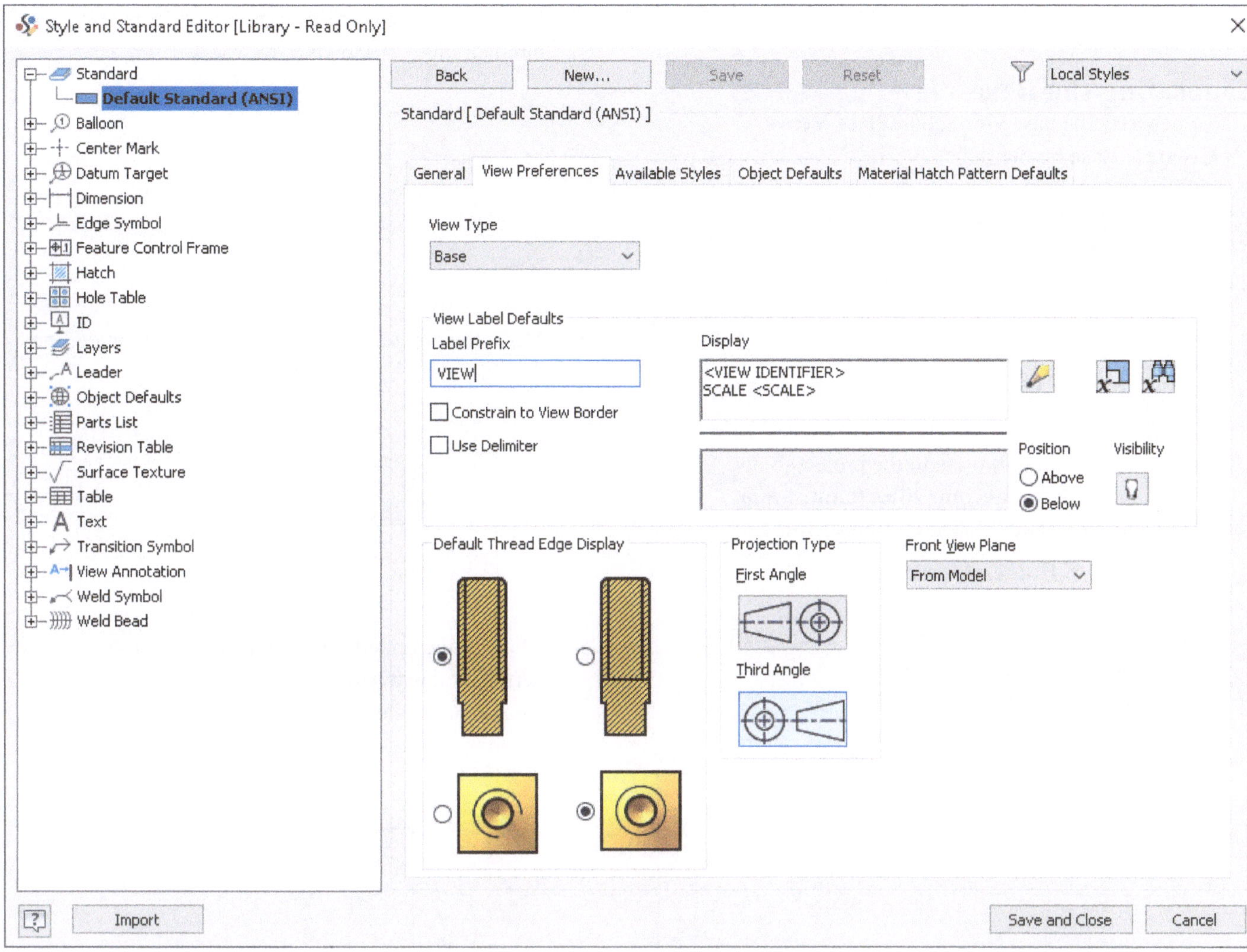

Style and Standard Editor [Library - Read Only]
Standard
Default Standard (ANSI)
Balloon
Center Mark
Datum Target
Dimension
Edge Symbol
Feature Control Frame
Hatch
Hole Table
ID
Layers
Leader
Object Defaults
Parts List
Revision Table
Surface Texture
Table
Text
Transition Symbol
View Annotation
Weld Symbol
Weld Bead
Back
New...
Save
Reset
Local Styles
Standard [Default Standard (ANSI)]
General
View Preferences
Available Styles
Object Defaults
Material Hatch Pattern Defaults
View Type
Base
View Label Defaults
Label Prefix
VIEW
Constrain to View Border
Use Delimiter
Display
<VIEW IDENTIFIER>
SCALE <SCALE>
Position
Above
Below
Visibility
Default Thread Edge Display
Projection Type
First Angle
Third Angle
Front View Plane
From Model
Import
Save and Close
Cancel

6. Click **Save and Close**.

Generating the Base View

1. To generate the base view, click **Place Views > Create > Base** on the ribbon.

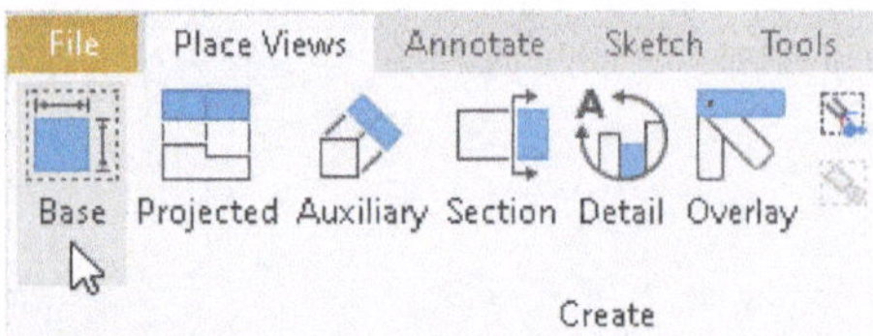

2. On the **Drawing View** dialog, click **Open existing file** .
3. On the **Open** dialog, browse to the project folder.
4. Set **Files of type** to **Inventor Files (*.ipt, *.iam, *.ipn)**, and then double-click on **Flange.ipt**.
5. Set the **Style** to **Hidden Line** .
6. Set **Scale** to **1:1**.
7. Click on the preview, drag, and place it at the left side on the drawing sheet, as shown.
8. Click **OK** on the dialog.

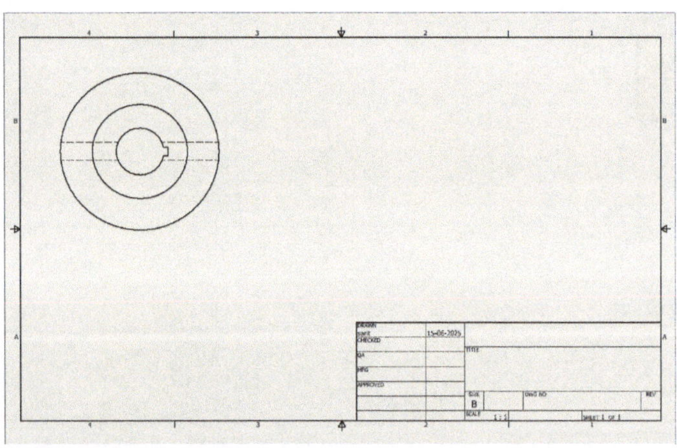

Generating the Section View

1. To create the section view, click **Place Views > Create > Section** on the ribbon.

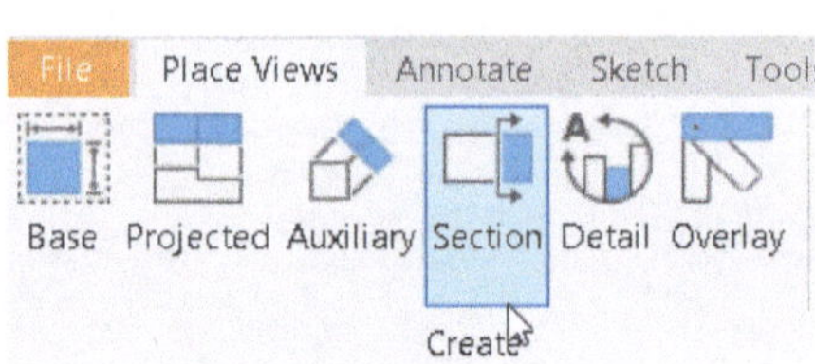

2. Select the base view.
3. Place the cursor on the top quadrant point of the circular edge, as shown.

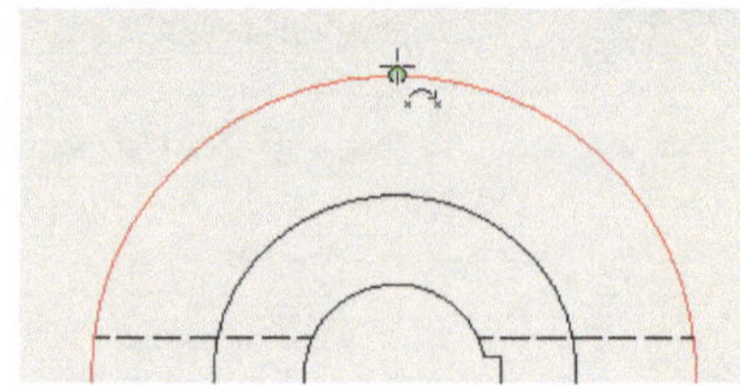

4. Move the pointer upward and notice the dotted line.

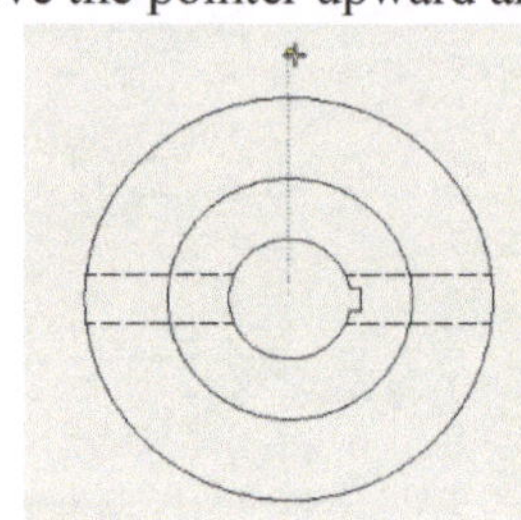

5. Click on the dotted line and move the cursor vertically downwards.
6. Click outside the bottom portion of the view, as shown.

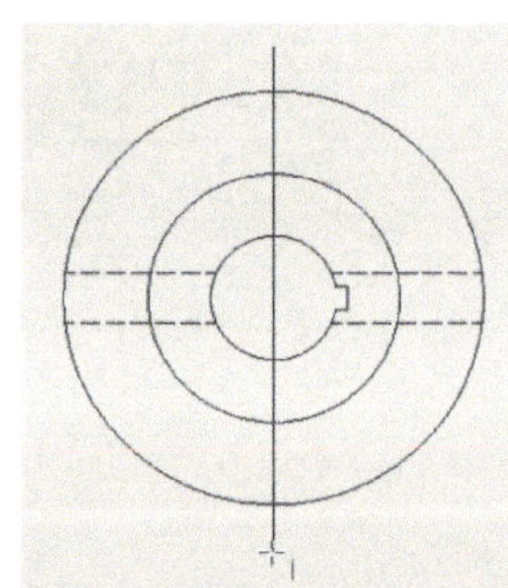

7. Right-click and select **Continue**.

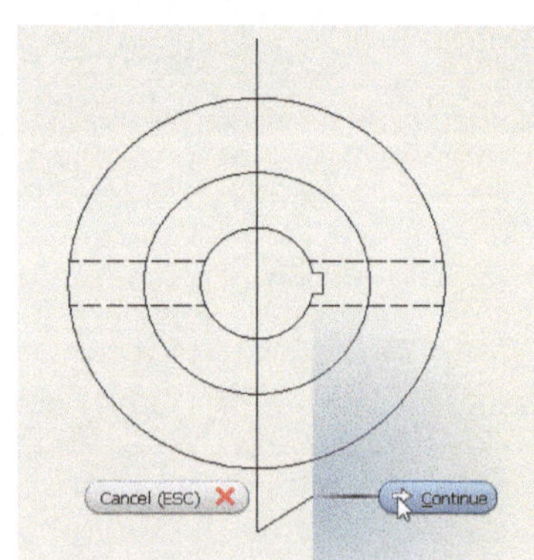

8. On the **Section View** dialog, click the **Hidden Line Removed** icon under the **Style** section.

9. Click the **Edit View Label**  icon. On the **Format Text** dialog, delete the three properties using the DELETE key, as shown. Also, delete the slash (/) and click **OK**.

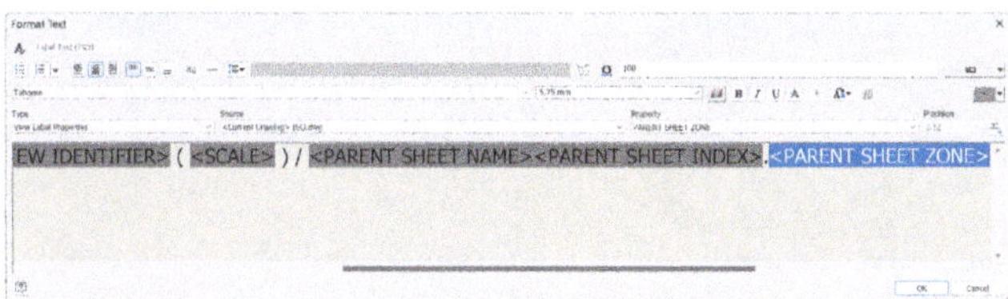

10. Move the cursor toward the right and click to place the section view.

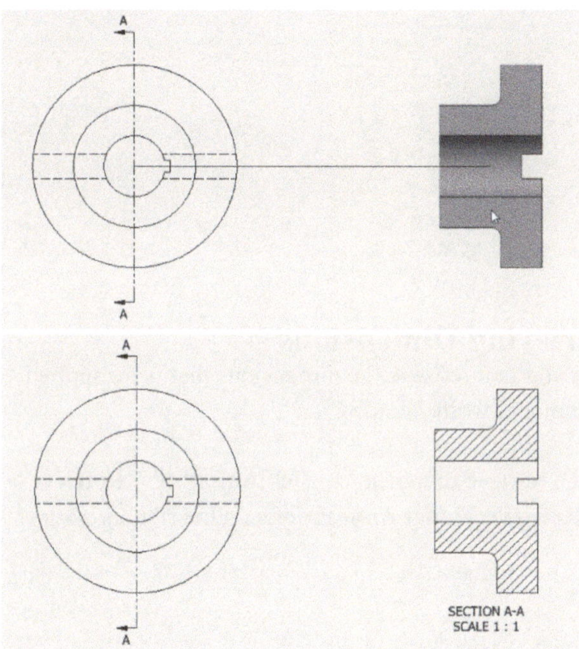

Creating Center marks and Centerlines

1. To create a center mark, click **Annotate > Symbols > Center Mark** on the ribbon.

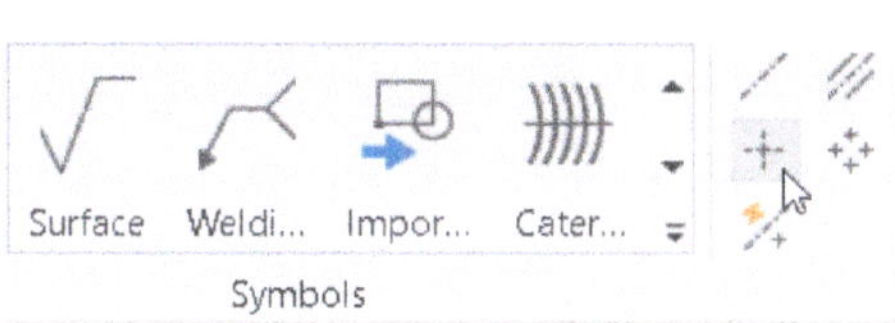

2. Click on the outer circle of the base view.

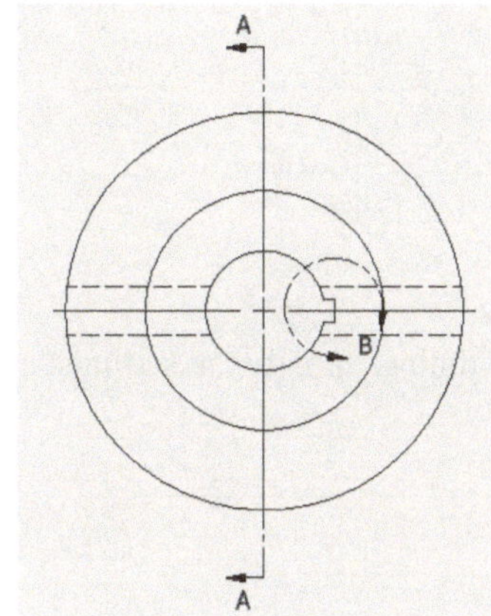

3. To create a centerline, click **Annotate > Symbols > Centerline Bisector** on the ribbon.

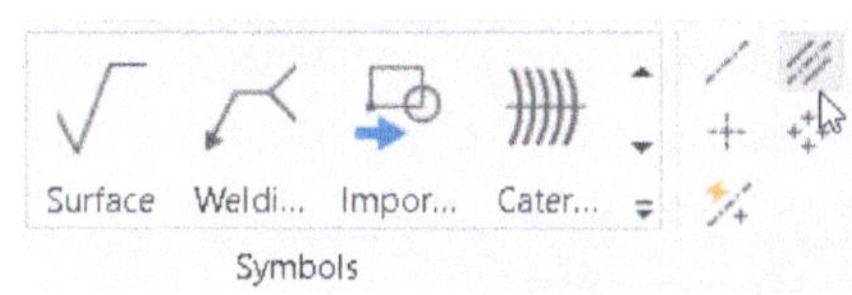

4. Click on the inner horizontal edges of the section view.

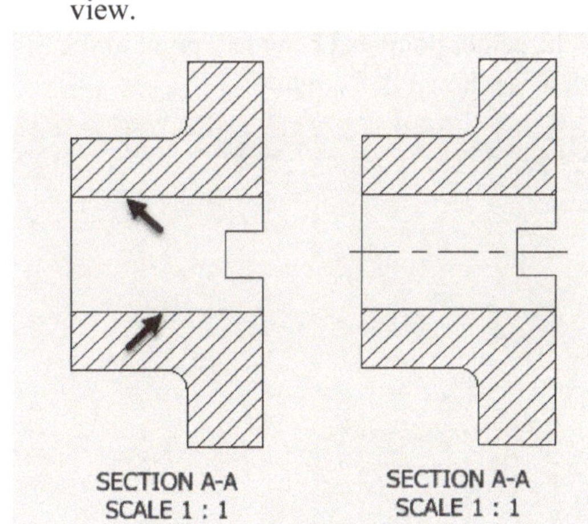

Creating the Detailed View

Now, you have to create a detailed view of the keyway, which is displayed, in the front view.

1. To create a detailed view, click **Place Views > Create > Detail** on the ribbon.

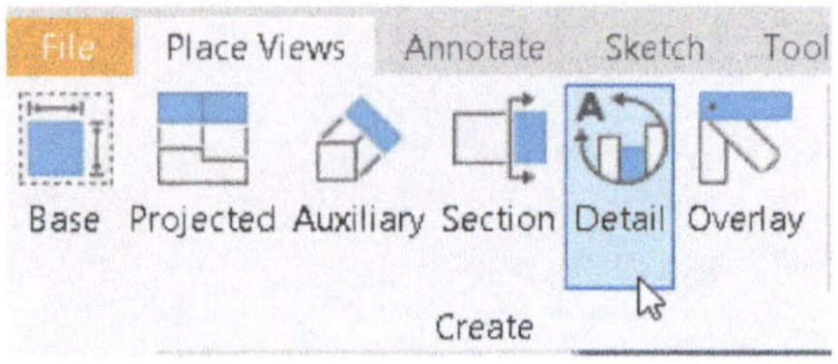

2. Select the base view.
3. On the **Detail View** dialog, specify the settings, as shown next.

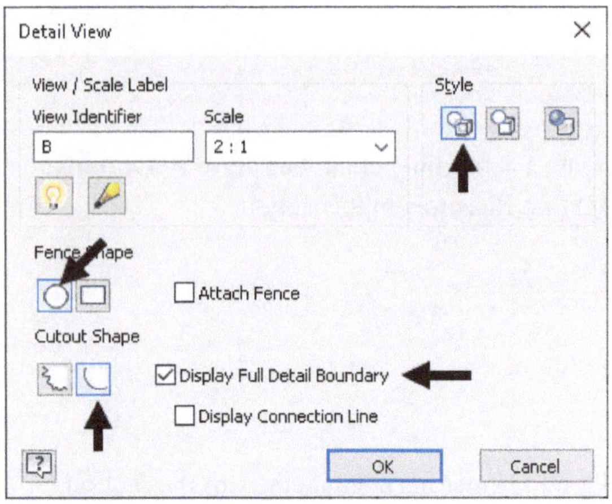

4. Specify the center point and boundary point of the detail view, as shown in the figure.

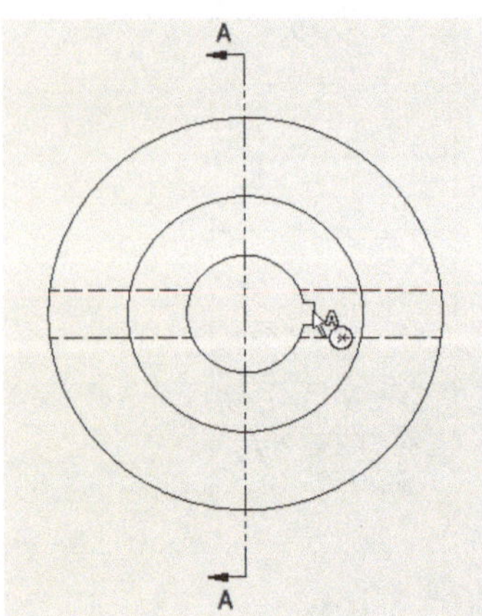

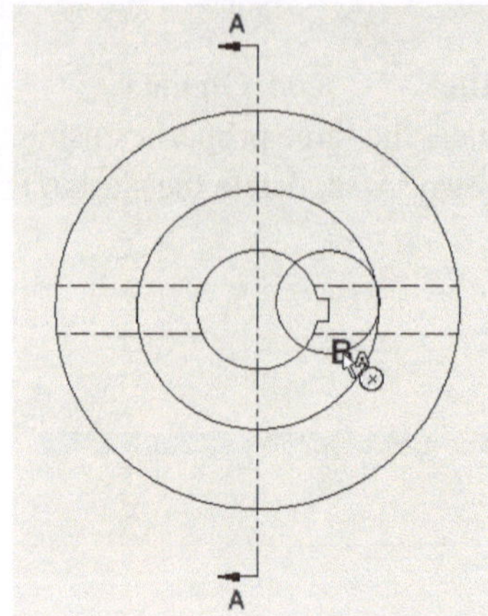

5. Place the detail view below the base view.

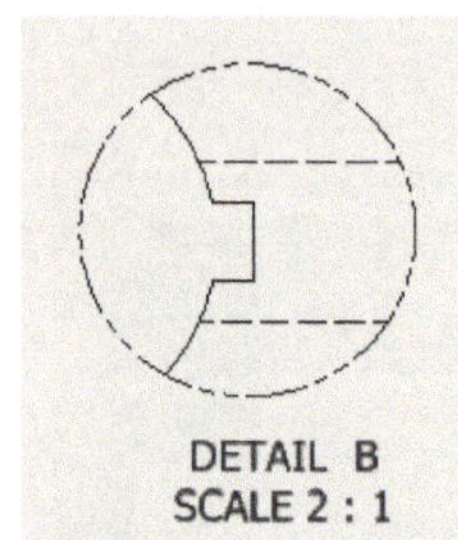

Retrieving Dimensions

Now, you will retrieve the dimensions that were applied to the model while creating it.

1. To retrieve dimensions, click **Annotate > Retrieve > Retrieve Model Annotations** on the ribbon.

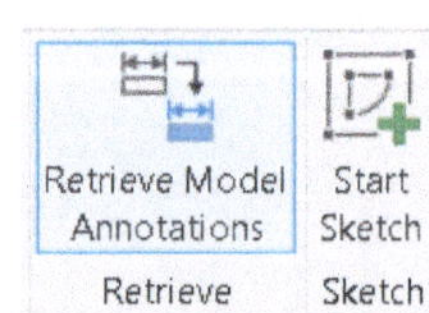

The **Retrieve Model Annotation** dialog appears.

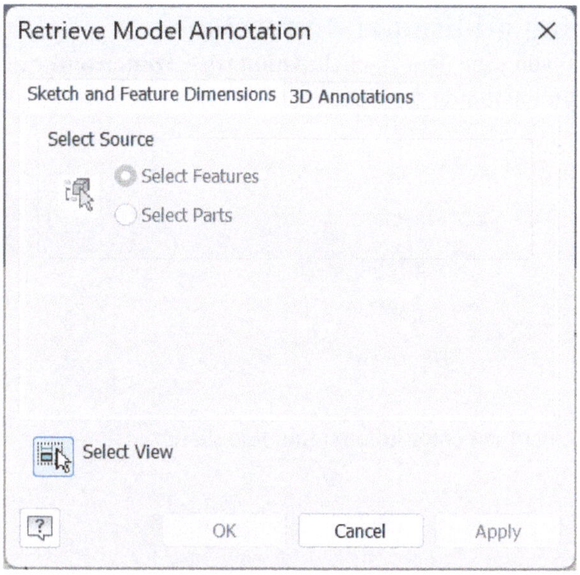

2. Select the section view from the drawing sheet.

Now, you must select the dimensions to retrieve.

3. Drag a window on the section view to select all the dimensions.

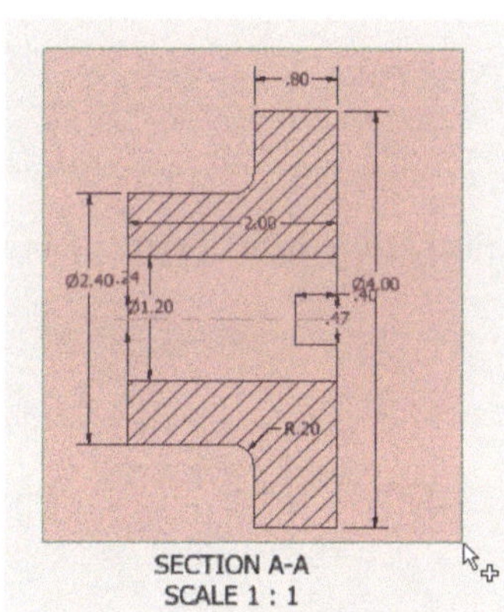

4. Click **Select Features** under the **Select Source** group.
5. Click **OK** to retrieve feature dimensions.

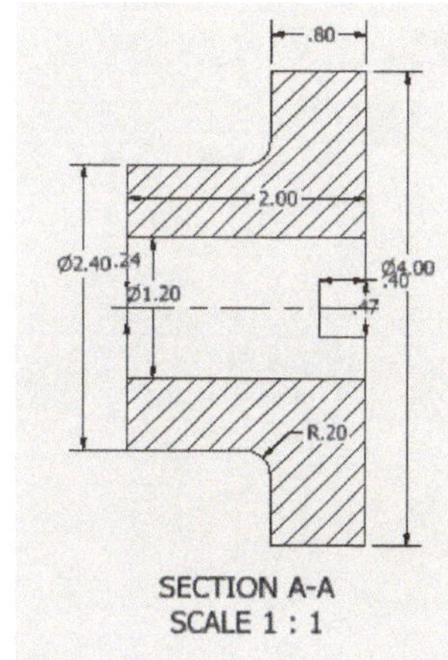

6. Click **Annotate > Dimension > Arrange** on the ribbon.

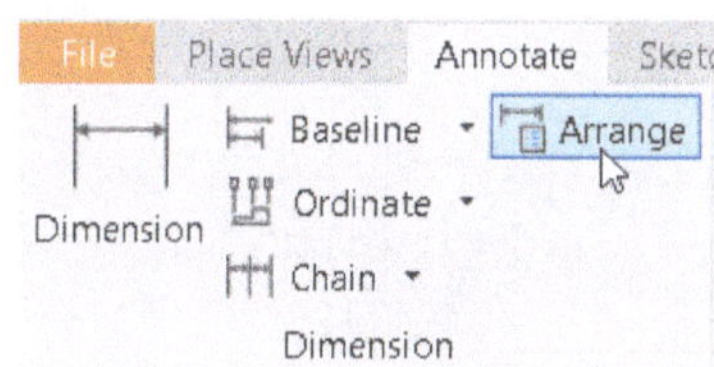

7. Drag a selection box and select all the dimensions of the section view.

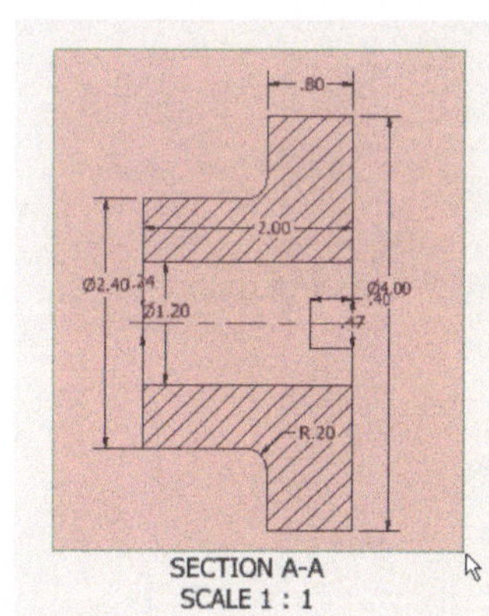

8. Click the right mouse button and select **OK**.

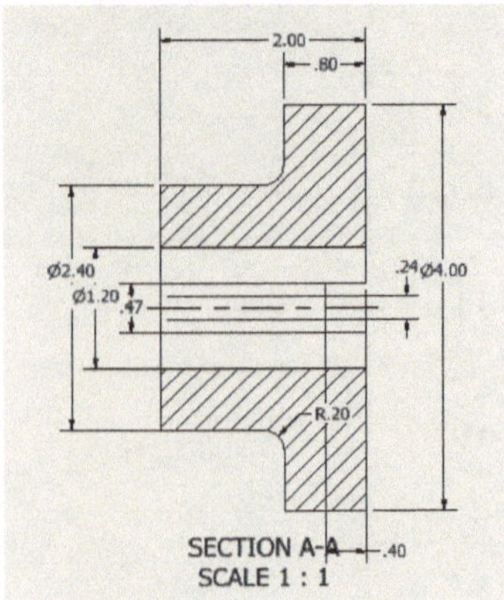

9. Select the unwanted dimensions and press Delete.

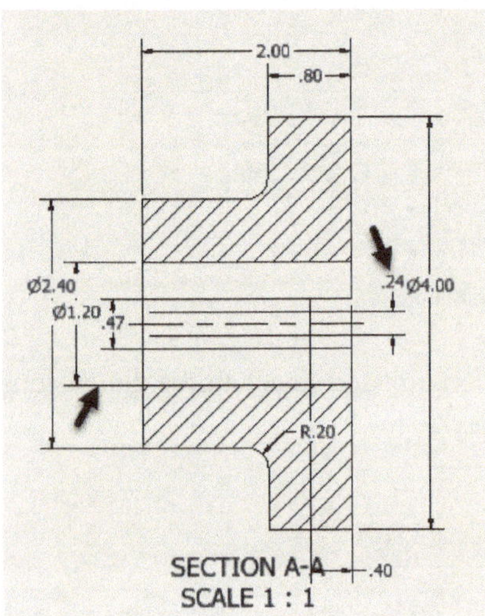

10. Click and drag the dimensions to arrange them correctly.

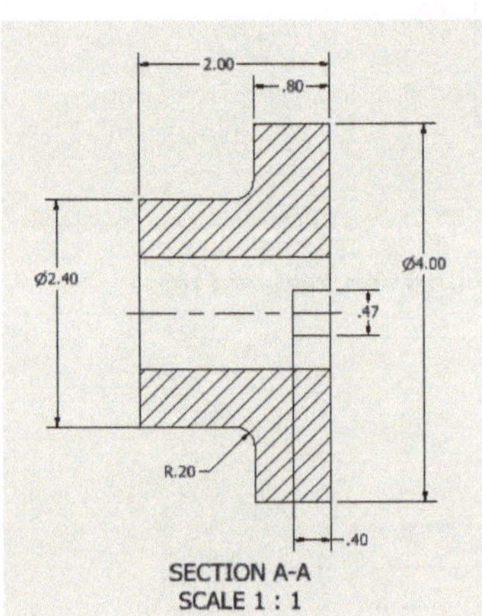

Adding additional dimensions

1. To add dimensions, click **Annotate > Dimension > Dimension** on the ribbon.

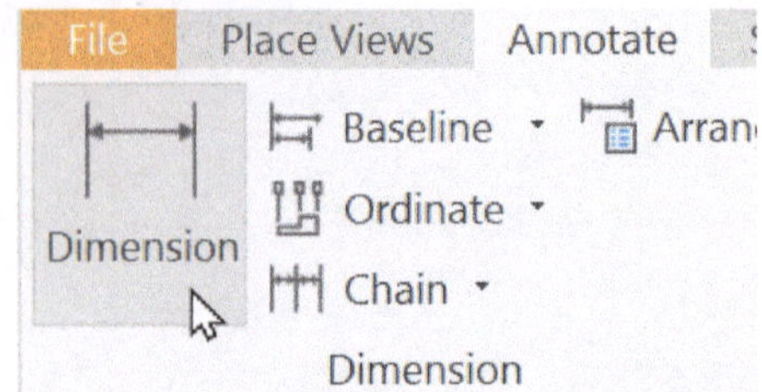

2. Select the center hole on the base view.

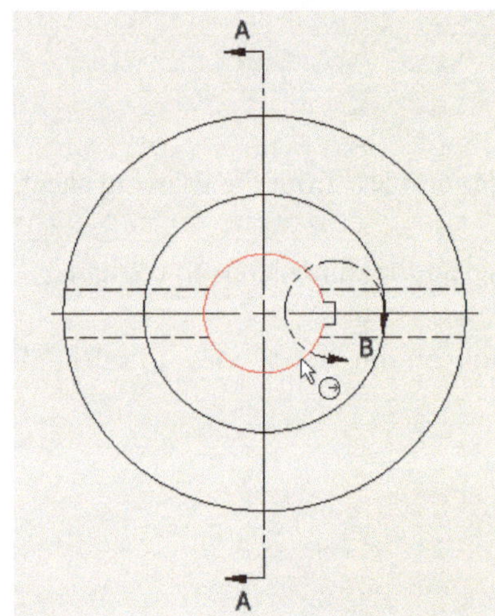

3. Right-click and select **Dimension Type > Diameter**.

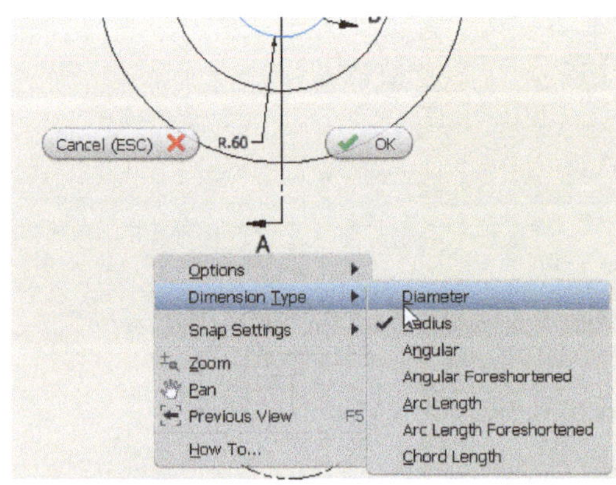

4. Place the dimension, as shown in the figure. The **Edit Dimension** dialog appears.

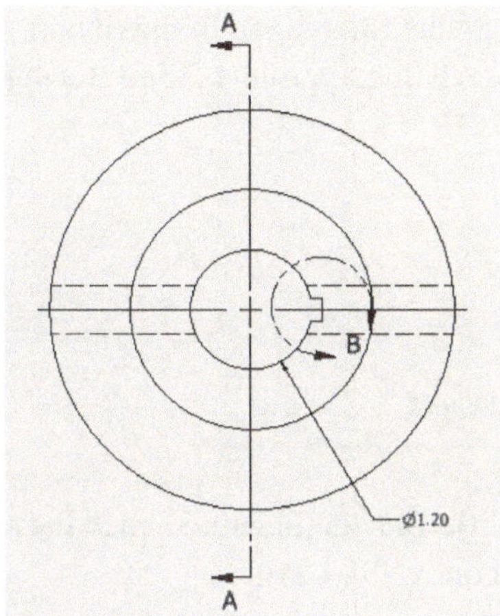

5. Click **OK**.
6. Create the dimensions on the detail view, as shown in the figure.

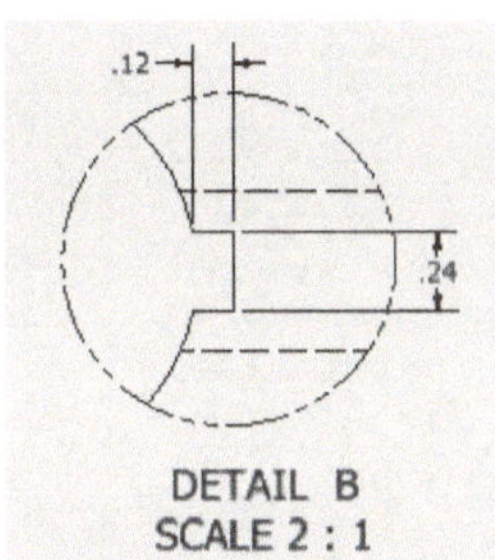

Populating the Title Block

1. To populate the title block, click **File Menu > iProperties**.

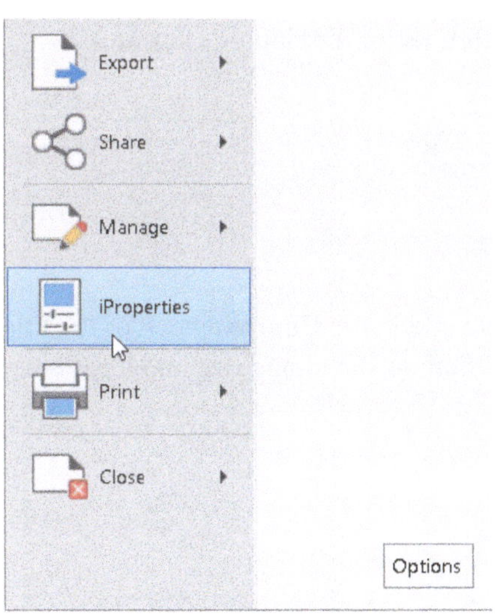

2. On the **Flange iProperties** dialog, click the tabs one-by-one and type-in data in respective fields.
3. Click **Apply** and **Close**.

Saving the Drawing

1. Click **Save** on the **Quick Access Toolbar**; the **Save As** dialog appears.
2. Type-in **Flange** in the **File Name** box.
3. Go to the project folder.
4. Click **Save** to save the file.
5. Click **File Menu > Close**.

TUTORIAL 2

In this tutorial, you will create a custom template, and then use it to create a new drawing.

Creating New Sheet Format

1. On the ribbon, click **Get Started > Launch > New**.
2. On the **Create New File** dialog, click the **Standard.idw** icon.

3. Click **Create** to start a new drawing file.
4. To edit the drawing sheet, right-click on **Sheet:1** in the **Browser window** and select **Edit Sheet** from the shortcut menu.

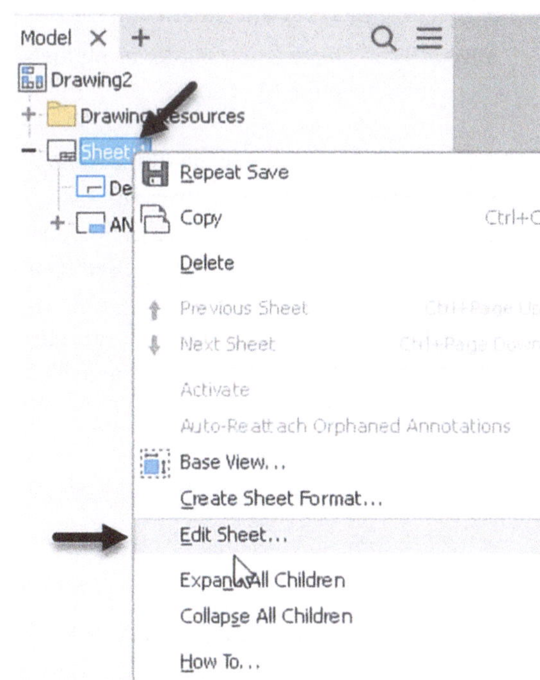

5. On the **Edit Sheet** dialog, set **Size** to **B**.

Under the **Orientation** section, you can change the orientation of the title block as well as the sheet orientation.

6. Click **OK**.
7. In the **Browser window**, expand the **Drawing Resources > Sheet Formats** folder to view different sheet formats available. Now, you will add a new sheet format to this folder.
8. Click the right mouse button on the **Borders** folder and select **Define New Border**.

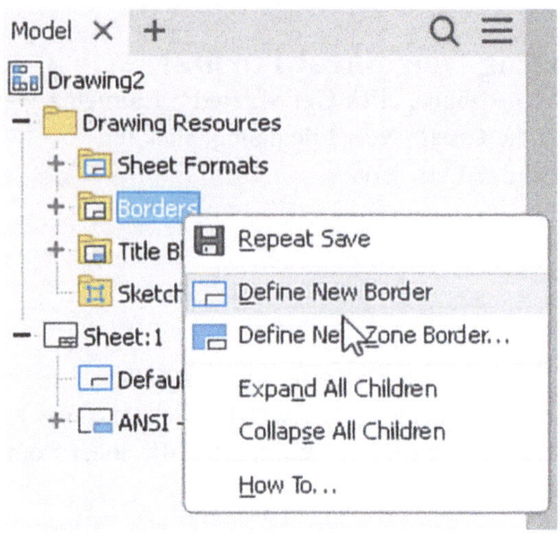

Now, you can create a new border using the sketch tools available in the **Sketch** tab.

9. Click **Finish** on the **Sketch** tab of the ribbon.
10. On the **Border** dialog, click **Discard**.
11. In the Browser window, click the right mouse button on the **Borders** folder and select **Define New Zone Border**.
12. On the **Default Drawing Border Parameters** dialog, type-in **4** in the **Vertical Zones** box and click **OK**.

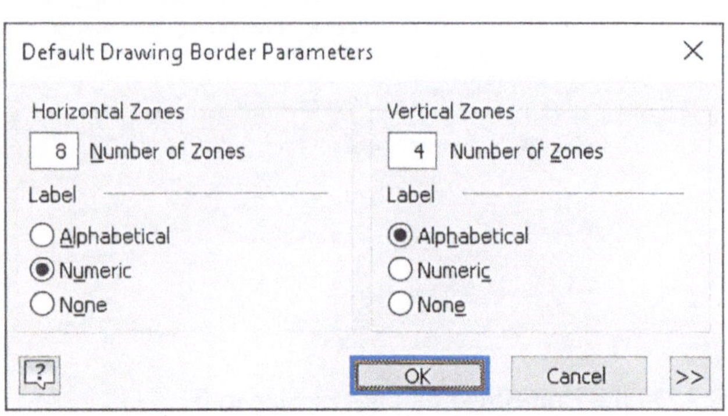

13. Click **Finish** on the **Sketch** tab of the ribbon.
14. On the **Border** dialog, type-in **4-Zone Border** and click **Save**.

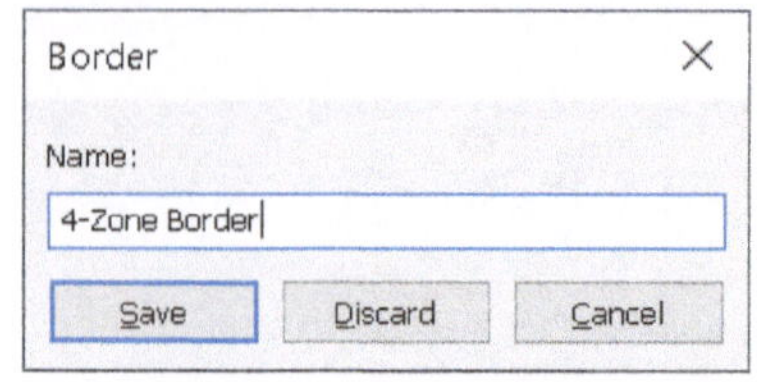

15. Expand the **Title Blocks** folder and click the right mouse button on **ANSI-Large**.
16. Select **Edit** from the shortcut menu.

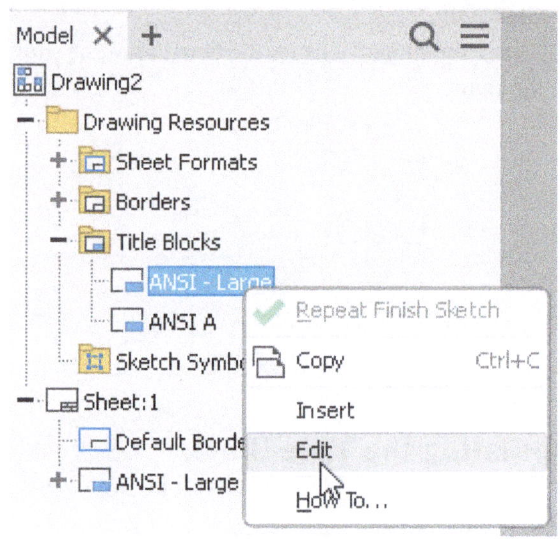

17. On the **Sketch** tab of the ribbon, click **Insert > Image**.

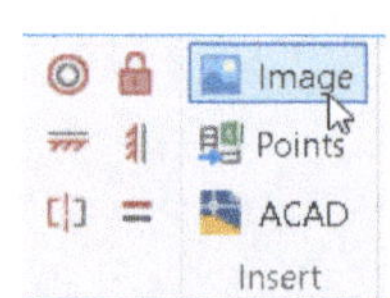

18. Draw a rectangle in the **Company** cell of the title block. This defines the image size and location.

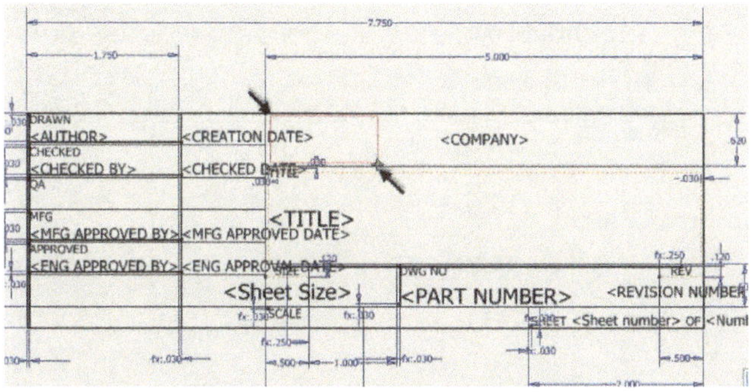

19. Go to the location of your company logo or any other image location. You must ensure that the image is located inside the project folder.
20. Select the image file and click **Open**. This will insert the image into the title block.

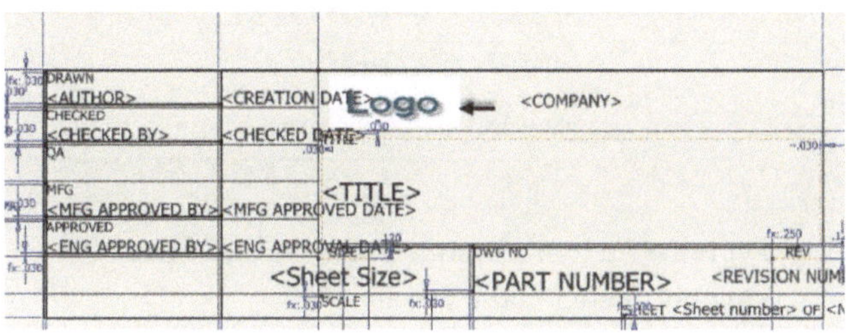

21. Click **Finish** on the ribbon.
22. Click **Save As** on the **Save Edits** dialog.
23. Type-in **ANSI-Logo** in the **Title Block** dialog.

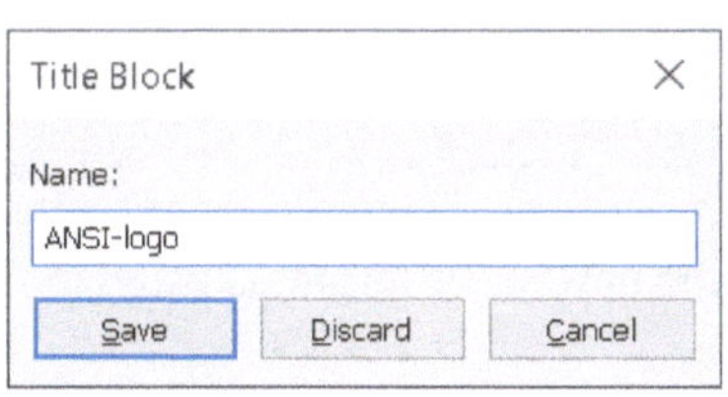

24. Click **Save**.
25. In the Browser window, expand **Sheet:1** and click the right mouse button on **Default Border**.
26. Select **Delete** from the shortcut menu.

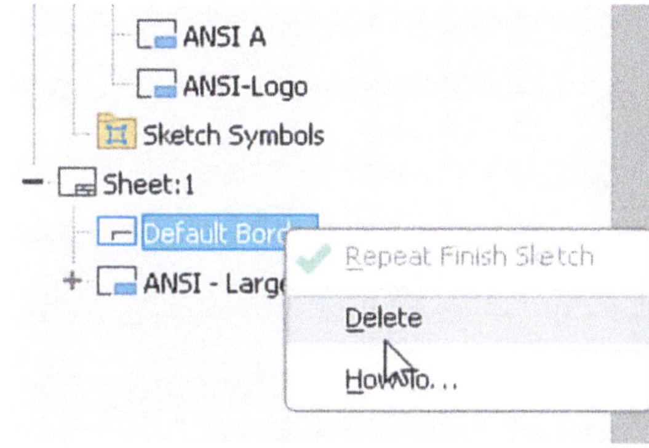

27. Expand the **Borders** folder and click the right mouse button on **4-Zone Border**.
28. Select **Insert** from the shortcut menu.

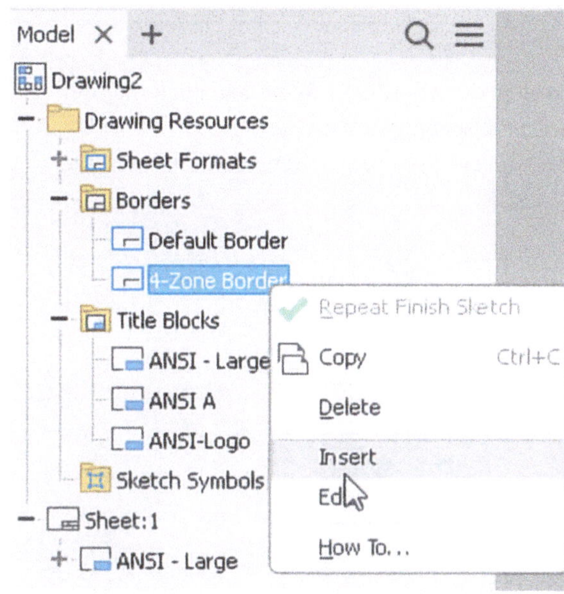

29. Click **OK** on the **Edit Drawing Border Parameters** dialog.
30. Expand **Sheet:1** and click the right mouse button on **ANSI-Large**.
31. Select **Delete** from the shortcut menu.

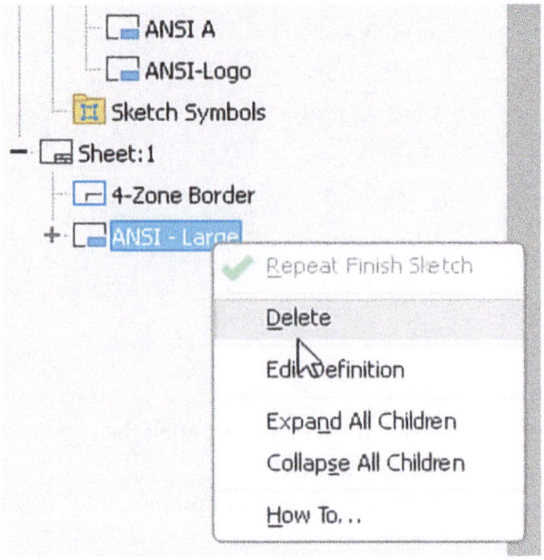

32. Expand the **Title Blocks** folder and click the right mouse button on **ANSI-Logo**.
33. Select **Insert** from the shortcut menu to insert the title block.

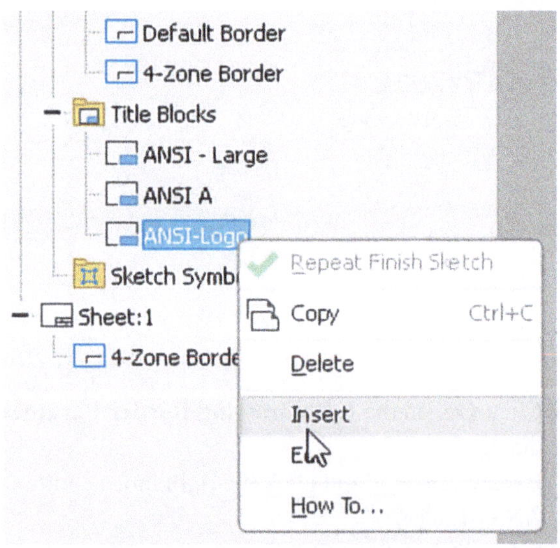

34. Click the right mouse button on **Sheet:1** and select **Create Sheet Format**.

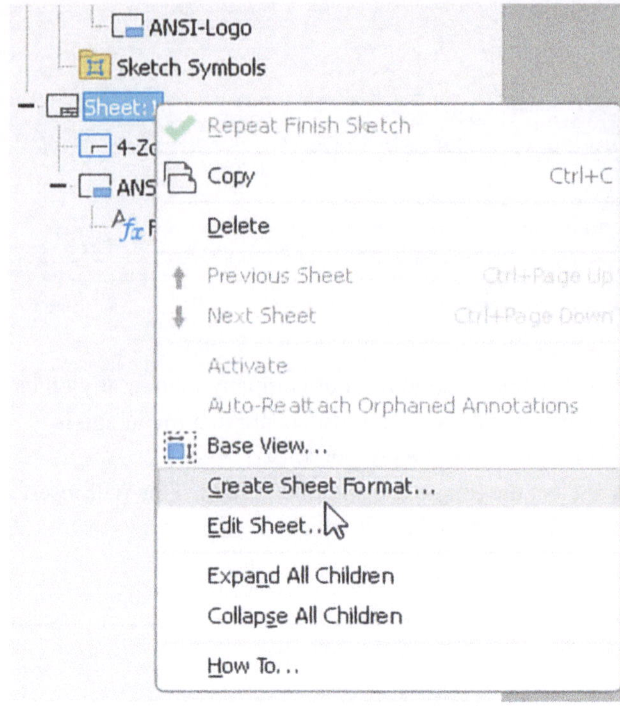

35. Type-in **Custom Format** in the **Create Sheet Format** dialog, and then click **OK**.

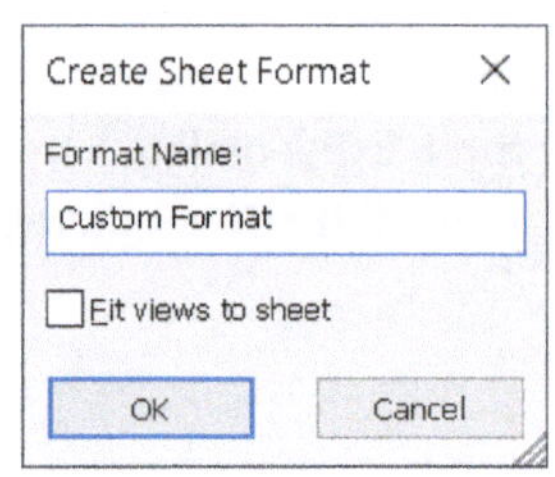

You will notice that the new sheet format is listed in the **Sheet Formats** folder.

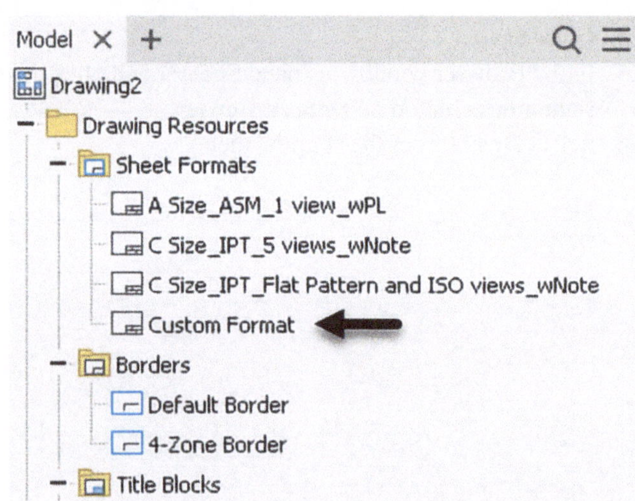

Creating a Custom Template

1. On the ribbon, click **Tools > Options > Document Settings**.

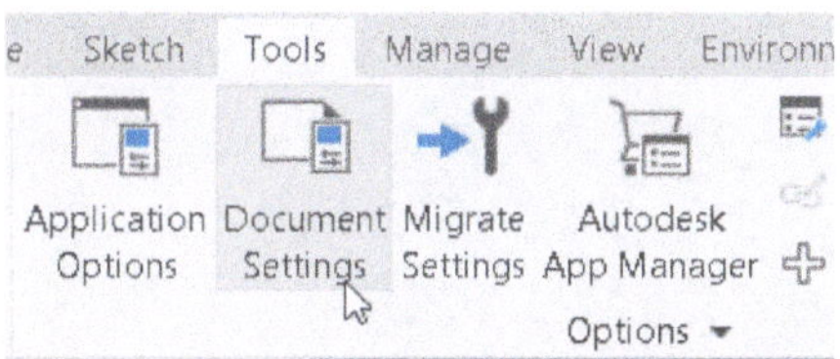

On **Document Settings** dialog, you can define the standard, sheet color, drawing view settings, and sketch settings.

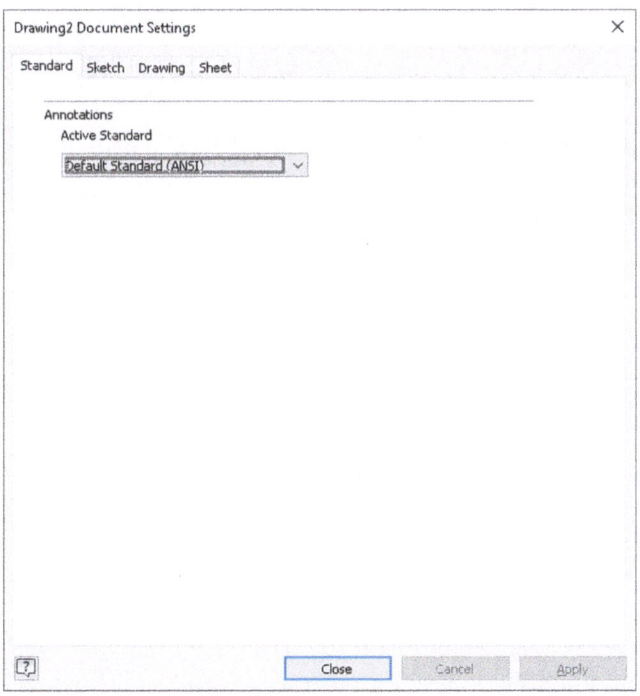

2. Leave the default settings on this dialog and click **Close**.
3. In the Browser window, expand the **Sheet Formats** folder and double-click on **Custom Format**.
4. Click the right mouse button on **Sheet: 2** and select **Delete** from the shortcut menu.

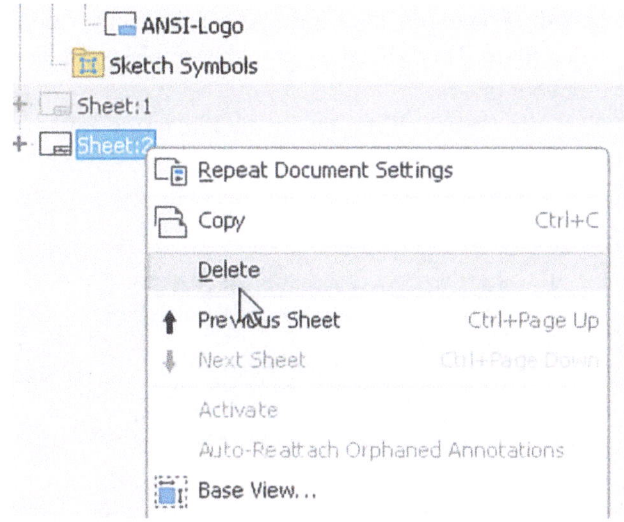

5. Click **OK**.
6. On the ribbon, click **Manage > Styles and Standards > Styles Editor**.
7. On the **Style and Standard Editor** dialog, select **Dimension > Default (ANSI)**.

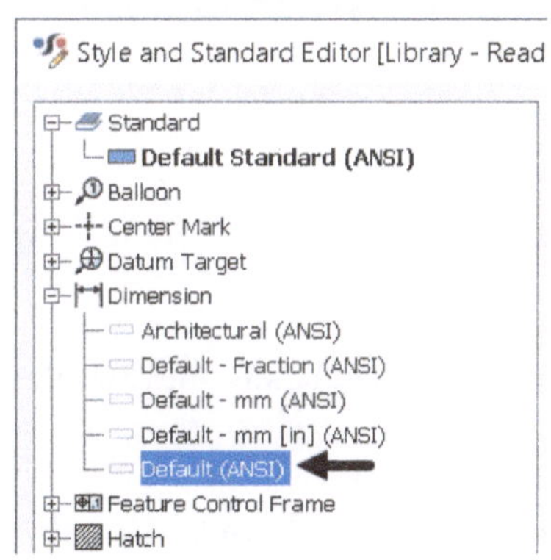

8. Click the **New** button located at the top of the dialog.
9. Type-in **Custom Standard** in the **New Local Style** dialog, and then click **OK**.
10. Click the **Units** tab and set **Precision** to **3.123**.

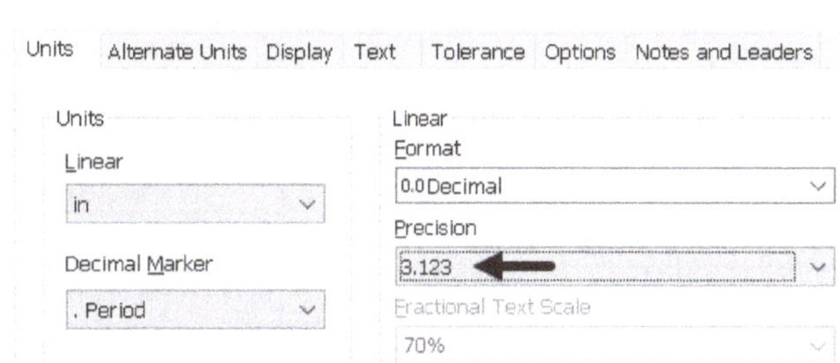

11. Click **Save and Close**.

12. On the **File menu**, click **Save As > Save Copy As Template**. This will take you to the templates folder on your drive.
13. Type-in **Custom Template** in the **File name** box.
14. Click **Save**.
15. Close the drawing file without saving it.

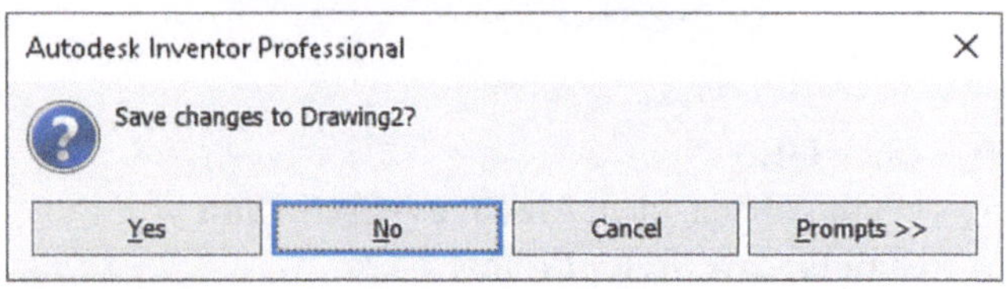

Starting a Drawing using the Custom template

1. On the ribbon, click **Get Started > Launch > New**.
2. On the **Create New File** dialog, click the **Custom Template.idw** icon.

3. Click **Create** and **OK** to start a new drawing file.

Generating the Drawing Views

1. To generate views, click **Place Views > Create > Base** on the ribbon.
2. On the **Drawing View** dialog, click **Open existing file**.
3. Go to the project folder and double-click on **Disc.ipt**.
4. Select **Front** from the ViewCube displayed on the sheet.

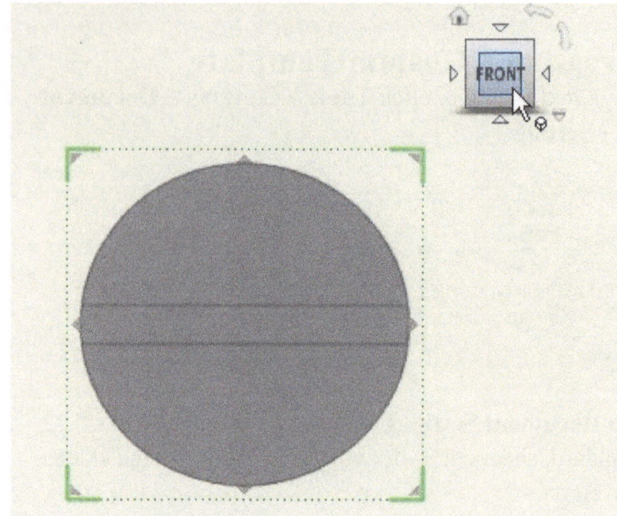

5. Set **Scale** to **1:1**.
6. Click and drag the view to the top-center of the drawing sheet.
7. Move the cursor downwards and click to place the projected view.
8. Right-click and select **OK**.

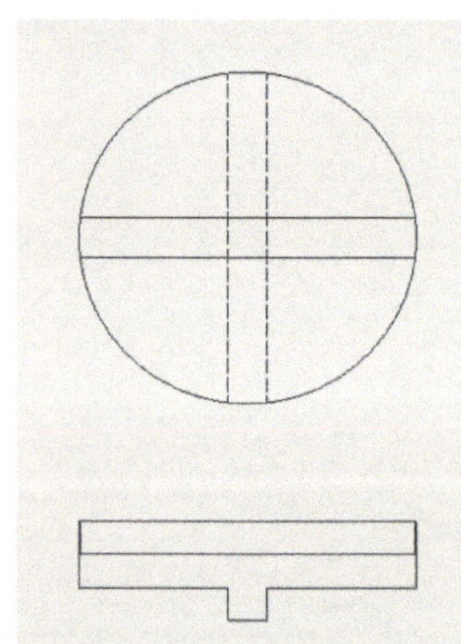

Adding Dimensions

1. On the ribbon, click **Annotate > Dimension > Dimension**.
2. Select the circular edge on the base view.
3. On the ribbon, click **Annotate > Format > Select Style > Custom Standard**.

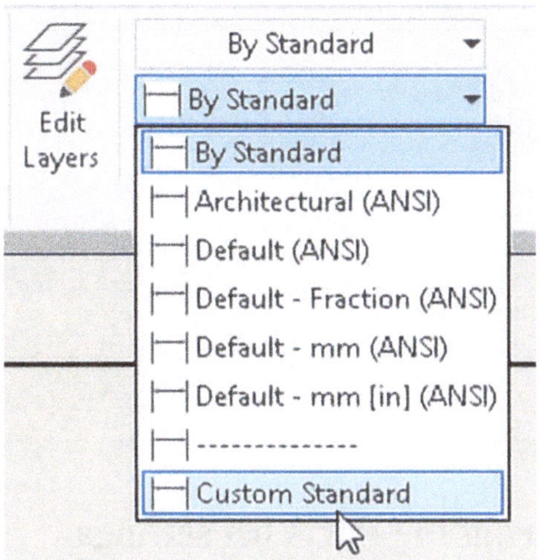

4. Right-click and select **Dimension Type > Diameter**.
5. Click to place the dimension.
6. Click **OK**.

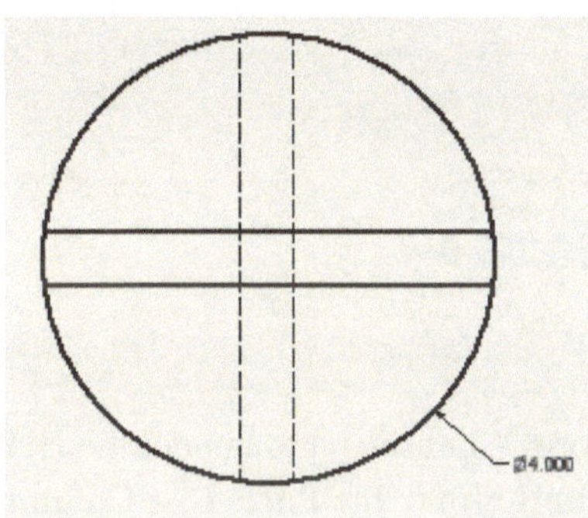

7. Select the horizontal edges on the base view.
8. Move the pointer toward the right and click to place the dimension.
9. Click **OK** on the **Edit Dimension** dialog.

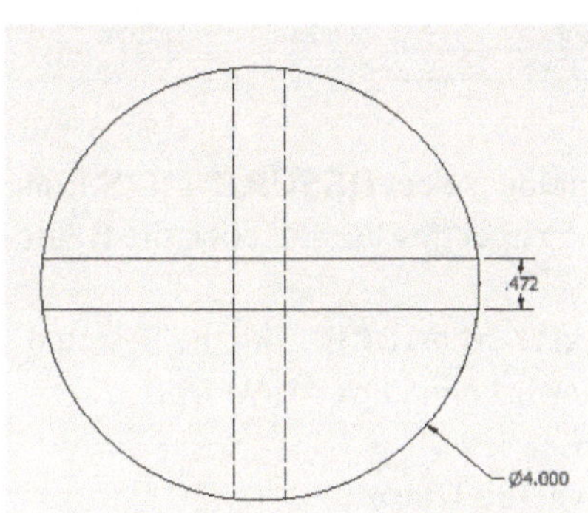

10. Add other dimensions to the drawing.

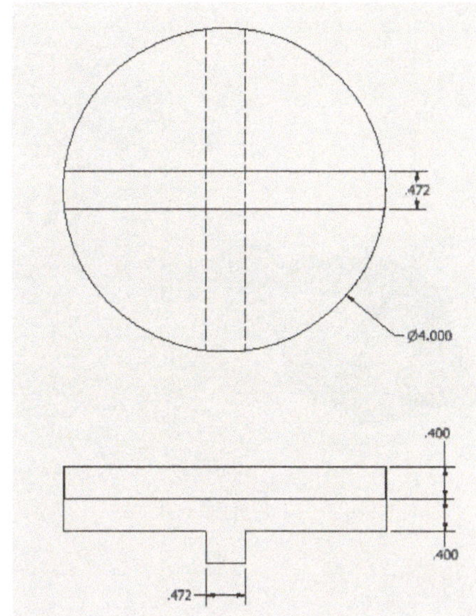

11. Right-click and select **OK** to deactivate the **Dimension** tool.
12. Save and close the drawing file.

Tutorial 3

In this tutorial, you will create the drawing of the Oldham coupling assembly created in the previous chapter.

Creating a New Drawing File

1. On the ribbon, click **Get Started > Launch > New**.
2. On the **Create New File** dialog, click the **Custom Template.idw** icon.

3. Click **Create** and **OK** to start a new drawing file.

Generating Base View

1. To generate the base view, click **Place Views > Create > Base** 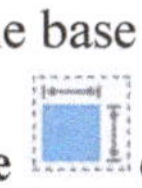 on the ribbon; the **Drawing View** dialog appears.
2. Click **Open existing file**  on this dialog; the **Open** dialog appears.
3. Go to the project folder and double-click on **Oldham_Coupling.iam**.
4. Click the **Home** icon located above the ViewCube.

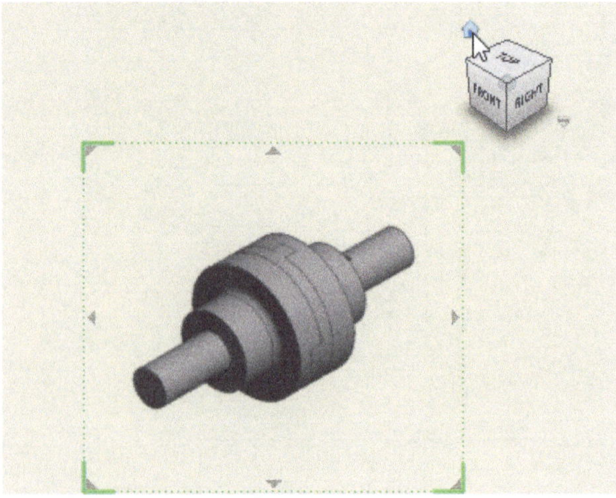

5. Set **Scale** to **1/2**.
6. Click and drag the view to the top left corner.
7. Right-click and select **OK**.

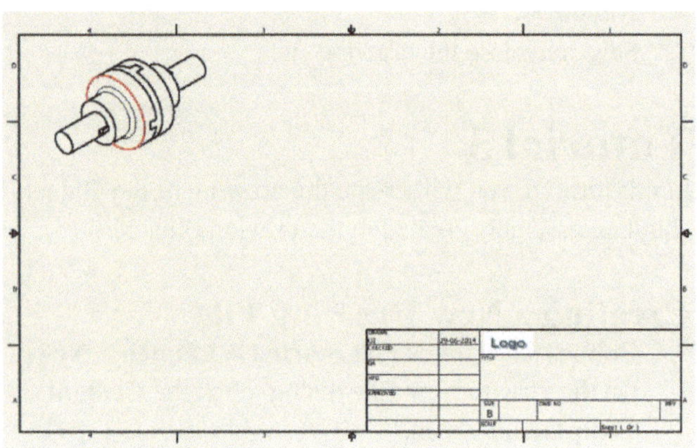

Generating the Exploded View

1. To generate the base view, click **Place Views > Create > Base** on the ribbon; the **Drawing View** dialog appears.
2. Click **Open existing file** on this dialog; the **Open** dialog appears.
3. Go to the project folder and double-click on **Oldham_Coupling.ipn**.
4. Click the **Home** icon located above the ViewCube.
5. Set **Scale** to **1/2**.
6. Click and drag the view to the center of the drawing sheet.
7. Right-click and select **OK**.

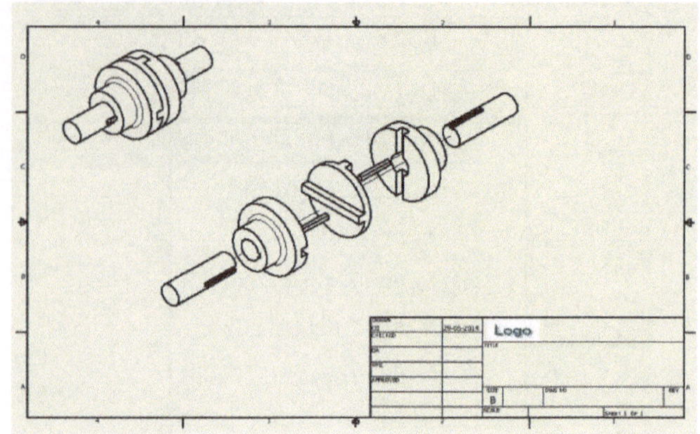

Configuring the Parts list settings

1. Click **Manage > Styles and Standards > Style Editor** on the ribbon; the **Style and Standard Editor** dialog appears.
2. Expand the **Parts List** node and select **Parts List (ANSI)**.

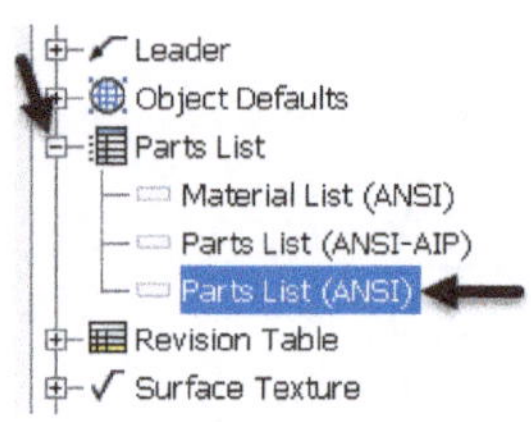

3. Click the **Column Chooser** button under the **Default Columns Settings** group; the **Parts List Column Chooser** dialog appears.

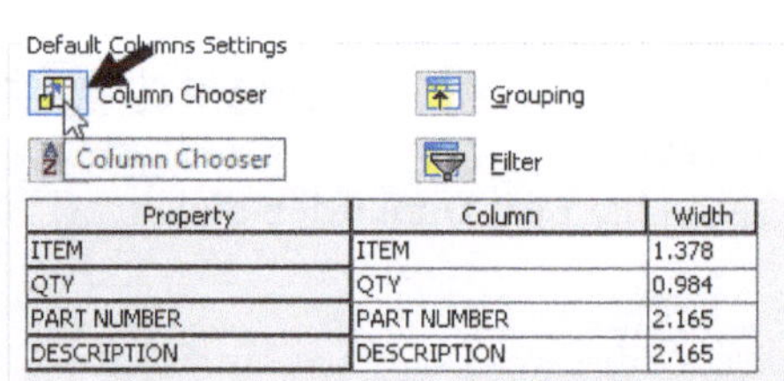

4. On this dialog, select **DESCRIPTION** from the **Selected Properties** list and click the **Remove** button.
5. Select **PART NUMBER** from the **Selected Properties** list and click **Move Up**.
6. Click **OK**.
7. Click **Save and Close**.

Creating the Parts list

1. To create a parts list, click **Annotate > Table > Parts List** on the ribbon; the **Parts List** dialog appears.

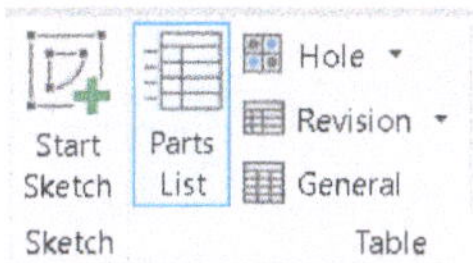

2. Select the exploded view from the drawing sheet.
3. Select **Parts Only** from the **BOM View** drop-down under the **BOM Settings and Properties** group.

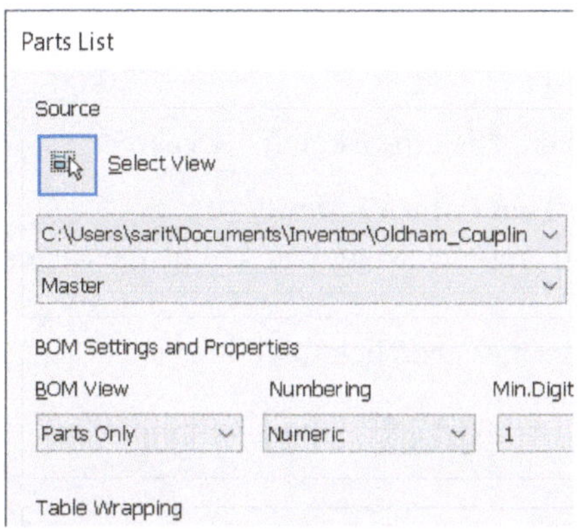

4. Click **OK**.
5. Place the part list above the title block.

PARTS LIST		
ITEM	PART NUMBER	QTY
1	Disc	1
2	Flange	2
3	Shaft	2
4	Key	2

Creating Balloons

1. To create balloons, click **Annotate > Table > Balloon > Auto Balloon** on the ribbon; the **Auto-Balloon** dialog appears.

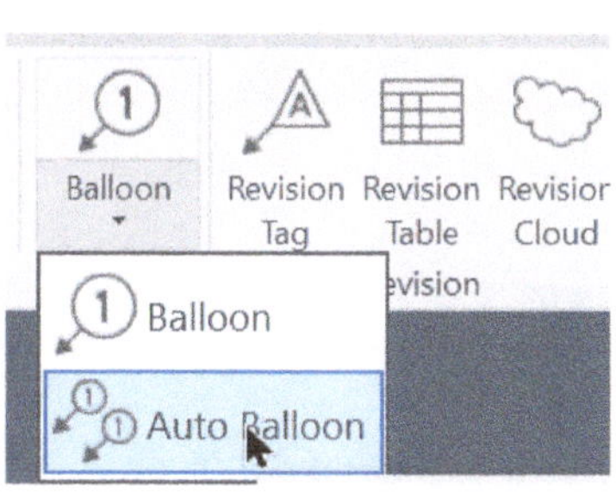

2. Select the exploded view from the drawing sheet.
3. Select all the parts in the exploded view.
4. Select **Horizontal** from the **Placement** group.
5. Click the **Select Placement** button in the **Placement** group.

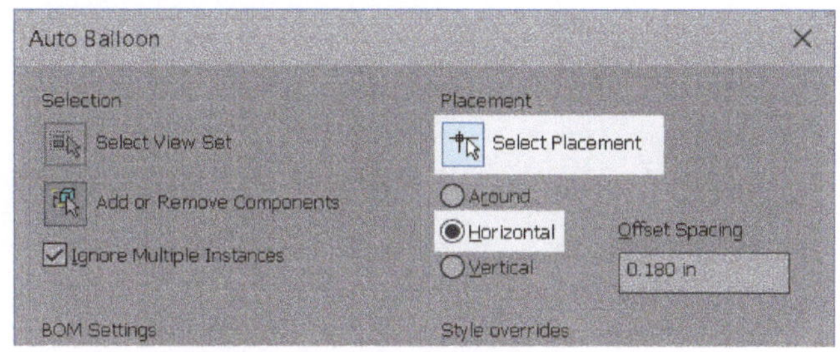

6. Click above the exploded view.
7. Click **OK** to place the balloons.

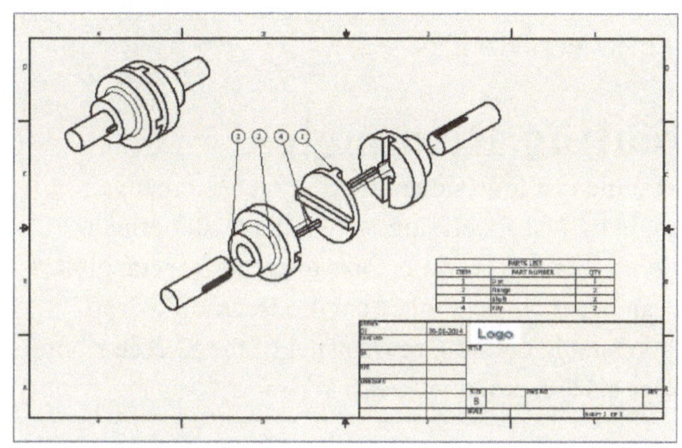

Saving the Drawing

1. Click **Save** on the **Quick Access Toolbar**; the **Save As** dialog appears.
2. Type-in **Oldham_Coupling** in the **File Name** box.
3. Go to the project folder.
4. Click **Save** to save the file.
5. Click **OK**.
6. Click **File Menu > Close**.

Chapter 5: Sketching

In this chapter, you will learn the sketching tools. You will learn to create:

- Rectangles
- Polygons
- Resolve Sketch
- Relations
- Splines
- Ellipses
- Move, rotate, scale, copy, and stretch entities
- Circles
- Arcs
- Circular pattern
- Trim Entities
- Fillets and Chamfers

Creating Rectangles

A rectangle is a four-sided object. You can create a rectangle by just specifying its two diagonal corners. However, there are various tools to create a rectangle. You can access these tools from the **Rectangle** drop-down available on the **Create** panel of the **Sketch** ribbon. These tools are explained next.

1. On the **My Home** page, click **New > Part**.
2. On the ribbon, click **3D Model > Sketch > 2D Sketch** and select the XY plane.

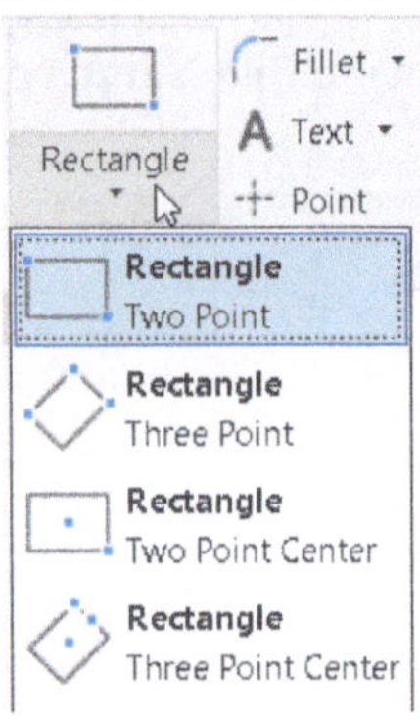

3. On the ribbon, click **Sketch > Create > Rectangle Drop-down > Rectangle Two Point**.
4. Select the origin point to define the first corner.
5. Move the pointer diagonally and click to define the second corner.

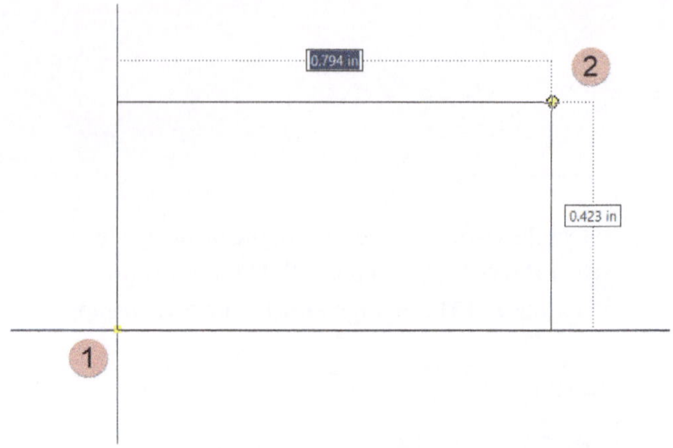

6. On the ribbon, click the **Sketch > Create > Rectangle Two Point Center**.
7. Click in the graphics window to define the center point.
8. Move the pointer and click to define the corner.

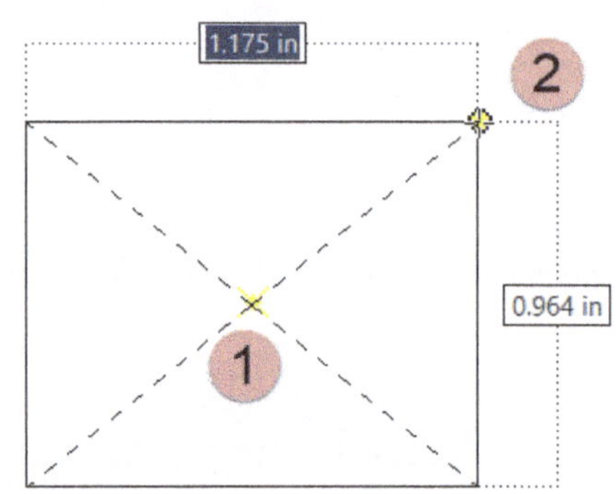

9. On the ribbon, click the **Sketch > Create > Rectangle** drop-down **> Rectangle Three Point**. This option creates a slanted rectangle.
10. Select two points to define the width and inclination angle of the rectangle.

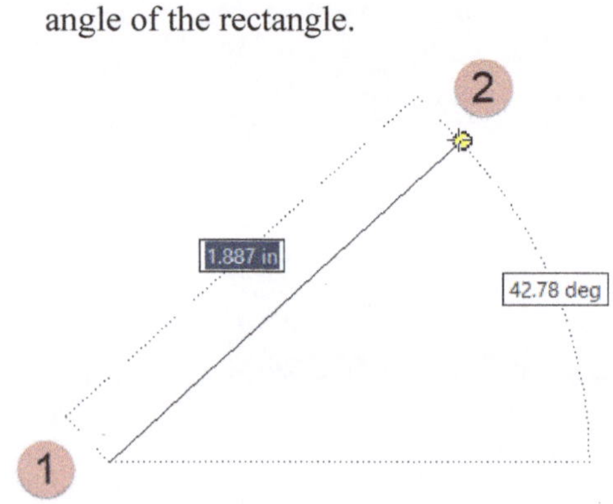

11. Select the third point to define its height.

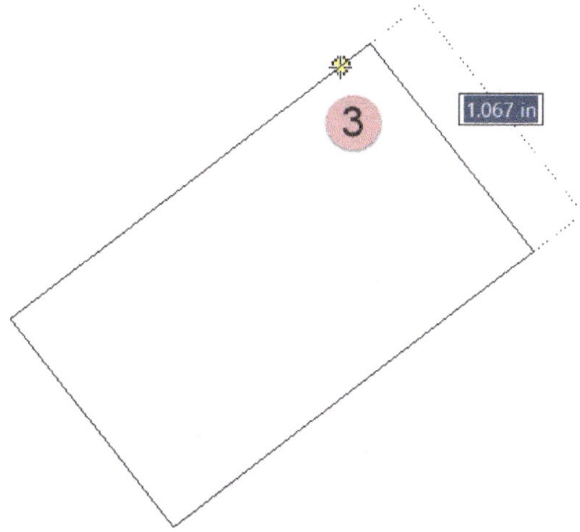

12. On the ribbon, click **Sketch > Create > Rectangle** drop-down **> Rectangle Three Point Center Rectangle** .
13. Click to define the center point of the rectangle.
14. Move the pointer and click to define the midpoint of one side.

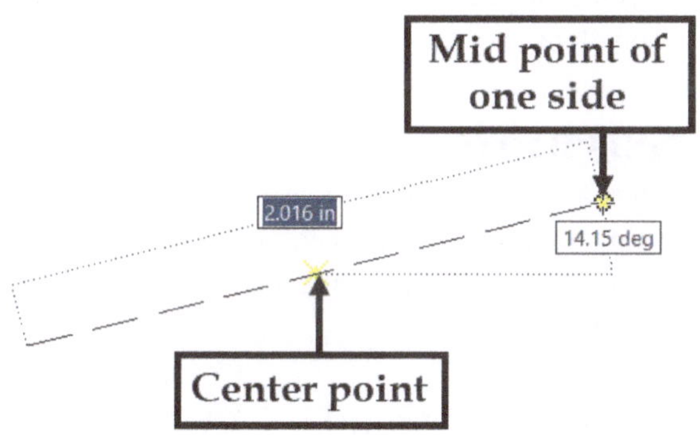

15. Move the pointer and click to define the height.

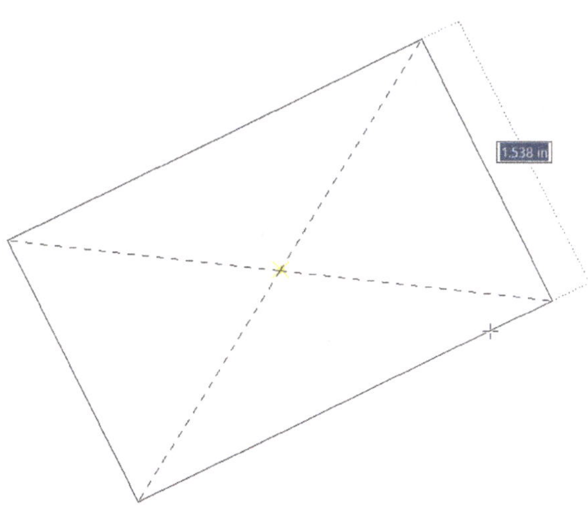

Creating Polygons

A Polygon is a shape having many sides ranging from 3 to 1024. In Inventor, you can create regular polygons having sided with equal length. Follow the steps given next to create a polygon.

1. Start a 2D sketch.
2. On the ribbon, click **Sketch > Create > Rectangle drop-down > Polygon** .
3. On the **Polygon** dialog, type **8** in the **Number of Sides** box.
4. Select **Inscribed circle**. This option creates a polygon with its vertices touching an imaginary circle. You can also select the **Circumscribed circle** option to create a polygon with its sides touching an imaginary circle.
5. Click to define the center of the polygon.
6. Move the pointer and click to define the size and angle of the polygon.

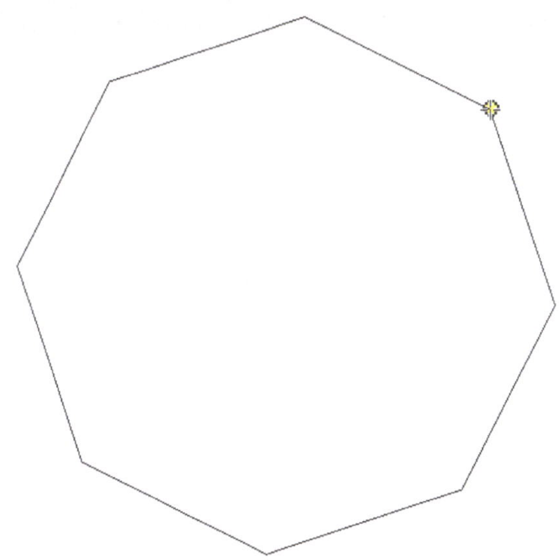

7. Click **Done** to deactivate the tool.

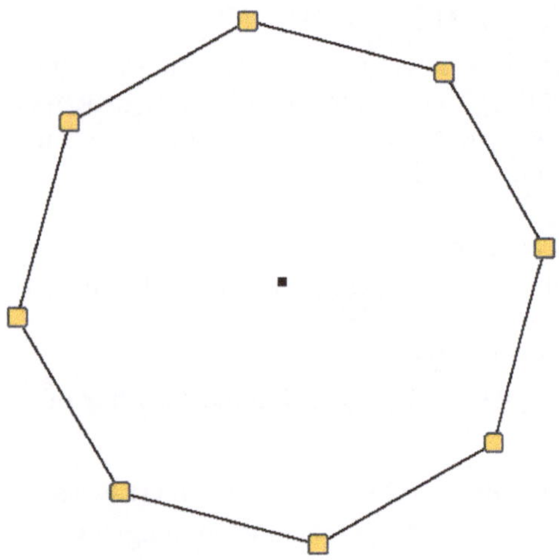

Driving and Driven Dimensions

When creating sketches for a part, Inventor will not allow you to over-constrain the geometry. The term 'over-constrain' means adding more dimensions than required. The following figure shows a fully constrained sketch. If you add another dimension to this sketch (e.g., diagonal dimension), the **Autodesk Inventor** dialog appears.

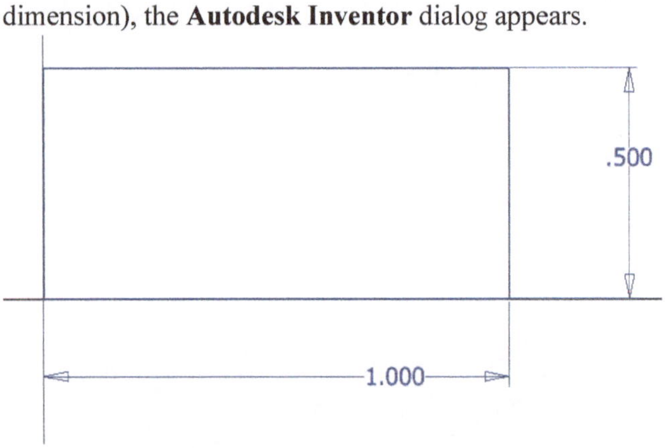

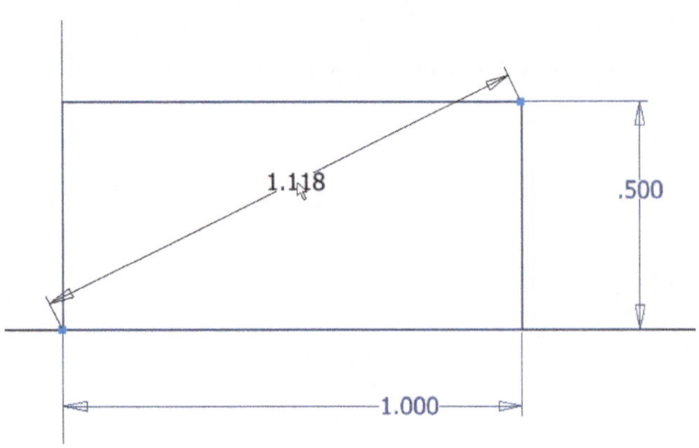

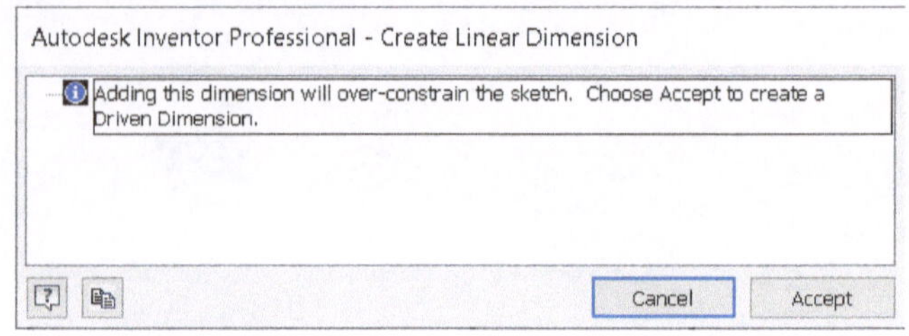

Now, click **Accept** to convert the new dimension into a driven dimension.

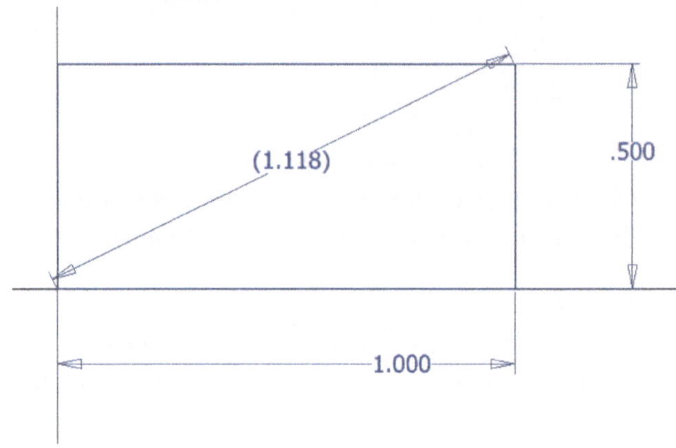

Now, if you change the value of the width, the reference dimension along the diagonal updates automatically.

Constraints

Constraints are used to control the shape of a sketch by establishing relationships between the sketch elements. You can add constraints using the tools available on the **Constrain** panel.

Coincident Constraint

This constraint connects a point to another point.

1. On the **Sketch** tab of the Ribbon, click **Constrain > Coincident Constrain** .
2. Select two points. The selected points are connected.

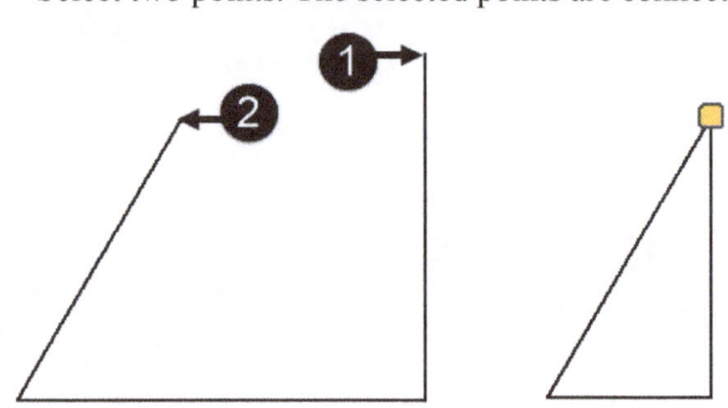

Horizontal Constraint

To apply the **Horizontal Constraint**, click on a line and click the **Horizontal Constraint** icon on the context toolbar.

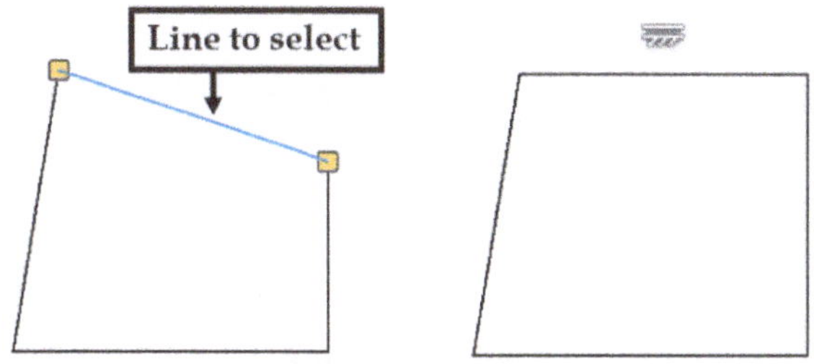

You can also align two points or vertices horizontally. Click the **Horizontal Constraint** icon on the **Constrain** panel, and then select the two points.

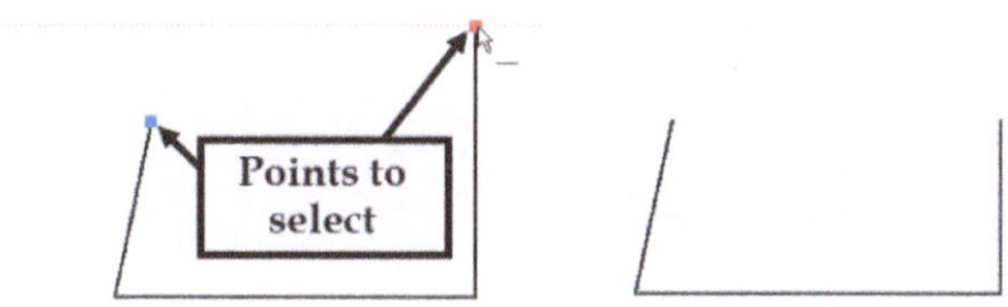

Vertical Constraint

Use the **Vertical Constraint** to make a line vertical. You can also use this constraint to align two points or vertices vertically.

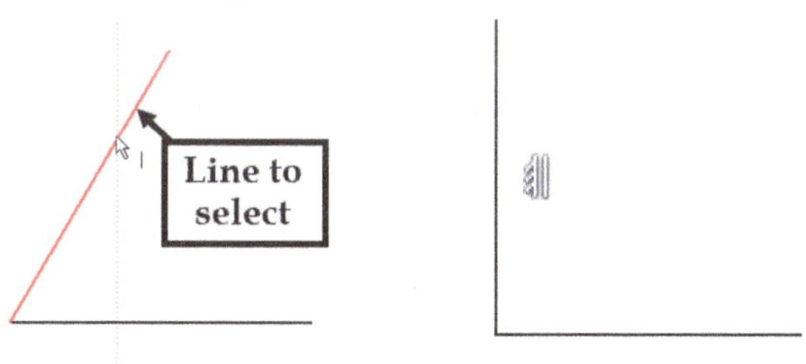

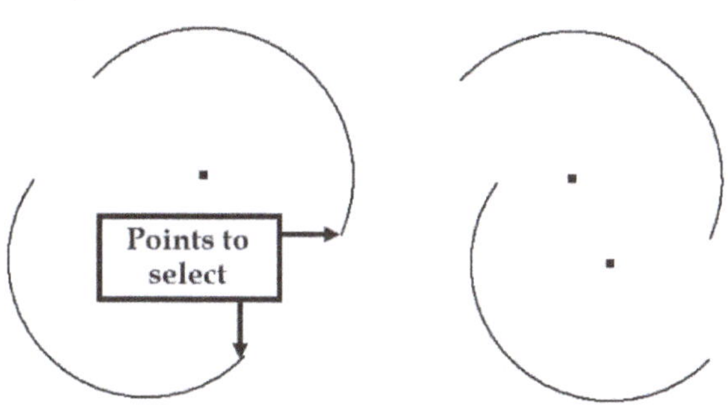

Tangent Constraint

This constraint makes an arc, circle, or line tangent to another arc or circle. Click the **Tangent Constraint** icon on the **Constrain** panel. Select a circle, arc, or line. Next, select another circle or arc; the two elements will be tangent to each other.

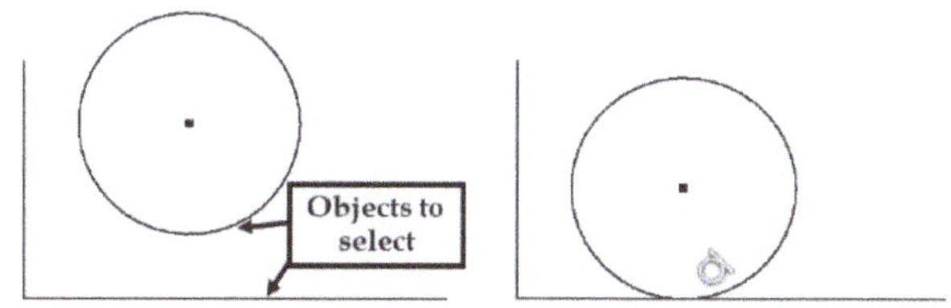

Parallel Constraint

Use the **Parallel Constraint** to make two lines parallel to each other. To do this, click the **Parallel Constraint** icon on the **Constrain** panel. Next, select the two lines to be parallel.

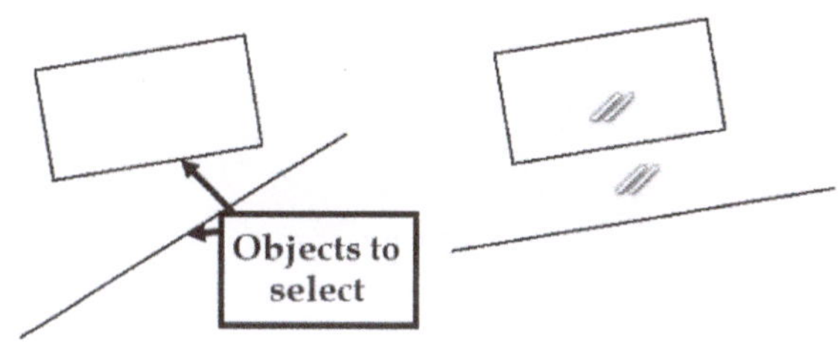

Perpendicular Constraint

Use the **Perpendicular Constraint** to make two entities perpendicular to each other.

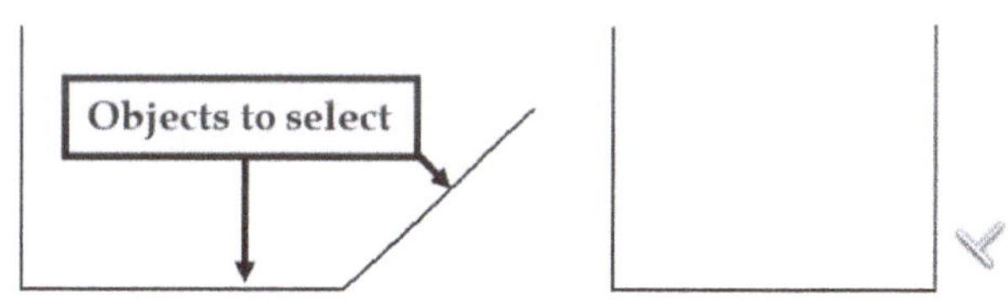

Automatic Constraints

Inventor automatically adds constraints when you create sketch elements.

1. Start a new sketch and activate the **Line** tool from the **Sketch** ribbon.
2. Click to specify the start point of the line.
3. Move the pointer in the horizontal direction and notice the **Horizontal** constraint flag.
4. Click to create a line with the **Horizontal** constraint.

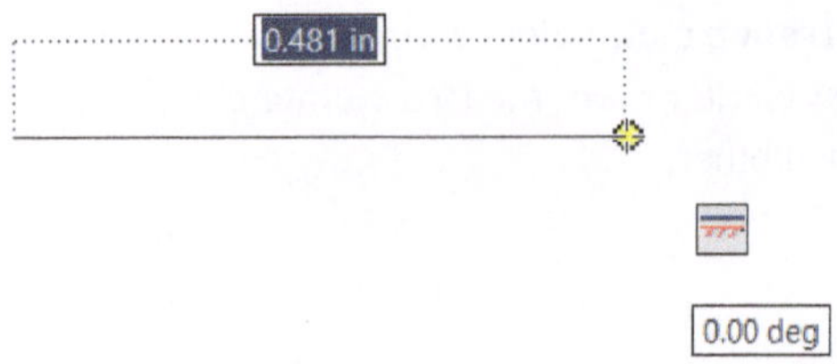

5. Move the pointer vertically in the upward direction and notice the **Perpendicular** constraint flag.
6. Click to create a line with the **Perpendicular** constraint.

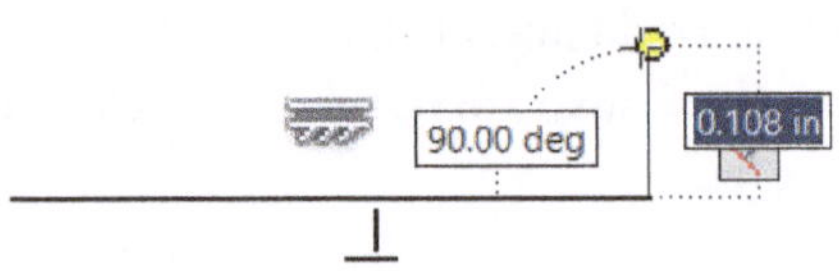

7. Create an inclined line, as shown.

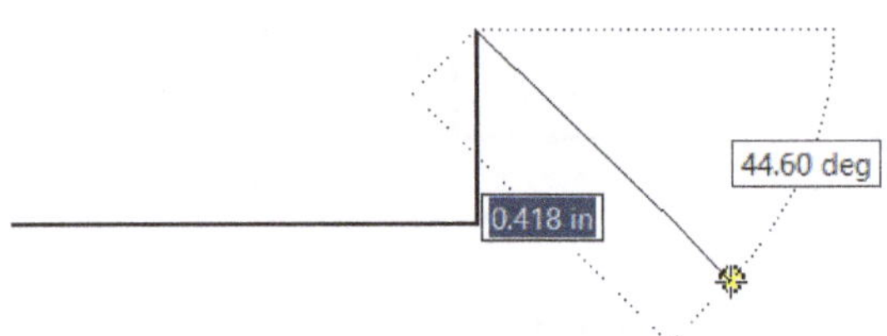

8. Move the pointer along the inclined line and notice the **Collinear** constraint flag.

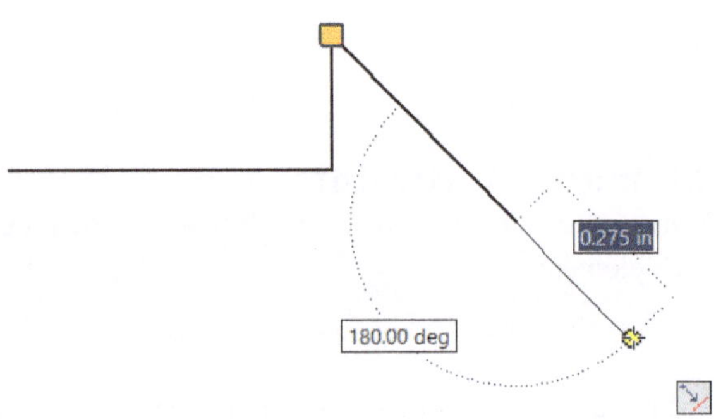

9. On the ribbon, click **Sketch** tab > **Create** panel > **Circle** 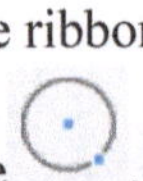, and then create a circle.
10. Activate the **Line** tool and click on the circle.
11. Move the pointer around the circle and notice that the line maintains the **Tangent** constraint with the circle.

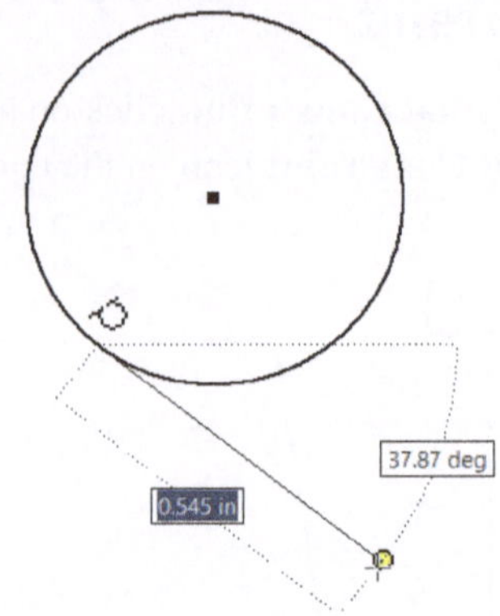

12. Click to create a line that is tangent and coincident to the circle. Right click and select **OK**.

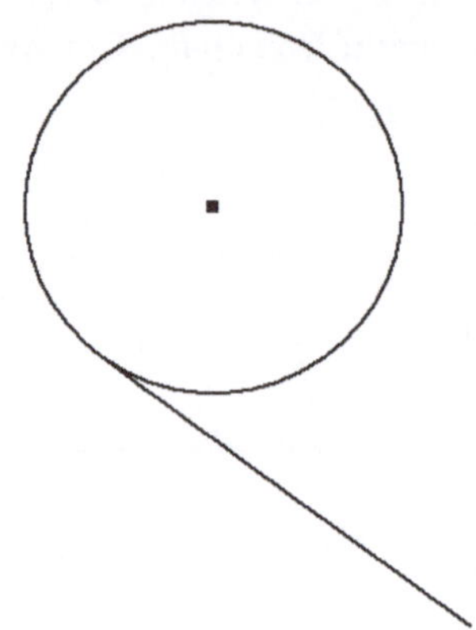

Deleting Constraints

You can delete constraints by using the following methods.

- On the status bar, click the **Show Constraints**  icon.
- Select the constraint and press **Delete** on your keyboard.

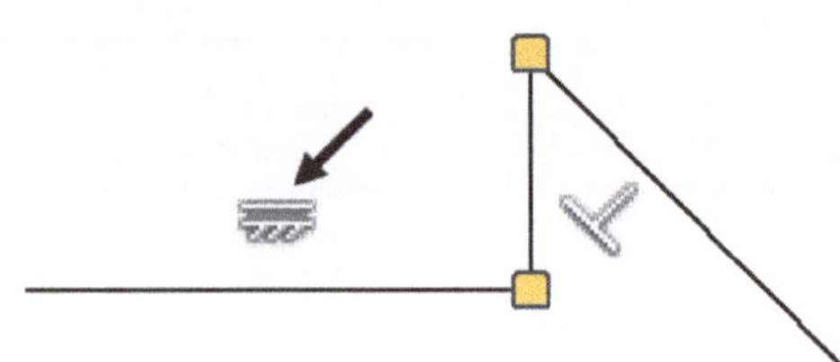

Hiding Constraints

To hide sketch constraints, click the **Hide All Constraints** icon located on the status bar.

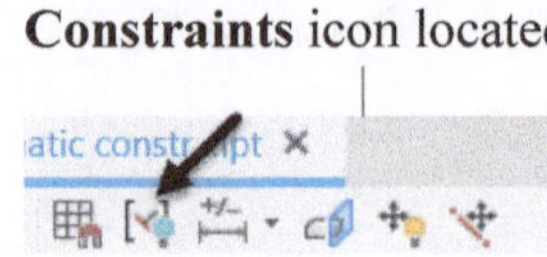

Project Geometry

The **Project Geometry** tool helps you to use the edges of the part geometry to create sketch elements.

1. Download Chapter 5: Sketching folder from the Companion website.
2. Open the Project_geomtry part file from the folder.
3. Start a sketch on the plane offset to the model face, as shown.
4. On the **Sketch** ribbon, click **Modify > Project Geometry**  .
5. Place the pointer on any one of the edges (or) Right-click on anyone of the edges and select **Select Other.**
6. Click the down-arrow next to fly out, and then select **Loop**.

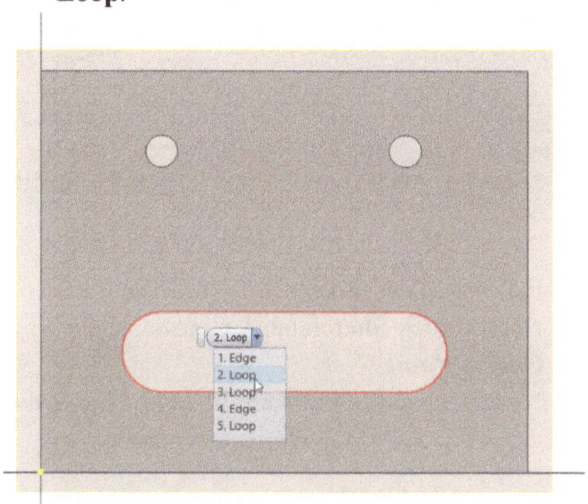

The loop is projected onto the sketch plane. The projected edges are displayed in yellow color.

7. Click on the round edges of the model.

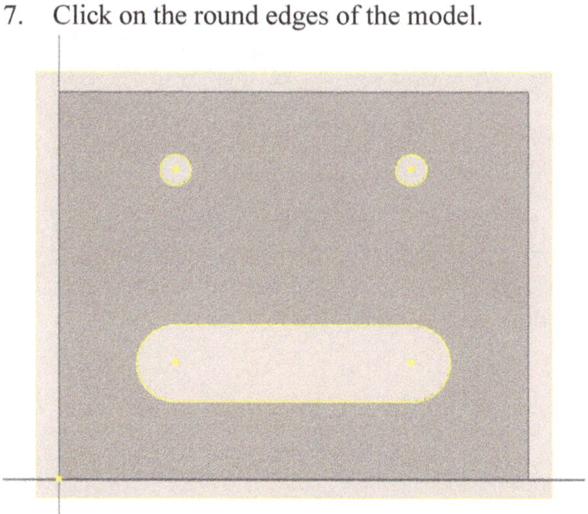

Tutorial 1

In this tutorial, you will create a sketch using the **Line**, **Three Point Arc**, and **Circle** tools.

1. Activate the **Sketch** Environment.
2. On the ribbon, click **Sketch > Create >Line.**
3. Click on the origin point to define the start point of the line.
4. Move the pointer horizontally toward the right and click.

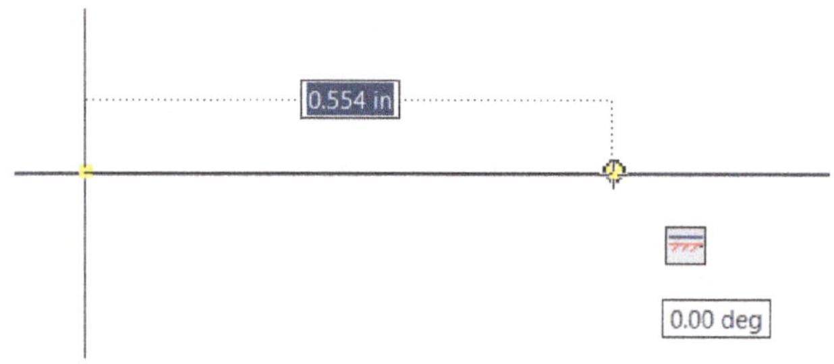

5. Move the pointer upward and click when a dotted line appears.

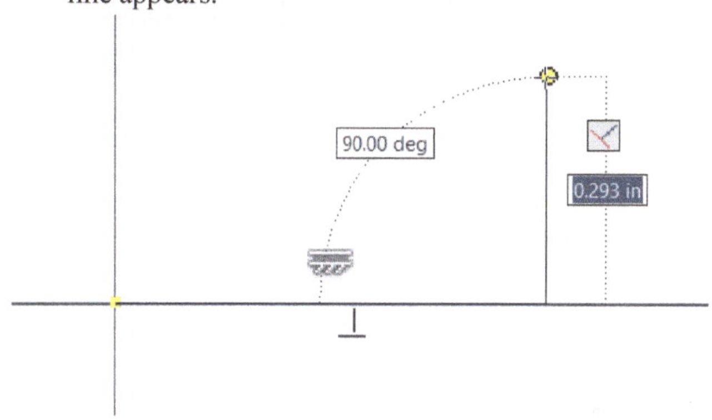

6. Move the pointer away from the endpoint of the vertical line.
7. Again, place the pointer on the endpoint of the vertical line.
8. Press and hold the left mouse button.
9. Move the pointer diagonally toward the top left corner and click. Next, right click and select **OK**.

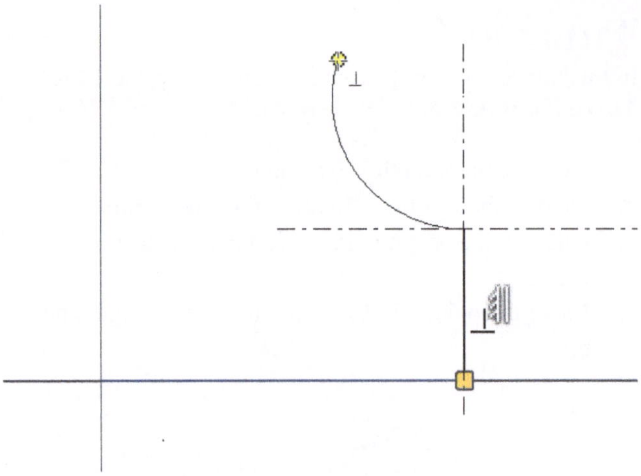

10. On the ribbon, click **Sketch > Format > Construction**.
11. Activate the **Line** tool.
12. Select the origin point of the sketch, move the pointer vertically upwards, and click. Press **Esc**.

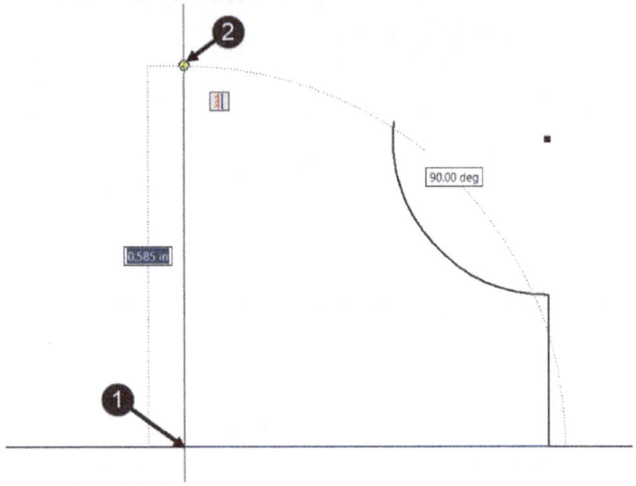

13. On the ribbon, click **Sketch > Pattern > Mirror**.
14. Select the arc, horizontal, and vertical lines.
15. On the **Mirror** dialog, click the **Mirror line** button and select the vertical construction line. Click **Apply** and **Done**.

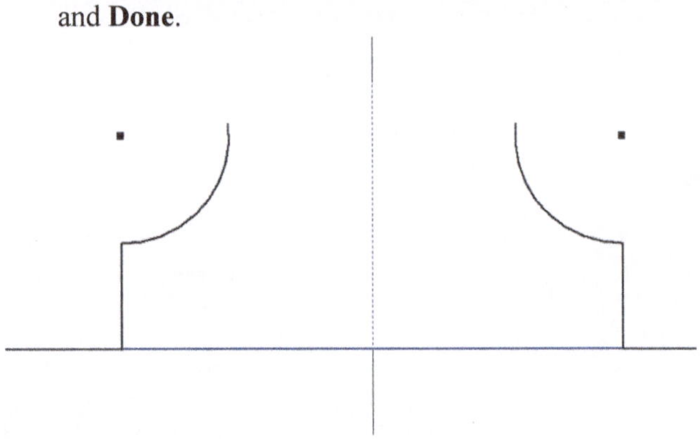

16. On the ribbon, click **Sketch > Format > Construction**.
17. On the ribbon, click **Sketch** tab > **Create** panel > **Arc Three Point**.
18. Select the endpoint of the left and right arc, and then move the pointer upward.
19. Click when the **Tangent** constraint appears.

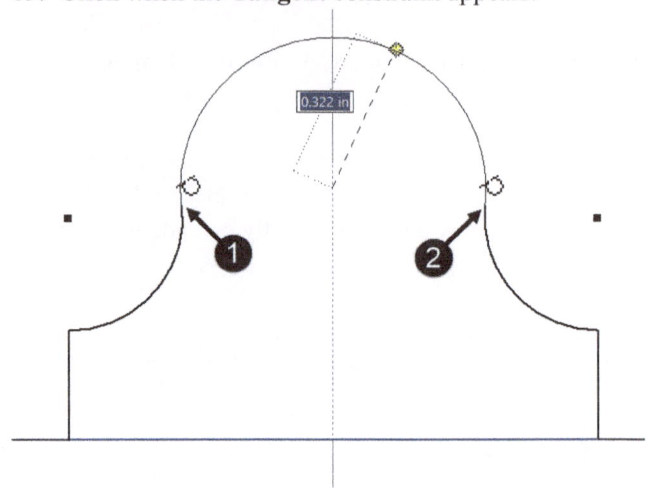

20. Right click and select **OK**.
21. On the ribbon, click **Sketch** tab > **Create** panel > **Circle Center Point**.
22. Select the centerpoint of the three-point arc, move the pointer outward, and click to create the circle.

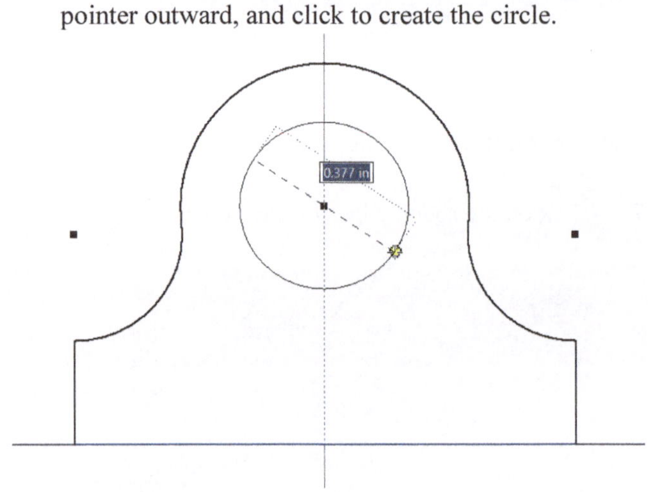

23. Add dimensions to the sketch, as shown.

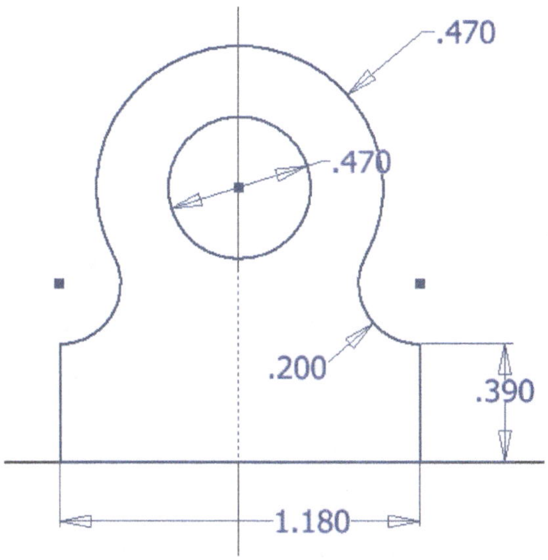

24. Click **Finish**.

Ellipses

Ellipses are also non-uniform curves, but they have a regular shape. They are actually splines created in regular closed shapes.

1. Activate the **Sketch** environment.
2. On the ribbon, click **Sketch** tab > **Create** panel > **Circle** drop-down > **Ellipse**.
3. Pick a point in the graphics window to define the center of the ellipse.
4. Move the pointer and click to define the radius and orientation of the first axis.

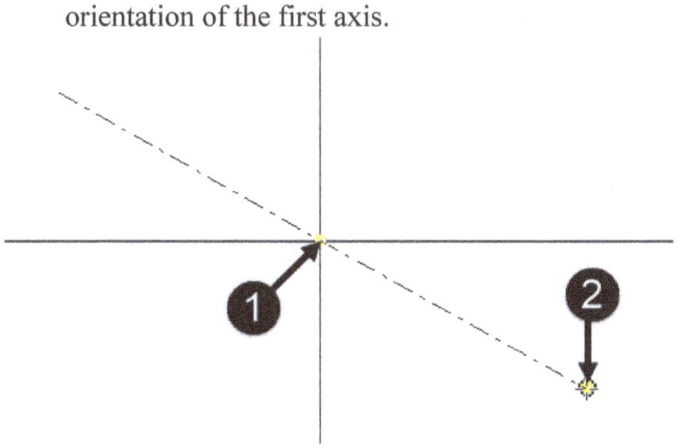

5. Move the pointer and click to define the radius of the second axis.

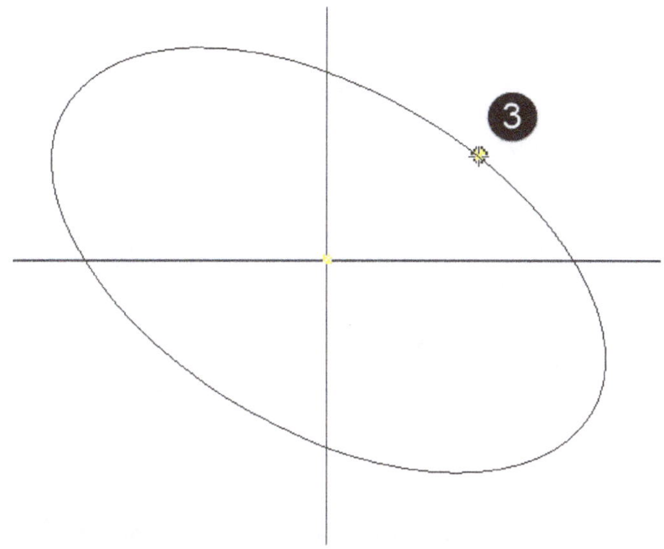

Click and drag the ellipse the notice that it is under-defined. You need to add dimensions and constraints to define the ellipse fully.

6. Activate the **Line** tool and select the centerpoint of the ellipse.
7. Move the pointer upward and select a point on the ellipse.

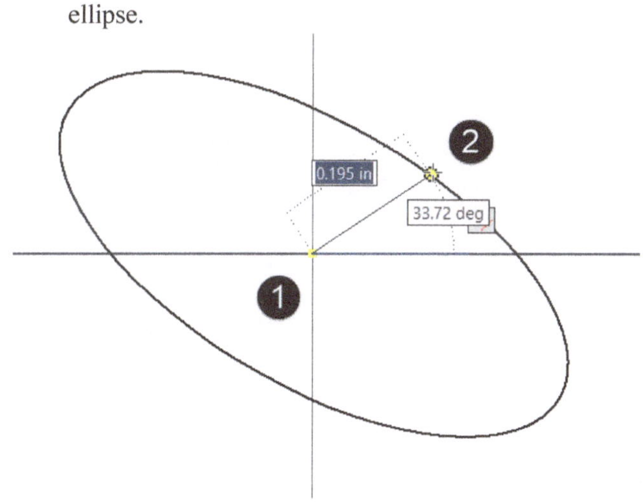

8. Select the centerpoint of the ellipse. Move the pointer toward the right and select a point on the ellipse.

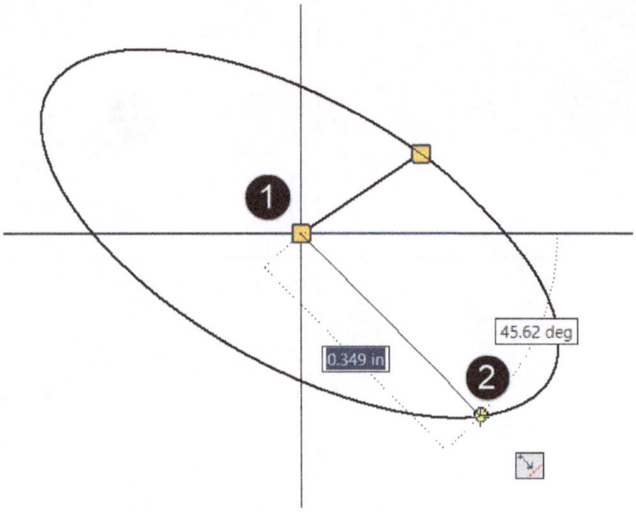

9. On the ribbon, click **Sketch** tab > **Constraint** panel > **Perpendicular**.
10. Select the two lines to make them perpendicular.

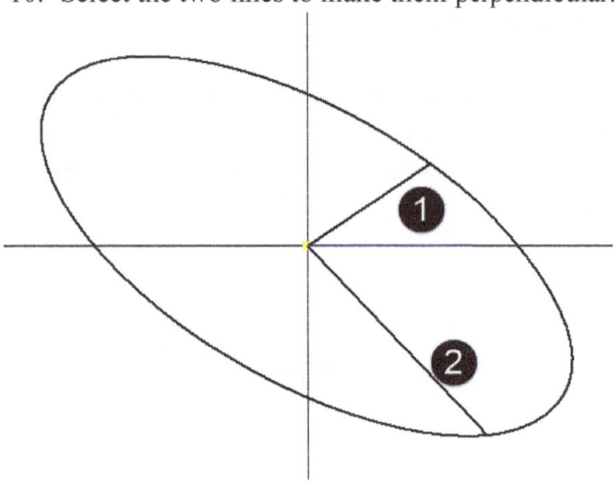

11. On the ribbon, click **Sketch** tab > **Constrain** panel > **Parallel Constraint**.
12. Select the line and the ellipse, as shown.

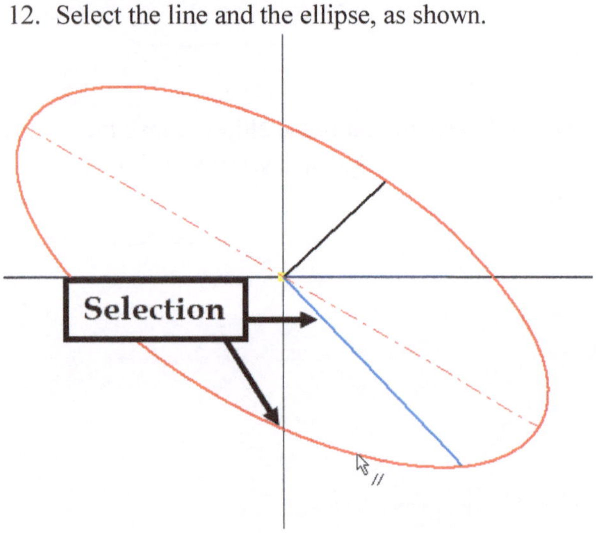

13. Create a horizontal line originating from the center point of the ellipse.

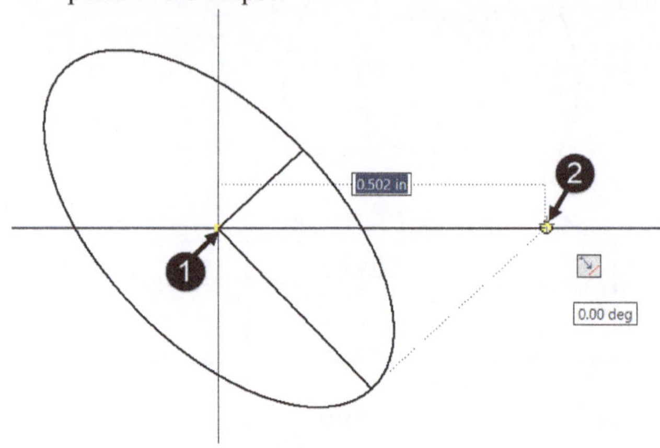

14. Right click and select **OK**.
15. Press and hold the Shift key and select the three lines.
16. On the ribbon, click **Sketch** tab > **Format** panel > **Construction**.
17. On the ribbon, click **Sketch** tab > **Constrain** panel > **Dimension**.
18. Select the lines, as shown.
19. Move the pointer between the selected lines and click to position the angled dimension.

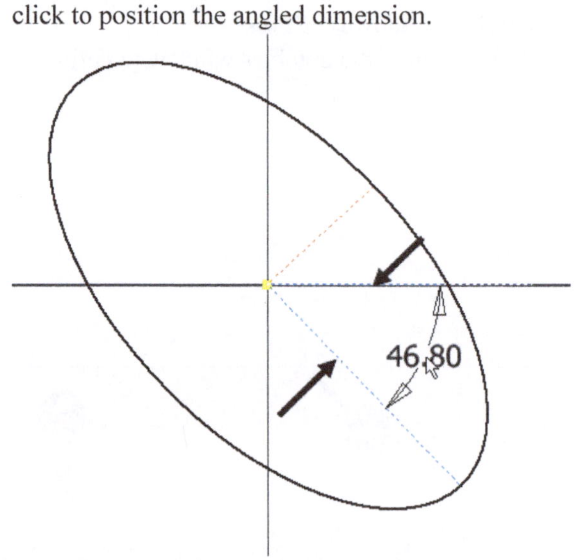

20. Type **15** and click the green check.
21. Select the major axis line.
22. Right click and select **Aligned**.
23. Move the pointer downward and click to position the dimension.
24. Type **0.98** and click the green check.

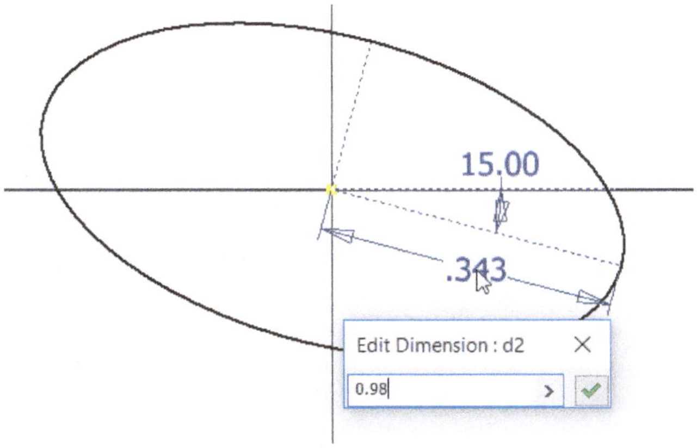

25. Likewise, add the dimension to the minor axis. This fully-defines the sketch.
26. Right-click and select **OK**.

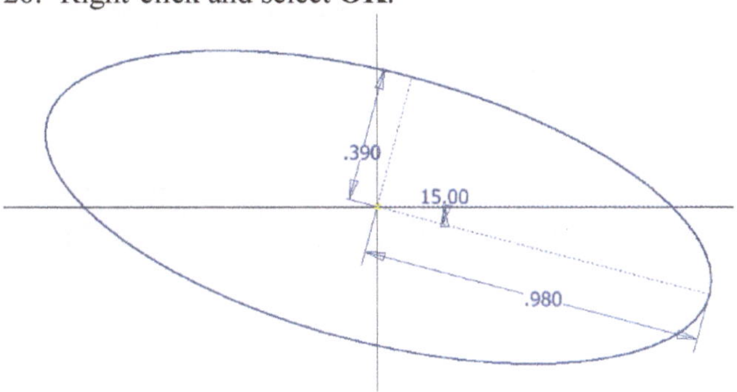

Bridge Curve

The **Bridge Curve** tool is used to create a curve connected to two open sketch elements.

1. Create a line and arc, as shown.

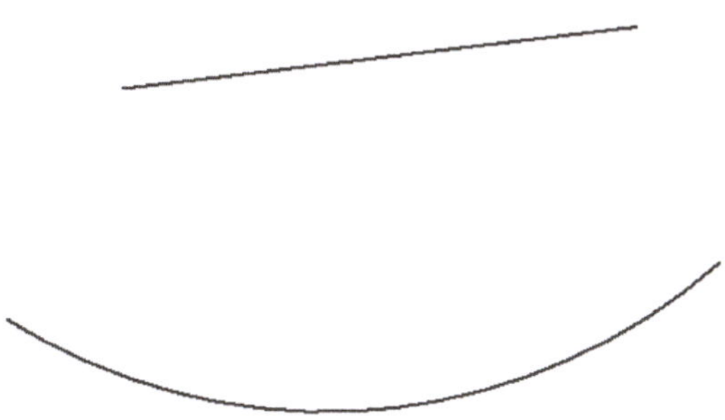

2. On the **Sketch** ribbon, click **Create** panel > **Line** drop-down > **Bridge Curve** .
3. Select the endpoints of the line and arc.

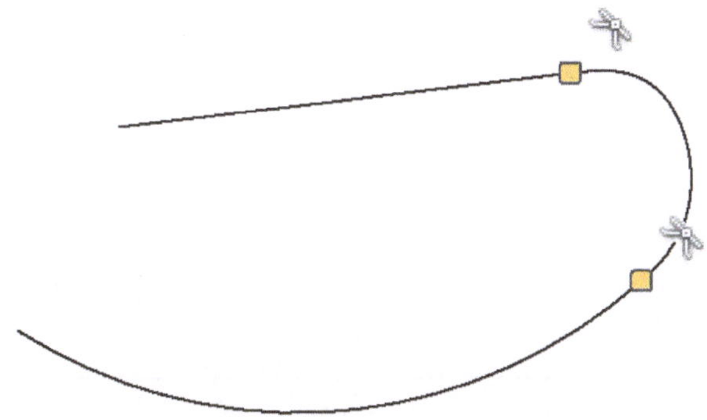

Extend

The **Extend** tool is similar to the **Trim** tool, but its use is the opposite of it. This tool is used to extend lines, arcs, and other open entities to connect to other objects.

1. Create a sketch, as shown below.

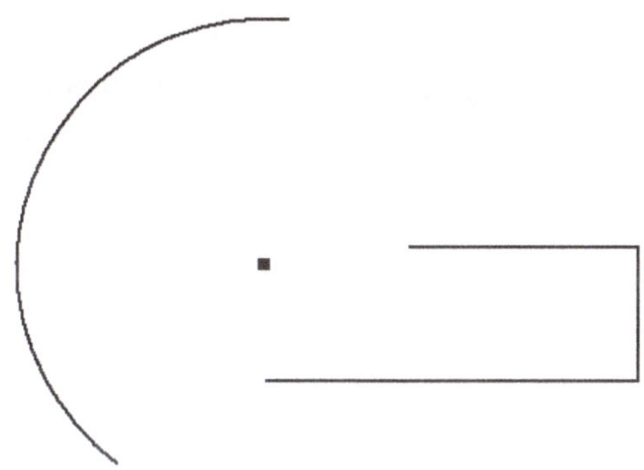

2. Click **Sketch > Modify > Extend** on the ribbon.
3. Select the horizontal open line. This will extend the line up to arc.

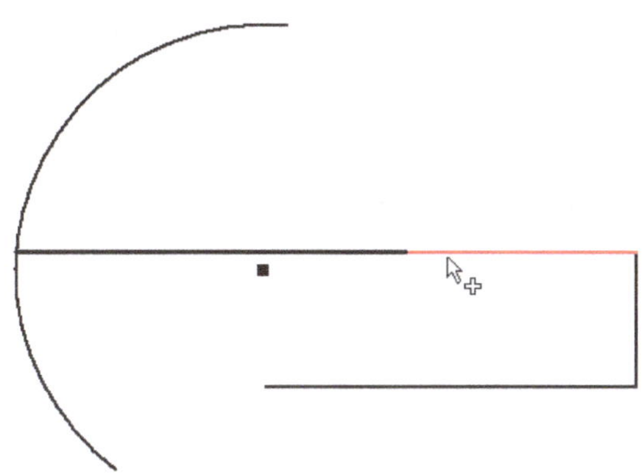

Likewise, extend the other elements, as shown.

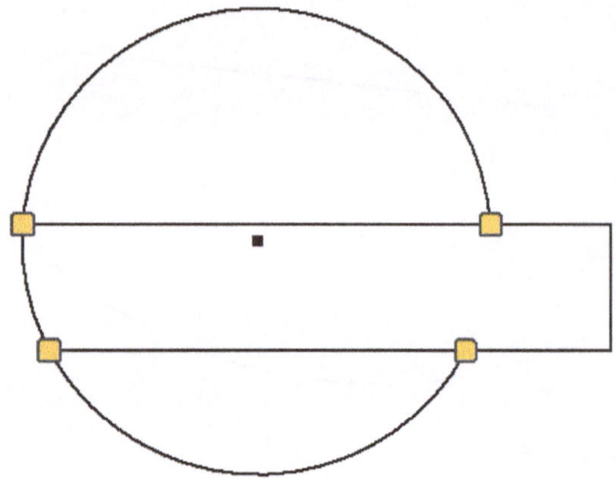

4. Trim the unwanted portions.

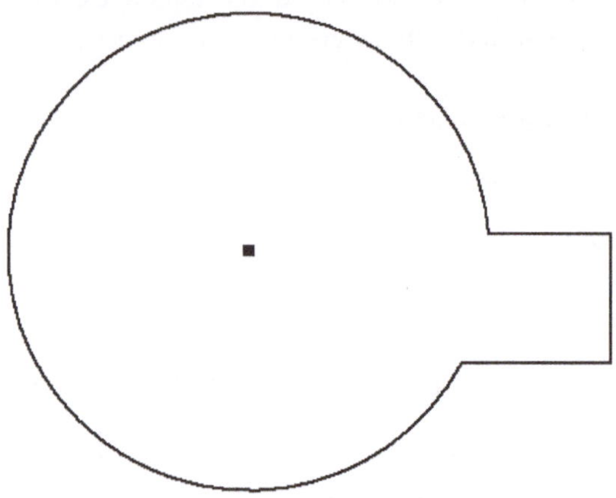

Offset

The **Offset** tool creates parallel copies of lines, circles, and arcs.

1. On the ribbon, click **Sketch** tab > **Modify** panel > **Offset** .
2. Select an entity and notice that all the connected entities are selected.
3. Type-in the offset distance in the value box attached to the offset copy.
4. Click inside or outside the sketch to define the offset side.

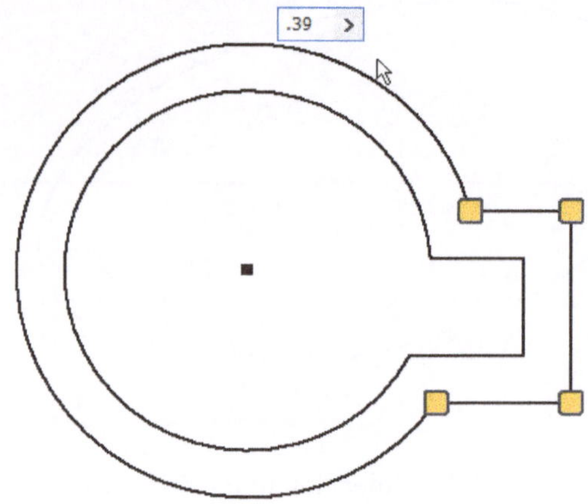

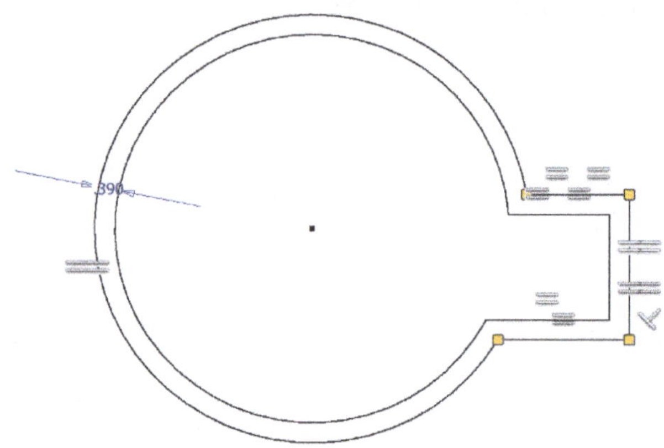

Concentric Constraint

Use the **Concentric Constraint** to make two center points of circles, arcs, or ellipses coincident with each other.

1. Create two circles, as shown.

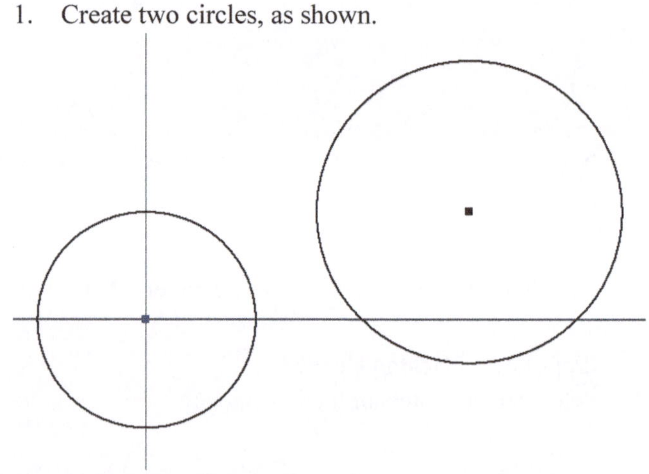

2. On the ribbon, click **Constrain** panel > **Concentric Constraint**.

3. Select the two circles to make them concentric.

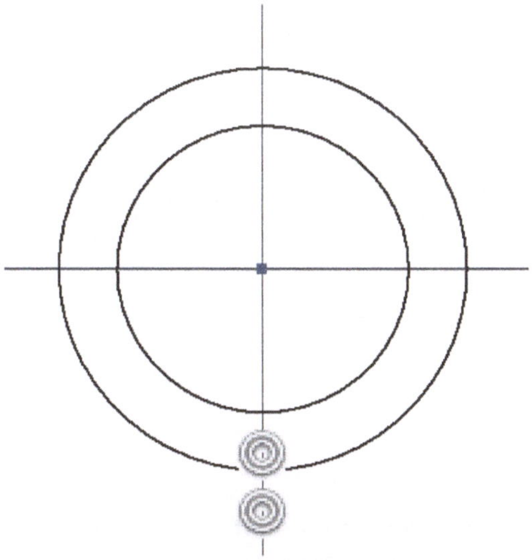

4. On the **Sketch** tab of the ribbon, click **Constrain > Dimension** .
5. Select the inner circle, move the point upward, and click to position the dimension.
6. Type **1.96** and click the green check on the **Edit Dimension** box.
7. Likewise, add dimension to the outer circle and change its value to **5.5**.
8. Right click and select **OK**.

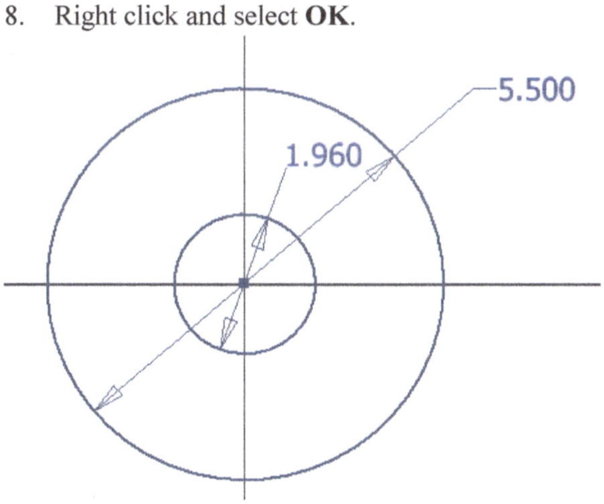

Center Point Arc

The Center Point Arc tool creates an arc by using three points (center, start, and endpoints).

1. On the ribbon, click **Sketch > Create > Arc drop-down > Arc Center Point**.
2. Select the quadrant point of the circle, as shown below.

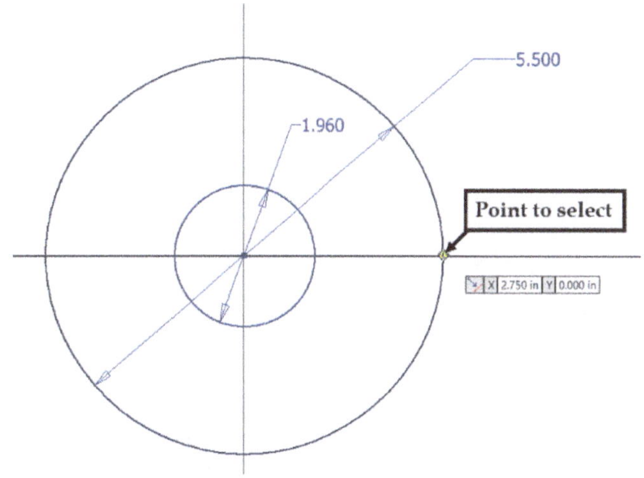

3. Move the pointer down and click on the circle.

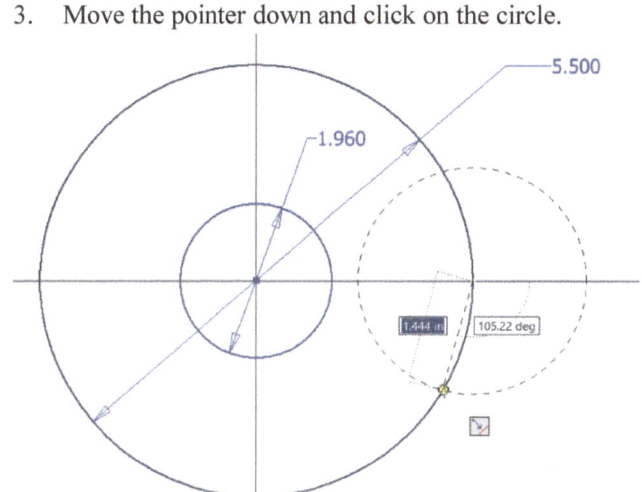

4. Move the pointer leftwards and up, and then click.

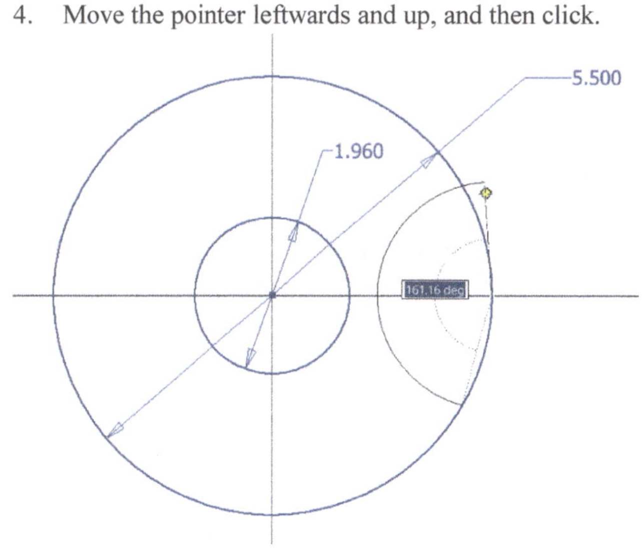

5. Right click and select **OK**.
6. On the ribbon, click **Sketch** tab > **Constrain** panel > **Coincident Constraint** .
7. Select the endpoint of the arc, and then click on the circle.

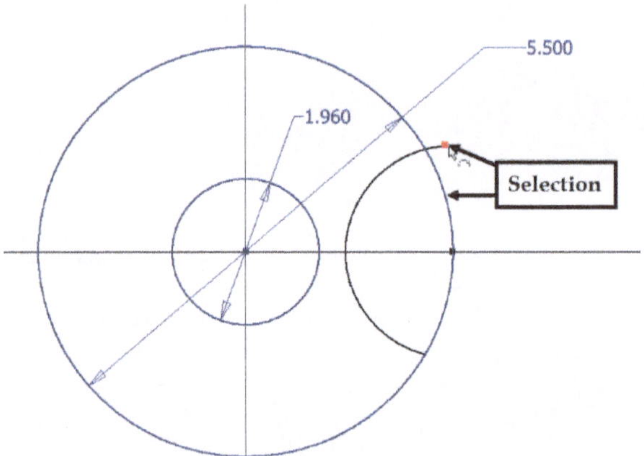

8. On the ribbon, click **Sketch** tab > **Constrain** panel > **Dimension**.
9. Select the arc, move the pointer, and then click to position the dimension.
10. Type **0.98** in the **Edit dimension** box, and then click the green check.

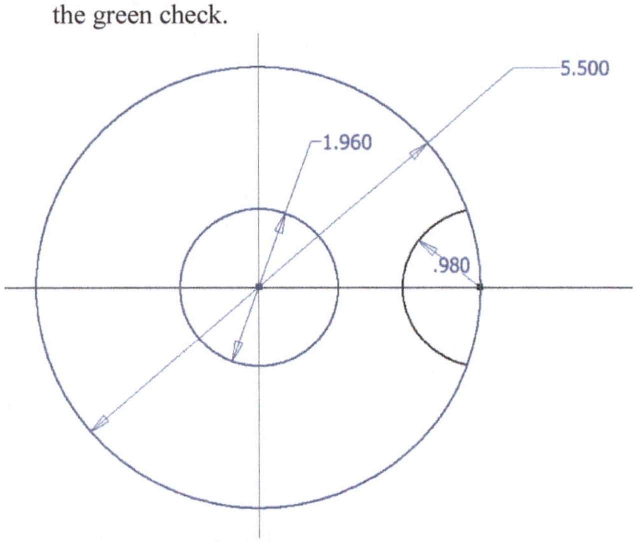

Circular Pattern

The **Circular Pattern** tool creates an arrangement of objects around a point in circular form.

1. On the ribbon, click **Sketch** tab > **Pattern** panel > **Circular Pattern**.
2. Select the arc.
3. Click the cursor button next to the **Axis** button.
4. Select the center of the circle; the preview of the circular pattern appears.

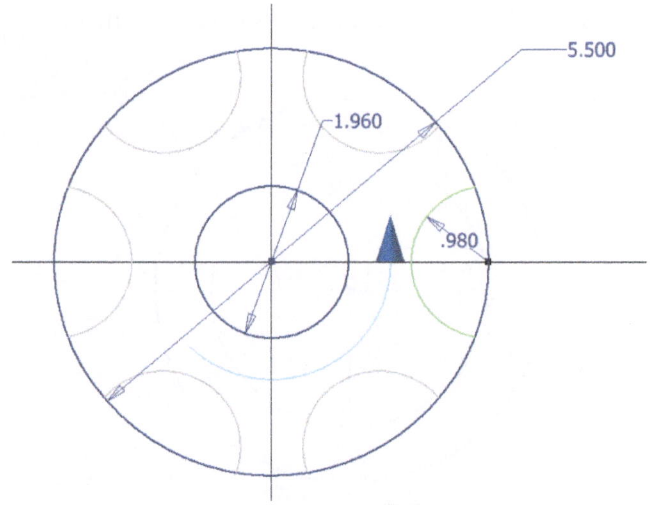

5. Type **4** and **360** in the **Count** and **Angle** boxes, respectively. Next, click **OK**.

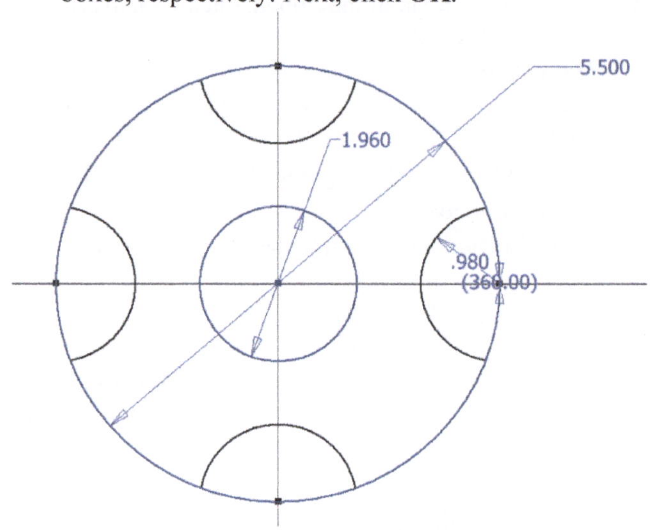

6. Trim the unwanted portions, as shown below.

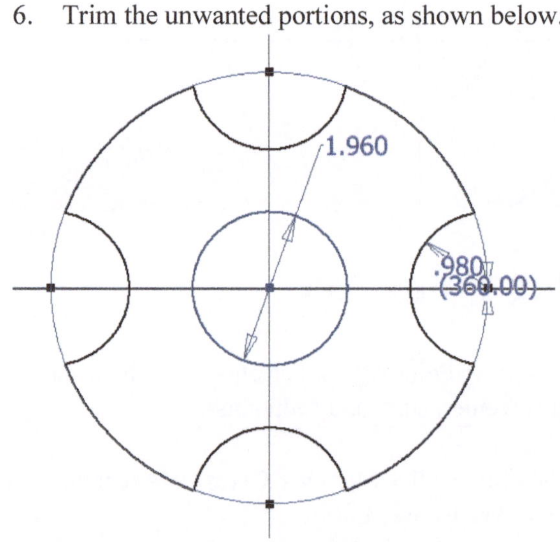

Next, you need to constrain the sketch fully.

7. Click and drag any one of the center points of the arcs. Notice that the arcs are moved freely.
8. On the ribbon, click **Sketch** tab > **Constrain** panel > **Coincident Constraint** .
9. Select the centerpoint of any one of the arcs.
10. Select the outer circle.

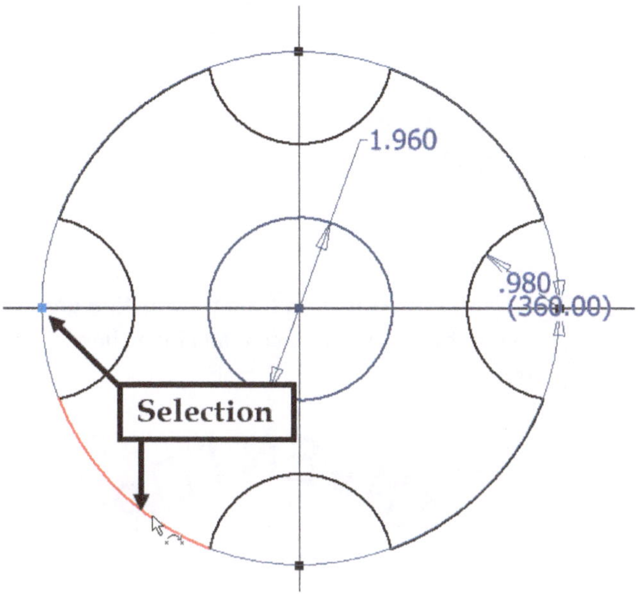

11. Right click and select **OK**.
12. Add dimension to the outer circle.
13. On the ribbon, click **Sketch** tab > **Constrain** panel > **Horizontal Constraint** .
14. Select the center points of the arc and circle, as shown.

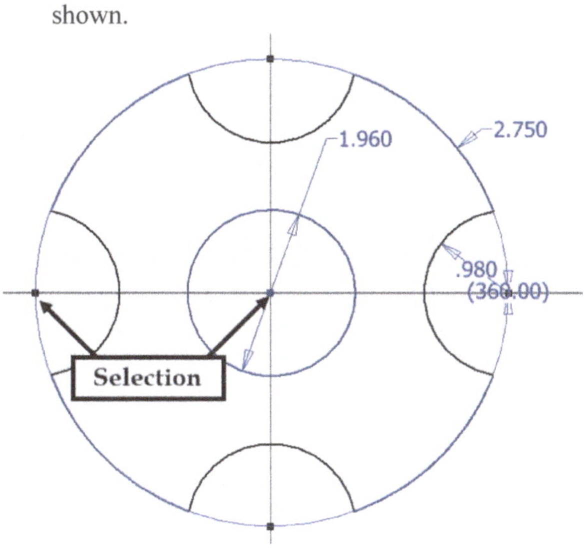

15. Right click and click **OK**.
16. Click **Finish Sketch**.

Text

Texts are used to provide information on the models such as company name, and model specifications.

1. Start a new sketch.
2. Create the circle and two lines perpendicular to each other, as shown.

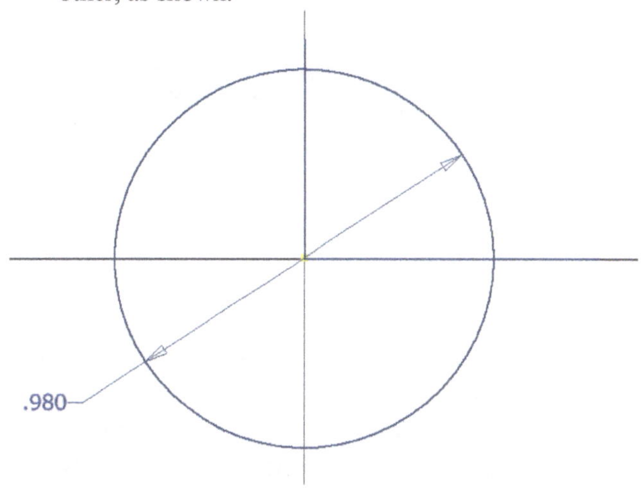

3. Press and hold the Shift key, and then select the circle and the lines.
4. On the ribbon, click **Sketch** tab > **Format** panel > **Construction** .

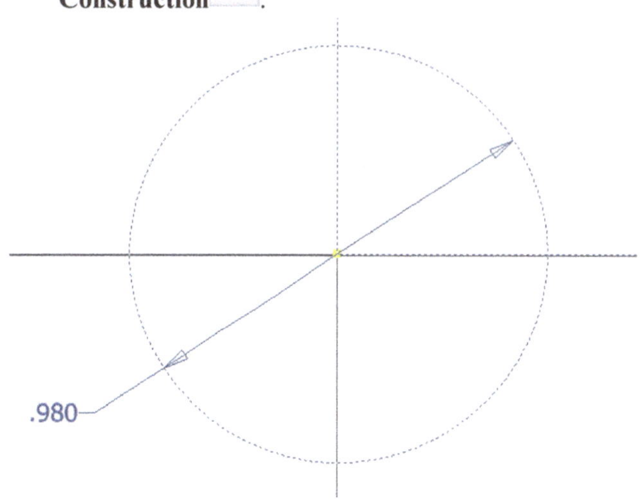

5. On the **Sketch** ribbon, click **Create** panel > **Text** drop-down > **Geometry Text** .
6. Select the horizontal line as the supporting curve.
7. Click in the text box in the **Geometry-Text** dialog, and then type INVENTOR. On the dialog, use the **Position** options (**Left Justification** , **Center Justification** , **Right Align**) to change the

alignment of the text. Use the **Outside**, **Inside** and **Direction options** to the flip the text.

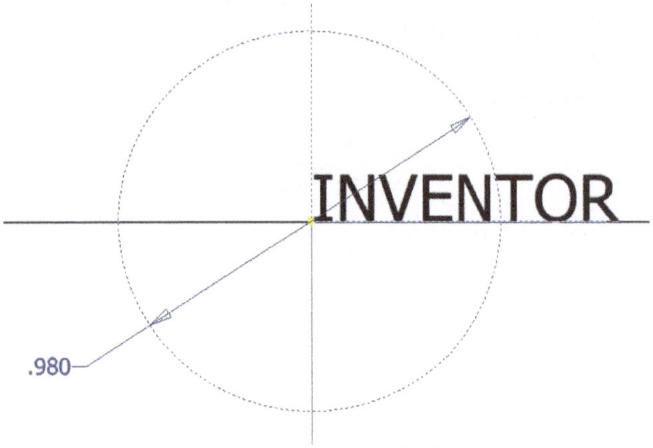

8. Click the **Launch Text Editor** icon to display the **Format Text** dialog
9. On the **Format Text** dialog, change the font type, size, font style, and spacing between the text. Also, you can apply effects such as strikeout and underline.
10. Click **OK** on the **Format Text** dialog.
11. Click the **Geometry** button and click on the vertical construction line.
12. Click the **Update** button.

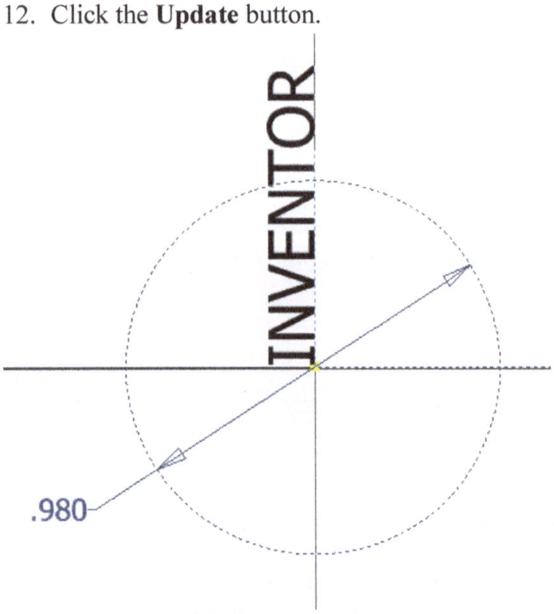

13. Click the **Geometry** button.
14. Select the circle as the alignment curve.
15. Type 0 in the **Start Angle** box.
16. Click **Update**.

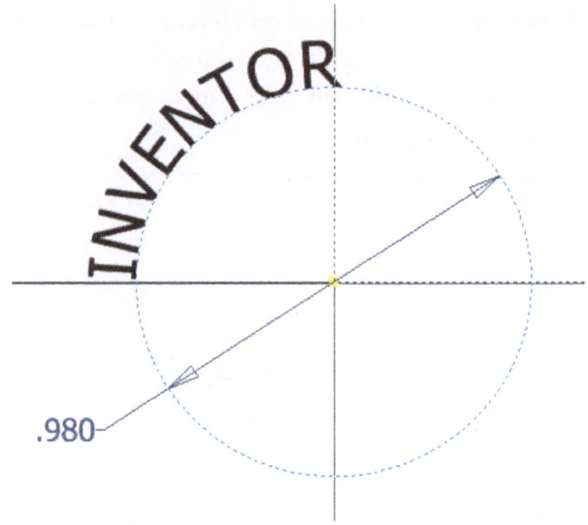

17. Select **Center Justification** from the **Position** group.
18. Type **90** in the **Start Angle** box, and then click **Update**.

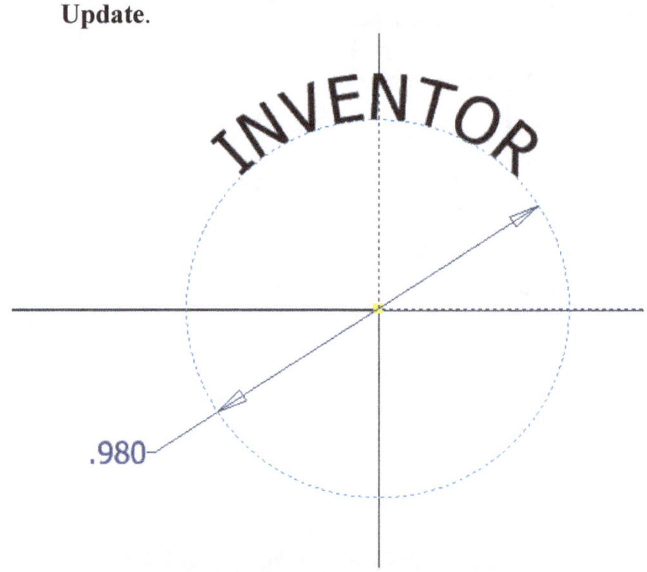

19. Click the **OK** on the **Geometry-Text** box.

Rectangular Sketch Pattern

The **Rectangular Pattern** tool creates an arrangement of objects around a point in linear form.

1. Download Chapter 5: Sketching folder from the Companion website.
2. Open the Rectangular pattern part file from the folder.
3. Right-click on the **Sketch1** in the **Browser** Window.
4. Select the polygon from the sketch.

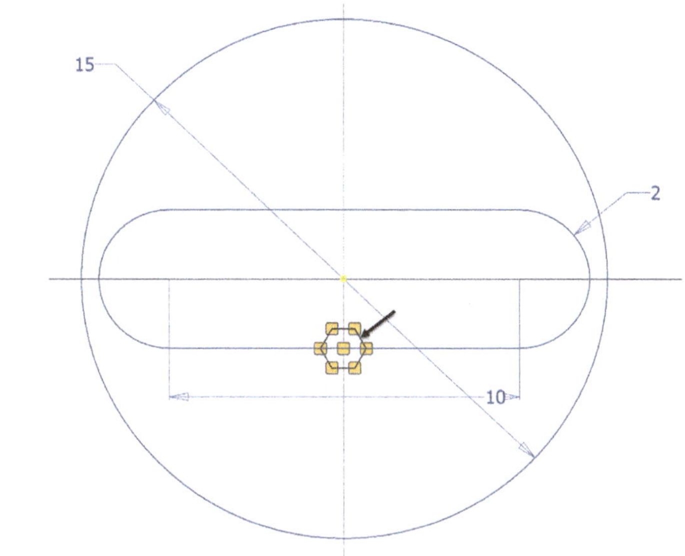

5. Click the **Cursor**  button in the **Direction 1** section and select the horizontal construction line, as shown.

6. Click the **Cursor**  button in the **Direction 2** section and select the vertical construction line, as shown.

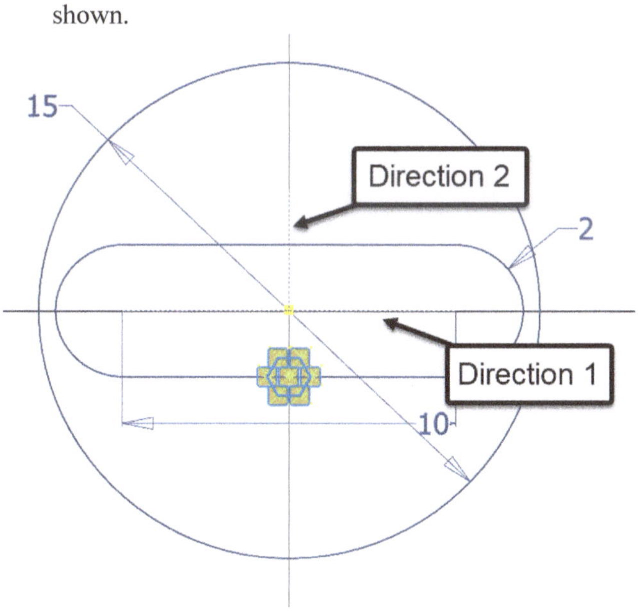

7. Type **7** and **2** in the **Count** and **Spacing** boxes in the **Direction 1** section, respectively.
8. Type **7** and **2** in the **Count** and **Spacing** boxes in the **Direction 2** section, respectively.
9. Click the **Symmetric** icon in the **Direction 1** and **Direction 2** sections.

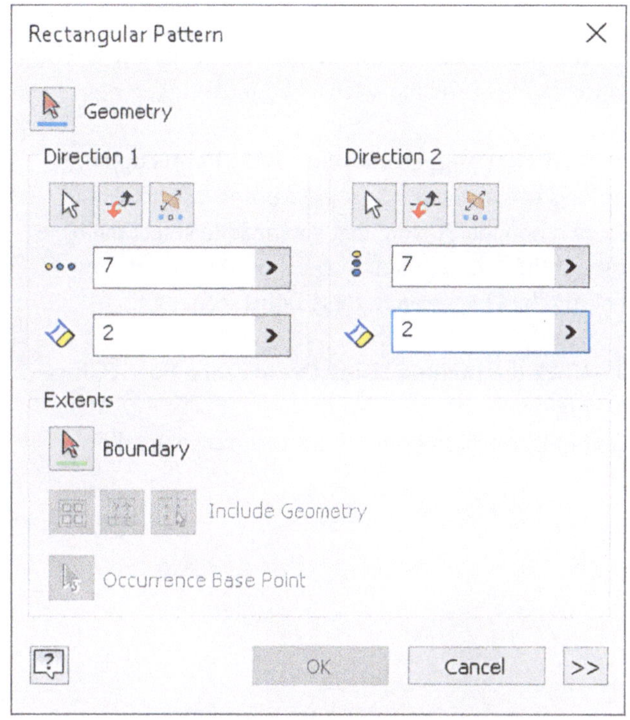

10. Click the **Boundary** icon in the **Extents** section and click in the slot.

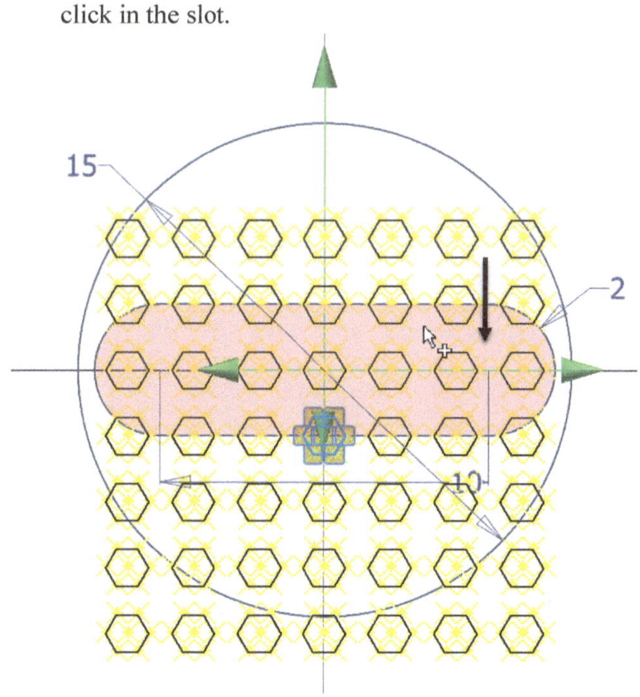

Notice three options in the **Extents** section: **Include Geometry**, **Include Centroid**, and **Include using occurrence base points**.

The **Include Geometry** option includes occurrences that are completely inside the selected boundary.

The **Include Centroid** option includes occurrences whose centroids are inside the selected boundary.

The **Include Using Occurrence Base Points** option includes occurrences whose base points are inside the selected boundary. Note that you need to select the base point of the original sketch object used to pattern by clicking the **Occurrence Base Point** icon.

11. Click the **Include Using Occurrence Base Points** option.
12. Select the base point of the occurrence, as shown.

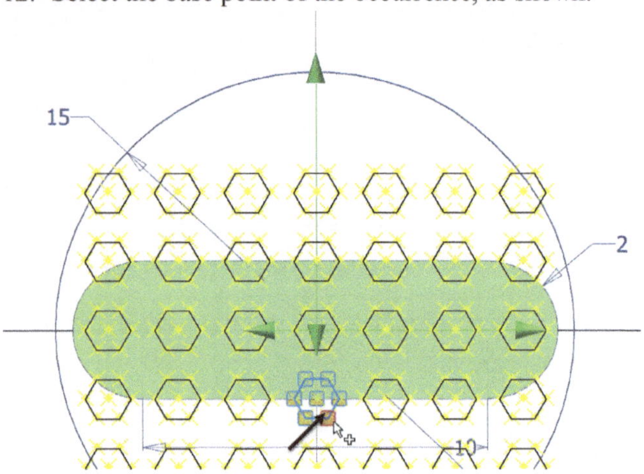

13. Click the arrow button on the bottom right corner of the **Rectangular Pattern** Properties panel to expand it.
14. Uncheck the **Associative** option.
15. Click **OK**.

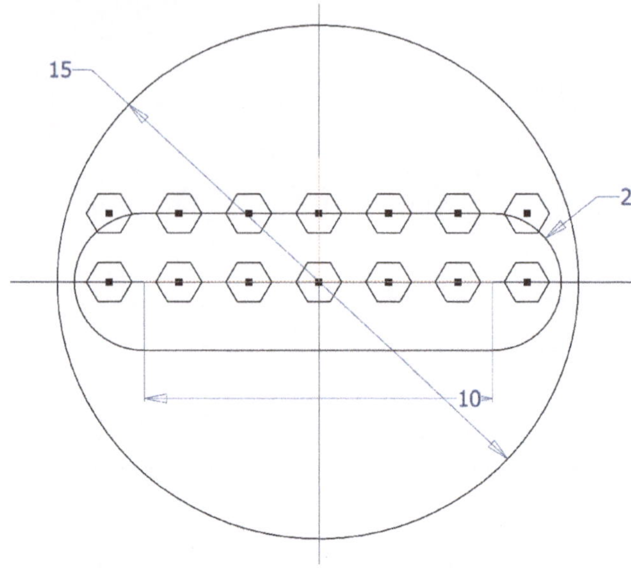

Chapter 6: Additional Modeling Tools

In this chapter, you create models using additional modeling tools. You will learn to:

- Create slots
- Create circular patterns
- Create holes
- Create chamfers
- Create shells
- Create rib features
- Create coils
- Create a loft feature
- Create an emboss feature
- Create a thread
- Create a sweep feature
- Create a grill feature
- Create a replace faces
- Create a face fillet
- Create a variable fillet
- Create a boss feature
- Create a lip feature

TUTORIAL 1

In this tutorial, you create the model shown in the figure:

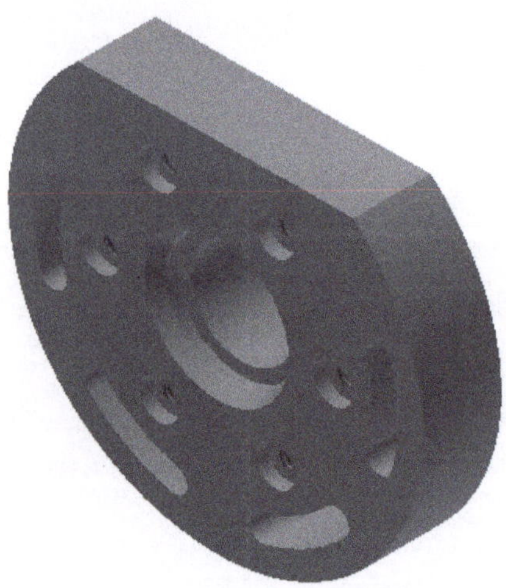

Creating the First Feature

1. Create a new project with the name **Autodesk Inventor 2026 Basics Tutorial** (See Chapter 2, Tutorial 1, Creating New Project section to learn how to create a new project).
2. Open a new Inventor part file using the **Standard.ipt** template (See Chapter 2, Tutorial 3, **Starting a New Part File** section).
3. Click the **Start 2D sketch** button on the ribbon and select the XY Plane.

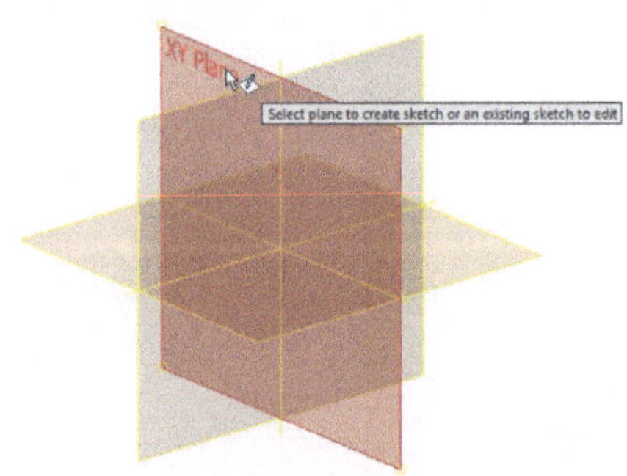

4. Click the **Circle Center Point** 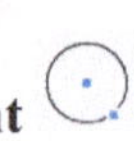 button and draw a circle (See Chapter 2, Tutorial 1, Starting a Sketch section to learn how to create a new project).
5. Click the **Line** 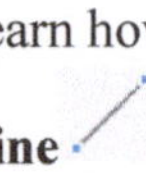 button.
6. Specify a point at the top left outside the circle.
7. Move the pointer horizontally and notice the Horizontal constraint symbol.
8. Click outside the circle — Press **Esc** to deactivate the **Line** tool.

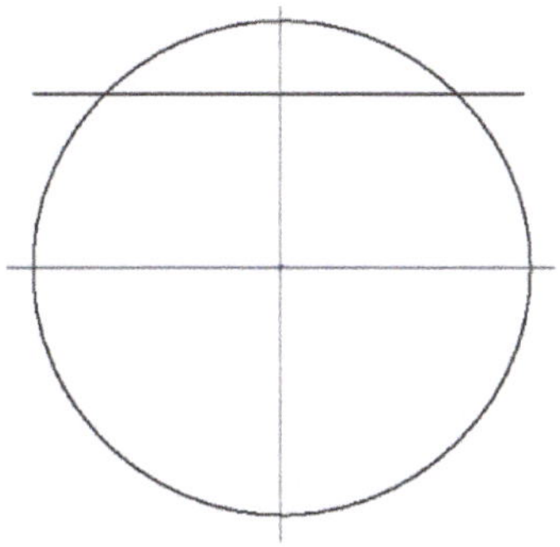

9. Click the **Trim** button on the **Modify** panel.
10. Click on the portions of the sketch to trim, as shown below.

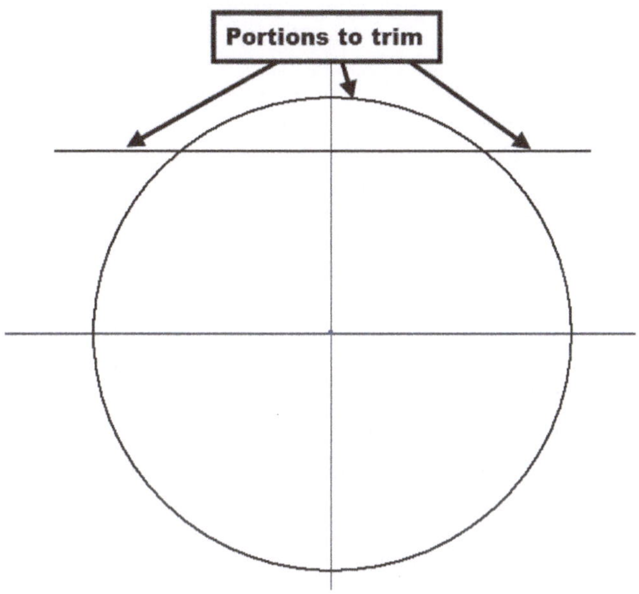

11. Apply dimensions to the sketch (Radius=0.63, vertical length=1.102). To apply the vertical length dimension, activate the **Dimension** tool, and select the horizontal line. Move the pointer downward and place the cursor on the bottom quadrant point of the arc. Click when the symbol appears. Move the pointer toward the left and click to place the dimension.

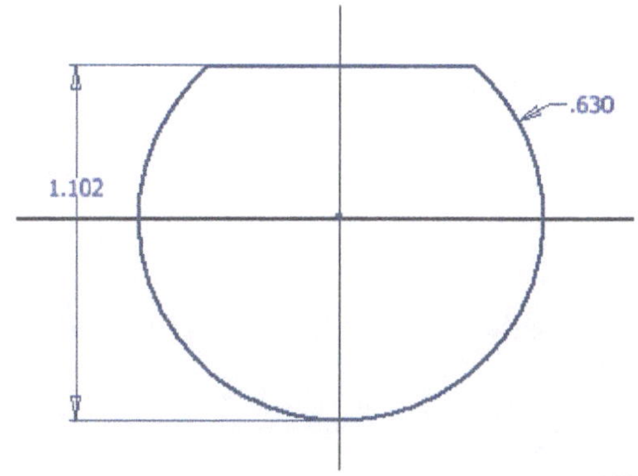

12. Click **Rectangle > Slot Center Point Arc** on the **Create** panel.
13. Select the origin as the center point.
14. Move the cursor outside and click in the first quadrant of the circle to specify the start point of the slot arc.
15. Move the cursor and click in the fourth quadrant of the circle to specify the endpoint of the slot arc.

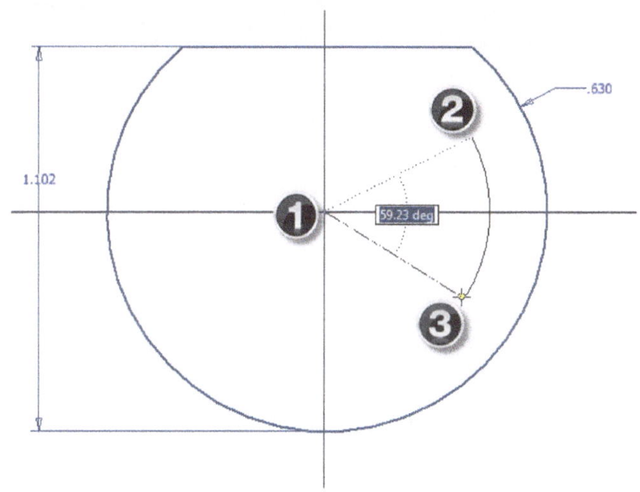

16. Move the cursor outward from the arc and click.

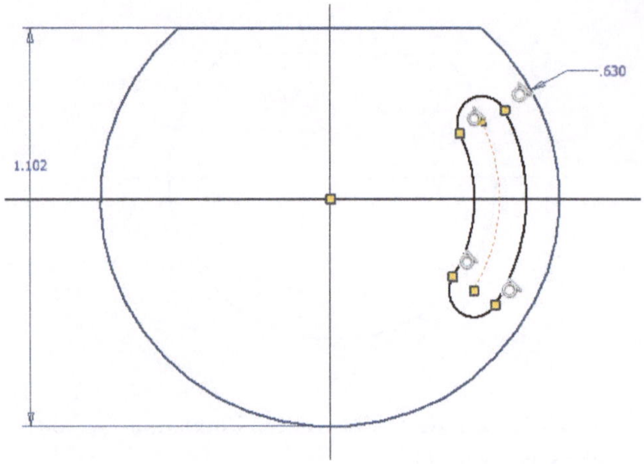

17. Click the **Dimension** button on the **Constrain** panel.
18. Select the start point of the slot arc.
19. Select the center point of the slot arc.
20. Select the endpoint of the slot arc.

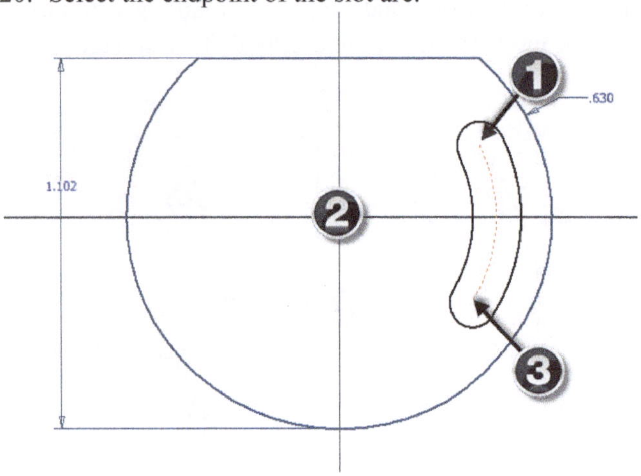

21. Place the angular dimension of the slot; the **Edit Dimension** box appears.
22. Enter **30** in the **Edit Dimension** box and click the green check.

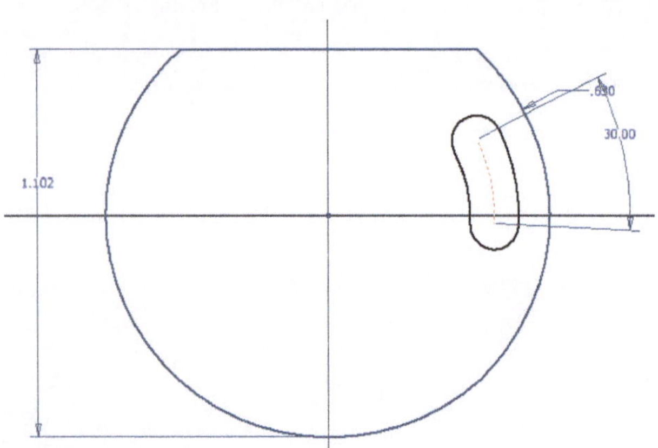

23. Click the **Construction** button on the **Format** panel.

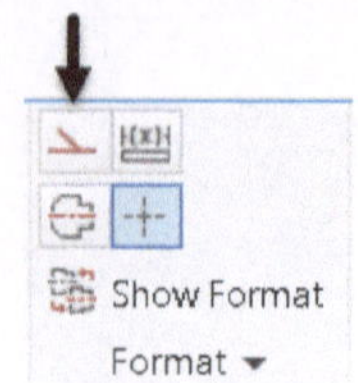

24. Click the **Line** button on the **Create** panel.
25. Draw a horizontal line passing through the origin.

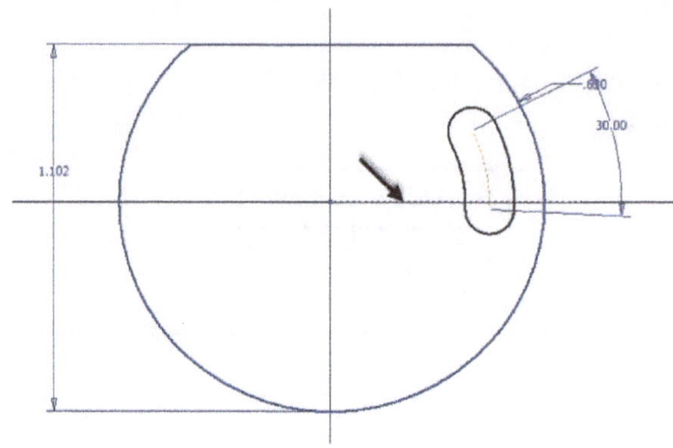

26. Click the **Construction** button on the **Format** panel to deactivate it.
27. Click the **Symmetric** button on the **Constrain** panel.
28. Select the end caps of the slot.
29. Select the construction line; the slot is made symmetric about the construction line.

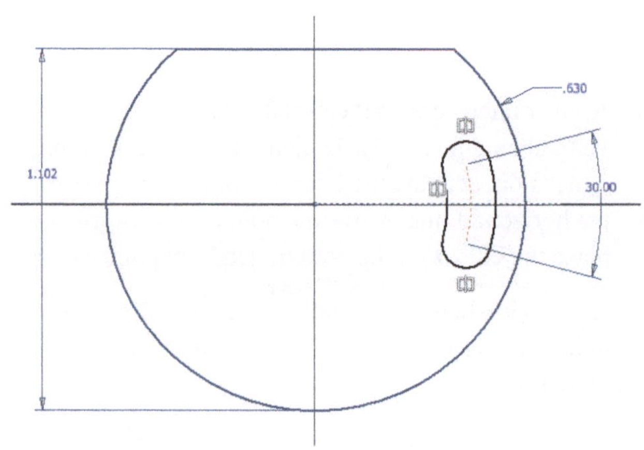

30. Apply other dimensions to the slot, as shown.

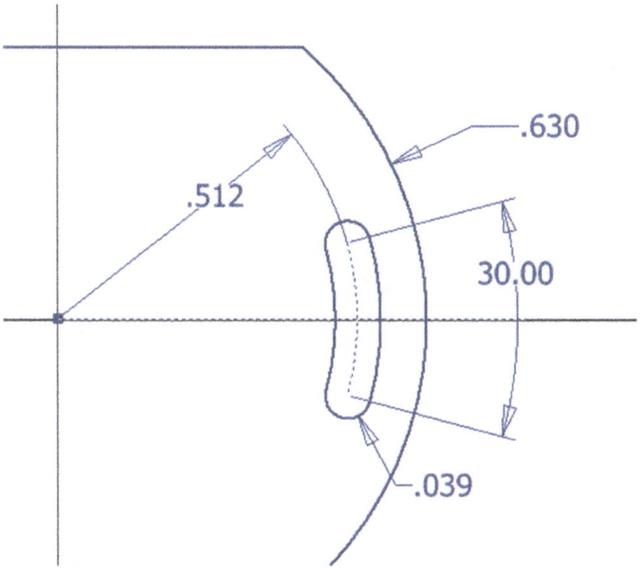

31. Click the **Circular Pattern** button on the **Pattern** panel; the **Circular Pattern** dialog appears.

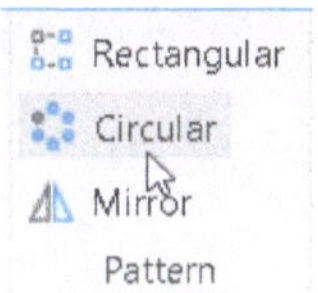

32. Select all the elements of the slot by creating a selection window.

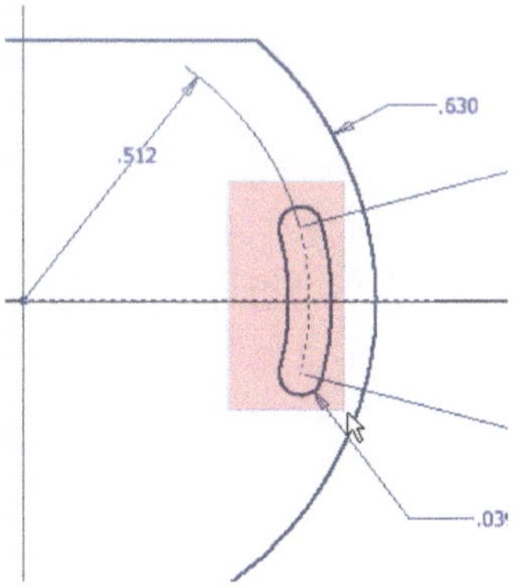

33. Click the cursor button located on the right side of the dialog.
34. Select the origin point of the sketch axis point.
35. Enter **4** in the **Count** box and **180** in the **Angle** box.
36. Click the **Flip** button.

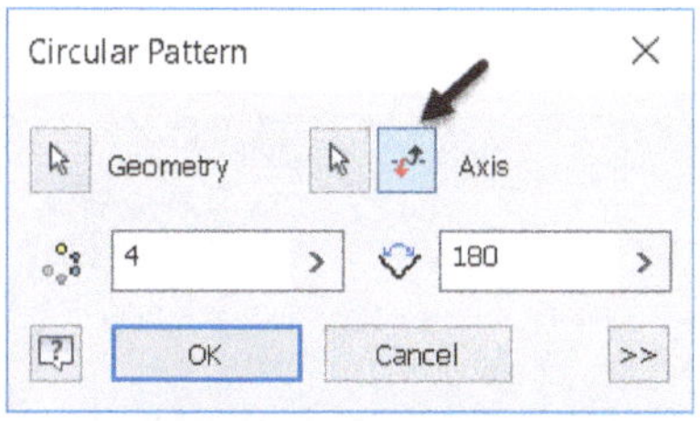

The preview of the circular pattern appears.

37. Click **OK** to create the circular pattern.

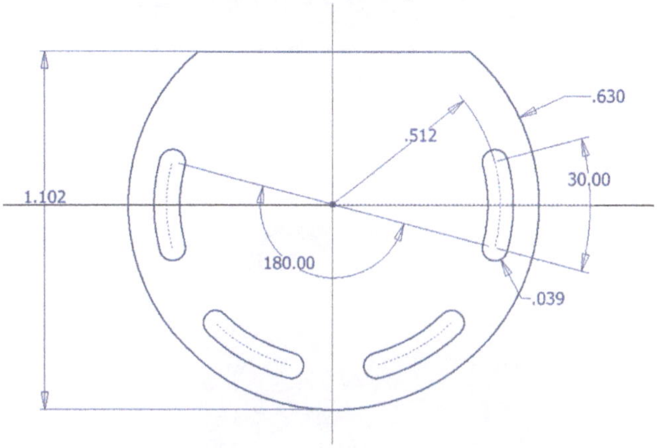

38. Click the **Finish Sketch** button on the ribbon.
39. Extrude the sketch up to **0.236** distance (See Chapter 2, Tutorial 1, Creating the Base Feature section to learn how to create a new project).

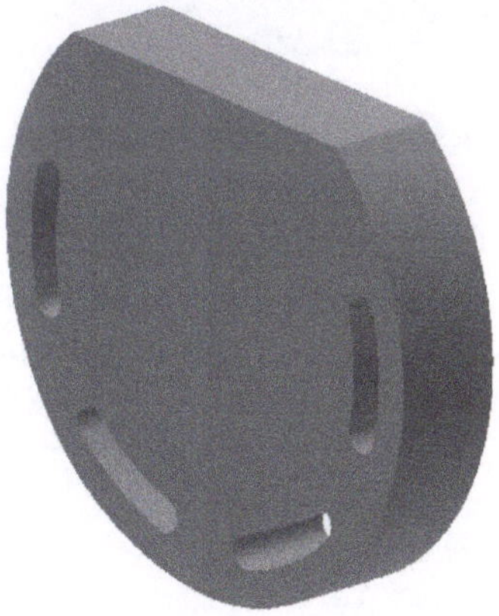

Adding the Second feature

1. Create a sketch on the back face of the model (use the Orbit tool available on the Navigate bar to rotate the model).

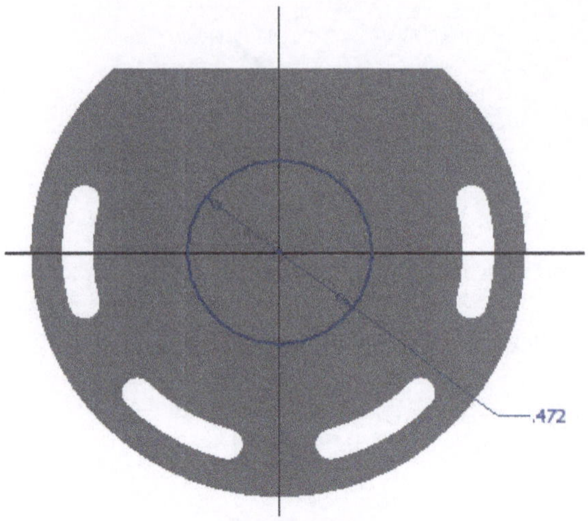

2. Extrude the sketch up to **0.078** distance.

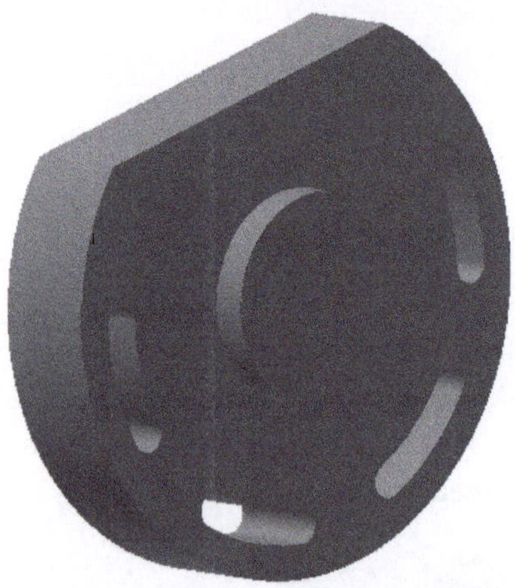

Creating a Counterbore Hole

In this section, you will create a counterbore hole concentric to the circular face.

1. Click the **Hole** button on the **Modify** panel; the **Properties panel** appears.

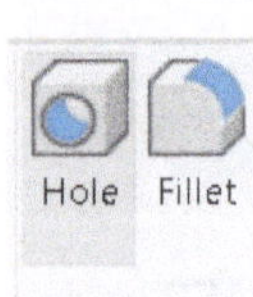

2. Set the parameters in the **Properties** panel, as shown in the figure.

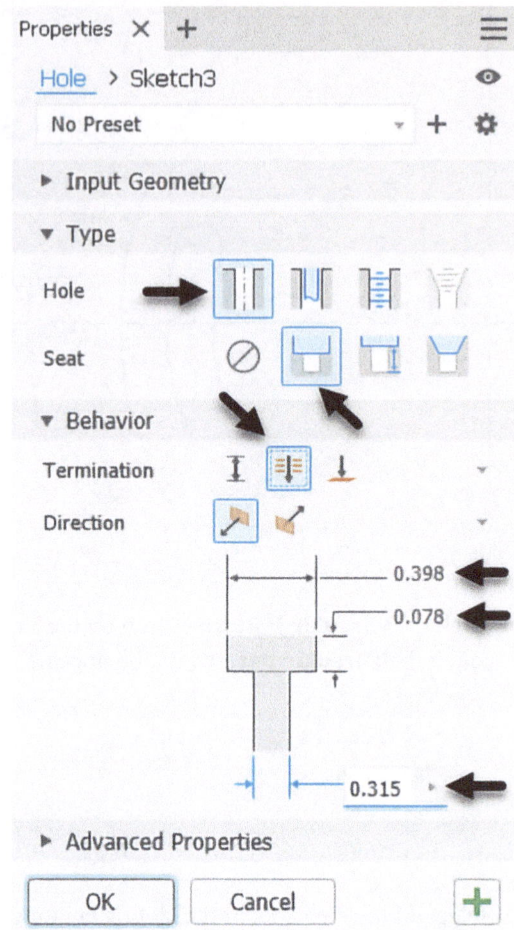

3. Click on the front face of the model; the preview of the hole appears.

Now, you need to specify the reference.

4. Select the circular face of the model; the hole is made concentric to the model.

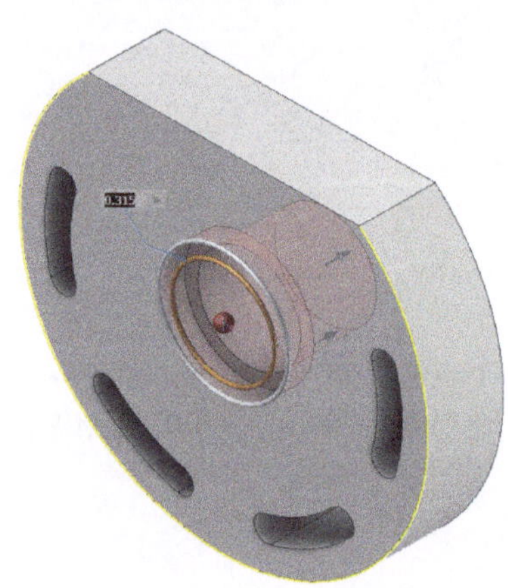

5. Click **OK** on the **Properties** panel; the counterbore hole is created.

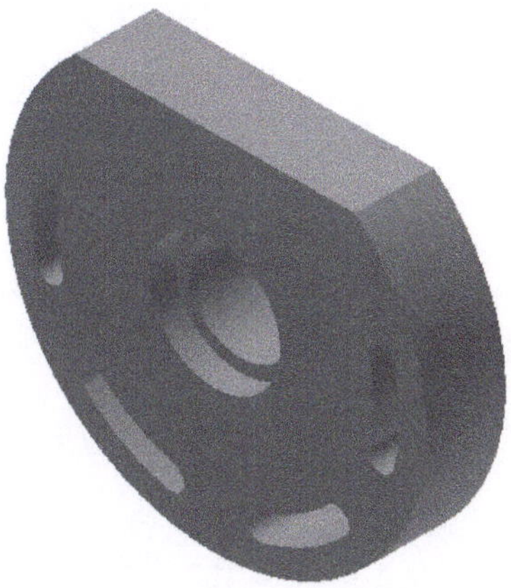

Creating a Threaded Hole

In this section, you will create a hole using a sketch point.

1. Click the **Start 2D Sketch** button and select the front face of the model.
2. Click the **Point** button on the **Create** panel.

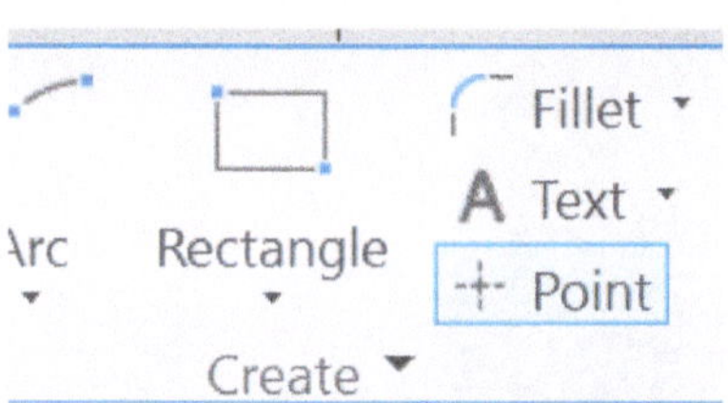

3. Place the point on the front face of the model.
4. Click the **Horizontal** button on the **Constrain** panel.
5. Select the point and sketch origin; the point becomes horizontal to the origin.
6. Create a horizontal dimension of **0.354** between point and origin.

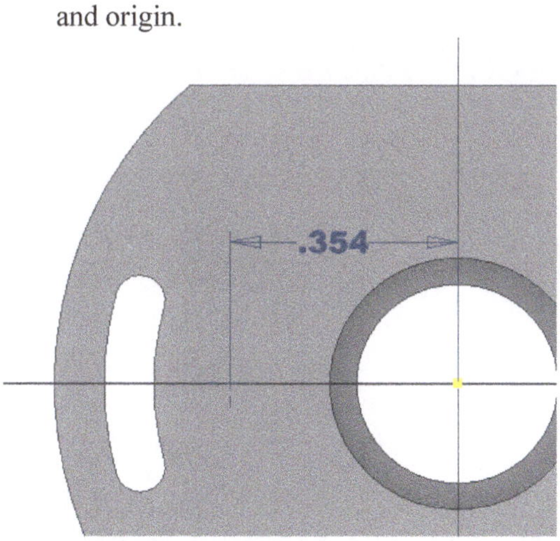

7. Click **Finish Sketch**.
8. Click the **Hole** button on the **Modify** panel; the **Properties** panel appears.
9. Select the sketch point, if not already selected.
10. Select the **Counterbore** option.
11. Select the **Tapped Hole** option.
12. Set the **Thread Type** to **ANSI Unified Screw Threads**.
13. Set the **Size** to **0.073**.
14. Select **Class > 2B**.
15. Set the **Designation** to **1-64 UNC**.
16. Select the **Full Depth** option.
17. Set the **Direction** to **Right Hand**.
18. Set the **Counterbore Diameter** to **0.118**.
19. Set the **Counterbore Depth** to **0.039**.

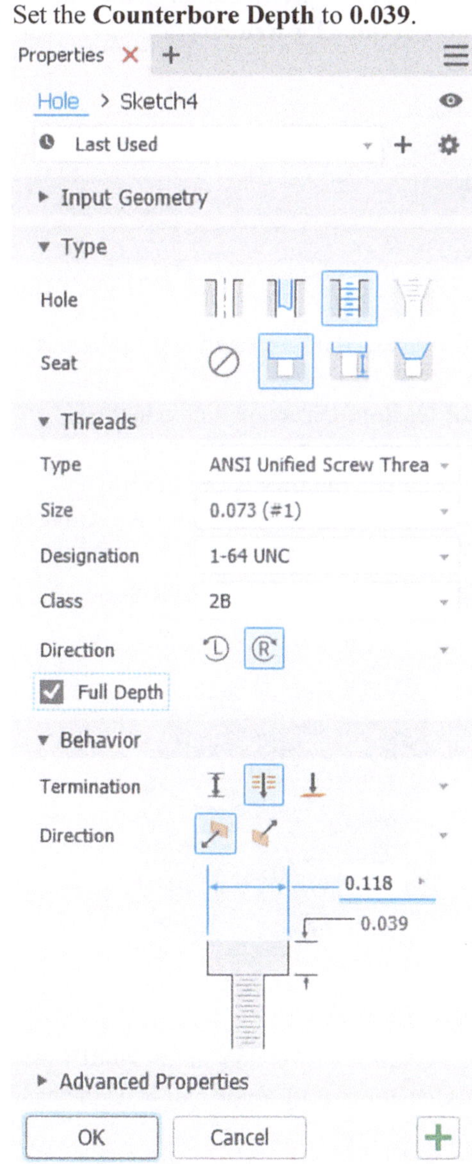

20. Click **OK** to create the hole.

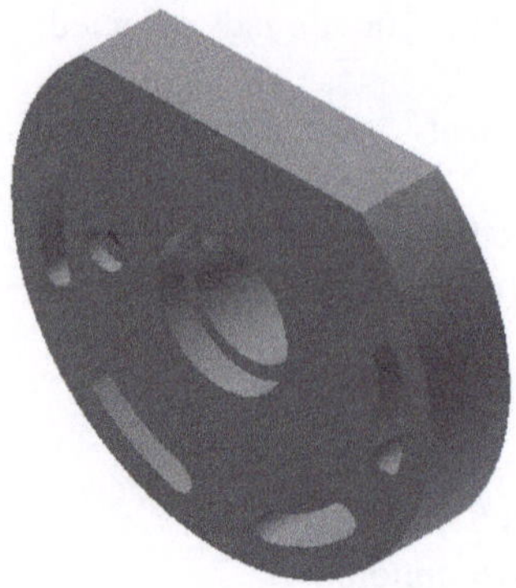

Creating a Circular Pattern

1. Click the **Circular Pattern** button on the **Pattern** panel; the **Circular Pattern** Properties panel appears.

2. Select the threaded hole created in the previous section.
3. Click the **Custom Direction** button in the **Orientation** section.
4. Select the outer cylindrical face of the model.
5. Enter **6** in the **Count** box and **360** in the **Angle** box.
6. Select **Distribution > Fitted**.
7. Click **OK** to create the circular pattern.

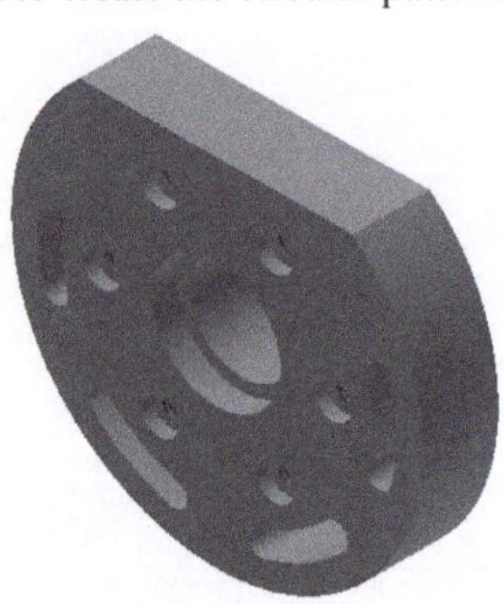

Creating Chamfers

1. Click the **Chamfer** button on the **Modify** panel.
2. Click the **Distance and Angle** button on the dialog.

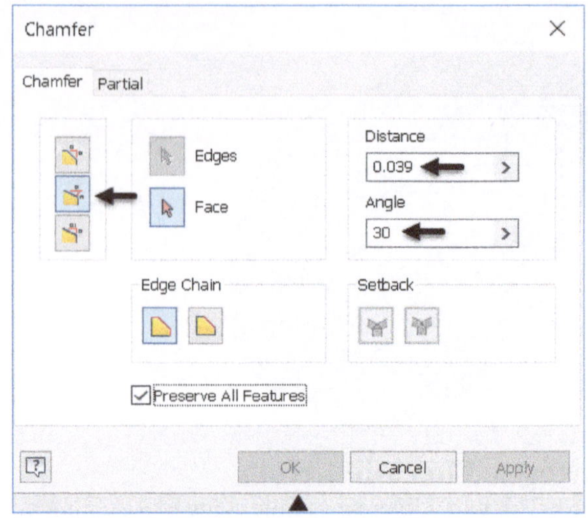

3. Select the circular face of the counterbore hole located at the center.

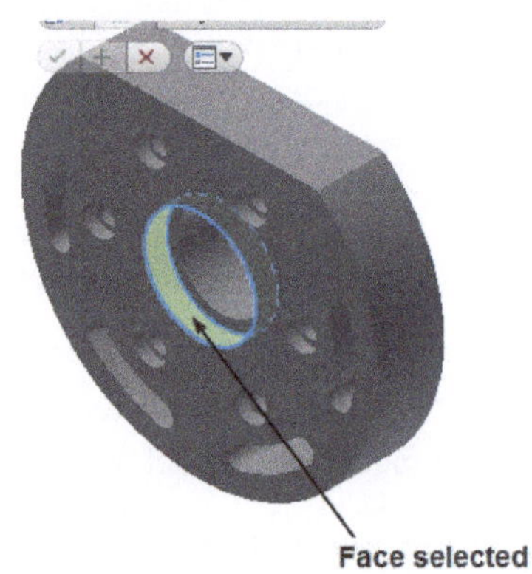

4. Select the circular edge of the counterbore hole.

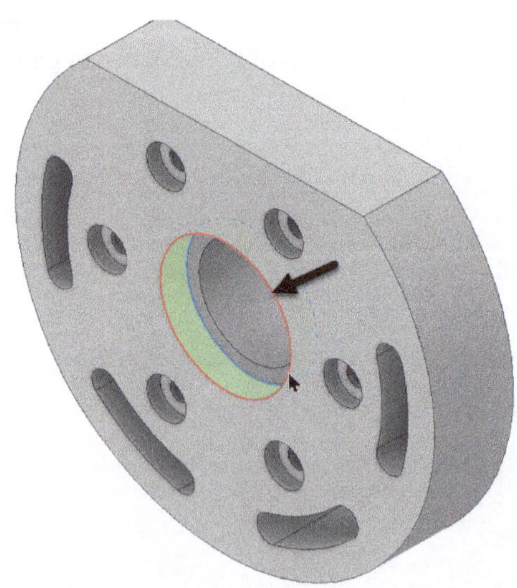

5. Enter **0.039** in the **Distance** box and **30** in the **Angle** box.

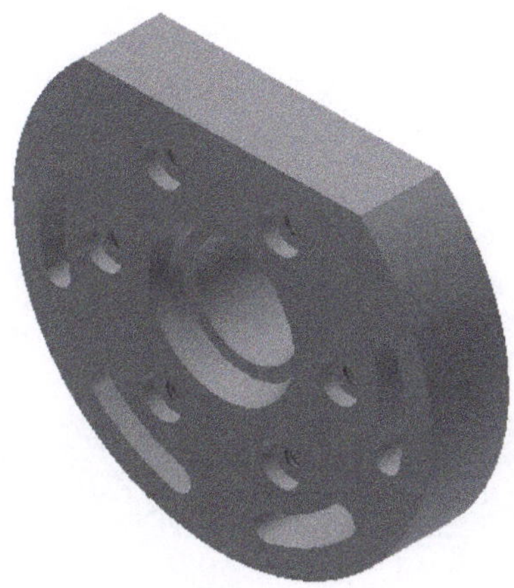

6. Click **OK** to create the chamfer.

Creating the Half Section View

1. In the Browse Window, right-click on the View node and select New. The new view representation is displayed under the View node in the Modeling browser.

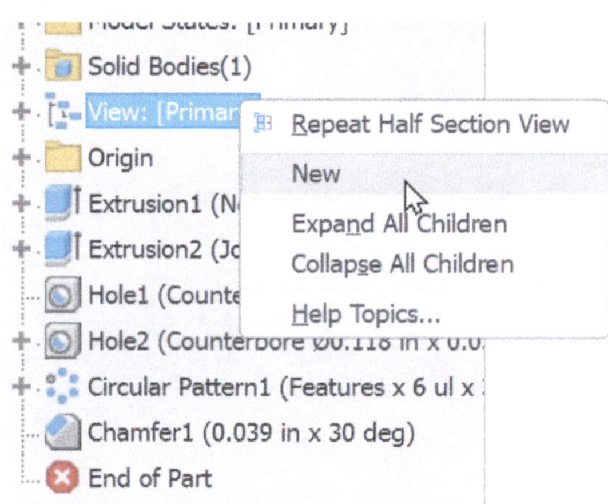

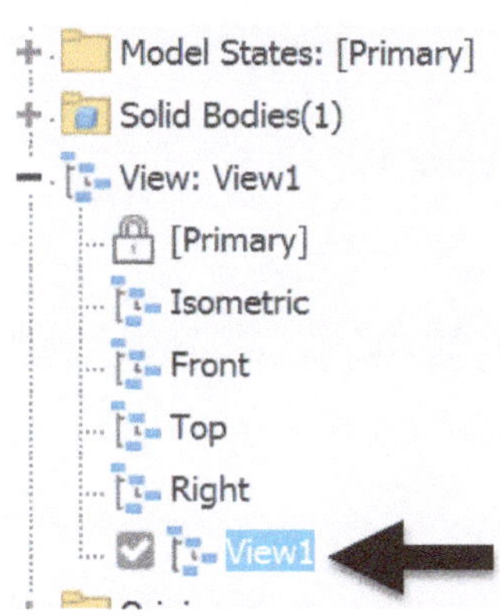

2. In the **Visibility** panel of the **View** tab, click **Section View** drop-down > **Half Section View**.

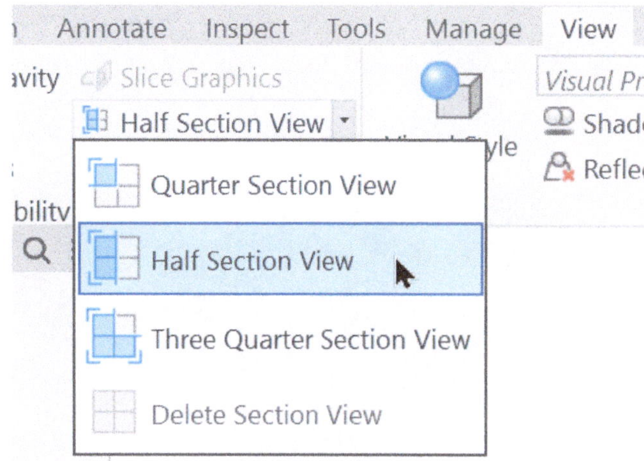

3. Select the top face of the model as the cutting plane.

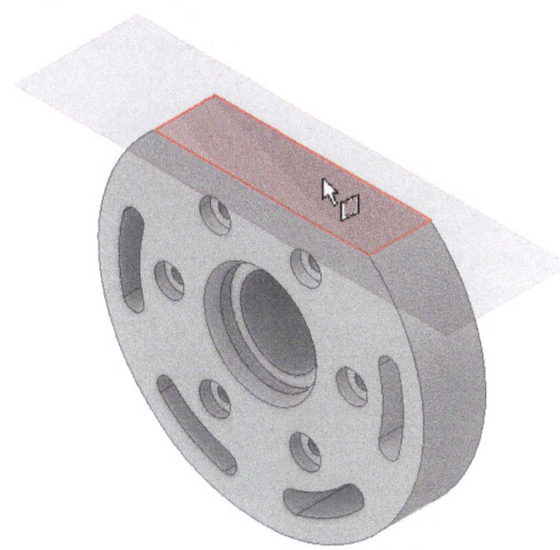

4. Click the **Flip** button to reverse the direction of the section view.
5. Drag the arrow displayed on the plane or input a value into the field; the postion of the section plane is changed.
6. Click **OK**.

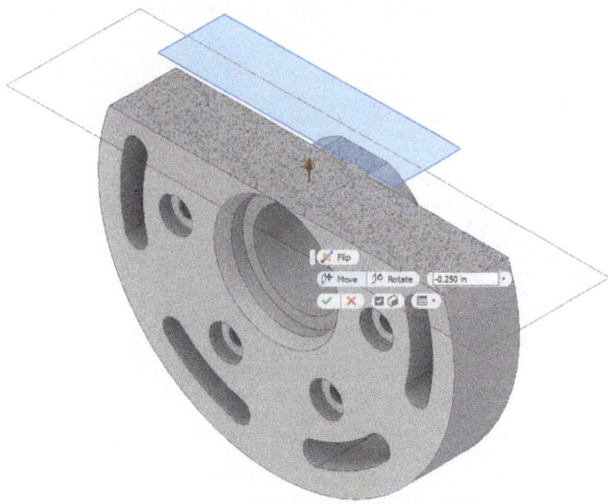

7. In the Modeling Browser, right-click on the current represection view and select **Section View > Edit**.

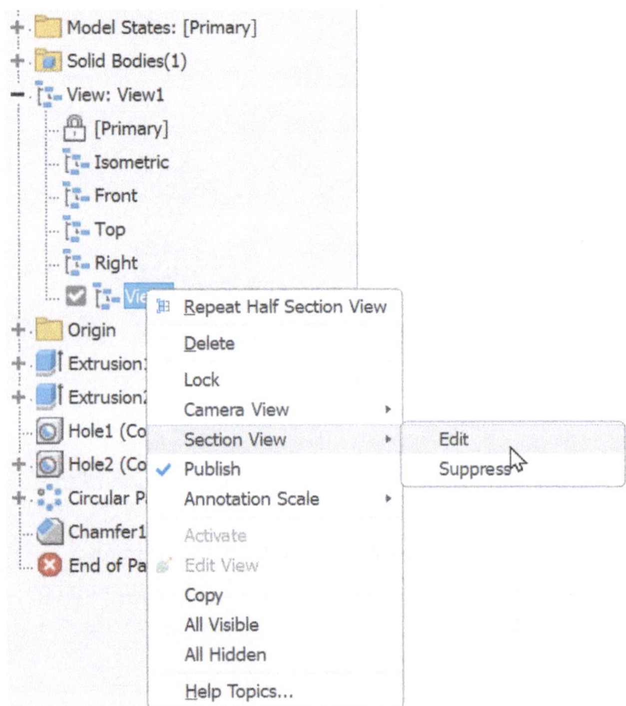

8. Click the **Rotate** button on the mini toolbar to display the rotate handle on section plane.
9. Select the rotate handle's left-facing angle manipulator by clicking on it.

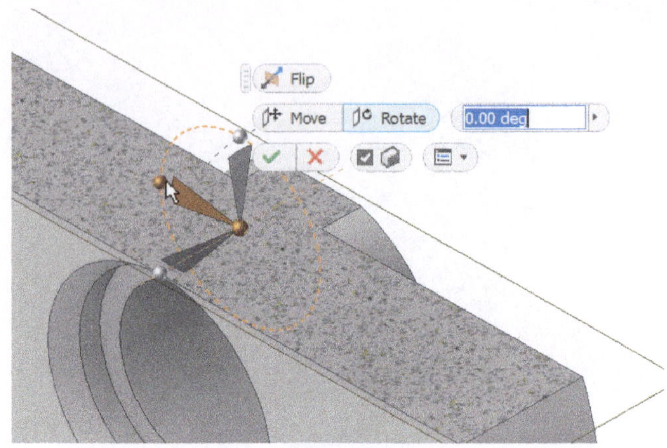

10. Press and hold the left mouse button and drag the pointer or input a value into the field to rotate the section plane.

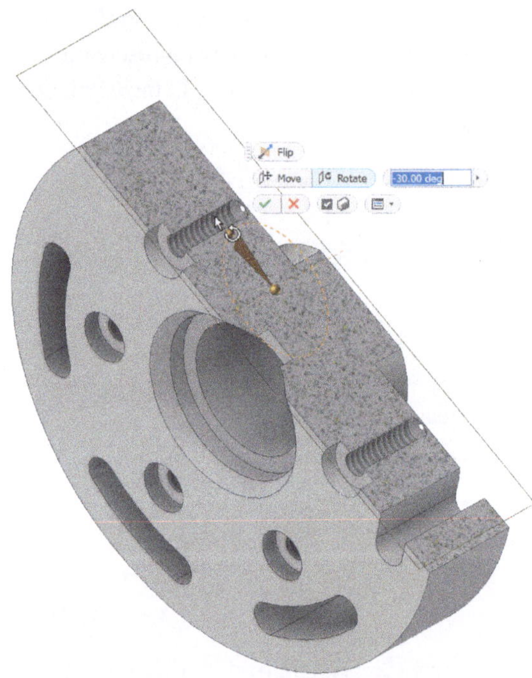

11. Click **OK**.
12. Save the model and close it.

TUTORIAL 2

In this tutorial, you will create the model shown in the figure.

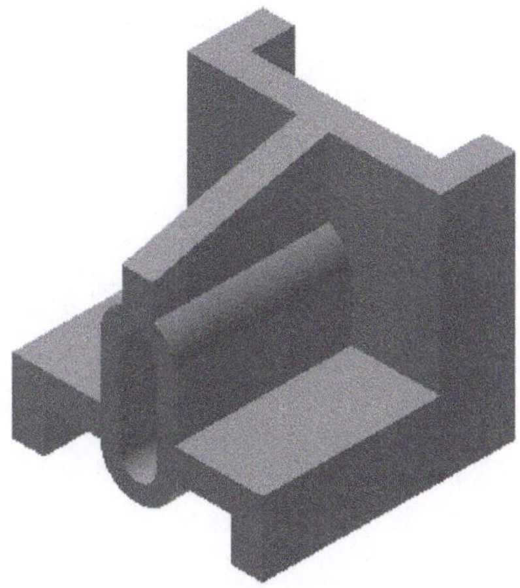

Creating the first feature

1. Open a new Inventor part file using the **Standard.ipt** template (See Chapter 2, Tutorial 3, Starting a New Part File section).
2. On the ribbon, click **3D Model > Sketch > Start 2D Sketch** .
3. Select the YZ plane.
4. Draw an L-shaped sketch using the **Line** tool and dimension it to be **1.575**, as shown in the figure.

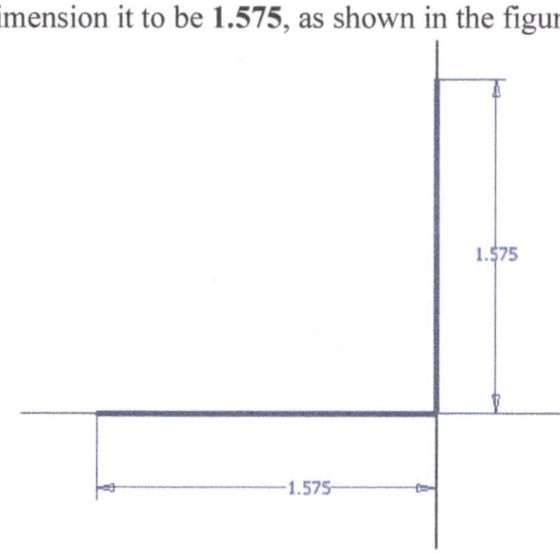

5. Click the **Offset** button on the **Modify** panel.

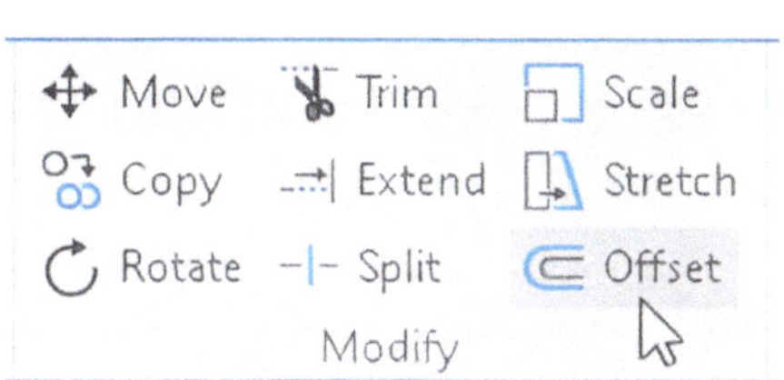

6. Select the sketch, and then specify the offset position at a random distance.

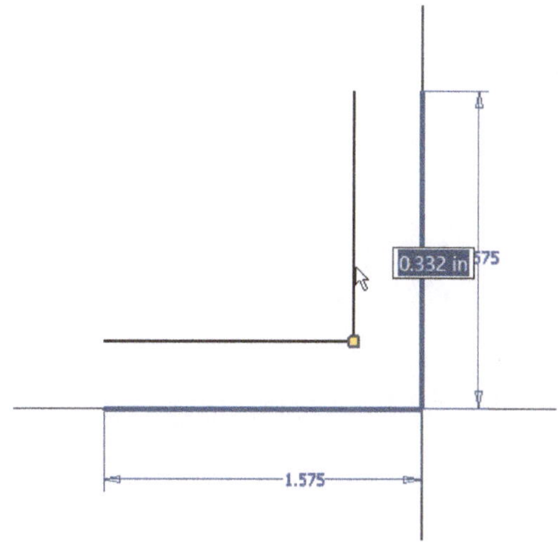

7. Click the **Line** button and draw lines closing the offset sketch.

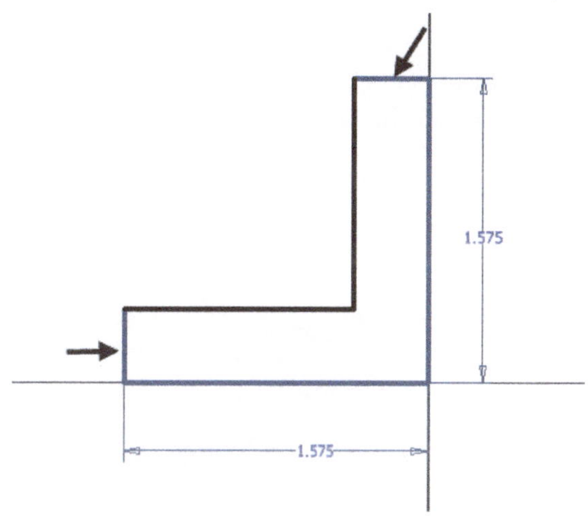

8. Add the offset dimension to the sketch.

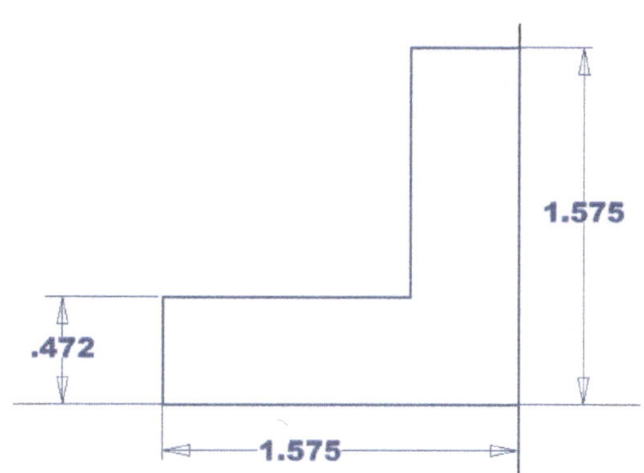

9. Click **Finish Sketch**.
10. Click **3D Model > Create > Extrude** on the ribbon.
11. Select the **Symmetric** option on the **Extrude**

Properties panel.

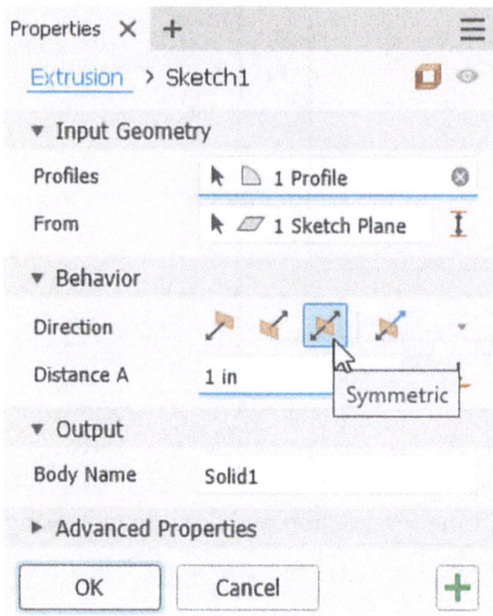

12. Set the **Distance A** to **1.575**.
13. Click **OK** to create the first feature.

Creating the Shell feature

You can create a shell feature by removing the face of the model and applying thickness to other faces.

1. Click **3D Model > Modify > Shell** on the ribbon; the **Shell** Properties panel appears. Click the down arrow to expand the dialog
2. Set **Thickness** to **0.197**.

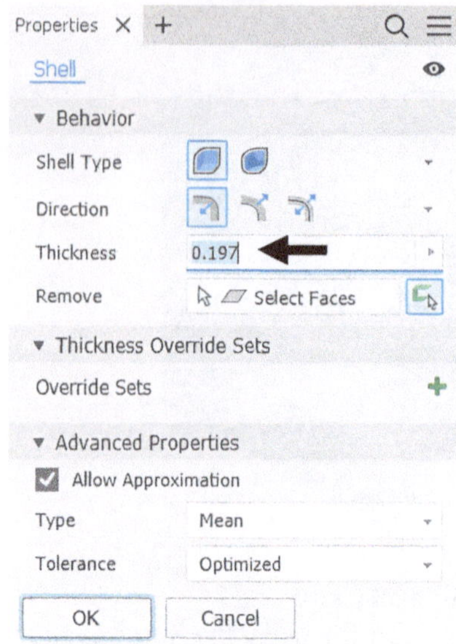

Now, you need to select the faces to remove.

3. Select the top face and the back face of the model.

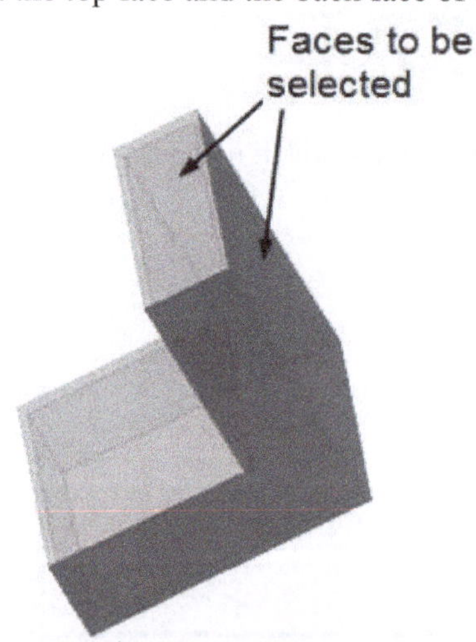

4. Select the front face and the bottom face of the model.

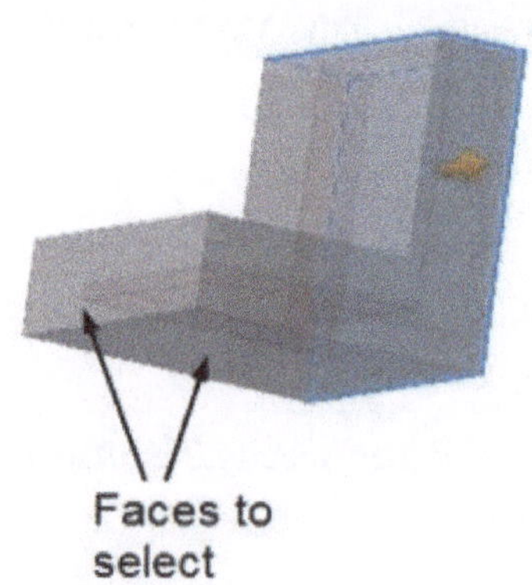

5. Click **OK** to shell the model.

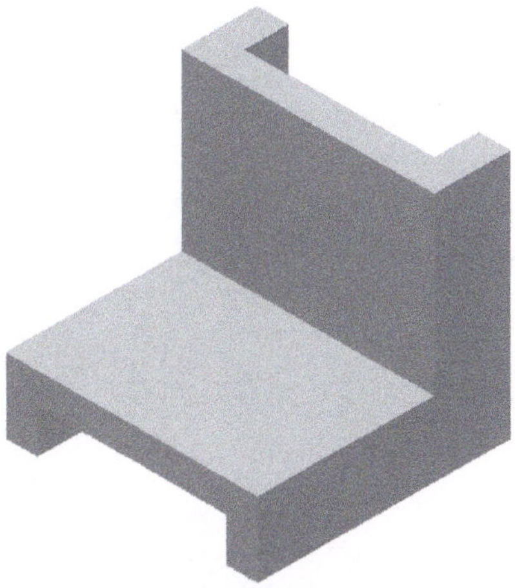

Creating the Third feature

1. Click **3D Model > Sketch > Start 2D Sketch** on the ribbon.

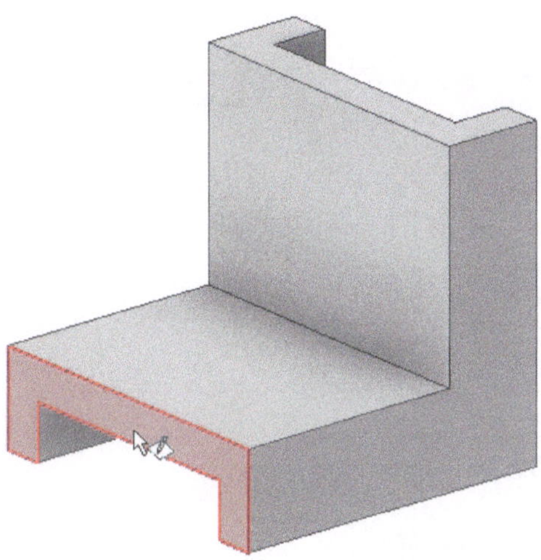

2. Select the front face of the model.
3. Click **Sketch > Create > Rectangle** drop-down > **Slot Center to Center** on the ribbon.

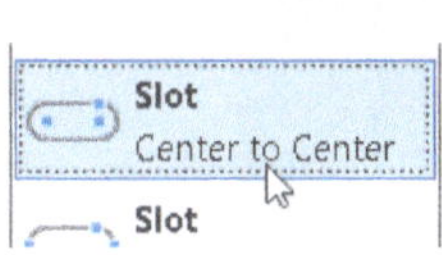

4. Draw a slot by selecting the first, second, and third points. Make sure that the second point is coincident with the lower horizontal edge.

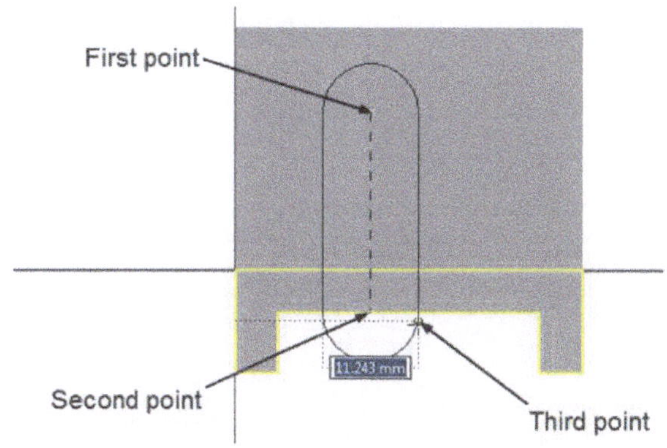

5. Apply dimensions to the slot.

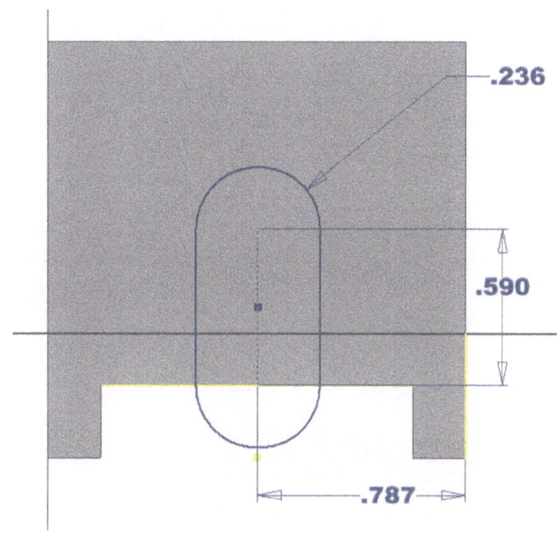

6. Click **Finish Sketch**.
7. Click **3D Model > Create > Extrude** on the ribbon.
8. Select the sketch.
9. Click the **To** button under the **Behavior** section.
10. Select the back face of the model.

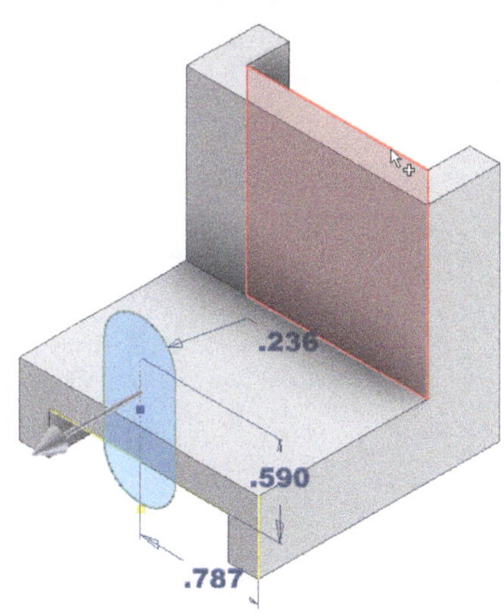

11. Click the **Join** button on the **Extrude Properties** panel.

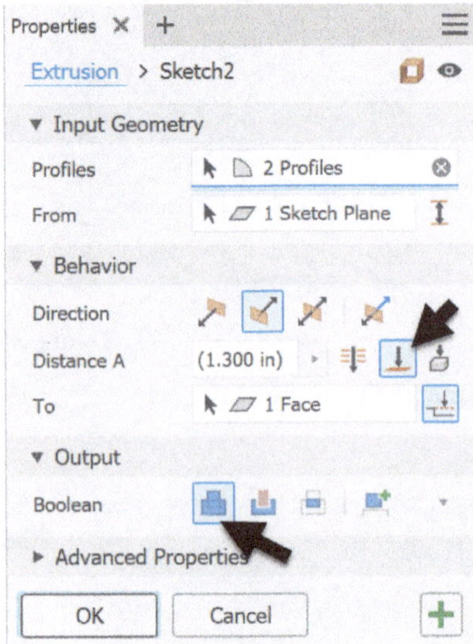

12. Click **OK** to create the feature.

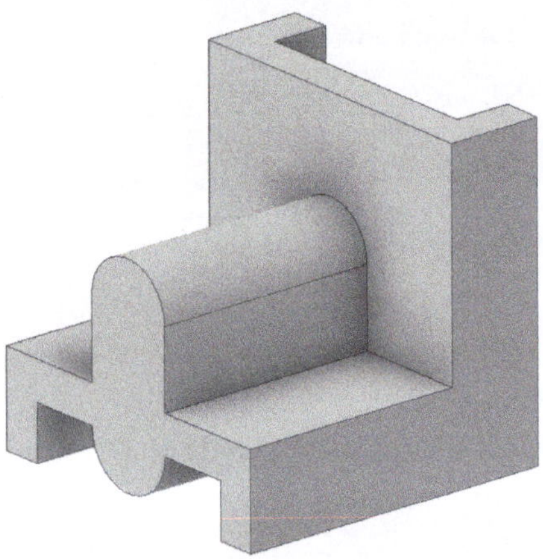

Creating a Cut Feature

1. Create the sketch on the front face of the model, as shown below.

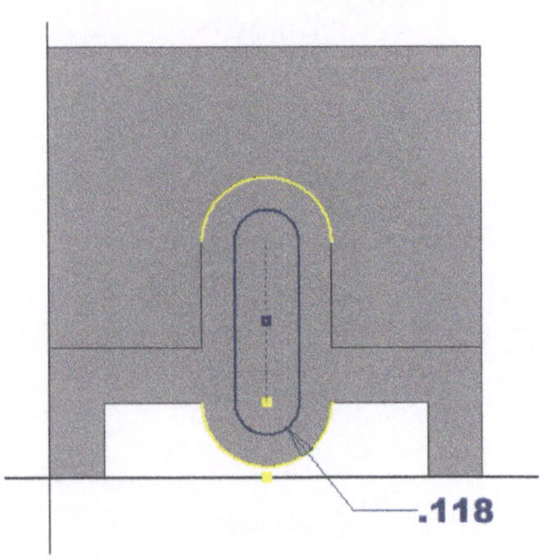

2. Finish the sketch.
3. Click **3D Model > Create > Extrude** on the ribbon.
4. Select the sketch.
5. Click the **Through All** button under the **Behavior** section.
6. Click the **Cut** button on the **Extrude Properties** panel.

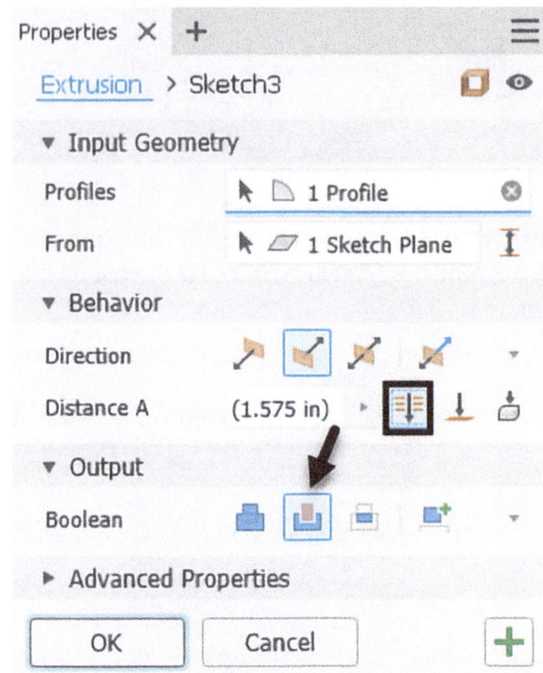

7. Click **OK** to create the cut feature.

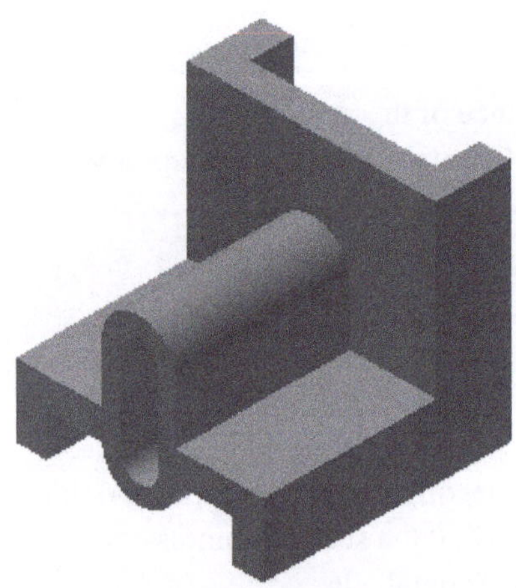

Creating the Rib Feature

In this section, you will create a rib feature in the middle of the model. To do this, you must create a mid-plane.

1. To create a mid-plane, click **3D Model > Work**

Features > Plane > Midplane between Two Planes on the ribbon.

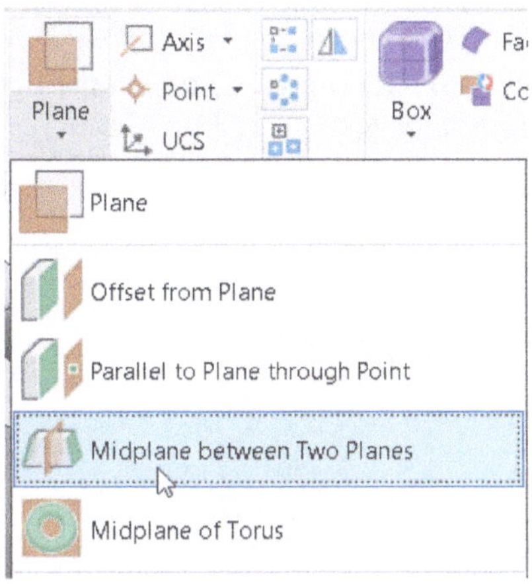

2. Select the right face of the model.
3. Select the left face of the model; the midplane is created.

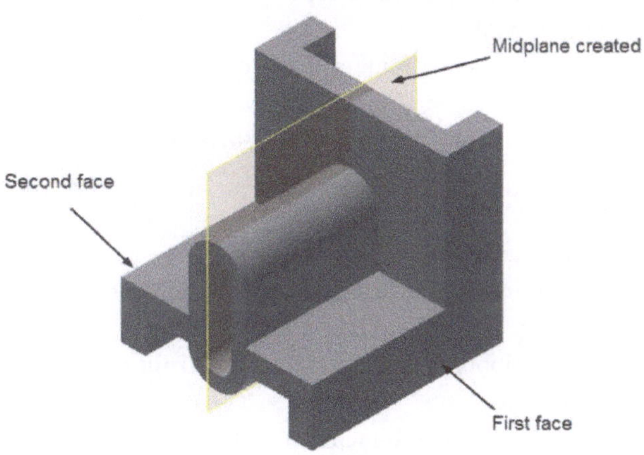

4. Click **3D Model > Sketch > Start 2D Sketch** on the ribbon.
5. Select the midplane.
6. Click the **Slice Graphics** button at the bottom of the window.

7. Click **Sketch > Create > Project Geometry > Project Cut Edges** on the ribbon; the edges cut by the sketch plane are projected.

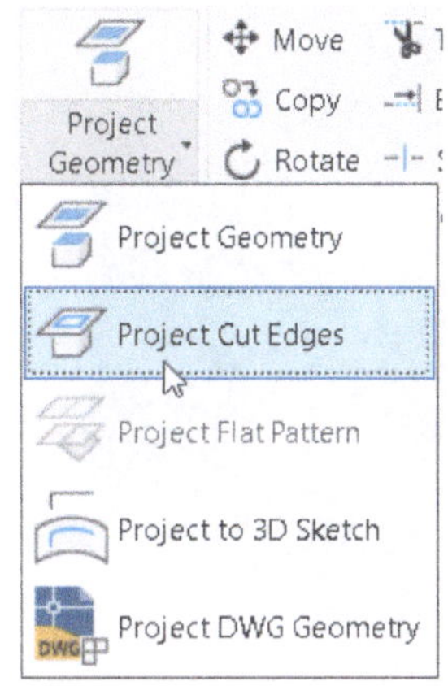

8. Draw the sketch, as shown below.

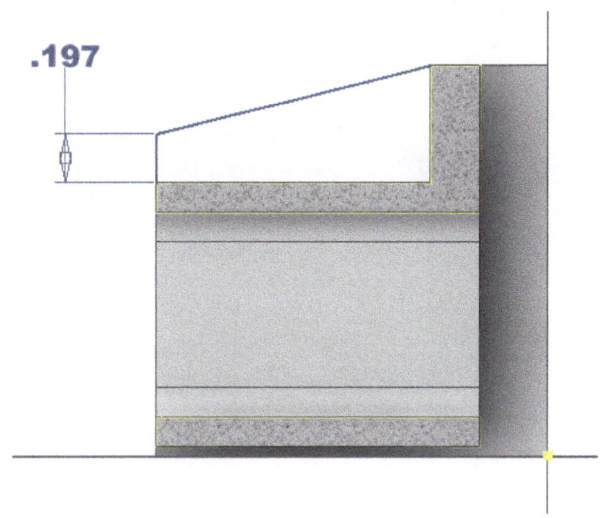

9. Finish the sketch.
10. Click **3D Model > Create > Rib**  on the ribbon; the **Rib** dialog appears.
11. Select the sketch.
12. Click the **Parallel to Sketch Plane**  button on the dialog.
13. Click the **Direction 1**  button.
14. Set **Thickness** to **0.197**.
15. Click the **To Next**  button.
16. Click the **Symmetric**  button below the **Thickness** box.
17. Click **OK** to create the rib feature.

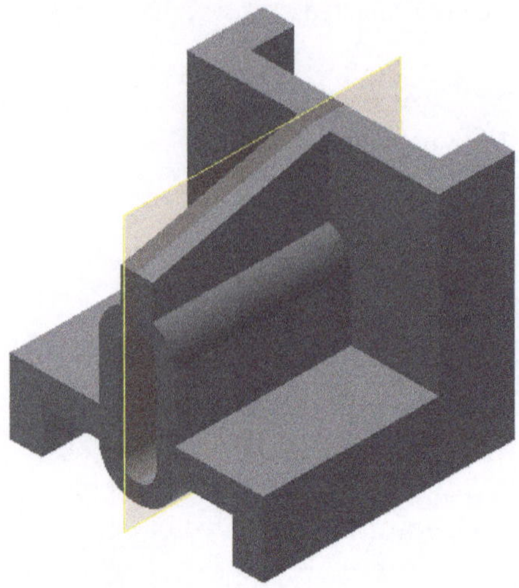

18. To hide the midplane, select it and right-click.
19. Click **Visibility** on the Marking Menu; the plane will be hidden.

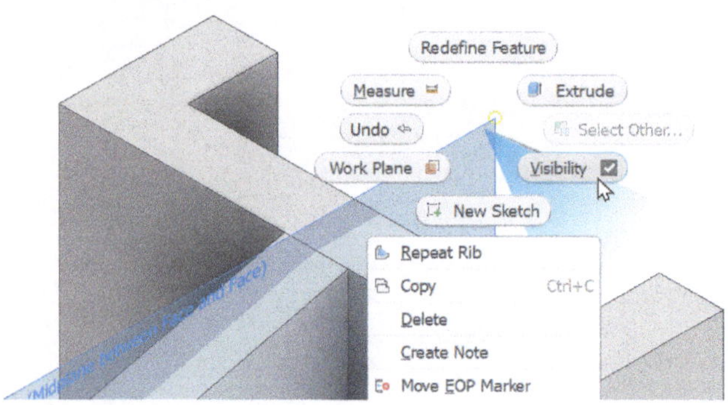

20. Save the model and close it.

TUTORIAL 3

In this tutorial, you will create a helical spring using the **Coil** tool.

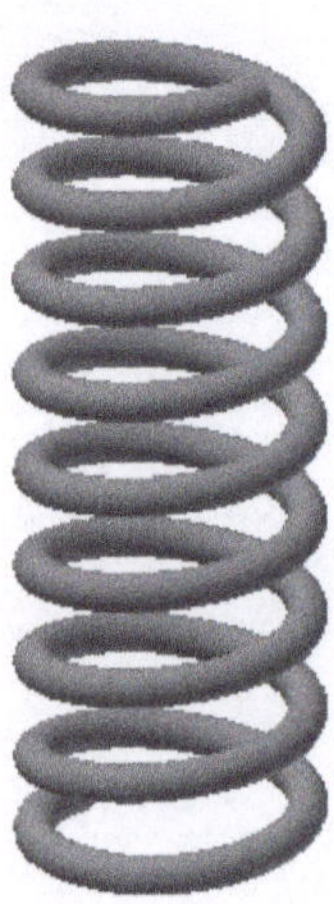

Creating the Coil

1. Open a new Inventor file using the **Standard.ipt** template (See Chapter 2, Tutorial 3, Starting a New Part File section).
2. Click the **Start 2D sketch** button on the ribbon and select the XY Plane.

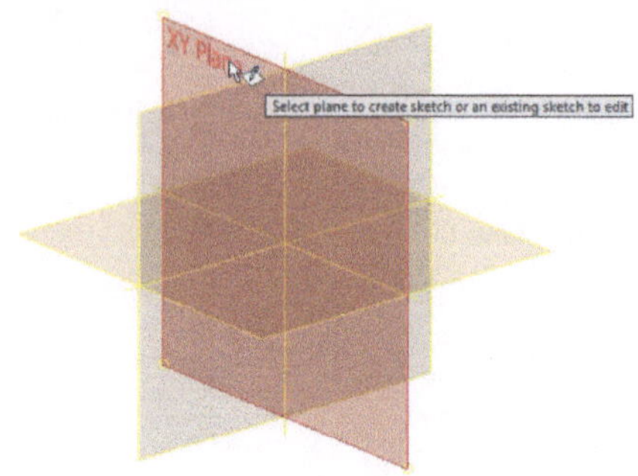

3. Click the **Circle Center Point** button.
4. Select a point on the left portion of the horizontal axis
5. Move the cursor outward and click to create a circle.
6. On the ribbon, click **Sketch > Constrain > Horizontal**.
7. Select the centerpoint of the circle and the sketch origin.
8. On the ribbon, click **Sketch > Format > Centerline** .
9. Click the **Line** button.
10. Select the origin point of the sketch, move the cursor upward, and click to create a centreline.
11. On the ribbon, click **Sketch > Constrain > Dimension**.
12. Add the diameter dimension to the circle, as shown.
13. Select the centreline and circle.
14. Move the pointer downward and click.
15. Type **1.575** and press Enter.

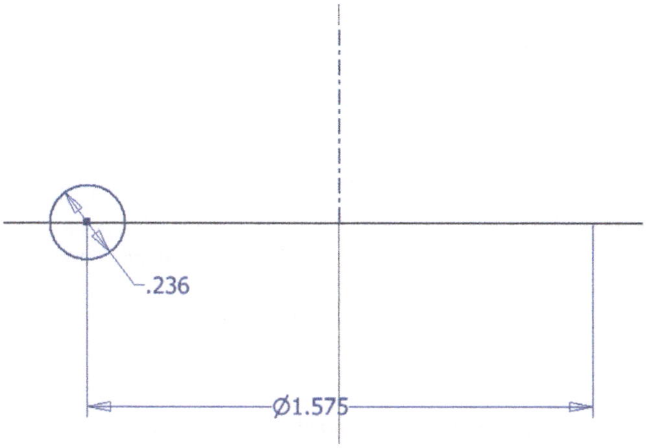

16. Finish the sketch.
17. To create a coil, click **3D Model > Create > Coil** on the ribbon; the **Properties** panel appears.

Also, the profile and the axis are automatically selected.

18. Click the **Reverse pitch direction along axis** button next to the **Axis** selection box, if the coil preview is downwards.
19. Under the **Behavior** section, select **Method > Pitch and Revolution**.
20. Type **0.590** in the **Pitch** box.
21. Type **8** in the **Revolution** box.
22. Check the **Close Start** option.
23. Type **90** in the **Flat Angle** and **Transition Angle** boxes.
24. Check the **Close End** option.
25. Type **0** in the **Flat Angle** and **Transition Angle** boxes.

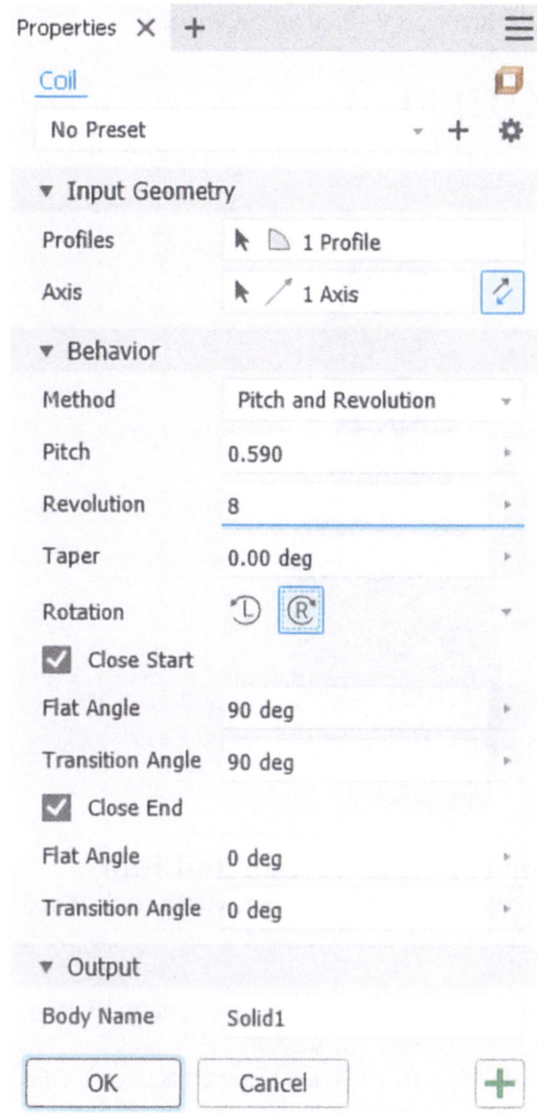

26. Click **OK** to create the coil.

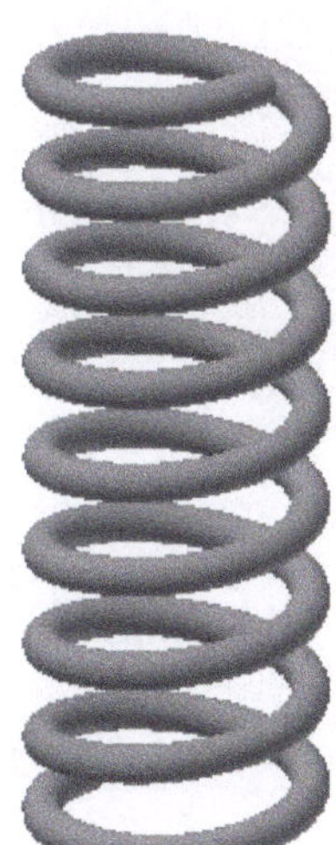

27. Save the model as **Coil.ipt** and close the file.

TUTORIAL 4

In this tutorial, you create a shampoo bottle using the **Loft**, **Extrude**, and **Coil** tools.

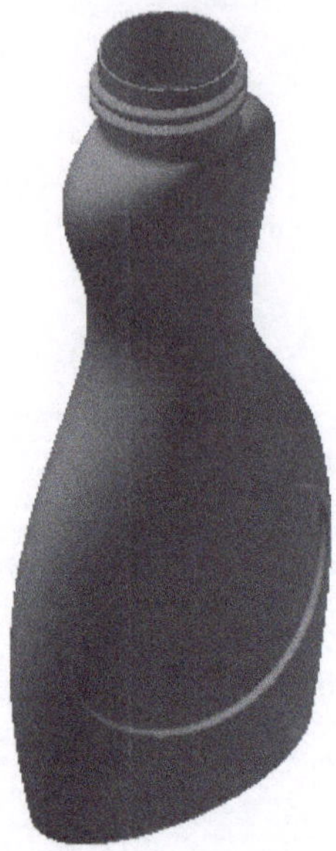

Creating the First Section and Rails

To create a swept feature, you need to create sections and guide curves.

1. Open a new Part file (See Chapter 2, Tutorial 3, Starting a New Part File section).
2. Click **3D Model > Sketch > Start 2D Sketch** on the ribbon.
3. Select the XZ plane.

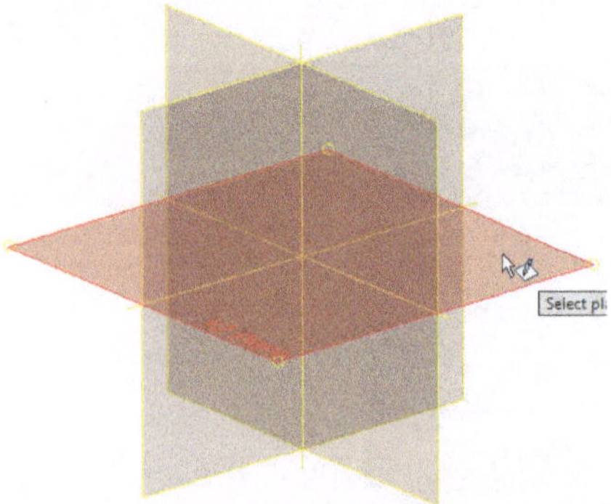

4. Click **Sketch > Create > Circle > Ellipse** on the ribbon.
5. Draw the ellipse by selecting the points, as shown.

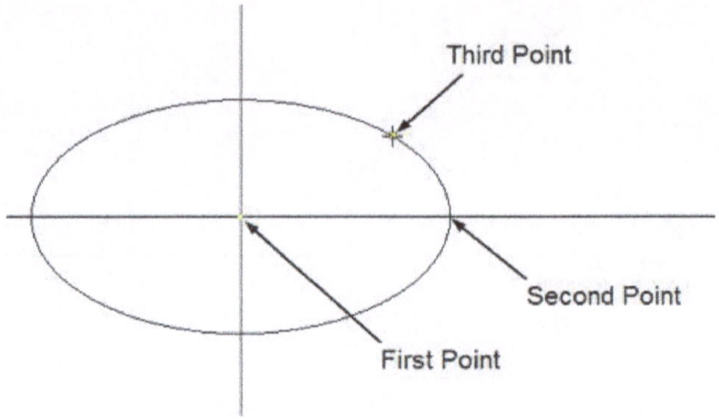

6. On the ribbon, click **Sketch > Constrain > Dimension**.
7. Select the ellipse, move the cursor downward, and click.
8. Type 1.968 and press Enter.
9. Select the ellipse, move the cursor toward left, and click.
10. Type 0.984 and press Enter.

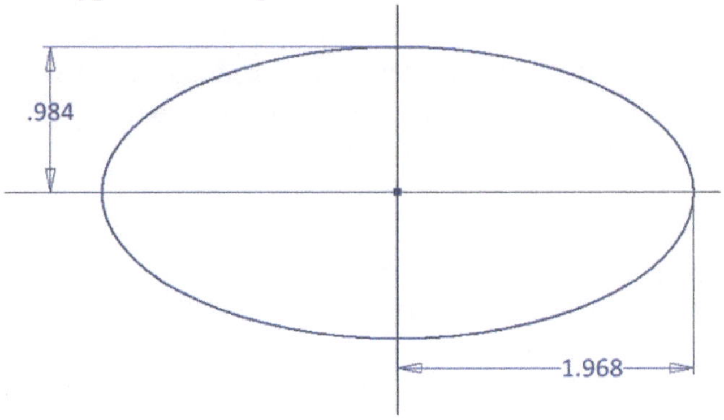

11. Click **Finish**.
12. Click **3D Model > Sketch > Start 2D Sketch** on the ribbon.
13. Select the YZ plane from the graphics window.
14. Click **Sketch > Create > Line> Spline Interpolation** on the ribbon.

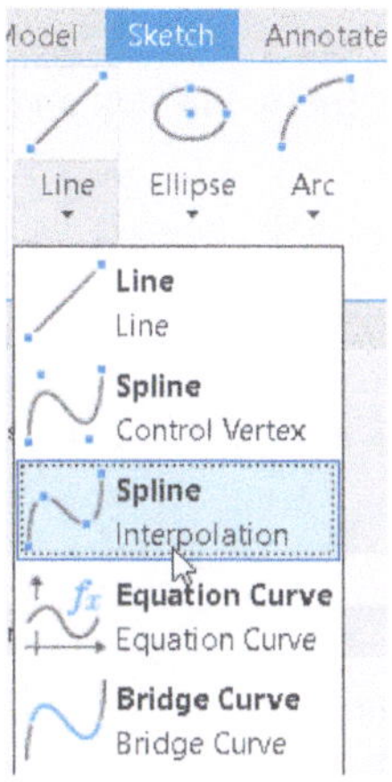

15. Select a point on the horizontal axis of the sketch; a rubber band curve is attached to the cursor

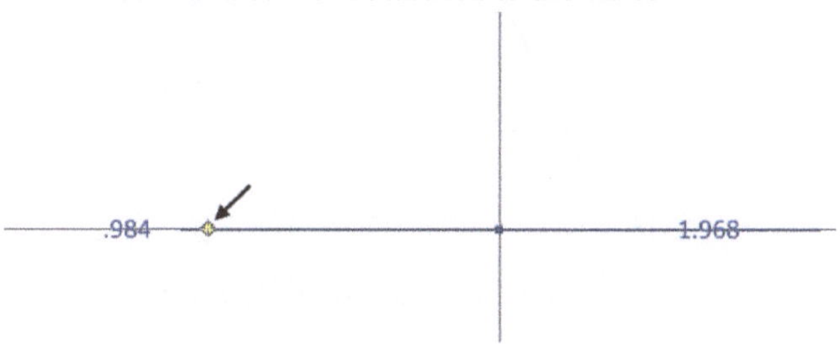

16. Move the cursor up and specify the second point of the spline; a curve is attached to the cursor.
17. Move the cursor up and specify the third point.
18. Likewise, specify the other points of the spline, as shown.
19. Click the right mouse button and select **Create**. The spline will be similar to the one shown in the figure.

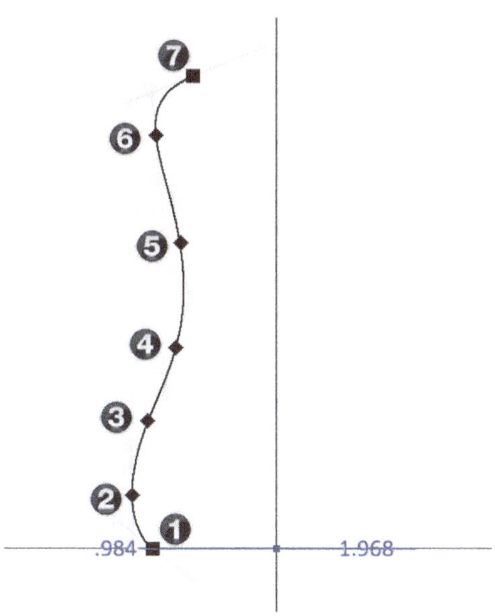

20. Right click and select **Line** from the Marking Menu.
21. On the ribbon, click **Sketch > Format > Construction** .
22. Select the origin point of the sketch, move the pointer vertically upward and click to create a vertical construction line.

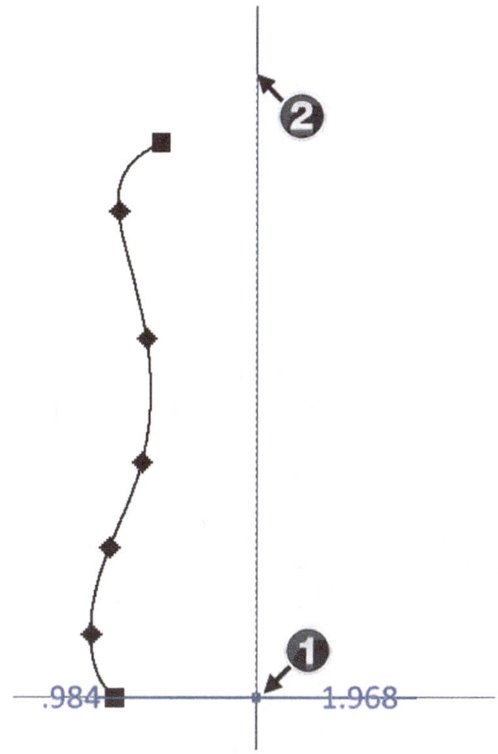

23. Deactivate the **Construction** icon on the **Format** panel.
24. On the ribbon, click **Sketch > Constrain > Vertical** .
25. Select the lower endpoints of the vertical construction line and the spline.

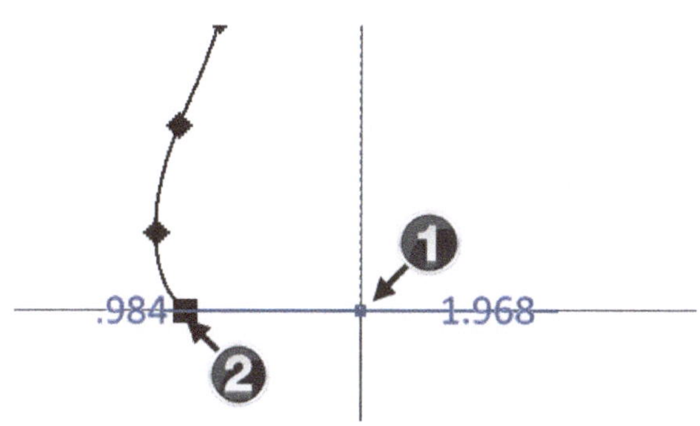

26. On the ribbon, click **Sketch > Constrain > Dimension**.
27. Select the lower endpoints of the construction line and spline.
28. Move the cursor downward and click.
29. Type the **1.968** in the **Edit Dimension** box and press

Enter.

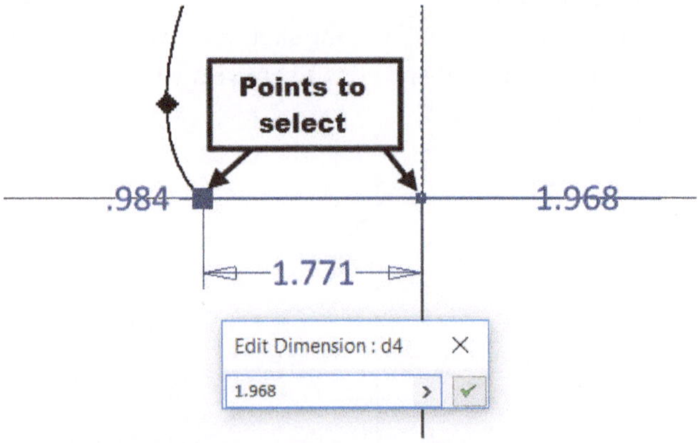

30. Select the second point of the spline and the construction line.
31. Move the cursor and click to place the dimension.
32. Type **2.362** in the **Edit Dimension** box and press **Enter**.

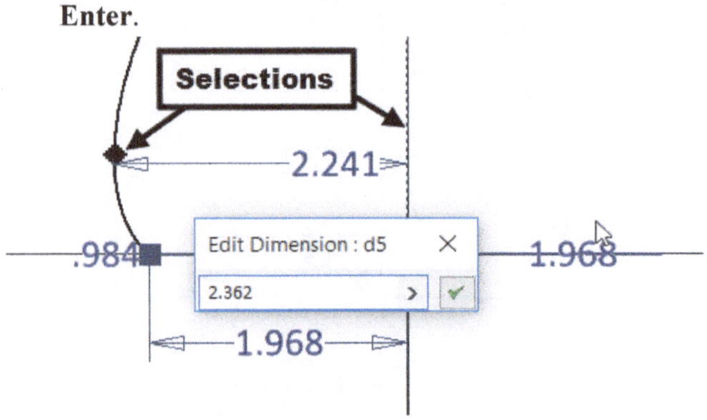

33. Apply the other horizontal dimensions to the spline, as shown in the figure.

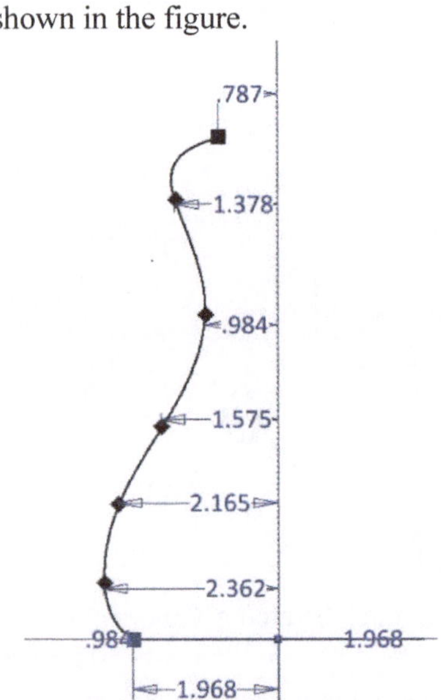

34. Select the origin point of the sketch and the top endpoint of the spline.
35. Move the pointer toward the right and click.
36. Type **8.858** in the **Edit Dimension** box and press Enter.

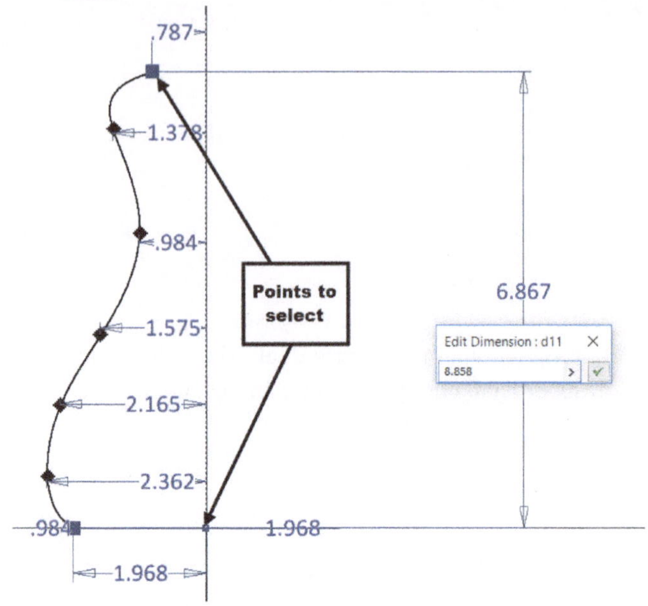

37. Likewise, create other dimensions, as shown.

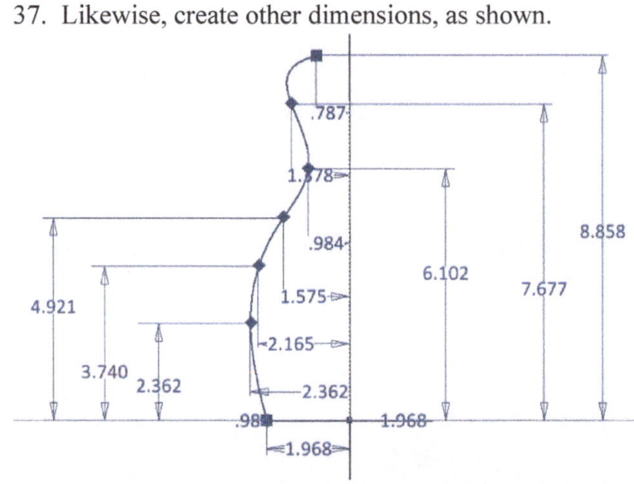

38. Click **Sketch > Pattern > Mirror** on the ribbon; the **Mirror** dialog appears.
39. Select the spline. Make sure that you select the curve and not the points.
40. Click **Mirror line** on the **Mirror** dialog, and then select the construction line.
41. Click **Apply**, and then click **Done**.

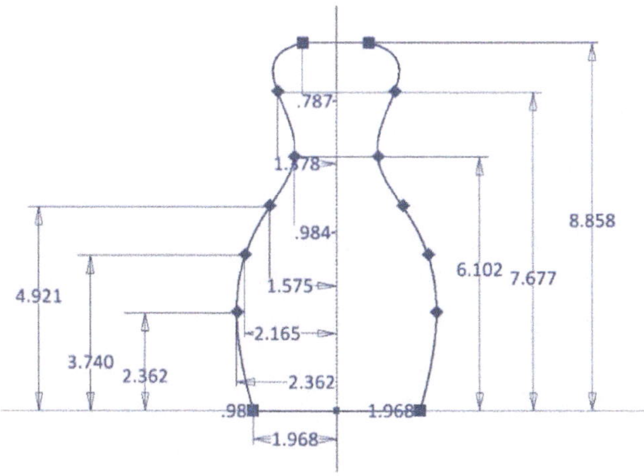

42. Click **Finish**.

Creating the second section

1. Click **3D Model > Work Features > Plane > Offset from Plane** on the ribbon.

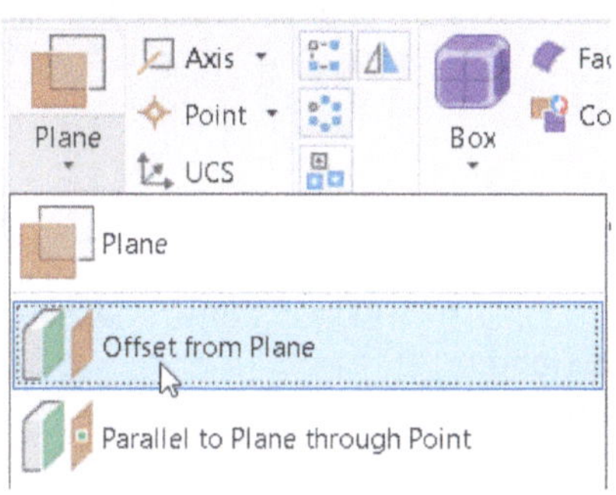

2. Select the XZ plane from the Browser window.

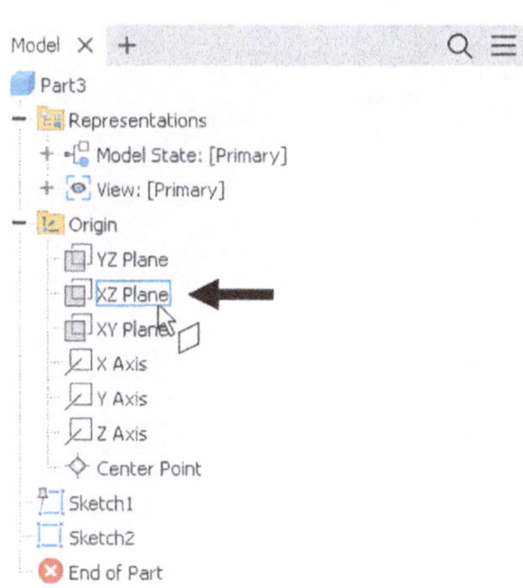

3. Enter **8.858** in the **Distance** box.

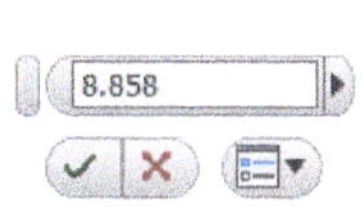

4. Click **OK**.
5. On the ribbon, click the **3D Model > Sketch > Start 2D Sketch**.
6. Select the newly created datum plane.
7. Right click and select **Center Point Circle** from the Marking Menu.
8. Select the origin point, move the cursor outside, and click to create a circle.
9. Right click and select **OK**.
10. Right click and select **General Dimension** from the Marking Menu.
11. Select the circle, move the cursor outward, and click.
12. Type **1.574** and press Enter.

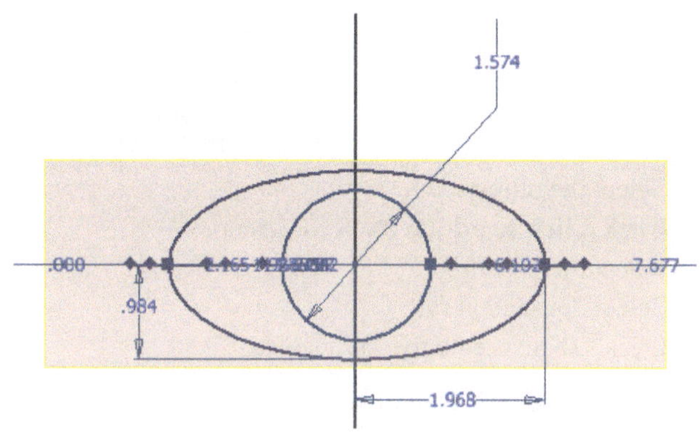

13. Click **Finish** on the ribbon.

Creating the Loft feature

1. To create a loft feature, click **3D Model > Create > Loft** on the ribbon; the **Loft** dialog appears.
2. Select the **Rails** option from the dialog.

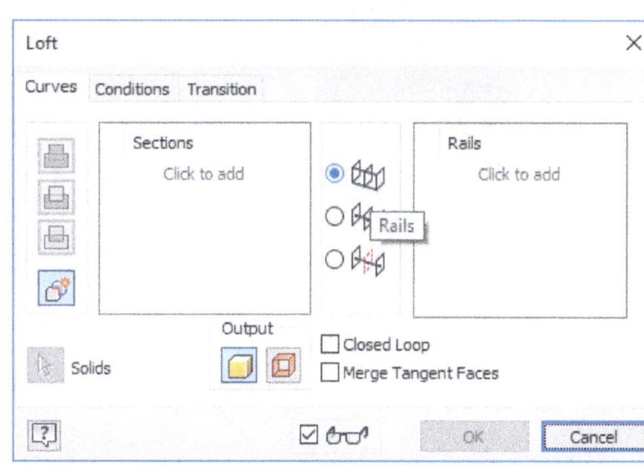

3. Click **Click to add** in the **Sections** group and select the circle.

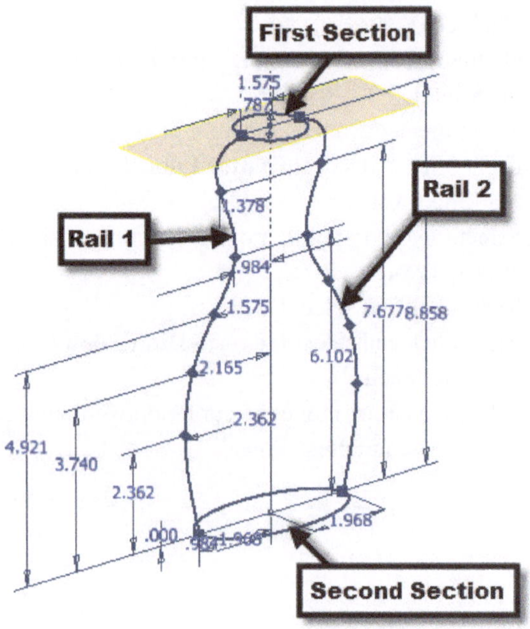

4. Select the ellipse.
5. Click **Click to add** in the **Rails** group.
6. Select the first rail.
7. Select the second rail.
8. Click **OK** to create the loft feature.

Creating the Extruded feature

1. Right click and select **New Sketch** from the Marking Menu.
2. Select the plane located at the top of the loft feature.
3. Right click and select **Center Point Circle** from the Marking Menu.
4. Select the origin point, move the cursor outside, and click to create a circle.
5. Right click and select **OK**.
6. Right click and select **General Dimension** from the Marking Menu.
7. Select the circle, move the cursor outward, and click.
8. Type **1.574** and press Enter.
9. Click **Finish** on the ribbon.
10. Click the **Extrude** button on the **Create** panel.
11. Extrude the circle up to **1** inch.

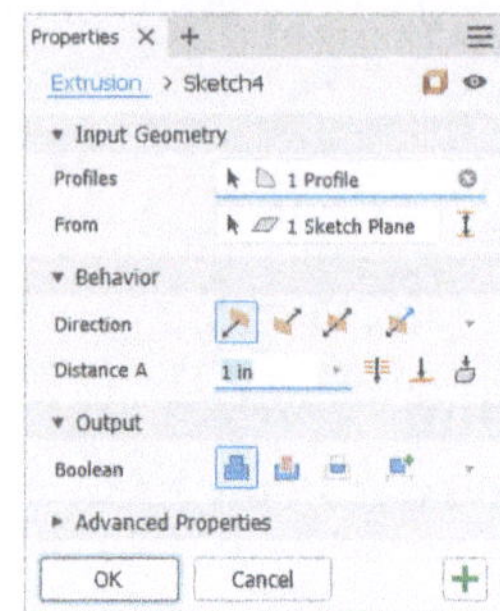

Creating the Emboss feature

1. Click **3D Model > Work Features > Plane > Offset from Plane** on the ribbon.
2. Select the **YZ Plane** from the Browser window.

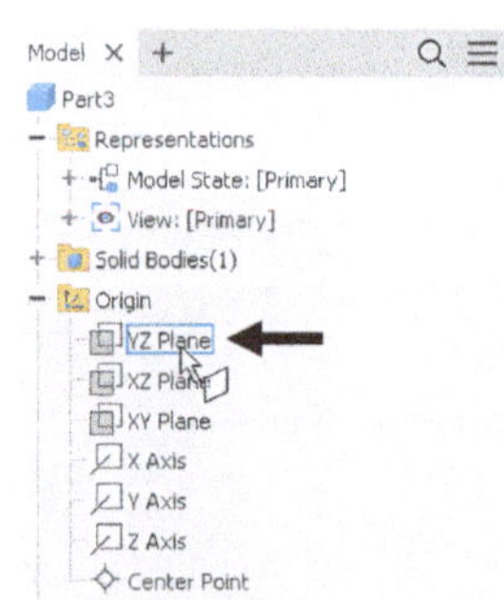

3. Enter **2** in the **Distance** box and click **OK**.

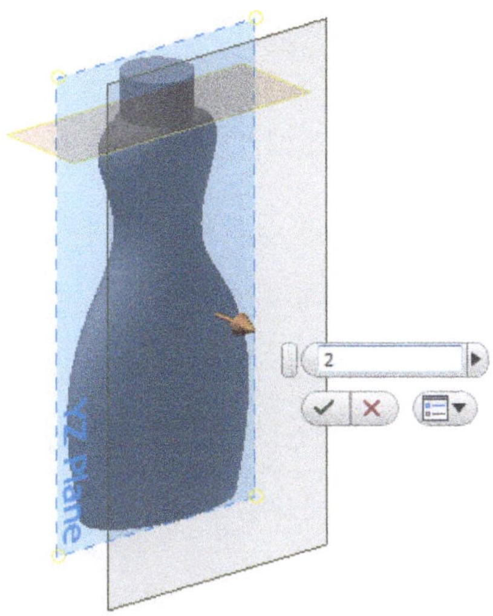

4. Click **3D Model > Sketch > Start 2D Sketch** on the ribbon.
5. Select the newly created datum plane
6. Click **Sketch > Create > Circle > Ellipse** on the ribbon.
7. Draw the ellipse by selecting the points, as shown.

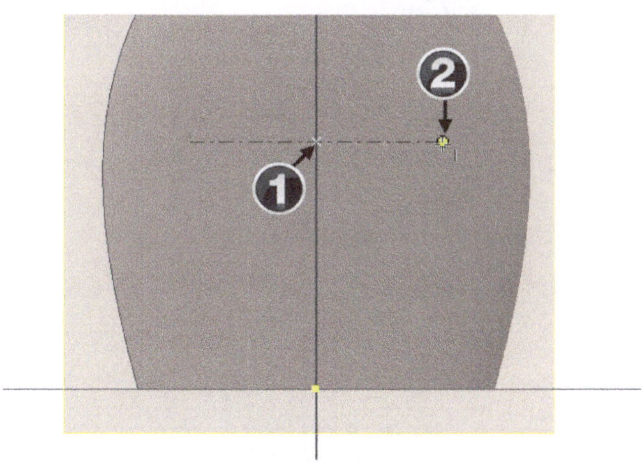

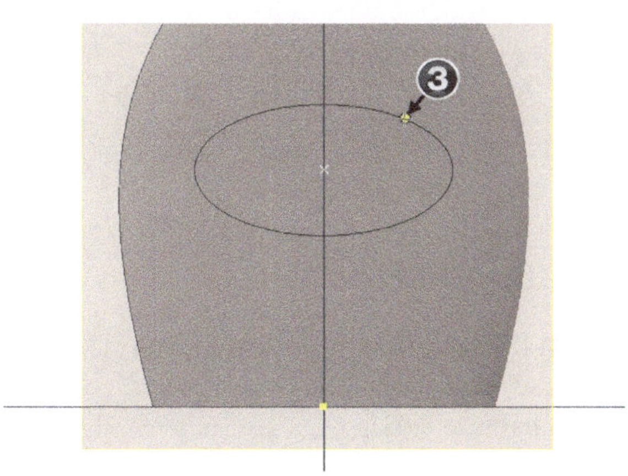

8. On the ribbon, click **Sketch > Constrain > Dimension**.
9. Select the ellipse, move the cursor downward, and click
10. Type **2** and press Enter.
11. Select the ellipse, move the cursor toward left, and click.
12. Type **1.35** and press Enter.
13. Select the origin point of the sketch and the center point of the ellipse.
14. Move the cursor toward the left and click to place the dimension between the selected point.
15. Type **2.55** and press Enter.
16. Right click and select **Line** from the Marking Menu.
17. Right click and select **Construction** from the Marking Menu.
18. Select the origin point of the sketch and the center point of the ellipse.
19. Right click and select **OK**; a construction line is created between the sketch origin and the ellipse. Also, the sketch is fully-constrained.
20. Click **Finish Sketch**.

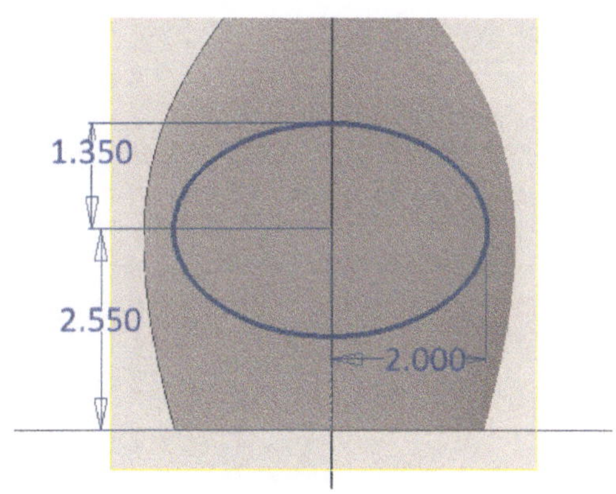

21. Click **3D Model > Create > Emboss** on the ribbon; the **Emboss** dialog appears.
22. Select the sketch, if not already selected.
23. Click the **Engrave from Face** button on the dialog.
24. Set the **Depth** to 0.125.
25. Click **OK** to create the embossed feature.

Mirroring the Emboss feature

1. Click **3D Model > Pattern > Mirror** on the ribbon.

2. Select the emboss feature from the model geometry.
3. On the **Mirror** dialog, click the **Mirror Plane** button, and then select the **YZ Plane** from the Browser window.
4. Click **OK** to mirror the emboss feature.

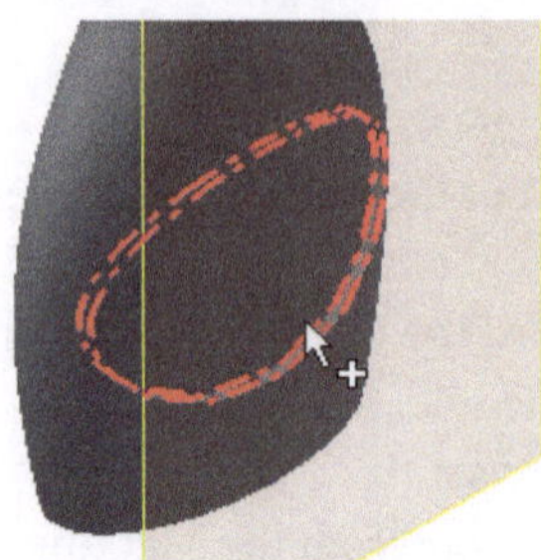

Creating Fillets

1. Click **3D Model > Modify > Fillet** on the ribbon; the **Fillet Properties panel** appears.
2. Click on the bottom and top edges of the swept feature.
3. Set **Radius** to **0.2**.

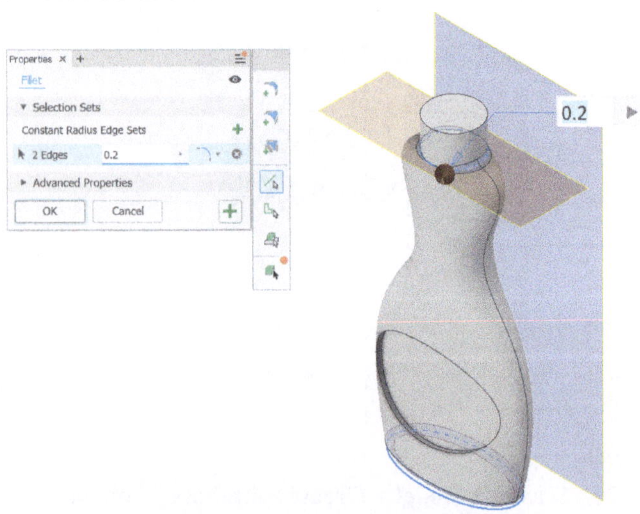

4. Under the **Selection Sets** section, click the **Add constant radius edge set** symbol on the Fillet Properties panel.
5. Set **Radius** to **0.04**.

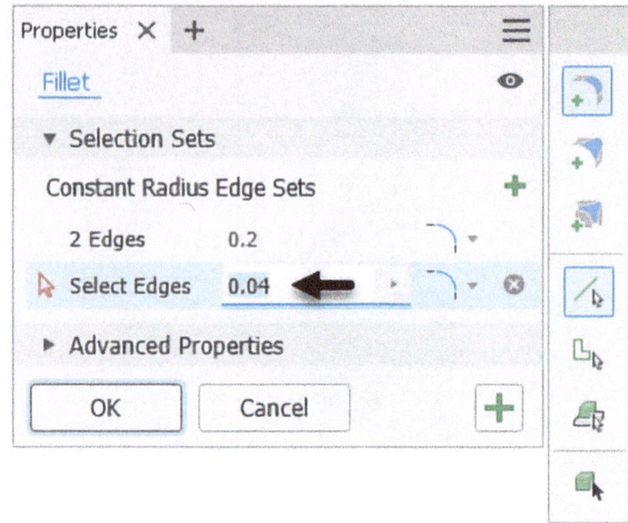

6. Select the edges of the emboss features, and click **OK**.

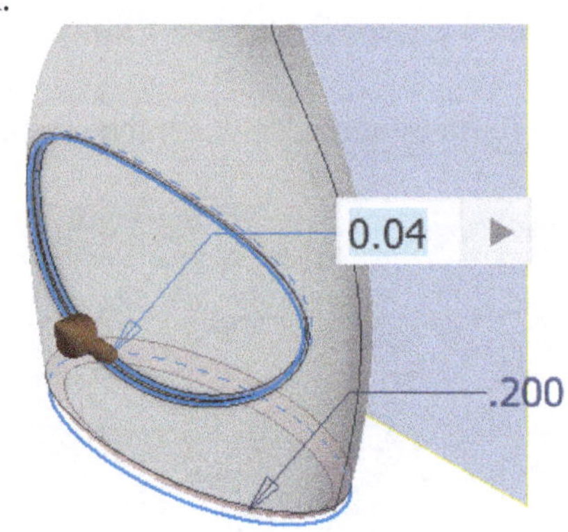

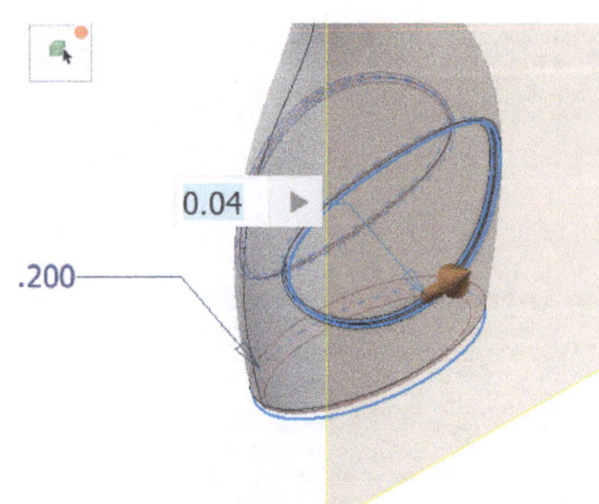

Shelling the Model

1. Click **3D Model > Modify > Shell** on the ribbon; the **Shell Properties panel** appears.
2. Set **Thickness** to 0.03.
3. Select the top face of the cylindrical feature.

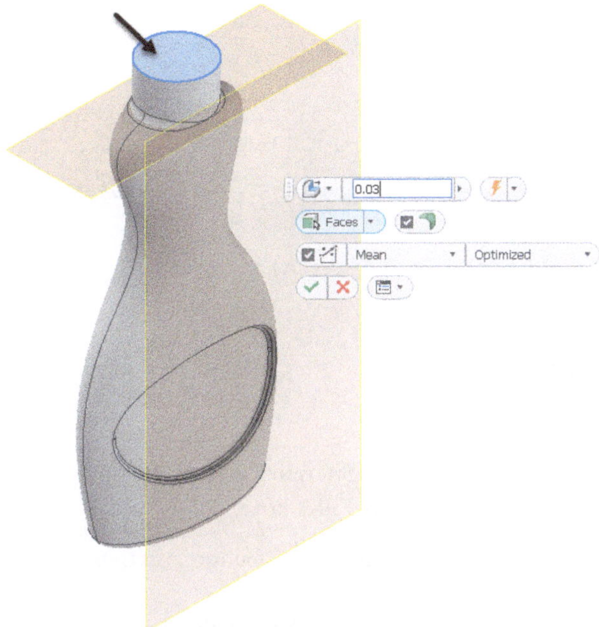

4. Click **OK** to create the shell.

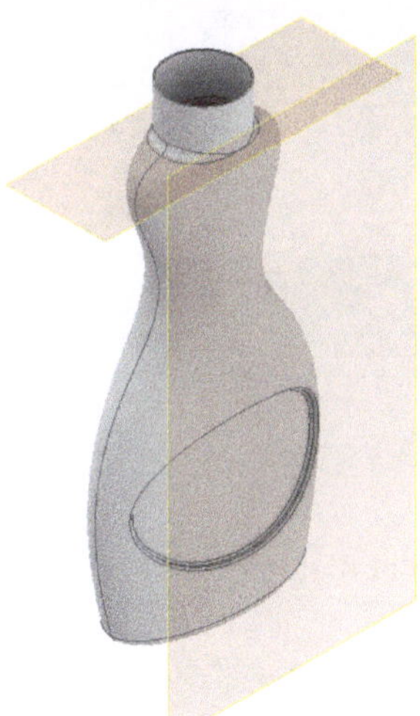

Adding Threads

1. Select the YZ Plane, and then click **Create Sketch**.

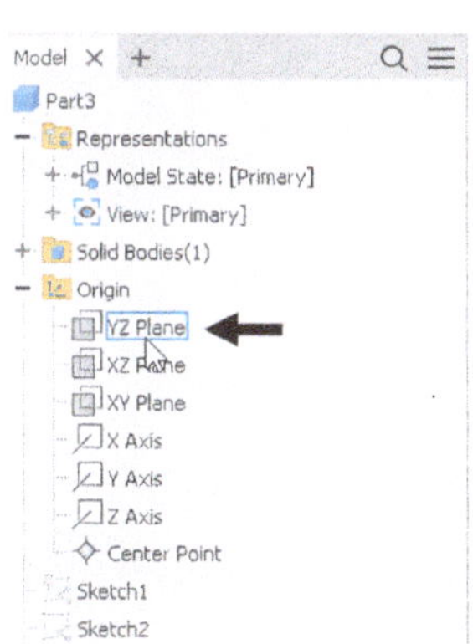

2. Click the **Slice Graphics** icon located at the bottom of the window.

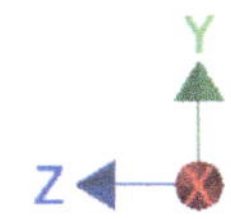

3. On the ribbon, click **Sketch > Create > Line**.
4. Right click and select **Centerline** from the Marking Menu.
5. Select the origin point of the sketch, move the cursor vertically upward and click to create a vertical centreline. Press **Esc**.
6. Deactivate the **Centerline** icon on the **Format** panel.
7. Right click and select **Create Line** from the Marking Menu.
8. Right click and select **Construction** from the Marking Menu.
9. Create a horizontal construction line, as shown.

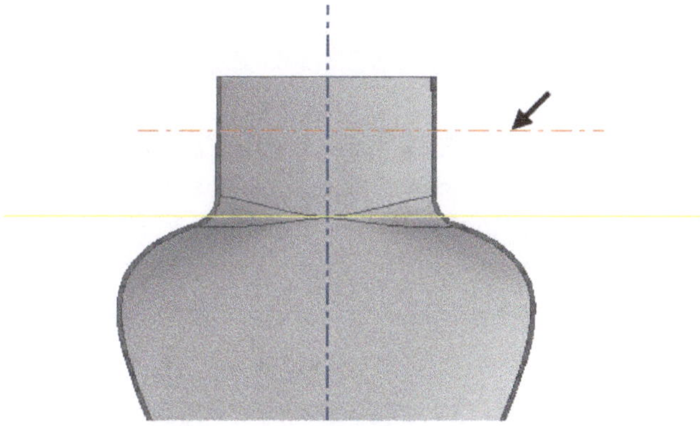

10. Deactivate the **Construction** icon on the **Format** panel of the **Sketch** ribbon tab.
11. On the ribbon, click **Sketch > Create > Line**.
12. Create a closed profile, as shown.

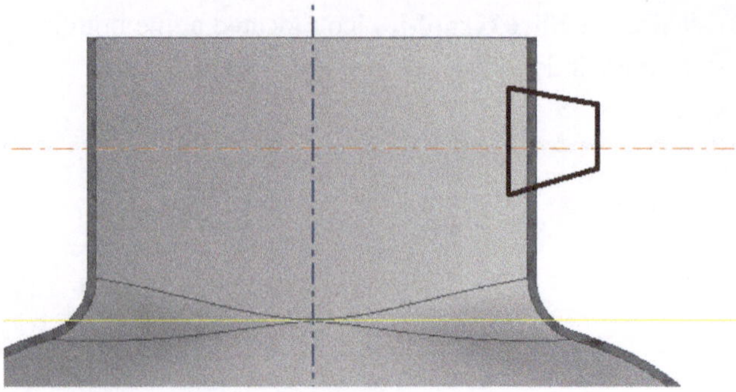

13. On the ribbon, click **Sketch > Constrain > Symmetric** .
14. Select the two inclined lines of the sketch, and then select the construction line; the two inclined lines are made symmetric about the construction line.

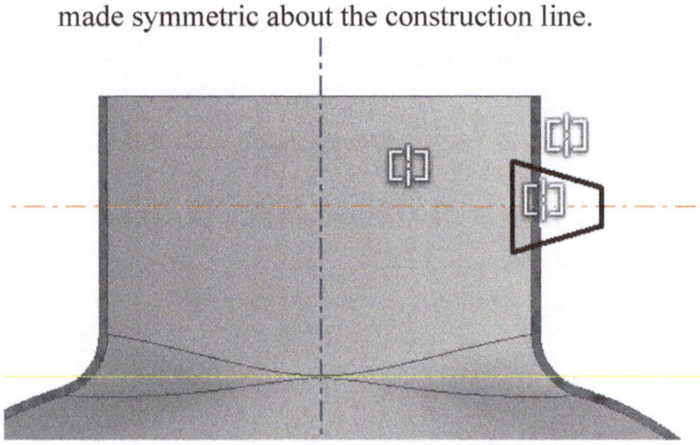

15. Click the **Dimension** button on the **Constrain** panel.
16. Select the two inclined lines, move the cursor horizontally toward left and click.
17. Type 60 in the **Edit Dimension** box and press Enter.

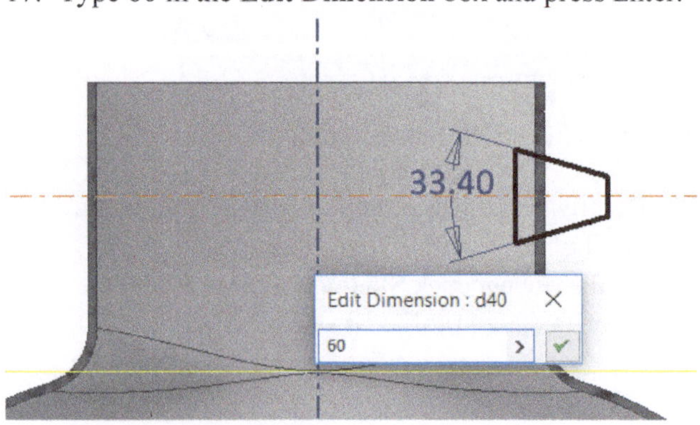

18. Draw the thread profile.

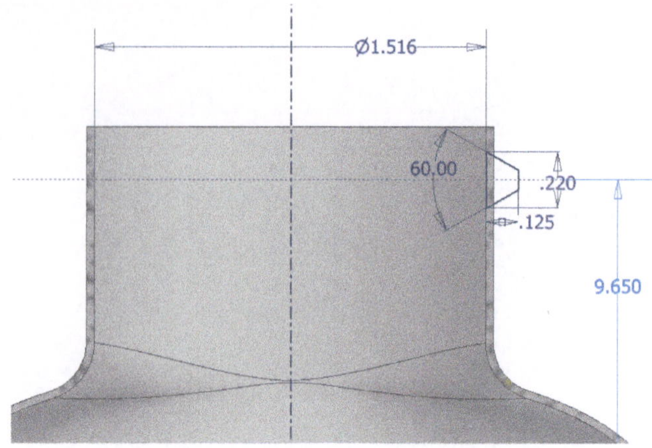

19. On the ribbon, click **Sketch > Create > Fillet** .
20. Type 0.04 in the **2D Fillet** box.
21. Make sure that the **Equal** button is active on the **2D Fillet** box.
22. Select the two corners of the sketch, as shown.

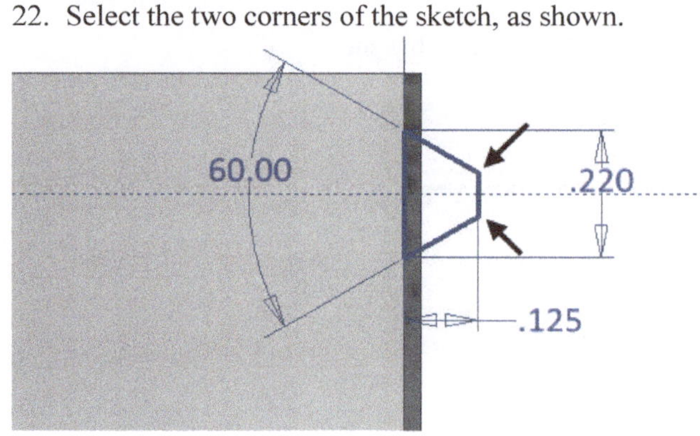

23. Close the **2D Fillet** dialog box.

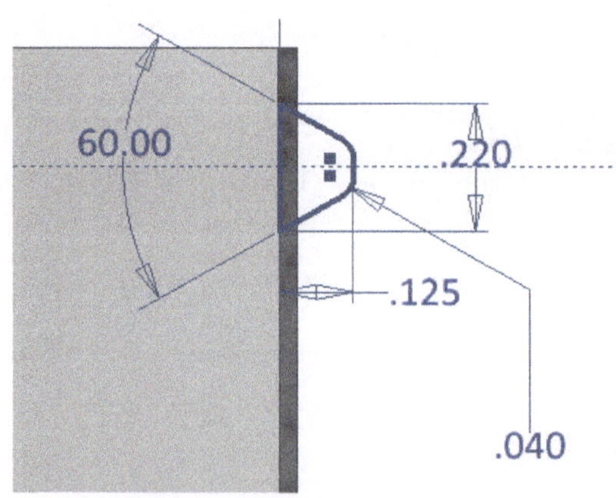

24. Click **Finish** on the ribbon.
25. On the ribbon, click **3D Model > Create > Coil** ; the closed profile of the sketch is selected

automatically.

26. Select the axis of the coil, if not already selected.

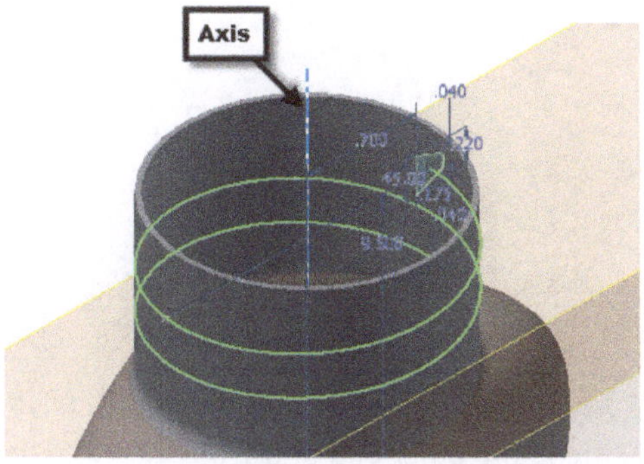

27. On the **Coil Properties panel**, select **Method > Pitch and Revolution** under the **Behavior** section.
28. Type-in **0.275** and **2** in the **Pitch** and **Revolution** boxes, respectively.

29. Click the **Reverse pitch direction** icon, if the preview of the coil is displayed in the upward direction.
30. Click **OK**.

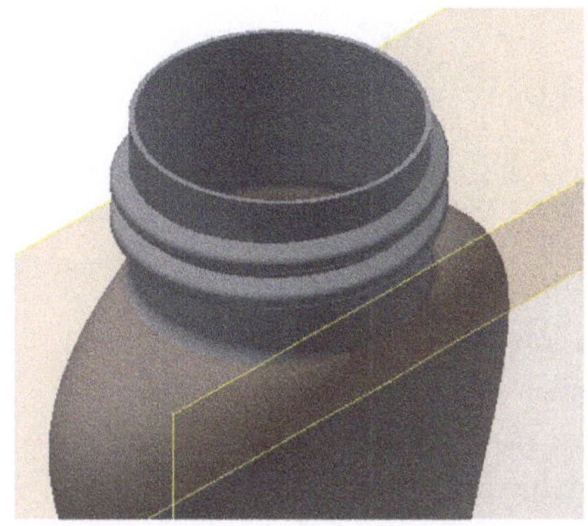

31. In the Browser Window, right click on the YZ Plane, and then select **New Sketch**.

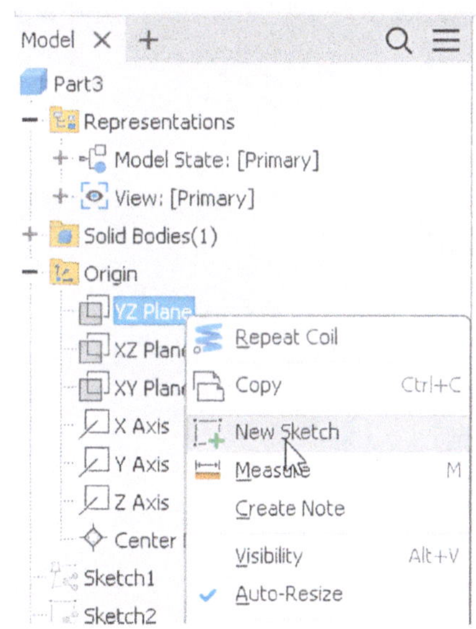

32. On the ribbon, click **Sketch > Create > Project Geometry**.
33. Select the edges of the end face of the thread.
34. Draw a straight line connecting the endpoints of the projected elements.

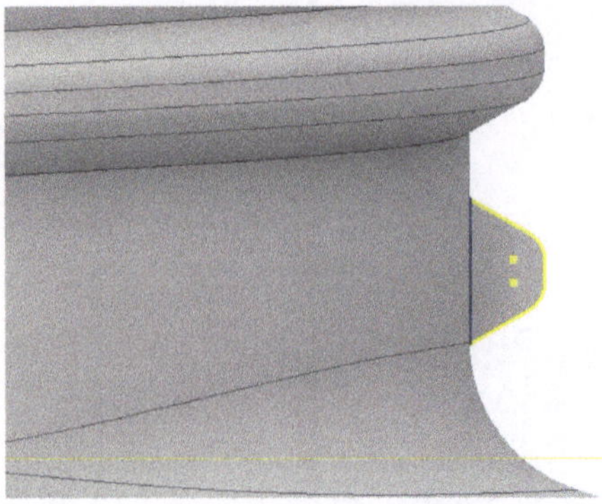

35. Click **Finish** on the **Exit** panel of the ribbon.
36. Activate the **Revolve** tool and click on the vertical line of the sketch.
37. On the Properties panel, type in **100** in the **Angle A** box under the **Behavior** section.

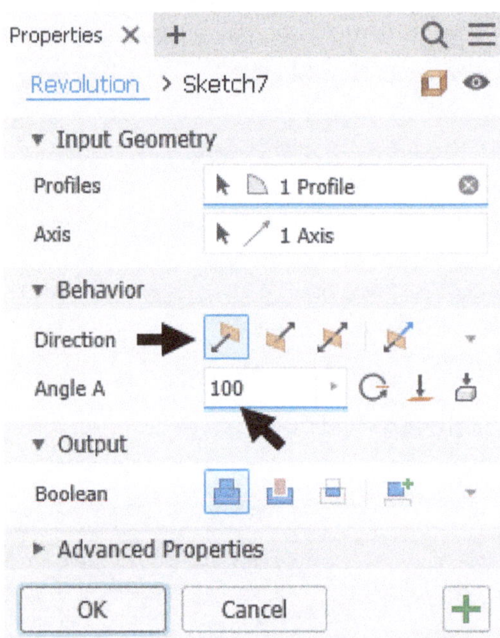

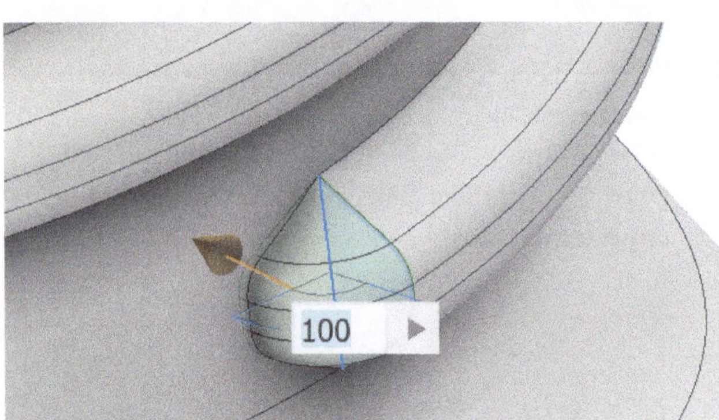

38. Click **OK**.

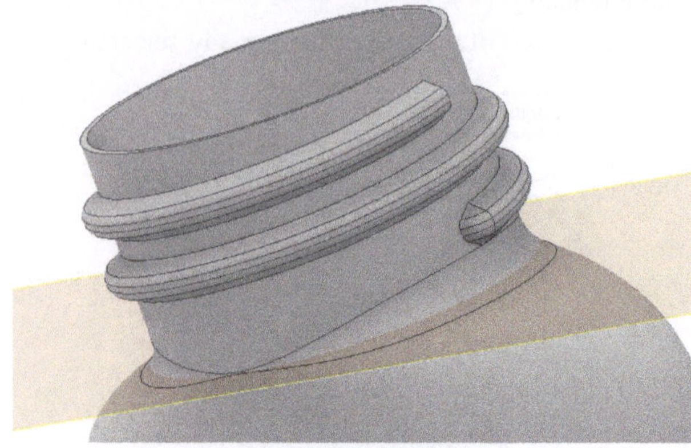

39. Likewise, blend the other end of the thread. Note that you need the reverse the direction of revolution.

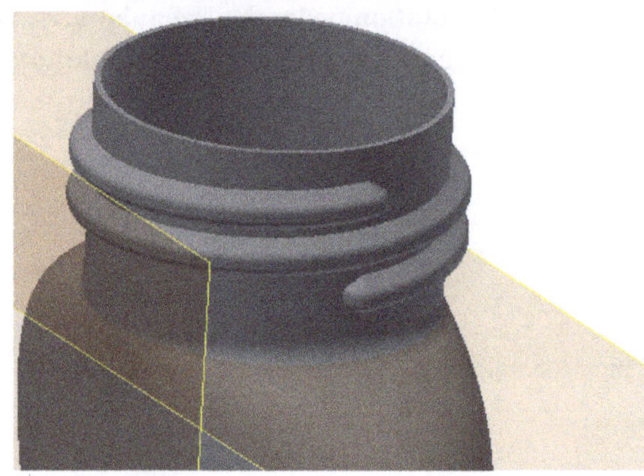

40. Save the model.

TUTORIAL 5

In this tutorial, you create a chair, as shown.

Creating a 3D Sketch

1. Open a new Inventor file using the Standard.ipt template (See Chapter 2, Tutorial 3, Starting a New Part File section).
2. Click the **Home** icon located above the ViewCube. This changes the view orientation to Home.

3. On the ribbon, click **3D Model > Sketch > Start 2D Sketch > Start 3D Sketch**.

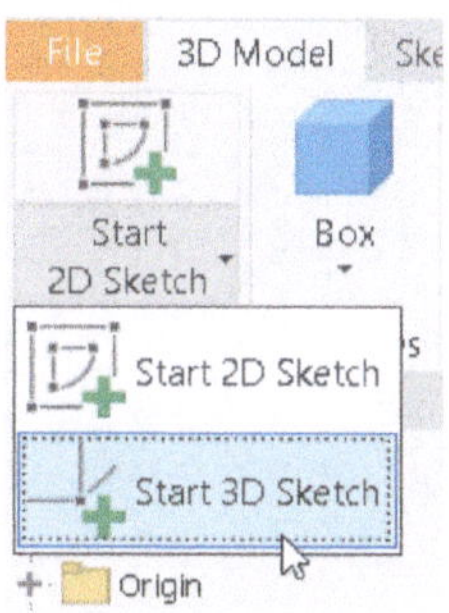

4. On the **3D Sketch** tab of the ribbon, click **Draw > Line**.

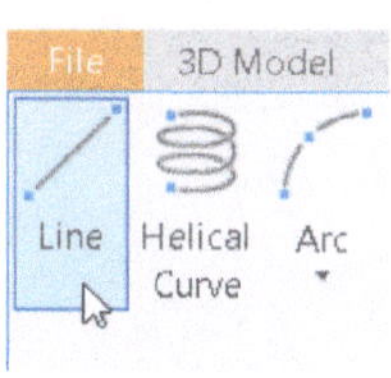

5. Expand the **Draw** panel on the ribbon and activate the **Precise Input** option.

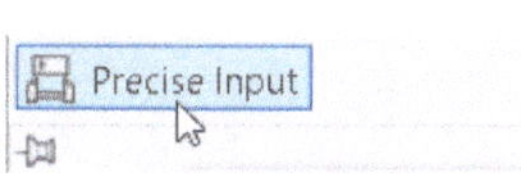

6. On the **Precise Input** toolbar, click the **Reset to Origin** button.
7. Select the **Relative** option from the drop-down available on the **Precise Input** toolbar.

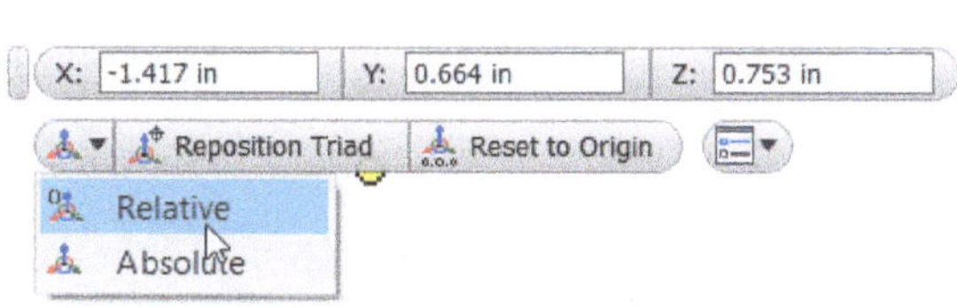

8. On the **Precise Input** toolbar, click in the X box and type 0.
9. Press the Tab key and type 0 in the Y box.
10. Press the Tab key and type 0 in the Z box.
11. Press Enter to specify the first point.

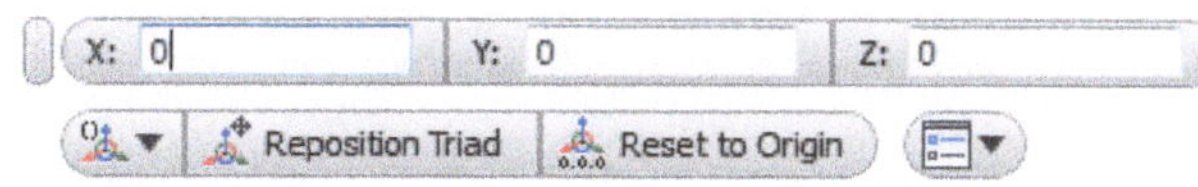

12. Type-in 12 in the **X** box and press Tab on your keyboard.
13. Likewise, type-in 0 in the **Y** and **Z** boxes, respectively. Press Enter to specify the second point.

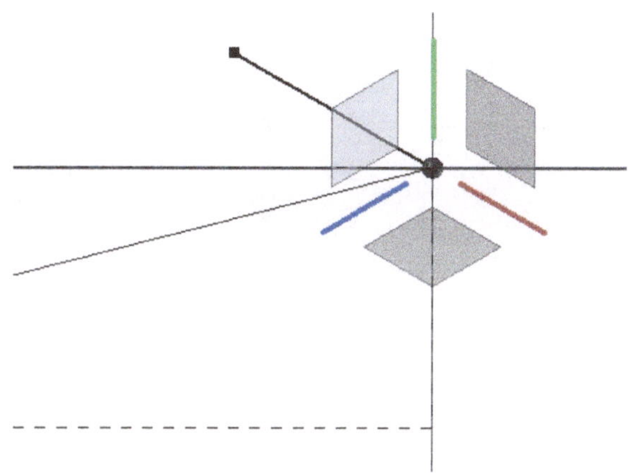

14. Type-in 0, 0, and 20 in the X, Y, and Z boxes, respectively. Press Enter.

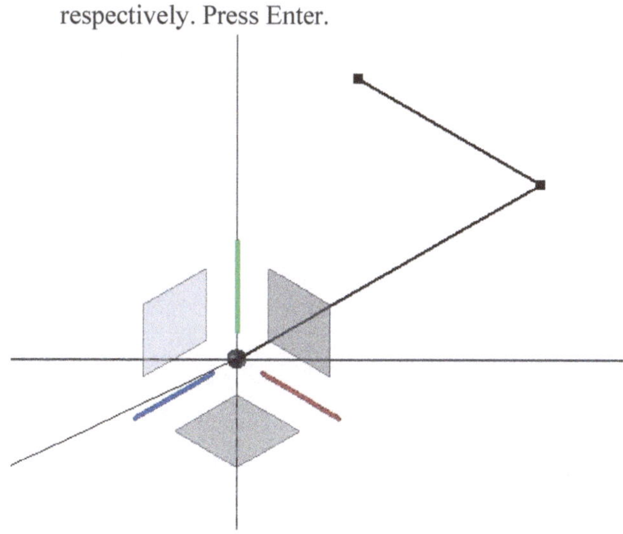

15. Type-in 0, 18, 0 in the X, Y, and Z boxes, respectively. Press Enter.

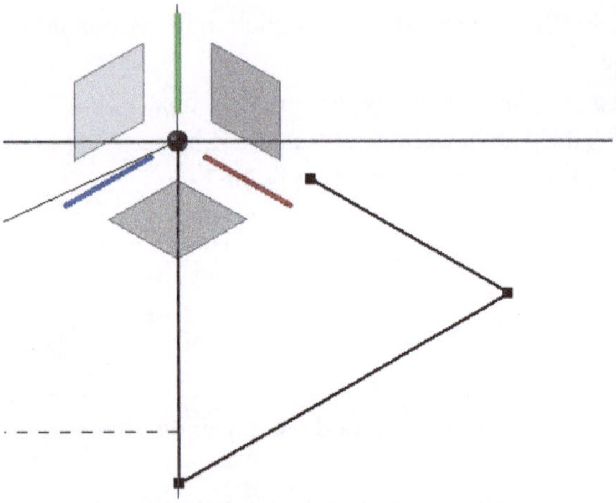

16. Type-in 0, 0, and -22 in the X, Y, and Z boxes, respectively. Press Enter.

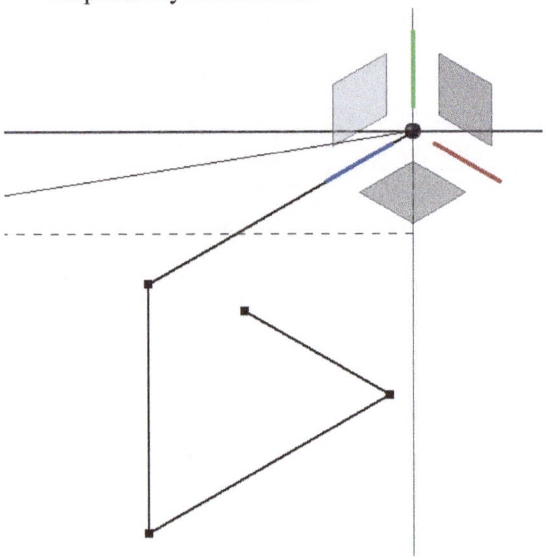

17. Type-in 0, 18, and 0 in the X, Y, and Z boxes, respectively. Press Enter.

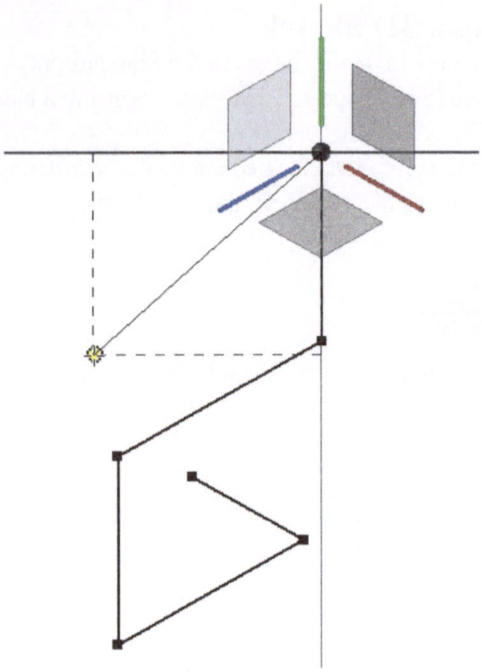

18. Type-in -12, 0, and 0 in the X, Y, and Z boxes, respectively. Press Enter.

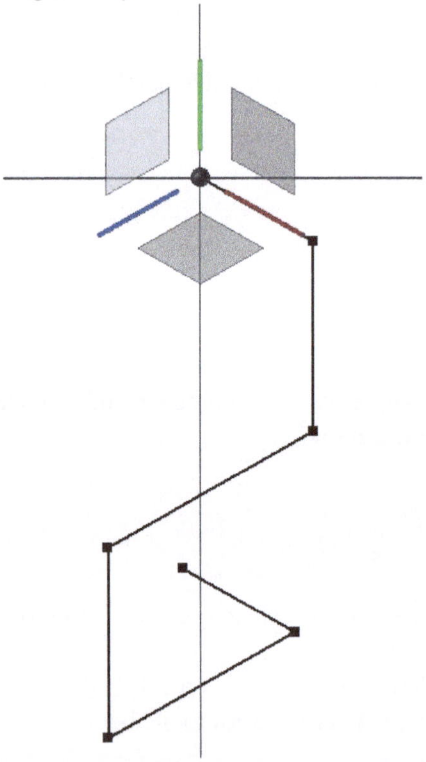

19. Click the right mouse button and select **OK**.
20. On the **3D Sketch** tab of the ribbon, click **Pattern > Mirror**.

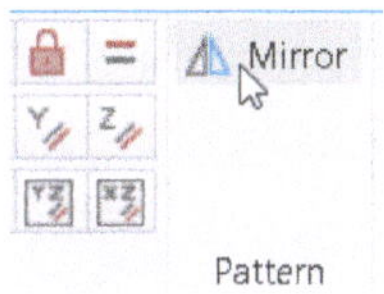

21. Drag a selection box and select all the sketch elements.

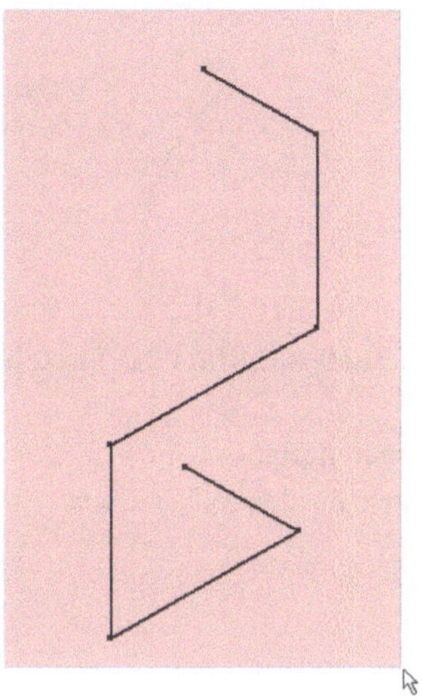

22. Click the **Mirror Plane** button on the dialog, and then select YZ Plane from the Browser window.
23. Click **Apply** and **Done** on the dialog.

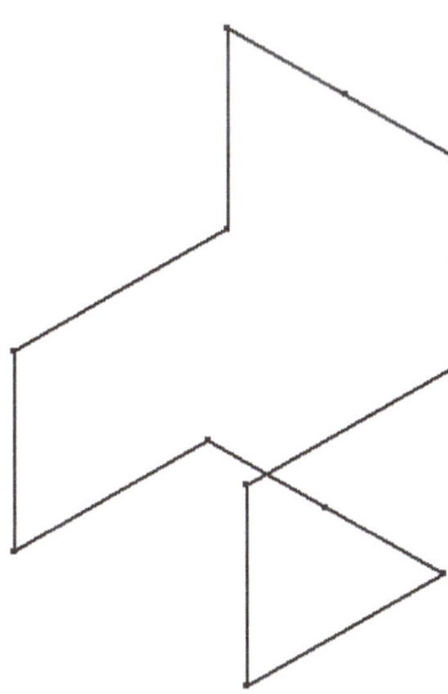

24. On the ribbon, click **3D Sketch > Draw > Bend**.

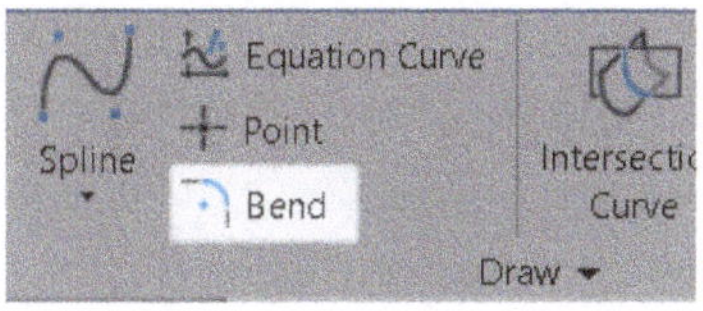

25. Type-in 3 in the **Bend** dialog and select the intersecting lines, as shown in the figure.

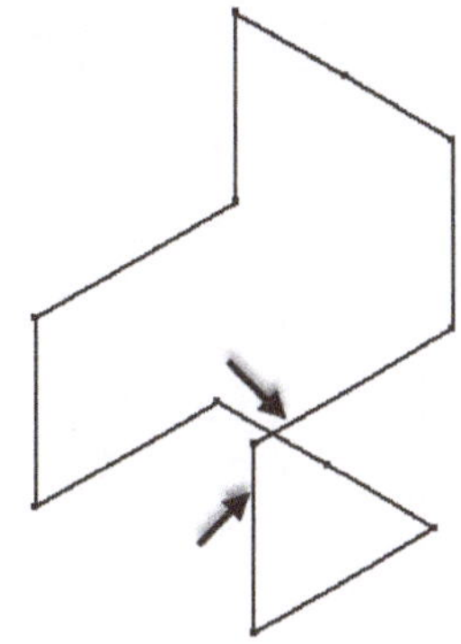

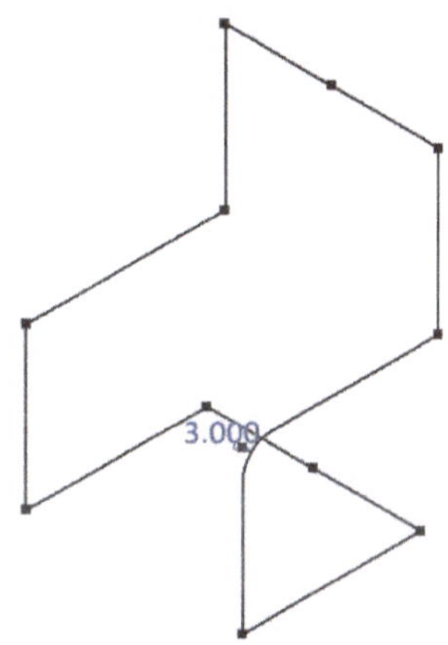

26. Likewise, bend the other corners of the 3D sketch.

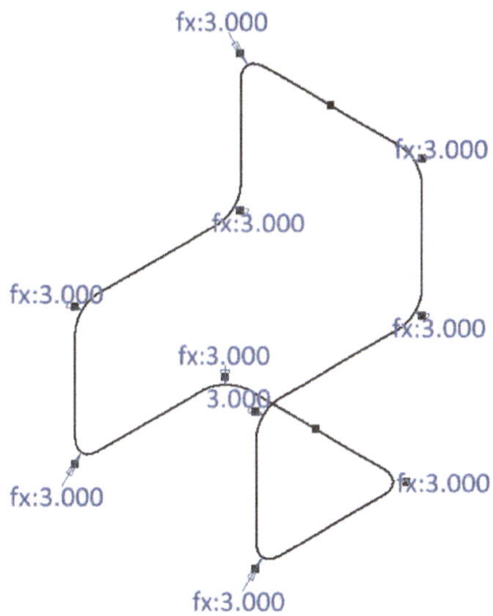

27. Click the right mouse button and select **OK**.
28. On the ribbon, click **3D Sketch > Constrain > Fix** .
29. Select the origin point of the sketch.

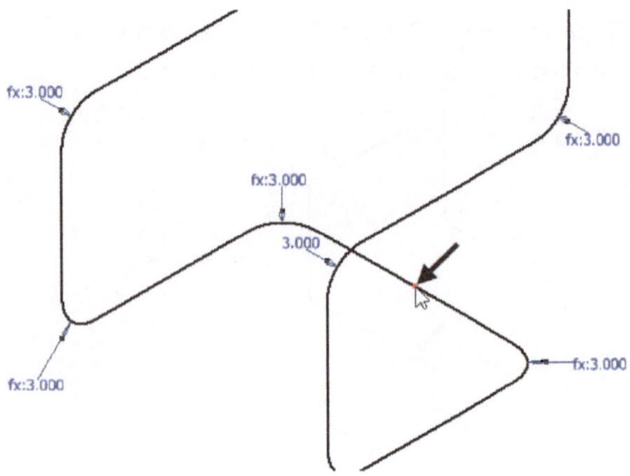

30. Add dimensions to define the sketch fully.

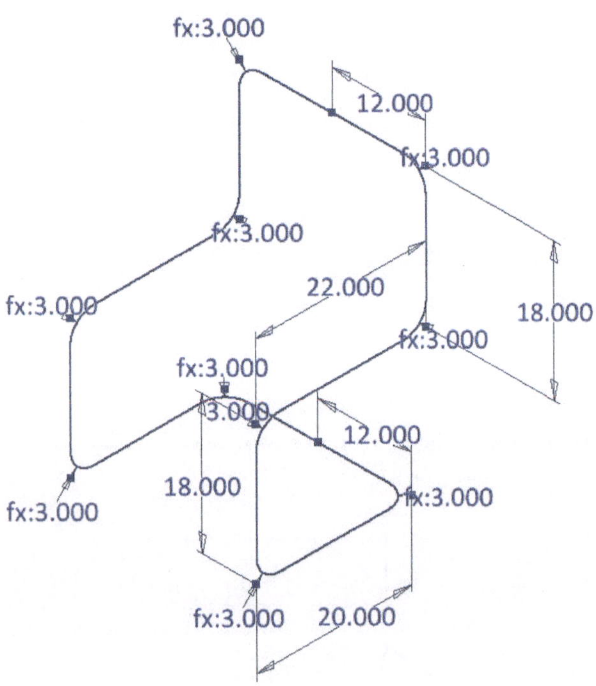

31. Click **Finish** on the ribbon.
32. On the ribbon, click **3D Model > Work Features > Plane > Normal to Axis through Point**.

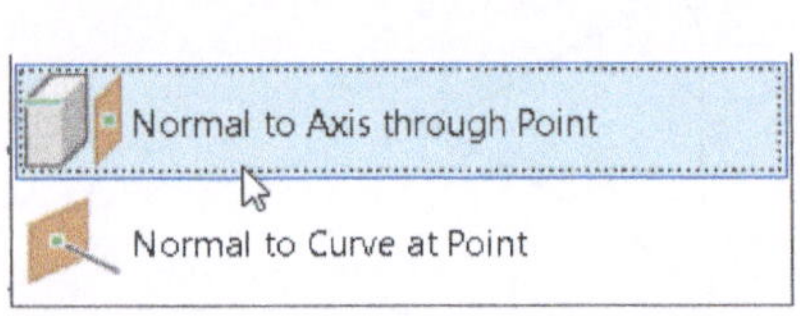

33. Click on the upper horizontal line of the sketch and its endpoint.

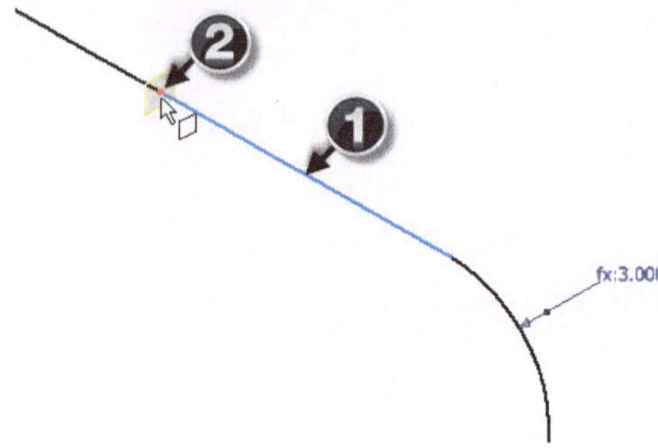

34. Click **3D Model > Sketch > Start 2D Sketch** on the ribbon.
35. Select the newly created plane.
36. Create two concentric circles of 1.250 and 1 diameters.

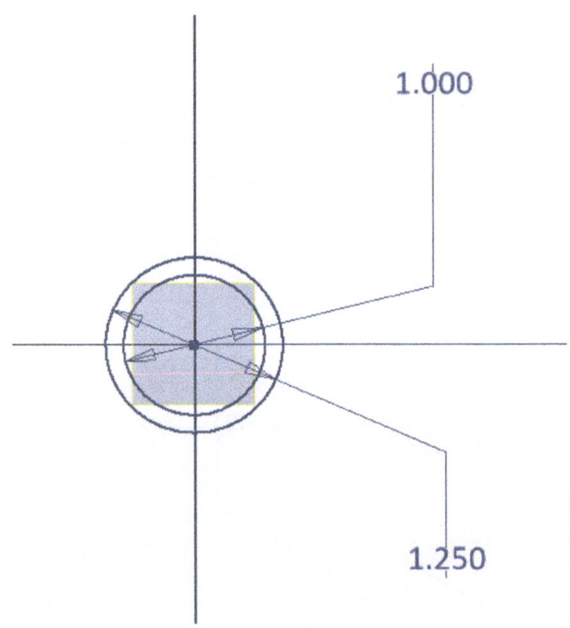

37. Add dimensions from the sketch origin to position the circles.

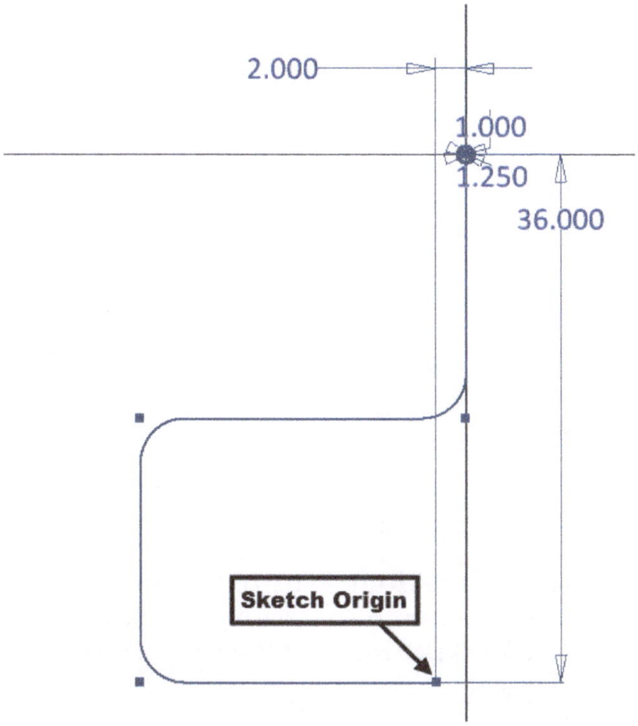

38. Click **Finish** on the ribbon.

Creating the Sweep feature

1. On the ribbon, click **3D Model > Create > Sweep**.

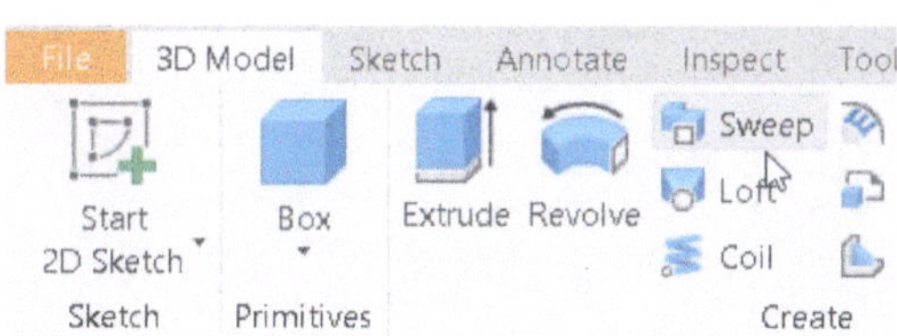

2. Zoom into the circular sketch and click in the outer loop.

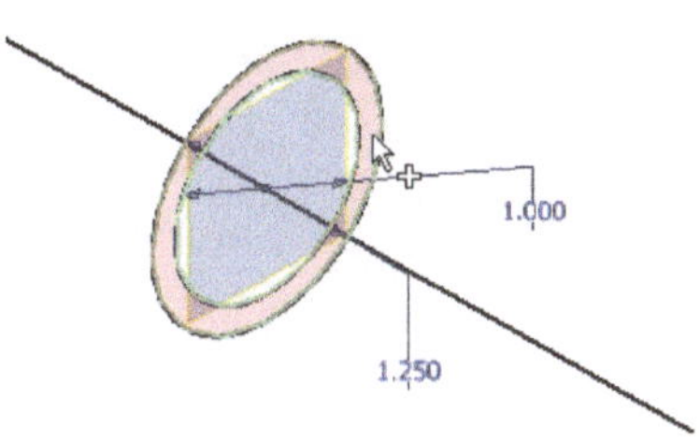

3. Click on the 3D sketch to define the sweep path.

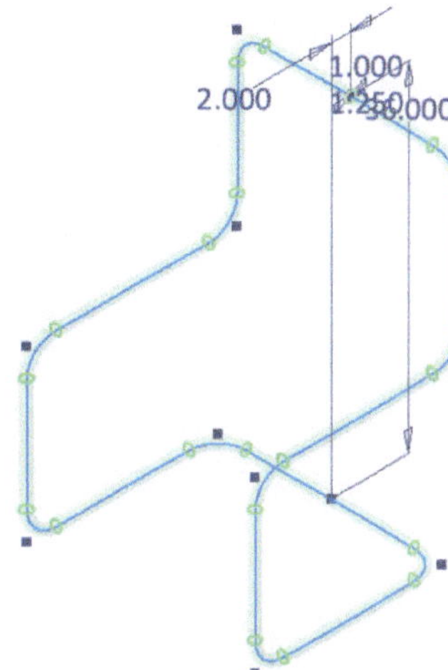

4. Click **OK** to sweep the profile.

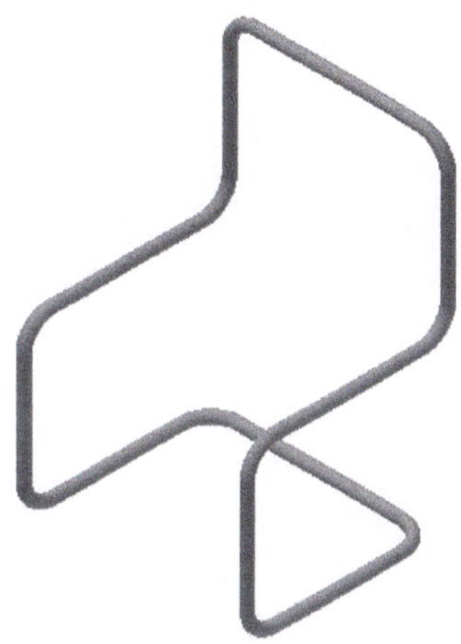

5. Start a sketch on the YZ Plane.
6. Click the **Slice Graphics** icon at the bottom of the graphics window.
7. Draw two concentric circles and dimension them.

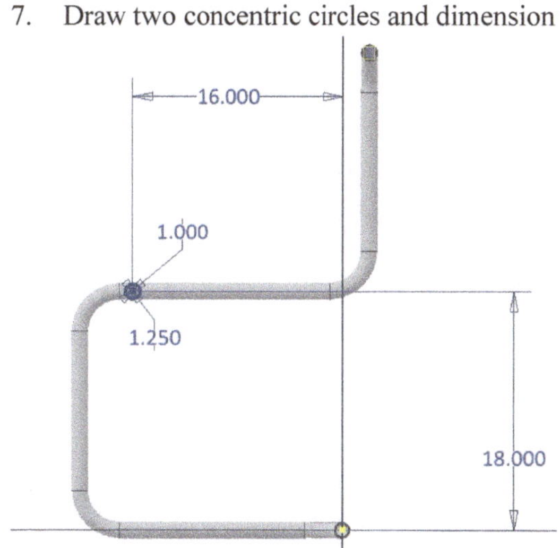

8. Click **Finish** on the ribbon.

9. Activate the **Extrude** tool and click in the outer loop of the sketch.

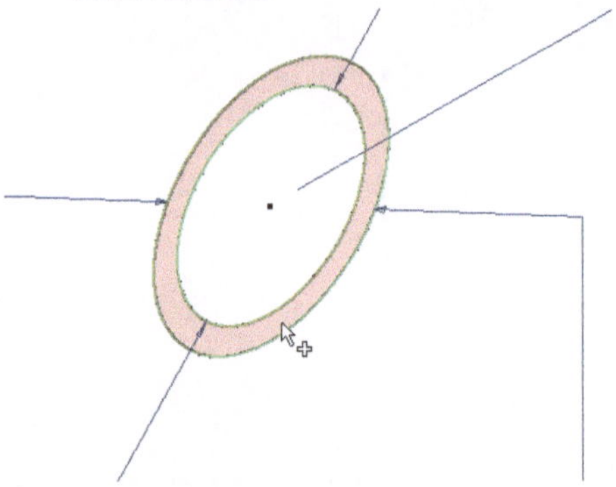

10. On the **Extrude Properties** panel, click the **Between** icon under the **Input Geometry** section.
11. Click on the tube, as shown.

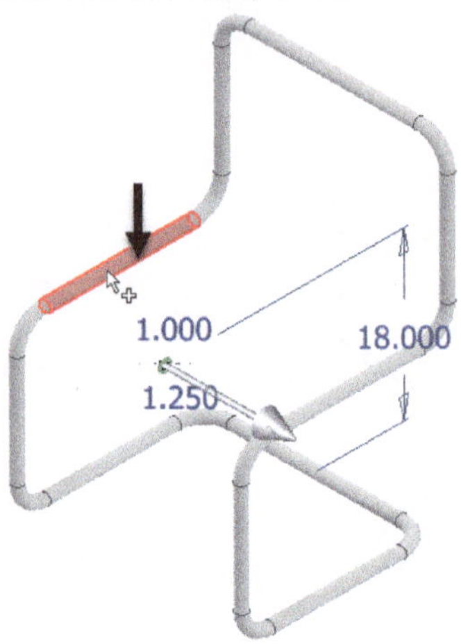

12. Click on the other side of the tube, as shown.

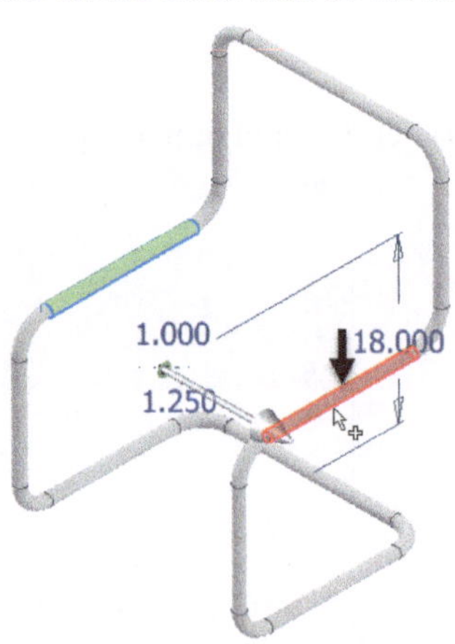

13. Click the **Alternate solution** icon.
14. Click **OK** to extrude the sketch.

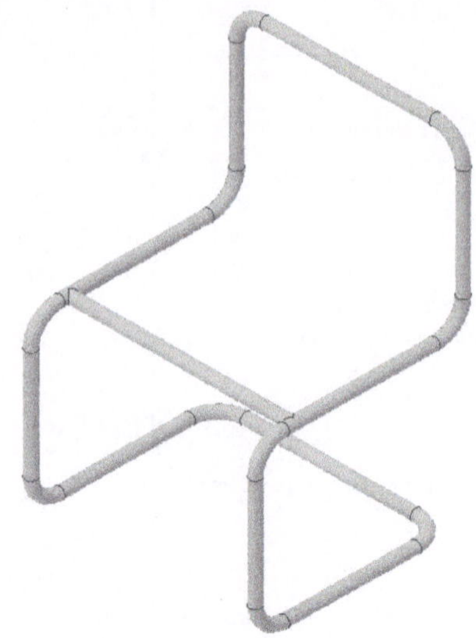

Creating the Along Curve pattern

1. On the Browser window, click the right mouse button on the **3D Sketch** and select **Visibility**; the 3D sketch is displayed.

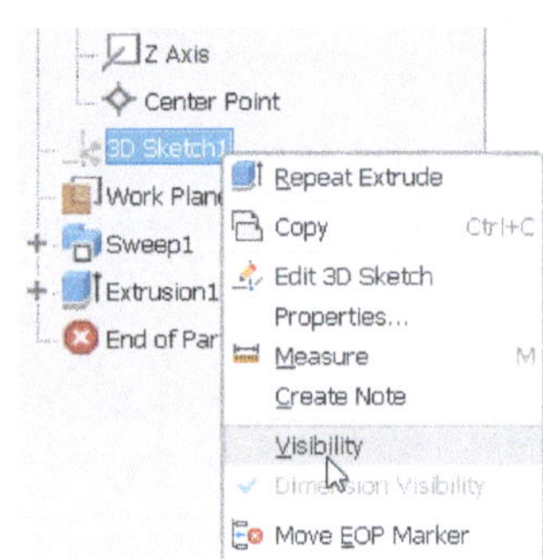

2. On the ribbon, click **3D Model > Pattern > Rectangular Pattern**.

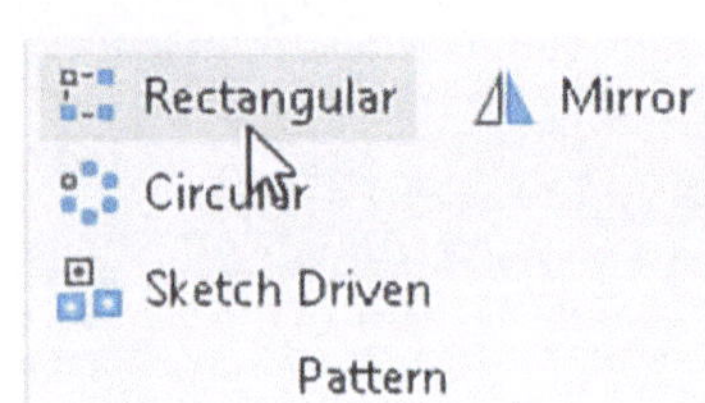

3. Click on the extrude feature.
4. On the **Rectangular Pattern** panel, click the **Custom Direction** selection button under the Direction A section.
5. Place the pointer on the sweep feature and then select the **3D sketch** option from the flyout.

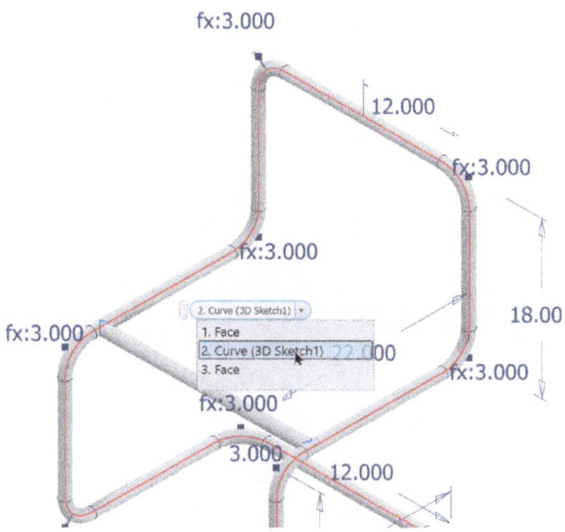

6. Type-in **3** and **23** in the **Number** and **Distance** boxes, respectively.
7. Select **Distribution > Fitted** .
8. Expand the **Output Geometry** section.
9. Set the **Orientation** to **Direction 1**.

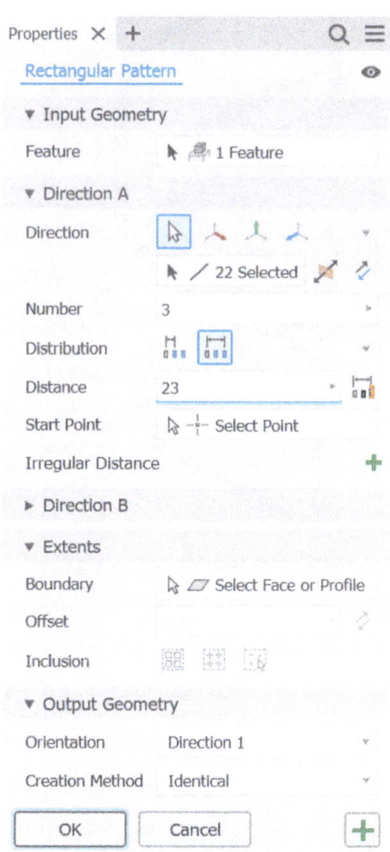

10. Click **OK** to pattern the extruded feature.
11. On the Browser window, click the right mouse button on the 3D sketch and select **Visibility**. This hides the 3D sketch.

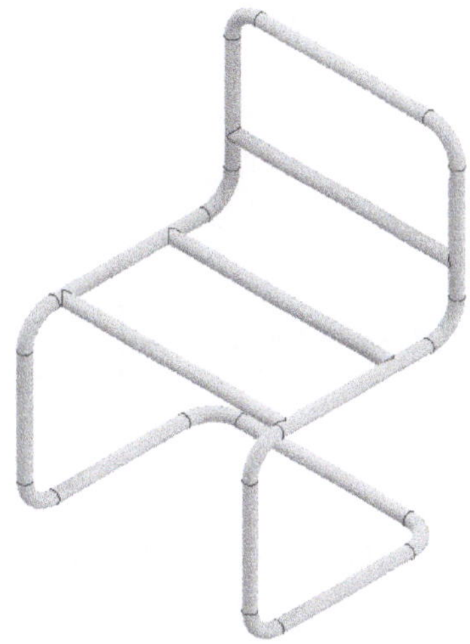

Creating the Freeform feature

1. On the ribbon, click **3D Model > Work Features > Plane**.

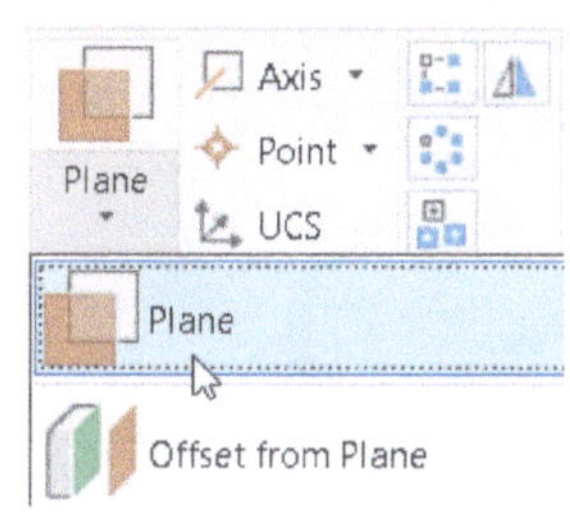

2. On the **Browser window**, click the XZ Plane. A plane appears on the XZ Plane.
3. Click on the top portion of the extruded feature. A plane appears tangent to the extruded feature.

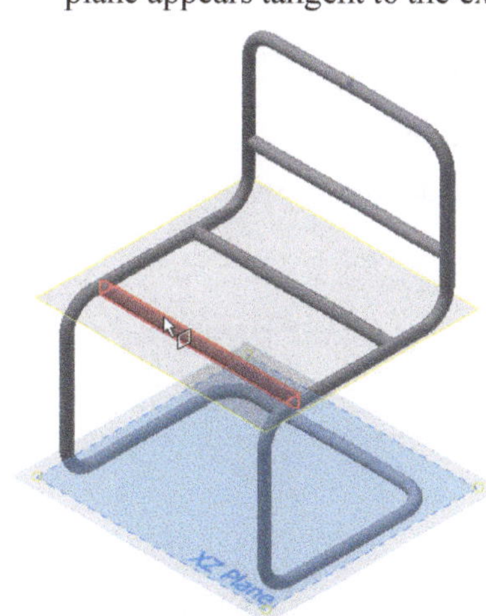

4. Start a sketch on the new plane.
5. Place a point on the sketch plane and add dimensions

to position it.

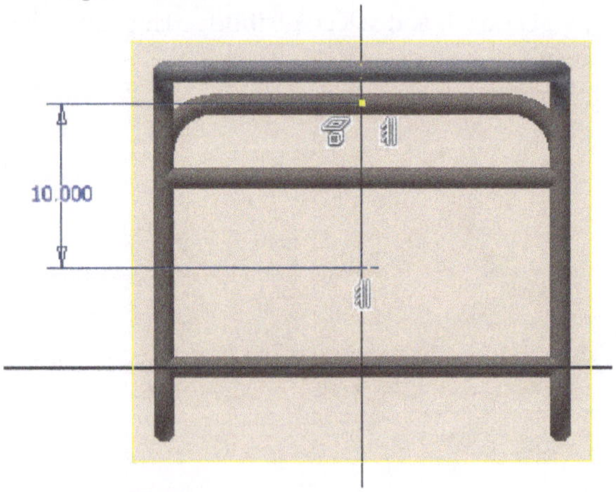

6. Click **Finish**.
7. On the ribbon, click **3D Model > Create Freeform > Box**  .
8. Select the plane tangent to the extruded feature.
9. Select the sketch point to define the location of the freeform box.
10. Click and drag the side-arrow of the freeform box.

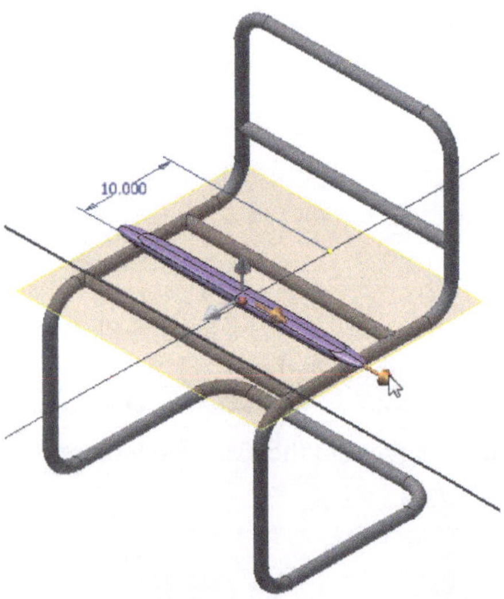

11. Click and drag the front arrow of the freeform box.

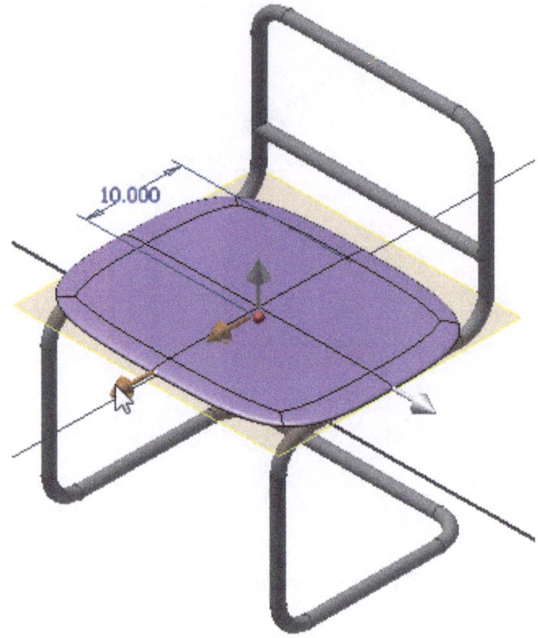

12. Click and drag the top arrow to increase the height of the freeform box.

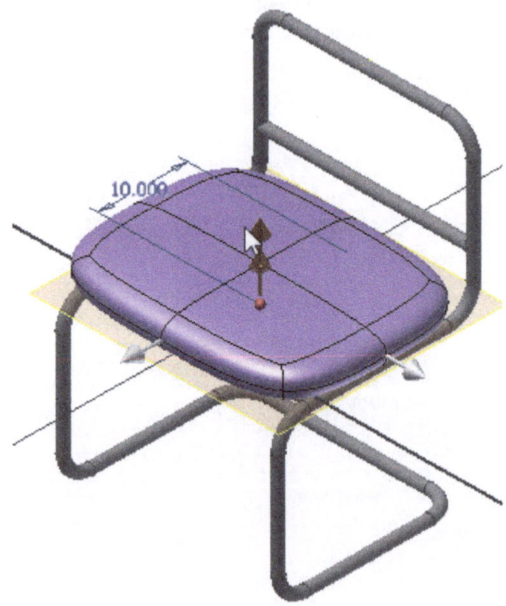

13. On the **Box** dialog, type in 4, 1, and 2 in the **Faces** boxes, respectively.

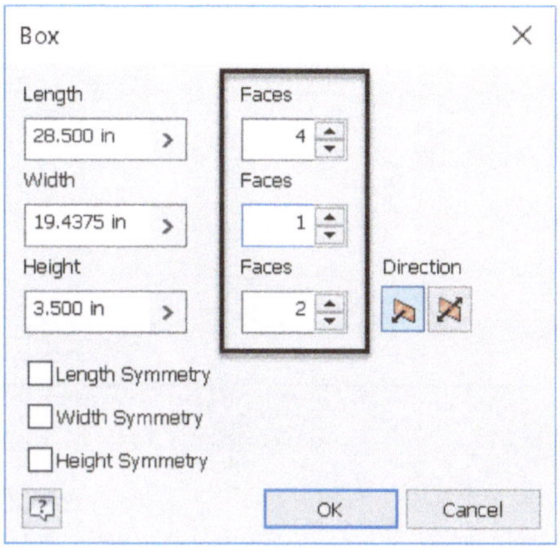

14. Click **OK** to create the freeform shape.

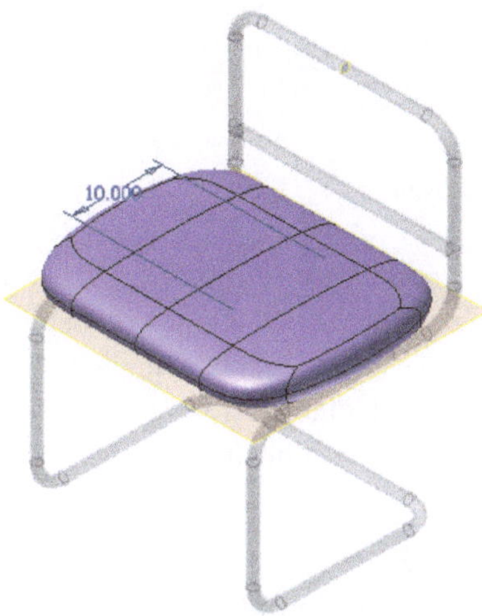

Editing the Freeform Shape

1. On the ribbon, click **Freeform > Edit > Edit Form**

.

2. Hold the Ctrl key and click on top faces of the freeform shape.

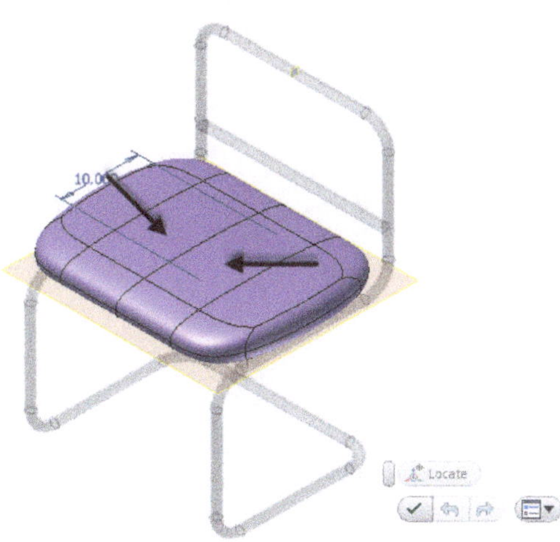

3. Click on the arrow pointing upwards.

4. Drag it downwards 1.6875 in as shown in the figure below.

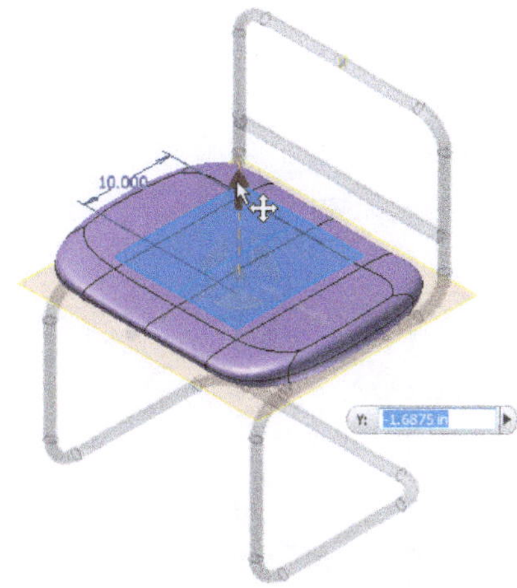

5. Click **OK** on the dialog.
6. On the ribbon, click **Freeform > Edit > Edit Form**

.

7. Hold the Ctrl key and click on the two edges at the front.

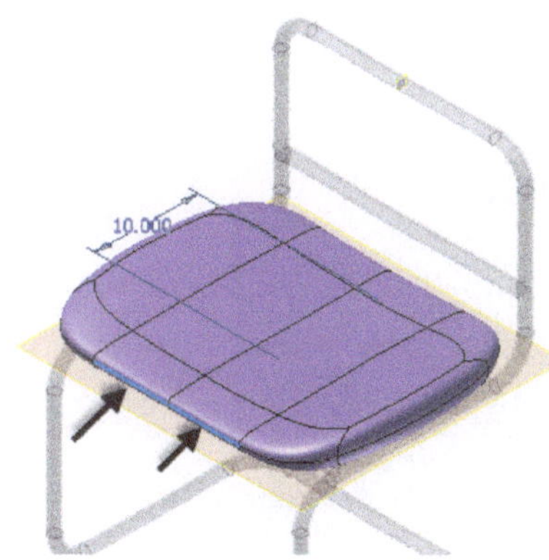

8. Drag the vertical arrow downwards.

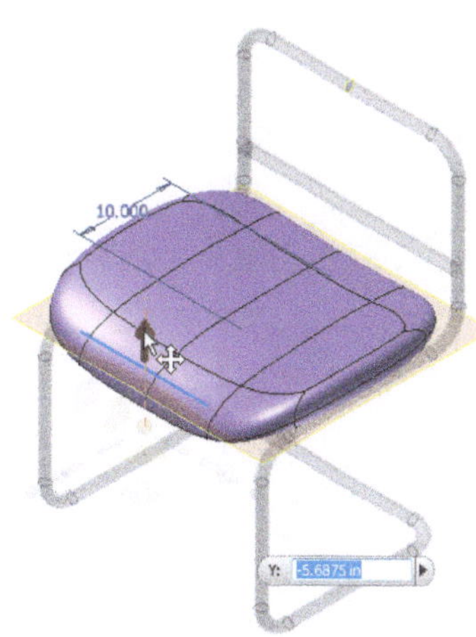

9. Click **OK** on the **Edit Form** dialog.

10. Click **Finish Freeform** on the ribbon.

Create another Freeform box

1. On the ribbon, click **3D Model > Work Features > Plane** 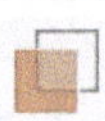 .
2. On the Browser window, click the XY Plane.
3. Click on the vertical portion of the sweep feature to create a plane tangent to it.

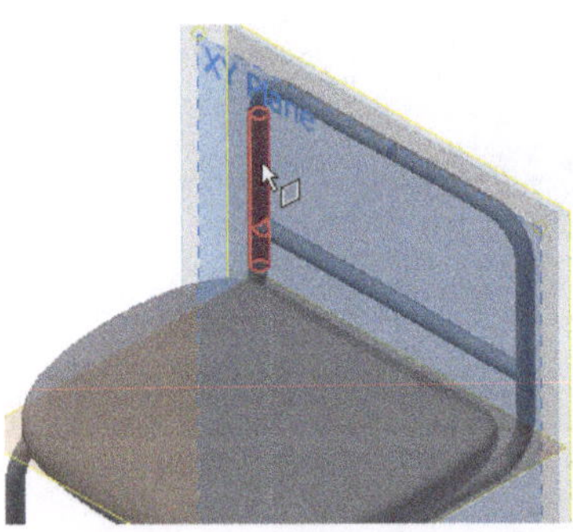

4. Start a sketch on the new plane.
5. Place a point and add dimensions to it.

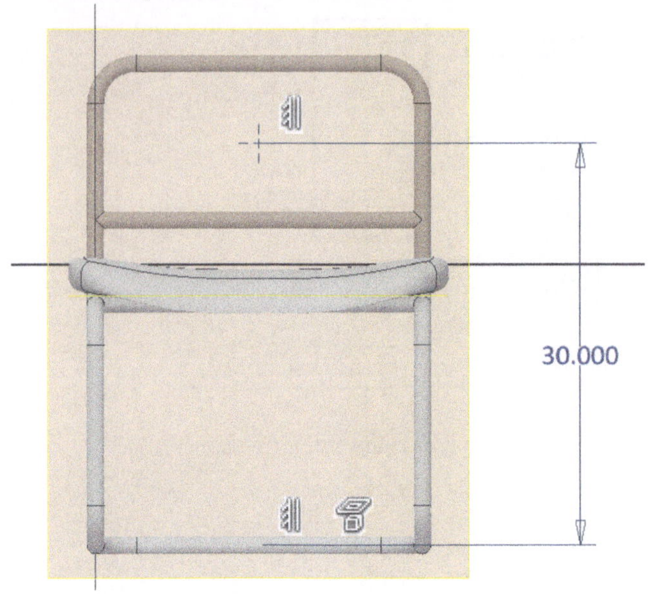

6. Click **Finish Sketch**.
7. Activate the Freeform **Box**  tool.
8. Select the new plane and click on the sketch point.
9. On the **Box** dialog, type in 27, 16, and 3 in the **Length**, **Width**, and **Height** boxes, respectively.
10. Click **OK**, and then click **Finish Freeform**.

11. Save and close the file.

TUTORIAL 6

In this tutorial, you create a bolt.

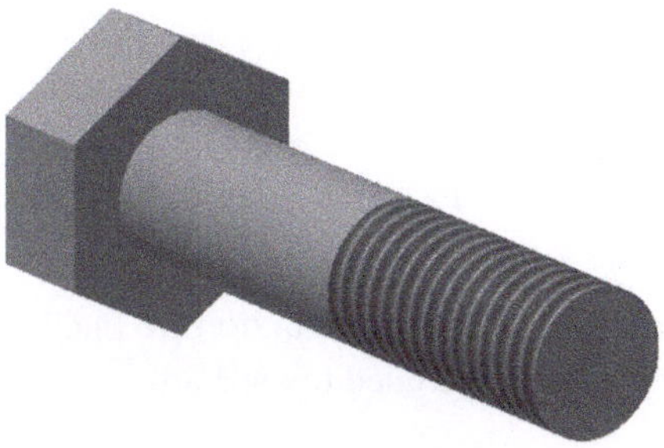

Start a new part file

1. Start a new part file using the **Standard.ipt** template (See Chapter 2, Tutorial 3, Starting a New Part File section).
2. On the ribbon, click **3D Model > Primitives > Primitive drop-down > Cylinder** .
3. Click on the YZ Plane.
4. Click the origin point of the sketch to define the center point of the circle.
5. Move the pointer and type in **0.75** in the box, and then press Enter.

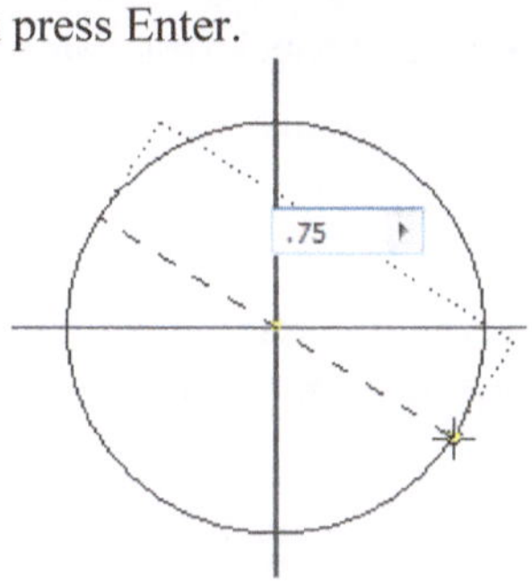

6. Type-in **3** in the **Distance A** box and press Enter.

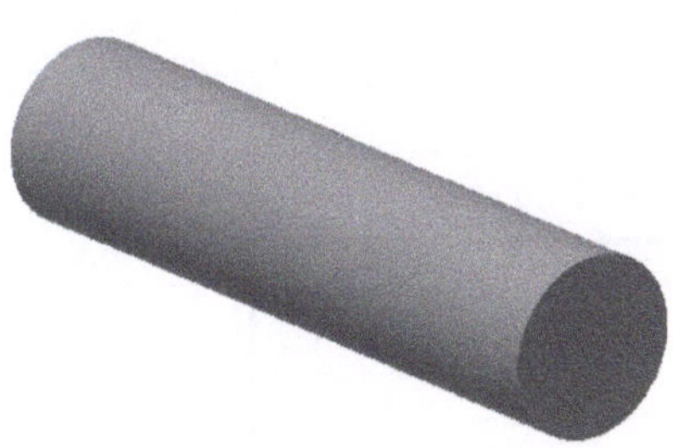

Creating the second feature

1. Start a sketch on the YZ Plane.

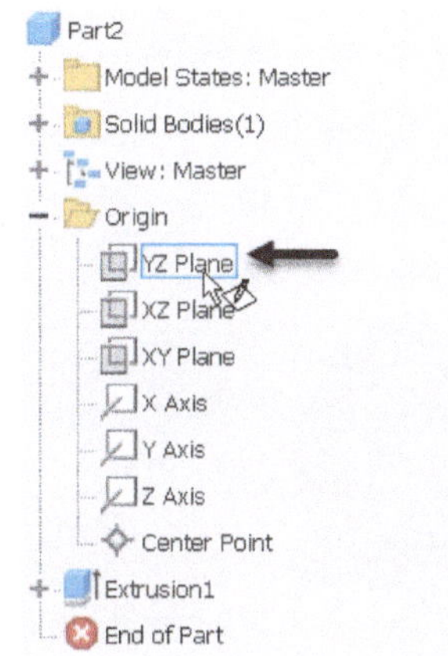

2. On the ribbon, click **Sketch > Create > Rectangle drop-down > Polygon.**

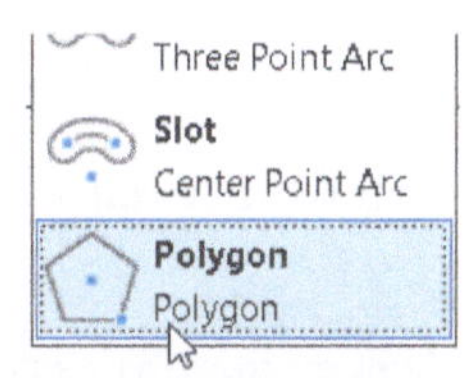

3. Click the sketch origin.

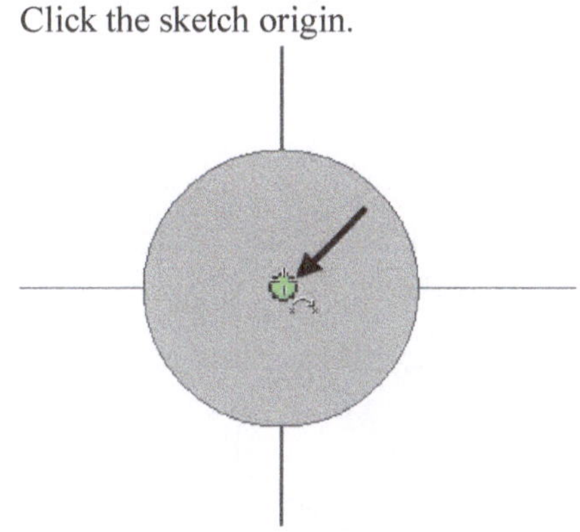

4. Type-in 6 in the **Polygon** dialog.

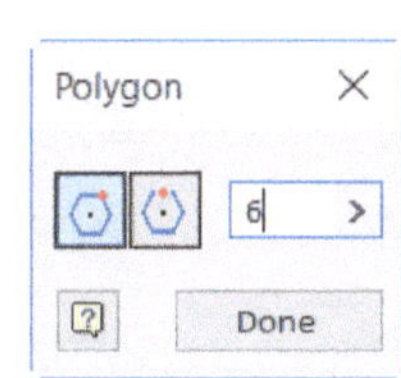

5. Move the pointer vertically upward. You will notice that a dotted trace line appears between the origin point and the pointer.

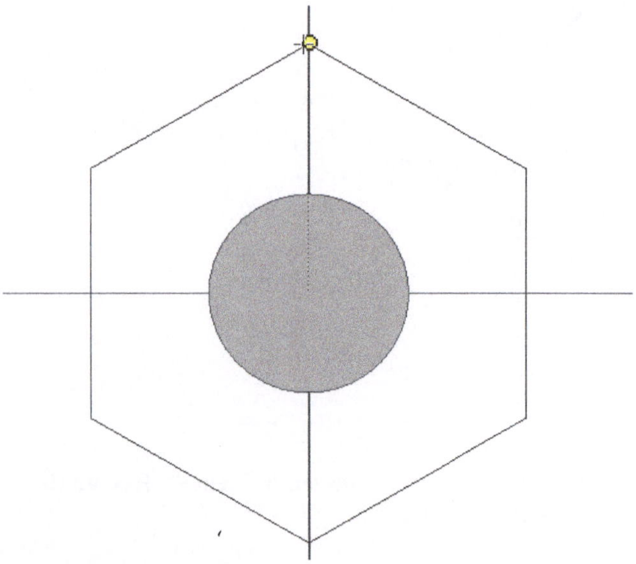

6. Click to create the polygon.
7. Click **Done** on the dialog.
8. On the ribbon, click the **Sketch > Format > Construction**.
9. Activate the **Line** tool and select the vertices of the polygon.

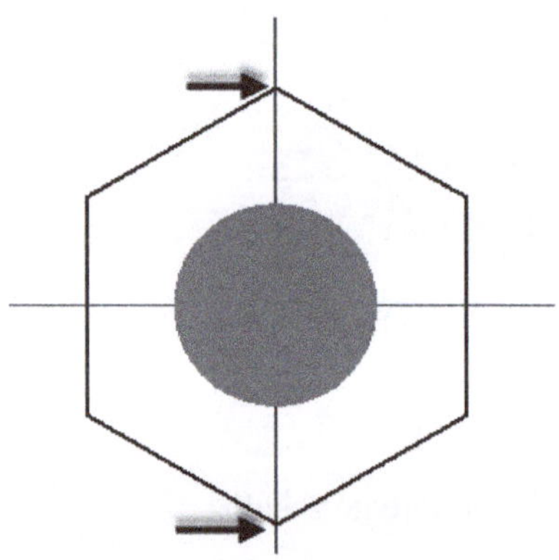

10. Activate the **Dimension** tool and create a dimension, as in the figure.

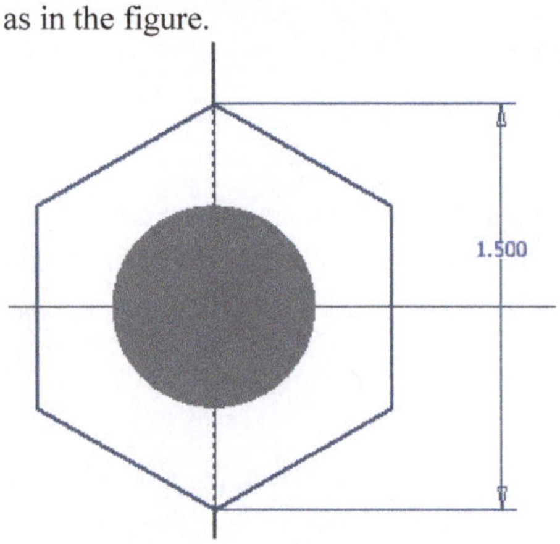

11. Finish the sketch.
12. Activate the **Extrude** tool and select the sketch, if not already selected.
13. On the **Extrude Properties** panel, type-in 0.5 in the **Distance A** box.
14. Use the **Default** or **Flipped** buttons to make sure that the polygon is extruded toward left.
15. Click **OK**.

Adding Threads

1. On the ribbon, click **3D Model > Modify > Thread**.
2. On the **Thread Properties** panel, deactivate the **Full Depth** icon under the **Behavior** section.
3. Type-in **1.5** in the **Depth** field and type in **0** in the **Offset** field.
4. Specify the thread settings under the **Threads** section on the **Thread Properties** panel, as shown in the figure.

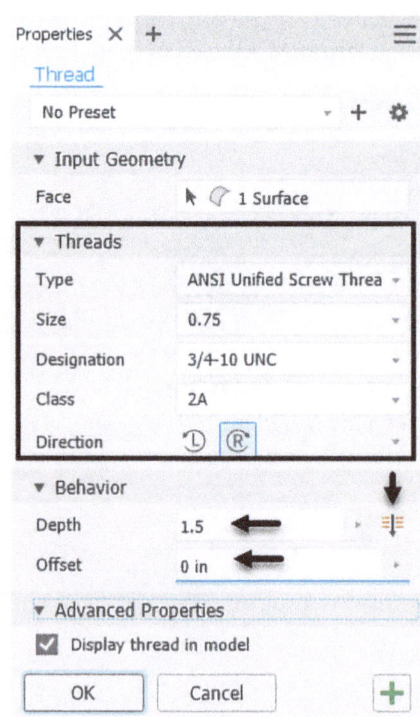

5. Select the circular face of the model by clicking near the end face.
6. Click **OK** to add the thread.

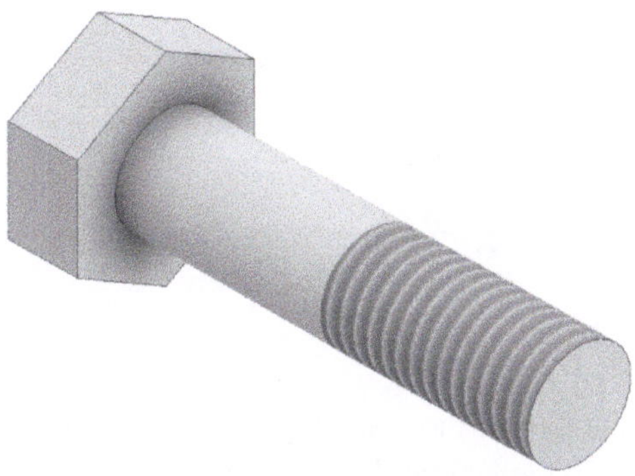

Creating iParts

The iParts feature allows you to design a part with different variations, sizes, materials, and other attributes. Now, you will create different variations of the bolt created in the previous section.

1. On the ribbon, click **Manage > Parameters > Parameters**. This opens the **Parameters** dialog.

2. On the **Parameters** dialog, click in the first cell of the **Model Parameters** table, and type-in **Diameter**.

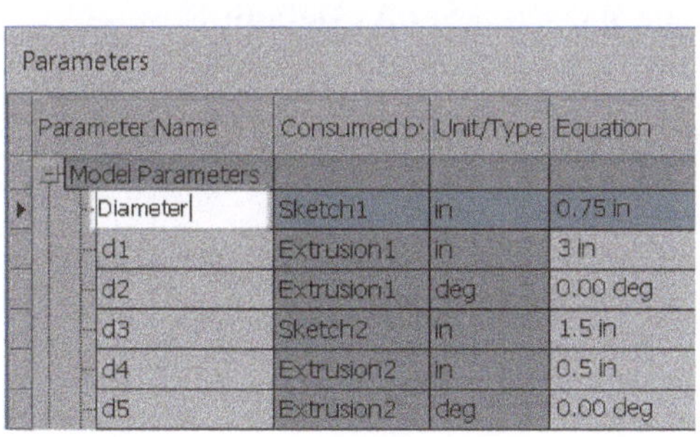

3. Likewise, change the names of other parameters.

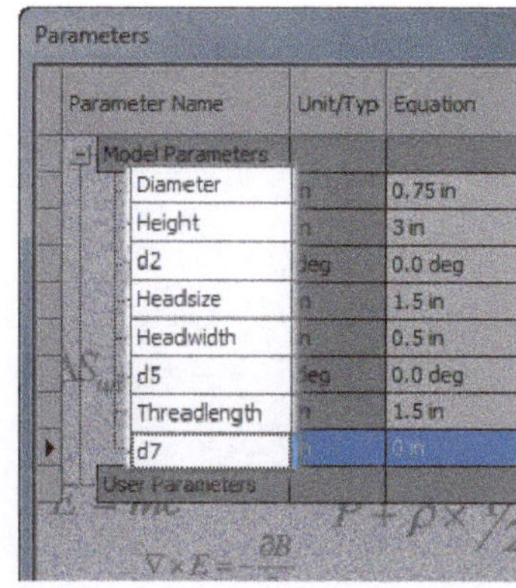

4. Click **Done** on the **Parameters** dialog.
5. Click the right mouse button in the graphics window and select **Dimension Display > Expression**.

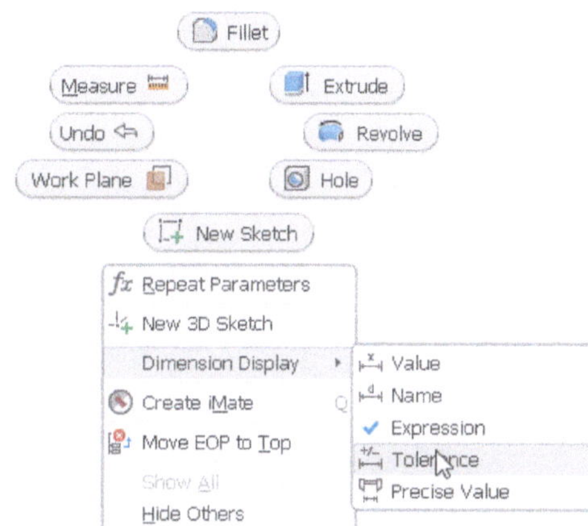

6. On the Browser window, click the right mouse button on the **Extrusion1** and select **Show Dimensions**. You will notice that the dimensions are shown along with the names.

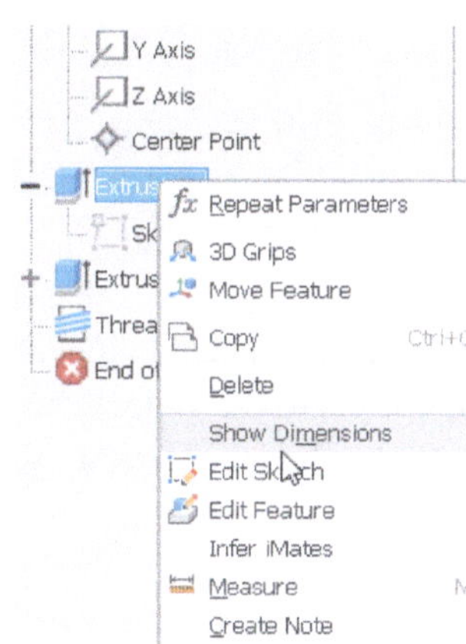

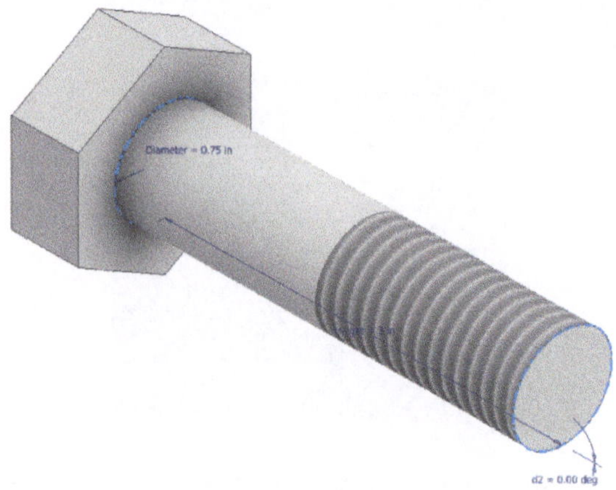

7. On the ribbon, click **Manage > Author > Create iPart**.

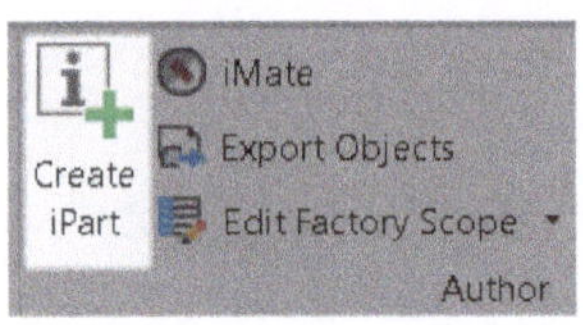

This opens the **iPart Table** dialog. In this dialog, you will define the parameters to create other versions of the model geometry.

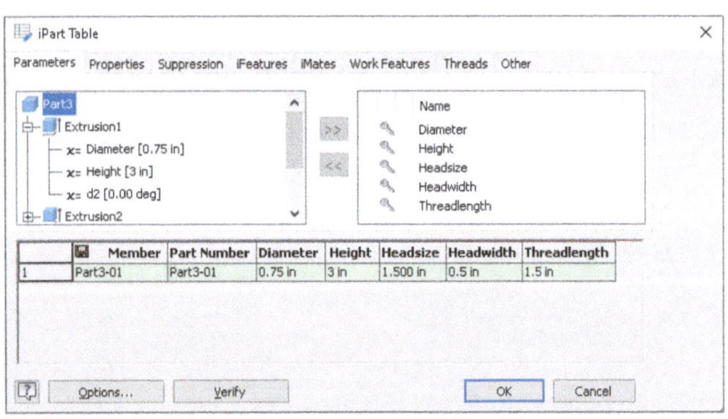

	Member	Part Number	Diameter	Height	Headsize	Headwidth	Threadlength
1	Part3-01	Part3-01	0.75 in	3 in	1.500 in	0.5 in	1.5 in

The table at the bottom of this dialog shows the parameters for the iPart factory. You will notice that the renamed parameters are automatically added to the table. If you want to add more parameters to the table, then select them from the section located on the left side. Click the arrow button pointing towards the right. Likewise, if you want to remove a parameter from the table, then select it from the right-side section and click the arrow pointing toward left.

8. Now, click the right mouse button on the table and select **Insert Row**. Notice that a new row is added to the table.

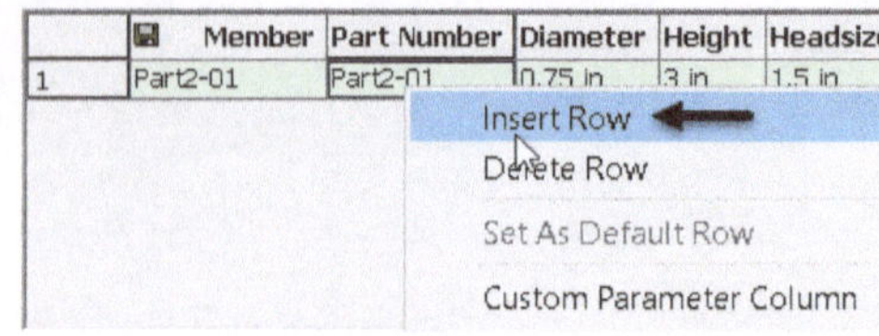

9. Likewise, insert another row.

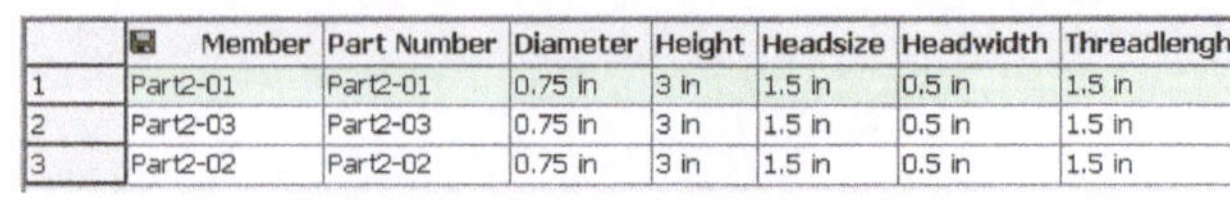

	Member	Part Number	Diameter	Height	Headsize	Headwidth	Threadlenght
1	Part2-01	Part2-01	0.75 in	3 in	1.5 in	0.5 in	1.5 in
2	Part2-03	Part2-03	0.75 in	3 in	1.5 in	0.5 in	1.5 in
3	Part2-02	Part2-02	0.75 in	3 in	1.5 in	0.5 in	1.5 in

10. In the second row of the table, type-in new values (5, 0.75, and 3) in the Height, Headwidth, and Threadlength boxes. This creates the second version of the bolt.

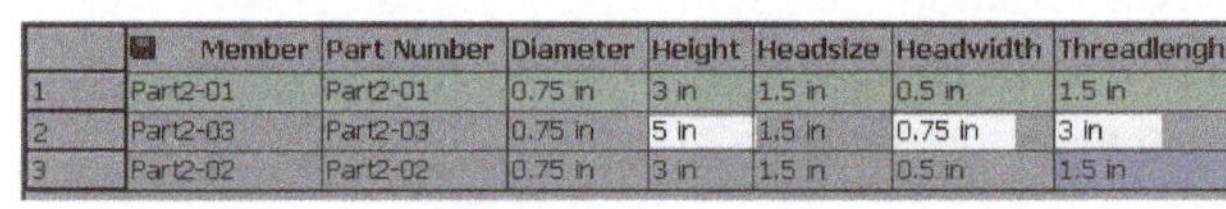

	Member	Part Number	Diameter	Height	Headsize	Headwidth	Threadlenght
1	Part2-01	Part2-01	0.75 in	3 in	1.5 in	0.5 in	1.5 in
2	Part2-03	Part2-03	0.75 in	5 in	1.5 in	0.75 in	3 in
3	Part2-02	Part2-02	0.75 in	3 in	1.5 in	0.5 in	1.5 in

11. In the third row of the table, type-in new values in (2, 0.75, and 3) the Headsize, Headwidth, and Threadlength boxes. This creates the third version of the bolt.

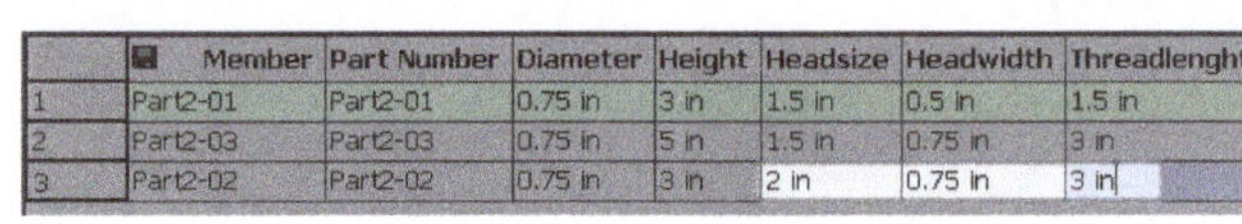

	Member	Part Number	Diameter	Height	Headsize	Headwidth	Threadlenght
1	Part2-01	Part2-01	0.75 in	3 in	1.5 in	0.5 in	1.5 in
2	Part2-03	Part2-03	0.75 in	5 in	1.5 in	0.75 in	3 in
3	Part2-02	Part2-02	0.75 in	3 in	2 in	0.75 in	3 in

Now, you have to set the default version of the bolt.

12. Click the right mouse button on the third row of the table and select **Set As Default Row**.

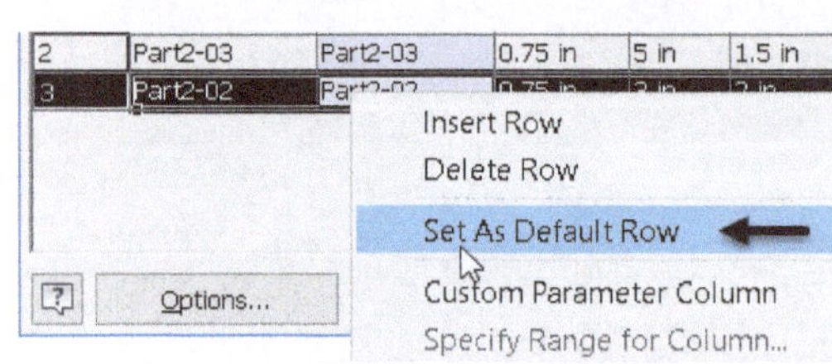

13. Click **OK** to close the dialog. Notice that the default version of the bolt changes.

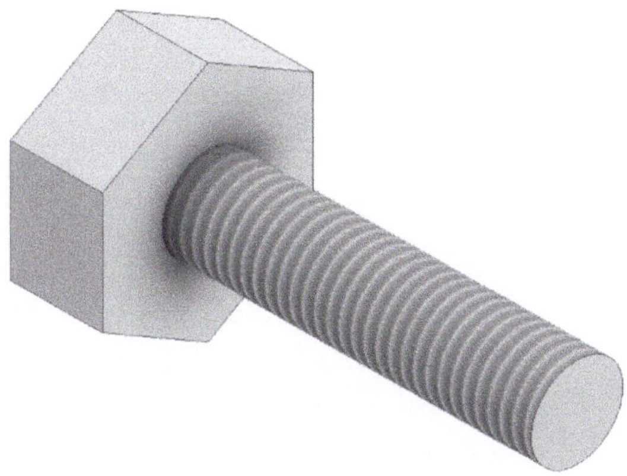

In the Bowser Bar, you will notice that the **Table** item is added.

14. Expand the **Table** item in the Browser Window to view the different variations of the iPart. Notice that a checkmark designates the activated version of the iPart.

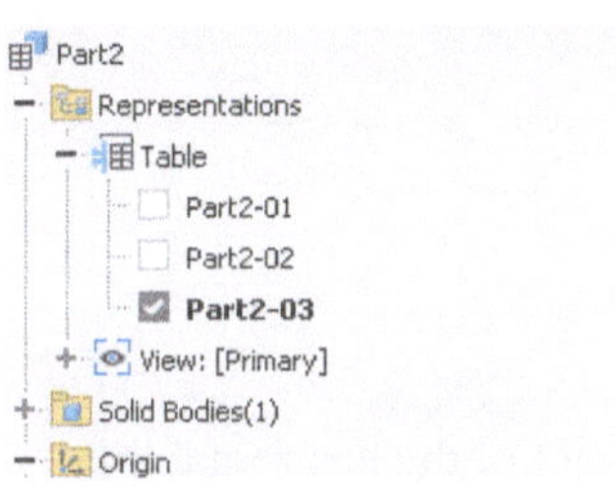

15. Double-click on any other version of the iPart to activate it.

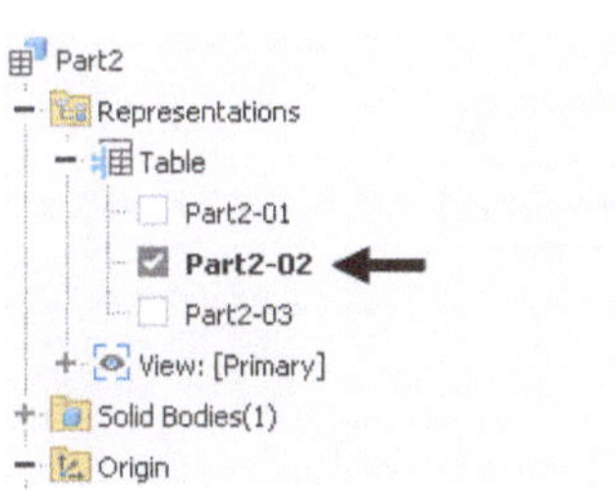

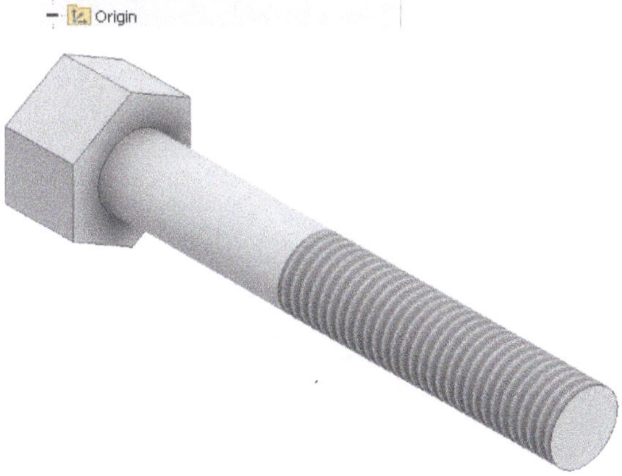

If you want to make changes to any version of the bolt, then click the right mouse button on it and select **Edit table**.

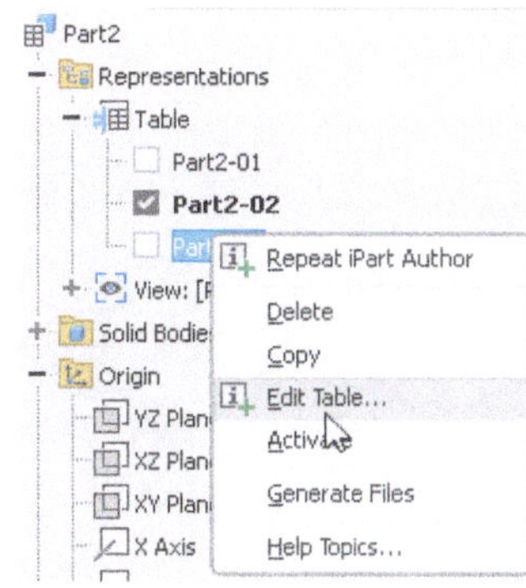

If you want to edit the table using a spreadsheet, then click the right mouse button on **Table** and select **Edit via Spreadsheet**. Click **OK** on the message box.

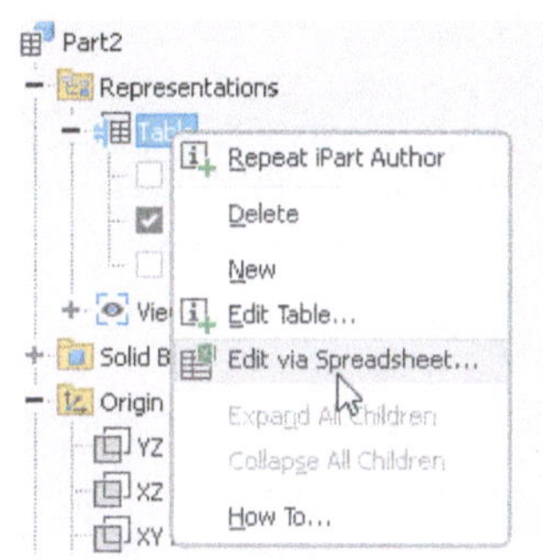

Now, modify the values in the spreadsheet and close it. A message pops up asking you to save the changes. Click **Save** to save the changes.

	A	B	C	D	E	F	G	H
1	Member<	Part Num!	Diameter	Height	Headsize	Headwidt	Threadler	Thread1
2	Part2-01	Part2-01	0.75 in	3 in	1.5 in	0.5 in	1.5 in	Compute
3	Part2-03	Part2-03	0.75 in	5	1.5 in	0.75 in	3	Compute
4	Part2-02	Part2-02	0.75 in	3 in	2	0.75 in	3	Compute

If you want to save anyone of the iPart versions as a separate part file, then click the right mouse button on it and select **Generate Files**.

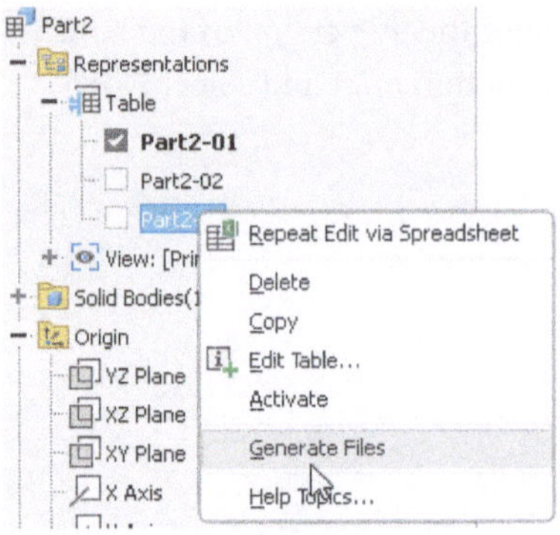

16. Save and close the file.

TUTORIAL 7

In this tutorial, you create a plastic casing.

Creating the First Feature

1. Open a new Autodesk Inventor part file using the **Standard.ipt** template (See Chapter 2, Tutorial 3, Starting a New Part File section).
2. On the ribbon, click **3D Model > Sketch > Start 2D Sketch**.
3. Select the XZ Plane.
4. On the ribbon, click **Sketch > Create > Line**.
5. Click on the second quadrant, move the cursor horizontally toward the right, and then click to create a horizontal line, as shown.

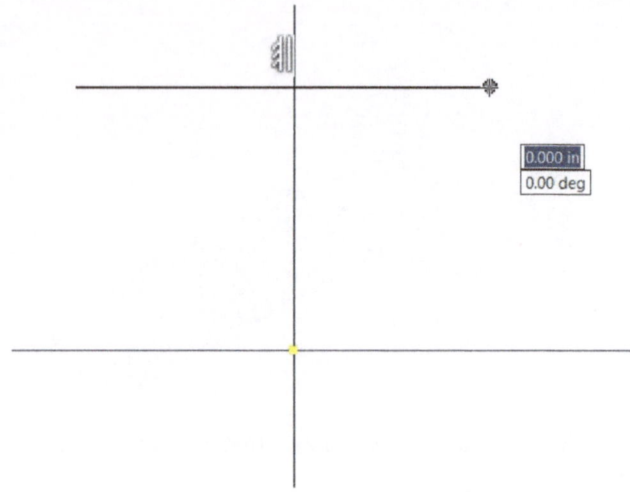

6. On the ribbon, click **Sketch > Create > Arc drop-down > Arc Three Point**.

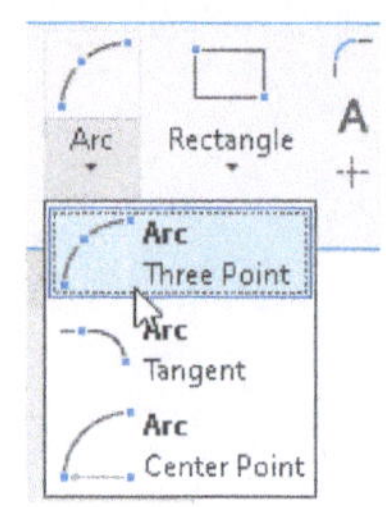

7. Select the right endpoint of the horizontal line.
8. Move the cursor vertically downwards and click to define the second point.
9. Move the pointer towards the right and click on the horizontal axis line.

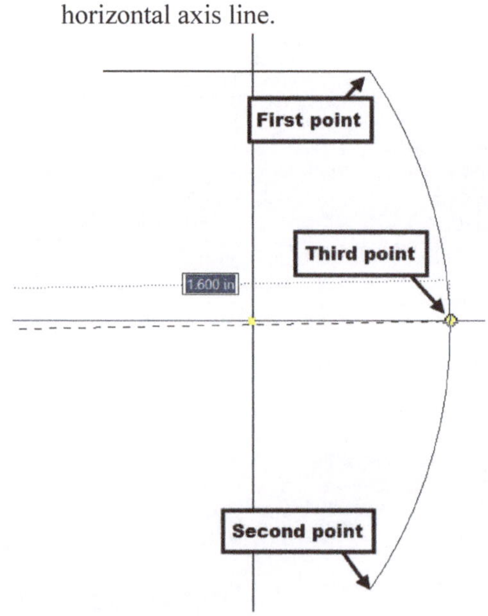

10. Likewise, create another three-point arc and

horizontal line, as shown.

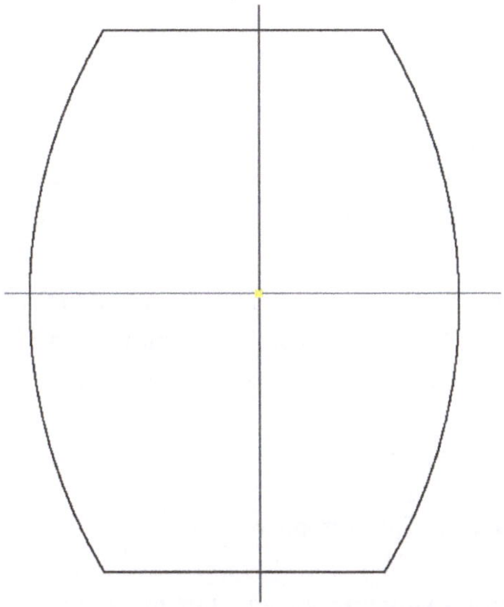

11. Create a vertical construction from the origin point.

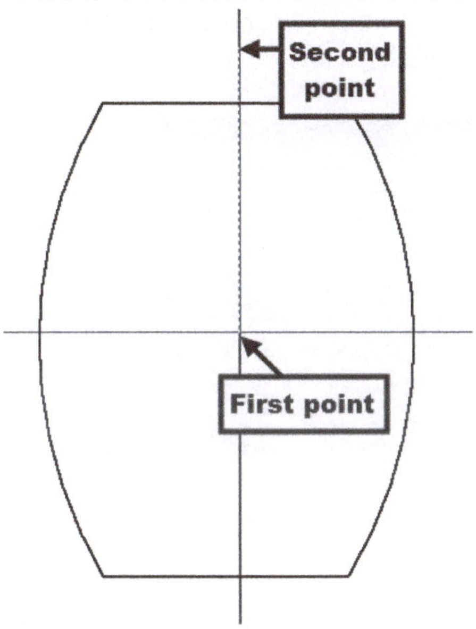

12. On the ribbon, click **Sketch > Constrain > Symmetric** .
13. Select the two arcs and the construction line.

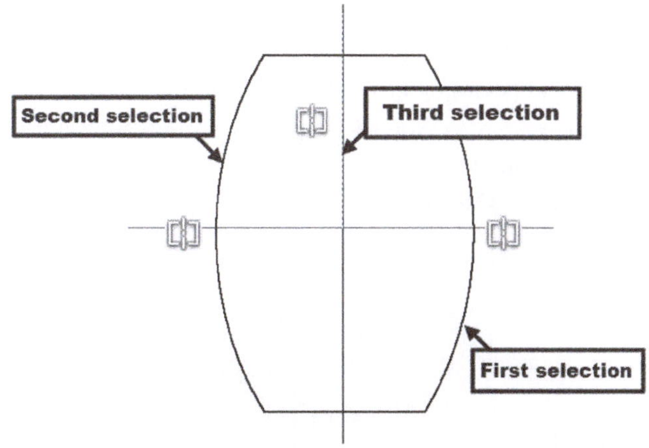

14. Likewise, create a horizontal construction line from the origin point, and then make the two horizontal lines symmetric about it.

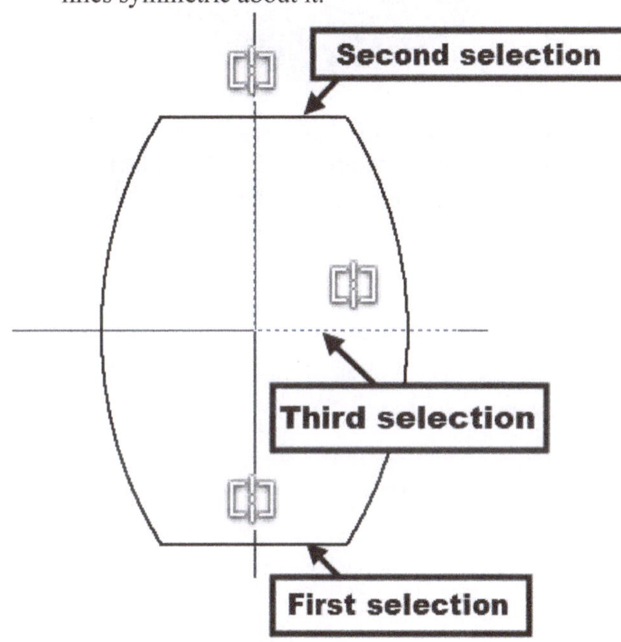

15. Add dimensions to the sketch. Also, add the **Vertical** constraint between the origin and the center point of the arc.

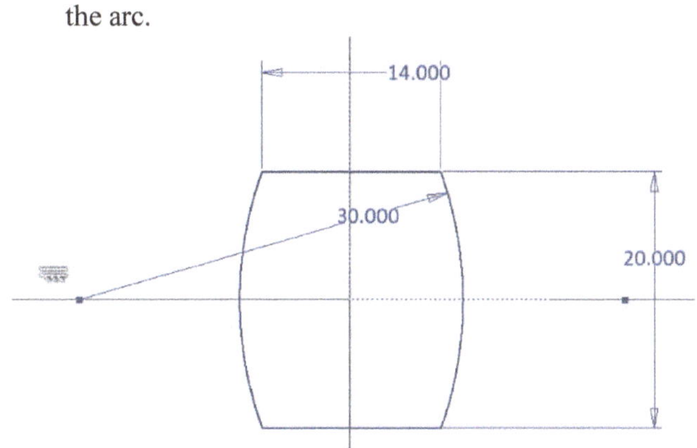

16. Click **Finish Sketch**.

17. Click the **3D Model > Create > Extrude** on the ribbon; the **Extrude Properties** panel dialog appears.
18. Set the **Distance A** to 3.15.
19. Expand the **Advanced Properties** section and set the Taper angle to -10.
20. Click the **OK** button.

Creating the Extruded surface

1. Click **3D Model > Sketch > Start 2D Sketch** on the ribbon, and then select the XY Plane.

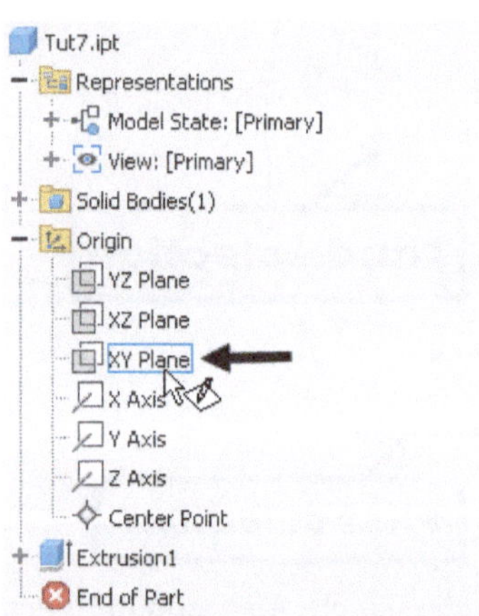

2. Click the **Slice Graphics** button at the bottom of the window or press **F7** on the keyboard.
3. Click **Sketch > Create > Line > Spline Interpolation** on the ribbon.
4. Create a spline, as shown in figure (See Chapter 5, Tutorial 4, Creating the First Section and Rails section).

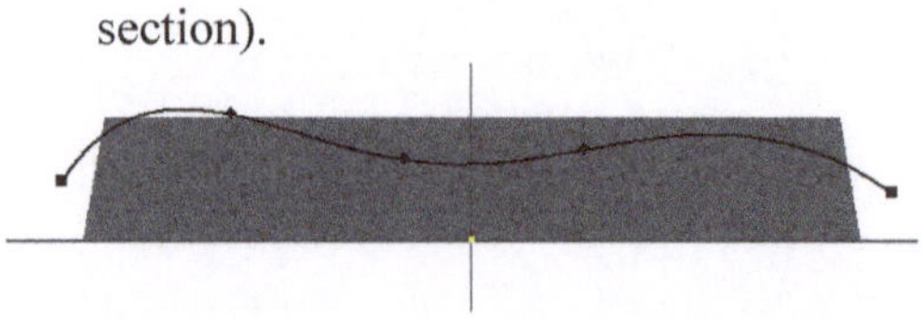

5. Apply dimensions to the spline, as shown below.

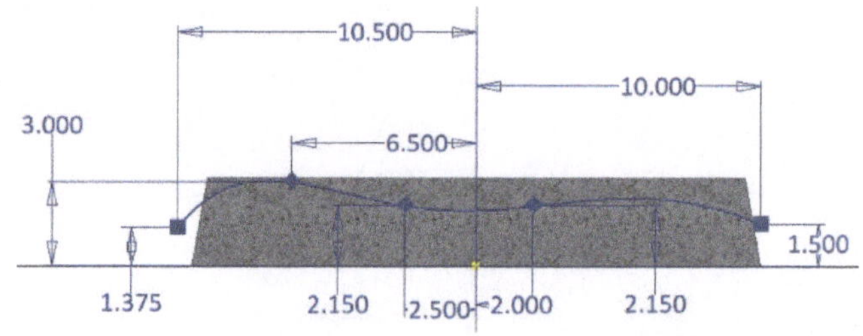

Adding a dimension between two points of a spline locks the distance between the two points. Also, removing the dimension will revert the spline to its original shape.

6. Click **Finish Sketch**.
7. Click the **Extrude** button.
8. On the **Extrude Properties** panel, click the toggle button on the top right corner of the **Extrude** Properties panel.

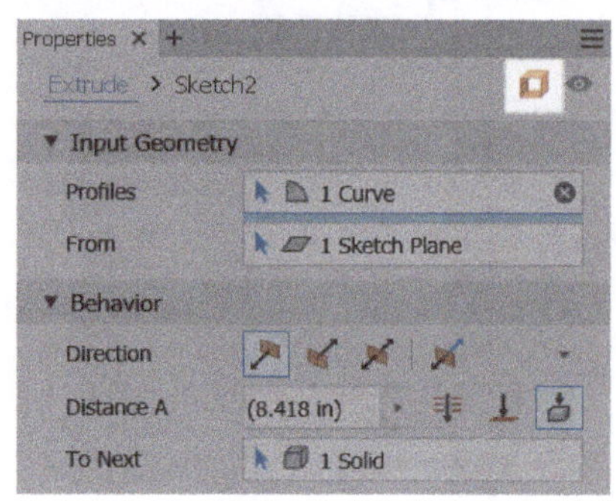

26. Select the sketch, if not already selected
27. Select the **Symmetric** button under the **Behavior** section.
28. Extrude the sketch up to 17 in **Distance A**. Next, click **OK**.

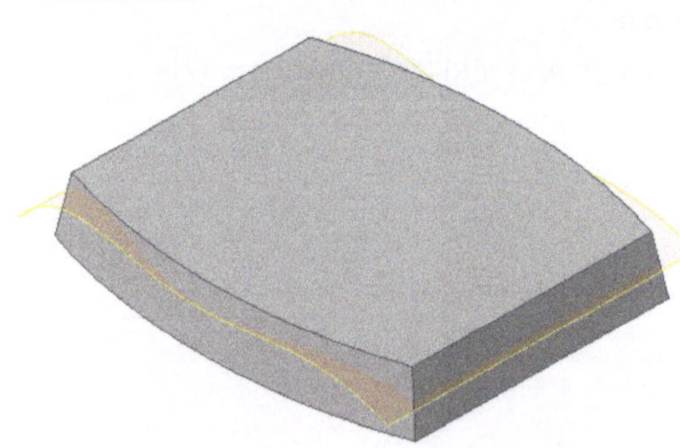

Replacing the top face of the model with the surface

1. On the **Surface** panel of the **3D Model** ribbon, click

the **Replace Face** button; the **Replace Face** dialog appears.

Now, you need to select the face to be replaced.

2. Select the top face of the model.

Next, you need to select the replacement face or surface.

3. Click the **New Faces** button on the dialog and select the extruded surface.

You can also use a solid face to replace an existing face.

4. Click **OK** to replace the top face with a surface.

5. Hide the extruded surface by clicking the right mouse button on it in the Browser Window and un-checking **Visibility**.

Creating a Face fillet

1. Click the **Fillet** drop-down > **Face Fillet** on the **Modify** panel.

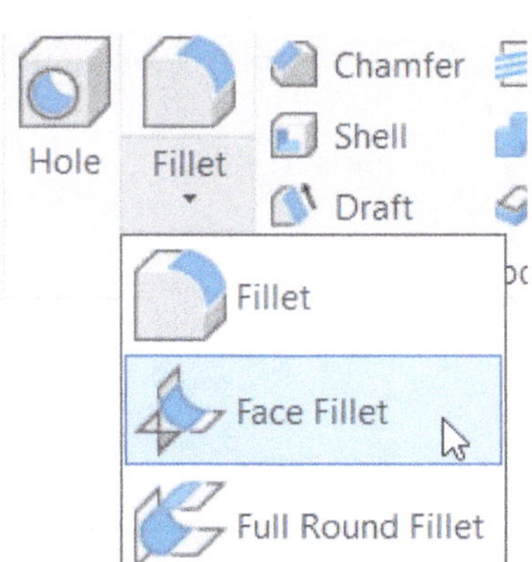

2. Select the top surface as the first face and the inclined front face as the second face.

3. Set the **Radius** to 1.5 and click the **OK** button to create the face fillet.

4. Likewise, apply a face fillet of 1.5 radius between the top surface and the inclined back face of the model.

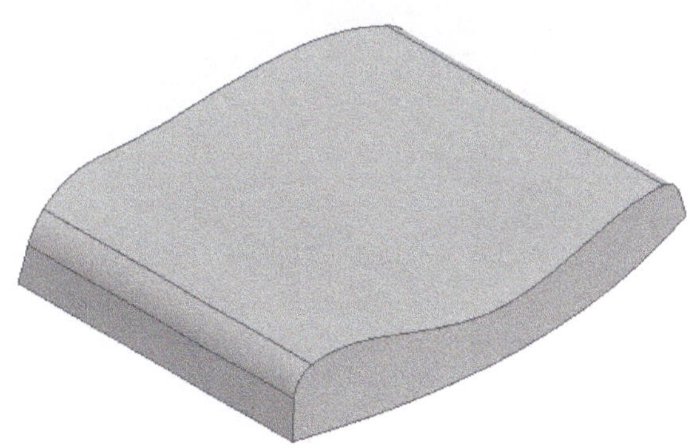

Creating a Variable Radius fillet

1. Click the **Fillet** button on the **Modify** panel.

2. Click the **Add variable radius fillet** icon on the **Fillet Properties panel**.

3. Select the curved edge on the model; the preview of the fillet appears.

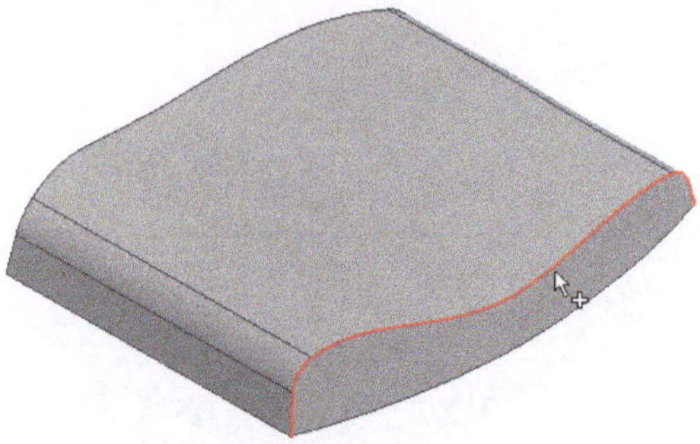

4. Select a point on the fillet, as shown in the figure.

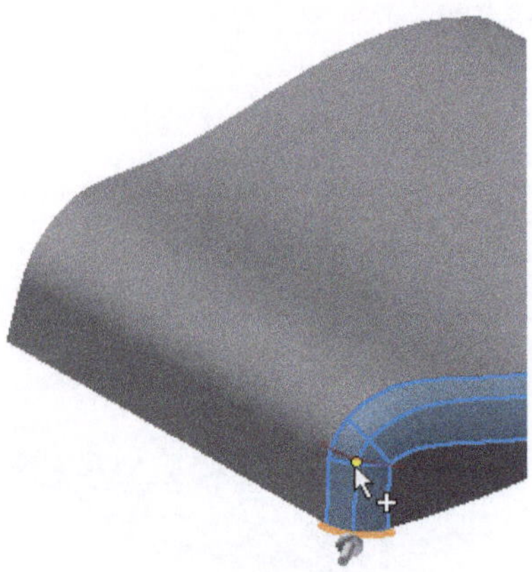

5. Select another point of the fillet, as shown in the figure.

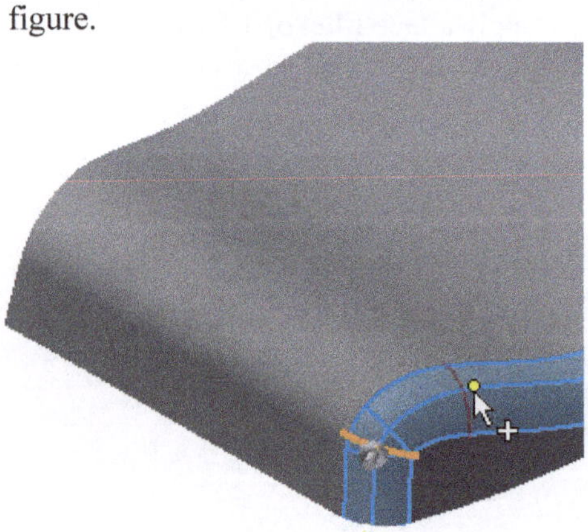

6. Set the radii of the **Start**, **End**, **Point 1,** and **Point 2**, as shown below.

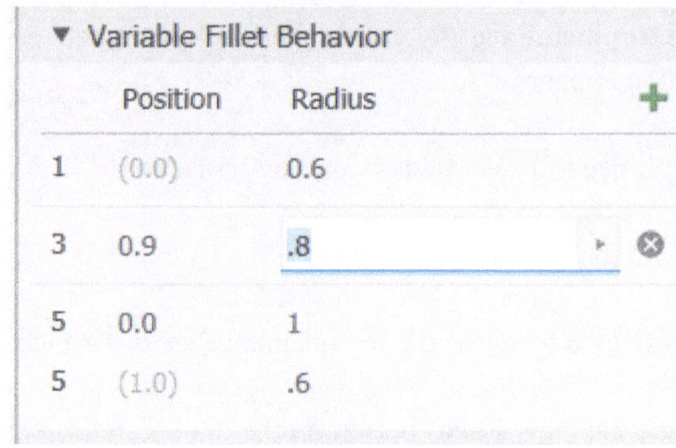

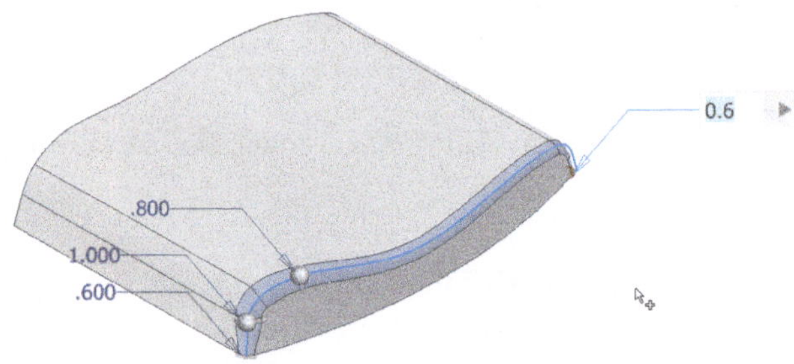

You can also specify the fillet continuity type. By default, the **Tangent** type is specified.

6. Select **Smooth (G2)** type from the drop-down, as shown.

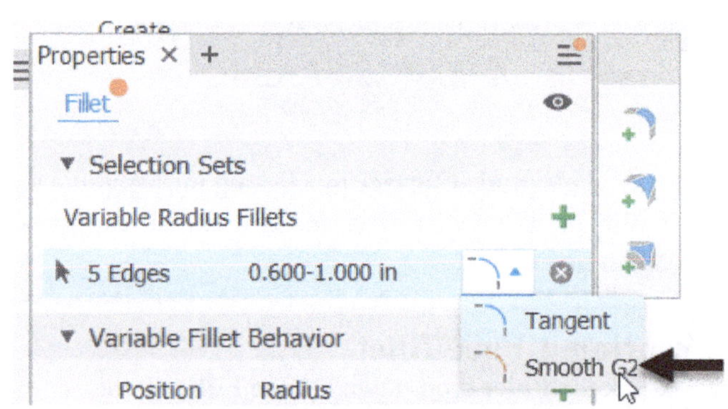

7. Expand the **Advanced Properties** section.
8. Make sure that the **Smooth Radius Transition** option is checked.
9. Click **OK** to create the variable fillet.

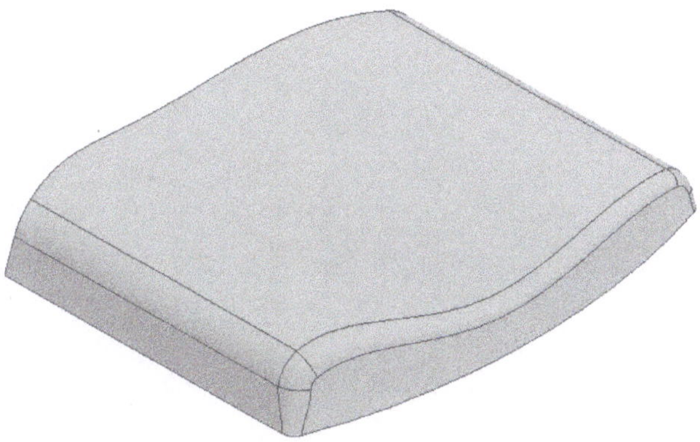

Mirroring the fillet

10. Click the **Mirror** button on the **Pattern** panel; the **Mirror** dialog appears.
11. Select the variable radius fillet from the model.
12. Click the **XY Plane** icon on the **Mirror** dialog.
13. Click **OK** to mirror the fillet.

Shelling the Model

1. Click the **Shell** button on the **Modify** panel; the **Shell Properties panel** appears.
2. Click the **Inside** button on the dialog under the **Behavior** section and set the **Thickness** to 0.2 in.
3. Click the **Remove** faces selection box, if not already selected.
4. Rotate the model and select the bottom face.

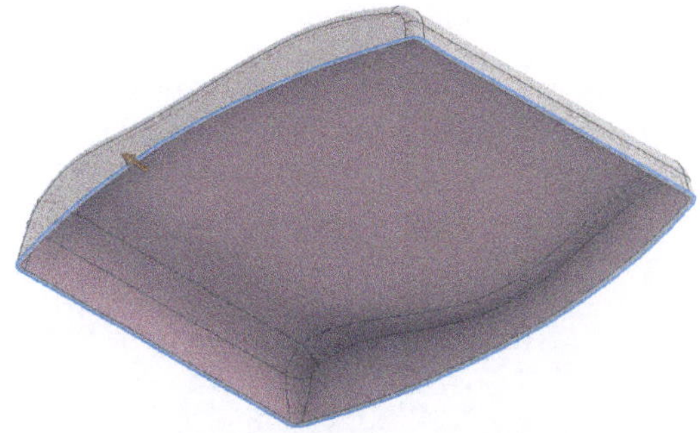

5. Click **OK**.

Creating the Boss Features

1. Click **3D Model > Sketch > Start 2D Sketch** on the ribbon and select the bottom face of the model.

2. Activate the **Construction** button on the **Format** panel.
3. On the ribbon, click **Sketch > Create > Rectangle drop-down > Rectangle Two Point Center**.

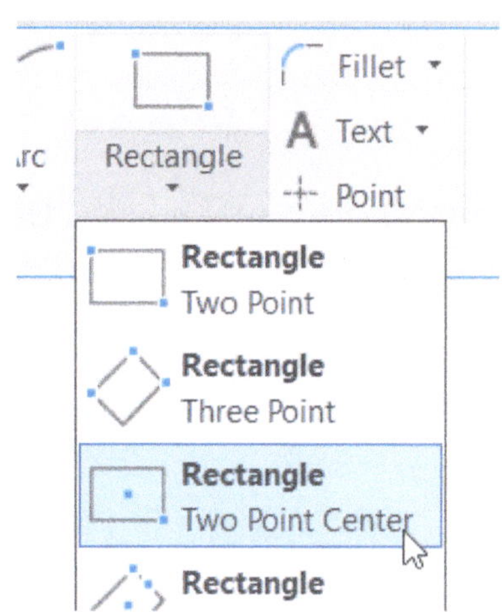

4. Select the origin point of the sketch.
5. Move the cursor outward and click to create the rectangle.

6. Apply dimensions to the rectangle.
7. Click the **Point** button on the **Create** panel.
8. Place four points at the corners of the rectangle.

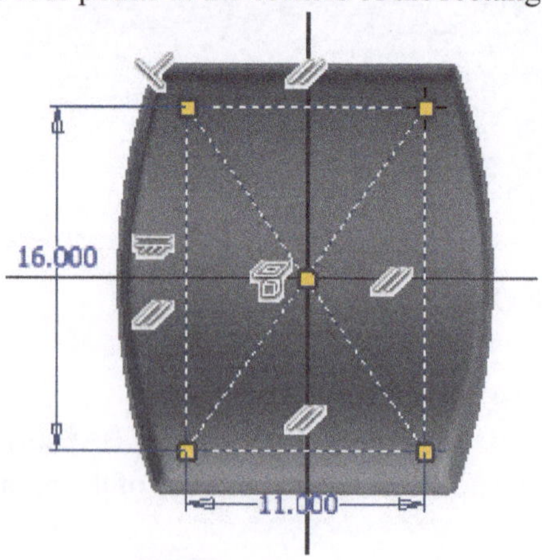

9. Click **Finish** on the ribbon.

Now, you will create bosses by selecting the points created in the sketch.

10. On the ribbon, click the **Show Panels** button located at the right side, and then select **Plastic Part** from the menu.
11. Click the **Boss** button on the **Plastic Part** panel; the **Boss** dialog appears.
12. Click the **Thread** button on the dialog.

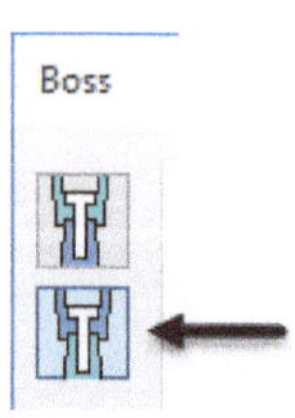

13. Select the **From Sketch** option from the **Placement** group.
14. Select the points located on the corners of the rectangle, if not already selected; the bosses are placed at the selected points.

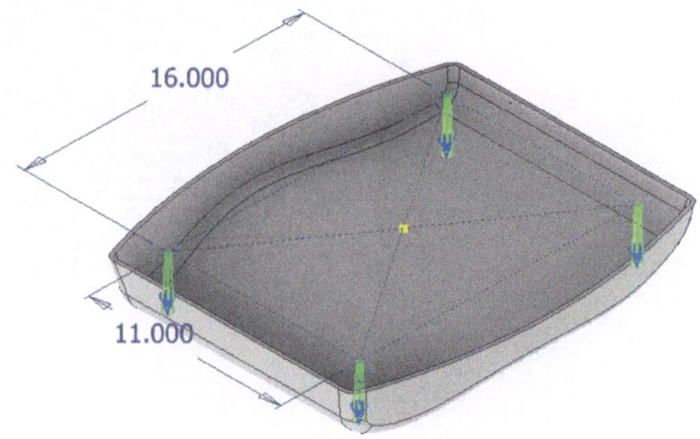

15. Click the **Thread** tab and specify the parameters, as shown below.

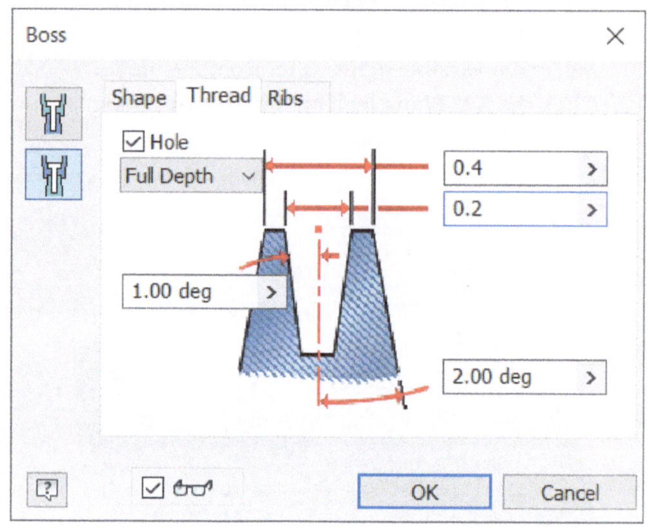

16. Click the **Ribs** tab and check the **Stiffening Ribs** option.
17. Set the rib parameters, as shown next.

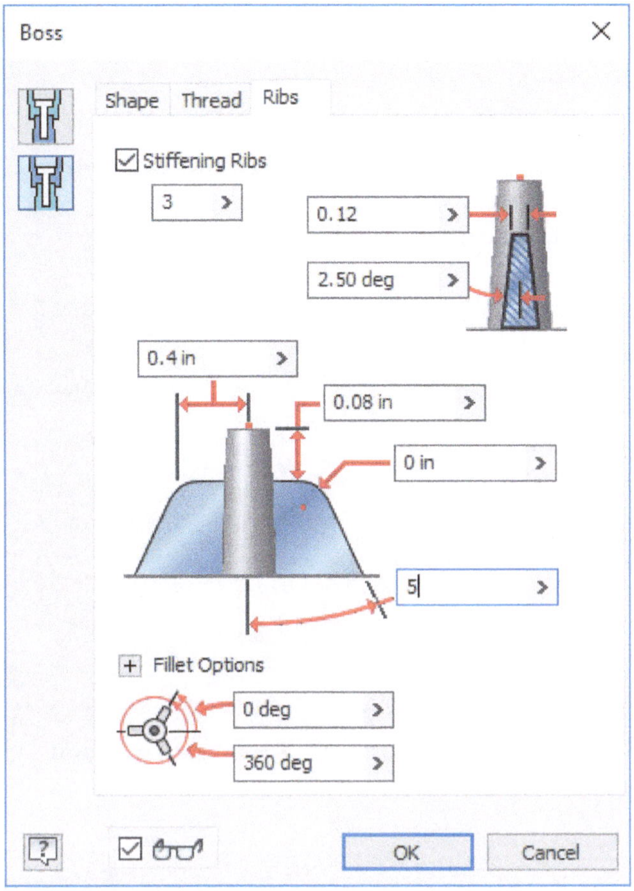

18. Expand the **Fillet options**.

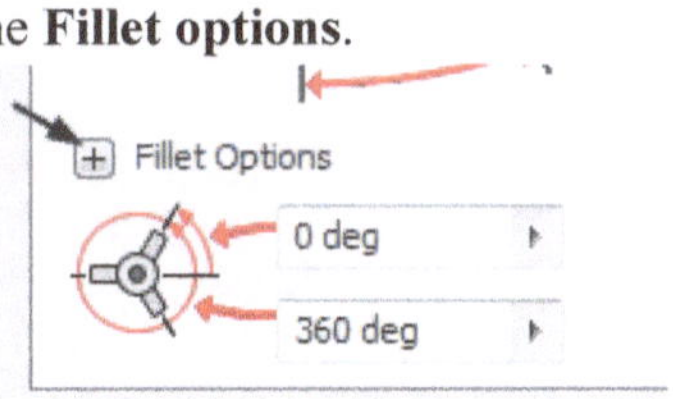

19. Specify the fillet options, as shown below.

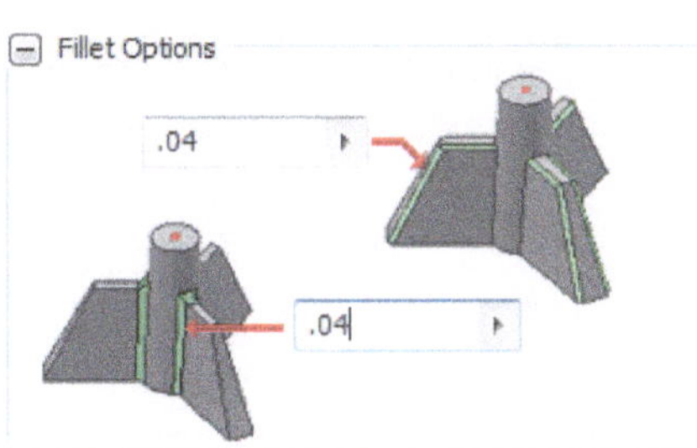

20. Click **OK** to create the bosses with ribs.

Creating the Lip feature

1. Click the **Lip** button on the **Plastic Part** panel of the ribbon; the **Lip** dialog appears.
2. Click the **Lip** button on the dialog.

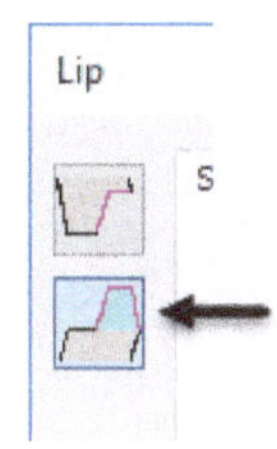

3. Select the outer edge of the bottom face.

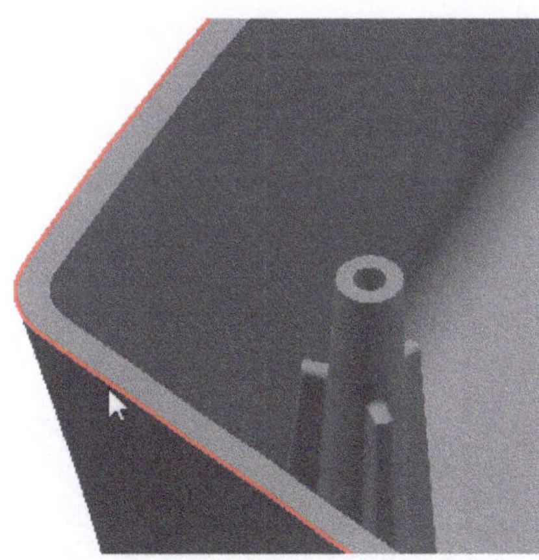

4. Click the **Guide Face** button on the dialog and select the bottom face of the model.

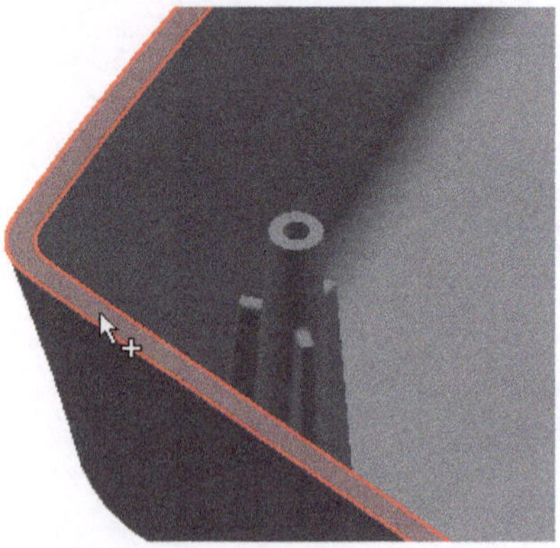

5. Click the **Lip** tab and set the parameters, as shown below.

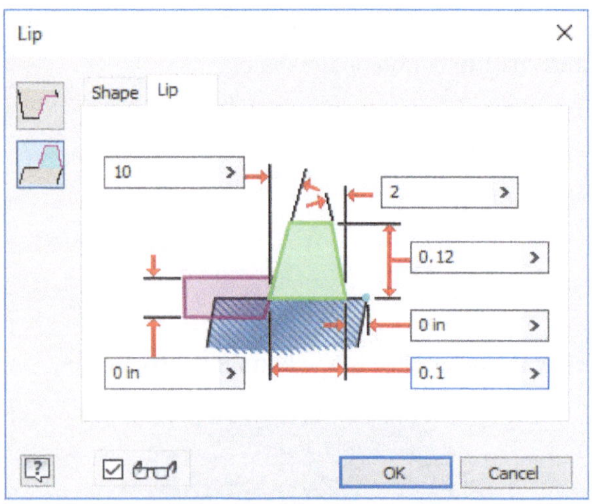

6. Click **OK** to create the lip.

Creating the Grill Feature

1. Click the **Home** button located at the top of the ViewCube.
2. Click the corner point of the ViewCube, as shown.

3. On the ribbon, click **3D Model > Sketch >> Start 2D Sketch**.
4. Select the inclined face, as shown.

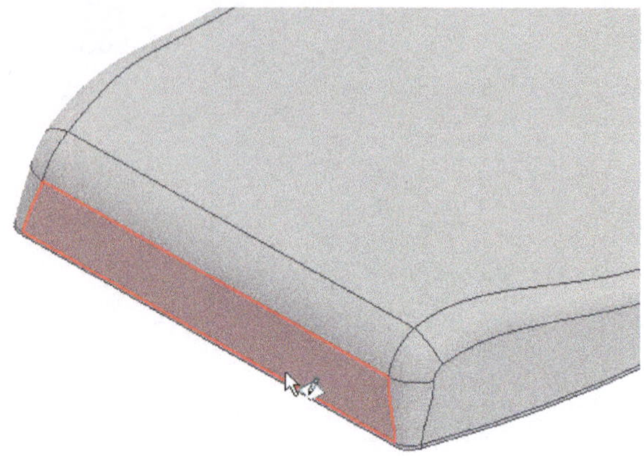

5. Create the sketch using the **Rectangle Two Point Center** and **Line** tools.

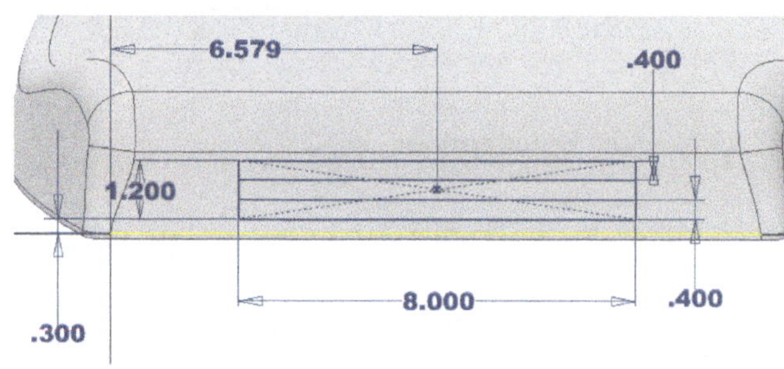

6. Click **Finish** on the ribbon.
7. Click the **Grill** button on the **Plastic Part** panel.
8. Select the rectangle as the boundary and set the **Boundary** parameters, as shown below.

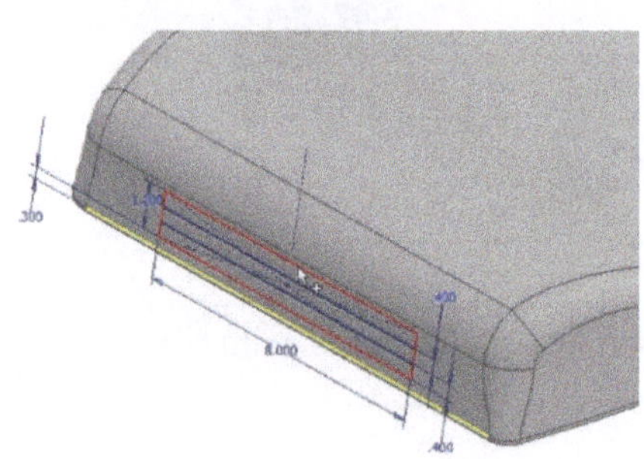

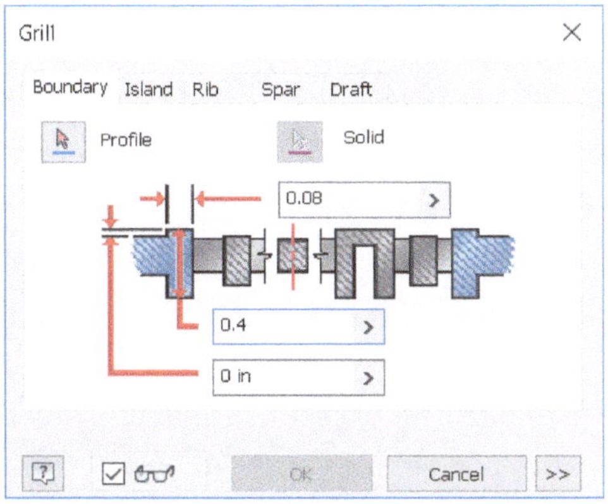

9. Click the **Rib** tab and select the horizontal lines.
10. Set the rib parameters, as shown below.

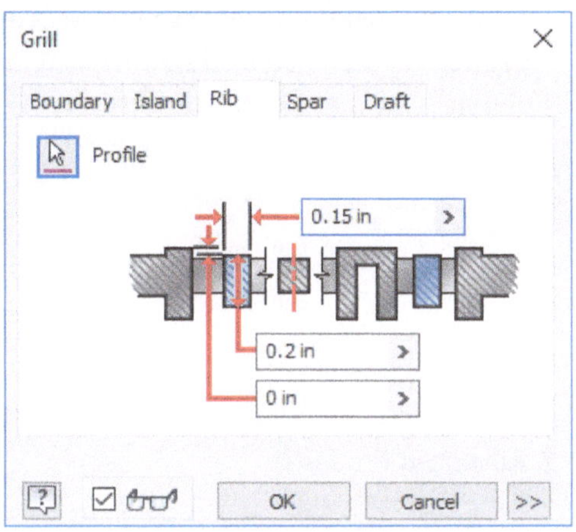

11. Click **OK** to create the grill.

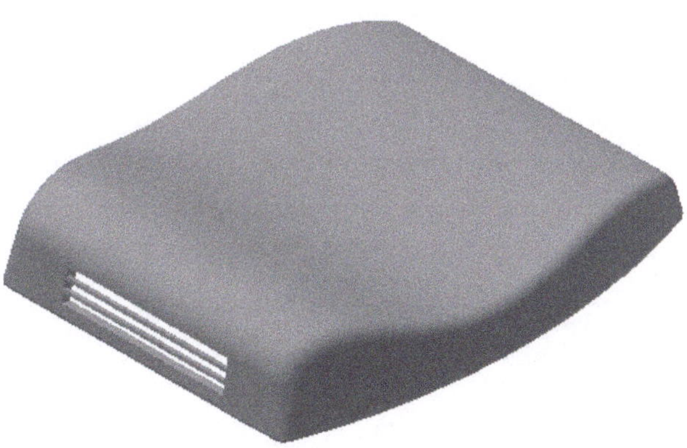

12. Save the model as Plastic Cover.ipt.

Creating Ruled Surface

1. Click **3D Model > Surface > Ruled Surface** on the ribbon and select the bottom edge of the model.

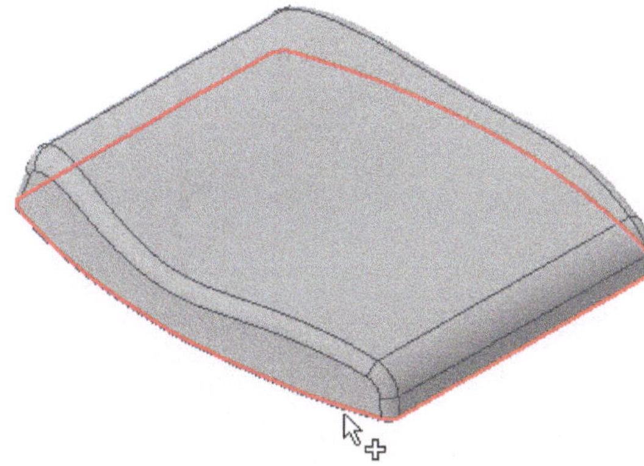

2. Click the **Normal** button on the **Ruled Surface** dialog.

   The preview of the ruled surface appears normal to the selected edge.

   You can click the **Alternate All Faces** button to change the direction of the ruled surface.

3. Type in 2 in the **Distance** box.
4. Click **OK** to create the ruled surface.

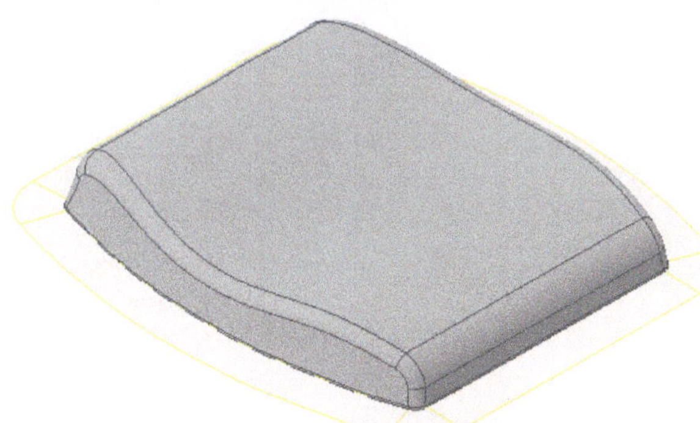

The ruled surface can be used as a parting split while creating a mold.

5. Close the part file without saving.

TUTORIAL 8 (The Extent Start option)

In this tutorial, you will learn the use of the **Extent Start** option in the **Hole** tool.

1. Download the Tutorial_9.ipt from the companion

website:
www.tutorialbook.weebly.com

2. Open the downloaded file.

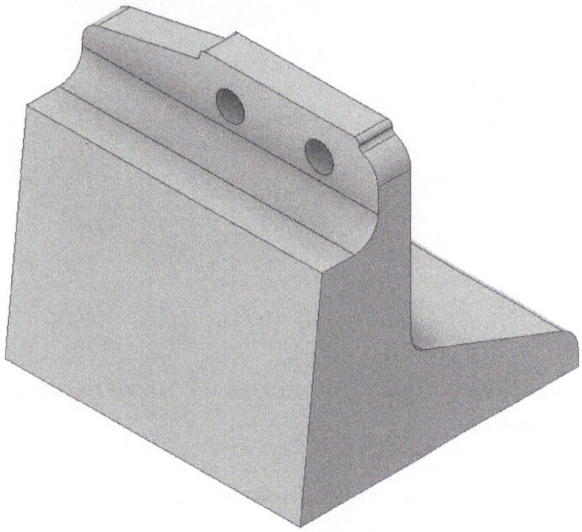

3. In the Browser Window, expand the **Hole** feature, and then right click on the **Sketch**.
4. Select **Edit Sketch** from the Shortcut Menu; the sketch is displayed.
5. Double click on the 0.19 dimension.
6. Type 0.12 in the **Edit Dimension** box, and then click the green check.

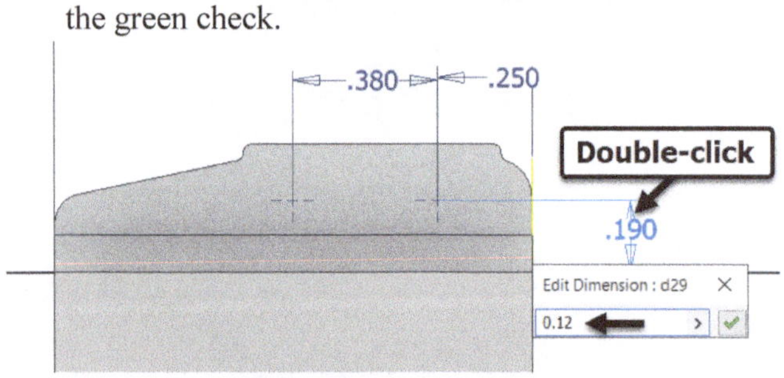

7. Click **Finish Sketch** on the ribbon.

Notice that the fillet overlaps with the holes.

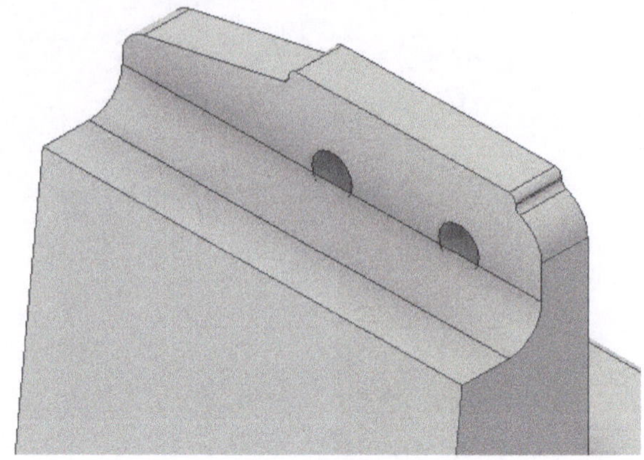

8. In the Browser Window, right click on the **Hole** feature, and then select **Edit Feature**.
9. On the **Properties** panel, expand the **Advanced Properties** section and check the **Extend Start** option.

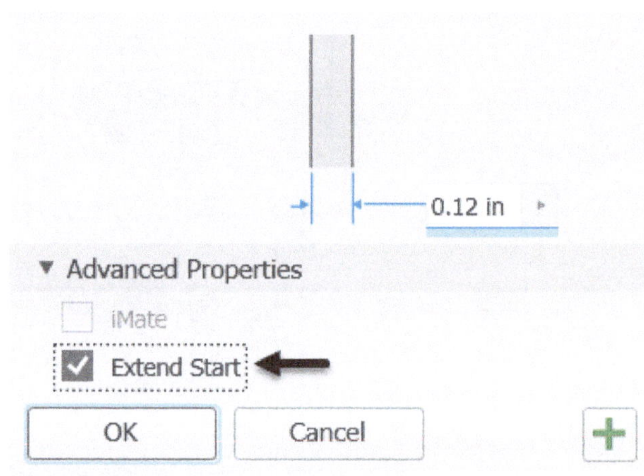

10. Click **OK** to close the dialog.

The **Extend Start** option removes the overlapping material.

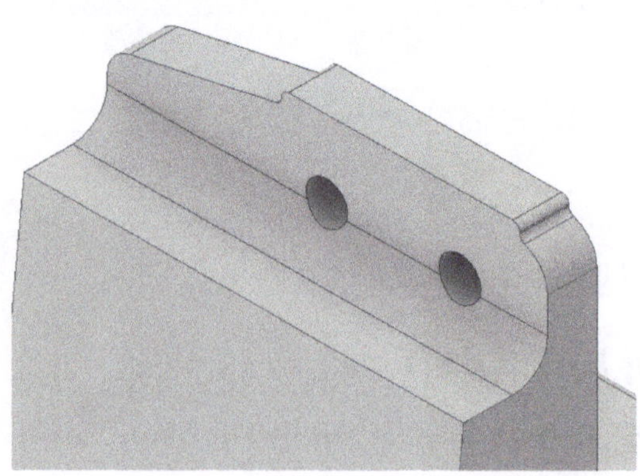

TUTORIAL 9 (Partial chamfer)

In this tutorial, you will learn to create a partial chamfer.

1. Start a new part file using the **Standard(in).ipt** template.
2. Create a 1 X 1 X 1 box using the Extrude tool, as shown.

3. On the ribbon, click **3D Model** tab > **Modify** panel > **Chamfer**.

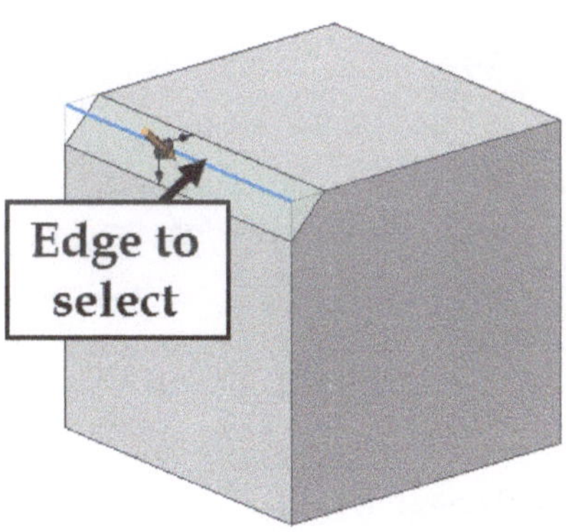

4. On the **Chamfer** dialog, click the **Partial** tab, and then click on the selected edge, as shown.

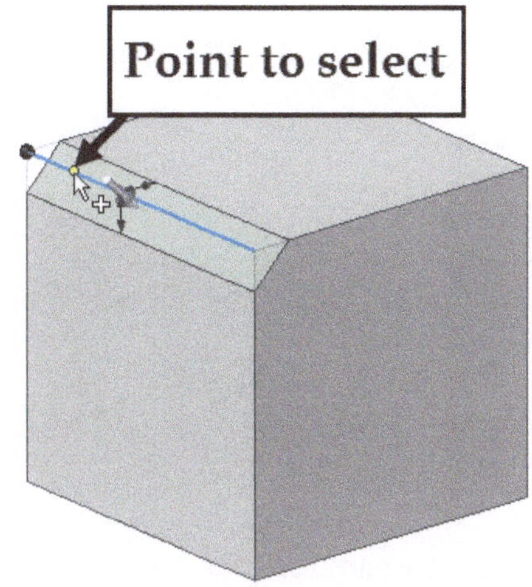

5. On the **Partial** tab, select **Set the Driven Dimension > To End**.
6. Change the **To Start**
7. and **Chamfer** values to 0.25 and 0.5, respectively.

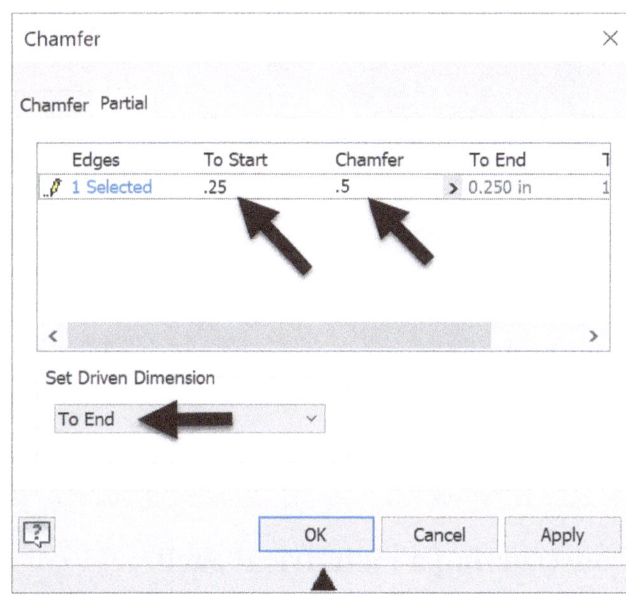

8. Click **OK**.

9. Save and close the part file.

TUTORIAL 10

In this tutorial, you construct a patterned cylindrical shell.

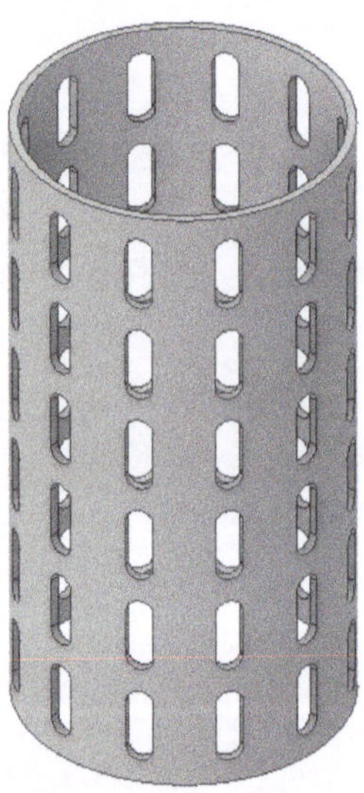

Constructing a cylindrical shell

1. Start a new part file.
2. Create a sketch on the XZ plane.

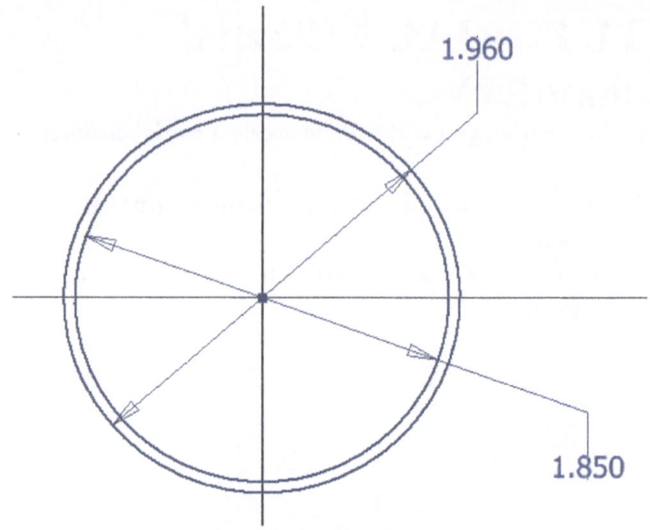

3. Extrude the sketch up to 3.93 depth.

Adding a Slot

1. Activate the **Start 2D Sketch** tool.
2. In the Browser Window, expand the **Origin** folder and select the XY Plane.
3. Click the **Slice Graphics** icon on the Status bar.

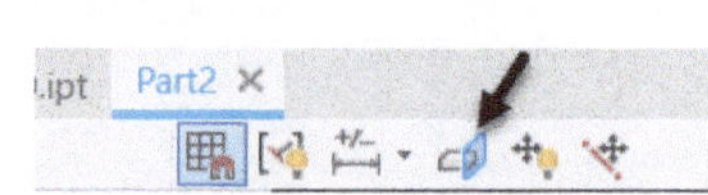

The model is sliced using the sketching plane.

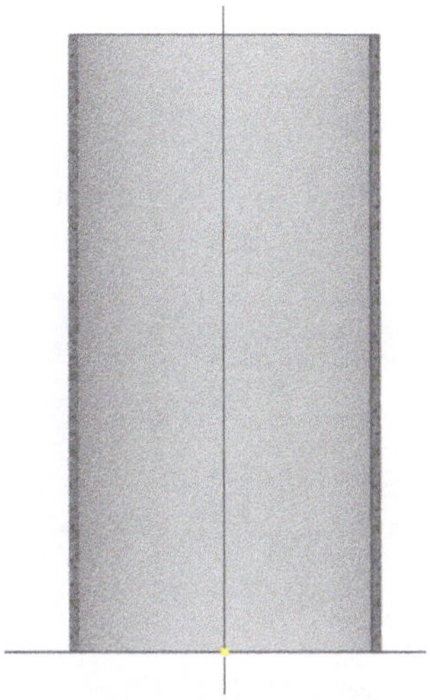

4. On the ribbon, click **Sketch** tab > **Create** panel > **Rectangle** drop-down > **Slot Center to Center** .
5. Click to define the first point of the slot.
6. Move the pointer up and click to define the second point.
7. Move the pointer outward and click to create a slot.

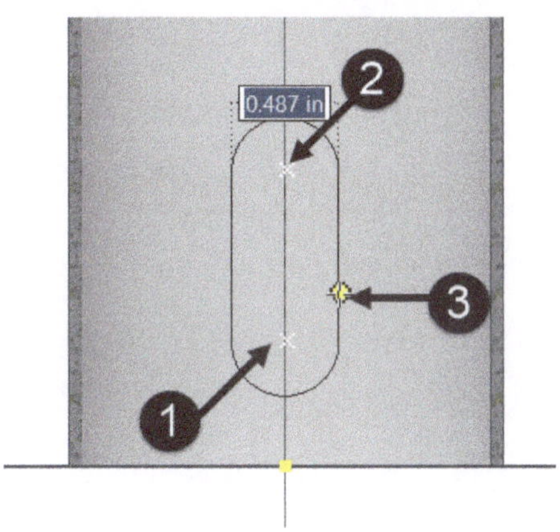

8. Apply the Vertical constraint between the Center point of the slot and the origin point.
9. Add dimensions to the slot.

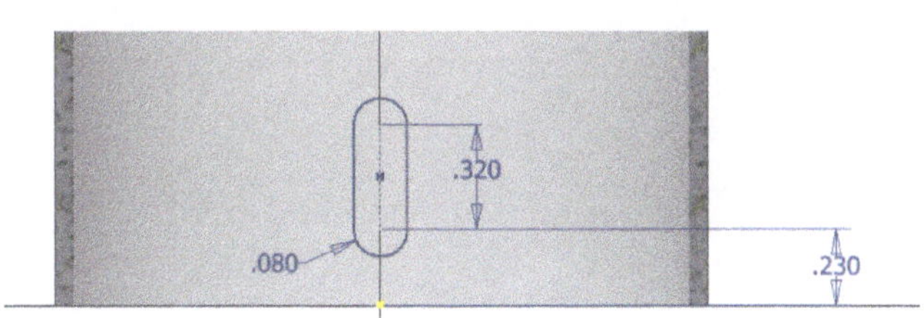

10. Click **Finish** on the ribbon.
11. On the ribbon, click **3D Model** tab > **Create** panel > **Extrude**.
12. On the **Extrude Properties** panel, click the **Through All** icon under the **Behavior** section.
13. Make sure that the arrow on the preview points in the forward direction.

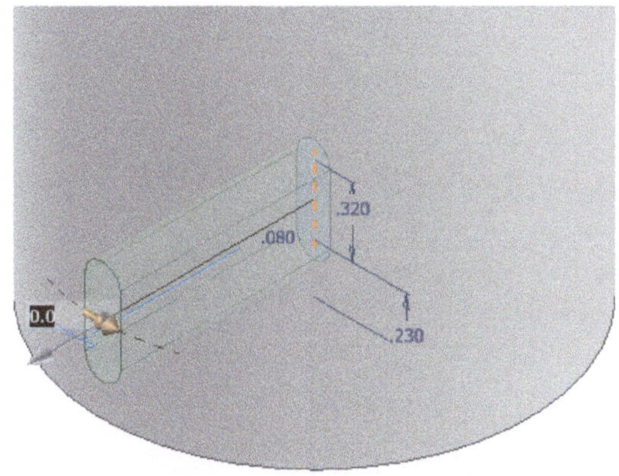

14. Click the **Cut** icon on the dialog.
15. Click **OK**.

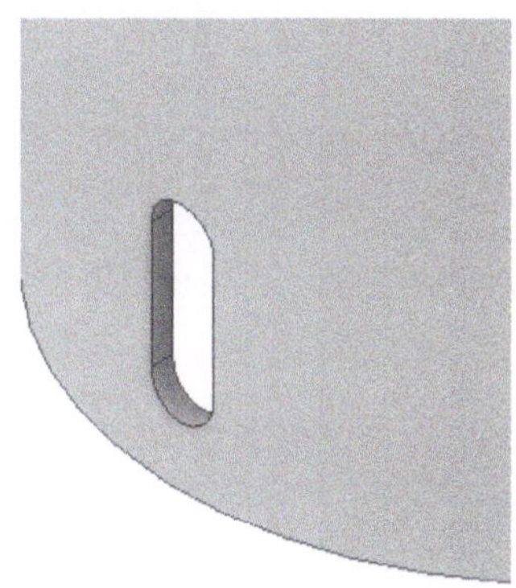

Constructing the Rectangular pattern

1. On the ribbon, click **3D Model > Pattern > Rectangular Pattern** .
2. On the **Rectangular Pattern** Properties panel, click the **Features** button, and then select the slot.
3. On the **Rectangular Pattern** Properties panel, click the cursor button in the **Direction A** section.
4. Select **Direction > Y Axis** icon under the **Direction A** section on the Properties panel.
5. Select the **Distribution > Incremental** icon.
6. Type **6** in the **Number** box.
7. Type **0.629** in the **Distance** box.

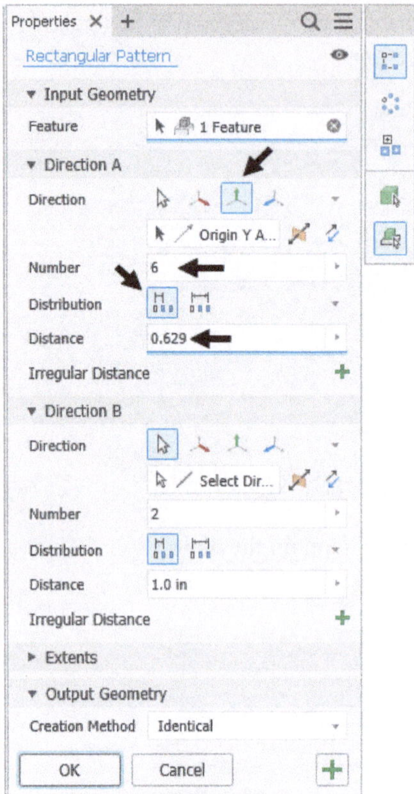

8. Click **OK**.

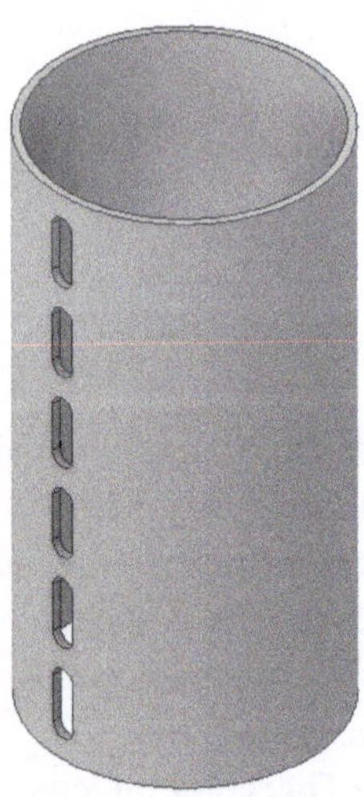

Constructing the Circular pattern

1. On the ribbon, click **3D Model > Pattern > Circular Pattern**.
2. In the Browser Window, select the rectangular pattern.
3. On the **Circular Pattern** Properties panel, click the **define axis of revolution** box and select the cylindrical face of the model.
4. Type-in **12** in the **Count** box.
5. Type **360** in the **Angle** box.
6. Click **Distribution > Fitted**.
7. Click the **Rotational** icon in the **Orientation** section.

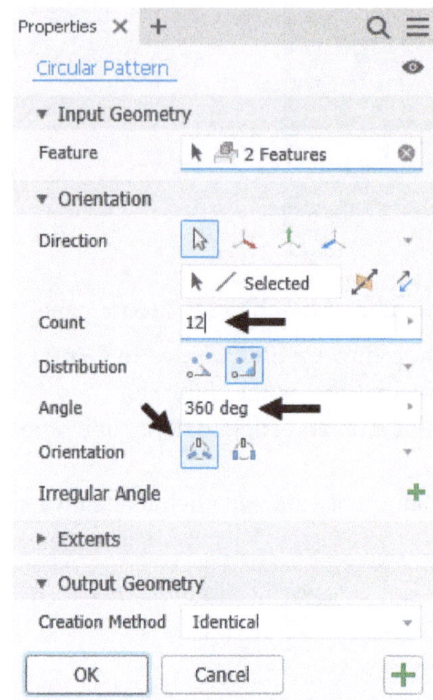

8. Click **OK** to make the circular pattern.

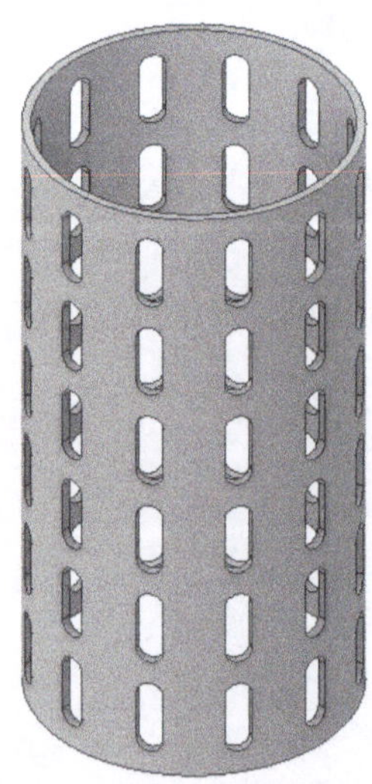

11. Save and close the model.

TUTORIAL 11

In this tutorial, you create the model shown in the figure.

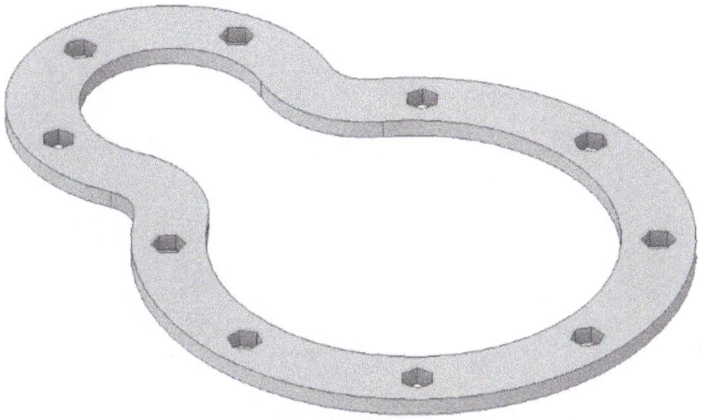

Constructing the first feature

1. Open a new part file.
2. On the ribbon, click **3D Model > Sketch > Start 2D Sketch**.
3. Click on the XZ plane.
4. Construct two circles and add dimensions to them.

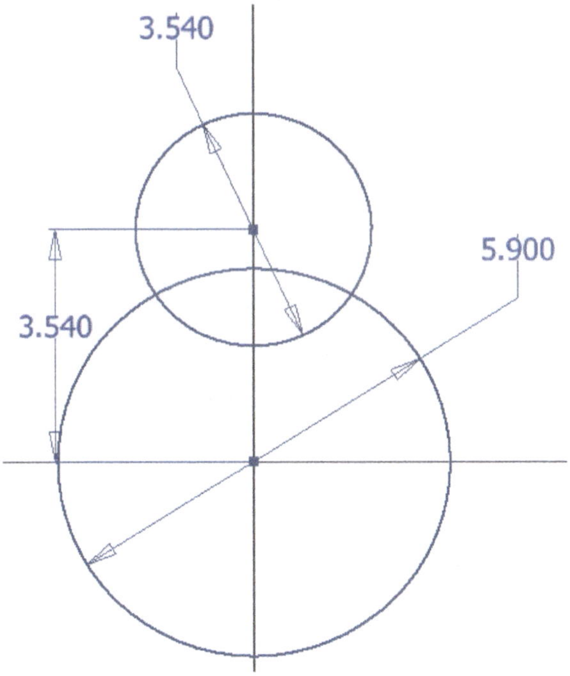

5. On the ribbon, click **Sketch > Modify > Trim**.
6. Click and drag the left mouse across the intersections of the two circles.

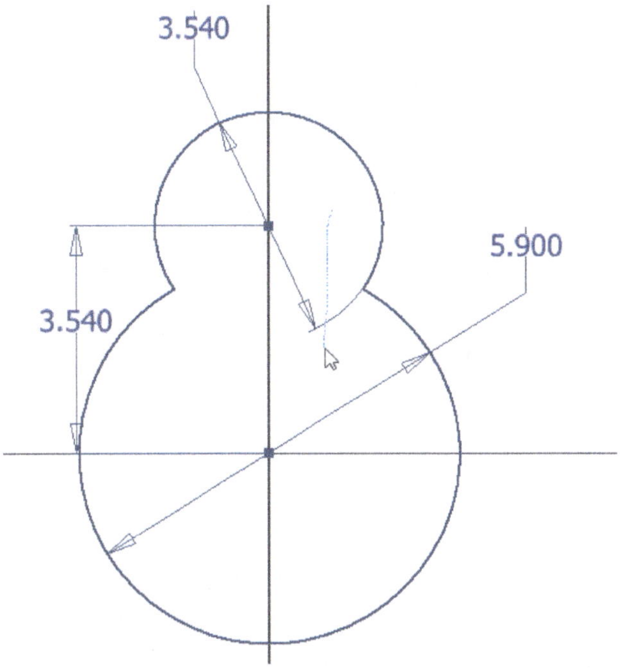

7. On the ribbon, click **Sketch > Create > Fillet** and set the **Radius** value to 0.39.
8. Make sure that the **equal to** button is pressed on the **2D Fillet** dialog.
9. Click on the two arcs; a fillet is created at one corner.
10. Again, click on the two arcs.
11. Right click and click **OK**.

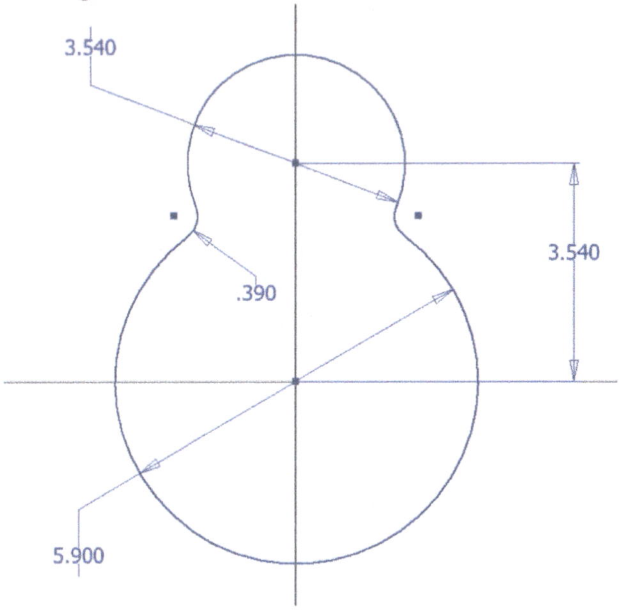

12. On the ribbon, click **Sketch** tab > **Modify** panel > **Offset**.
13. Click on the sketch, and then move the pointer inward.

14. Type 0.78 in the box attached to the offset element.
15. Press Enter.
16. Click **Finish** on the ribbon.
17. On the ribbon, click **3D Model > Create > Extrude**.
18. Click inside the region enclosed by the sketch and its offset.

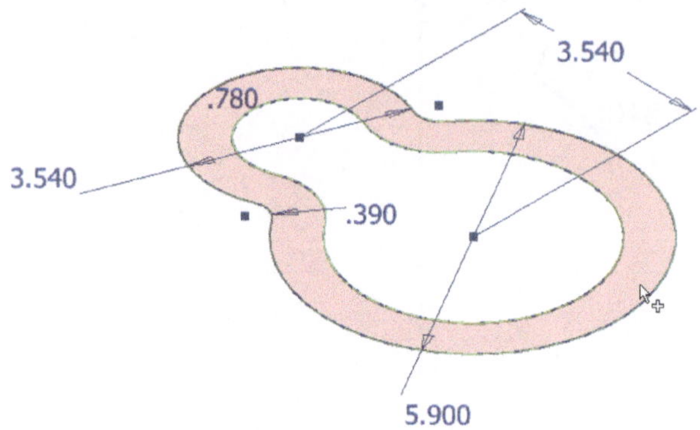

19. On the **Extrude** Properties panel, type 0.196 in the **Distance A** box.
20. Click **OK**.

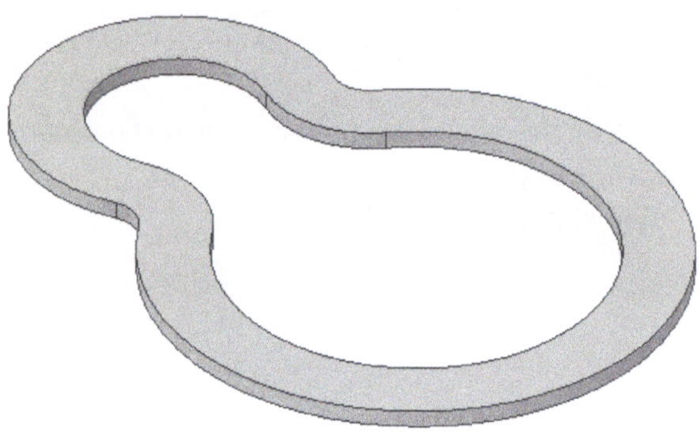

Constructing the Extruded cut

1. On the ribbon, click **3D Model > Sketch > Start 2D Sketch**.
2. Click on the top face of the model geometry.
3. On the ribbon, click **Sketch > Create > Rectangle** drop-down > **Polygon** .
4. On the dialog, type-in 6 in the **Number of Sides** box.
5. Click the **Inscribed** icon.
6. Click to define the center point of the polygon.

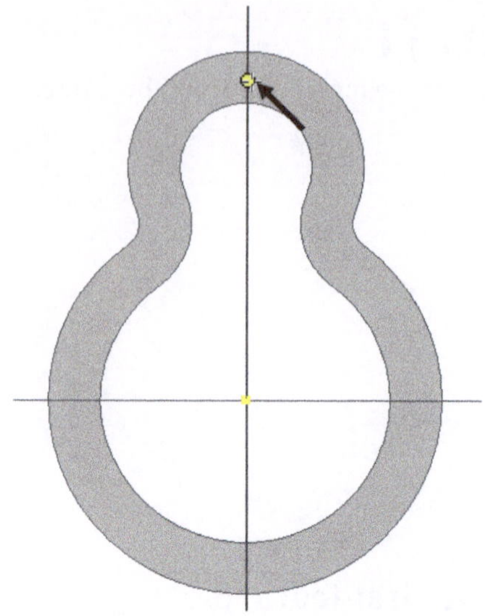

7. Move the pointer and click to construct the polygon.
8. Right click and select **OK**.
9. On the ribbon, click **Sketch > Constrain > Horizontal**.
10. Click on the line of the polygon, as shown.

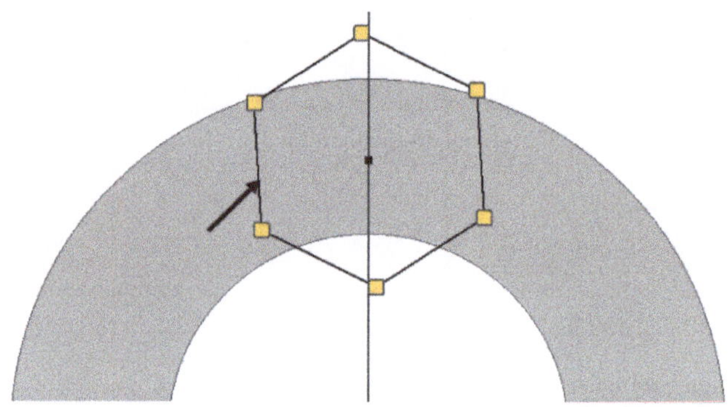

11. Select the center point of the polygon and the sketch origin.

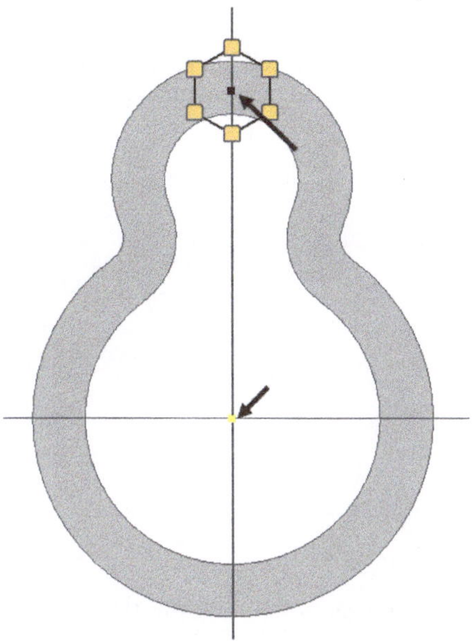

12. Activate the **Dimension** command, zoom into the polygon, and select the two lines, as shown.

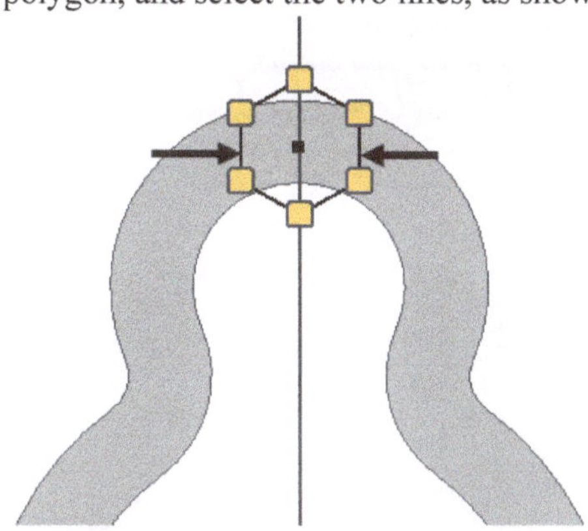

13. Place the dimension, type 0.31, and press Enter.
14. Select the center point of the polygon and the sketch origin.
15. Place the dimension, and type 4.92. Next, press Enter.

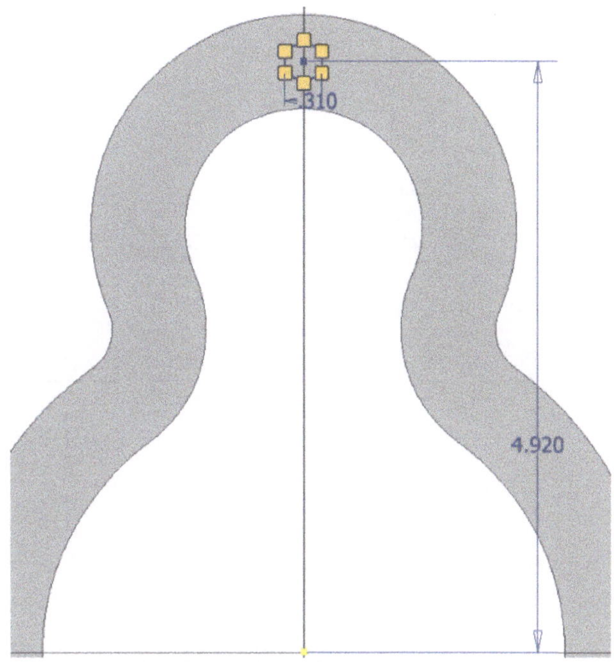

16. Click **Finish** on the ribbon.
17. On the ribbon, click **3D Model > Create > Extrude**.
18. Click on the region enclosed by the polygon.
19. Click the **Cut** icon on the **Extrude Properties** panel.
20. Click the **Through All** icon under the **Behavior** section.
21. Click **OK**.

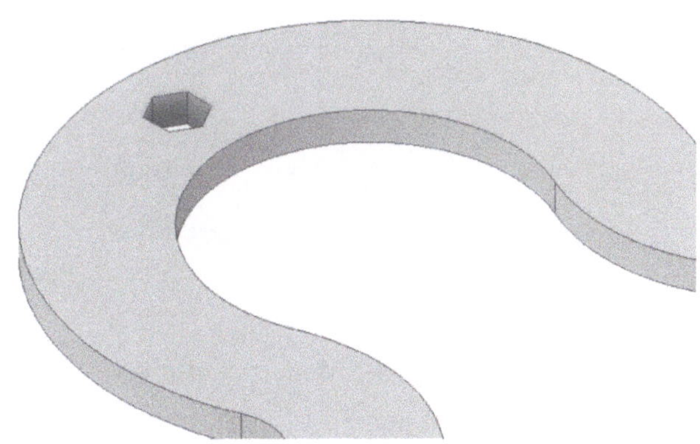

Making the Path Pattern

1. On the ribbon, click **3D Model > Sketch > Start 2D Sketch**.
2. Click on the top face of the model.
3. On the ribbon, click **Sketch > Create > Project Geometry** 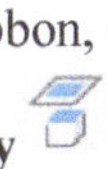 .
4. Right click on the outer edge of the model, and then select **Select Tangencies**.

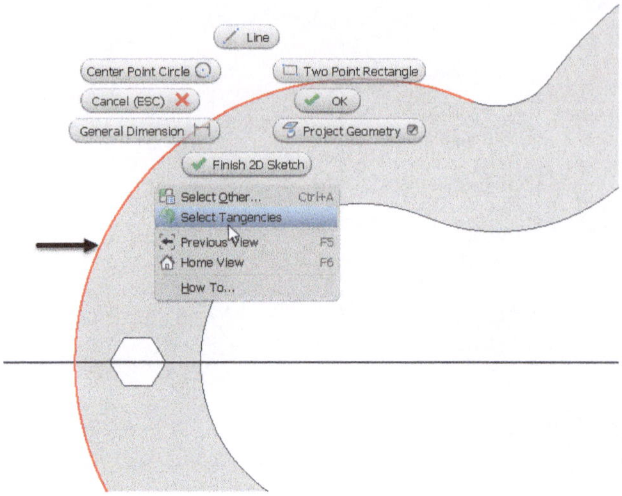

5. On the ribbon, click **Sketch > Create > Point**.
6. Specify the point, as shown.

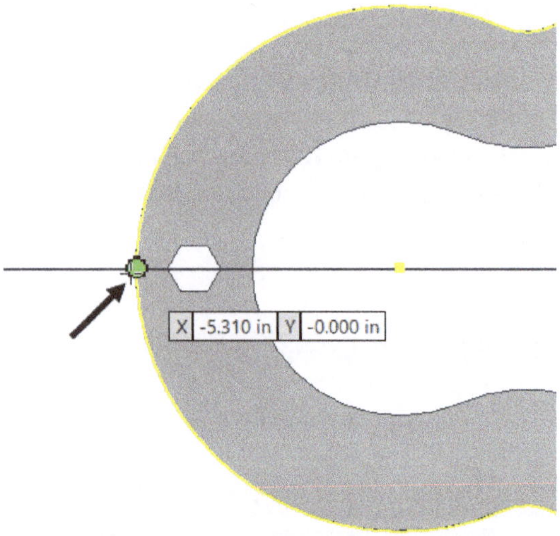

7. Right click and select **OK**.
8. Click **Finish**.
9. On the ribbon, click **3D Model > Pattern > Rectangular Pattern** .
10. Select the Extruded cut feature from the model.

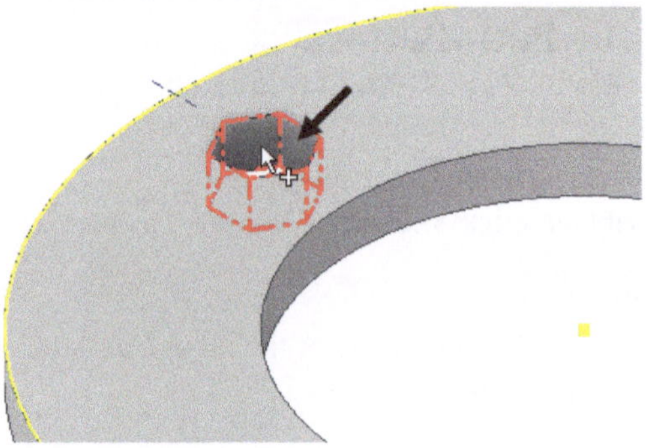

11. Click the cursor button in the **Direction A** section.
12. Place the pointer on the projected curve, and then click when all its edges are highlighted in red.

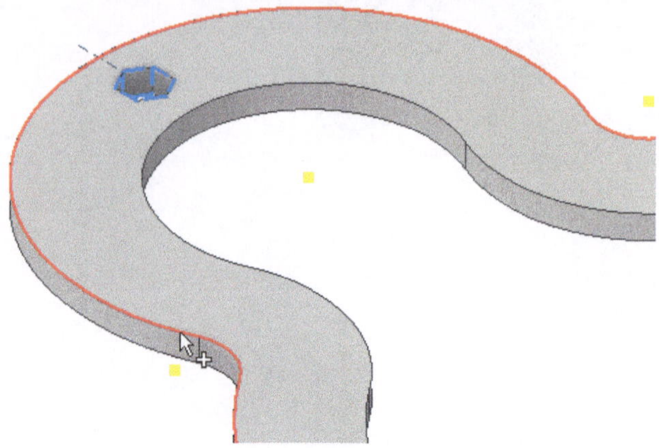

13. Click the **Start Point** selection box in the **Direction A** section.
14. Select the point created in the sketch to define the start point of the pattern.

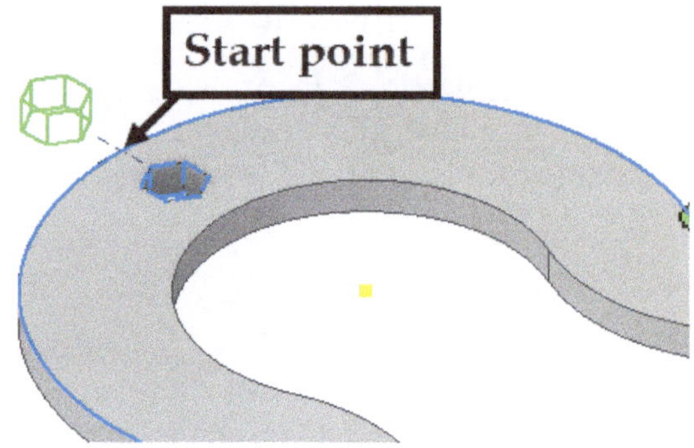

15. Type 10 in the **Number** box.
16. Select **Distribution > Fitted** icon in the **Direction A** section.
17. Click the **Curve Length** icon next to the **Distance** box in the **Direction A** section.
18. Select **Direction 1** from the **Orientation** drop-down in the **Output Geometry** section.

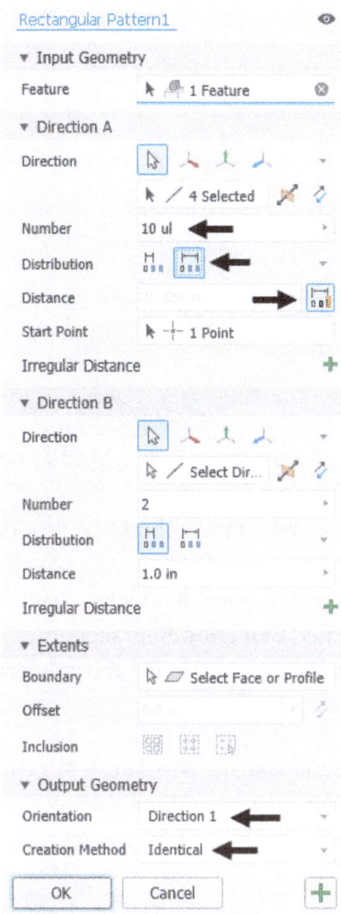

19. Click **OK** to create the pattern along a path.

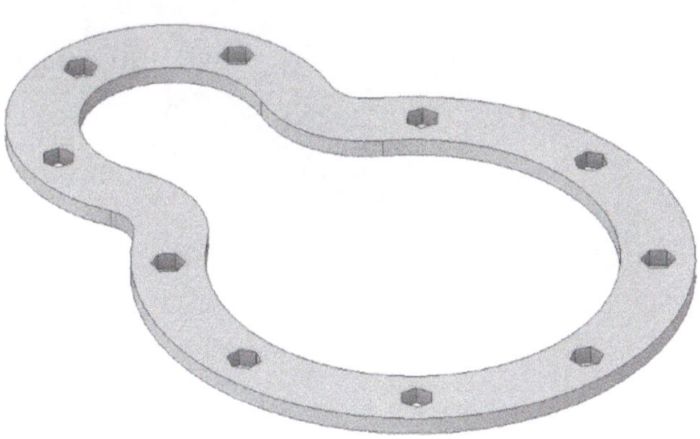

20. Save and close the file.

TUTORIAL 12

In this tutorial, you add markings to a model using the Mark tool. The **Mark** tool allows you add of laser markings, etchings, and engravings on parts. Here are some examples of what you can achieve using the Mark tool:

Laser Markings:

- Add a serial number or unique identifier on a component for traceability.
- Apply a barcode or QR code for automated scanning and tracking purposes.
    - Include part numbers or manufacturing dates for easy identification.

Etchings:

- Engrave safety instructions or warning labels on a product.
- Incorporate legal or regulatory information, such as certifications or compliance marks.
- Include assembly instructions or part orientation indicators.

Engravings:

- Personalize products with customer names, logos, or customized designs.
- Add decorative patterns or artistic engravings for aesthetic purposes.
- Include branding elements, such as company names or trademarks.

1. Download the Chapter 6 part files and open the Tutorial_12.ipt file.
2. On **3D Model** tab of the ribbon, in the **Modify** panel, click the **Mark** button.

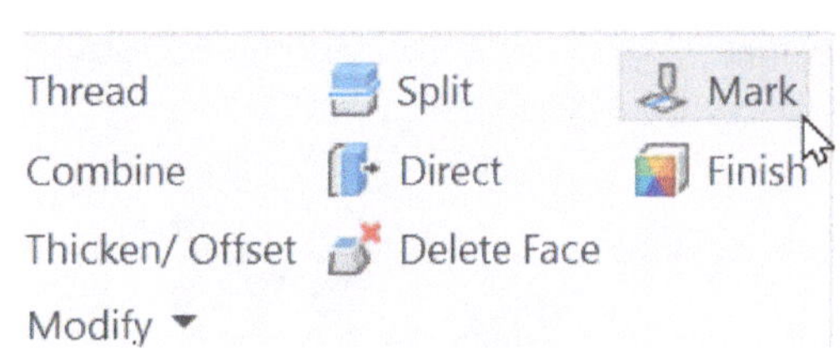

3. Select the circle displayed on the horizontal face of the model.

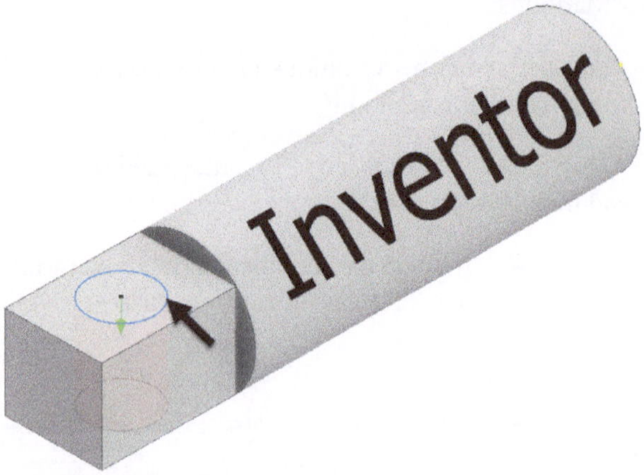

4. In the **Selection Sets** section, select **Mark through** from the drop-down on the **Properties** panel.
5. In the **Behavior** section, select **Method > Project** .
6. Select **Direction > Default** .

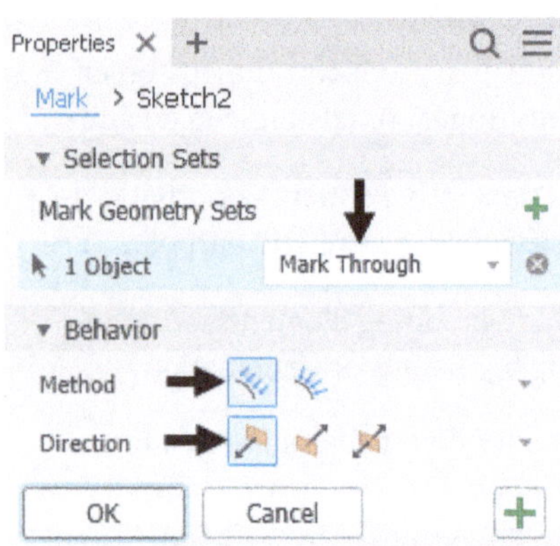

7. Click **OK**. Notice that the circle is marked through the 3D geometry. As a result, the marking is created on both sides of the 3D geometry.

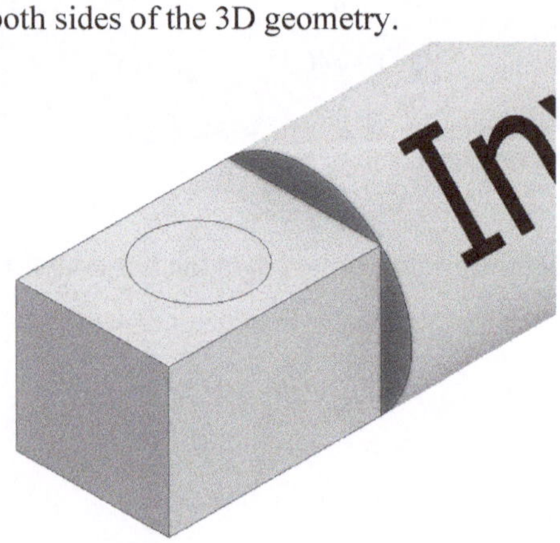

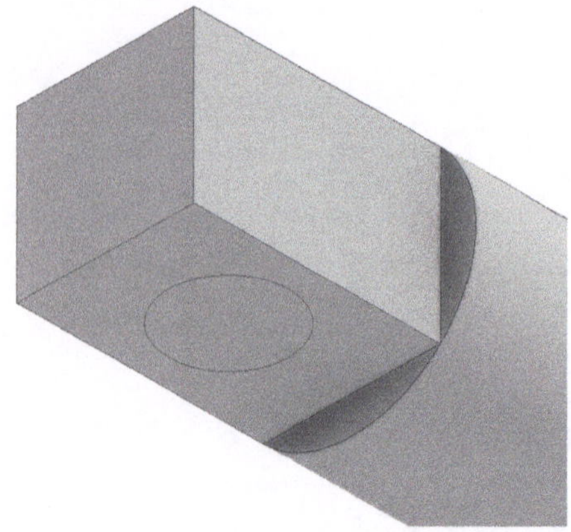

8. On **3D Model** tab of the ribbon, in the **Modify** panel, click the **Mark** button.
9. Select the text displayed on the cylindrical face of the model.
10. On the **Properties** panel, select **Mark Surface** from the drop-down located **Selection Sets** section.
11. Select the text that is wrapped around the cylindrical face.
12. In the **Behavior** section, select **Method > Wrap** .
13. Click the **Select Face** under the **Behavior** section and then select the cylindrical face of the model.

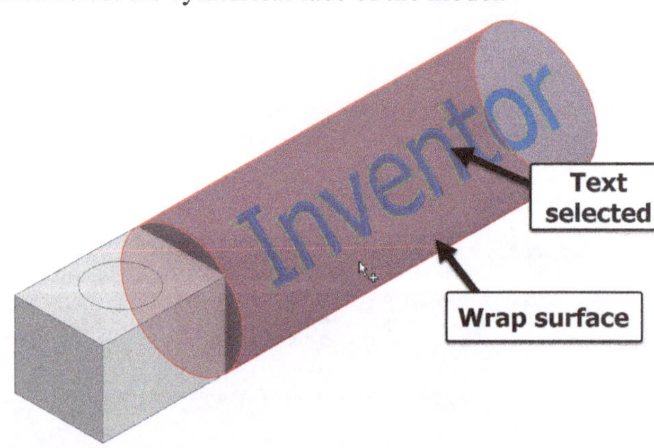

14. Click **OK** to mark the text on the cylindrical face.

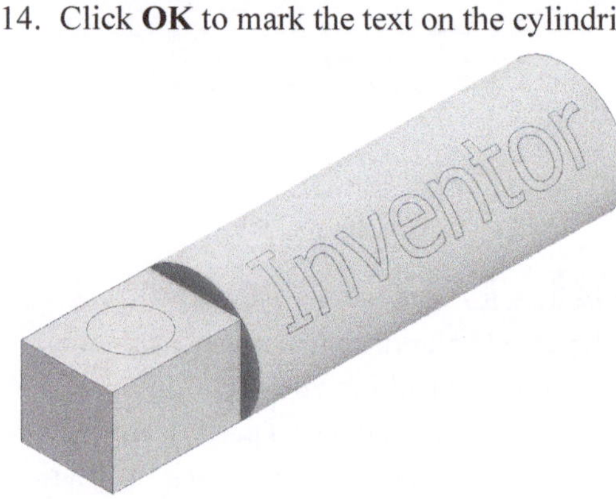

TUTORIAL 13

In this tutorial, you construct the model shown in the figure.

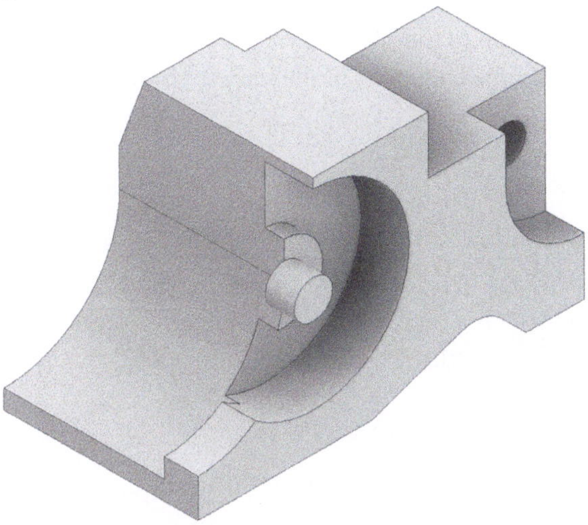

Creating the Base Feature

1. Open a new Part file using the Standard.ipt template.
2. Click the **Start 2D Sketch** icon on the **Sketch** panel of the **3D Model** tab of the ribbon.
3. Select the YZ Plane from the graphics window.
4. Click the **Two Point Rectangle** icon on the **Create** panel of the **Sketch** tab of the ribbon.
5. Specify the first and second corners of the rectangle, as shown.

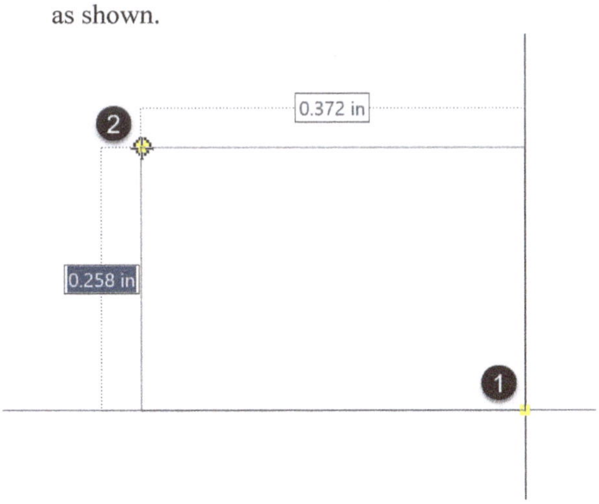

6. Create another rectangle by specifying its first and second corners, as shown.

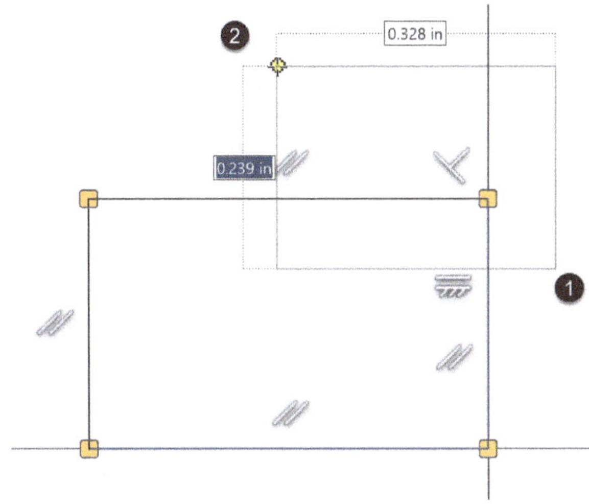

7. Click the **Trim** icon on the **Modify** panel.
8. Select the elements of the rectangles to be trimmed, as shown.

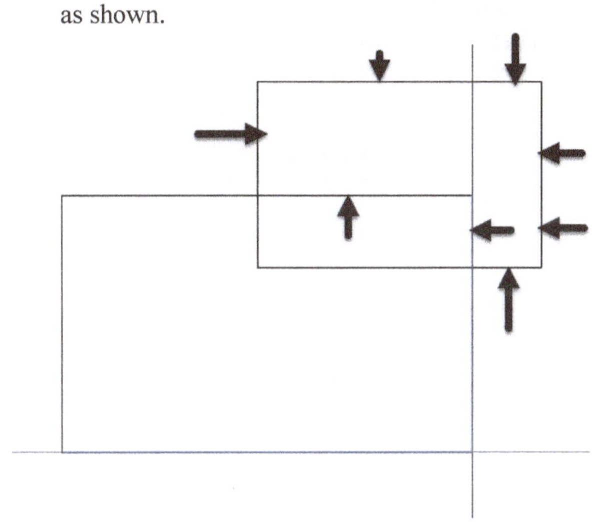

9. Add vertical and horizontal distance dimensions to the sketch, as shown.

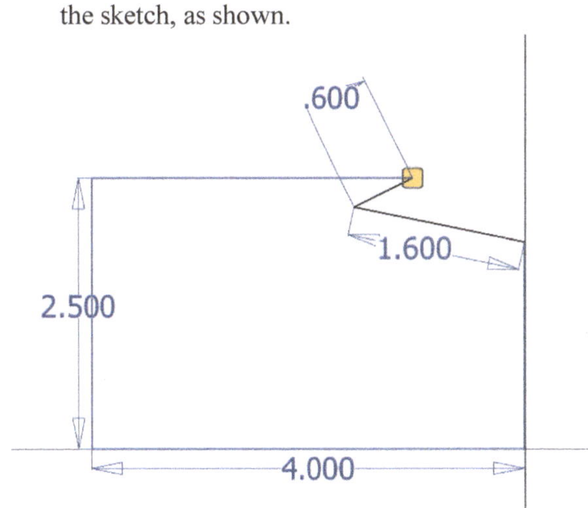

10. Apply the horizontal and vertical constraints to the lines, as shown.

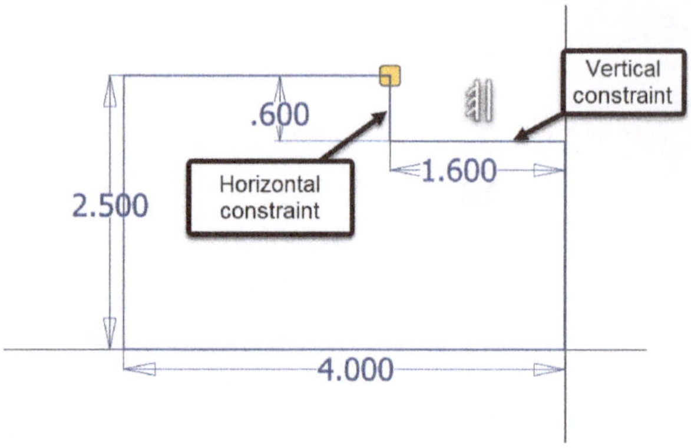

11. Click **Finish** on the **Exit** panel of the **Sketch** tab of the ribbon.
12. On the ribbon, click **3D Model > Create > Extrude**; the sketch is selected automatically.
13. Select the **Symmetric** option on the **Extrude Properties** panel.
14. Set the **Distance A** to **2**.
15. Click **OK** to create the first feature.

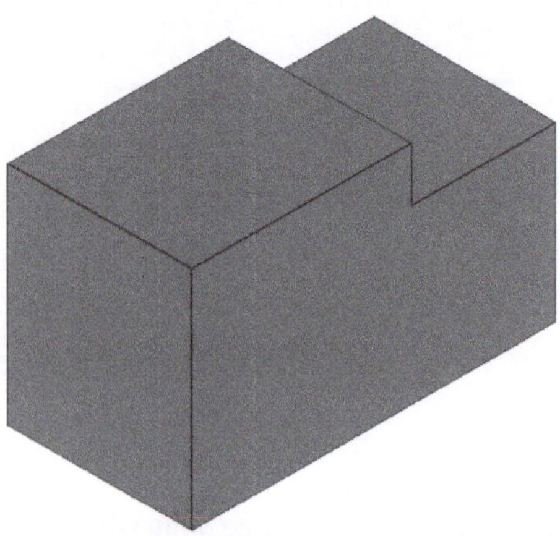

Creating the Cut Features

1. On the ribbon, click **3D Model > Sketch > Start 2D Sketch** .
2. Select the YZ plane from the **Origin** folder of the **Model** Browser.

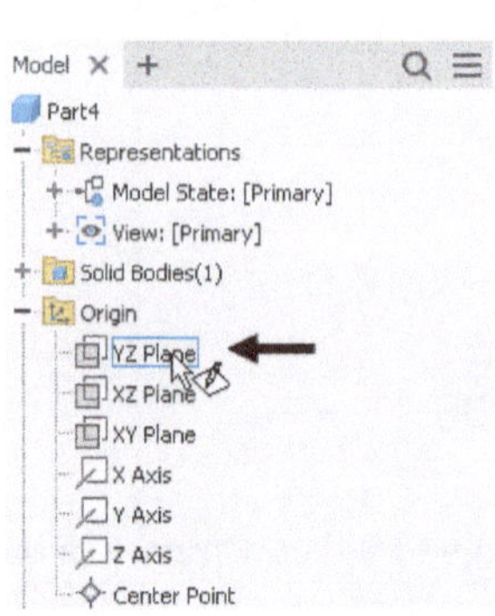

3. Click the **Slice Graphics** button at the bottom of the window.
4. Click the **Line** icon on the **Create** panel of the **Sketch** tab of the ribbon.
5. Specify the endpoints of the line, as shown.

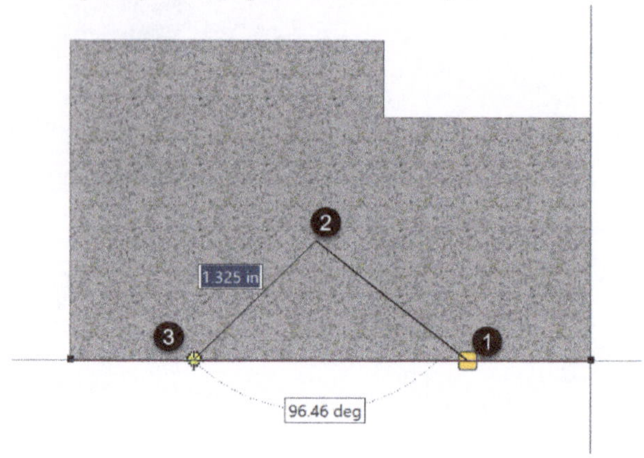

6. Right-click and select **OK**.
7. Click the **Fillet** icon on the **Create** panel on the **Sketch** tab of the ribbon.
8. Type **0.4** in the **2D Fillet** dialog.

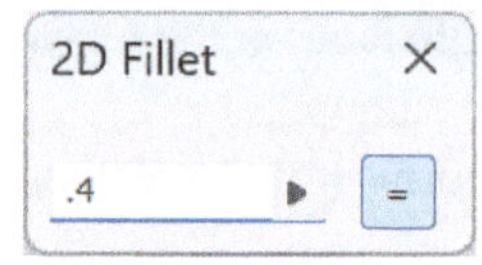

9. Select the corner point of the sketch, as shown.

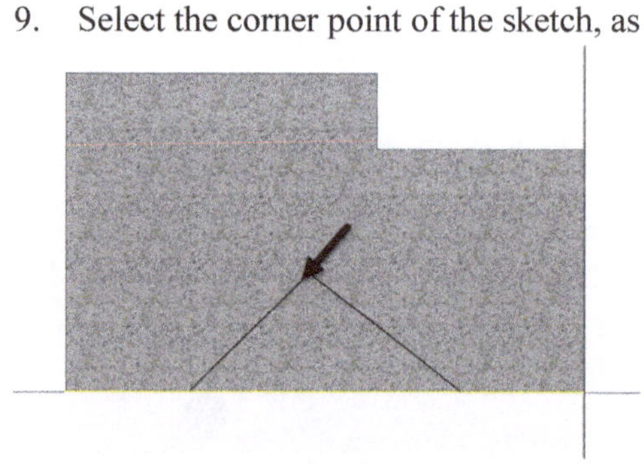

10. Click the **Dimension** icon on the **Constrain** panel.
11. Select the inclined line and the horizontal axis of the sketch.
12. Move the pointer and click to position the dimension.
13. Type **20** in the **Edit Dimension** box and click **OK**.

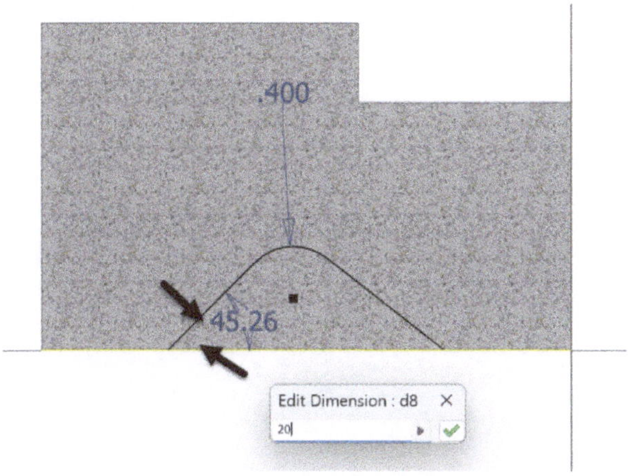

14. Select the other inclined line and the horizontal axis of the sketch, as shown.
15. Position the dimension on the right side.
16. Type **135** in the **Edit Dimension** box and click **OK**.

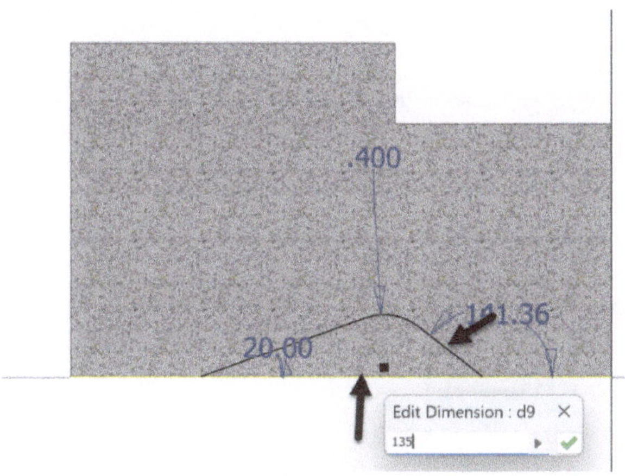

17. Add vertical and horizontal dimensions to the sketch, as shown.

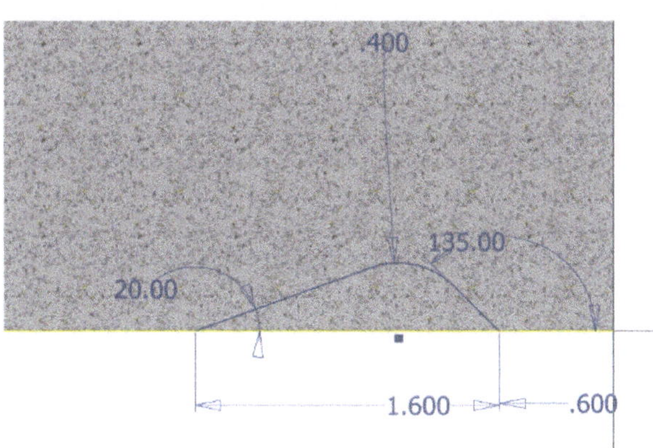

18. Click **Finish** on the **Exit** panel of the **Sketch** tab of the ribbon.
19. On the ribbon, click **3D Model > Create > Extrude**; the sketch is selected automatically.
20. Click the **Through All** icon under the **Behavior** section.
21. Select the **Symmetric** option on the **Extrude Properties** panel.
22. Click the **Cut** icon under the **Output** section on the **Extrude** Properties panel.
23. Click **OK** to create the cut feature.

24. Click on the right side face of the model.
25. Click the **Create Sketch** icon.

26. Click the **Rectangle** drop-down > **Slot Center point** icon on the **Create** panel of the **Sketch** tab of the ribbon.

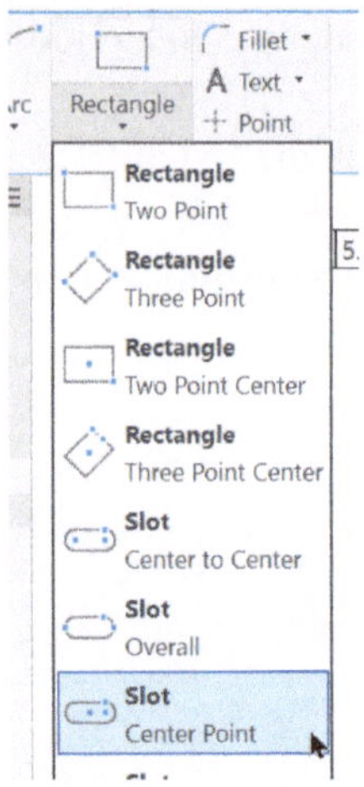

27. Select the top-right corner point of the selected face, as shown.
28. Move the pointer downward and click on the vertical edge.

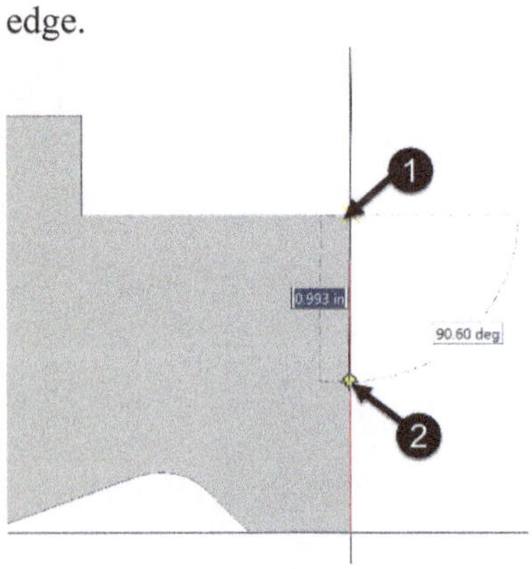

29. Move the pointer outward and click to create slot.

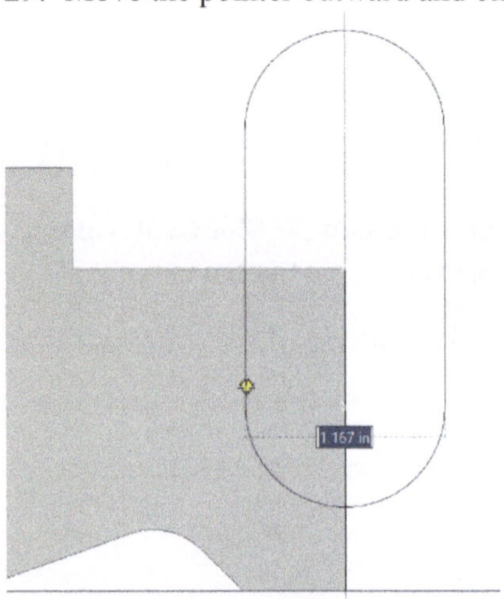

30. On the ribbon, click **Sketch > Create > Project geometry**.
31. Select the horizontal edge of the model, as shown.

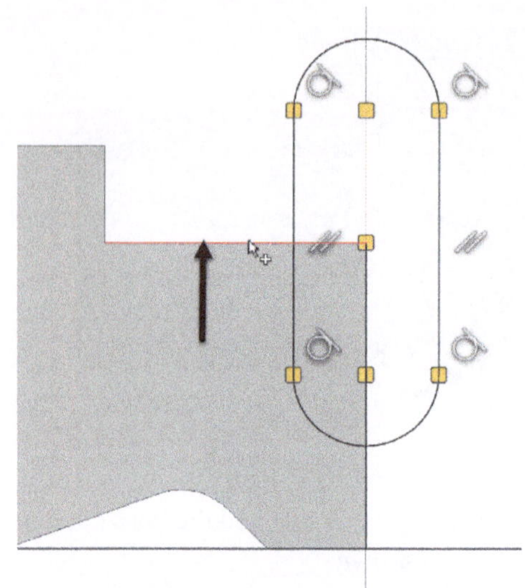

32. Click the **Trim** icon on the **Modify** panel.
33. Select the elements of the rectangles to be trimmed, as shown.

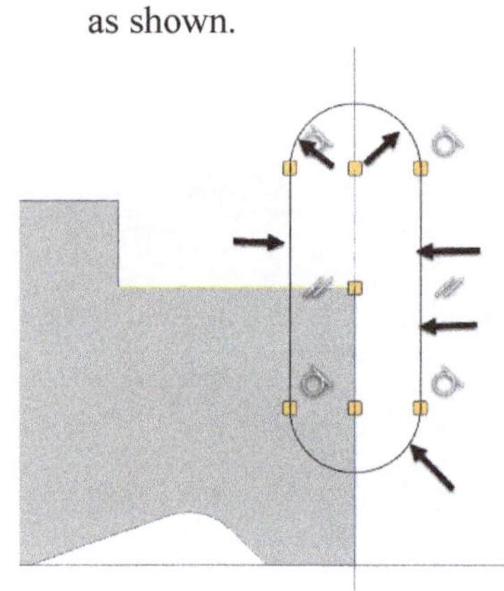

34. Click the **Dimension** tool on the **Constrain** panel of the **Sketch** tab of the ribbon.
35. Select the arc and place the dimension.
36. Type **0.8** and click **OK**.
37. Select the centerpoint of the arc and the sketch origin.
38. Place the dimension on the right side.
39. Type 1.4 in the **Edit dimension** box and click **OK**.
40. On the ribbon, click **Sketch > Constrain > Horizontal Constraint**.
41. Select the endpoint and centerpoint of the arc.

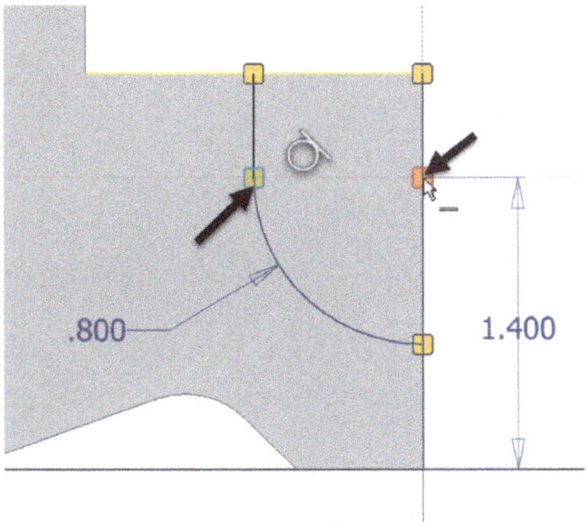

42. Click **Finish** on the **Exit** panel of the **Sketch** tab of the ribbon.
43. On the ribbon, click **3D Model > Create > Extrude**; the sketch is selected automatically.
44. Click the **Cut** icon under the **Output** section on the **Extrude** Properties panel.
45. Type **0.4** in the **Distance A** box.
46. Click **OK** to create the cut feature.

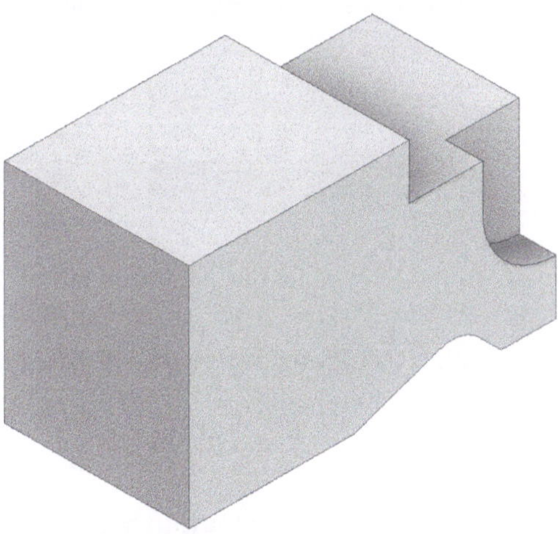

47. Select the flat face of the cut feature.
48. Click the **Create Sketch** icon.

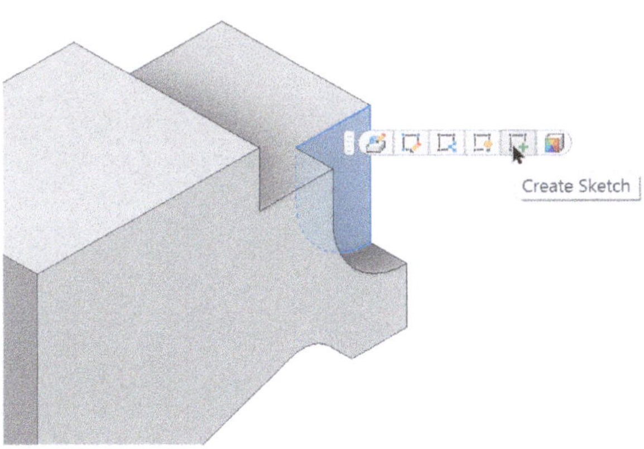

49. Create a circle.
50. On the ribbon, click **Sketch > Constrain > Vertical Constraint**.
51. Select the centerpoint of the circle and the midpoint of the top edge of the model, as shown.

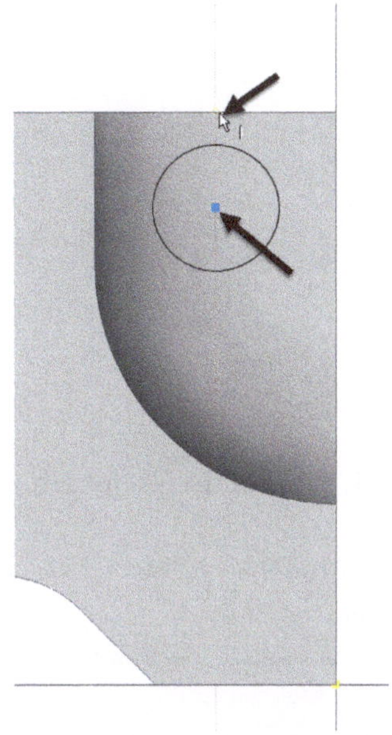

52. On the ribbon, click **Sketch > Constrain > Horizontal Constraint**.
53. Select the centerpoint of the circle and the endpoint of the curved edge, as shown.

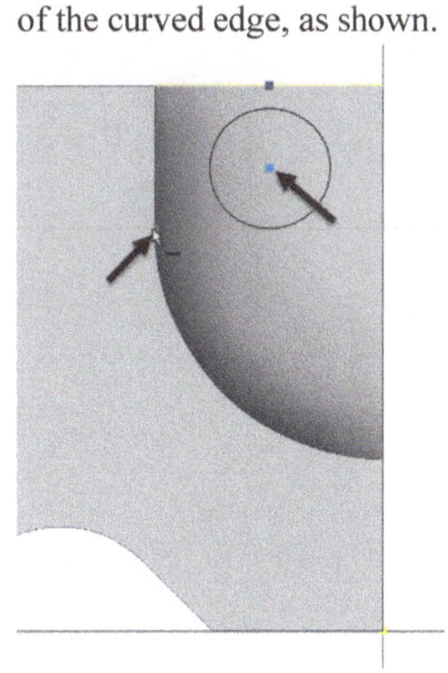

54. Add the diameter constraint to the circle.

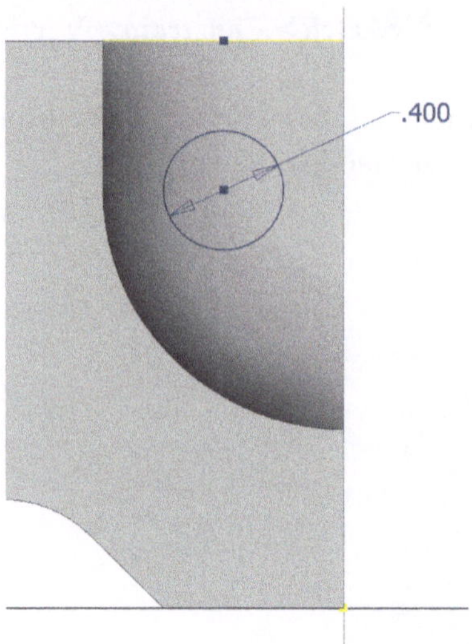

55. Click **Finish** on the **Exit** panel of the **Sketch** tab of the ribbon.
56. On the ribbon, click **3D Model > Create > Extrude**; the sketch is selected automatically.
57. Click the **Through All** icon under the **Behavior** section.
58. Click the **Cut** icon under the **Output** section on the **Extrude** Properties panel.
59. Click **OK** to create the cut feature.

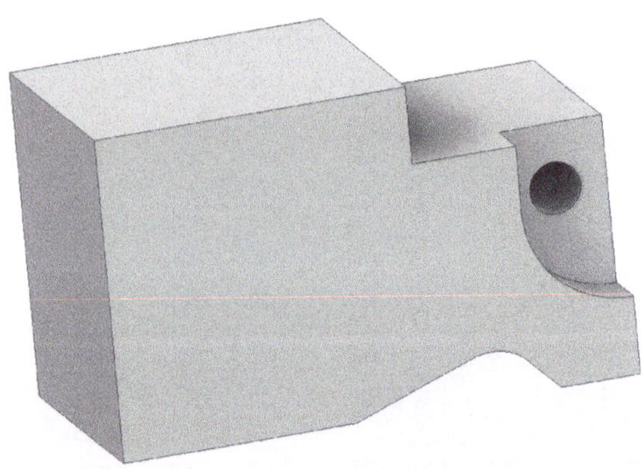

Creating the Cut Feature on the left side

1. Click on the top face of the model.

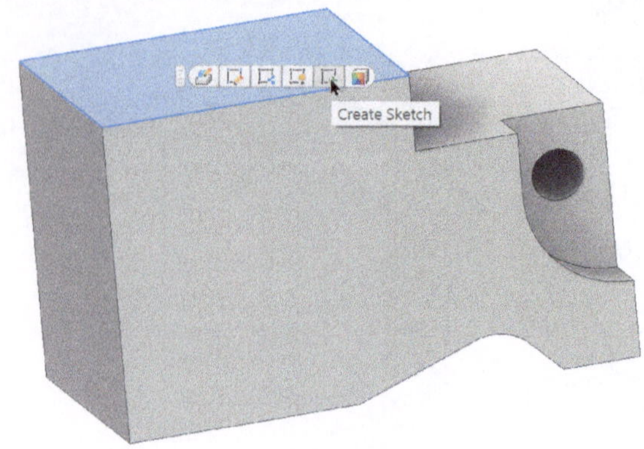

2. Click the **Create Sketch** icon.
3. On the ribbon, click **Sketch** tab > **Create** panel > **Rectangle Two Point**.
4. Select the top-right corner point of the model.
5. Move the pointer toward lower corner and click.
6. Add dimensions to the sketch.

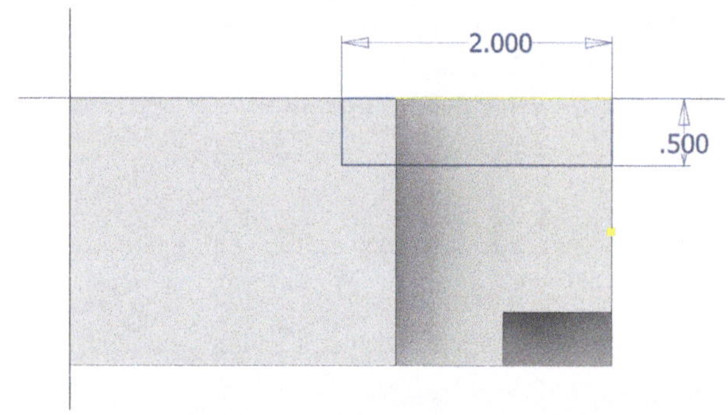

60. Click **Finish** on the **Exit** panel of the **Sketch** tab of the ribbon.
61. On the ribbon, click **3D Model > Create > Extrude**; the sketch is selected automatically.
62. Click the **Through All** icon under the **Behavior** section.
63. Click the **Cut** icon under the **Output** section on the **Extrude** Properties panel.
64. Click **OK** to create the cut feature.

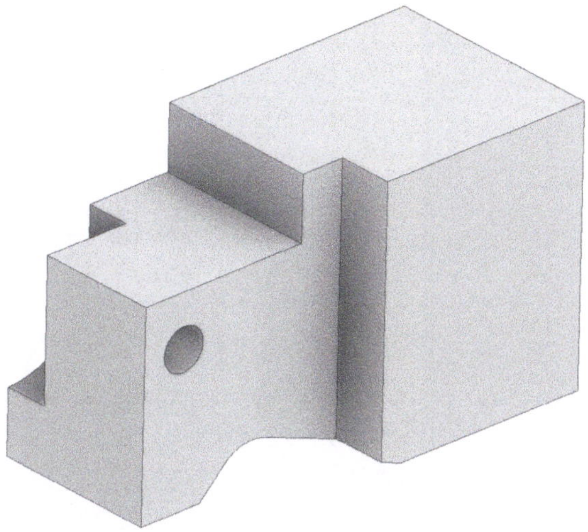

Creating the Angled Cut

1. Click on the front face of the model.
2. Click the **Create Sketch** icon.

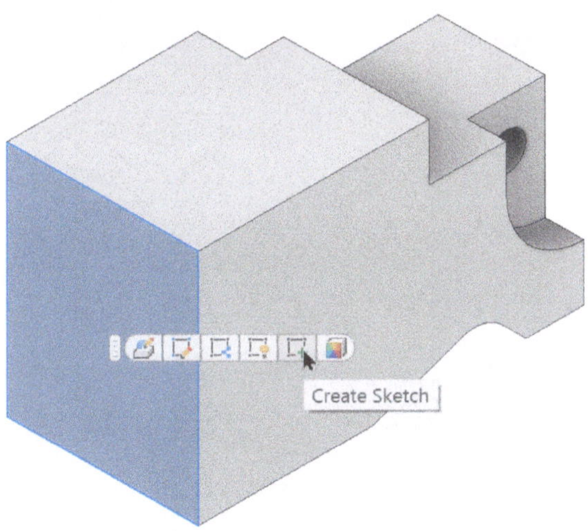

3. Create a line by specifying its endpoints on the left vertical edge and top horizontal edge, as shown.

4. Create horizontal distance and angle constraints, as shown.

5. Click **Finish** on the **Exit** panel of the **Sketch** tab of the ribbon.
6. On the ribbon, click **3D Model > Create > Extrude**; the sketch is selected automatically.
7. Click the **Through All** icon under the **Behavior** section.
8. Click the **Cut** icon under the **Output** section on the **Extrude** Properties panel.
9. Click **OK** to create the cut feature.

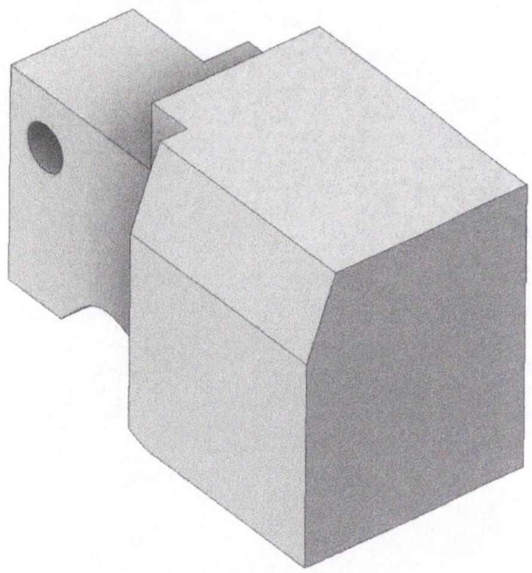

Creating the Cut feature on the left

1. Click on the top-left corner of the ViewCube, as shown.

2. Click on the left face of the model.
3. Click the **Create Sketch** icon.

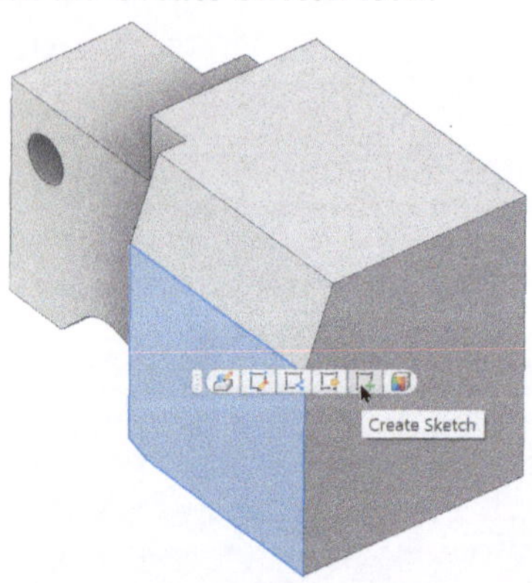

4. Click the **Rectangle** drop-down > **Slot Center point** icon on the **Create** panel of the **Sketch** tab of the ribbon.
5. Select the top-right corner point of the selected face, as shown.
6. Move the pointer downward and click on the vertical edge.
7. Move the pointer outward and click to create slot.

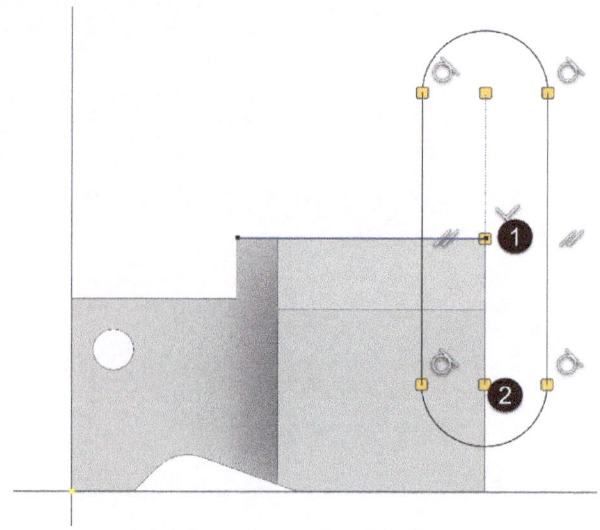

8. Click the **Trim** icon on the **Modify** panel.
9. Select the elements of the rectangles to be trimmed, as shown.

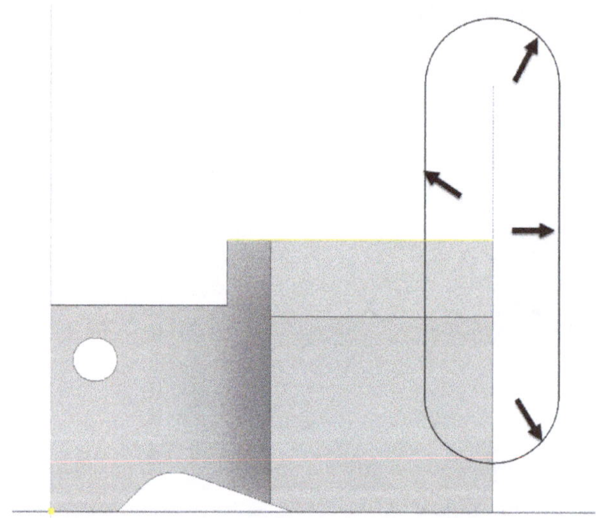

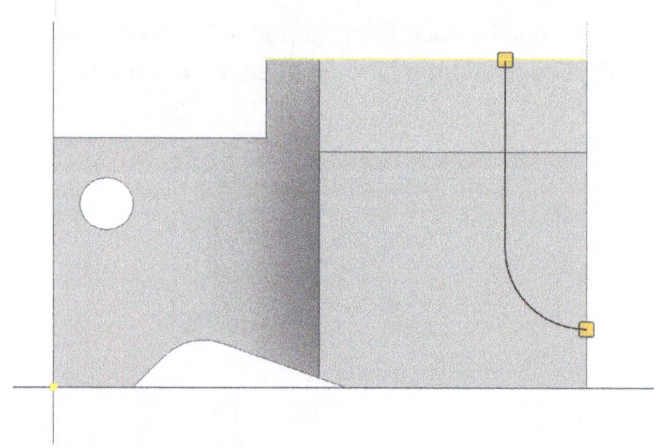

10. Click the **Dimension** tool on the **Constrain** panel of the **Sketch** tab of the ribbon.
11. Select the arc and place the dimension.
12. Type **1.2** and click **OK**.

13. Select the vertical line.
14. Place the dimension on the left side.
15. Type 1.1 in the **Edit dimension** box and click **OK**.

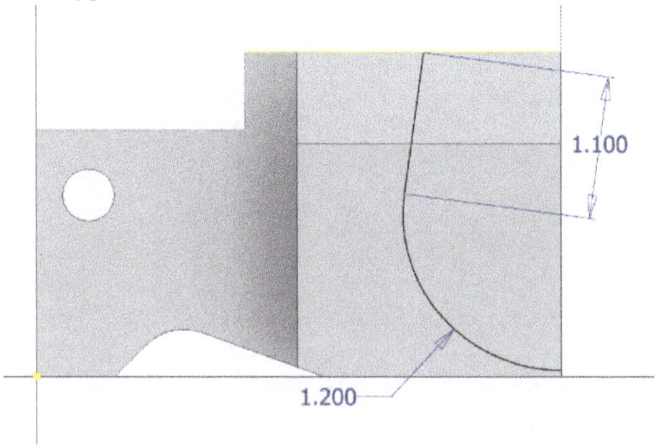

16. On the ribbon, click **Sketch > Constrain > Vertical Constraint**.
17. Select the line.

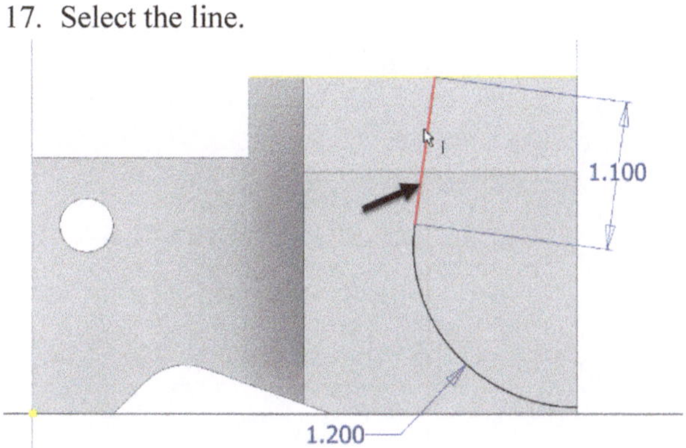

18. Click **Finish** on the **Exit** panel of the **Sketch** tab of the ribbon.
19. On the ribbon, click **3D Model > Create > Extrude**.
20. Select the sketch.
21. Click in the region, as shown.

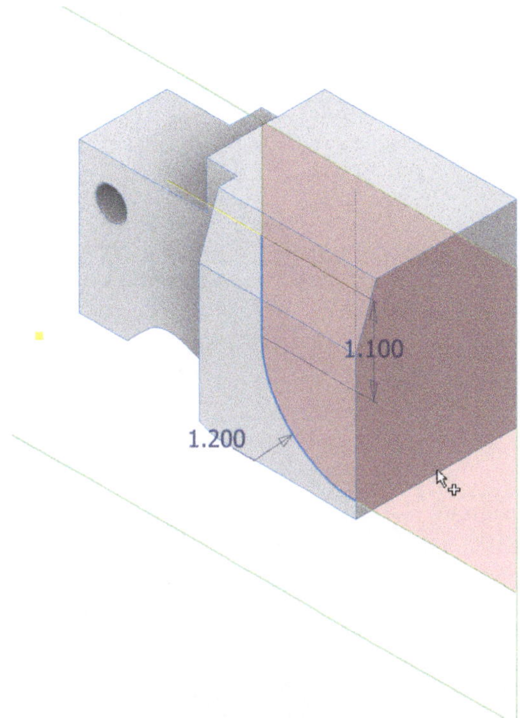

22. Click the **Cut** icon under the **Output** section on the **Extrude** Properties panel.
23. Type **1.65** in the **Distance A** box.
24. Click **OK** to create the cut feature.

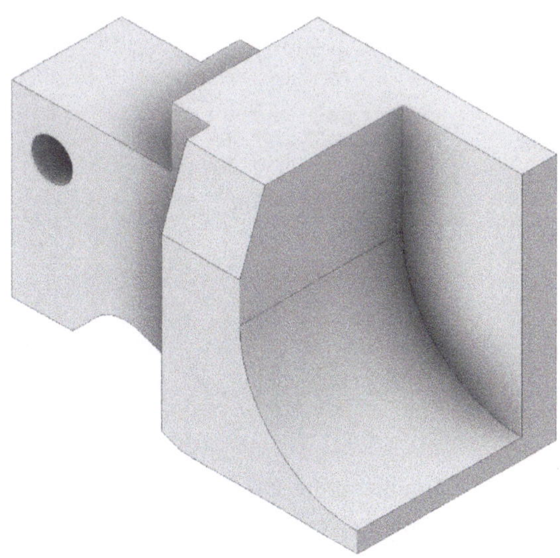

Creating the Cut feature on the right

1. Click the **Home** icon next to the ViewCube.
2. Click on the right face of the model.
3. Click the **Create Sketch** icon.

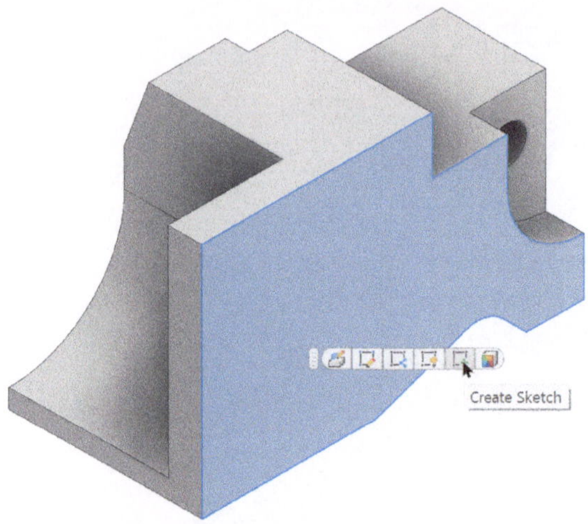

4. Create a circle.
5. Add the diameter and vertical distance constraint, as shown.

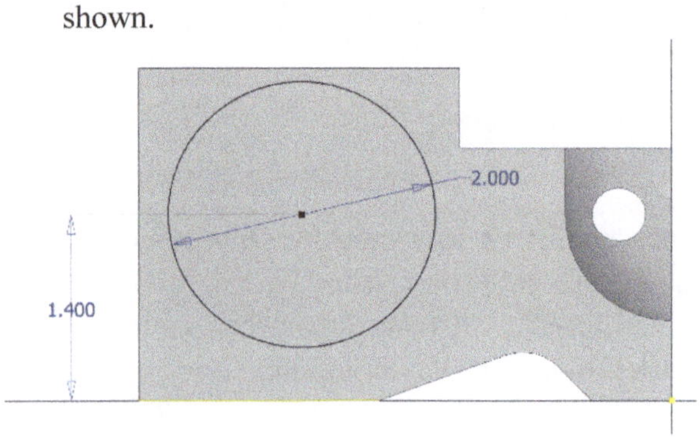

6. Create a vertical line, as shown.

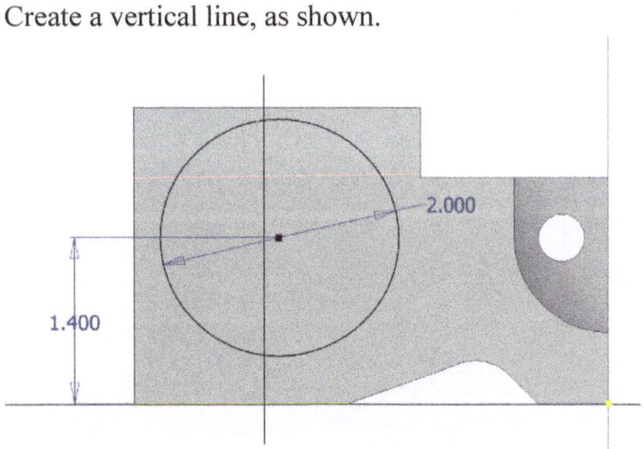

25. Click the **Trim** icon on the **Modify** panel.
26. Select the left side portion of the circle.

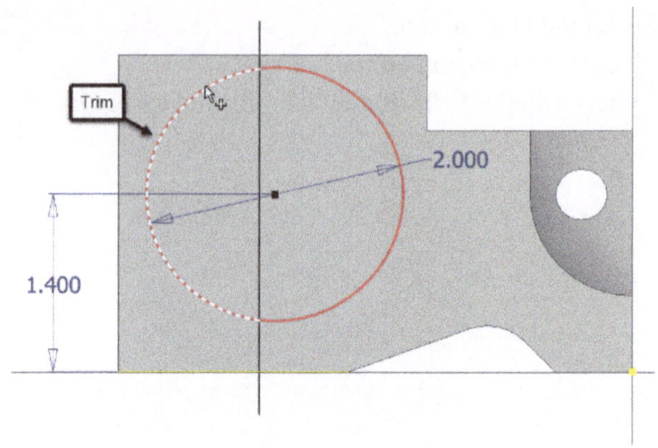

27. Click the **Coincident Constraint** icon on the **Constrain** panel.
28. Select endpoint the vertical line and the horizontal edge.

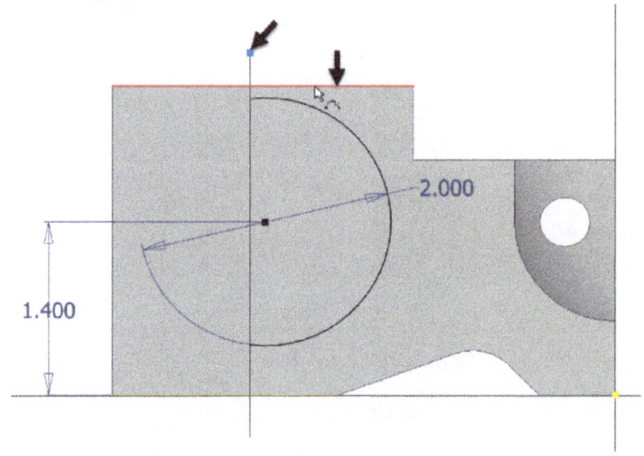

29. Trim the bottom and middle portions of the vertical line.

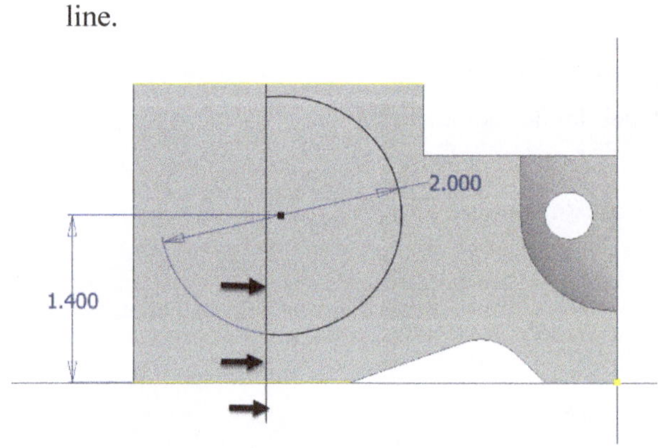

30. Click the **Arc** drop-down > **Arc Three Point** on the **Create** panel.

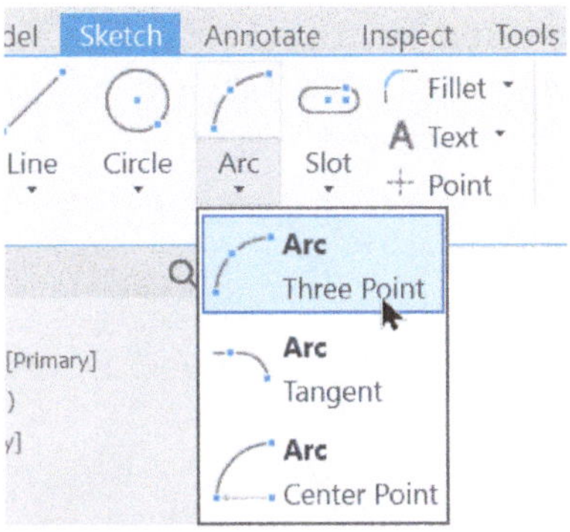

31. Select the endpoint of the arc.
32. Move the pointer toward the left and click on the extracted edge.
33. Move the pointer downward and click to create the arc.

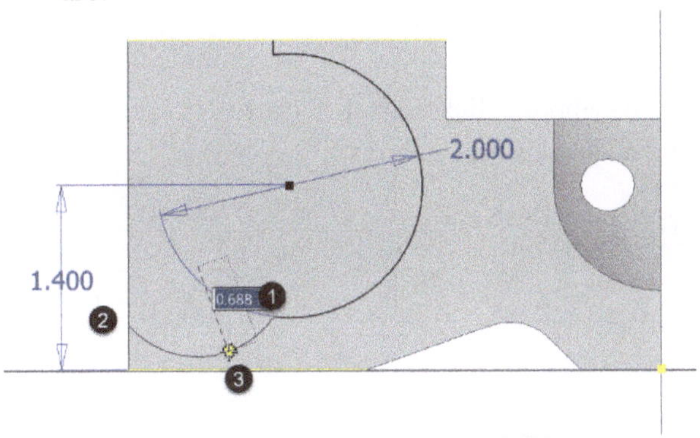

34. Click the **Coincident Constraint** icon on the **Constrain** panel.
35. Select the centerpoint of the new arc.
36. Select the vertical edge.

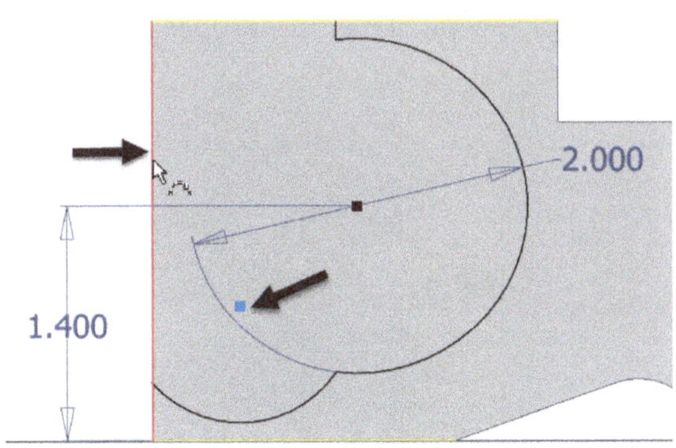

37. Click the **Horizontal Constraint** icon on the **Constrain** panel.
38. Select the centerpoints of the two arcs.

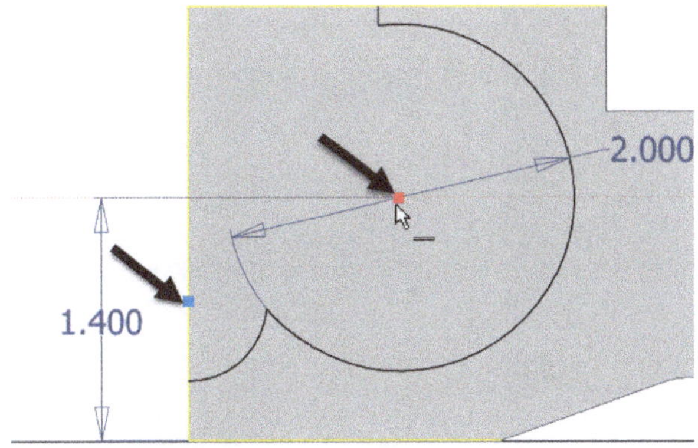

39. Click the **Equal Constraint** icon on the **Constrain** panel.
40. Select the two arcs to make their radius equal.

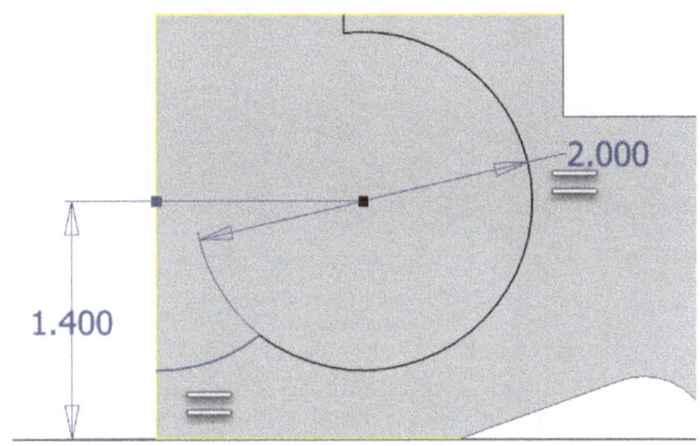

41. Create a horizontal dimension between the centerpoint of the large arc and the vertical edge, as shown.

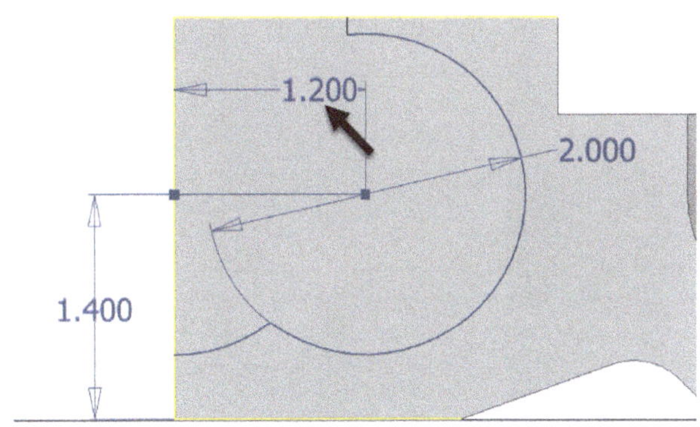

42. Click the **Vertical Constraint** icon on the **Constrain** panel.
43. Select the center point and endpoint of the arc, as shown.

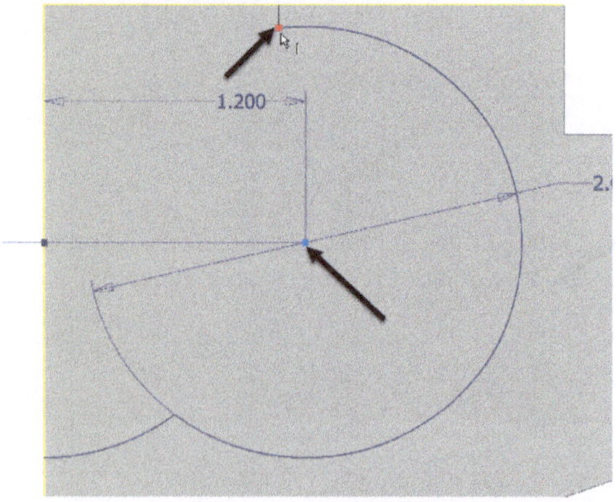

44. Make sure that the **Conicident Constraint** is applied between the endpoint of the small arc and the vertical edge.

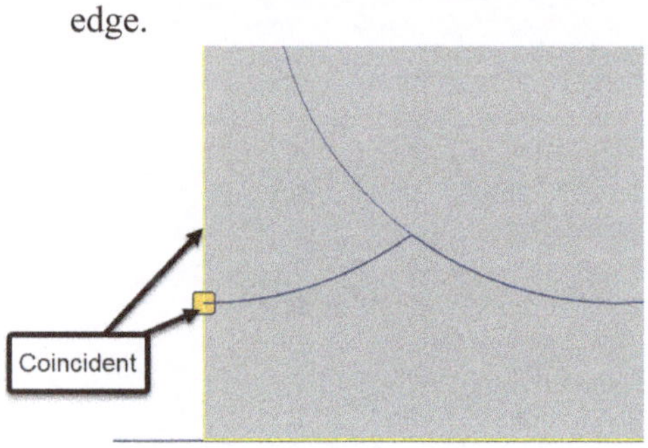

45. Click **Finish** on the **Exit** panel of the **Sketch** tab of the ribbon.
46. On the ribbon, click **3D Model > Create > Extrude**.
47. Click the **Cut** icon under the **Output** section on the **Extrude** Properties panel.
48. Type **0.5** in the **Distance A** box.
49. Click **OK** to create the cut feature.

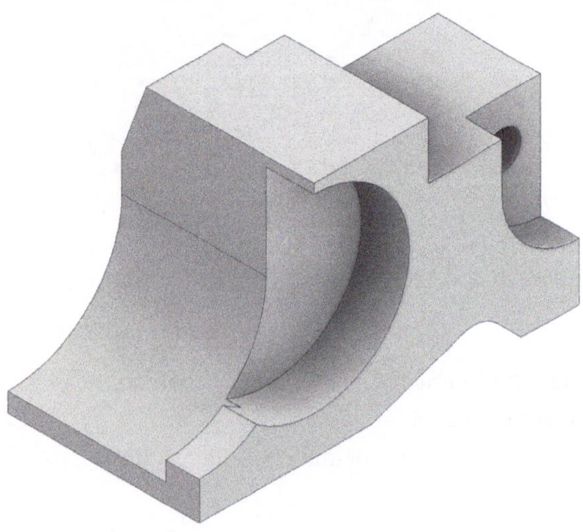

Adding the Extruded Features

1. Click on the flat face of the cut feature.
2. Click the **Create Sketch** icon.

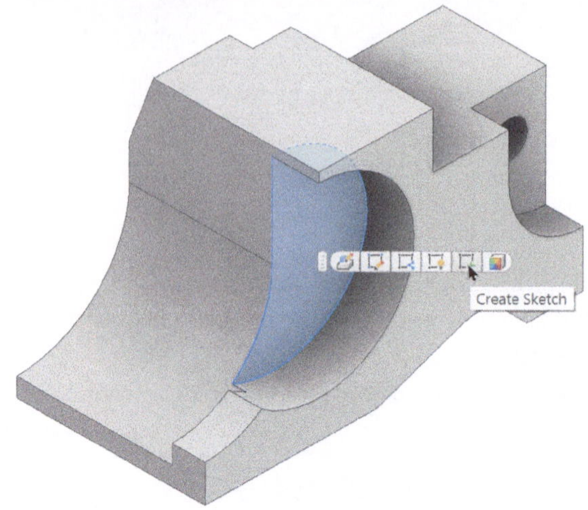

3. On the ribbon, click **Sketch > Create > Arc drop-down > Arc Center Point**.

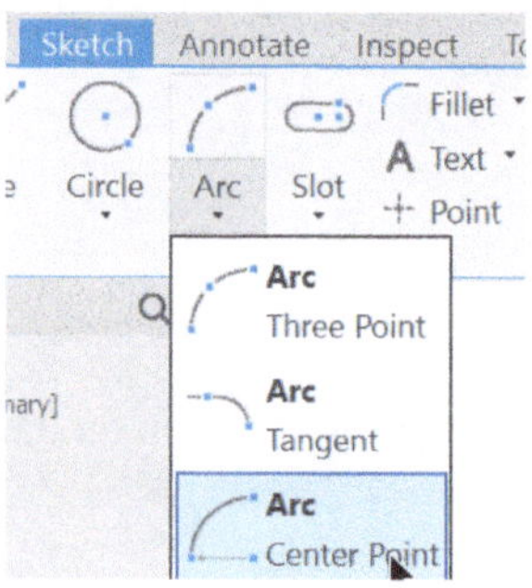

4. Place the pointer on the large circular edge.
5. Select the centerpoint of the circular edge.
6. Click on the vertical edge.

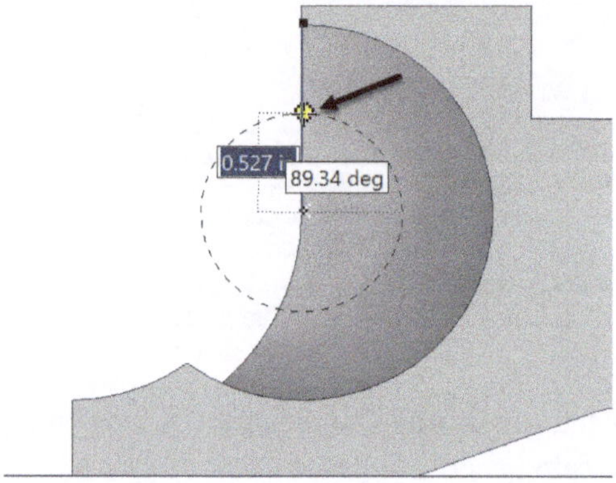

7. Move the pointer toward right and click on the inclined edge.

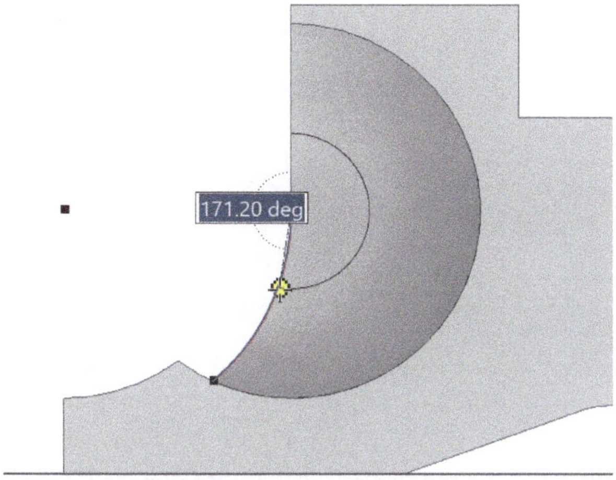

8. Add the radius dimension of value 0.4 to the arc.

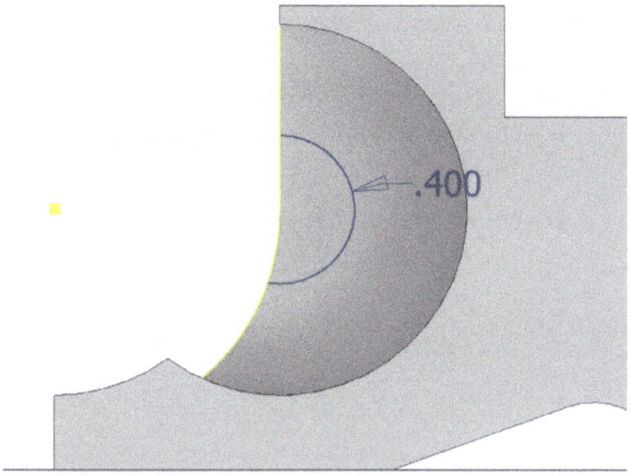

9. Click **Finish** on the **Exit** panel of the **Sketch** tab of the ribbon.
10. On the ribbon, click **3D Model > Create > Extrude**.
11. Type **0.2** in the **Distance A** box.
12. Click **OK** to create the extruded feature.

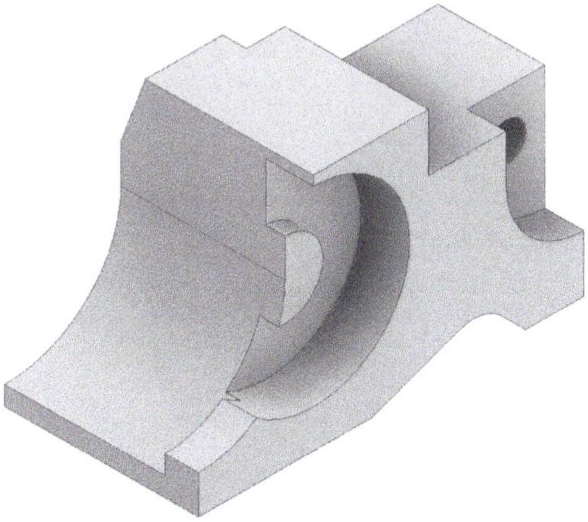

13. Click on the face of the extruded feature, as shown.
14. Click the **Create Sketch** icon.

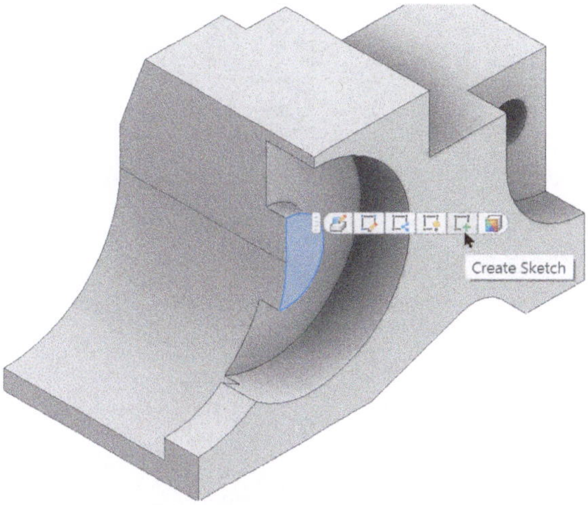

15. On the ribbon, click **Sketch > Create > Circle** drop-down **> Circle Center Point**.
16. Place the pointer on the circular edge.
17. Select the centerpoint of the circular edge.
18. Move the pointer outward.
19. Type 0.4 in the dimension box and press ENTER.
20. Click **Finish** on the **Exit** panel of the **Sketch** tab of the ribbon.
21. On the ribbon, click **3D Model > Create > Extrude**.
22. Click the **To** icon next to the **Distance A** box.
23. Select the right face of the model, as shown.

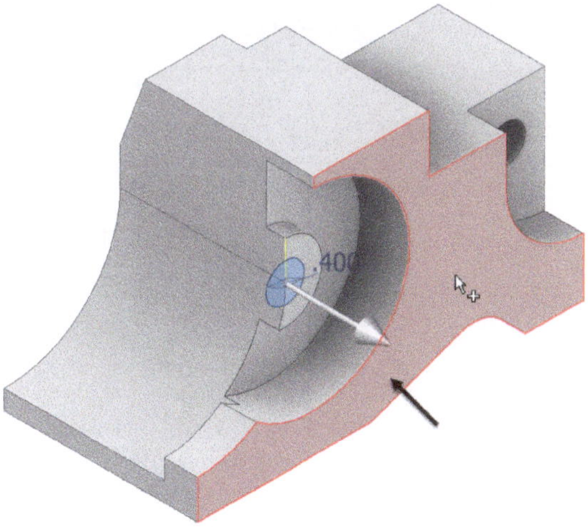

24. Click **OK** to create the extruded feature.

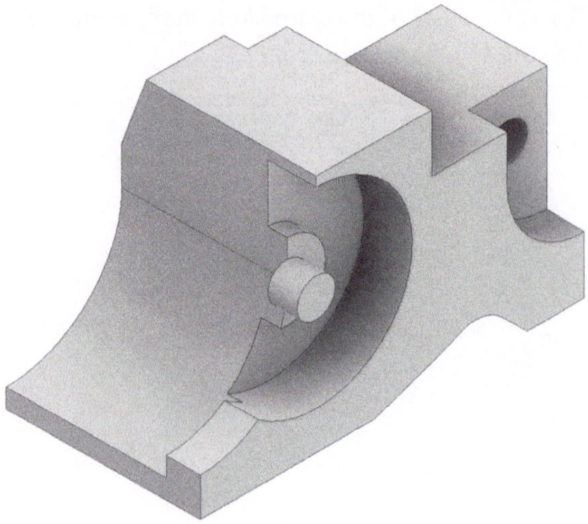

25. Save and close the model.

TUTORIAL 14

In this tutorial, you create the model shown in the figure:

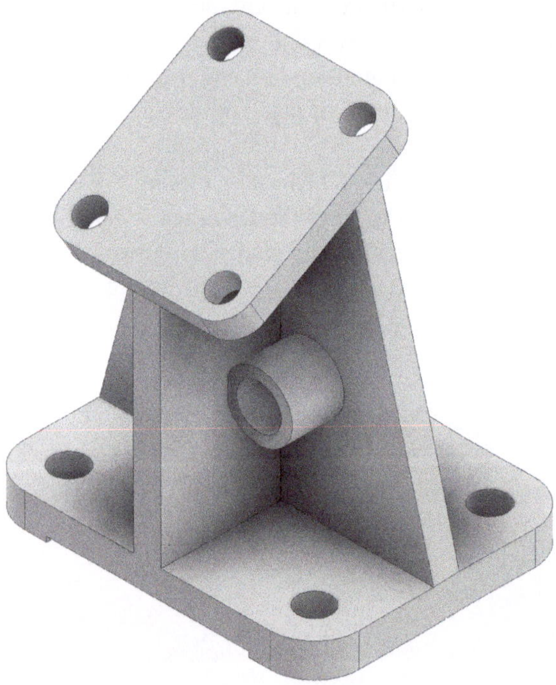

Creating the Base

1. Open a new Part file using the Standard.ipt template.
2. Click the **Start 2D Sketch** icon on the **Sketch** panel of the **3D Model** tab of the ribbon.
3. Select the XZ Plane from the graphics window.

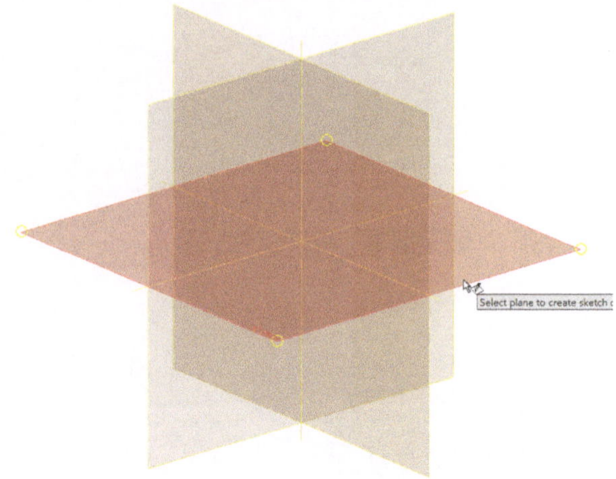

4. Click the **Rectangle** drop-down > **Rectangle Two Point Center** icon on the **Create** panel of the **Sketch** tab of the ribbon.
5. Specify the first and second corners of the rectangle, as shown.
6. Select the sketch origin, move the pointer outward and click. Next, add dimensions to the sketch.

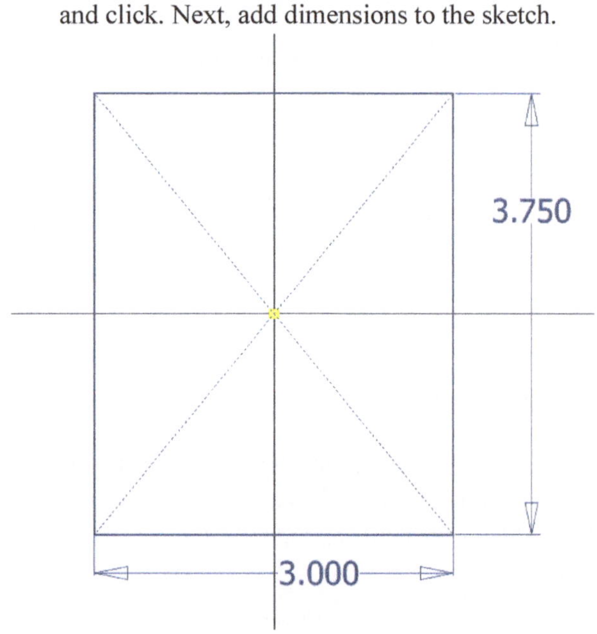

7. Click **Finish** on the **Exit** panel of the **Sketch** tab of the ribbon.
8. On the ribbon, click **3D Model > Create > Extrude**.
9. Set the **Distance A** to **0.38**.
10. Click **OK** to create the first feature.

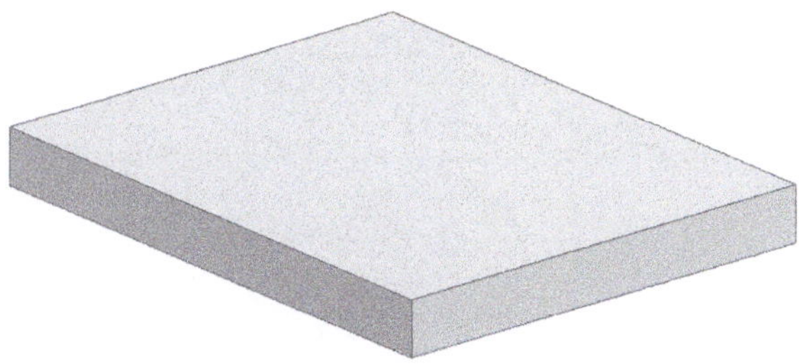

11. Select the front right edge, as shown.
12. Click the **Create fillet** icon.

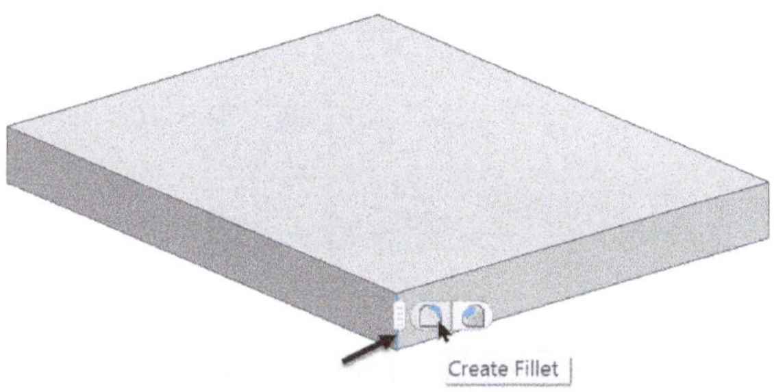

13. Select the front left edge.
14. Likewise, select the back vertical edges of the pad features.
15. Type-in **0.50** in in the **Radius** box.
16. Click **OK** on the **Properties** panel.

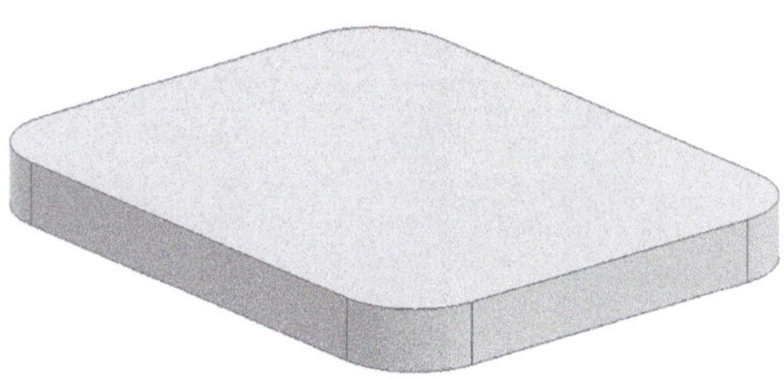

17. On the ribbon, click **Hole** icon on the **Modify** panel.
18. On the **Hole Properties** panel, select **Hole > Simple Hole** from the **Type** section.
19. Select **Seat > None**.
20. Select **Termination > Through all**.
21. Select **Direction > Default**.
22. Set **Diameter** to **0.38**.

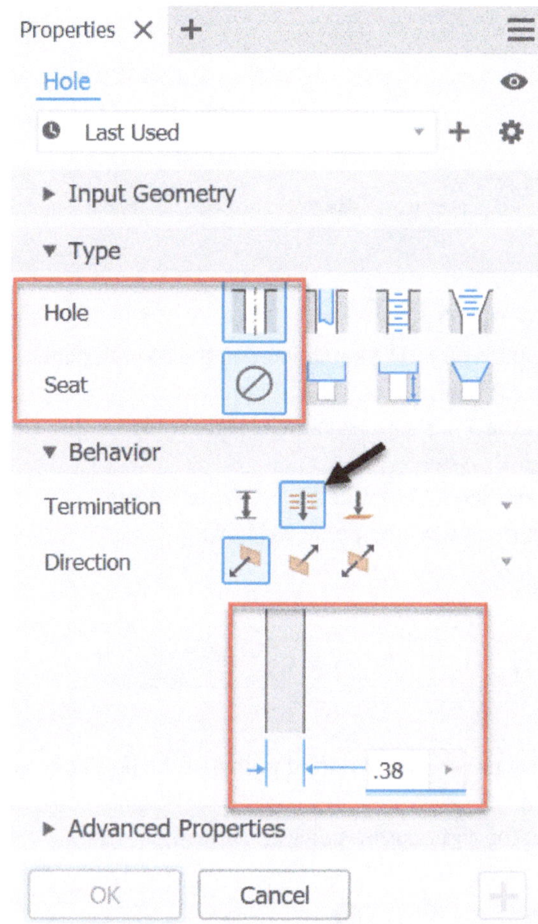

23. Click on the top face of the first feature.
24. Select anyone of the cicular edges; the hole is made concentric to the selected edge.
25. Place another hole and select anyone of the three remaining circular edges. The hole is made concentric to the selected edge.
26. Likewise, place two mode holes concentric to the two remaining circular edges.

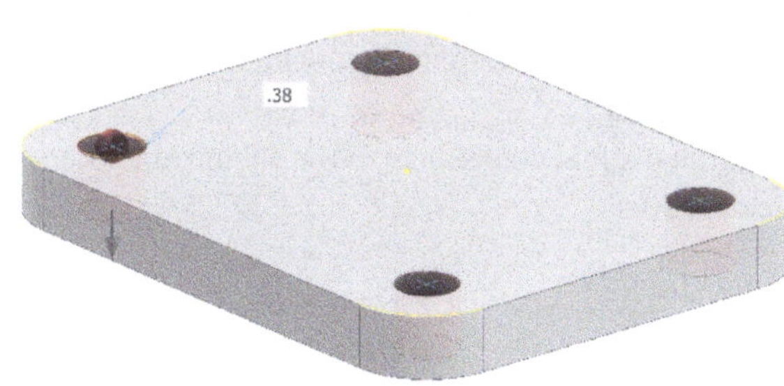

27. Click **OK**.

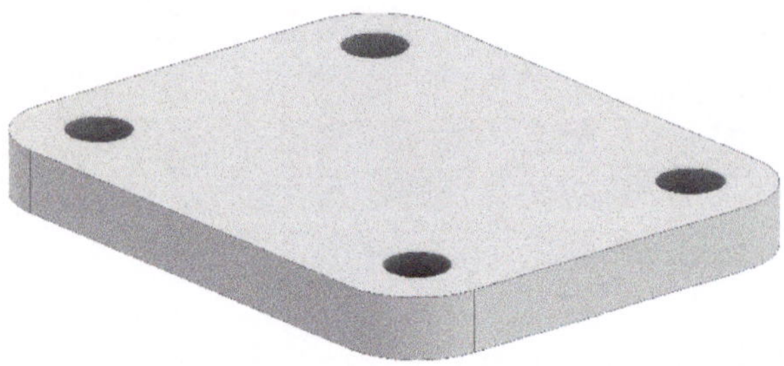

Creating the Rib

1. Click the **Start 2D Sketch** icon on the **Sketch** panel of the **3D Model** tab of the ribbon.
2. Select the XY Plane from the **Origin** folder in the **Model** Browser.
3. On the ribbon, click **Sketch > Create > Line**.
4. Select the left corner point, as shown.

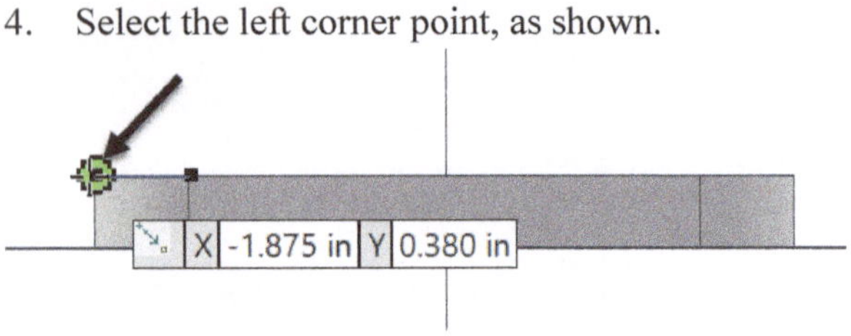

5. Specify the second and third points of the polyline, as shown.
6. Select the right corner point, as shown.

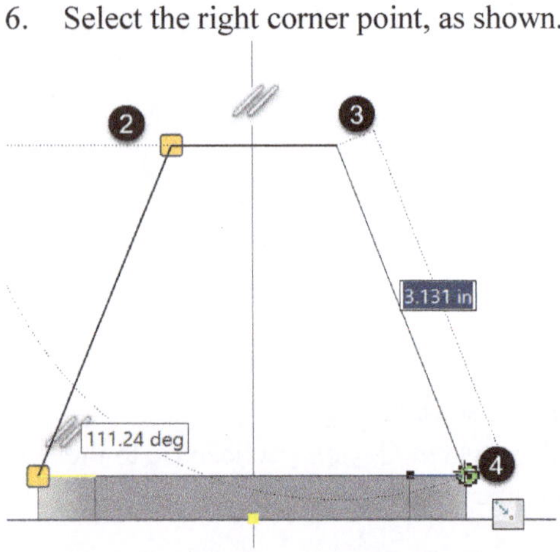

7. Move the pointer horizontally toward left and select the left corner.
8. Add dimensional constraints to the sketch, and then click **Finish**.

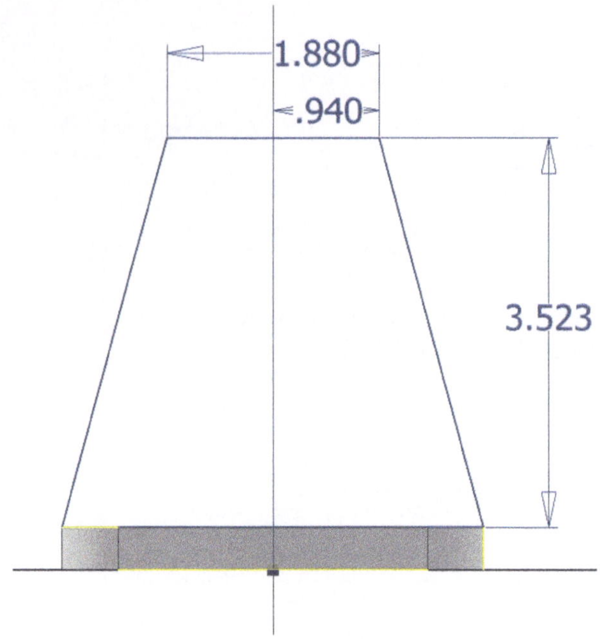

9. On the ribbon, click **3D Model > Create > Extrude**.
10. Click in the region enclosed by the sketch.
11. Select the **Symmetric** option on the **Extrude Properties** panel.
12. Set the **Distance A** to **0.31**.
13. Click **OK** to create the first feature.

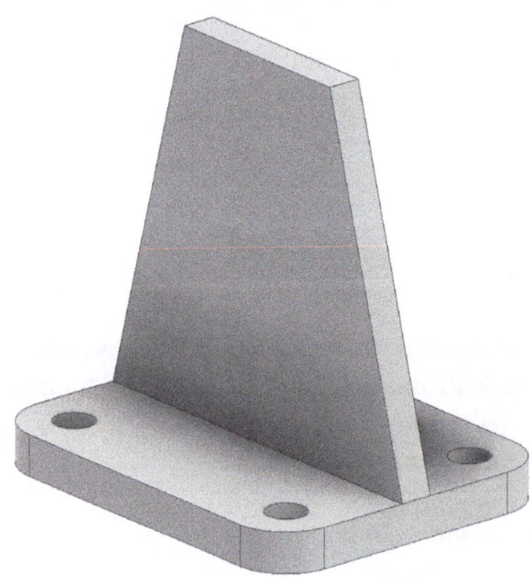

14. Click on the horizontal face of the model, as shown.
15. Click **Create Sketch**.

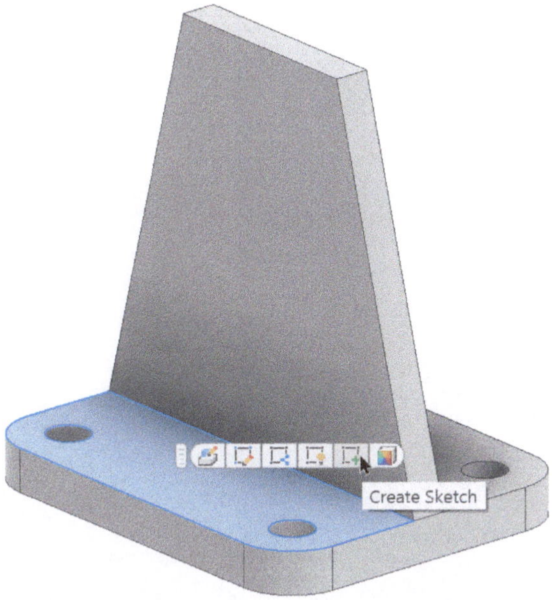

16. On the ribbon, click **Sketch > Create > Rectangle** drop-down **> Rectangle Two Point Center**.
17. Click on the vertical axis of the sketch to define the center of the rectangle.
18. Move the pointer and click on the edge of the second extruded feature.

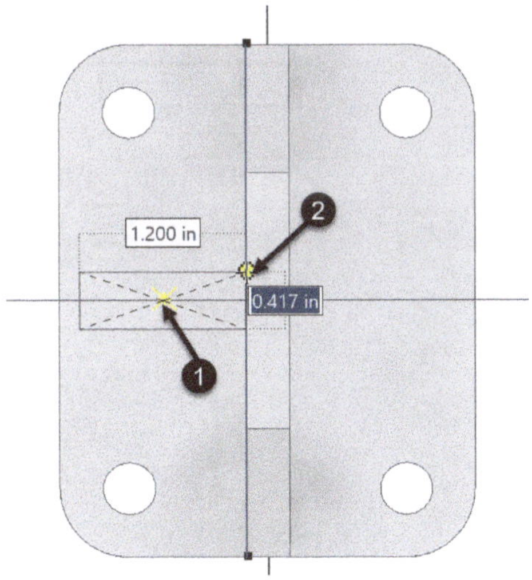

19. On the ribbon, click **Sketch > Constrain > Coincident Constraint**.
20. Select the edge of the base feature and the corner point of the rectangle.

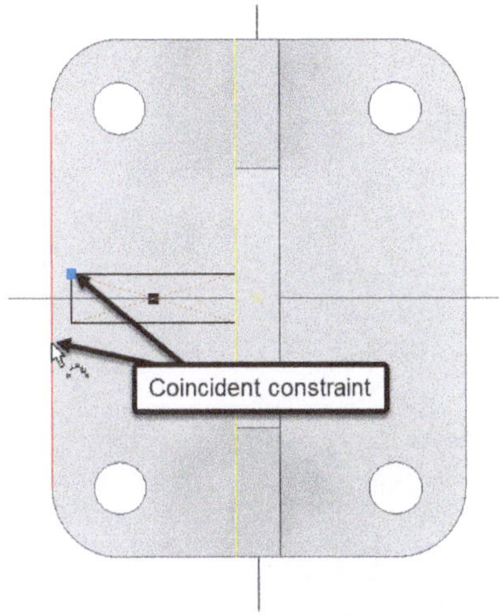

21. Click the **Dimension** icon on the **Constraint** panel and select the width of the rectangle.
22. Place the dimension, type 0.31 and click the green check.
23. On the ribbon, click **Sketch > Constrain > Vertical Constraint**.
24. Select the center of the rectangle and the sketch origin.

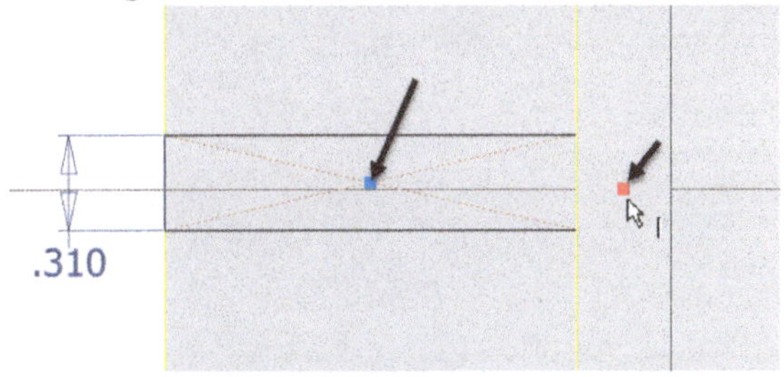

25. Click **Finish** on the **Exit** panel of the **Sketch** tab of the ribbon.
26. On the ribbon, click **3D Model > Create > Extrude**.
27. Click the **To** icon next to the **Distance A** box.
28. Select the top face of the model, as shown.

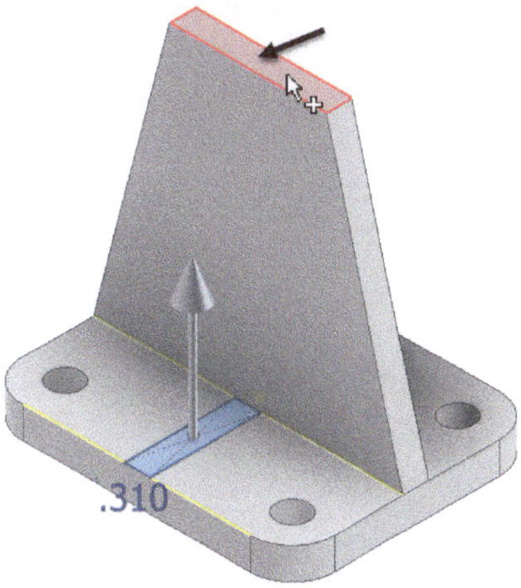

29. Click **OK** to create the extruded feature.

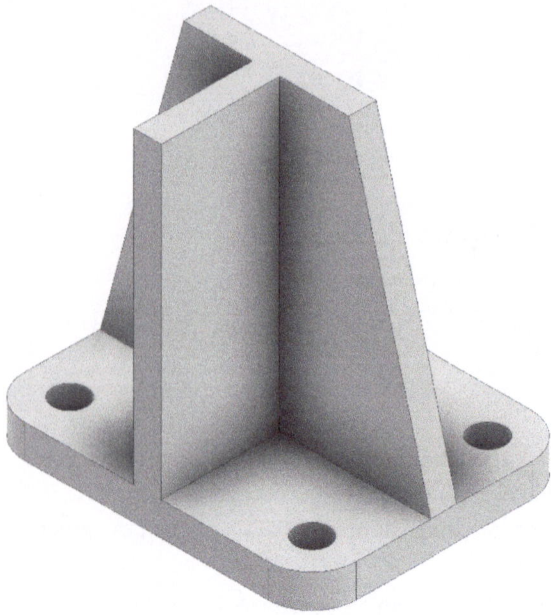

30. In the Model Browser, right-click on the **YZ Plane** and select **New Sketch**.

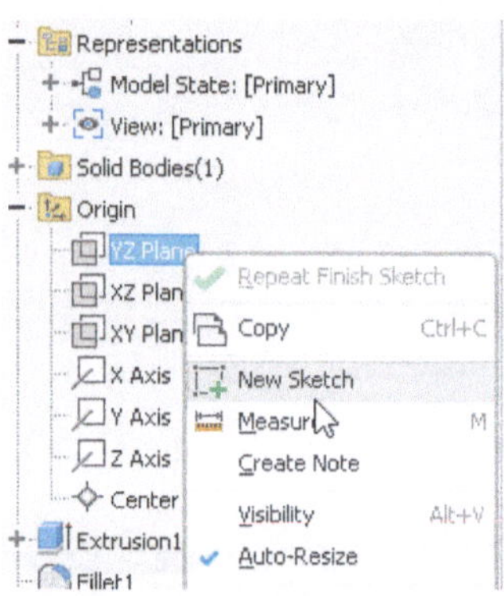

31. Click the **Slice Graphics** button at the bottom of the window.
32. Click the **Line** icon on the **Create** panel of the **Sketch** tab of the ribbon.
33. Create a closed sketch, as shown.

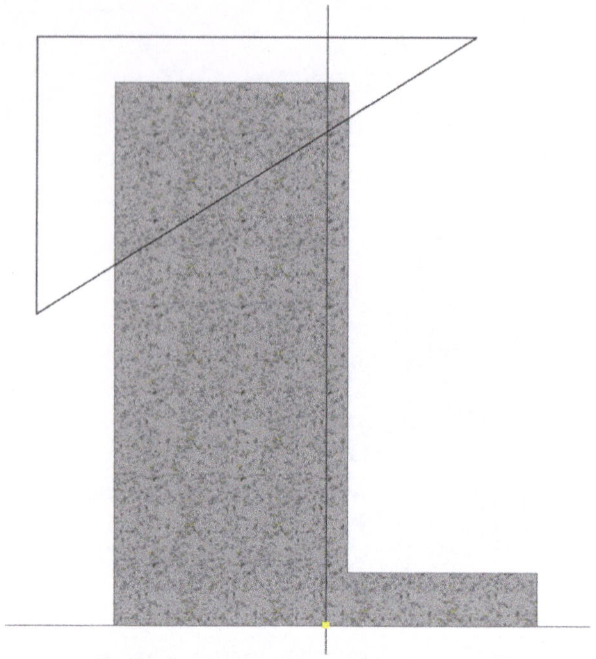

34. Add the Collinear constraint between the horizontal line and the top horizontal edge of the model.
35. Add the Collinear constraint between the vertical line and the left vertical edge of the model.
36. Add the Coincident constraint between the corner point of the sketch and the right vertical edge of the model.

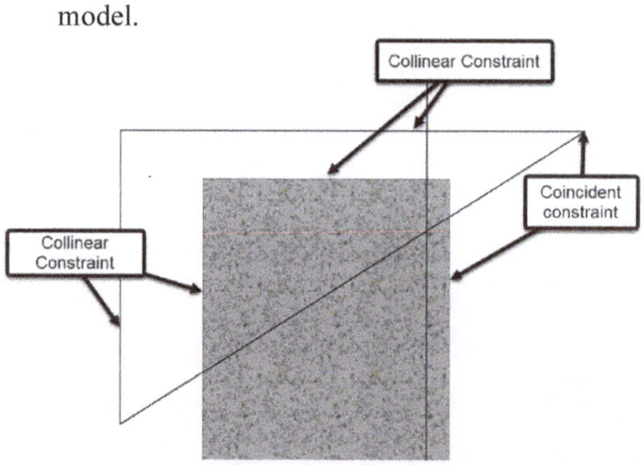

37. Add angular dimension between the inclined and horizontal line, as shown.

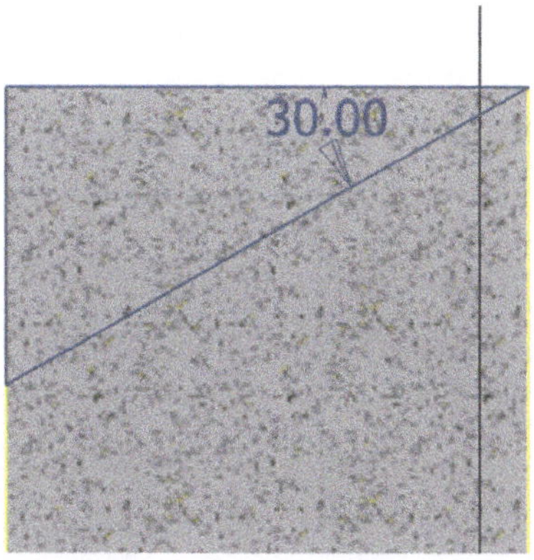

38. Click **Finish** on the **Exit** panel of the **Sketch** tab of the ribbon.
39. On the ribbon, click **3D Model > Create > Extrude**.
40. Click the **Cut** icon under the **Output** section on the **Extrude** Properties panel.
41. Select **Direction > Symmetric**.
42. Click the **Through all** icon next to the **Distance A** box.
43. Click **OK** to create the cut feature.

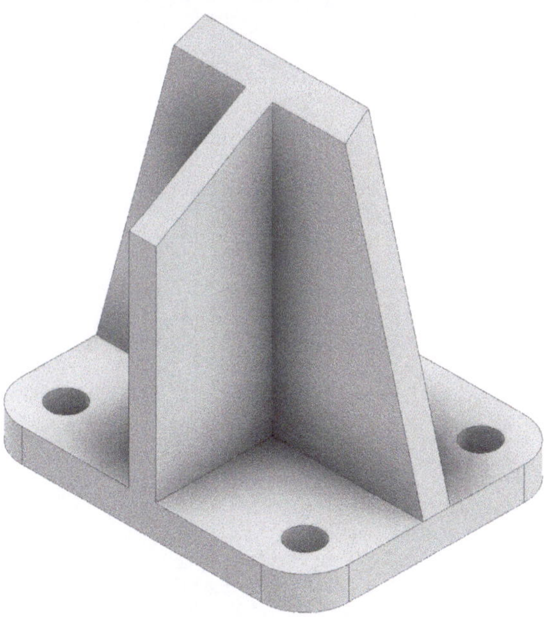

Creating the Third feature

1. Click on the inclined face of the model, as shown.
2. Click the **Create Sketch** icon.

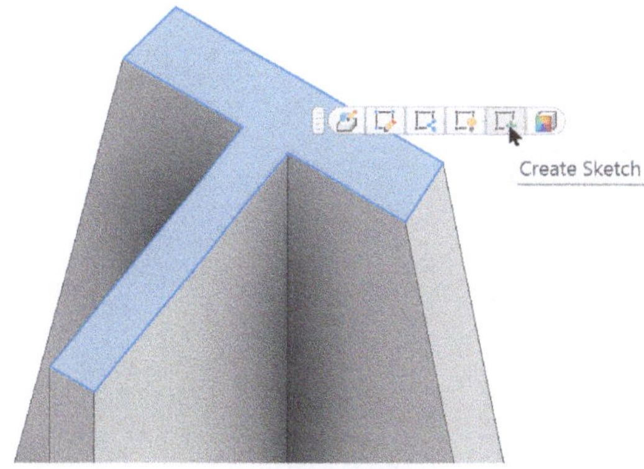

3. Create the rectangle and add dimensions to it, as shown.

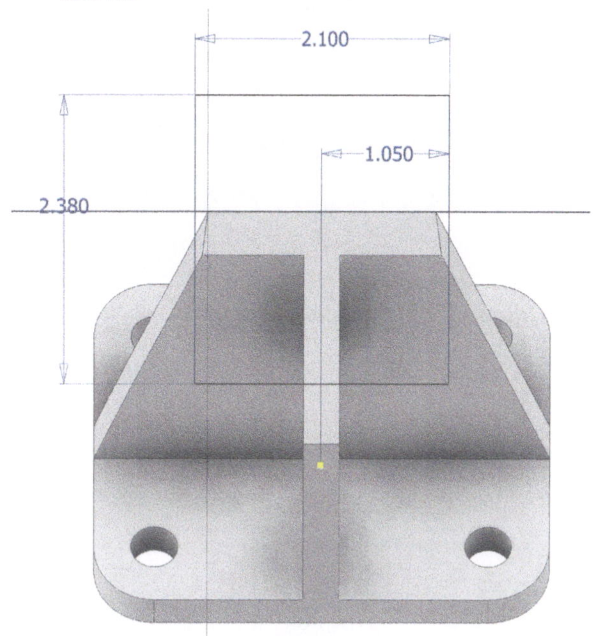

4. On the ribbon, click **Sketch > Constrain > Collinear Constraint**.
5. Select the lower horizontal line of the sketch.
6. Select the horizontal edge of the model, as shown.

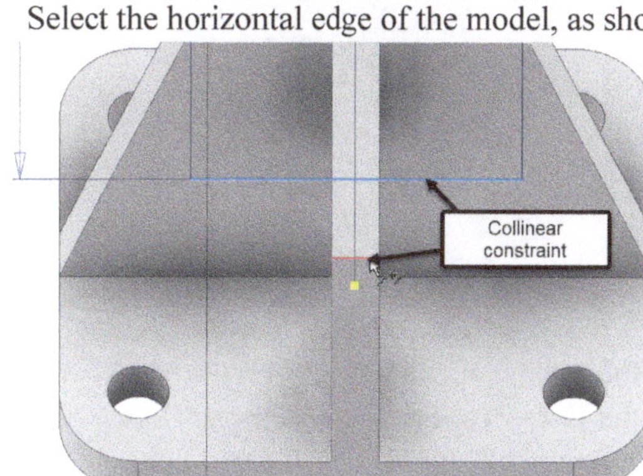

7. Right-click and select **Finish 2D Sketch**.
8. On the ribbon, click **3D Model > Create > Extrude**.

9. Set the **Distance A** to **0.31**.
10. Click **OK** to create the first feature.

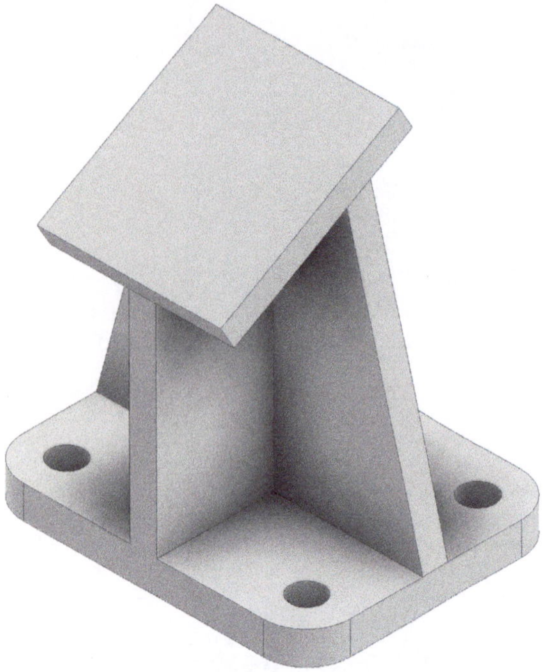

11. Add fillets of 0.31 in radius, as shown.

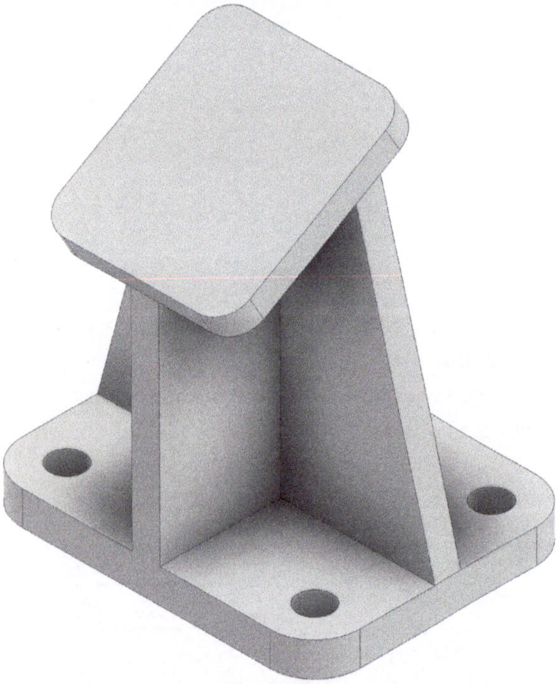

12. On the ribbon, click **Hole** icon on the **Modify** panel.
13. On the **Hole Properties** panel, select **Hole > Simple Hole** from the **Type** section.
14. Select **Seat > None**.
15. Select **Direction > Default**.
16. Set **Diameter** to **0.31**.
17. Click on the inclined face, as shown.
18. Select anyone of the circular edges; the hole is made concentric to the selected edge.
19. Place another hole and select anyone of the three remaining circular edges. The hole is made concentric to the selected edge.
20. Likewise, place two mode holes concentric to the two remaining circular edges.

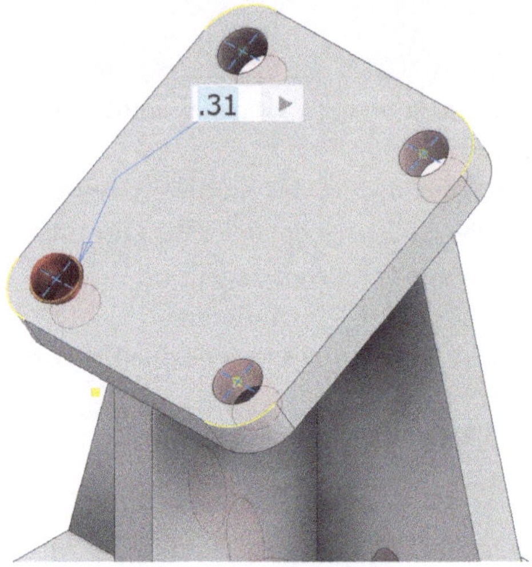

21. Select **Termination > To**.
22. Select the bottom face of the inclined extruded feature.

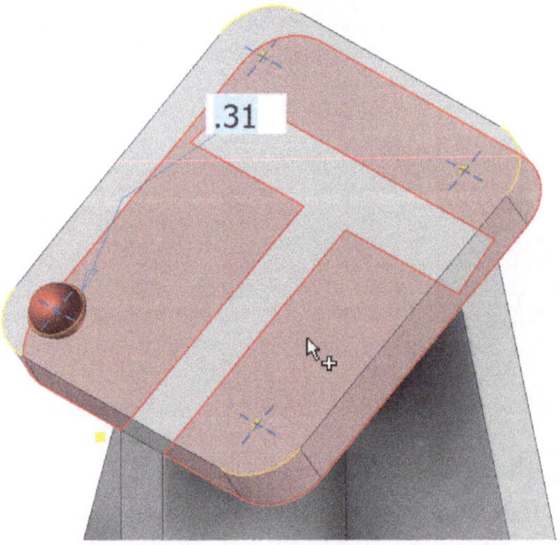

Notice various **Drill Point** options on the Hole Properties panel.

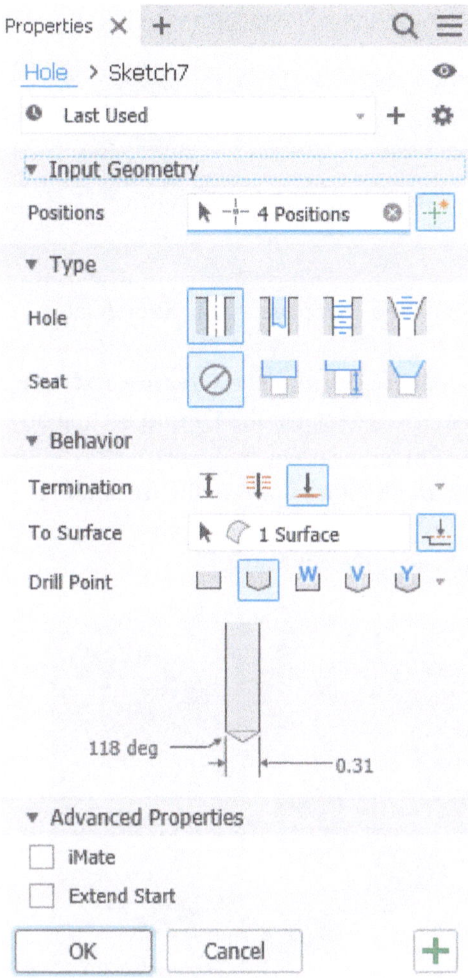

23. Leave the default **Drill Point** option and click **OK**.

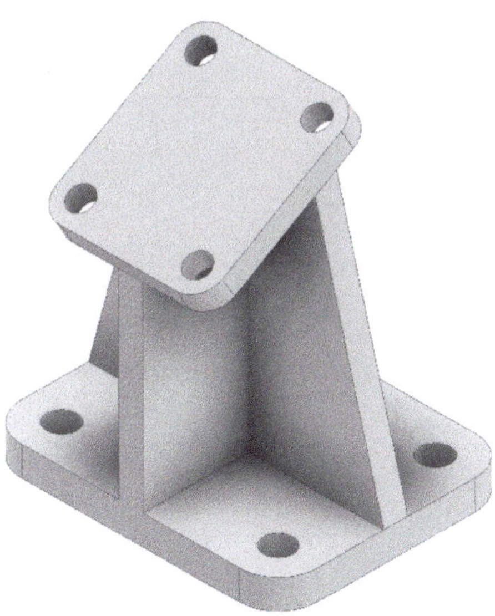

24. Click on the vertical face, as shown.

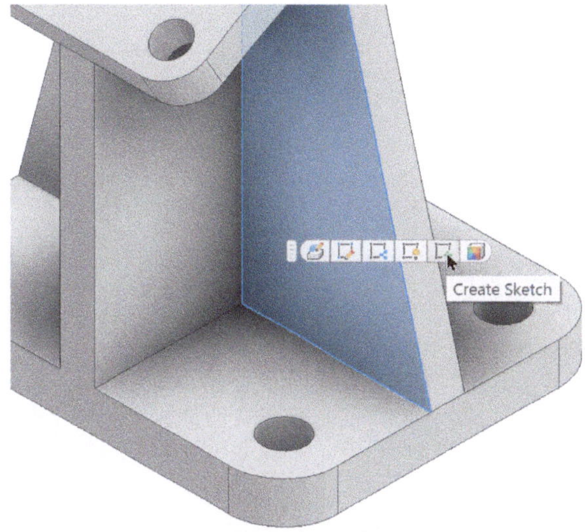

25. Click the **Create Sketch** icon.
26. Create two circles and add dimensions to it, as shown.

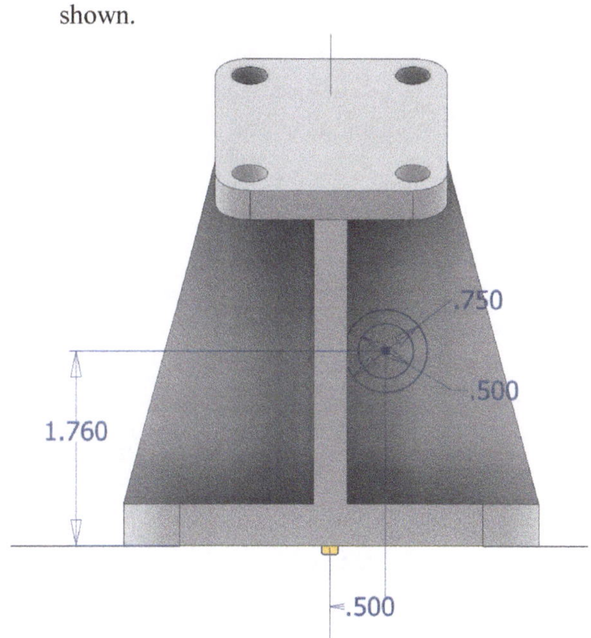

27. Click **Finish** on the **Exit** panel of the **Sketch** tab of the ribbon.
28. On the ribbon, click **3D Model > Create > Extrude**.
29. Click in the region enclosed by the two circles.
30. Select **Direction > Asymmetric**.
31. Type **0.59** in the **Distance A** box.
32. Type **0.79** in the **Distance B** box and click **OK**.

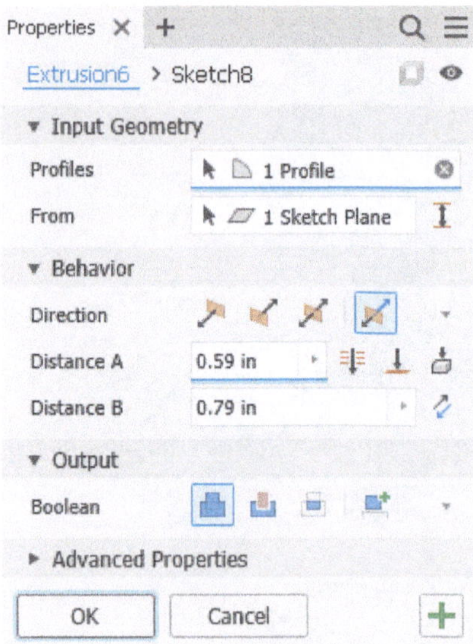

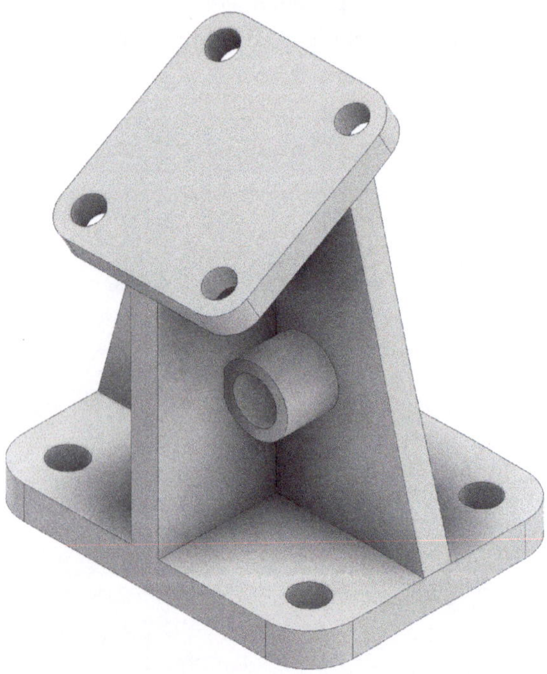

Creating the Cut Feature

1. Click on the vertical face, as shown.
2. Click the **Create Sketch** icon.

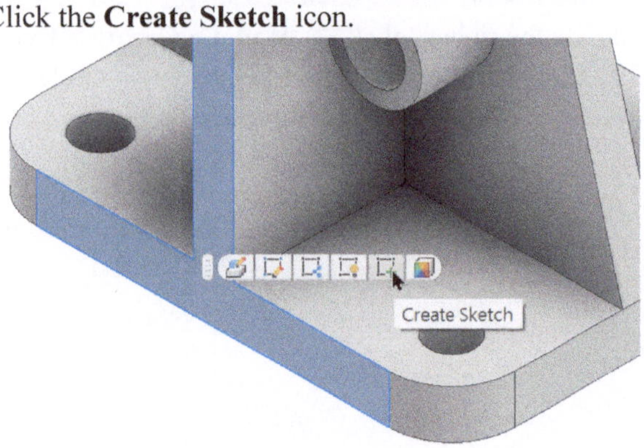

3. Create a rectangle and add dimensions to it.

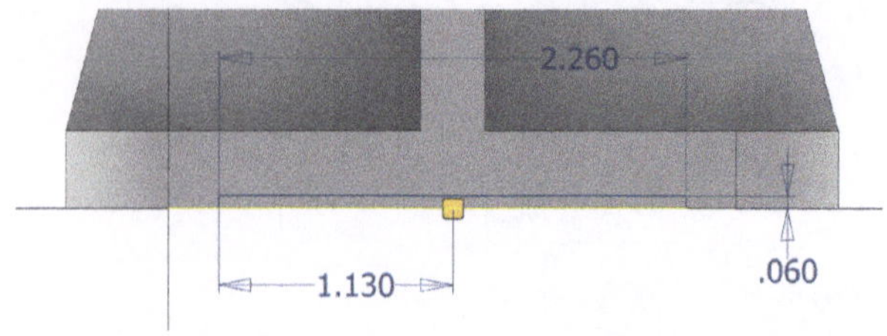

4. Click **Finish** on the **Exit** panel of the **Sketch** tab of the ribbon.
5. On the ribbon, click **3D Model > Create > Extrude**.
6. Click the **Cut** icon under the **Output** section on the **Extrude** Properties panel.
7. Click the **Through all** icon next to the **Distance A** box.
8. Click **OK** to create the cut feature.

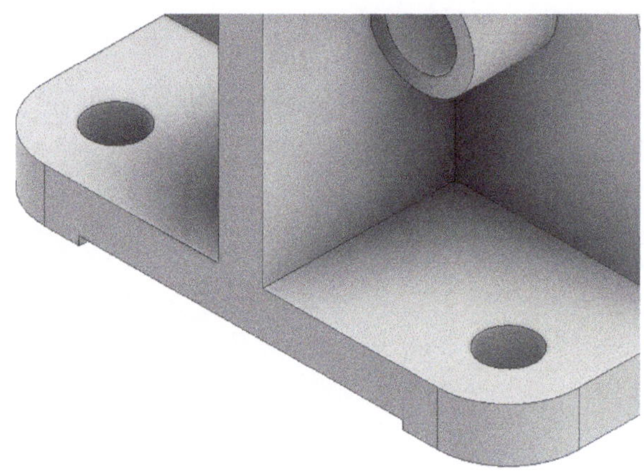

9. Save and close the file.

Chapter 7: Sheet Metal Modeling

This chapter will show you:

- Create a face feature
- Create a Flange
- Create a Contour Flange
- Create a Corner Seam
- Create Punches
- Create a Bend Feature
- Create Corner Rounds
- Flat Pattern

TUTORIAL 1

In this tutorial, you create the sheet metal model shown in the figure.

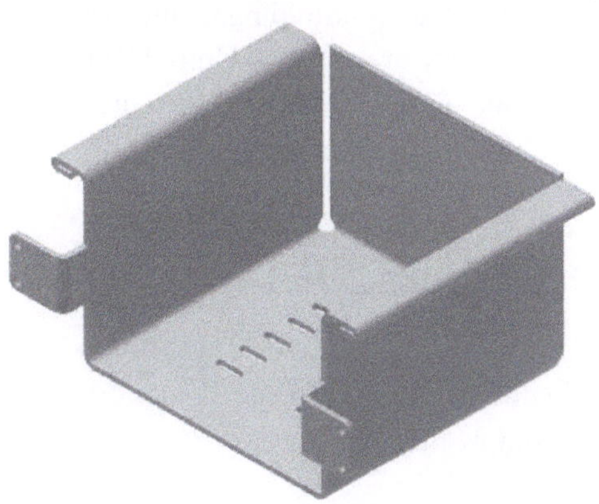

Starting a New Sheet metal File

1. To start a new sheet metal file, click **Get Started Launch > New** on the ribbon.
2. On the **Create New File** dialog, click the **Sheet Metal.ipt** icon, and then click **Create**.

Setting the Parameters of the Sheet Metal part

1. To set the parameters, click **Sheet Metal > Setup > Sheet Metal Defaults** on the ribbon; the **Sheet Metal Defaults** dialog appears.

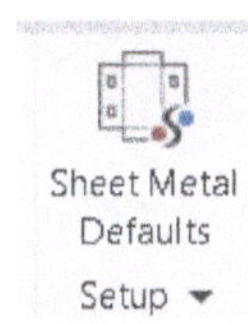

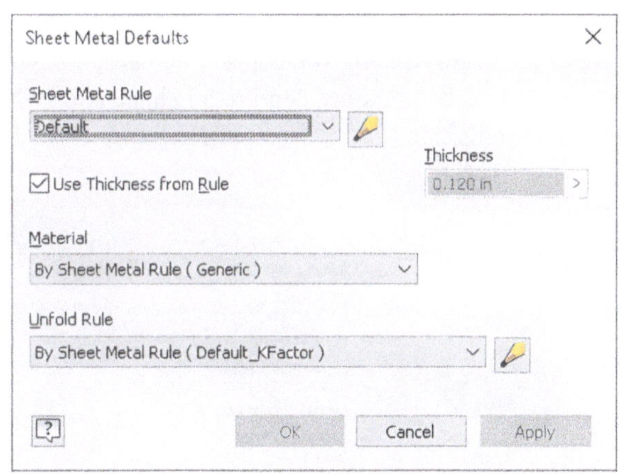

This dialog displays the default preferences of the sheet metal part, such as sheet metal rule, thickness, material, and unfold rule. You can change these preferences as per your requirement.

2. To edit the sheet metal rule, click the **Edit Sheet Metal Rule** button on the dialog.

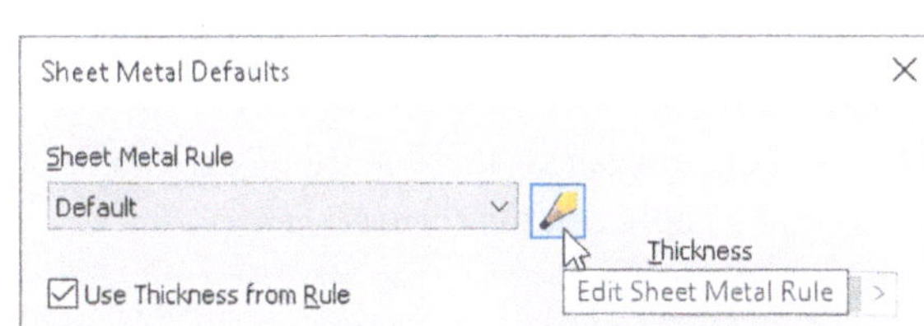

In the **Sheet** tab of the **Style and Standard Editor** dialog, you can set the sheet preferences such as sheet thickness, material, flat pattern bend angle representation, flat pattern punch representation, and gap size.

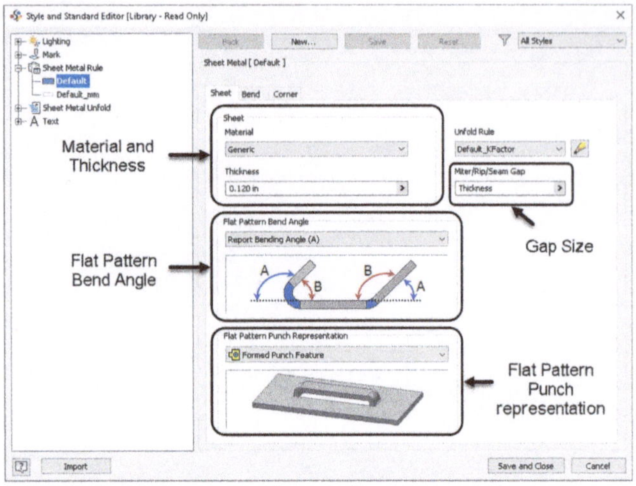

3. In the **Sheet** tab, set the **Thickness** to **0.12** and leave all the default settings.
4. Click the **Bend** tab.

In the **Bend** tab of this dialog, you can set the bend preferences such as bend radius, bend relief shape and size, and bend transition.

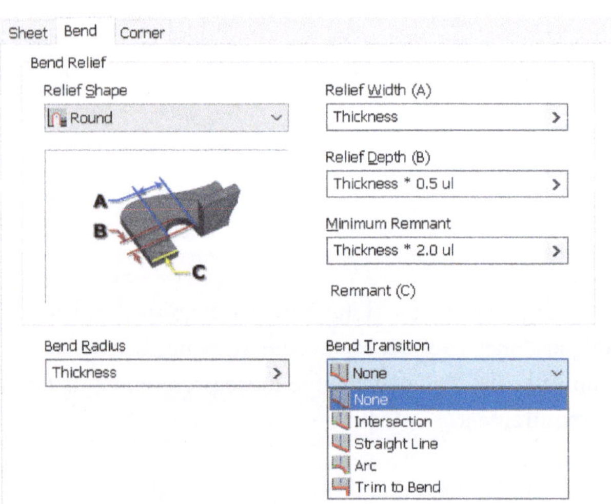

5. Set the **Relief Shape** to **Round**.
6. Click the **Corner** tab.

In the **Corner** tab, you can set the shape and size of the corner relief to be applied at the corners.

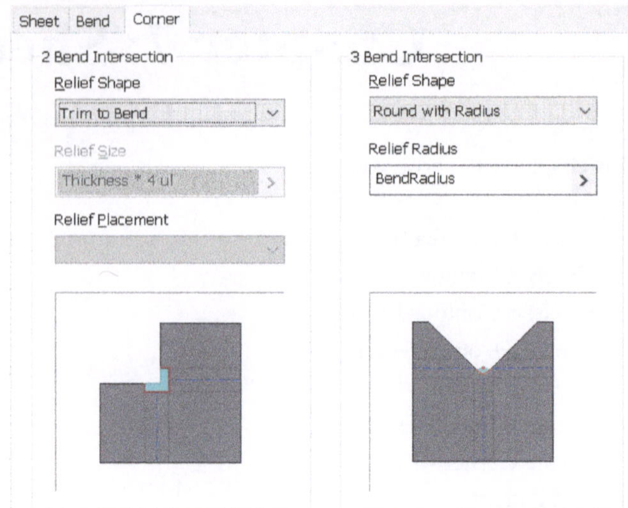

7. After setting the required preferences, click the **Save and Close** button.

The **Unfold Rule** option on the **Sheet Metal Defaults** dialog defines the folding/unfolding method of the sheet metal part. To modify or set a new Unfold Rule, click the **Edit Unfold Rule** button on the **Sheet Metal Defaults** dialog.

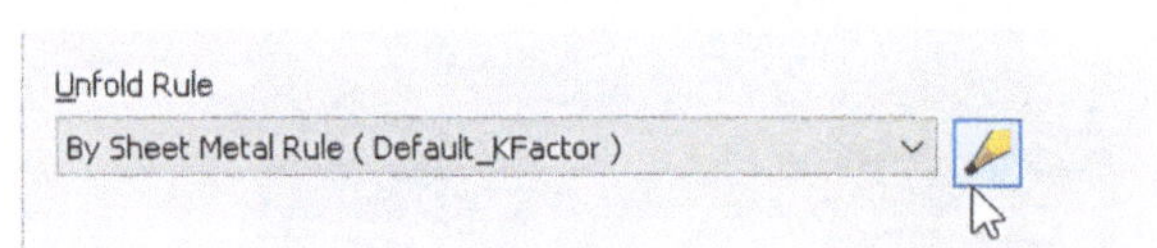

On the **Style and Standard Editor** dialog, select the required **Unfold Method**.

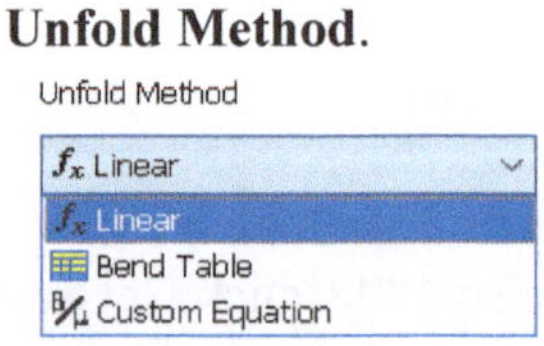

You can define the Unfold rule by selecting the **Linear** method (specifying the K factor), selecting a **Bend Table**, or entering a custom equation. Click **Save and Close** after setting the parameters.

8. Close the **Sheet Metal Defaults** dialog.

Creating the Base Feature

1. Create the sketch on the XZ Plane, as shown in figure (Use the **Rectangle Two Point Center** tool).

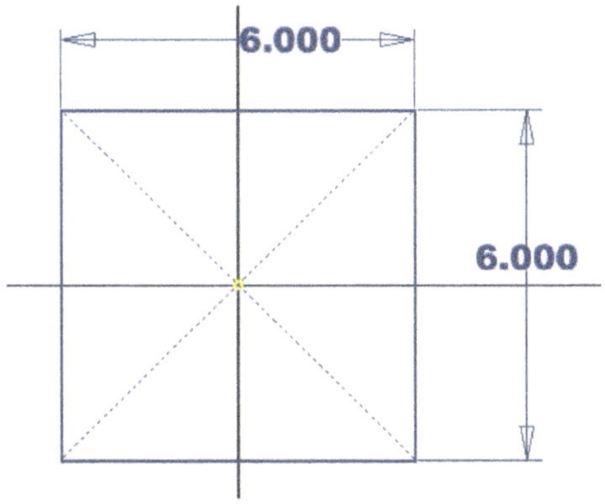

2. Click **Finish** on the ribbon.
3. To create the base component, click **Sheet Metal > Create > Face** on the ribbon; the **Face** dialog appears.

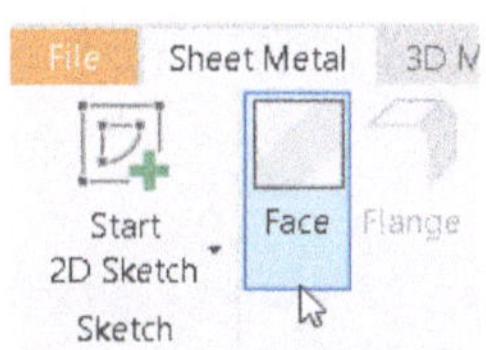

4. Click **OK** to create the tab feature.

Creating the flange

1. To create the flange, click **Sheet Metal > Create > Flange** on the ribbon; the **Flange** dialog appears.

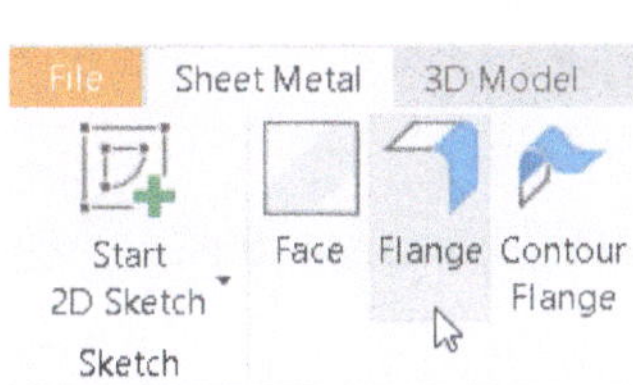

2. Select the edge on the top face, as shown.

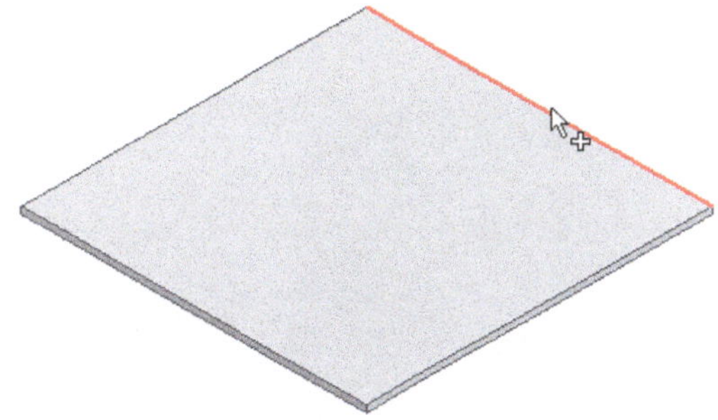

3. Set the **Distance** to 4.
4. Click on the **From the intersection of the two outer faces** icon. This measures the flange height from the outer face.
5. Under the **Angle and Placement** section, click **Placement > Plane through partner edge**.
6. Select **Position > Outer face through plane**.

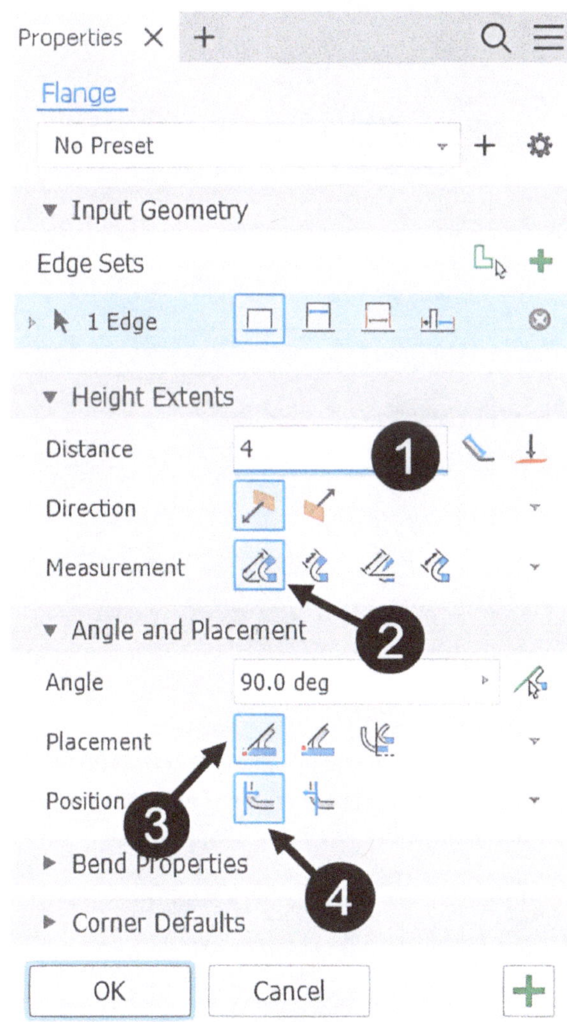

7. Click **OK** to create the flange.

Creating the Contour Flange

1. Draw a sketch on the front face of the flange, as shown in the figure.

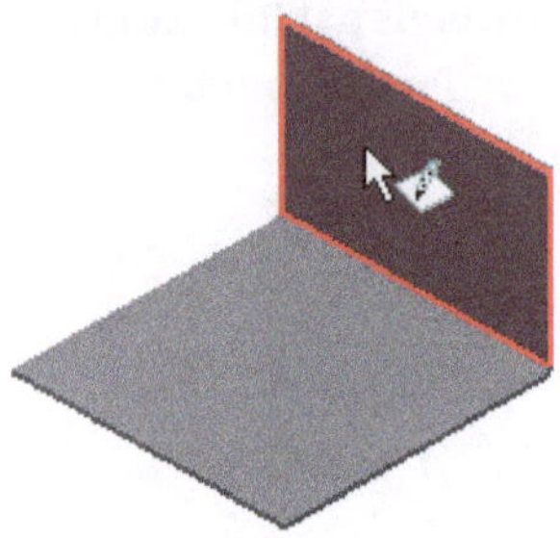

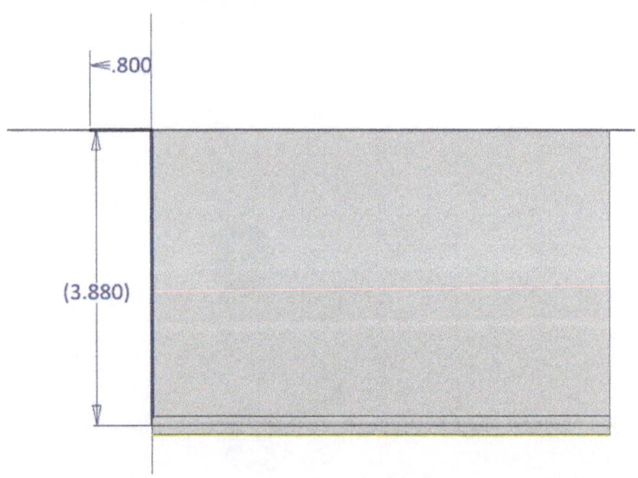

2. Click **Finish** on the ribbon.
3. To create the contour flange, click **Sheet Metal > Create > Contour Flange** on the ribbon; the **Contour Flange** Properties panel appears.

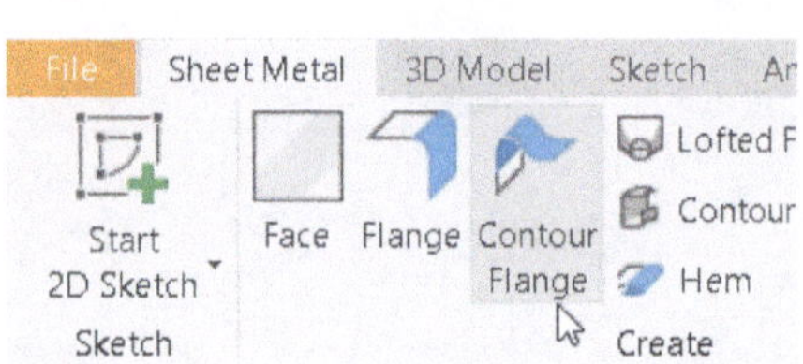

4. Select the sketch from the model.
5. Select **Along selected edge** icon of **Width Extents** under the **Behavior** section.

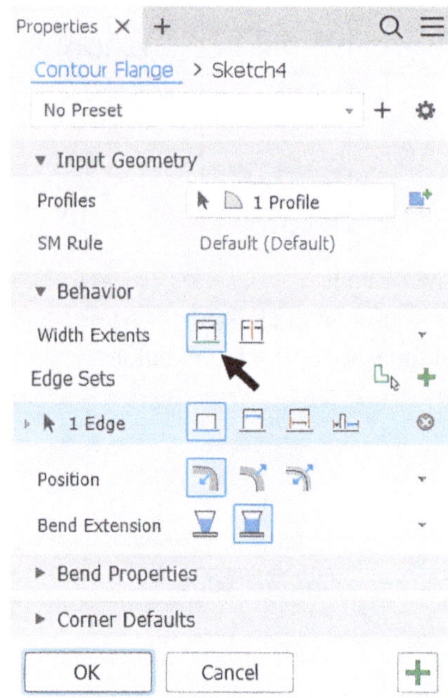

6. Select the edge on the left side of the top face; the contour flange preview appears.

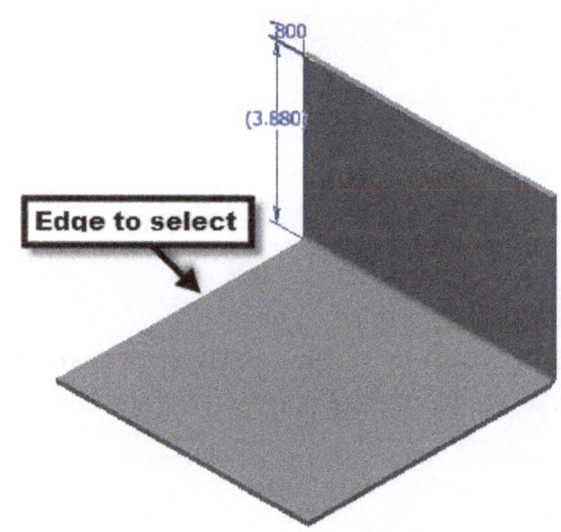

7. Select **Position > Flipped** icon under the **Behavior** section.

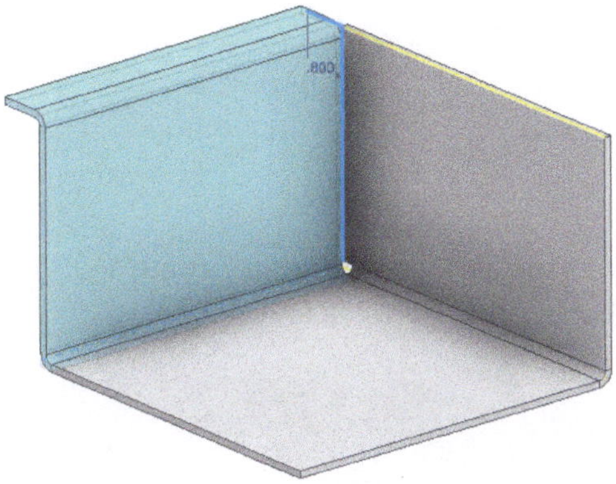

8. Click **OK** to create the contour flange.

Creating the Corner Seam

1. To create the corner seam, click **Sheet Metal> Modify > Corner Seam** on the ribbon; the **Corner Seam** dialog appears.

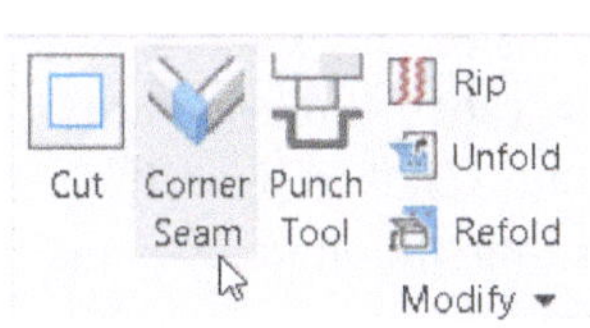

2. Rotate the model.
3. Select the two edges forming the corner.

4. Set the parameters in the **Shape** tab of the dialog, as shown.

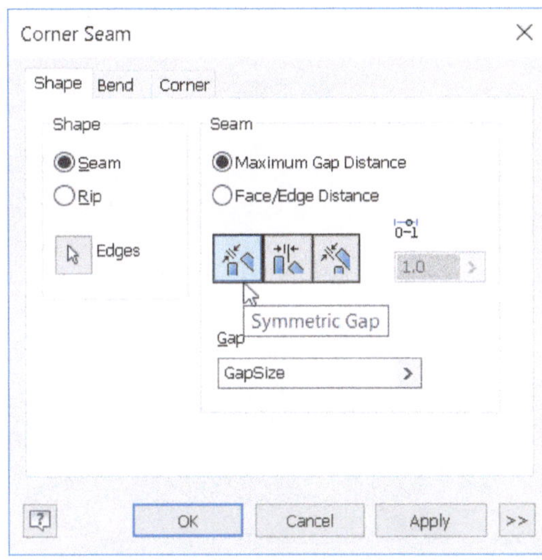

5. Click the **Bend** tab and make sure that the **Default** option is selected in the **Bend Transition** drop-down.
6. Click the **Corner** tab and set the **2 Bend Relief Shape** to **Round**.

You can also apply other types of relief using the options in the **Relief Shape** drop-down.

7. Click **OK**.

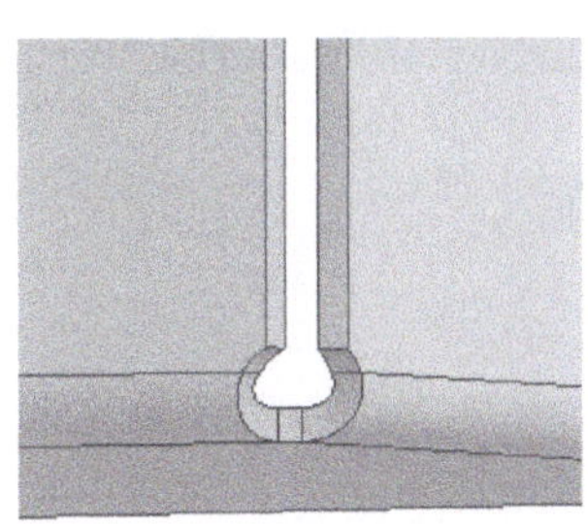

Creating a Sheet Metal Punch iFeature

1. Open a new sheet metal file using the **Sheet Metal.ipt** template.

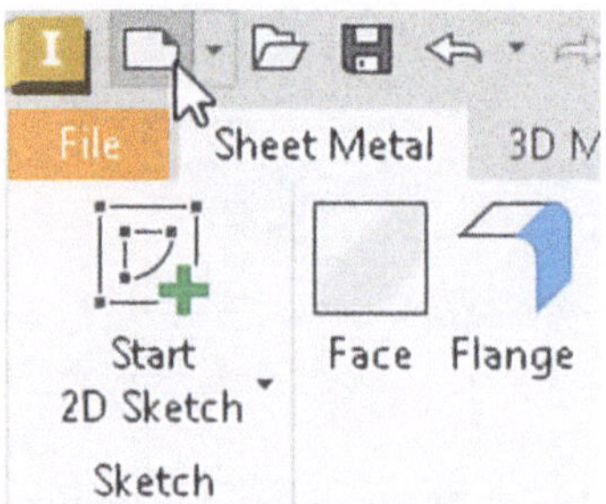

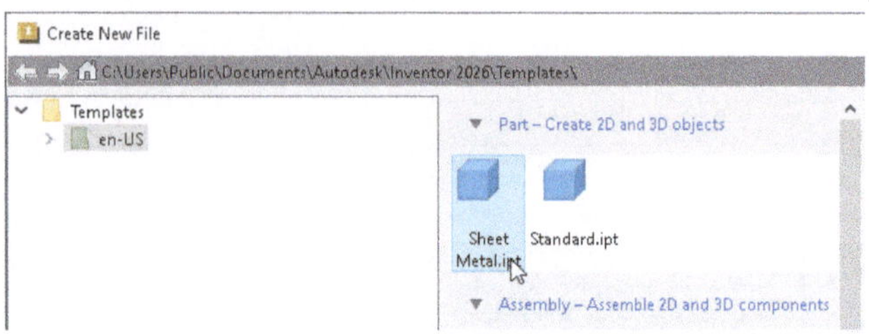

2. Create a sheet metal face of the dimensions 4x4.

3. Click **Manage > Parameters > Parameters** *fx* on the ribbon; the **Parameters** dialog appears.
4. Select the **User Parameters** row and click the **Add Numeric** button on the dialog. This adds a new row.

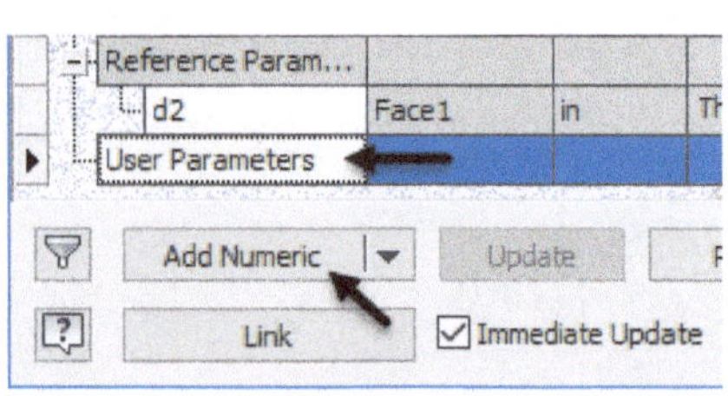

5. Enter **Diameter** in the new row.
6. Set **Unit Type** to **in** and type-in 0.04 in the **Equation** box.

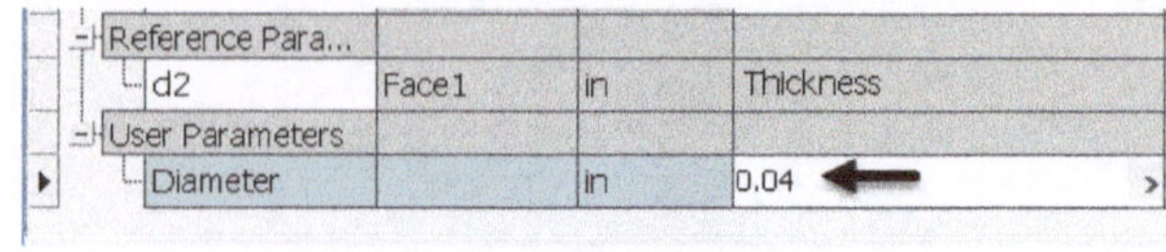

7. Likewise, create a parameter named **Length** and specify its values, as shown below.

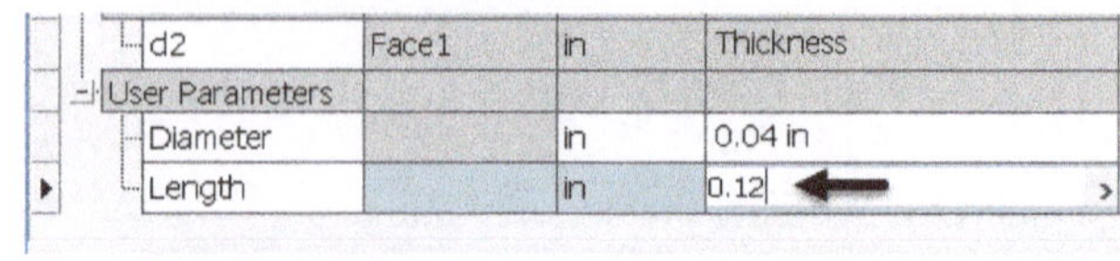

8. Click **Done**.
9. Click **Sheet Metal > Sketch > Start 2D Sketch** on the ribbon.
10. Select the top face of the base feature.
11. On the ribbon, click **Sketch > Create > Rectangle** drop-down **> Slot Center to Center**.
12. Click anywhere to define the first center point of the slot.
13. Move the cursor horizontally and click to define the second center point of the slot.
14. Move the cursor outward and click to define the slot radius.

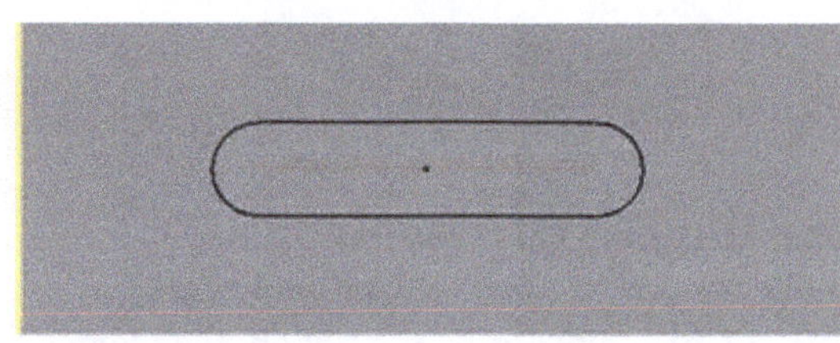

15. Click **Dimension** on the **Constrain** panel and select the round end of the slot.
16. Click to display the **Edit Dimension** box.
17. Click the arrow button on the box and select **List User Parameters** from the shortcut menu; the **Parameters** list appears.

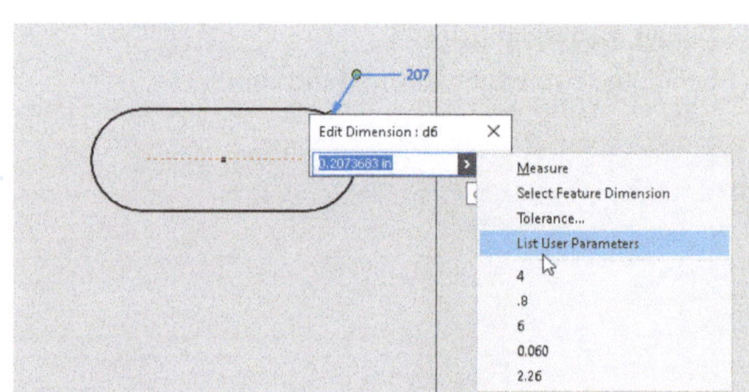

18. Select **Diameter** from the list and click the green check on the **Edit Dimension** box.

19. Likewise, dimension the horizontal line of the slot and set the parameter to **Length**.

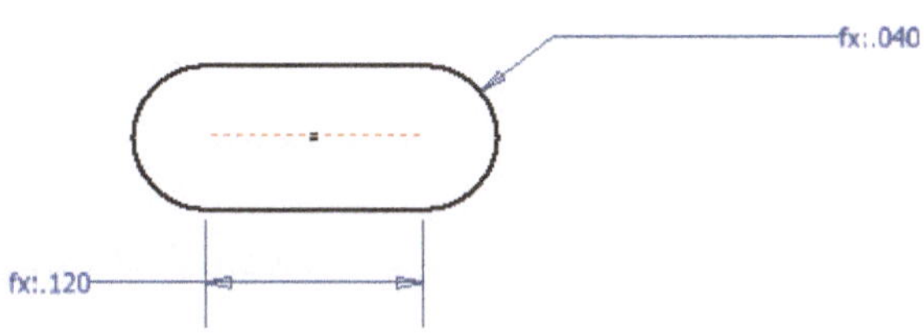

20. Click the **Point** button on the **Create** panel and place it at the center of the slot.
21. Delete any projected edges (yellow lines) from the sketch.
22. Click **Finish** on the ribbon.
23. Click **Sheet Metal > Modify > Cut** on the ribbon; the **Cut** Properties panel appears.

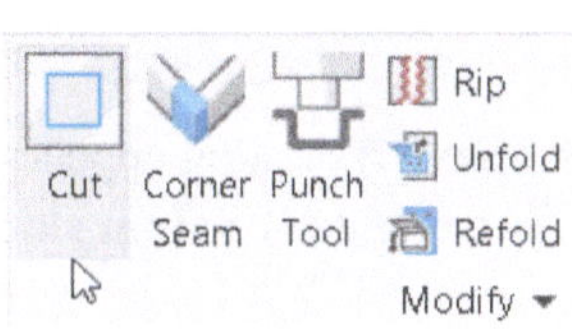

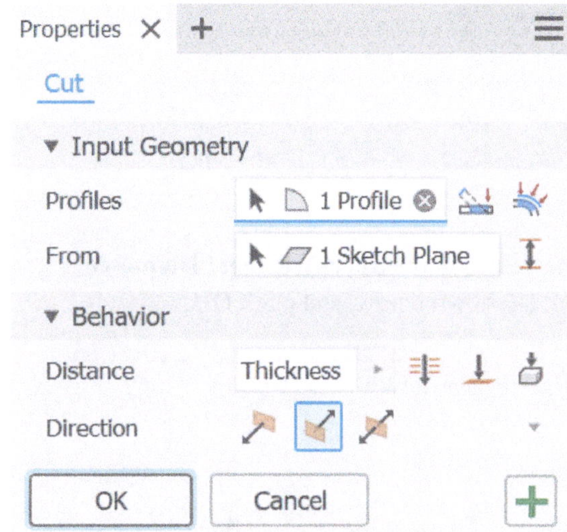

24. Accept the default values and click **OK** to create the cut feature.

25. Click **Manage > Author > Extract iFeature** on the ribbon; the **Extract iFeature** dialog appears.

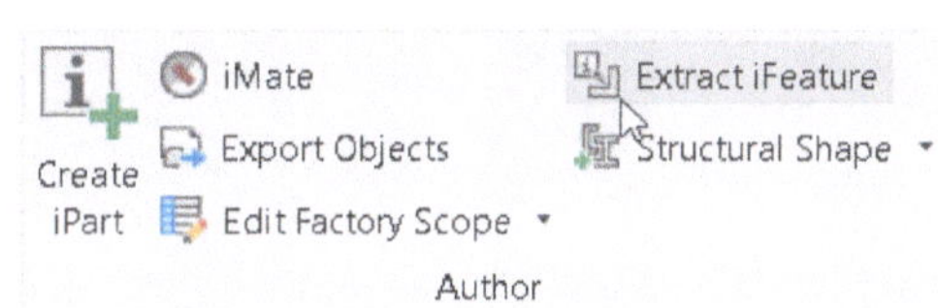

26. On the dialog, select **Type > Sheet Metal Punch iFeature**.
27. Select the cut feature from the model geometry or the Browser window. The parameters of the cut feature appear in the **Extract iFeature** dialog.

Next, you must set the **Size Parameters** of the iFeature.

28. Set the **Limit** of the **Diameter** value to **Range**. The **Specify Range** dialog appears.

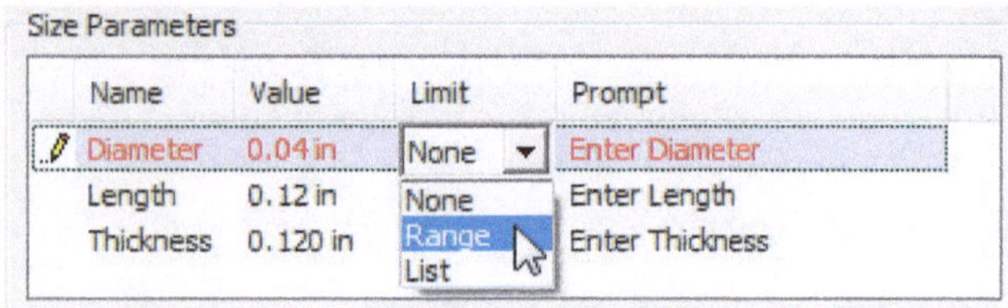

29. Set the values in the **Specify Range: Diameter** dialog, as shown below, and click **OK**.

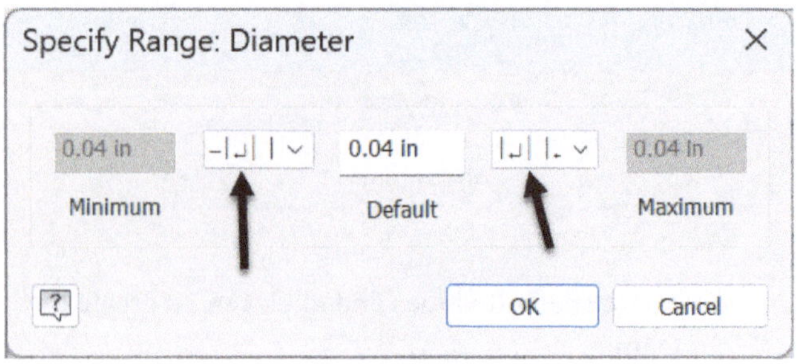

30. Set the **Limit** of the **Length** value to **List**. The **List Values: Length** dialog appears.
31. Click on **Click here to add value** and enter 0.2 as value.
32. Likewise, type-in values in the **List Values**: **Length** dialog, as shown below.

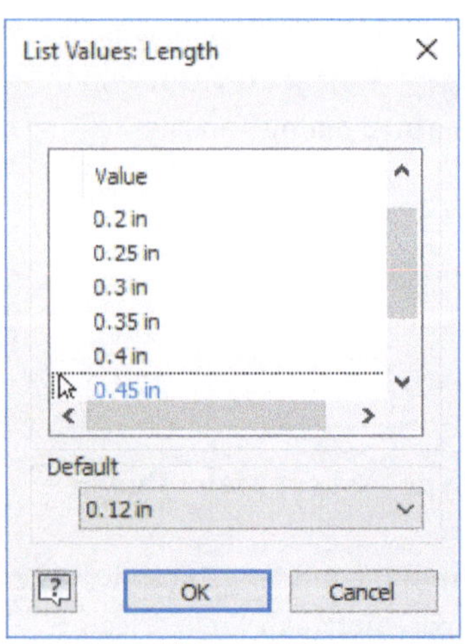

33. Click **OK**.
34. Set the **Limit** of the **Thickness** value to **Range**. The **Specify Range: Thickness** dialog appears.
35. Set the values in the **Specify Range: Thickness** dialog, as shown below. Next, click **OK**.

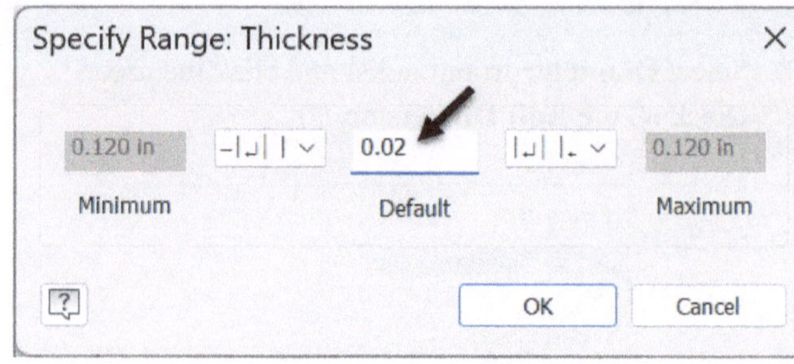

Next, you need to select the center point of the slot. This point will be used while placing the slot.

36. Click the **Select Sketch** button on the **Extract iFeature** dialog.

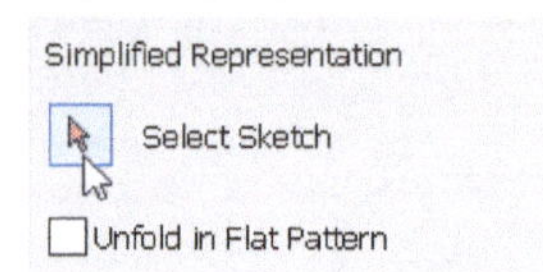

37. Select the sketch of the cut feature from the Browser window.

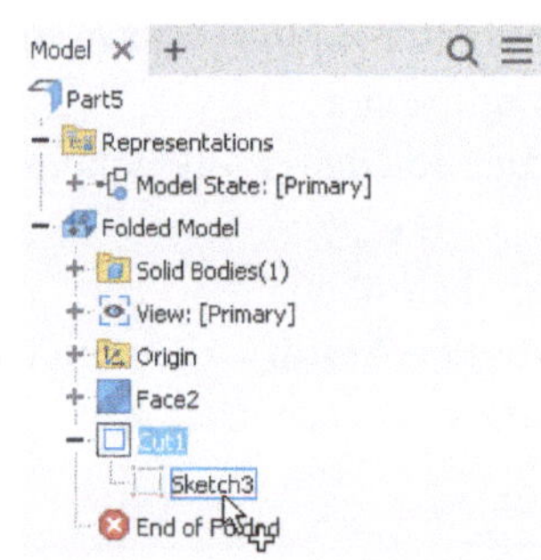

38. Click **Save** on the dialog; the **Save As** dialog appears.
39. Browse to the **Punches** folder and enter **Custom slot** in the **File name** box.

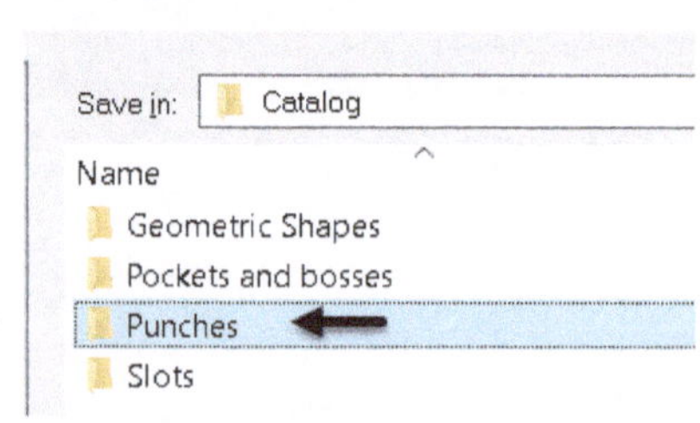

40. Click **Save** and **Yes**.
41. Click **File Menu > Save**.
42. Save the sheet metal part file as Custom slot.
43. Switch to the sheet metal file of the current tutorial.

Creating a Punched feature

1. Start a sketch on the top face of the base sheet.
2. On the ribbon, click **Sketch > Create > Point**.
3. Place a point and add dimensions to it, as shown below.

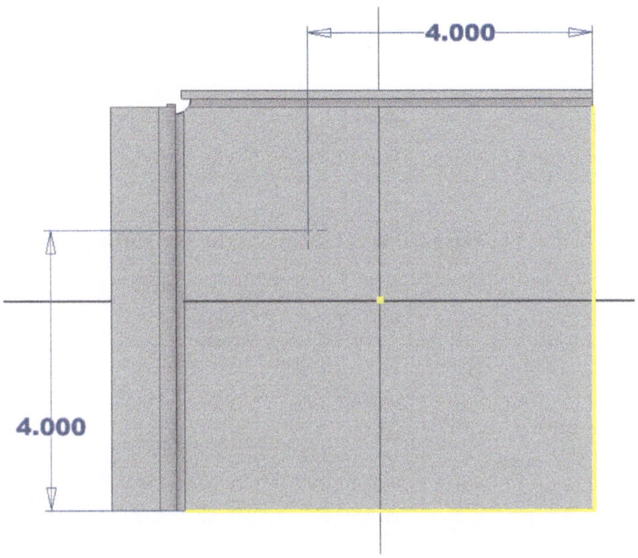

4. Click **Finish** on the ribbon.
5. To create the punch, click **Sheet Metal > Modify > Punch Tool** on the ribbon; the **iFeature7** Properties panel appears.

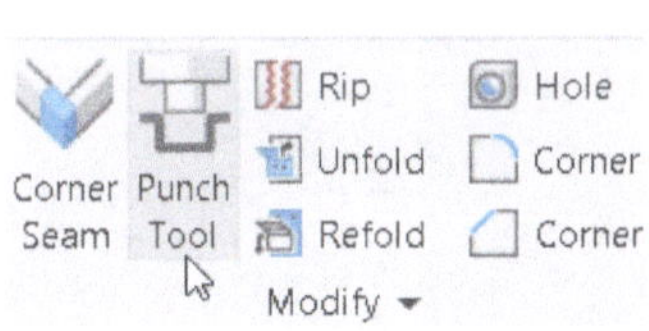

6. On the dialog, click the **Browse** icon under the **Punch Tool** section.
7. Select the Custom slot.ide from the **Select Punch Tool** dialog and click **Open**.
8. Set **Diameter** to 0.1 and **Length** to 0.45 under **Size Parameter** section.

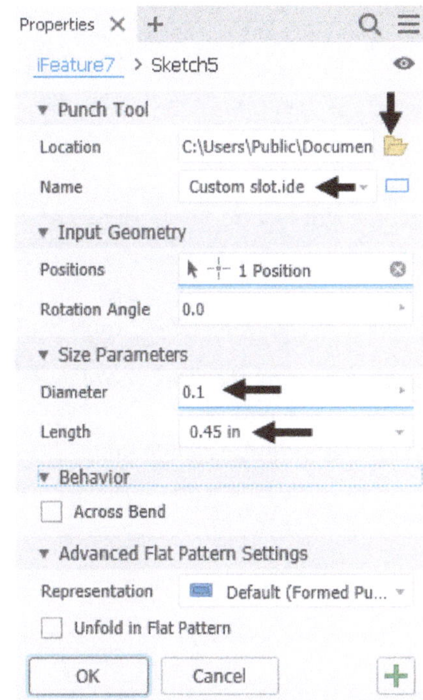

9. Click **OK** to create the slot.

Note: If the slot is not oriented as shown in the figure, then on the **iFeature7** dialog and type in **0** in the **Rotation Angle** box under the **Input Geometry** section.

Creating the Rectangular Pattern

1. Click **Sheet Metal > Pattern > Rectangular Pattern** on the ribbon. The **Rectangular Pattern** Properties panel appears.

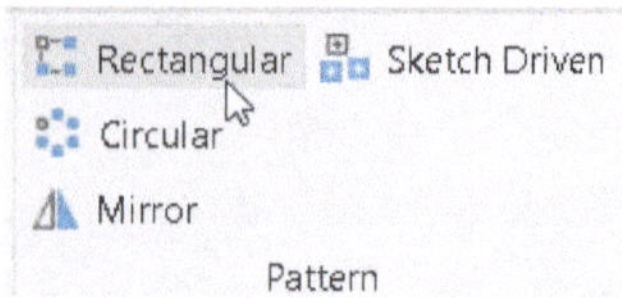

2. Select the slot feature.

*You can also select multiple solid bodies from the graphics window using the **Pattern Solids** option.*

3. Click the **Direction A** button on the Properties panel.

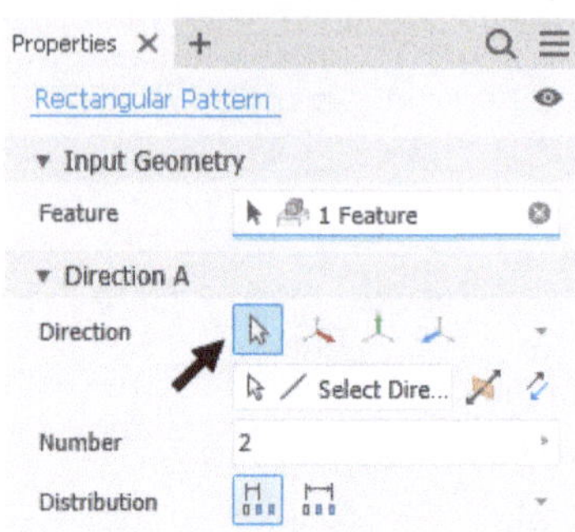

4. Select the edge of the base feature, as shown below.

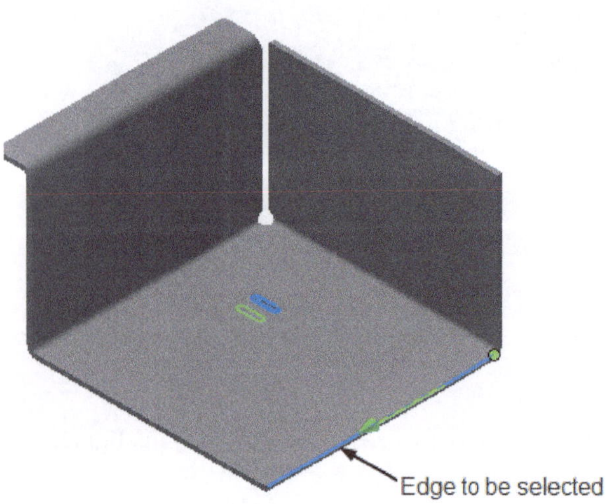

5. Click **Distribution > Incremental** icon in the **Direction A** section.
6. Specify **Number** as **5**.
7. Specify **Distance** as **0.6**.

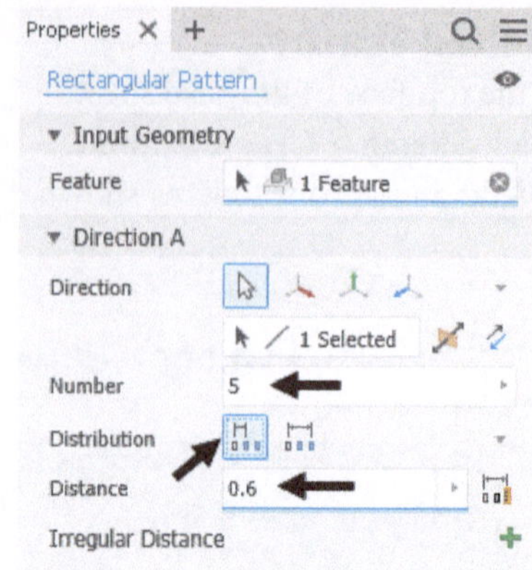

8. Click the **Direction B** button on the Properties panel.

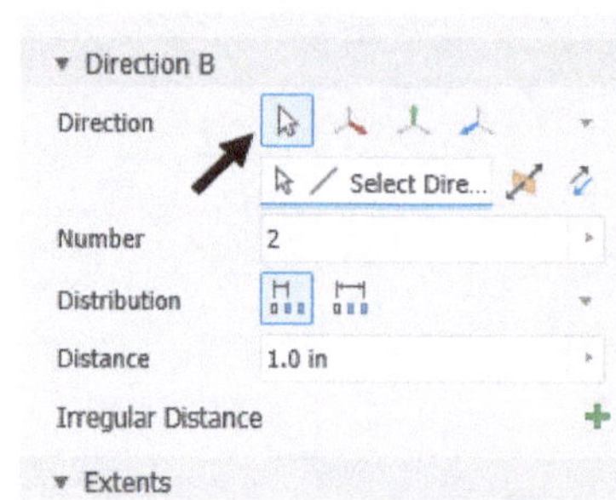

9. Select the edge of the base feature, as shown below.

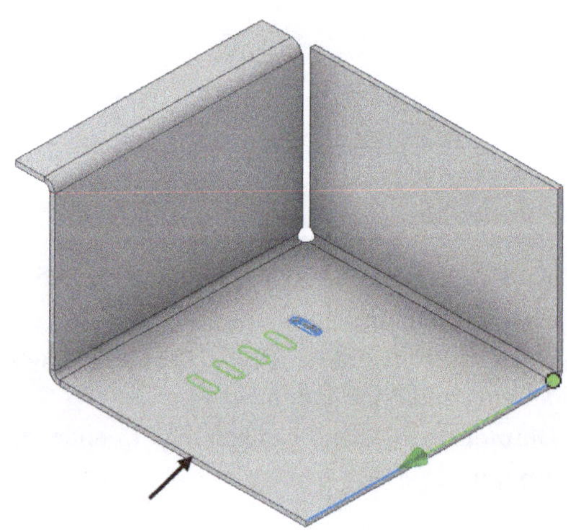

10. Click the **Flip direction** button in the **Direction B** section to make sure the arrow is pointed toward the right.
11. Click **Distribution > Incremental** icon in the **Direction B** section.
12. Specify **Number** as **2**.
13. Specify **Distance** as **2**.

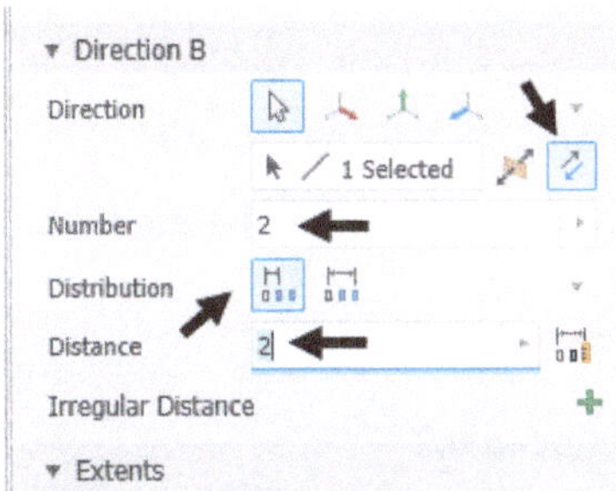

14. Click **OK** to create the pattern.

Creating the Bend Feature

1. Create a plane parallel to the front face of the flange feature. The offset distance is 6.3.

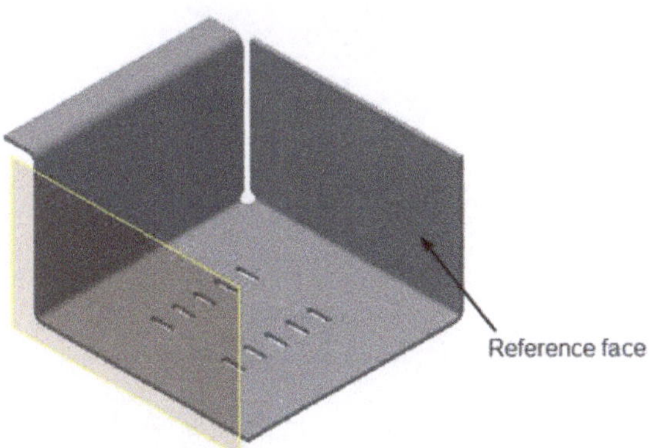

2. Create a sketch on the new work plane.

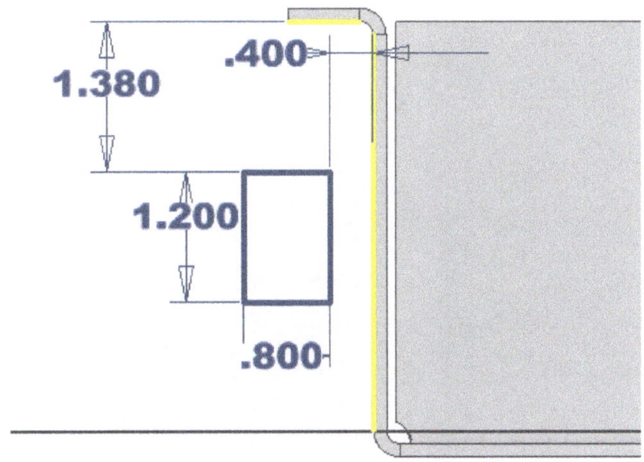

3. Click **Finish** on the ribbon.
4. Click **Sheet Metal > Create > Face** on the ribbon and create a face feature.

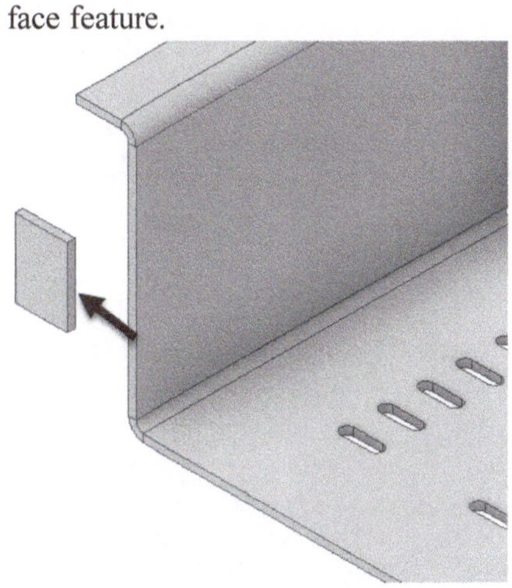

5. Click **Sheet Metal > Create > Bend** on the ribbon. The **Bend** dialog appears.

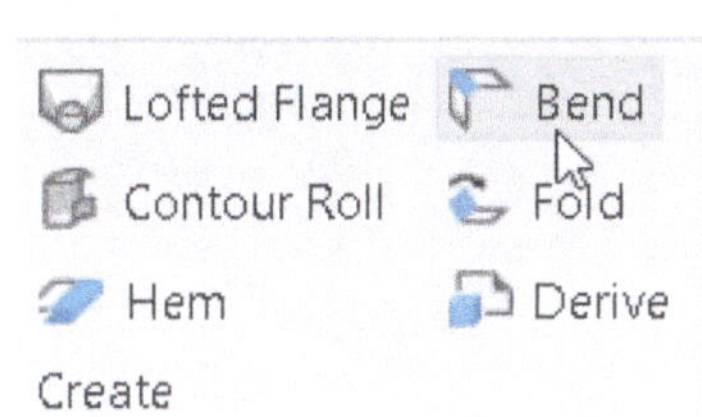

6. Select the edges from the model, as shown below.

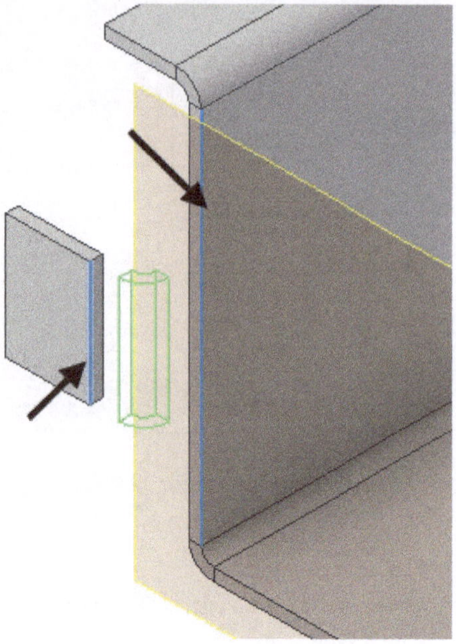

7. Make sure the **Bend Extension** is set to perpendicular.

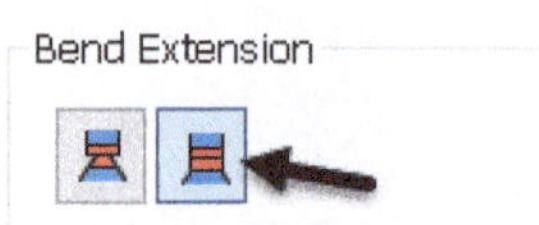

8. Click **OK** to create the bend feature.

9. Hide the work plane (Right-click on it and uncheck **Visibility**).

Applying a corner round

1. To apply a corner round, click **Sheet Metal > Modify > Corner Round** on the ribbon; the **Corner Round** dialog appears.

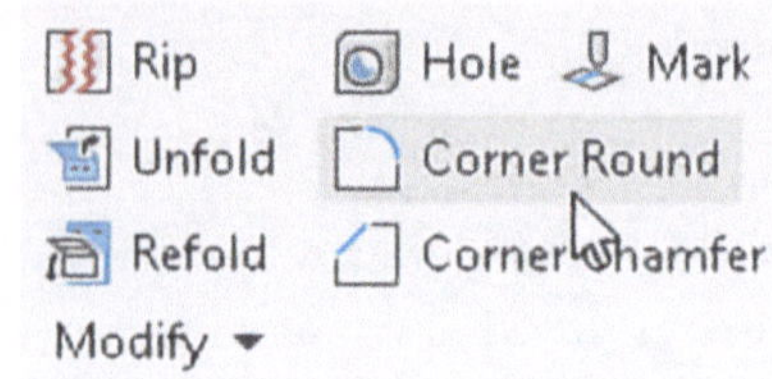

2. Set the **Radius** value to **0.2**.
3. Click the **Sets selection priority to features** icon on the **Corner Round** panel.

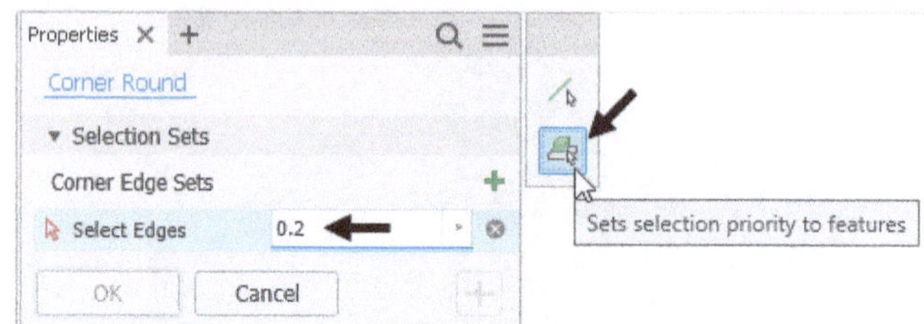

4. Select the face feature from the model.

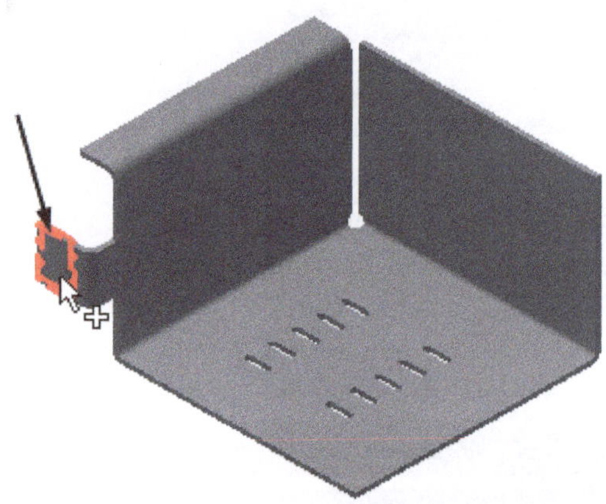

5. Click **OK** to apply the rounds.

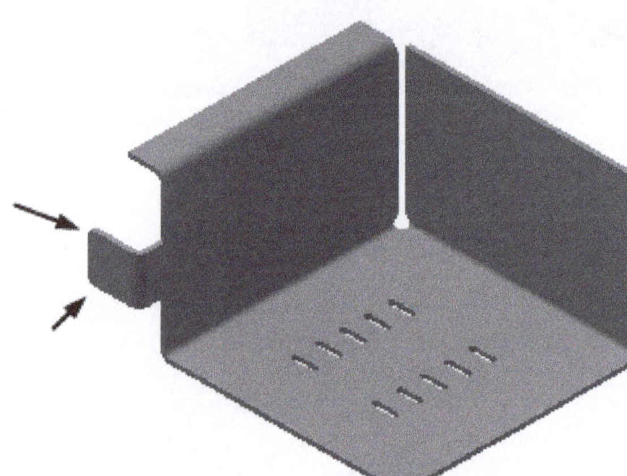

Creating Countersink holes

1. Click **Sheet Metal > Modify > Hole** on the ribbon; the **Properties panel** appears.

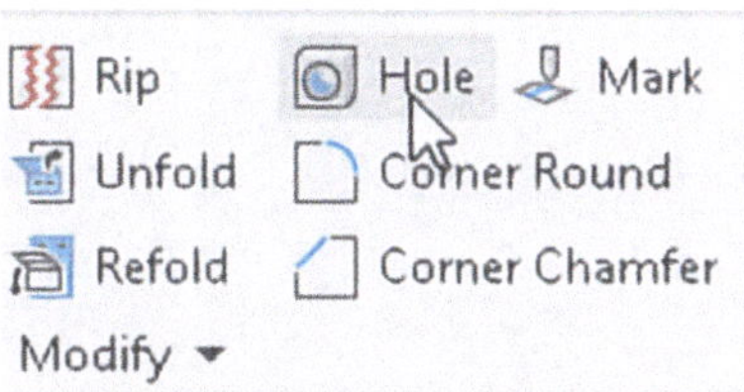

2. Click on the front face of the flange.
3. Select the circular edge of the fillet, as shown.
4. Set the hole type to **Countersink**.
5. Set the other parameters on the **Hole Properties** panel, as shown below.

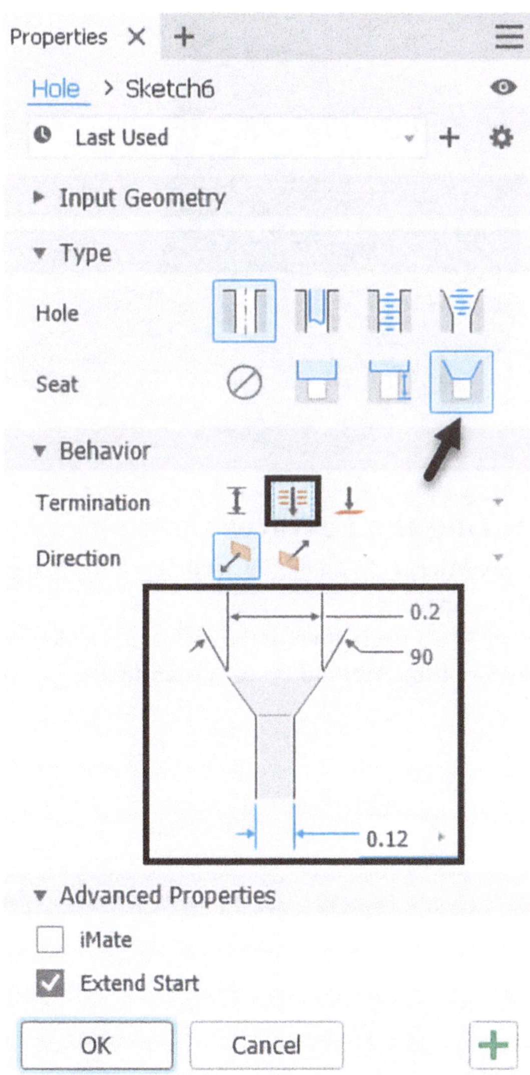

6. Click on the face of the flange, as shown below.

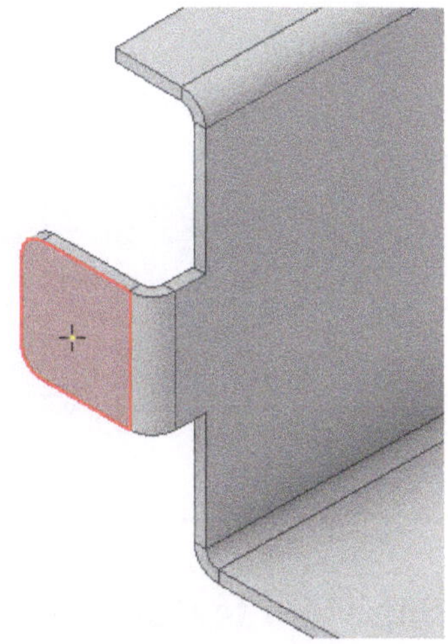

7. Select the corner round as the concentric reference.

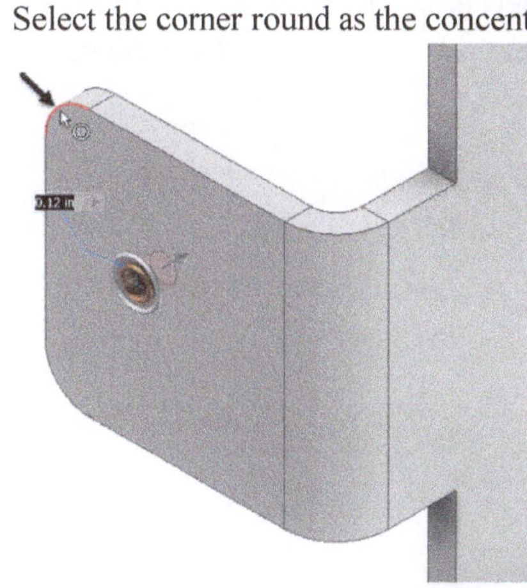

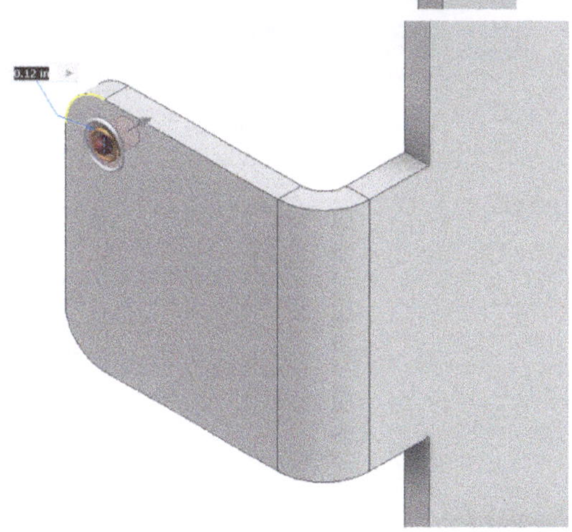

8. Again, click on the flange face and select the other rounded corner as the concentric reference.

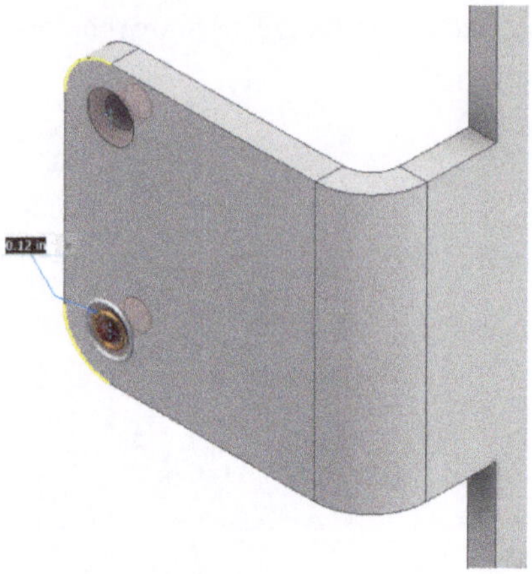

9. Click **OK** to create the countersink.

Creating Hem features

1. To create the hem feature, click **Sheet Metal > Create > Hem** on the ribbon; the **Hem** dialog appears.

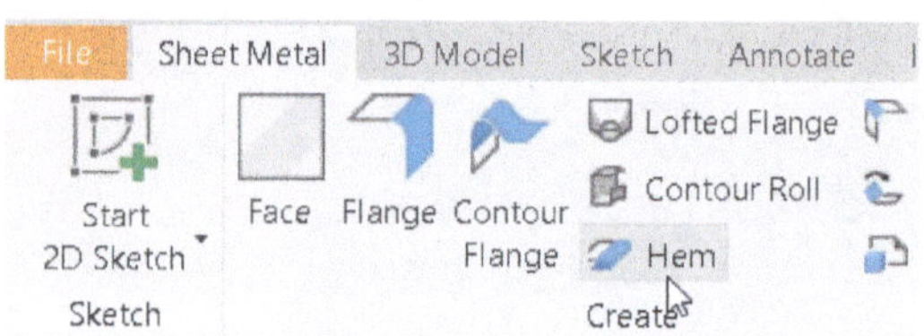

2. Set the **Type** to **Single**.

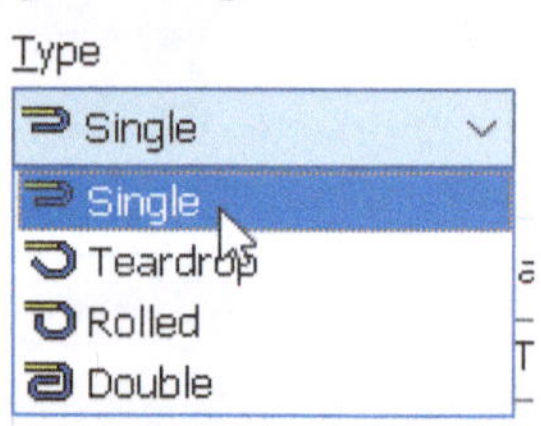

3. Select the edge of the contour flange, as shown below.

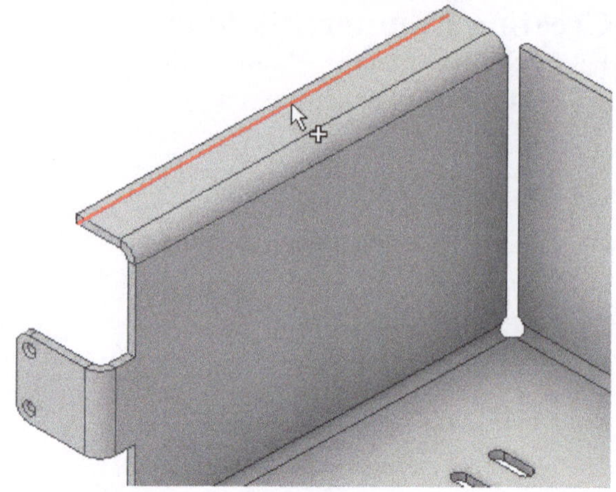

4. Leave the default settings of the dialog and click **OK** to create the hem.

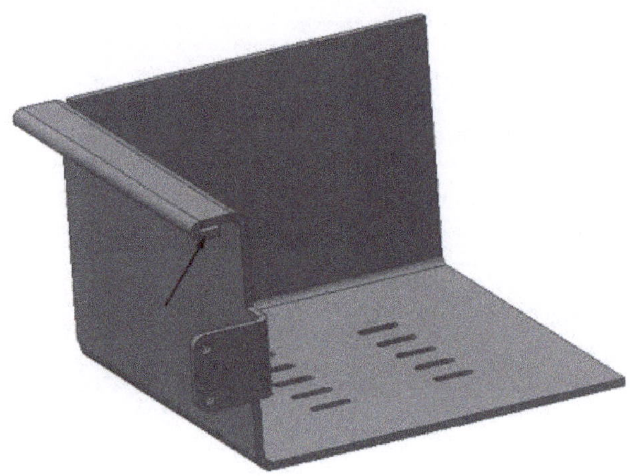

Mirroring the Features

1. Click **Mirror** on the **Pattern** panel; the **Mirror** dialog appears.
2. Click >> at the bottom of the dialog and make sure the **Creation Method** is set to **Identical**.

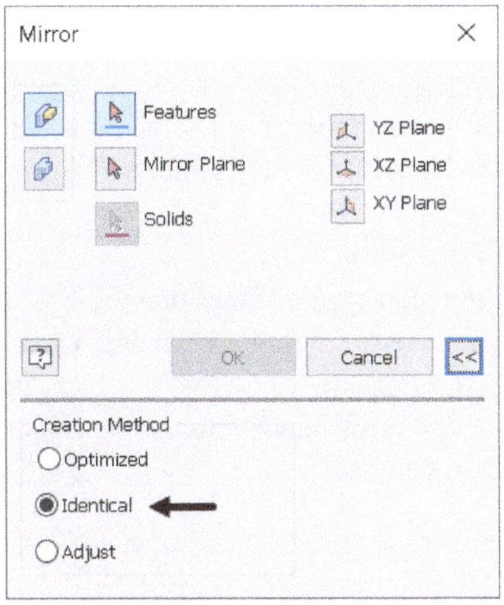

3. Select the features from the Browser window, as shown below.

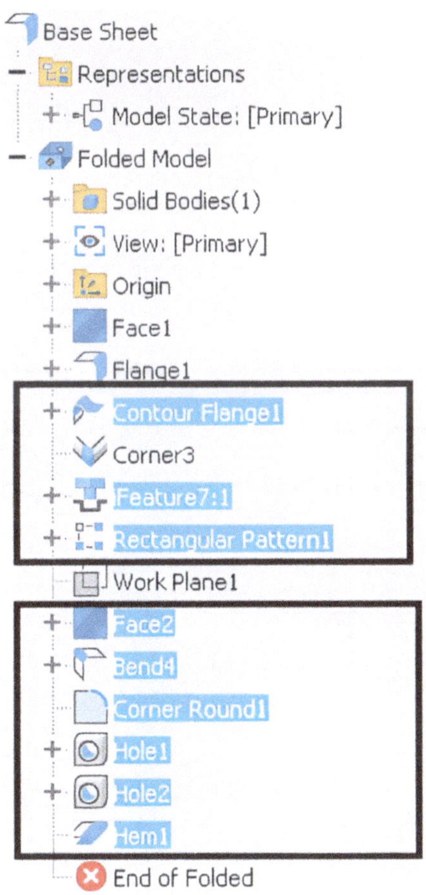

4. Click the **Origin YZ Plane** button on the dialog
5. Click **OK** to mirror the feature.
6. Create a corner seam between the mirrored counter flange and flange.

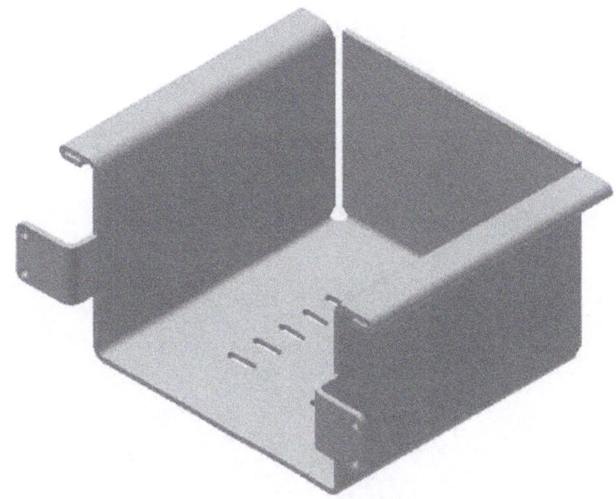

Creating the Flat Pattern

1. To create a flat pattern, click **Sheet Metal > Flat Pattern > Create Flat Pattern** on the ribbon.

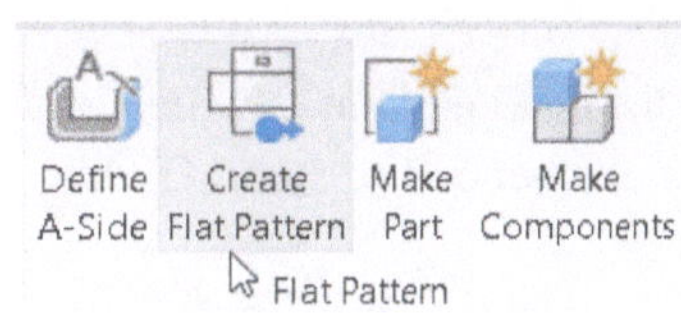

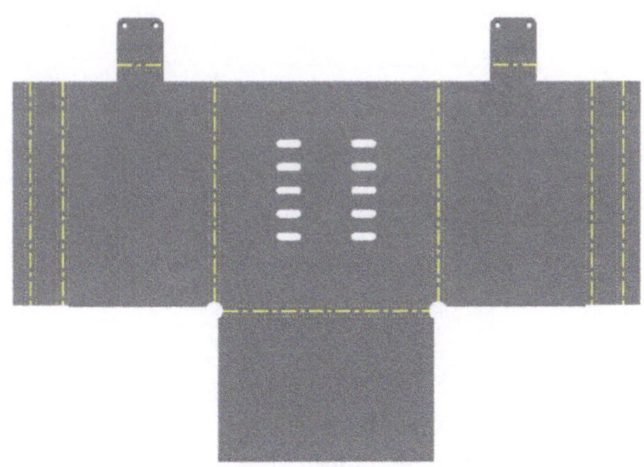

You can set the order in which the bends will be annotated.

2. Click the **Bend Order Annotation** button on the **Manage** panel of the **Flat Pattern** tab. The order in which the bends will be annotated is displayed.

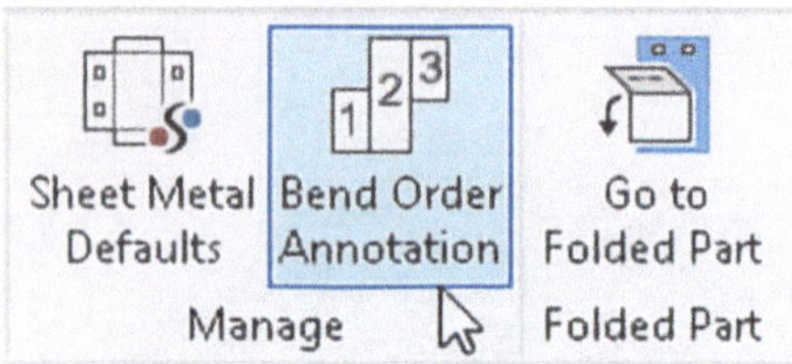

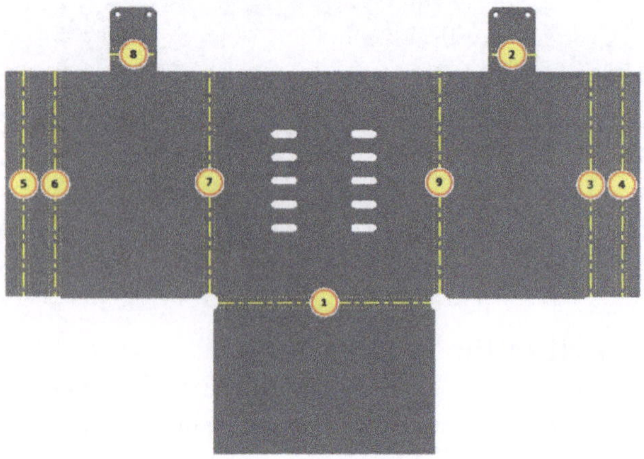

3. To change the order of the bend annotation, click on the balloon displayed on the bend. The **Bend Order Edit** dialog appears.
4. Select the **Bend Number** checkbox and enter a new number in the data field.

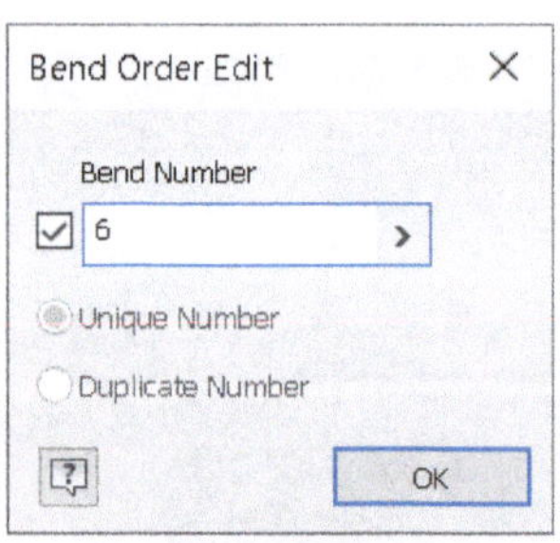

5. Click **OK** to change the order.
6. To switch back to the folded view of the model, click **Go to Folded Part** on the **Folded Part** panel.

7. Save the sheet metal part.

Creating 2D Drawing of the sheet metal part

1. On the **Quick Access toolbar**, click the **New** button.
2. On the **Create New File** dialog, double-click on **Standard.idw**.
3. Activate the **Base View** tool.
4. Click the **Home** icon on the ViewCube.
5. Leave the default settings on the **Drawing View** dialog and click **OK.**
6. Click and drag the drawing view to the top right corner of the drawing sheet.

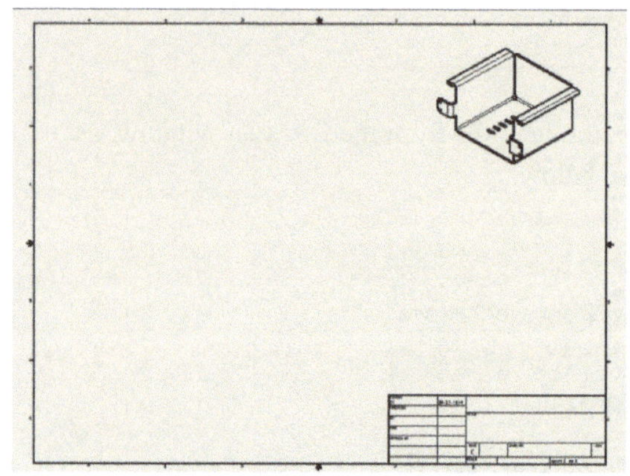

7. Likewise, create the front and top views of the sheet metal part.

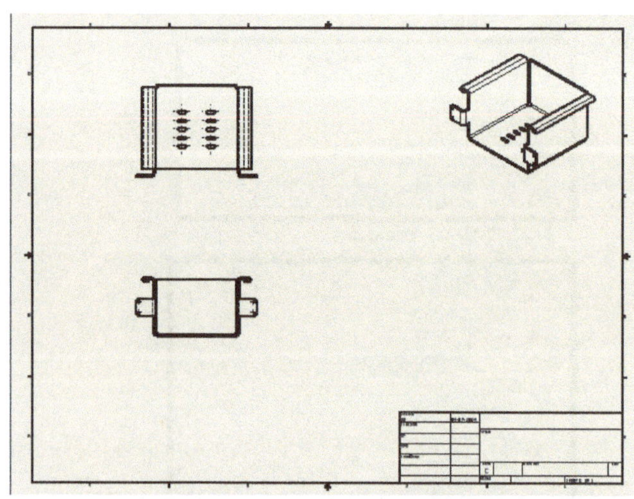

8. Activate the **Base View** tool and select **Sheet Metal View > Flat Pattern** on the **Drawing View** dialog.

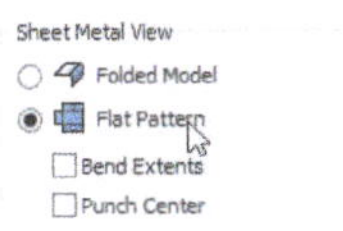

9. Place the flat pattern view below the Isometric view.

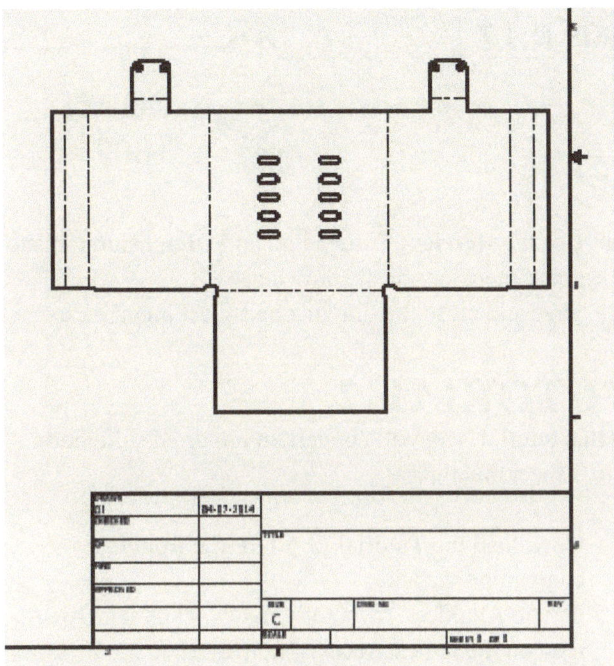

10. To add bend notes to the flat pattern, click **Annotate > Feature Notes > Bend** on the ribbon.

11. Click the horizontal bend line on the flat pattern to add the bend note.

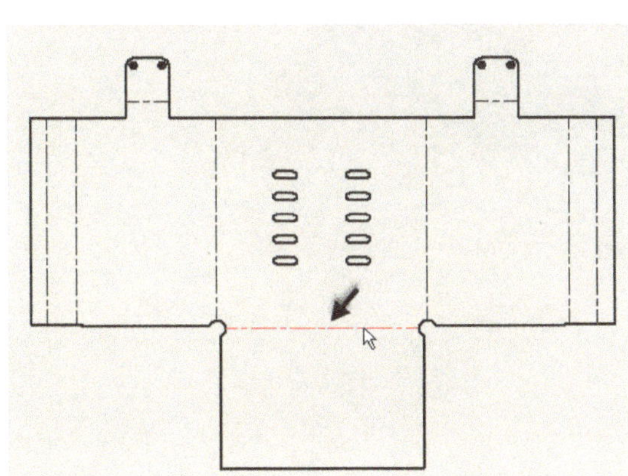

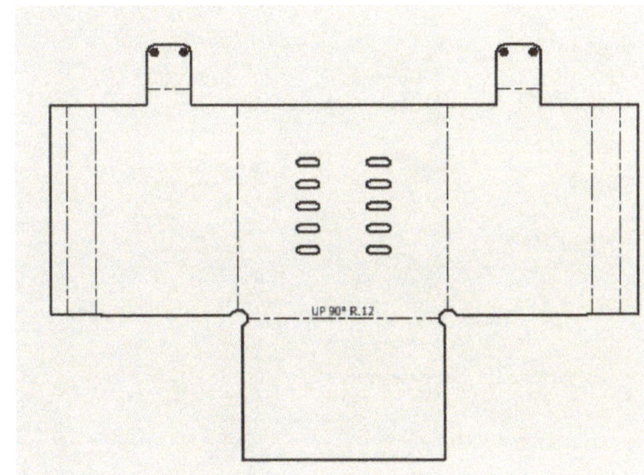

12. Likewise, select other bend lines on the flat pattern. You can also drag a selection box to select all the bend lines from the flat pattern view.

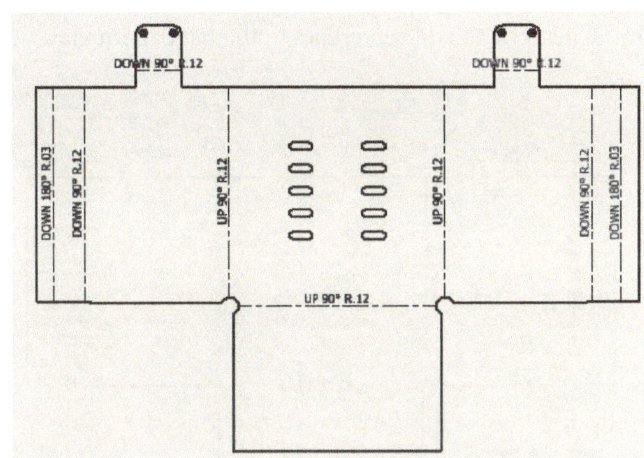

13. To add centerlines to the flat pattern view, click the right mouse button on it, and select **Automated Centerlines**.

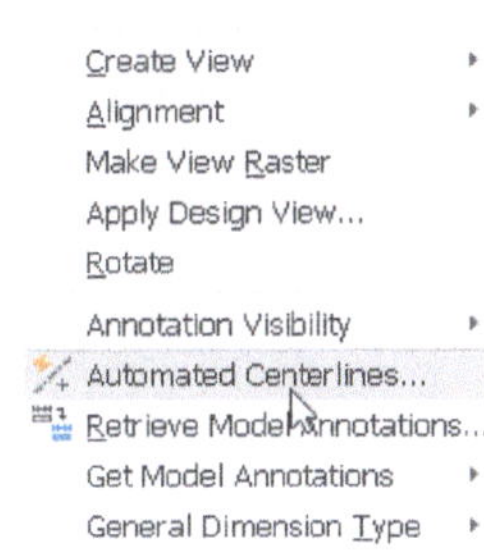

14. On the **Automated Centerlines** dialog, click the **Punches** button under the **Apply To** section.

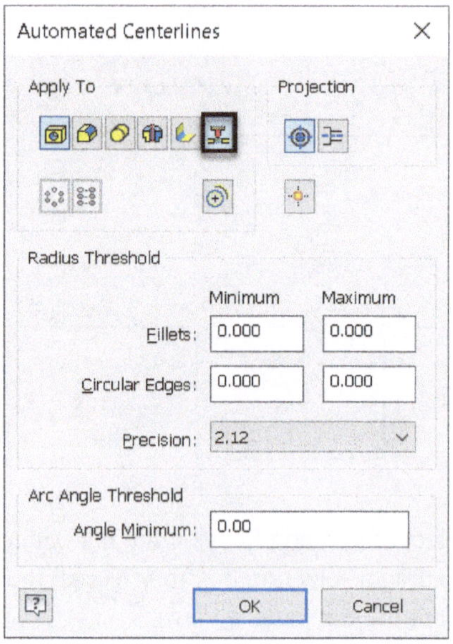

15. Click **OK** to add centerlines to the flat pattern view.

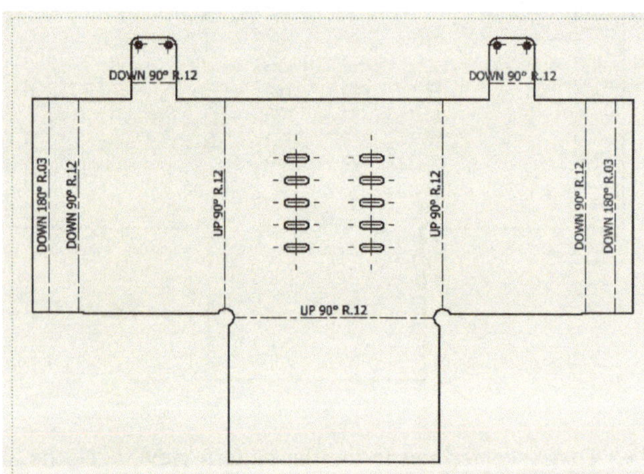

16. Likewise, add centerlines to other views on the drawing sheet.
17. To add a punch note, click **Annotate > Feature Notes > Punch** on the ribbon.

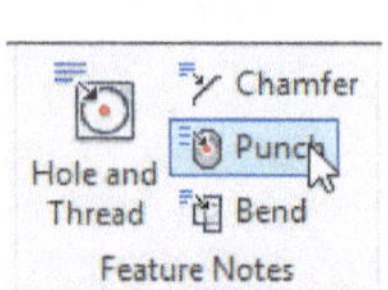

18. Zoom into the flat pattern view and click on the arc of the slot.
19. Move the pointer and click to create an annotation.

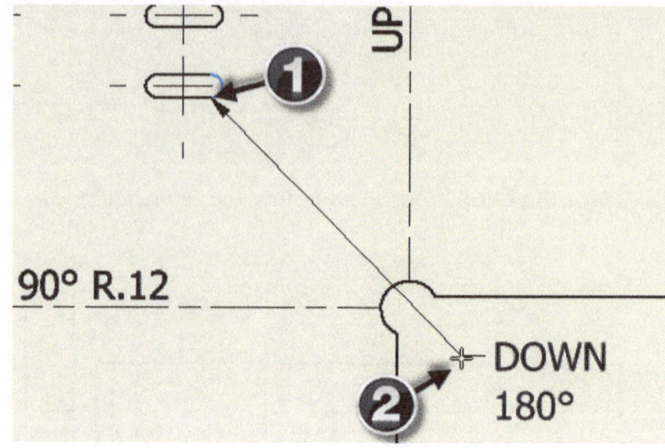

20. Use the **Retrieve Dimension** and **Dimension** tools to add dimensions to the drawing.
21. Save and close the drawing and sheet metal part.

TUTORIAL 2

In this tutorial, you will convert an imported solid body into a sheet metal part.

1. Download the Tutorial_2. STEP file from the companion website.
2. On the Autodesk Inventor window, click the **Open** icon on the Quick Access Toolbar.
3. Browse to the location of the downloaded file, and then double-click on it.
4. On the **Import** dialog, select **Import Type > Convert Model**.
5. Click **OK** on the **Import** dialog.
6. On the ribbon, click the **3D Model** tab > **Convert** > **Convert to Sheet Metal** .
7. Click on the flat sheet metal face, as shown; the fixed face is defined.

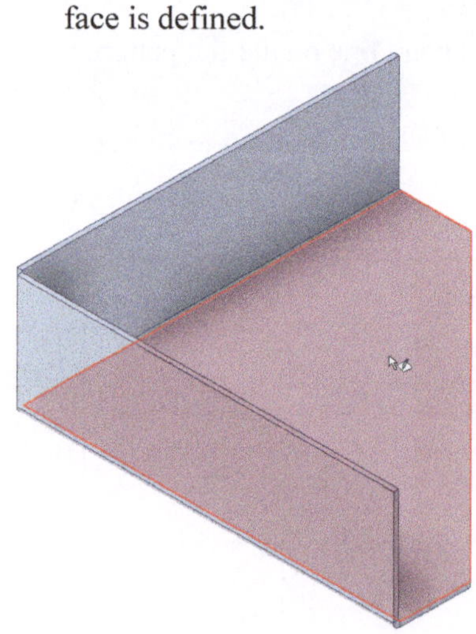

8. Set **Thickness** to 2
9. Click **OK**.
10. On the ribbon, click **Sheet Metal** tab > **Flat Pattern** panel > **Create Flat Pattern** .

TUTORIAL 3

In this tutorial, you will create a multi-body sheet metal part.

1. Start a new Inventor sheet metal part file using the **Sheet Metal.ipt** template.
2. Create a new face feature, as shown. The sheet metal thickness is 0.0787.

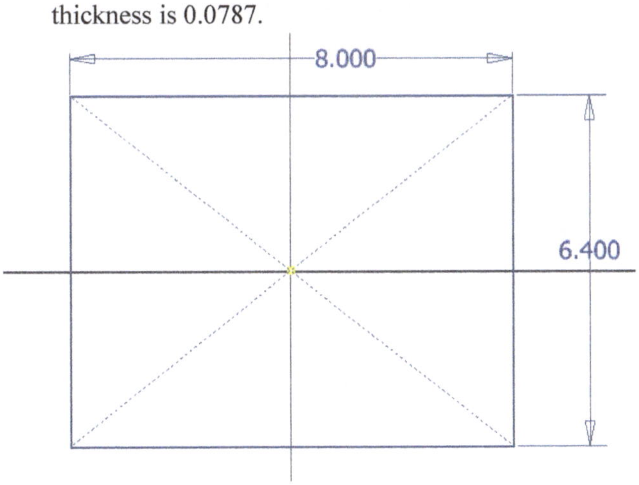

3. Create edge flanges of 1.575 inches' length, as shown.

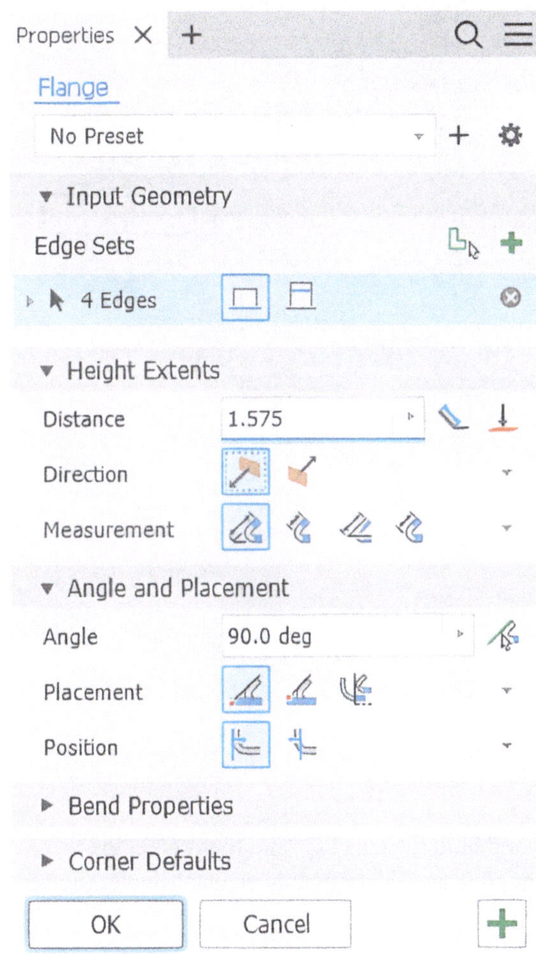

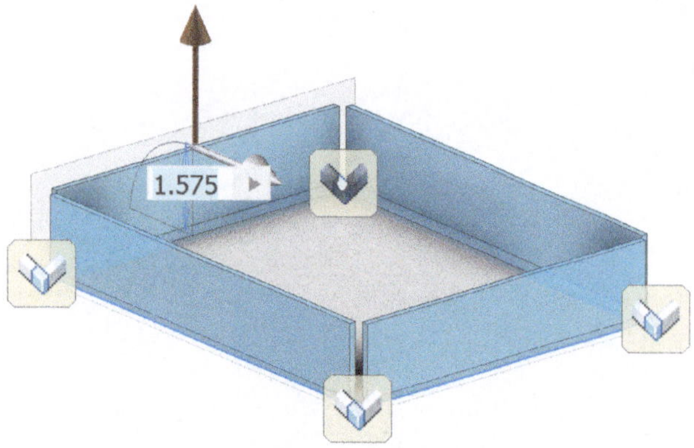

4. Activate the **Start 2D Sketch** tool, and then click on the outer face of the edge flange.

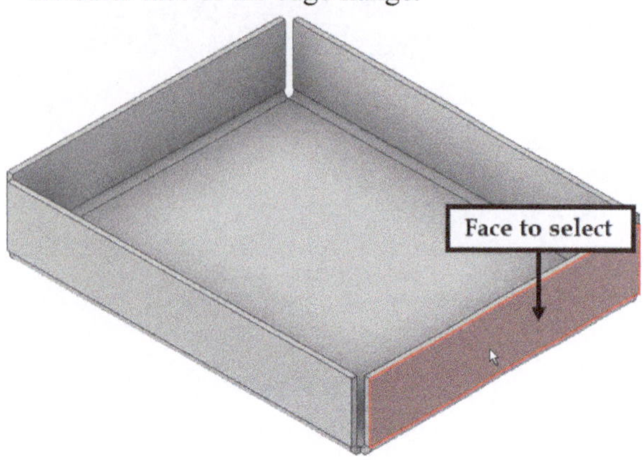

5. Create a rectangle, as shown.

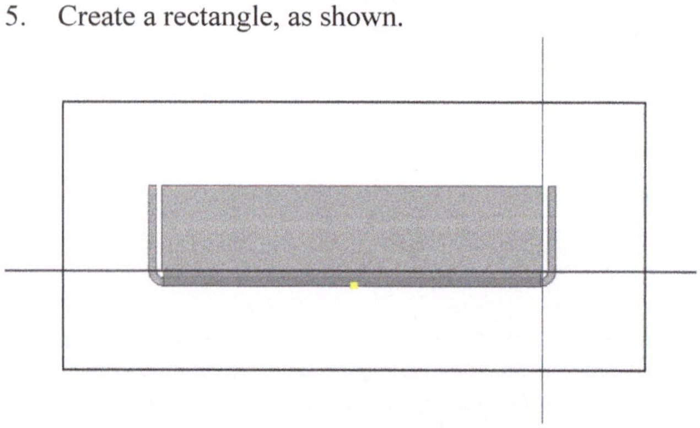

6. Press and hold the Ctrl key, and then select the bottom edge and the bottom horizontal line of the rectangle.

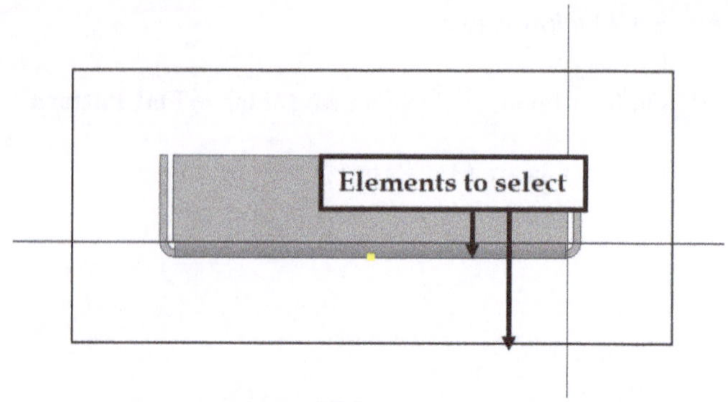

7. Click the **Collinear** icon the **Constrain** panel of the **3D Model** tab of the ribbon; the line is made collinear with the horizontal edge of the bend.
8. Likewise, make the vertical line collinear with the side edges, as shown.

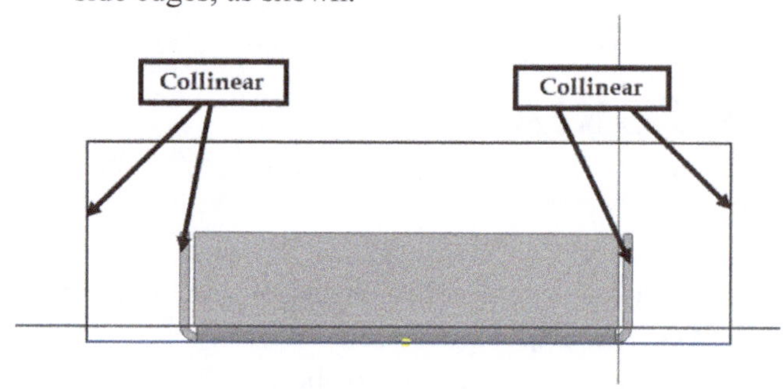

9. Add dimension to the vertical line, as shown.

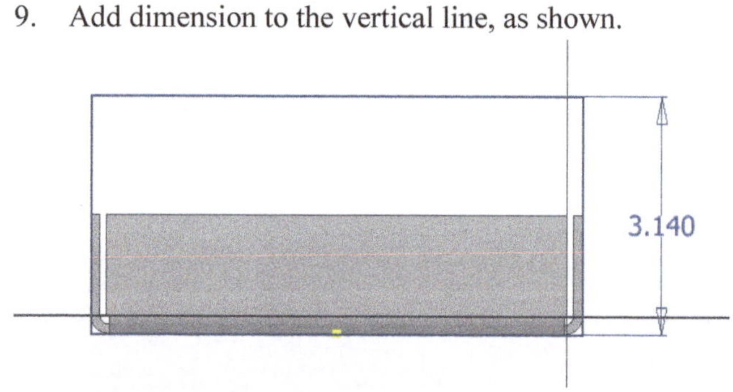

10. Click **Finish** on the ribbon.
11. Activate the **Face** command.
12. On the **Face** properties panel, click the **New Solid** icon under the **Output** section.
13. Make sure that the arrow on the face feature points outwards. Click the **Flipped** icon, if it points inwards.
14. Click **OK**; the face feature is created as a separate body.

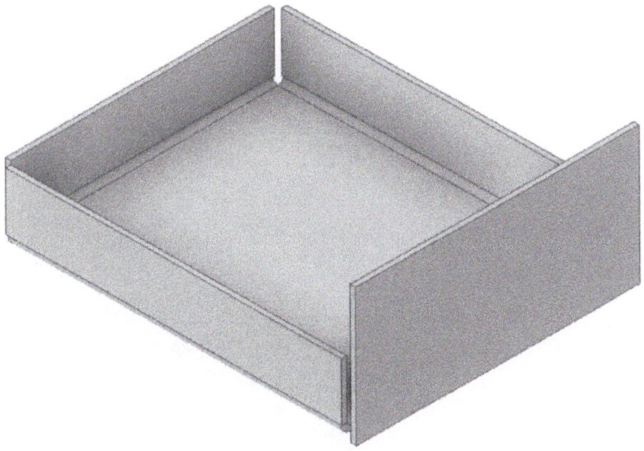

15. Expand the **Solid Bodies** folder; notice the two bodies.

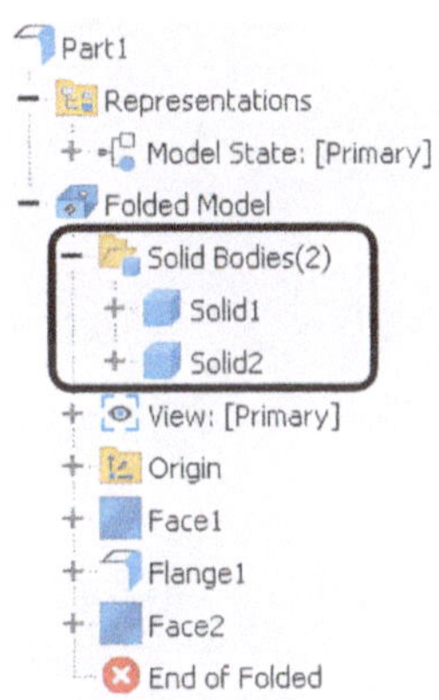

16. Click the top left corner of the ViewCube, as shown.

17. Activate the **Start 2D Sketch** tool.
18. Click on the flange face.

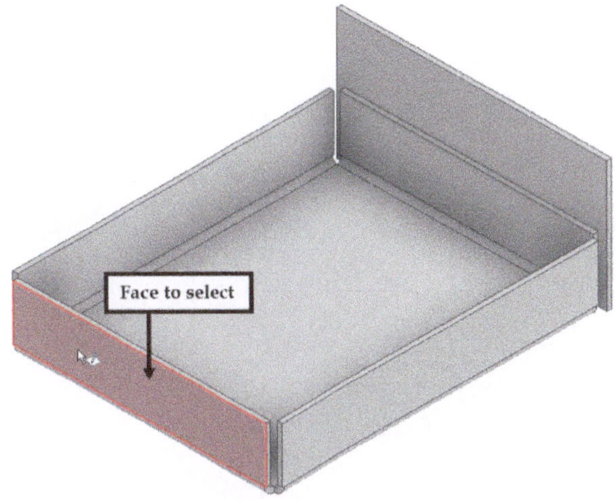

19. Activate the **Two Point Rectangle** tool.
20. Click on the first and second corners, as shown.

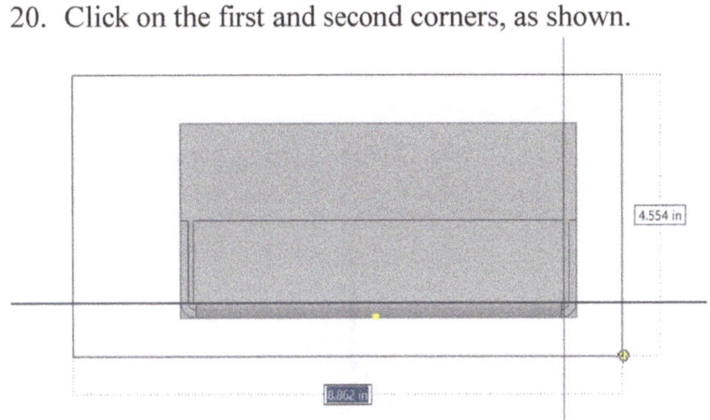

21. On the ribbon, click **Sheet Metal** tab > **Constrain** panel > **Coincident**.
22. Make the points coincident, as shown.

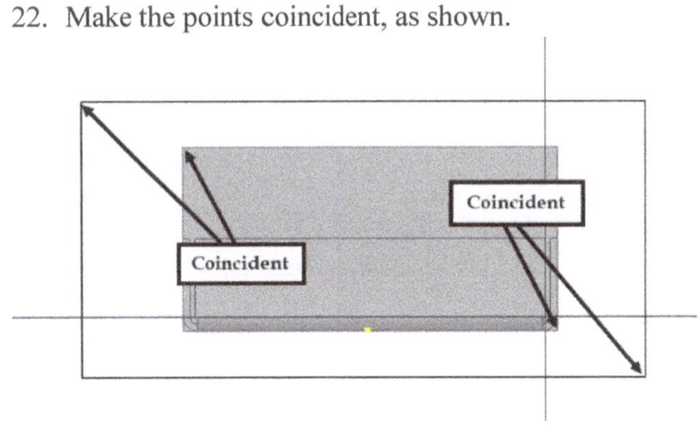

23. Click **Finish** on the ribbon.
24. Activate the **Face** command.
25. On the **Face** Properties panel, click the **New Solid** icon.
26. Click **OK**.

Notice three bodies inside the **Solid Bodies** folder in the **Model** tab of the Browser Window.

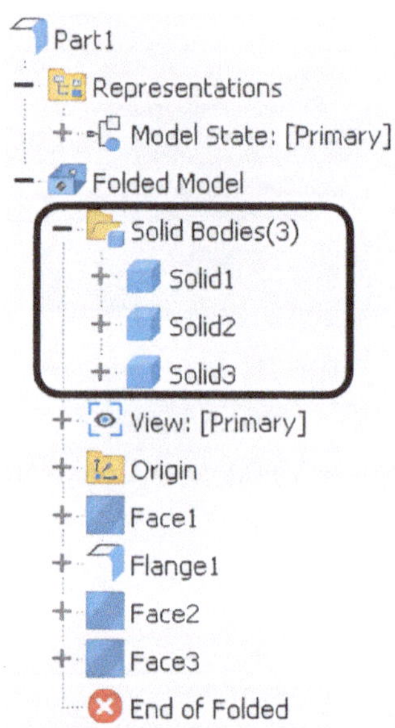

27. Right click and select **Home View**.
28. On the ribbon, click **Sheet Metal** tab > **Create** panel > **Bend** .
29. Click on the edges of the second and third sheet metal bodies, as shown.

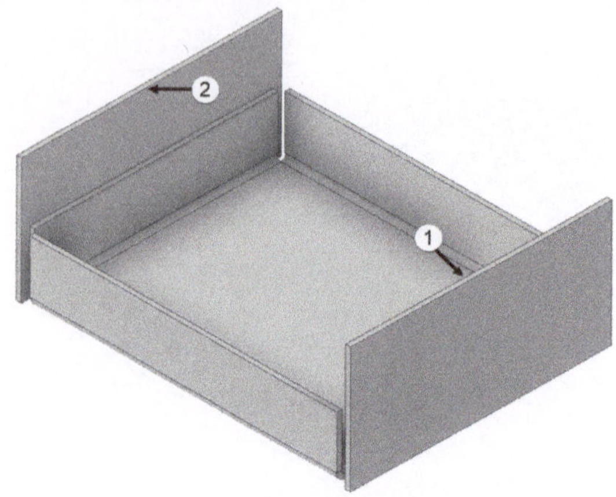

30. On the **Bend** dialog, select **Double Bend > 90 Degree**.
31. Click **OK** on the **Bend** dialog.

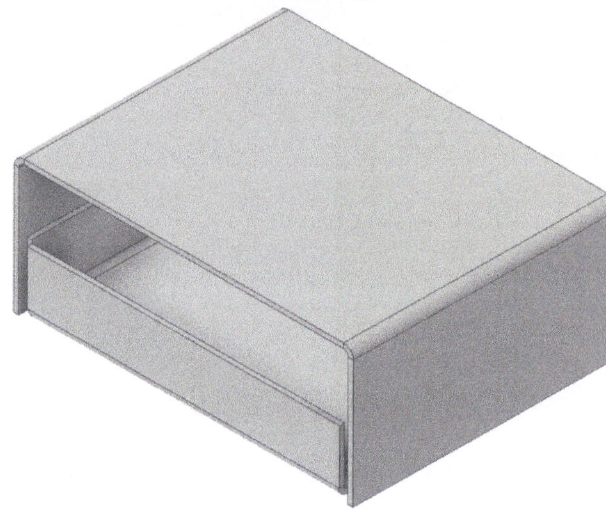

32. On the ribbon, click **Sheet Metal > Create > Flange** .
33. Click on the edge of the previously created edge flange, as shown.

34. On the **Flange** Properties panel, click the **To** icon under the **Height Extents** section.
35. Zoom to the bottom portion of the sheet metal part, and then select the vertex of the flange, as shown.

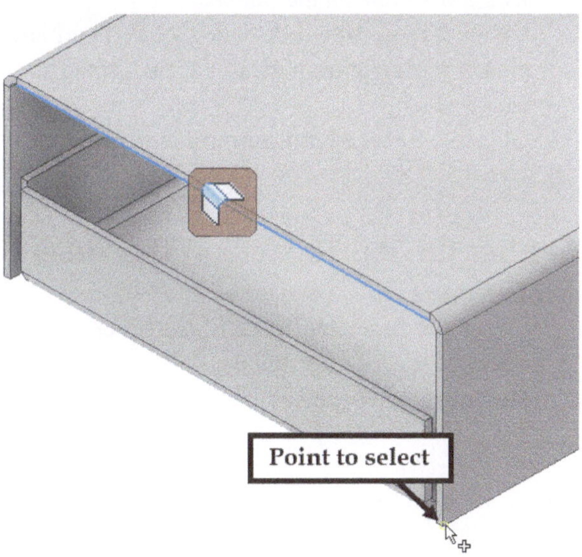

36. Click **Position > Inner face through plane** under the **Angle and Placement** section.

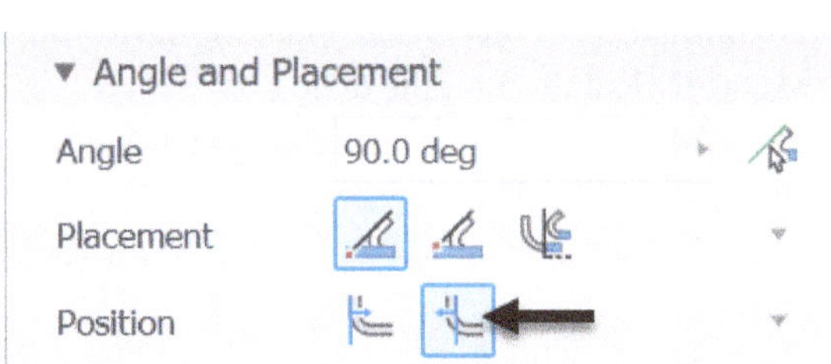

37. Click **OK**.
38. Likewise, create a flange on the opposite side.

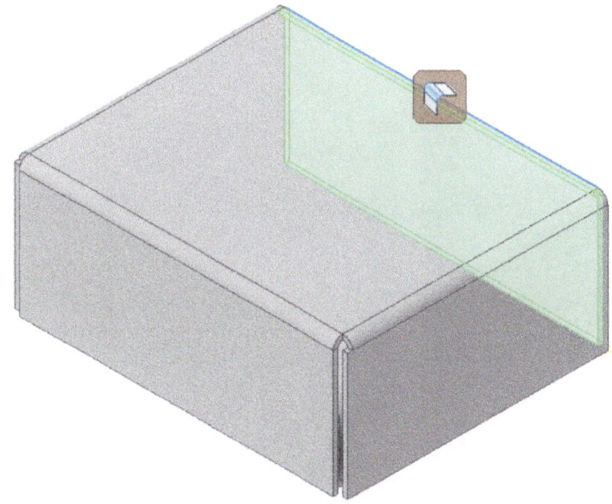

39. Save and close the sheet metal file.

TUTORIAL 4

In this tutorial, you will create a **Contour Roll** feature. The **Contour Roll** tool allows you to create a sheet metal feature by sweeping a profile about an axis.

1. Open a new Autodesk Inventor sheet metal file using the Sheet metal.ipt template.
2. On the ribbon, click **Sheet Metal** tab > **Start 2D Sketch**.
3. Click on XY Plane.
4. Draw the sketch profile, as shown.

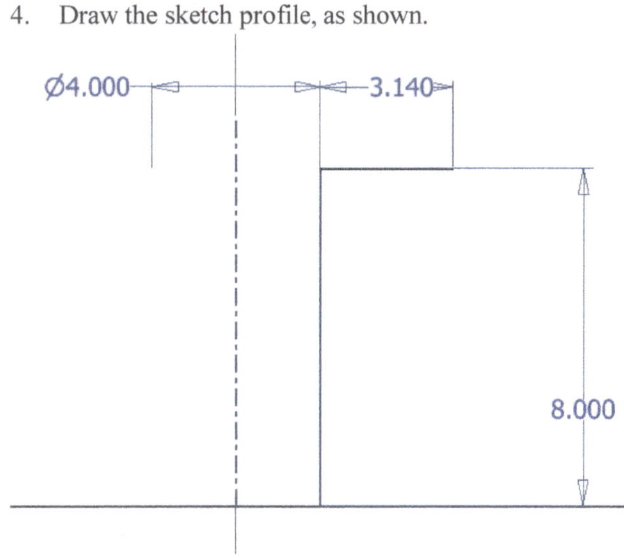

5. Click **Finish** on the ribbon.
6. On the ribbon, click **Sheet Metal > Create > Contour Roll** ; the profile and the axis are selected automatically.

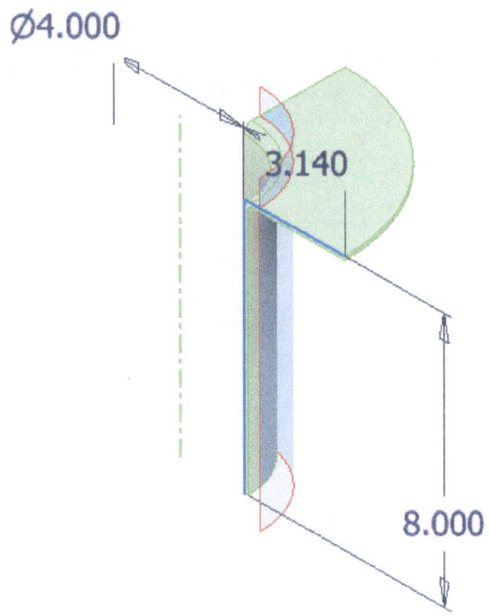

7. Specify the **Offset Direction** of the sheet metal (select **Both Sides** in this case).
8. Type **355** in the **Rolled Angle** box.
9. Specify the **Unroll Method**. There are four options **Centroid Cylinder**, **Custom Cylinder**, **Developed Length**, and **Neutral Radius** (select **Centroid Cylinder** in this case).
10. Click **OK** to create the swept flange.

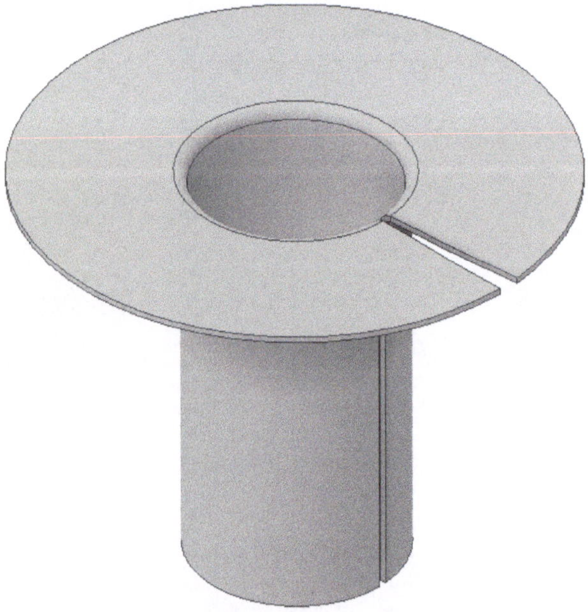

11. Save and close the part file.

TUTORIAL 5

In this tutorial, you will create the sheet metal part given below:

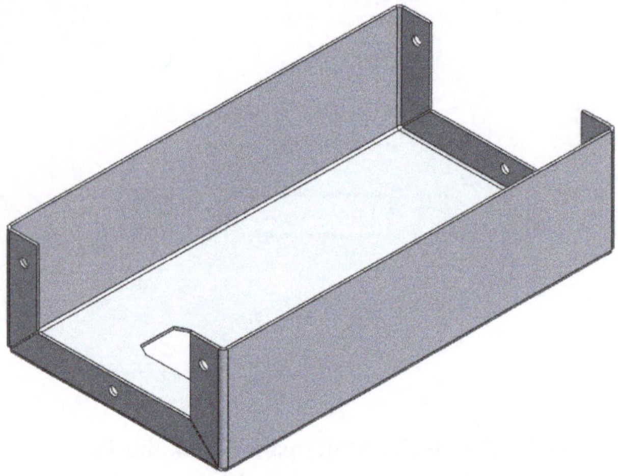

Starting a New Sheet metal File

1. To start a new sheet metal file, click **Get Started Launch > New** on the ribbon.
2. On the **Create New File** dialog, click **Templates > en-US > Metric** from the tree view located at the left side.
3. Click the **Sheet Metal(mm).ipt** icon, and then click **Create**.

Setting the Parameters of the Sheet Metal part

1. To set the parameters, click **Sheet Metal > Setup > Sheet Metal Defaults** on the ribbon; the **Sheet Metal Defaults** dialog appears.

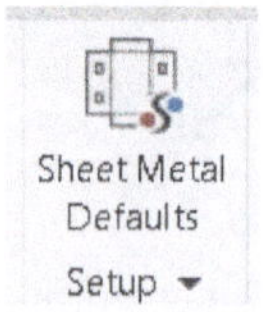

2. To edit the sheet metal rule, click the **Edit Sheet Metal Rule** button on the dialog.
3. In the **Sheet** tab, set the **Thickness** to **1.2** and leave all the default settings.
4. Click the **Bend** tab and type **1** in the **Bend Radius** box.
5. Click **Save & Close**.
6. Close the **Sheet Metal Defaults** dialog.
7. Click **Manage > Parameters > Parameters** f_x on

the ribbon; the **Parameters** dialog appears.

8. Select the **User Parameters** row and click the **Add Numeric** button on the dialog. This adds a new row.

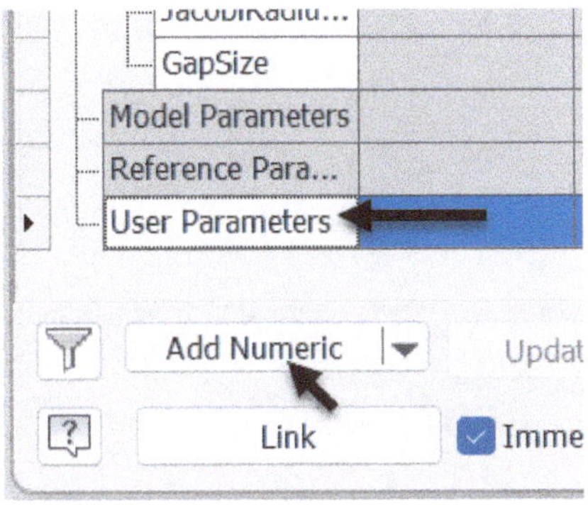

9. Enter **a1** in the new row.
10. Set **Unit Type** to **mm** and type-in **180** in the **Equation** box.

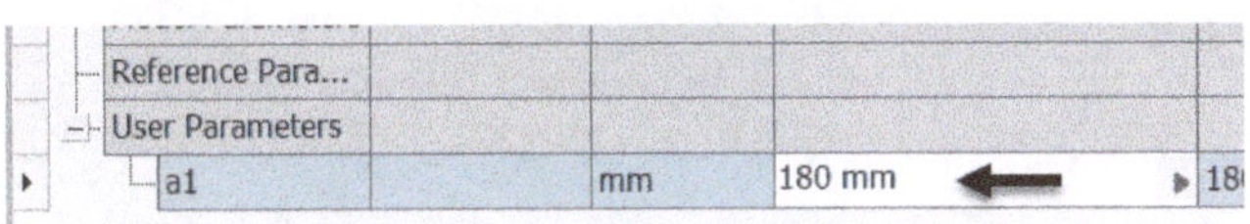

4. Likewise, create a parameter with the values, as shown, as shown below.

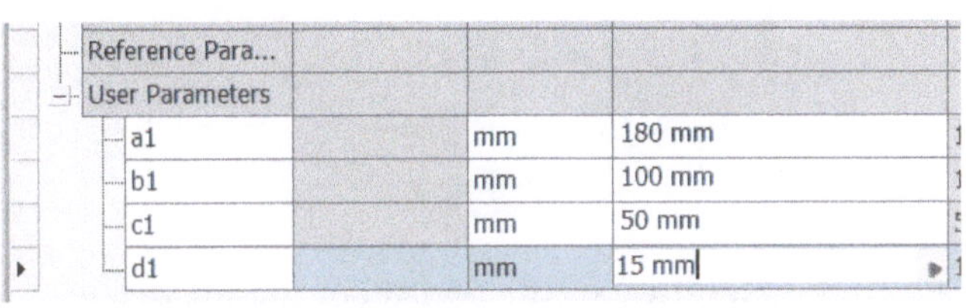

5. Click **Done** on the **Parameters** dialog.

6. On the ribbon, click **Sheet Metal** tab > **Start 2D Sketch**.
7. Click on XY Plane.
8. Activate the **Line** command and create a horizontal and vertical line, as shown.

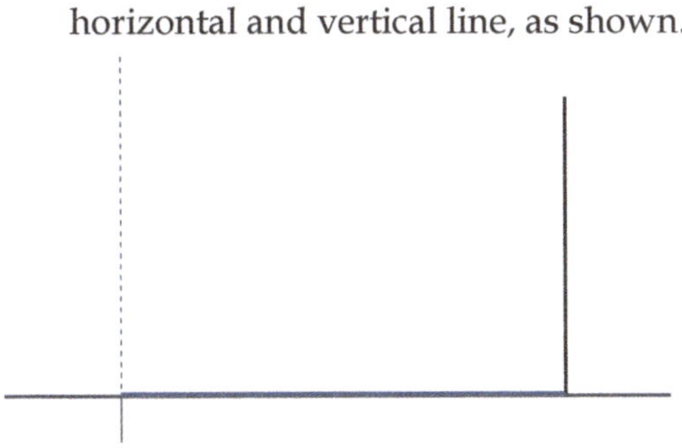

9. On ribbon, click **Sketch > Constrain > Dimension**.
10. Select the horizontal line.
11. Move the pointer downward and click to place the dimension.
12. On the **Edit Dimension** dialog, click the arrow button and select **List User Parameters**.

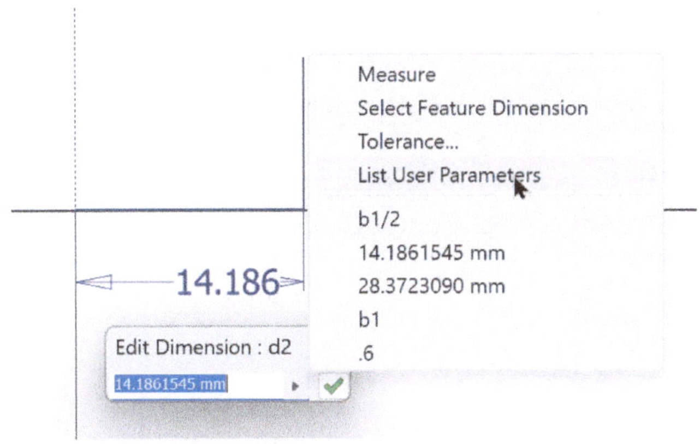

13. Select the **b1** parameter from the **Parameters** list.

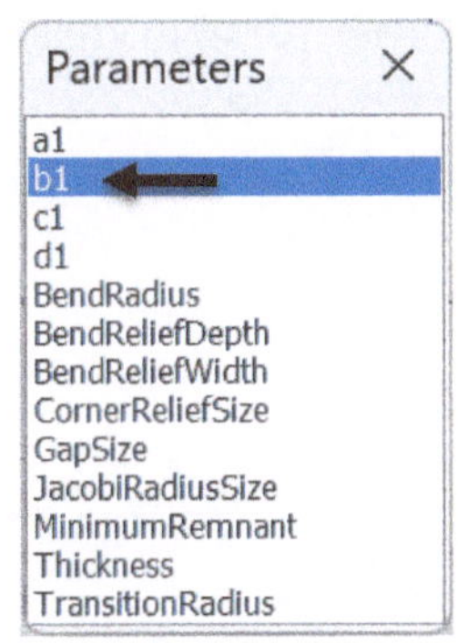

14. Type **/2** and click the green check.

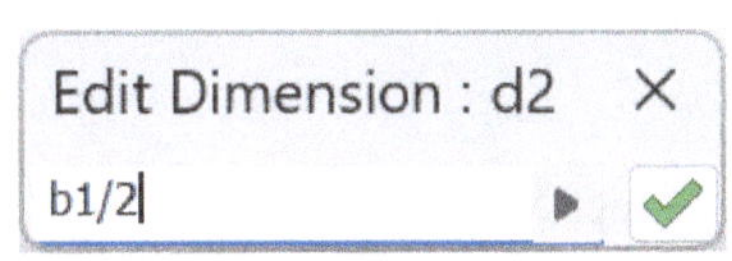

15. With the **Dimension** command active, select the vertical line.
16. Move the pointer toward right and click.
17. On the **Edit Dimension** dialog, select the dimension value and type **c1**.

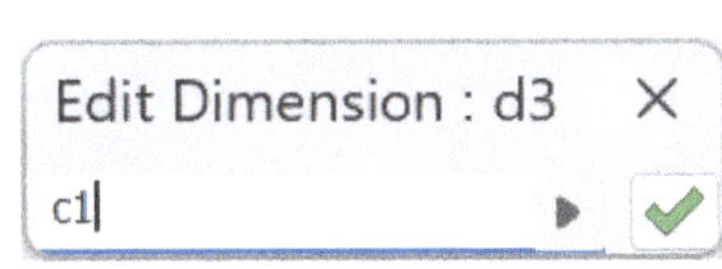

18. Click the green check on the **Edit Dimension** dialog.
19. Click **Finish** on the ribbon.

20. On the ribbon, click **Sheet Metal > Create > Contour Flange**.
21. Select the sketch from the graphics window.
22. Click **Position > Flipped** to make sure that the material is inside the sketch.
23. Click the arrow next to the Distance A box and select **List User Parameters**.

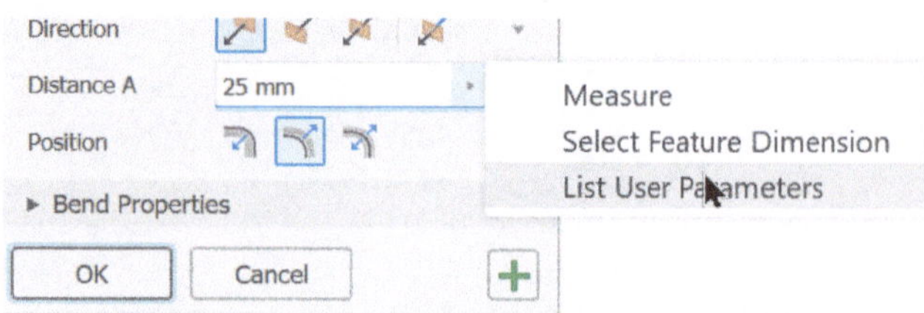

24. Select a1 from the parameter list.
25. Type **/2** to divide the a1 value by two.
26. Click the **OK** on the Properties panel to create the base flange.

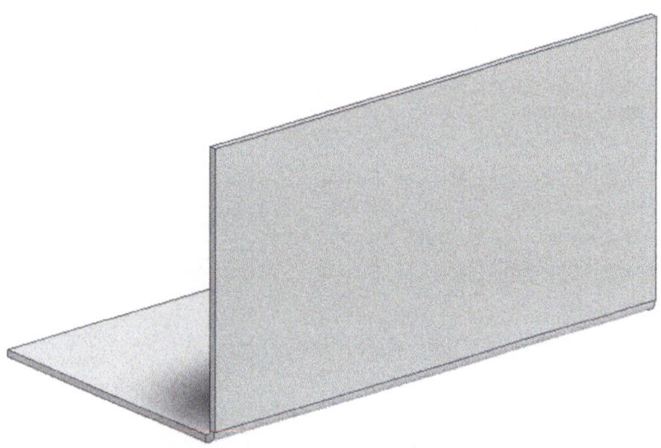

27. On the ribbon, click **Sheet Metal > Create > Flange**.
28. Select the inside edge of the vertical portion of the sheet metal.

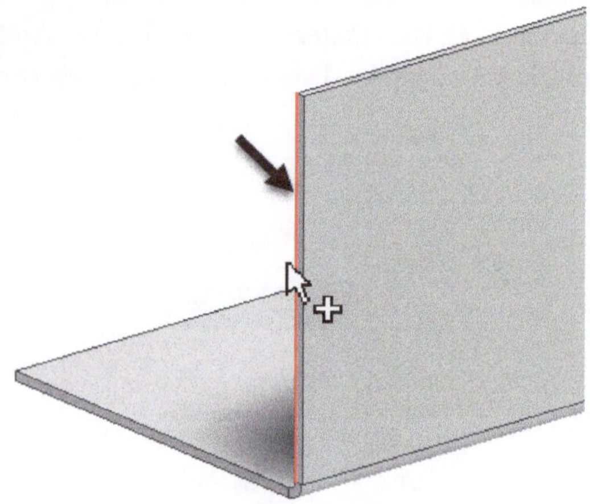

29. Likewise, select thee inside edge of the horizontal portion.

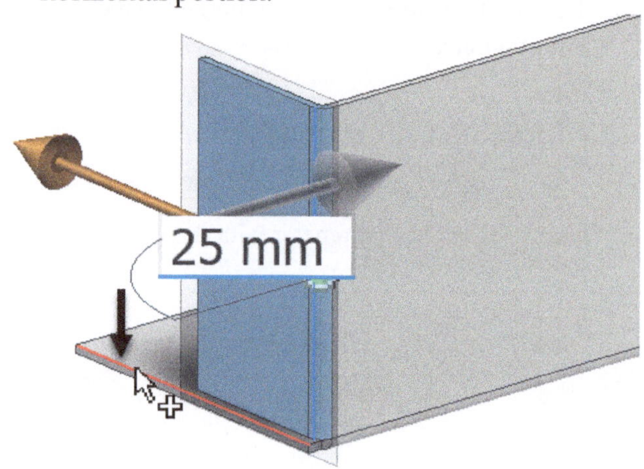

30. In the **Height Extents** section of the Properties panel, click the arrow button next to the **Distance** box and select **List User Parameters.**
31. Select **d1** from the parameters list.
32. Expand the **Corner Defaults** section, and type **0.5** in the **Miter Gap** box.

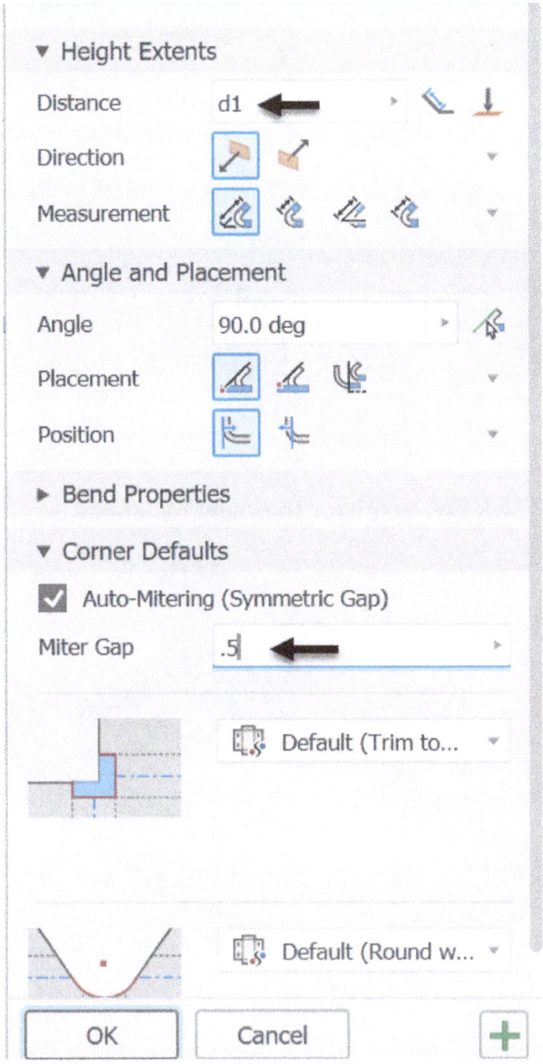

33. Click the **OK** on the Properties panel to create the edge flanges.

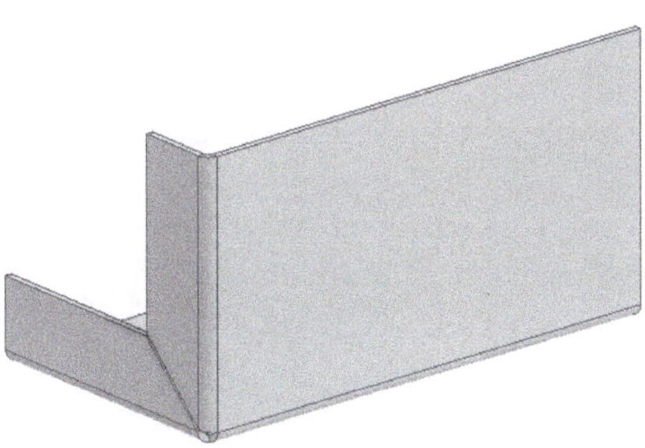

34. On the ribbon, click **Sheet Metal > Modify > Cut**.
35. Select the outer face of anyone of the edge flange.
36. Create two circles and add dimensions to it, as shown.

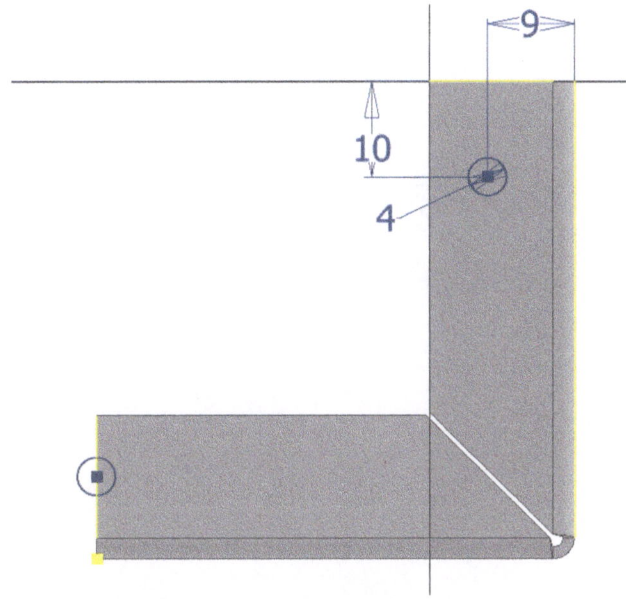

37. Click **Finish** on the ribbon.
38. Click in the regions enclosed by the circles.
39. Click **OK** on the Properties panel.

40. On the ribbon, click **Sheet Metal > Pattern > Mirror**.
41. Click the **Mirror solids**  icon on the **Mirror** dialog.
42. Click the **YZ Plane** icon on the **Mirror** dialog.

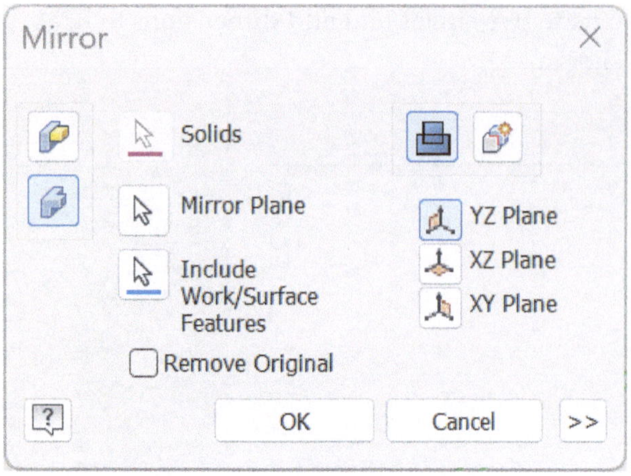

43. Click **OK** to mirror the sheet metal body.

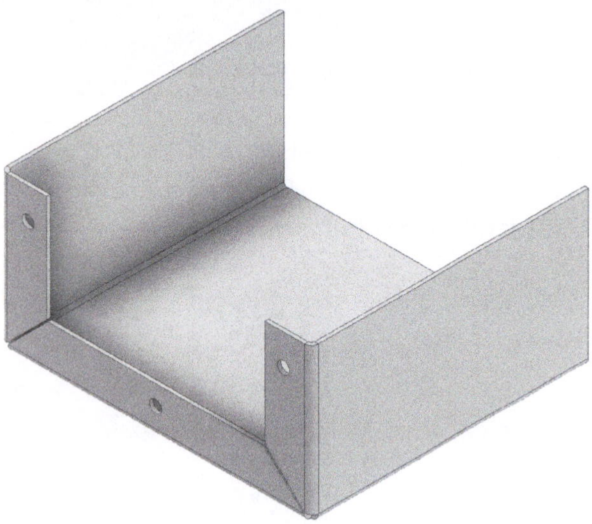

44. On the ribbon, click **Sheet Metal > Pattern > Mirror**.

45. Click the **Mirror solids**  icon on the **Mirror** dialog.
46. Click the **XY Plane** icon on the **Mirror** dialog.

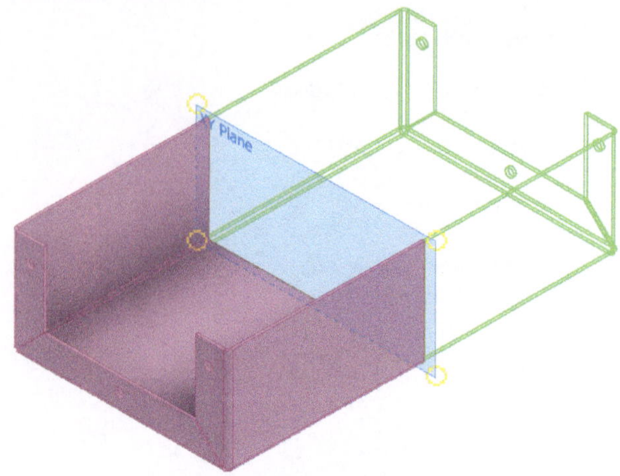

47. Click **OK** to mirror the sheet metal body.

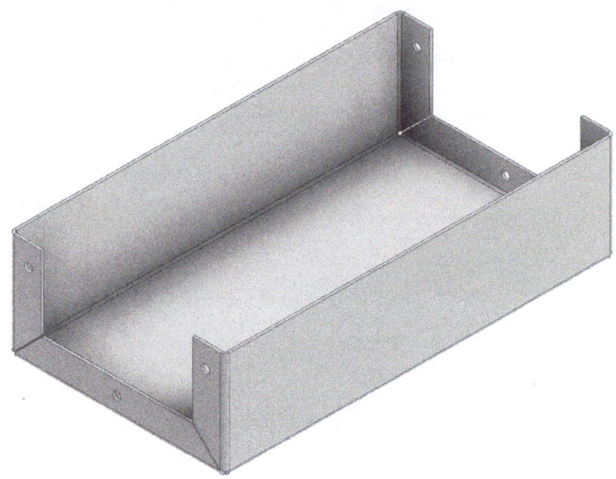

48. On the ribbon, click **Sheet Metal > Sketch > Start 2D Sketch**.
49. Rotate the model and select the bottom face.
50. Create a centered rectangle and add dimensions to it, as shown.

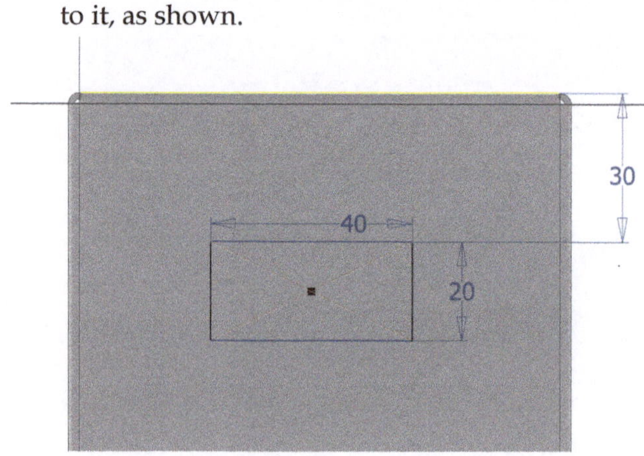

51. Click the **Vertical** icon under the **Constrain**

section of the ribbon.

52. Select the center point of the rectangle and the sketch origin.
53. On the ribbon, click **Sketch > Create > Fillet** drop-down > **Chamfer**.
54. On the **2D Chamfer** dialog, select **Distance-distance**  icon.
55. Type **5** and **2.5** in the **Distance 1** and **Distance 2** boxes, respectively.

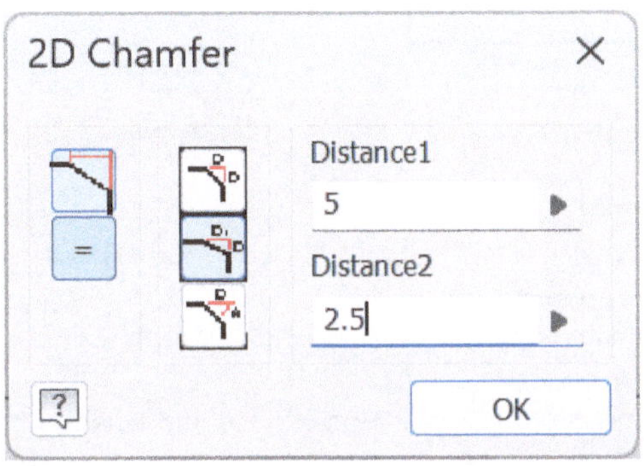

56. Select the lower horizontal line of the rectangle.
57. Select the left vertical line of the rectangle; a chamfer is created at the lower left corner.
58. Likewise, create three more chamfers by selecting the horizontal and vertical lines, as shown.

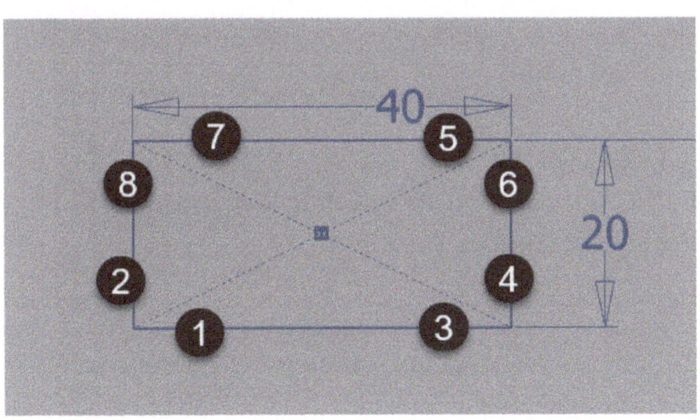

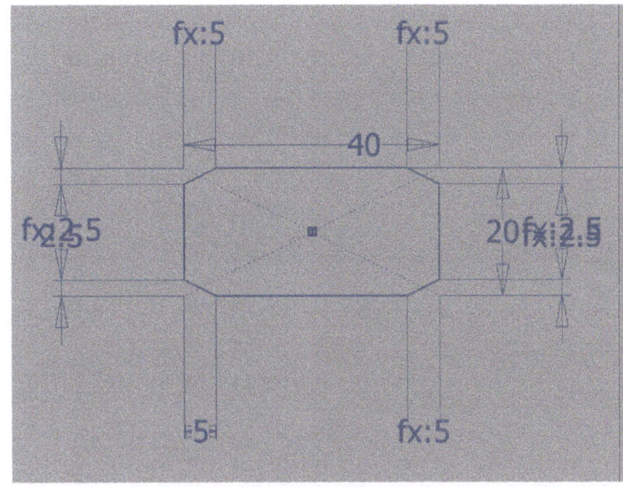

59. Click **OK** on the **2D Chamfer** dialog.
60. Click **Finish** on the ribbon.
61. On the ribbon, click **Sheet Metal > Modify > Cut**.
62. Click in the region enclosed by the sketch.
63. Click **OK** on the Properties panel.

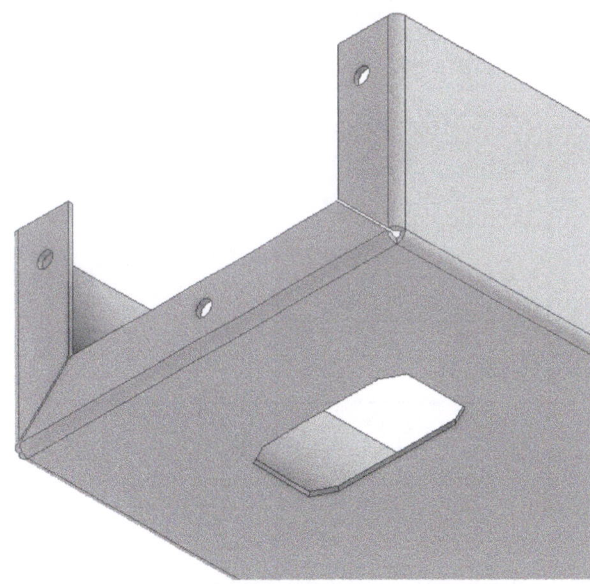

64. In the **Model** tab of the Browser, select the part node.

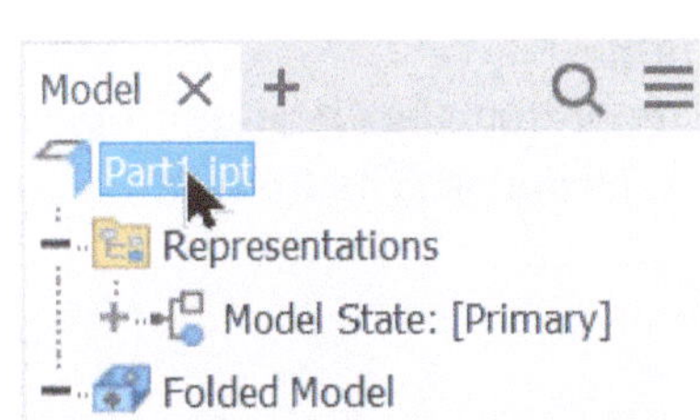

65. On the Quick Access Toolbar, click the **Material** drop-down and select the **Autodesk Material Library** option; the materials in the Autodesk material library are displayed.

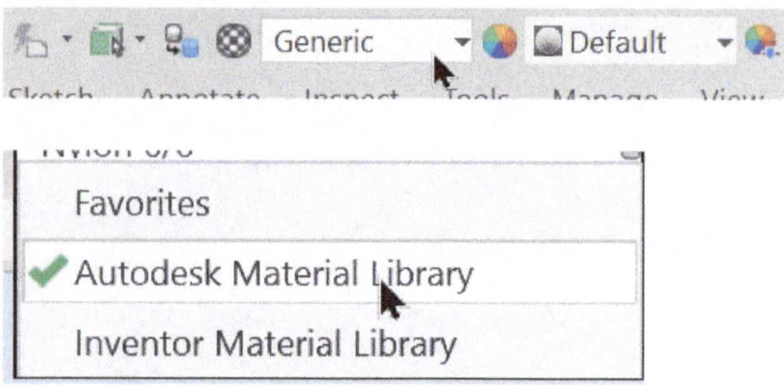

66. Select the **Aluminium 1100-H14** from the **Material** drop-down.

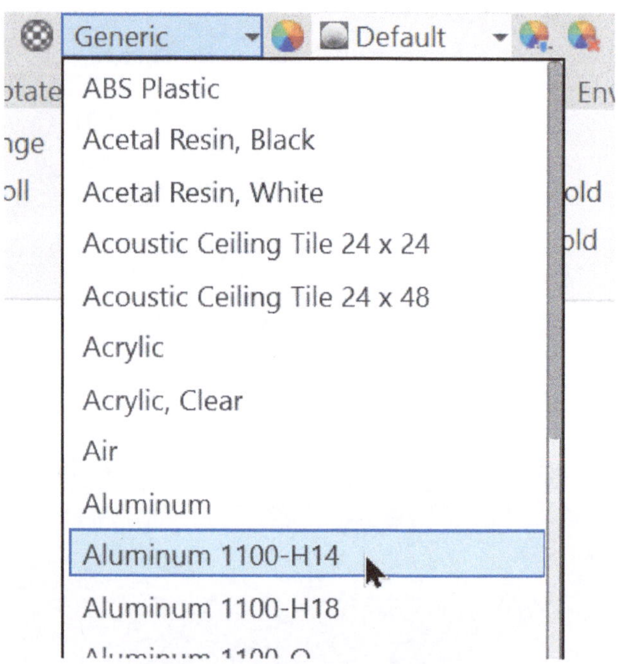

67. In the **Model** tab of the Browser, right-click on the part node and select iProperties.
68. On the iProperties dialog, select **Requested Accuracy > High**.
69. Click the **Update** button; the General Properties are updated on the dialog. The Mass is displayed as 0.126 kg.

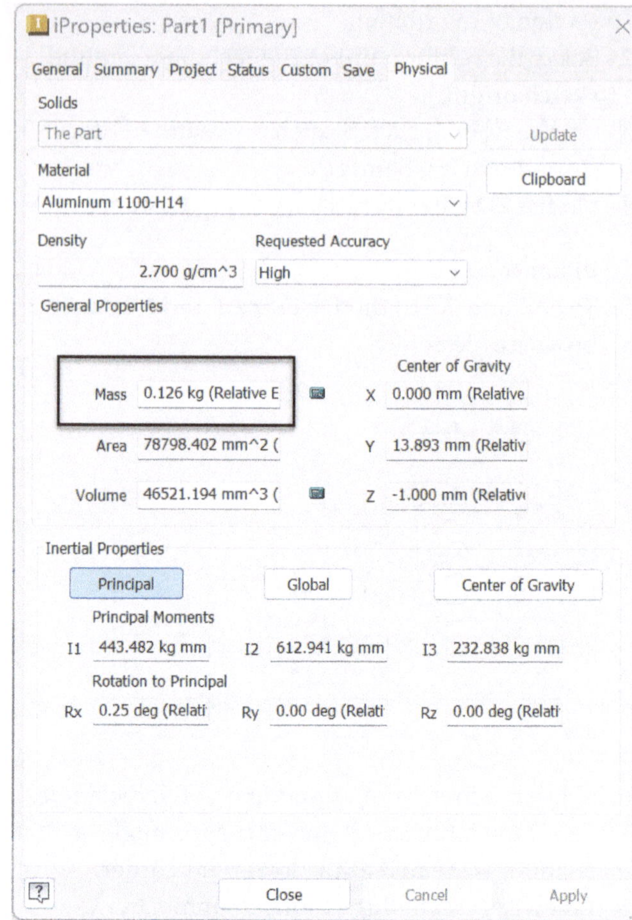

70. Close the **iProperties** dialog.
71. Click **Save** on the Quick Access Toolbar.
72. Type **C7_Tutorial5** in the **File name** box and click **Save.**

TUTORIAL 6

In this tutorial, you will update the parameters of the part created in Tutorial 15.

1. Open the file created in Tutorial 5.
2. On the ribbon, click **Manage > Parameters > Parameters.**
3. On the **Parameters** dialog, select the value in the **Equation** box next to the **a1** User Parameters.
4. Type **200.**
5. Likewise, change the **b1**, **c1**, and **d1** values to **110**, **40**, and **18**, respectively.

d4	Flange1, Co...	mm	Thickness	1
User Parameters				
a1	d9	mm	200 mm	2
b1	d2	mm	110 mm	1
c1	d3	mm	40 mm	4
d1	d19	mm	18 mm	1

6. Click **OK**; the model is updated.

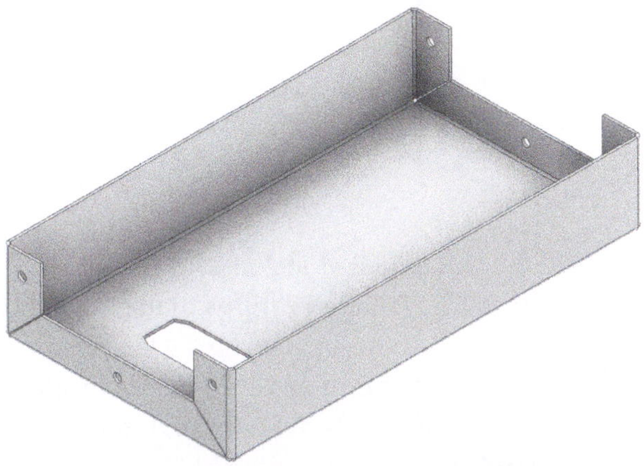

7. In the **Model** tab of the Browser, right-click on the part node and select iProperties.
8. On the iProperties dialog, select **Requested Accuracy > High**.
9. Click the **Update** button; the General Properties are updated on the dialog. The Mass is displayed as 0.133 kg.
10. Close the **iProperties** dialog.
11. Save the file as C7_tutorial6 and close it.

TUTORIAL 7

In this tutorial, you will create the flat pattern of the part created in Tutorial 5.

1. Open the file created in Tutorial 5.
2. Click **Sheet Metal > Setup > Sheet Metal Defaults** on the ribbon; the **Sheet Metal Defaults** dialog appears.

3. To edit the sheet metal unfold rule, click the **Edit Unfold Rule** button on the dialog.
4. Type 0.4 in the **KFactor Value** box.

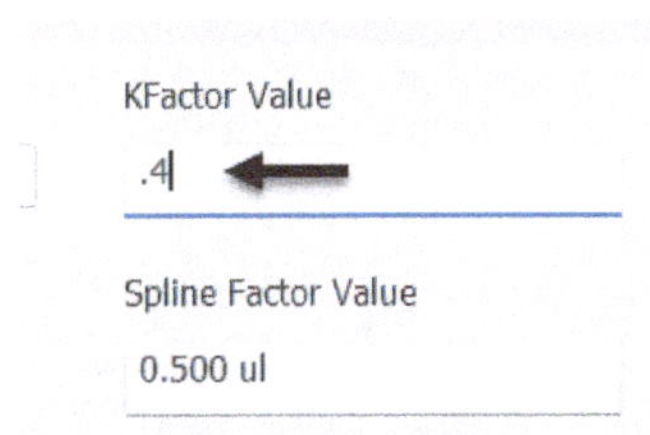

5. Click **Save & Close.**
6. Close the **Sheet Metal Defaults** dialog.
7. To create a flat pattern, click **Sheet Metal > Flat Pattern > Create Flat Pattern** on the ribbon.

8. On the ribbon, click **Inspect > Measure > Measure**.
9. Select the vertices of the flatten pattern. The 195.85 is displayed.

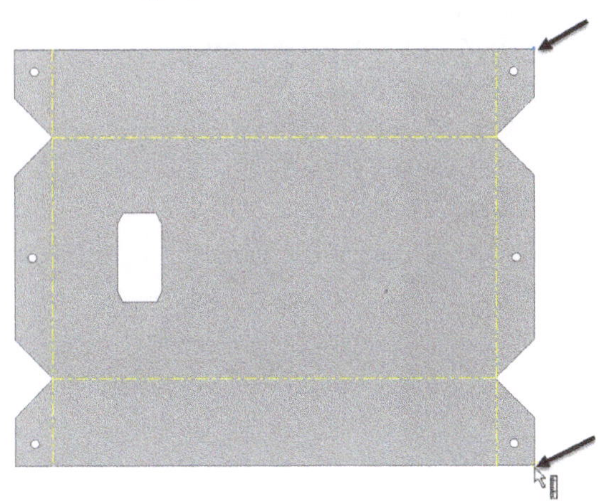

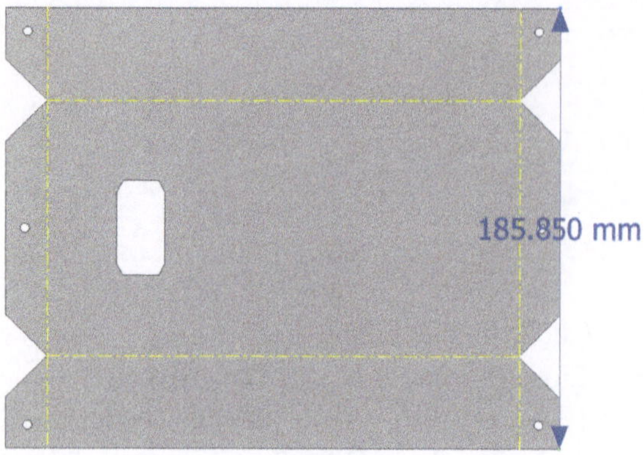

10. Save it as C7_tutorial7 and close the file.

TUTORIAL 8

In this tutorial, you will create the flat pattern of the Tutorial 6 part file.

1. Open the file created in Tutorial 16.
2. Click **Sheet Metal > Setup > Sheet Metal Defaults** on the ribbon; the **Sheet Metal Defaults** dialog appears.

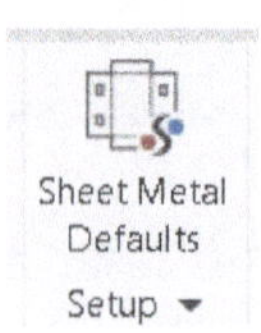

3. To edit the sheet metal unfold rule, click the **Edit Unfold Rule** button on the dialog.
4. Type 0.32 in the **KFactor Value** box.
5. Click **Save & Close.**
6. Close the **Sheet Metal Defaults** dialog.
7. Type 0.32 in the **K** box.
8. Click **OK.**
9. In the Model tab of the Browser, right-click on the **Cut** feature and select **Delete.**

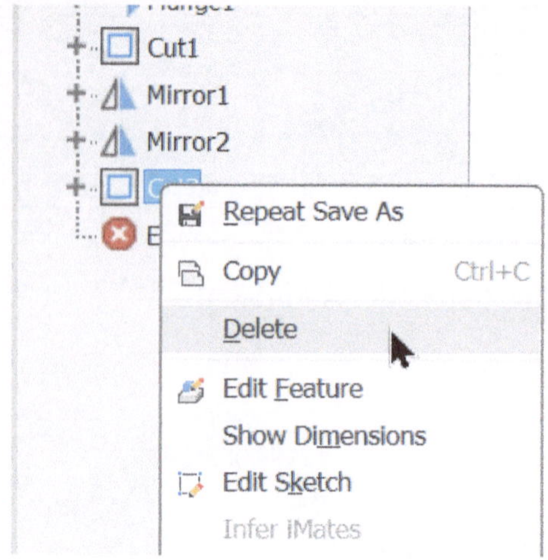

10. Check the **consumed sketches and features** option from the **Delete Features** dialog and click **OK.**
11. Click and drag the **End of Folded** node located at the bottom of the **Model** tab. Next, release it above the **Cut1** feature.

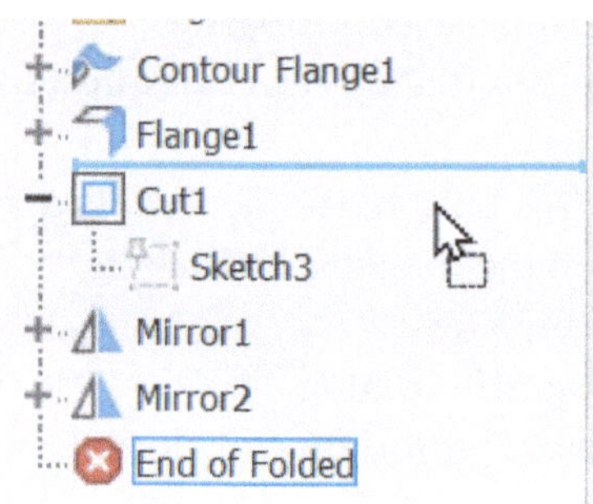

12. On the ribbon, click **Sheet Metal > Create > Hem** .
13. Select the inner edge of the flange, as shown.

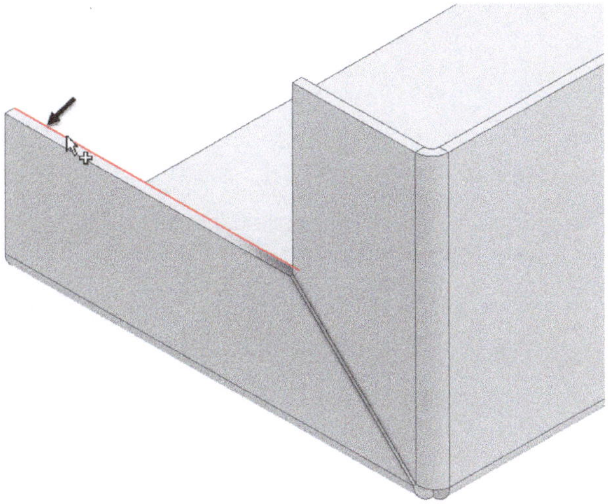

14. Select **Type > Single**.
15. Type **10** and **1** in the **Length** and **Gap** boxes, respectively.
16. Click the **Expand** button to expand the Hem dialog.
17. In the **Width Extents** section, select **Type > Offset**.
18. Type **0** and **2** in the **Offset1** and **Offset2** boxes, respectively.

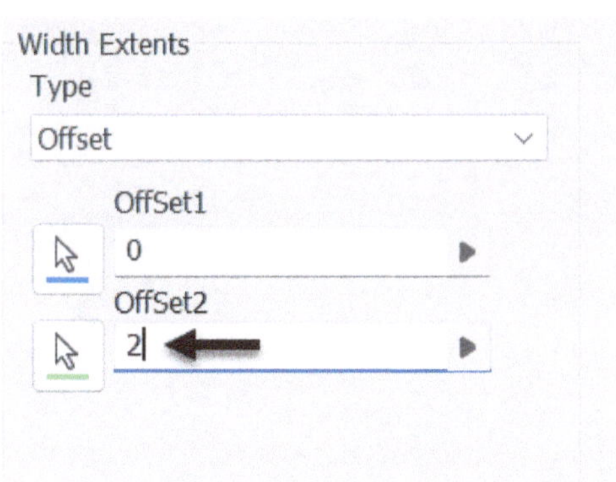

19. Click the **Bend** tab and select **Relief Shape > Tear**.

20. Click **OK**.

21. Click and drag the bar located at the bottom of the Model tab. Next, release it below the last feature.

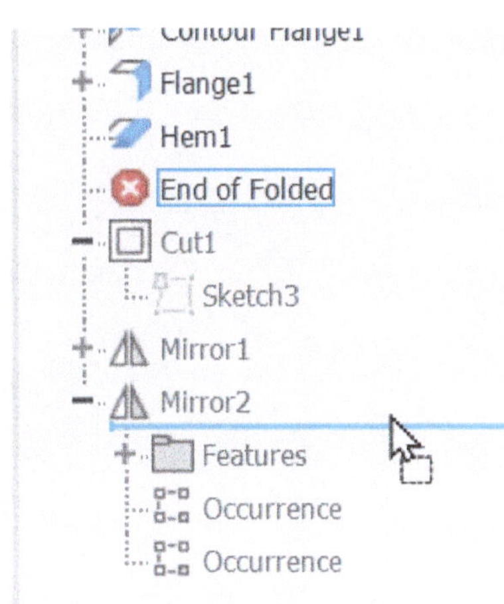

The model is updated, as shown.

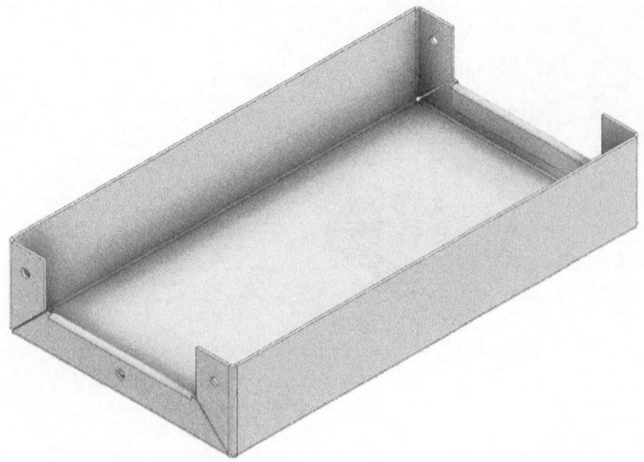

22. In the **Model** tab, right-click on the part node and select **iProperties**.
23. Click the **Physical** tab, and then click the **Update** button. The Mass is displayed as 0.140 kg.
24. Close the **iProperties** dialog.
25. Save and close the file.

Chapter 8: Top-Down Assembly and Joints

In this chapter, you will learn to

- Create a top-down assembly
- Insert Fasteners using Design Accelerator
- Export to 3D PDF
- Create assembly joints

TUTORIAL 1

In this tutorial, you will create the model shown in the figure. You use a top-down assembly approach to create this model.

Creating a New Assembly File

1. To create a new assembly, click **New** > **Assembly** on the Home screen.

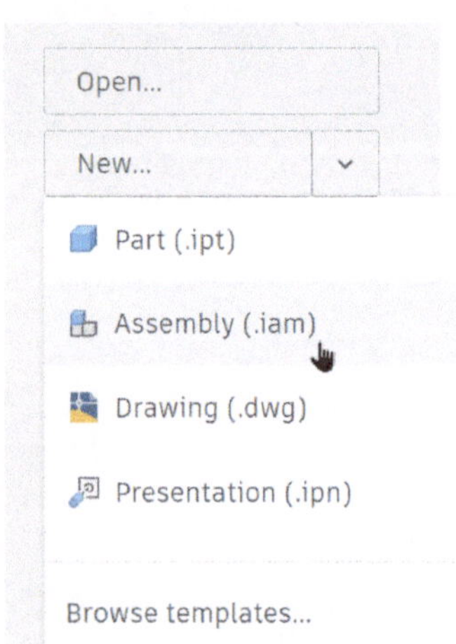

Creating a component in the Assembly

In a top-down assembly approach, you create components of an assembly directly in the assembly by using the **Create** tool.

1. Click **Create** on the **Component** panel of the **Assembly** tab. The **Create In-Place Component** dialog appears.

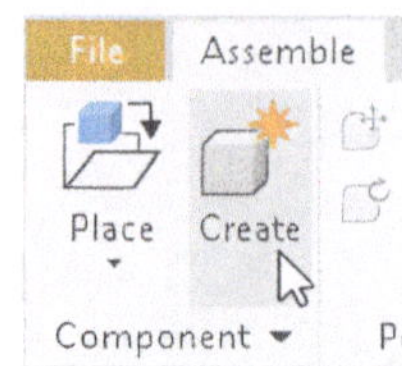

2. Enter **Base** in the **New Component Name** field.

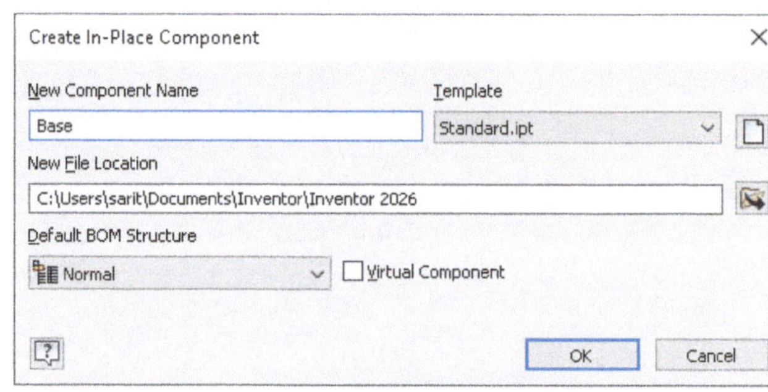

3. In the **Create In-Place Component** dialog, set the **New File Location** to the current project folder.
4. Click the **Browse to New File Location** icon.
5. On the **Save As** dialog, click the **Create New Folder** icon.
6. Type **C08_Tut_01** as the name of the folder.
7. Double-click on the new folder and click **Save**.
8. Click **OK** on the **Create In-Place Component** dialog.
9. Expand the **Origin** folder in the **Browser window** and select the **XZ Plane**. The **3D Model** tab is activated in the ribbon.

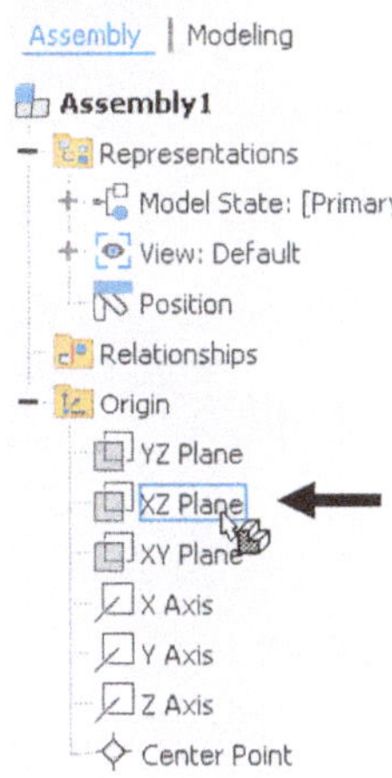

10. Click **Sketch > Start 2D Sketch** on the ribbon.
11. Select the **XY Plane**.
12. Create a sketch, as shown below.

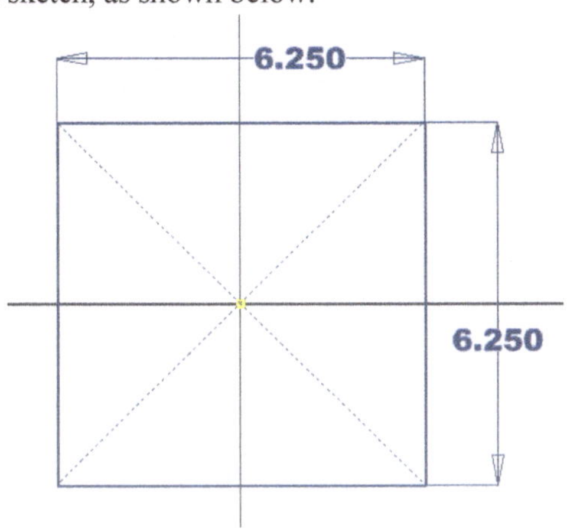

13. Click **Finish** on the ribbon.
14. Click **3D Model > Create > Extrude** on the ribbon and extrude the sketch up to 1.5 in.

15. Start a sketch on the top face and draw a circle of **2** in diameter.

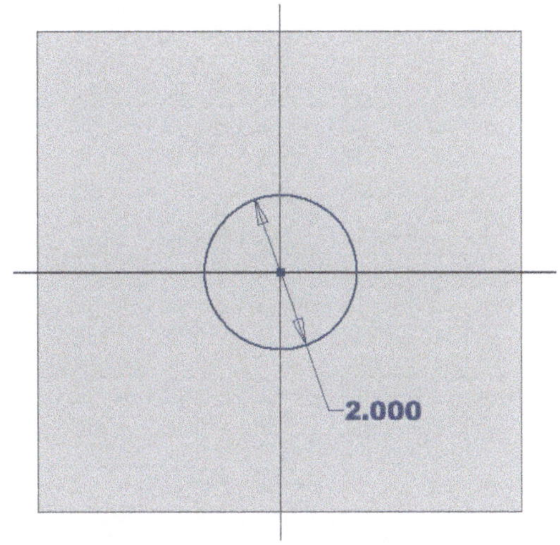

16. Click **Finish.**
17. Extrude the sketch up to **3.75** inches' distance.
18. Create a counterbore hole on the second feature (See Chapter 5, Tutorial 1, Create a Counterbore Hole section). The following figure shows the dimensions of the counterbore hole.

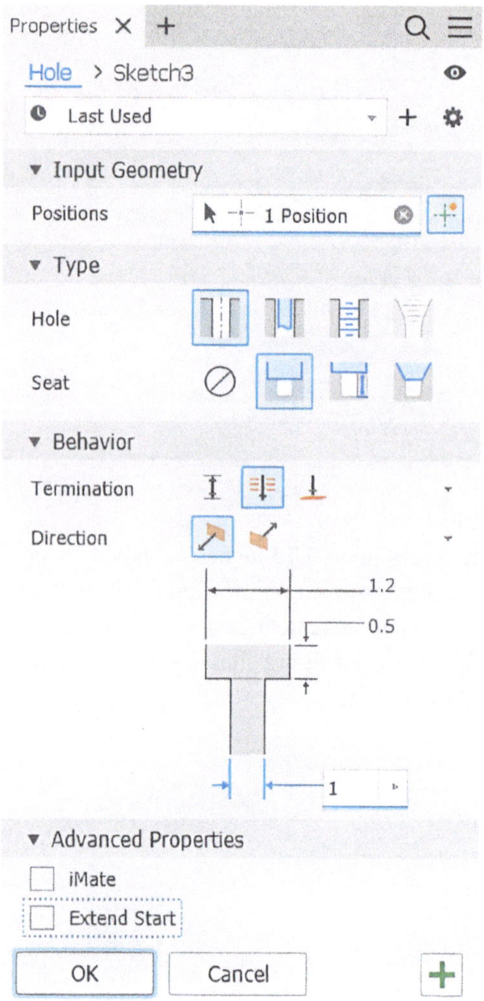

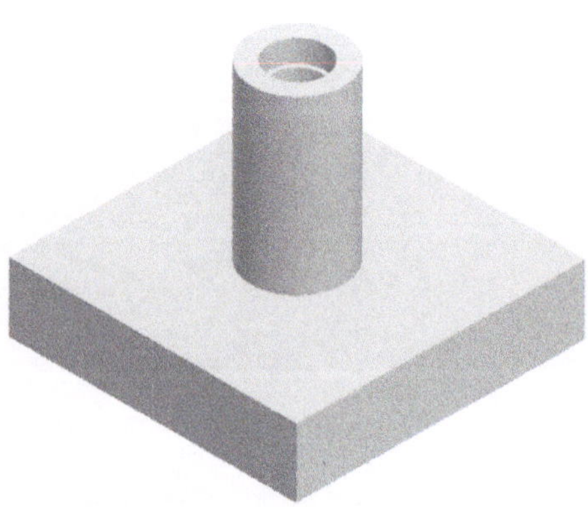

19. Start a new sketch on the top face of the first feature.
20. Create a **3.5** diameter circle with the **Construction** button active.

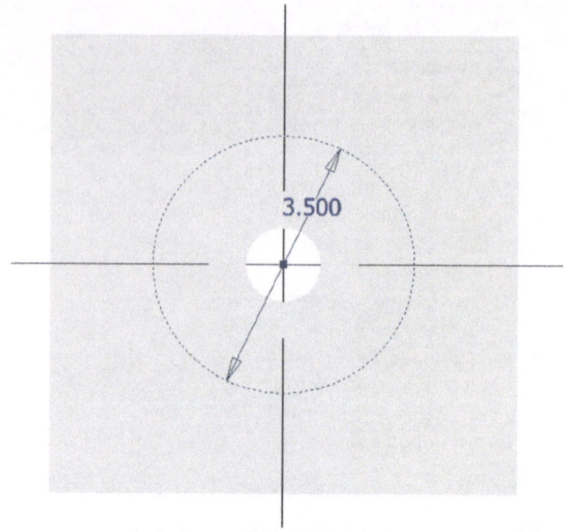

21. On the ribbon, click **Sketch > Create > Point**.
22. Place a point on the circle, as shown.

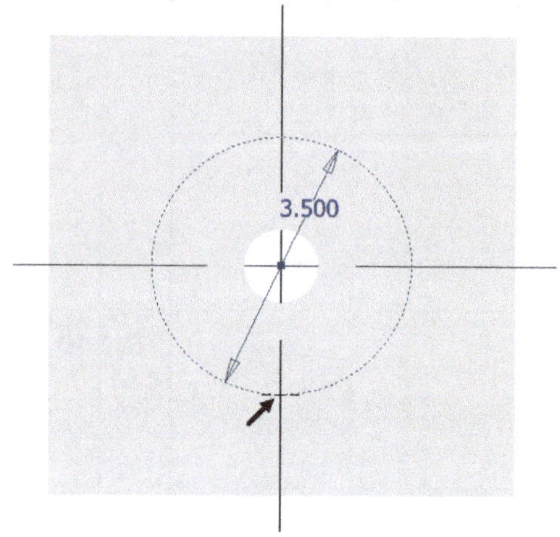

23. Click **Finish**.
24. On the ribbon, click **3D Model > Modify > Hole**.
25. On the **Properties** panel, specify the settings, as shown.

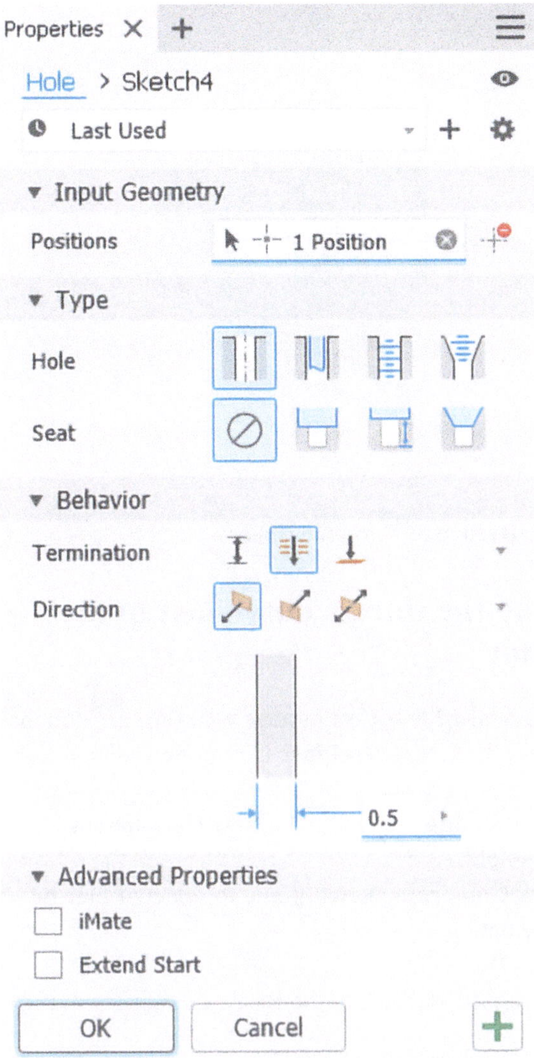

26. Make sure that the sketch point is selected.

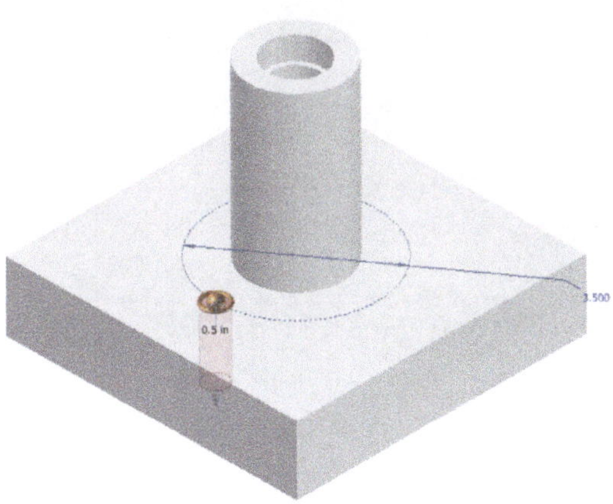

27. Click **OK** to create the hole.
28. Create a circular pattern of the hole (See Chapter 5, Tutorial 1, Create a Circular Pattern).

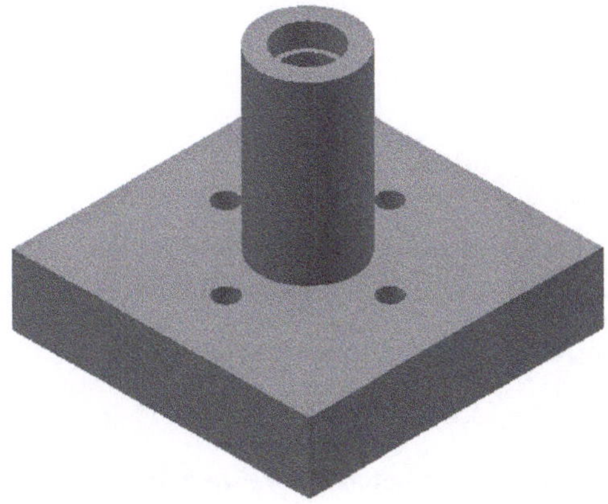

29. Click the **Return** button on the ribbon.

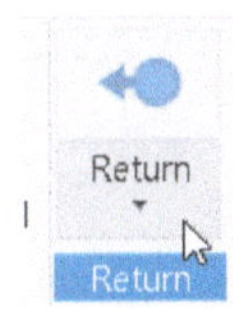

Creating the Second Component of the Assembly

1. Click **Assemble > Component > Create**  on the ribbon; the **Create In-Place Component** dialog appears.
2. Enter **Spacer** in the **New Component name** field.
3. Check **Constrain sketch plane to selected face or plane** option.
4. Click **OK**.
5. Select the top face of the Base.

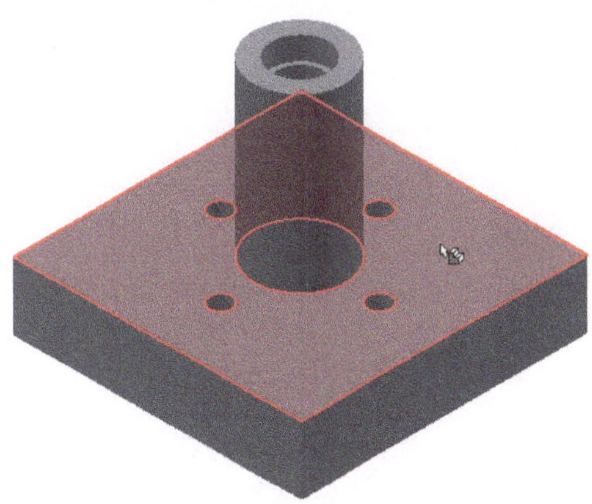

6. Click **Sketch > Start 2D Sketch** on the ribbon.
7. Select the top face of the Base.

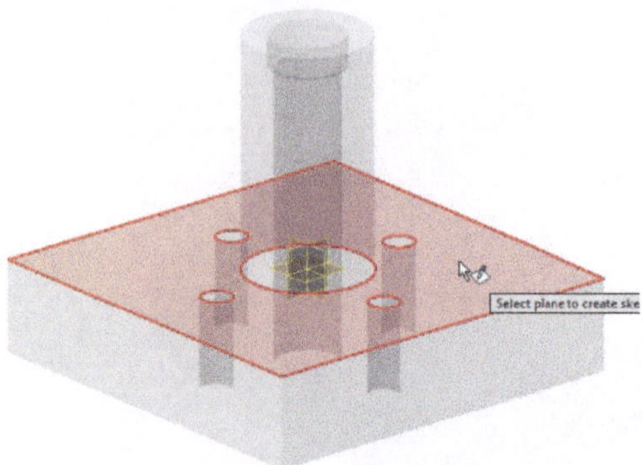

8. On the ribbon, click **Sketch > Create > Project Geometry** and select the circular edges of the Base.

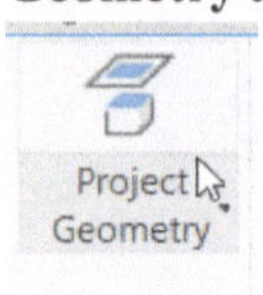

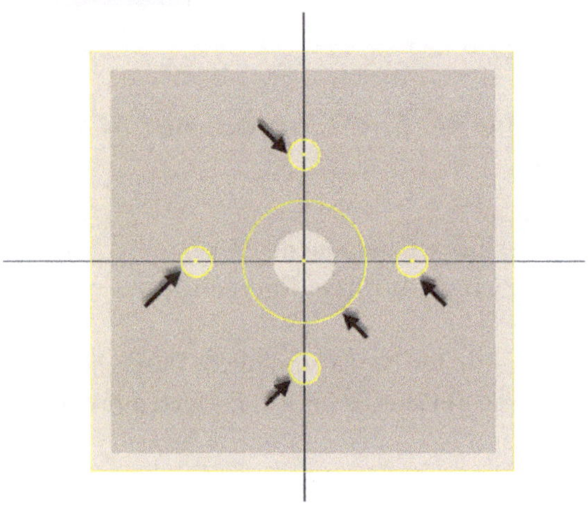

9. Draw a circle of **4.5** in diameter.

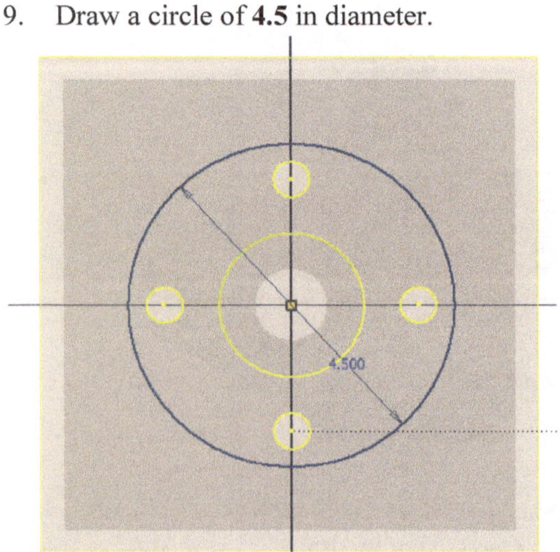

10. Click **Finish**.
11. Extrude the sketch up to **1.5** in.

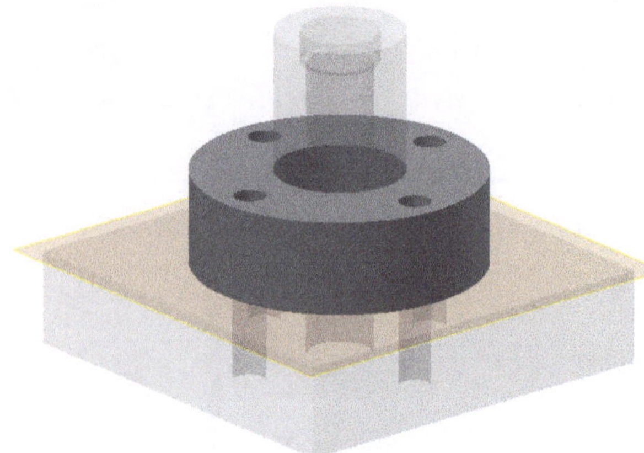

12. Click **Return**  on the ribbon.

Creating the third Component of the Assembly

1. Click **Assemble > Component > Create**  on the ribbon; the **Create In-Place Component** dialog appears.
2. Enter **Shoulder Screw** in the **New Component name** field.
3. Check **Constrain sketch plane to selected face or plane** option.
4. Click **OK**.
5. Click on the top face of the Base.

6. Start a sketch on the YZ Plane.

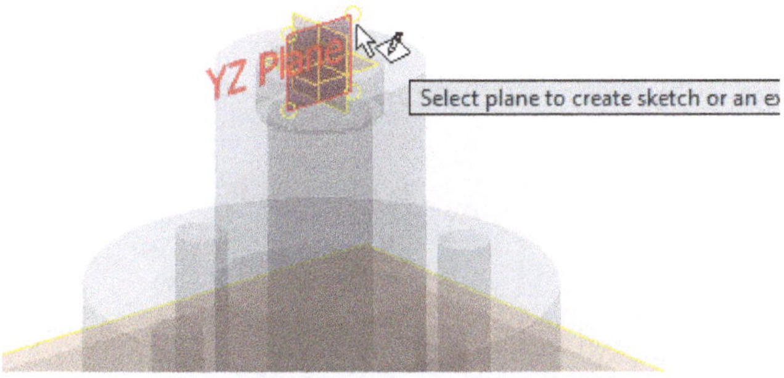

7. Draw a sketch, as shown in the figure.

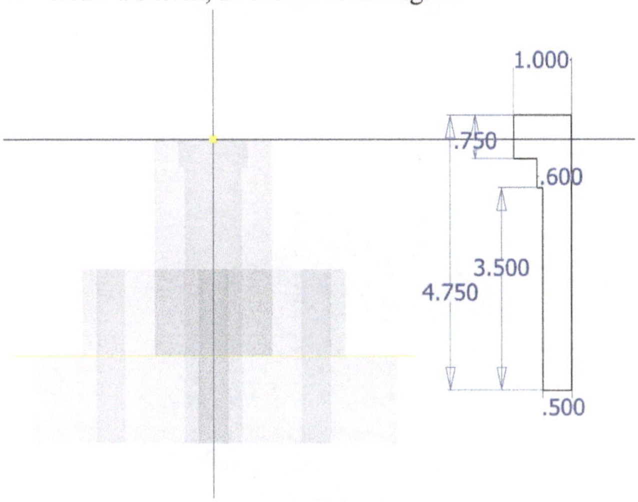

8. On the ribbon, click **Sketch > Create > Project Geometry**.
9. Select the top edge of the model, as shown.

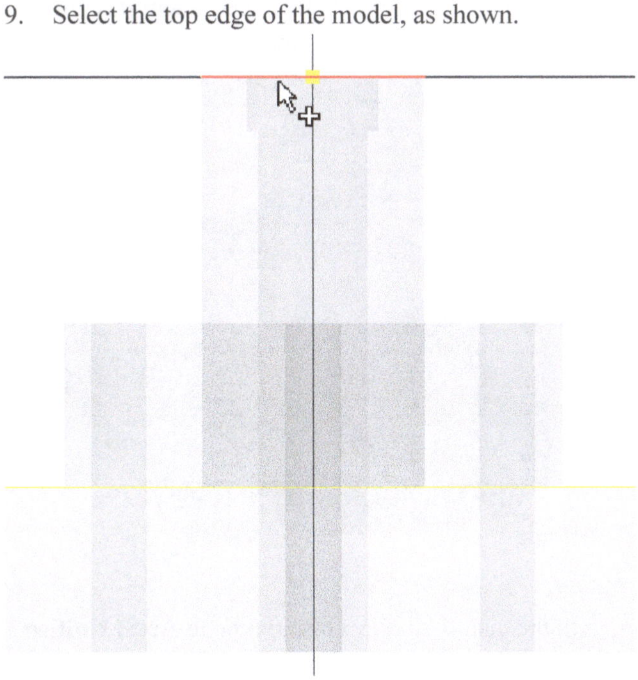

10. Apply the Coincident constraint between the corner point of the sketch and the left-end point of the projected edge.

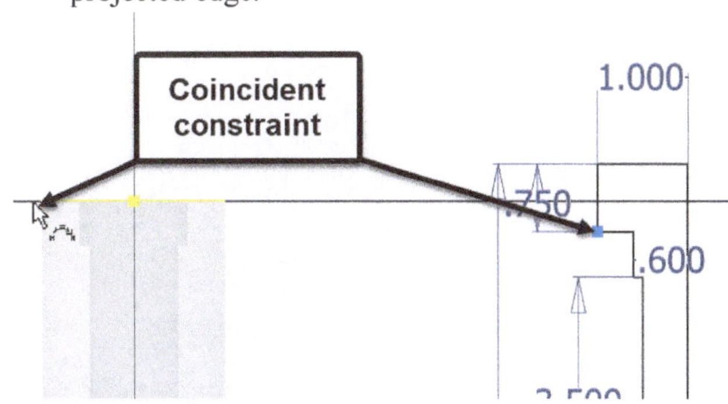

11. Click **Finish**.
12. Activate the **Revolve** tool and revolve the sketch.

13. Activate the **Chamfer** tool and chamfer the edges, as shown in the figure.

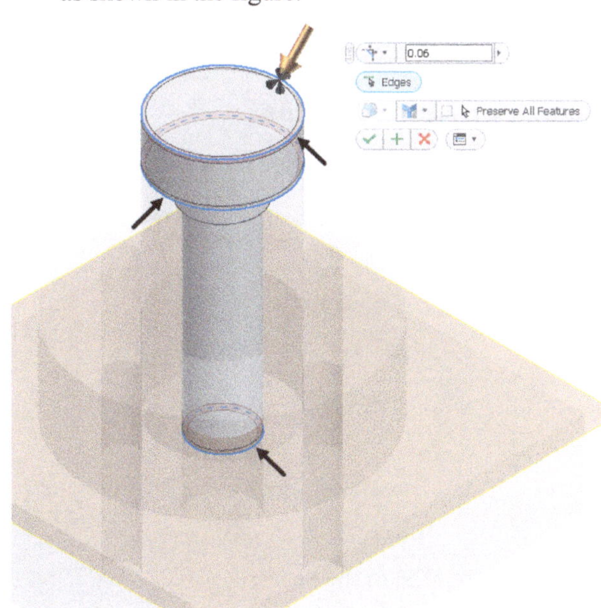

14. Activate the **Fillet** tool and round the edges, as shown in the figure.

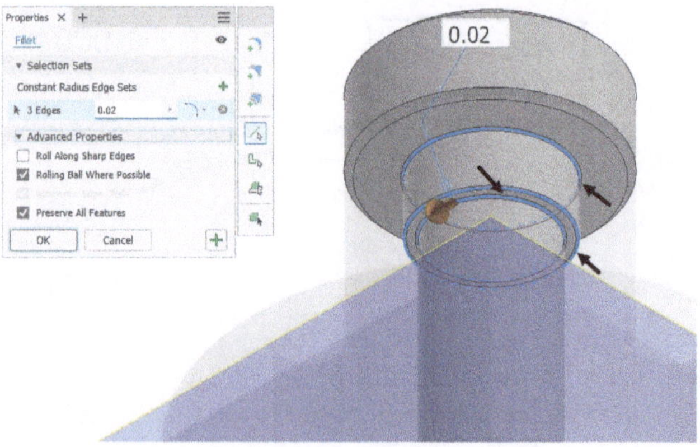

15. Click **Return**  on the ribbon.
16. Save the assembly.

Adding Bolt Connections to the assembly

1. On the ribbon, click **Design > Fasten > Bolt Connection**.

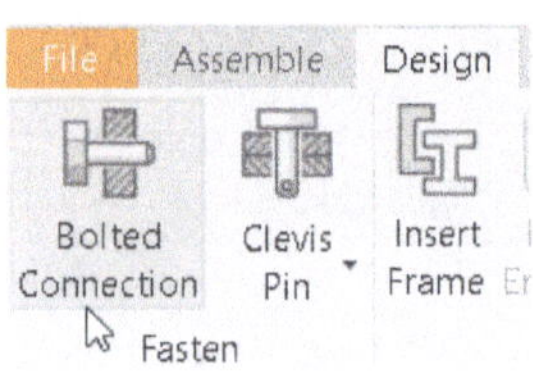

2. On the **Bolted Connection Component Generator** dialog, under the **Design** tab, select **Type > Through All.**
3. Select **Placement > Concentric**.

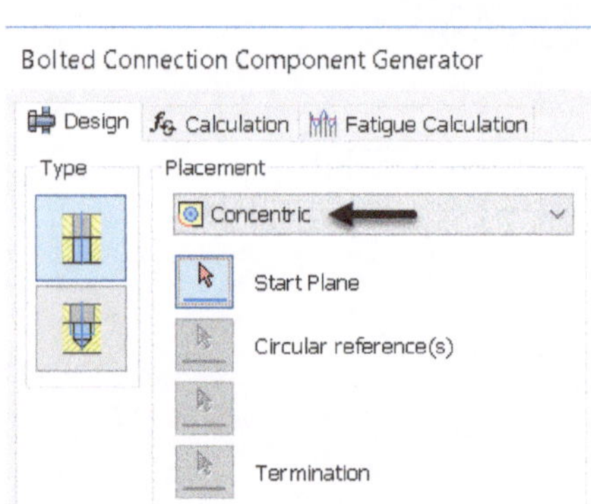

4. Select the top face of the Spacer.

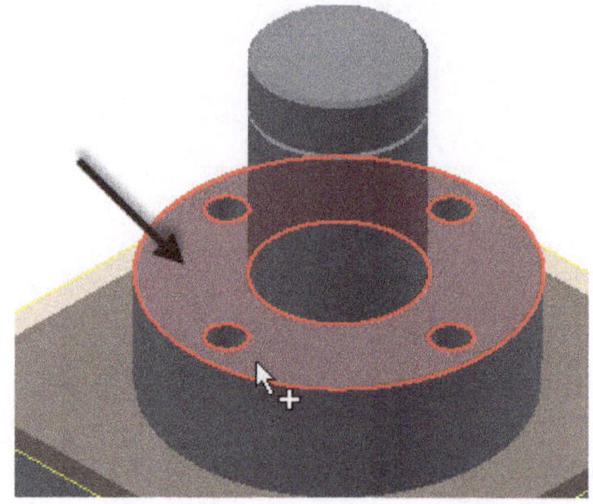

5. Click on the hole to define the circular reference.

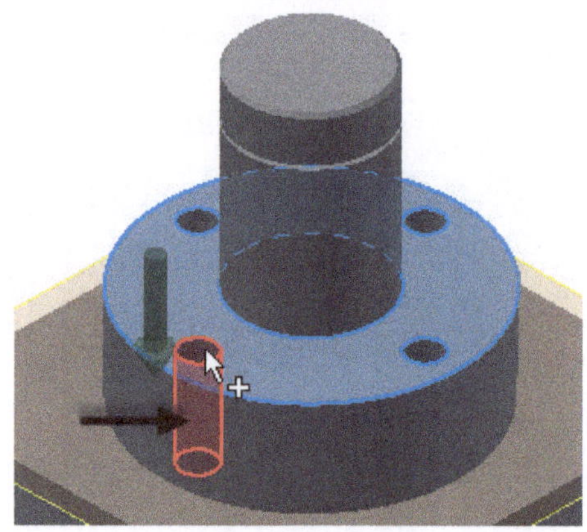

6. Rotate the model and click on the bottom face of the base. This defines the termination.

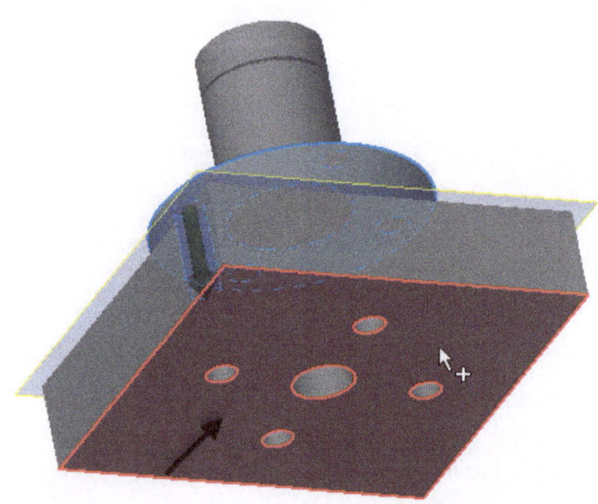

7. On the dialog, set the **Thread** type to **ANSI Unified Screw Threads**.
8. Make sure that the **Diameter** is set to **0.5** in.

9. On the dialog, click **Click to add a fastener**.

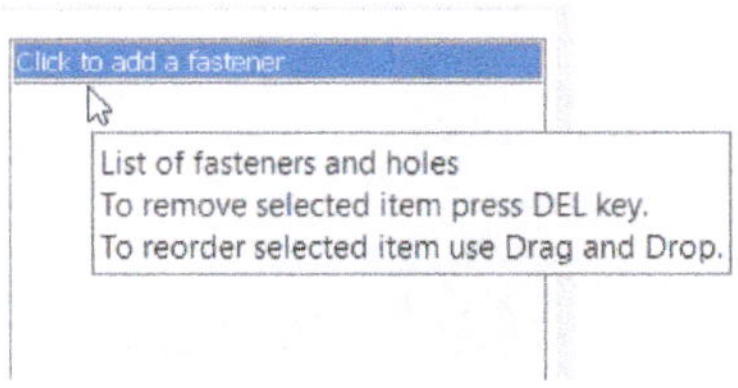

10. On the pop-up dialog, set the **Standard** to **ANSI** and **Category** to **Hex Head Bolts**.
11. Select **Hex Bolt-Inch**. This adds a hex bolt to the list.

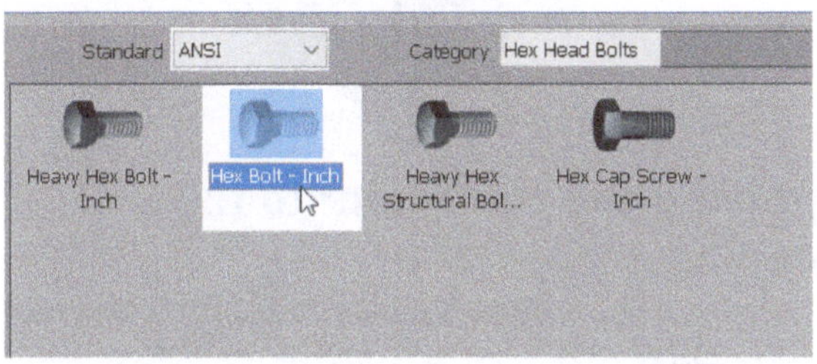

12. On the list, click **Click to add a fastener** below the Hex Bolt.
13. On the pop-up dialog, scroll down and select **Plain Washer (Inch)**.

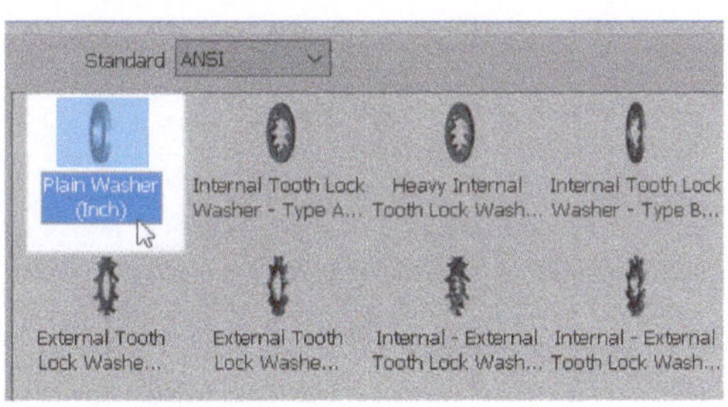

14. Click **Click to add a fastener** at the bottom of the list.

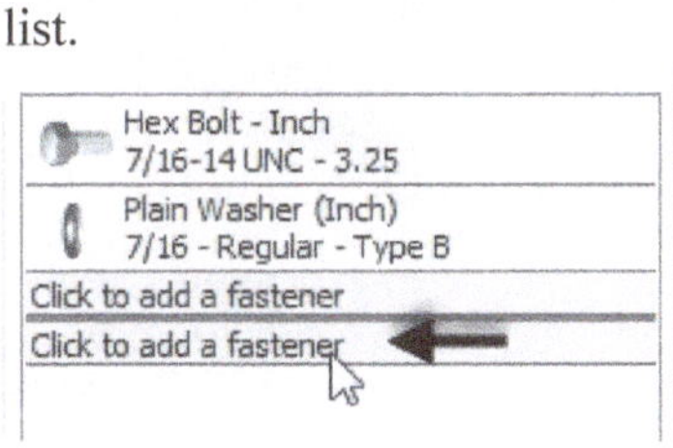

15. On the pop-up dialog, scroll down and select **Plain Washer (Inch)**.
16. Click **Click to add a fastener** at the bottom of the list.
17. On the pop-up dialog, set the **Category** to **Nuts** and select **Hex Nut –Inch**.

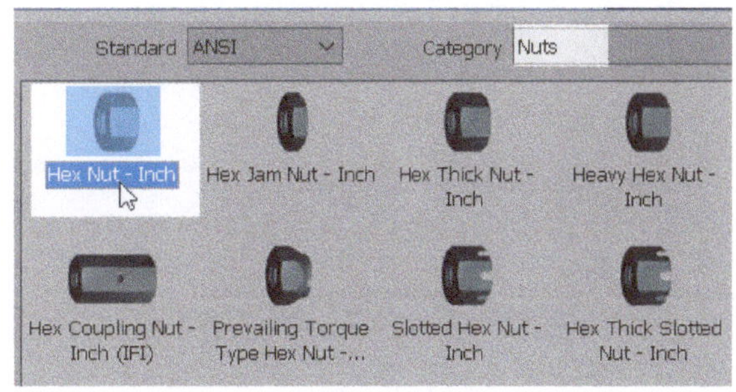

18. Click **OK** twice to add a bolt connection subassembly.

Patterning components in an assembly

1. On the ribbon, click **Assemble > Pattern > Pattern**.

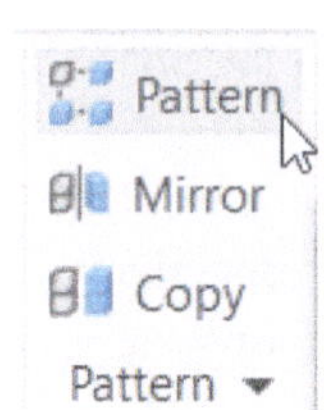

2. Select the components of the **Bolt connection** from the Browser window.

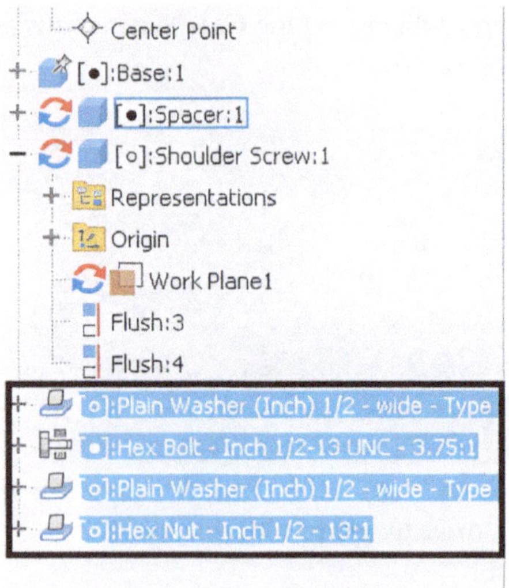

3. On the **Pattern Component** dialog, click the **Circular** tab and select the **Axis Direction** button.

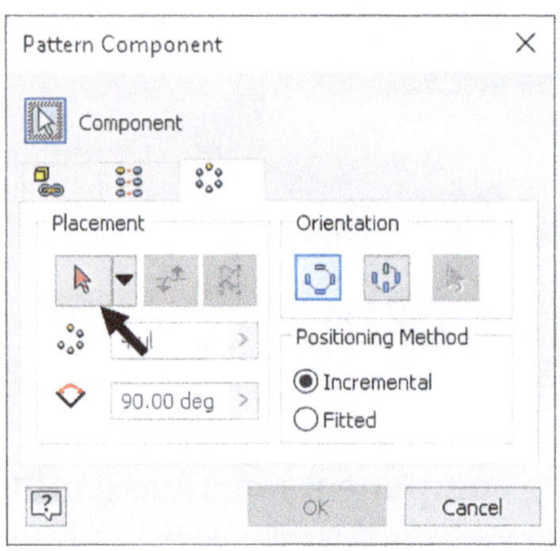

4. Click on the large cylindrical face of the Spacer to define the axis of the circular pattern.
5. On the dialog, type in **4** and **90** in the **Circular Count** and **Circular Angle** boxes, respectively.
6. Click **OK** to pattern the bolt connection.

Applying the constraint to the components

1. On the ribbon, click **View > Visibility > Degrees of Freedom**.

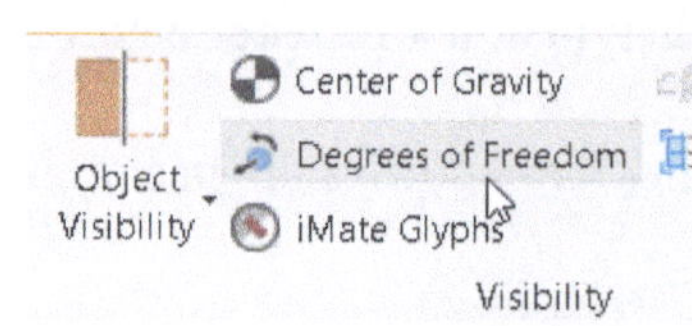

2. On the ribbon, click **Assemble > Relationships > Constrain**.
3. On the dialog, click the **Mate** icon and click on the round faces of the Spacer and Base.

4. Click the **Aligned** 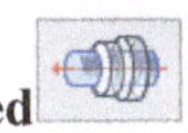 icon in the **Solution** group.
5. Click **Apply**.
6. Click on the round faces of the Shoulder Screw and Base.

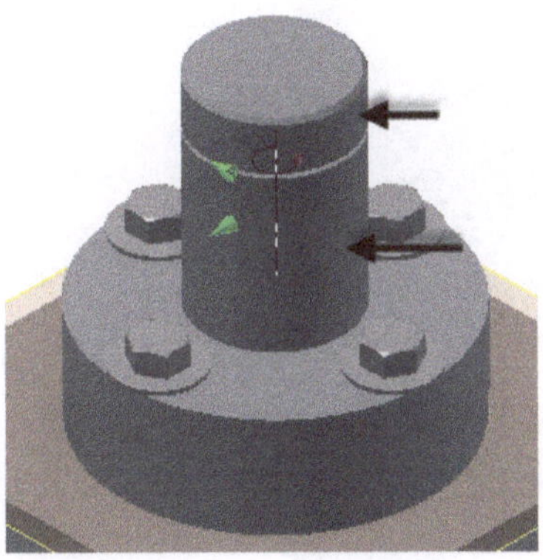

7. Click **Apply**.
8. On the dialog, select **Flush** from the **Solution** section.
9. In the Browser Window, expand the **Origin** folder and select **XY Plane**.

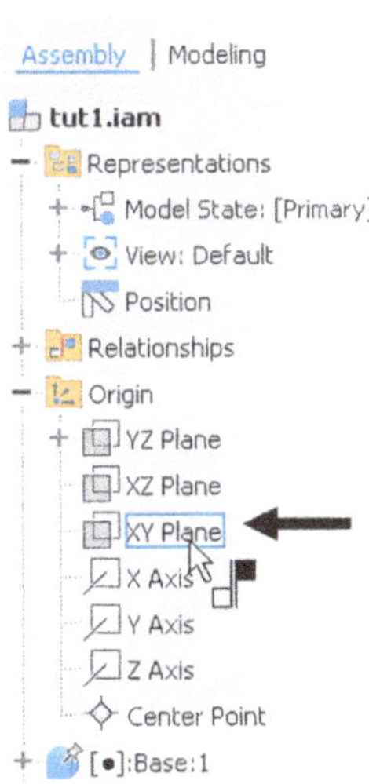

10. Expand the **Origin** folder of the Shoulder Screw and select XZ Plane.

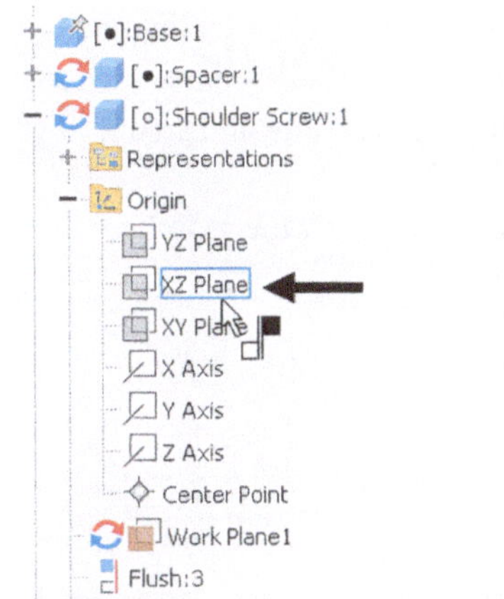

11. Click **OK** to fully-constrain the assembly.
12. Save the assembly and all its parts.

Using the Search tool in the Browser window

Autodesk Inventor provides you with the search tool to locate the components or features very quickly.

1. In the Browser Window, click the **Search** 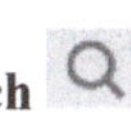 icon.
2. Type 'hex' in the search bar; all the hexagonal bolts appear in the browser window.

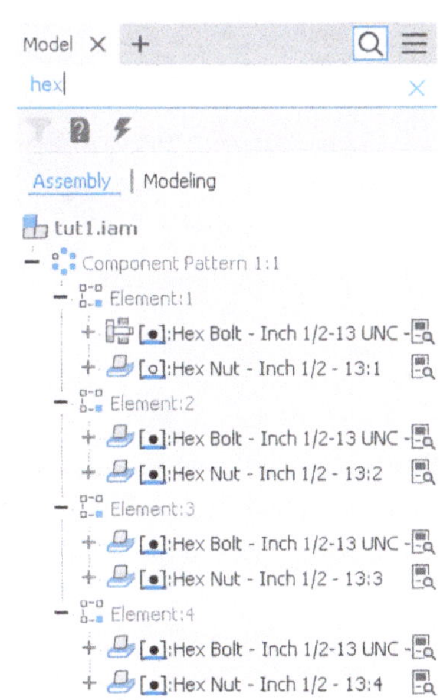

3. Place the pointer on the hexagonal bolts in the

browser window; they are highlighted in the graphics window.

You can select all the hexagonal bolts by pressing the Shift key and clicking on them. After selecting them, you can perform a variety of operations at a time, such as hiding, deleting, solving, suppressing, and so on.

4. Click **Clear Search** to clear all the searched components.

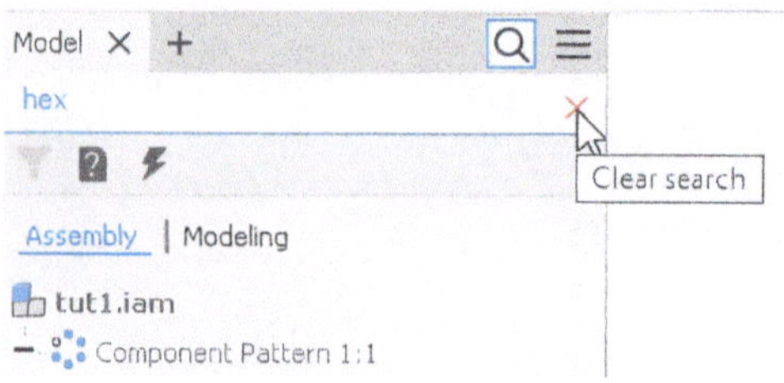

Editing Values in the Browser window

Autodesk Inventor 2026 allows you to edit the values of the assembly components directly in the Browser Window.

1. In the Browser Window, click the Drop-down menu next to the Search box, and then select **Edit Values in Browser**.

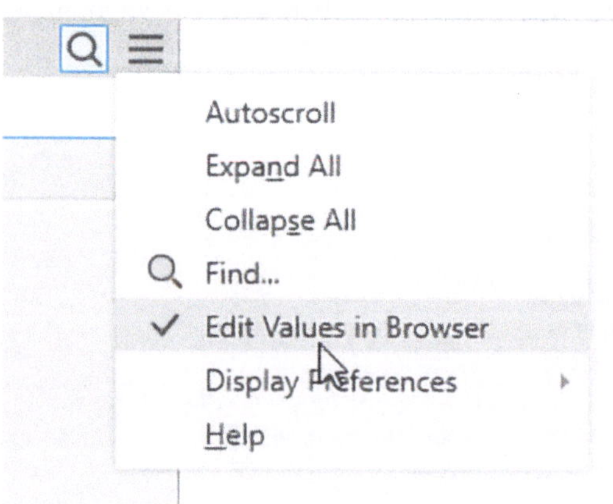

2. In the Browser Window, expand the **Shoulder Screw** part, and then click on the **Flush** relation, as shown; the selected relation is highlighted in the graphics window, as shown.

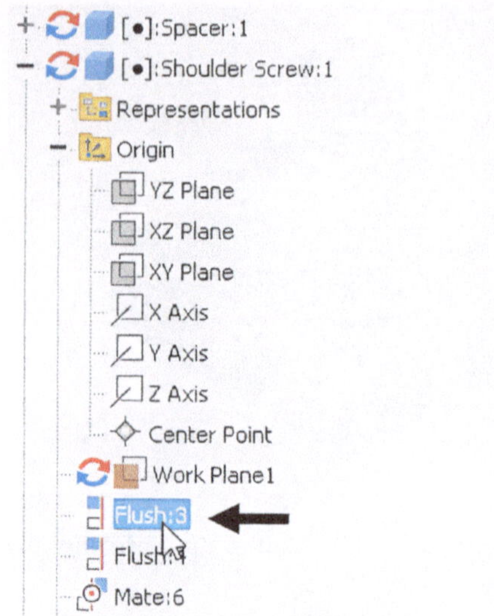

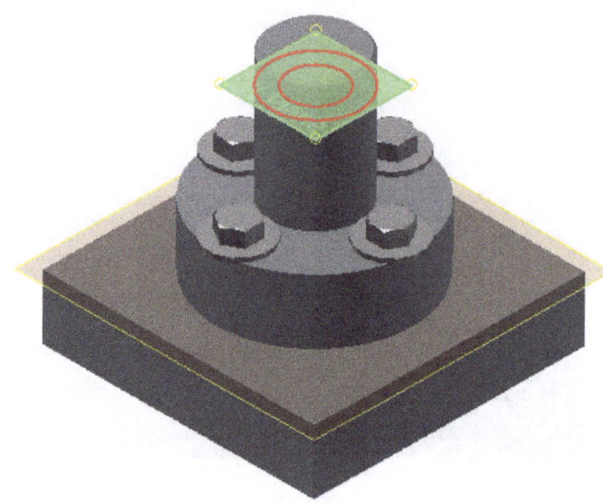

3. Type 1 in the box that appears next to the selected relation, and then press Enter; the relation is updated in the graphics window.

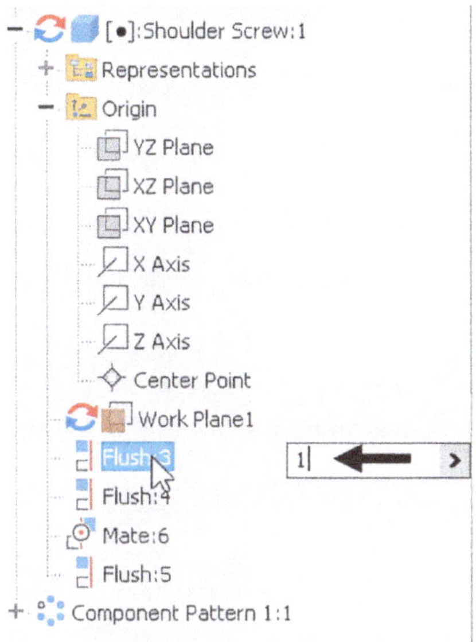

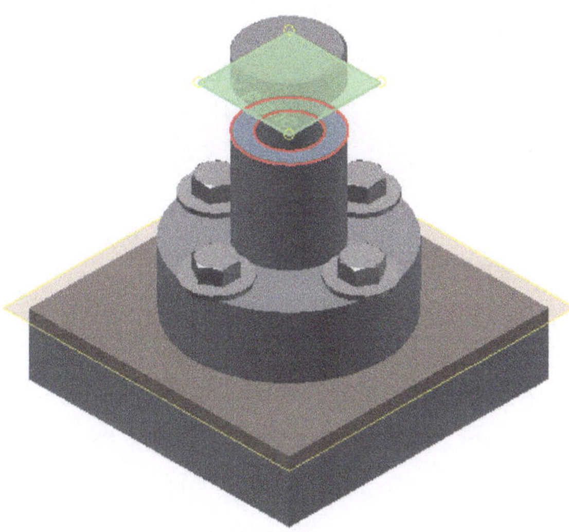

4. Click **Undo** on the Quick Access Toolbar.

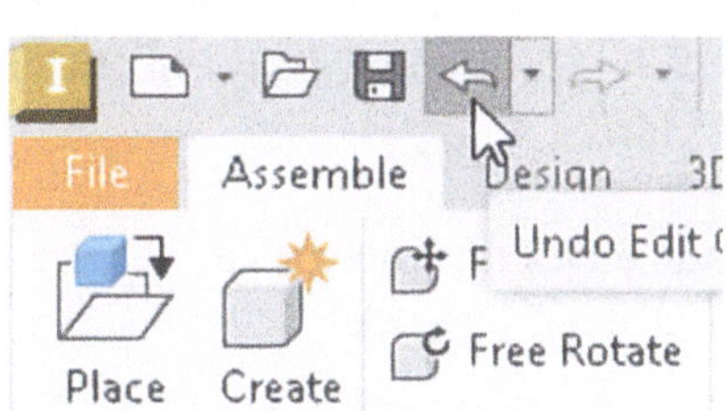

Changing the Display Preferences of the Browser window

Autodesk Inventor allows you to hide or display items to reduce the clutter in your Browser Window. For example, you can hide or display the work features such as plane and UCS in the Browser Window.

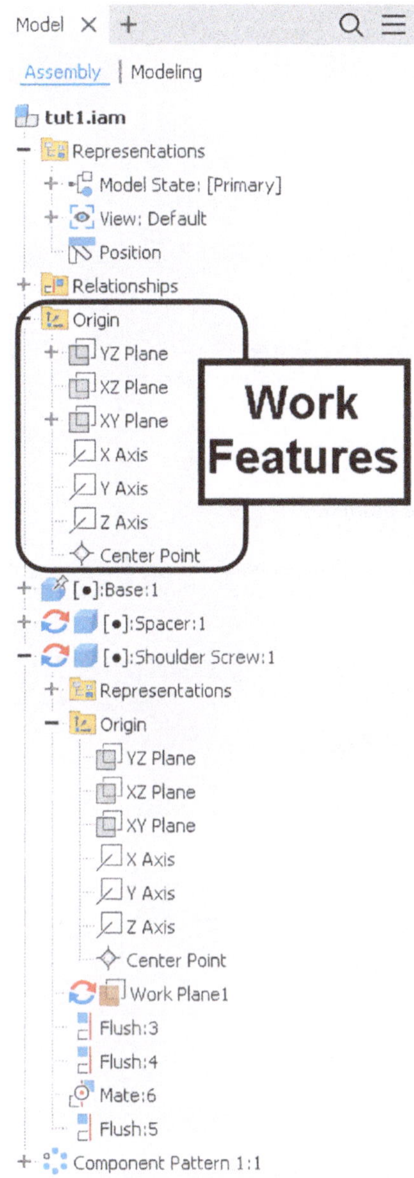

1. In the Browser Window, click the Drop-down menu next to the **Search** box, and then select **Display Preferences > Hide Work Features**.

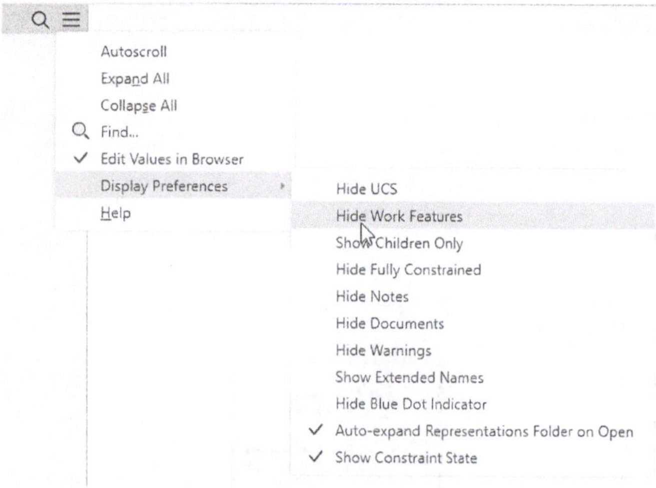

The work features are hidden.

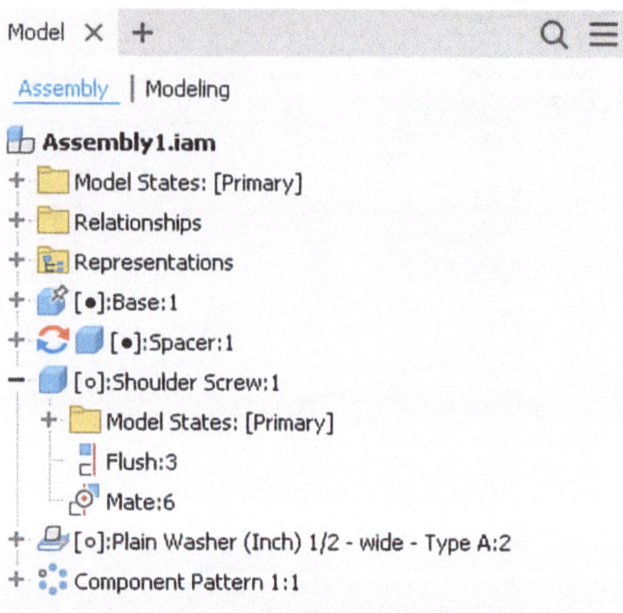

Using the Measure tool

The **Measure** tool helps you measure the size and position of the model. You can measure the various parameters of the model, such as length, angle, and radius.

1. On the ribbon, click **Inspect** tab > **Measure** panel > **Measure** ; the **Measure** floating window appears on the screen.

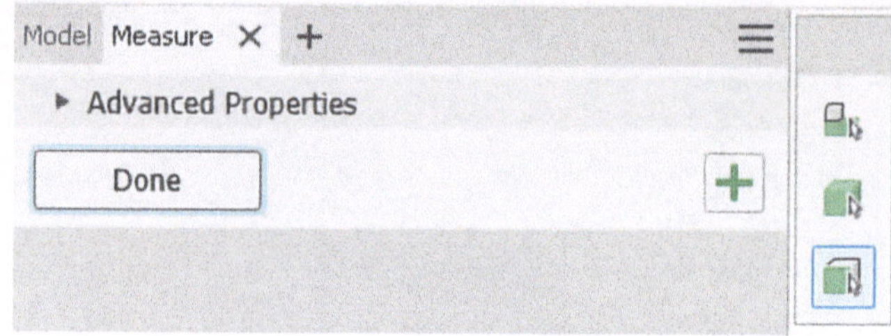

2. Click and drag the **Measure** floating window, and then release it on to the Browser Window; the Measure window is docked to the Browser Window.

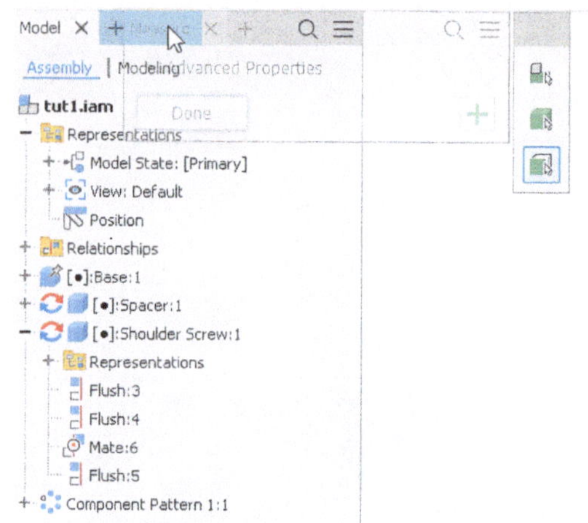

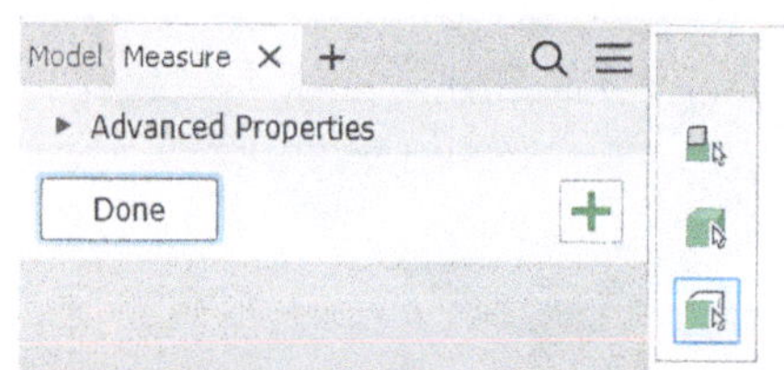

The **Measure** Window has three selection filters (shown from right to left): **Select faces and edges**, **Part Priority**, and **Component Priority**.

The **Select faces and edges** filter allows you to select only the faces and edges of the model.

The **Part Priority** filter allows you to select the part geometry for measurement.

The **Component Priority** filter allows you to select the part geometry and assemblies. This filter is used to select subassemblies from the main assembly.

3. Select the **Select faces and edges** filter and select the straight edge, as shown.

The length of the selected edge is displayed in the **Measure** window.

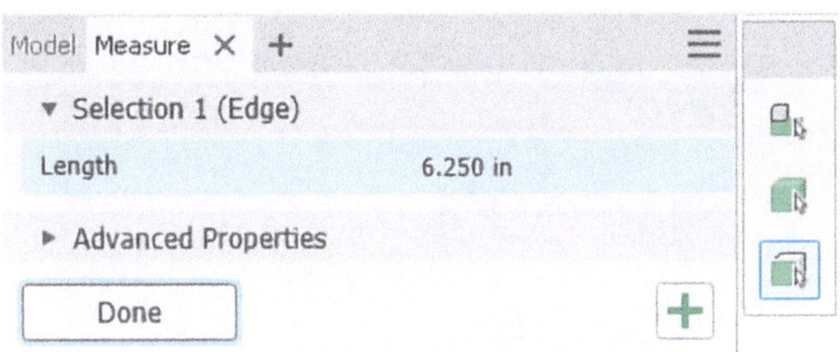

4. Expand the **Advanced Properties** section in the **Measure** window.

In the **Advanced Properties** section, you can change the **Precision**, **Angle Precision** of the displayed measurement. In addition to that, you can display the measurement in dual units by specifying the **Dual Units** type.

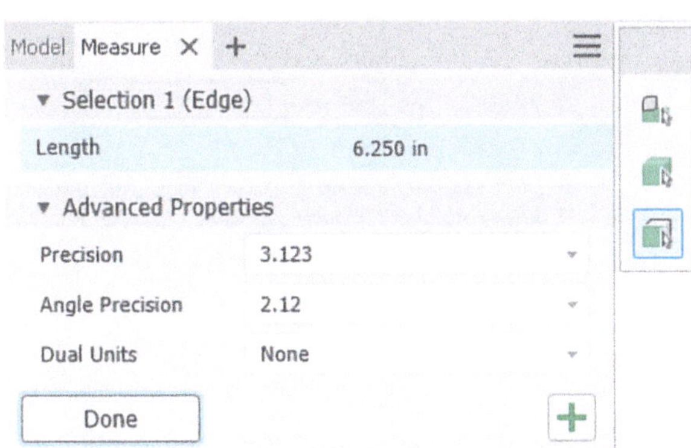

5. Select the round face, as shown; the Measure window displays results.

The Measure results section displays the results of the first and second selections separately. In addition to that, the distance between the two selected entities is displayed.

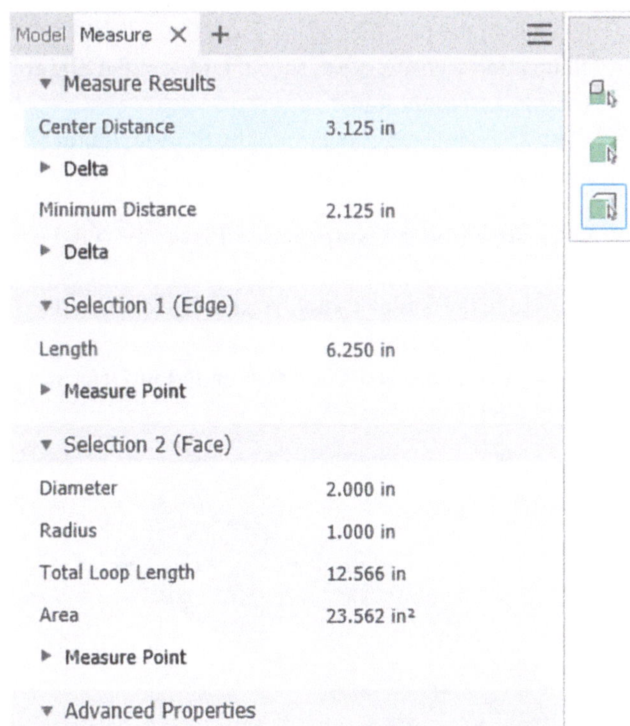

6. Save and close the assembly and its parts.

TUTORIAL 2

In this tutorial, you create a slider-crank mechanism by applying Joints.

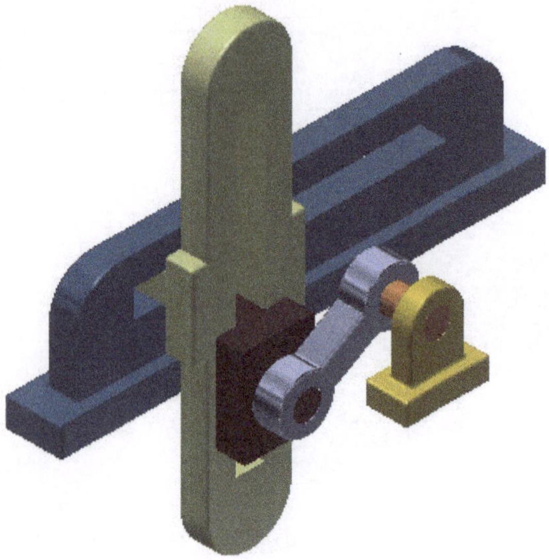

1. Create the **Slider Crank Assembly** folder inside the project folder.
2. Download the part files of the assembly from the companion website. Next, save the files in the **Slider Crank Assembly** folder.
3. Start a new assembly file using the **Standard.iam** template.
4. Click **Assemble > Component > Place** on the ribbon.
5. Browse to the **Slider Crank Assembly** folder and double-click on **Base**.
6. Right-click and select **Place Grounded at Origin**.
7. Right click and select **OK**.

8. Click **Assemble > Component > Place** on the ribbon.
9. Browse to the **Slider Crank Assembly** folder and select all the parts except the **Base**.
10. Click **Open** and click in the graphics window to place the parts.
11. Right click and select **OK**.
12. Click and drag the parts if they are coinciding with each other.

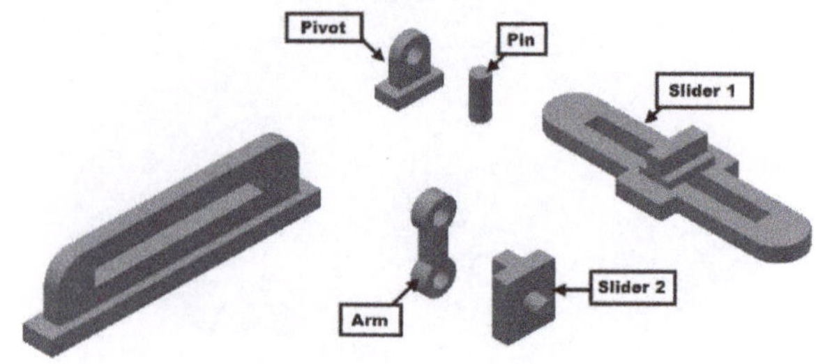

Creating the Slider Joint

1. Click **Assemble > Relationships > Joint** on the ribbon; the **Place Joint** dialog appears.

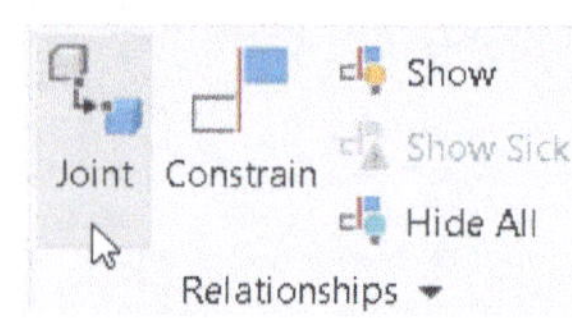

2. Set the **Type** to **Slider**.

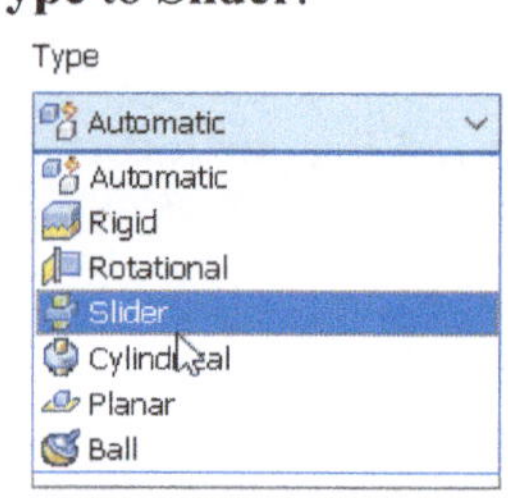

3. Select the face on the Slider1, as shown below.

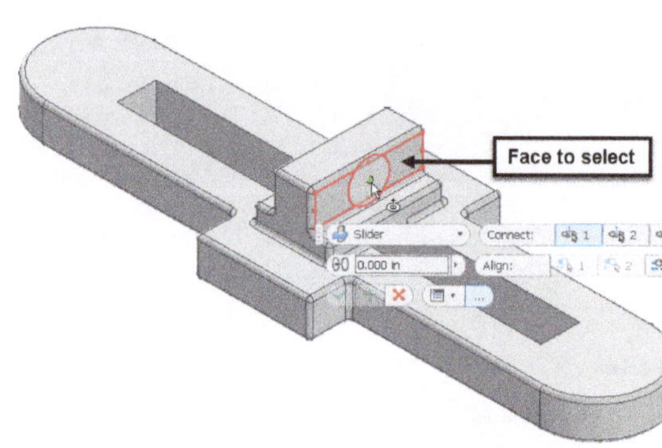

4. Select the face on the Base, as shown below; the two faces are aligned.

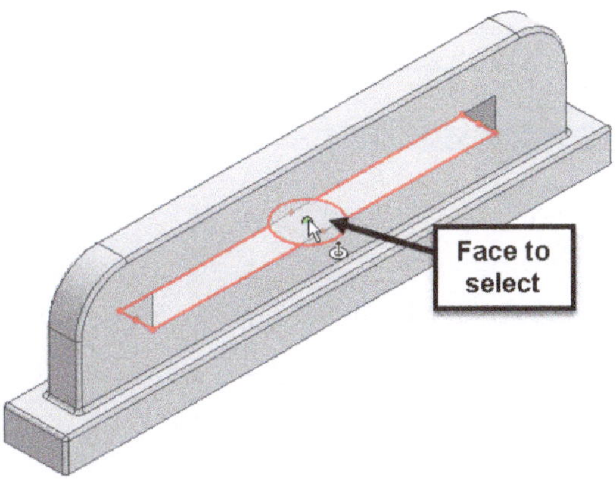

5. On the dialog, click the **First Alignment** button.
6. Select the face of the Slider1, as shown.

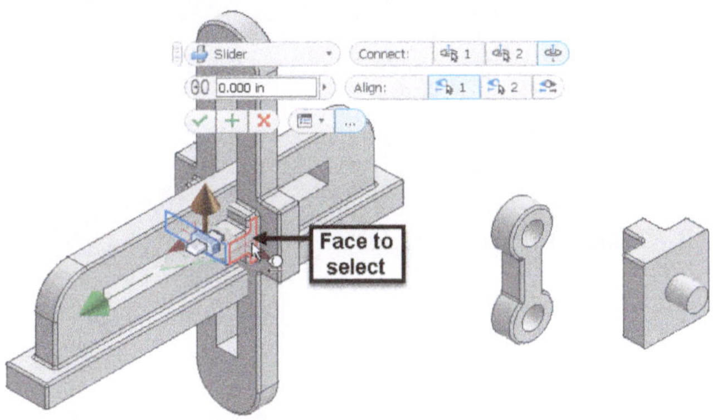

7. Select the face of the Base, as shown; the Slider 1 is aligned to the selected face.

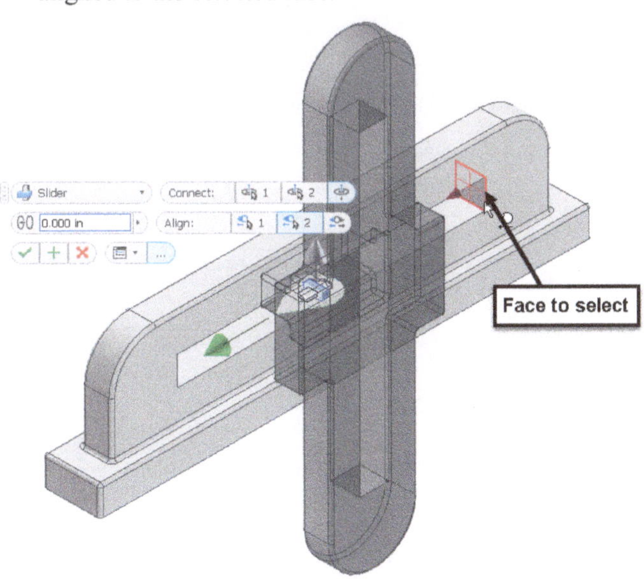

5. Click the **Limits** tab on the **Place Joint** dialog.
6. Check the **Start** and **End** options under the **Linear** group.
7. Set the **Start** value to 1.5 in and **End** to -1.5 inches.

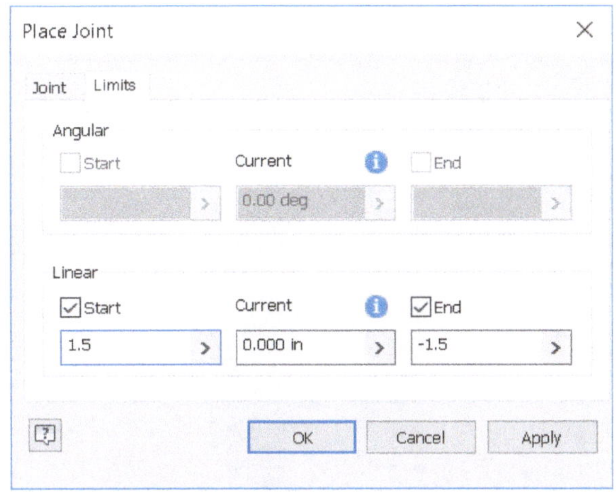

8. Click **OK**.
9. Select the Slider1 and drag the pointer; the Slider1 slides in the slot of the Base. Also, the slider motion is limited up to the end of the slot.

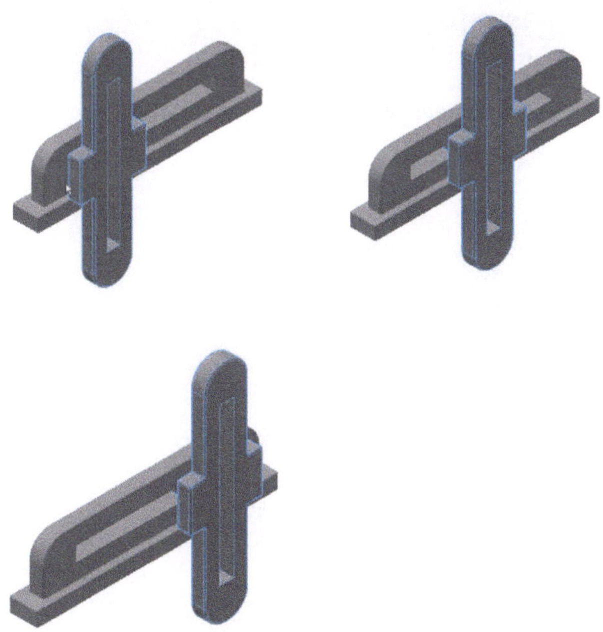

10. Click the corner of the ViewCube, as shown; the orientation of the assembly is changed.

11. Click **Assemble > Relationships > Joint** on the ribbon.

12. On the dialog, set the **Type** to **Slider**.
13. Select the face on the Slider2, as shown below.

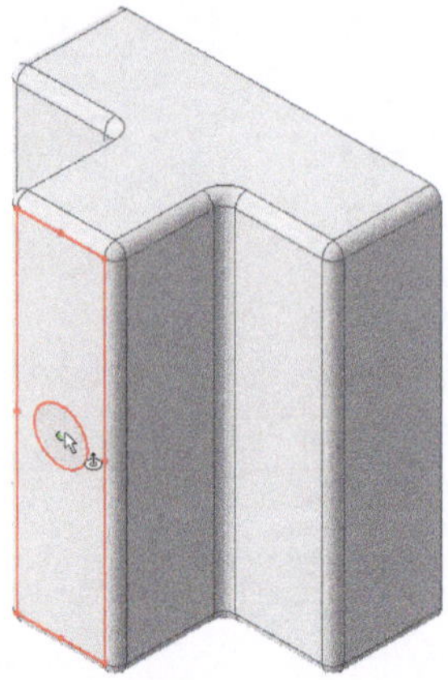

14. Select the right edge of the top face of the ViewCube; the orientation of the assembly changes.

15. Select the face on the Slider1, as shown below. Next, click **OK**.

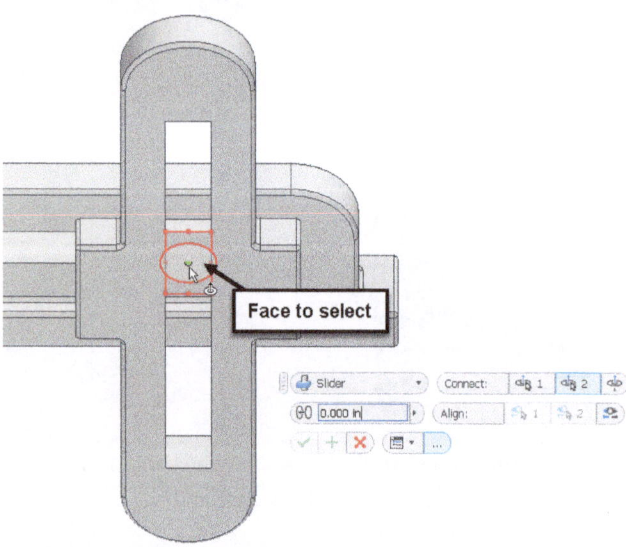

Creating the Rotational Joint

1. Click **Assemble > Relationships > Joint** on the ribbon.
2. Set **Type** to **Rotational**.

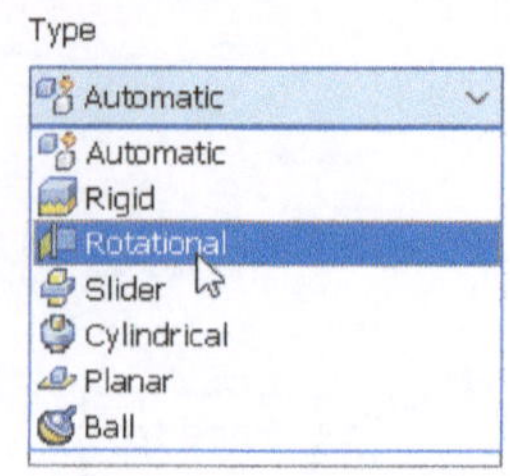

3. Select the circular edge of the arm, as shown below.

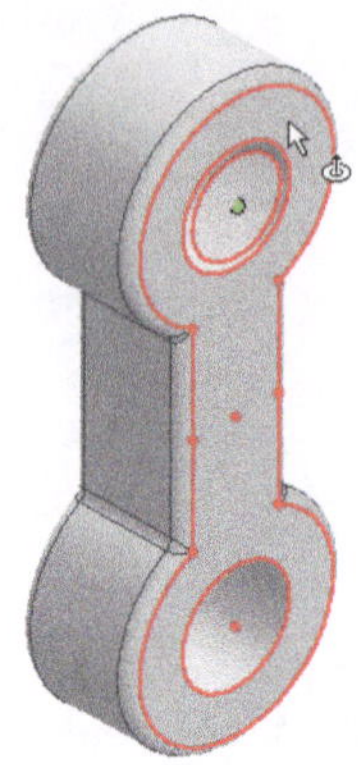

4. Select the circular edge of the Slider2.

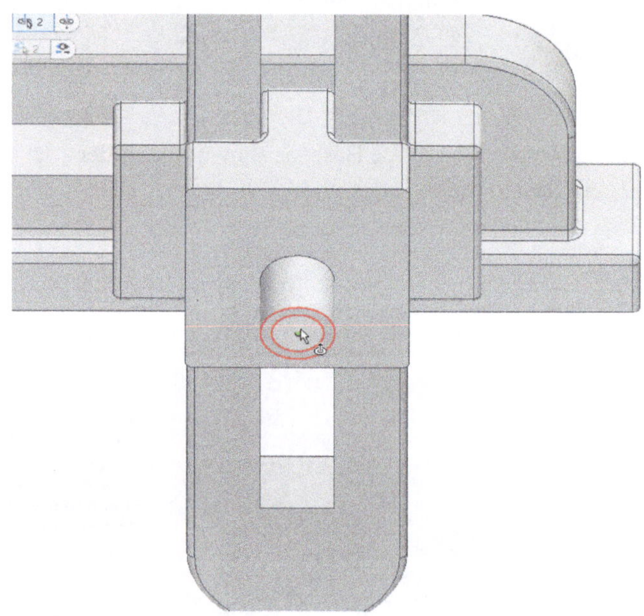

6. Click the **Flip Component** button under the **Connect** group.

7. Click **OK**

Creating the Rigid Joint

1. Click **Assemble > Relationships > Joint**  on the ribbon.
2. Set the **Type** to **Rigid**.

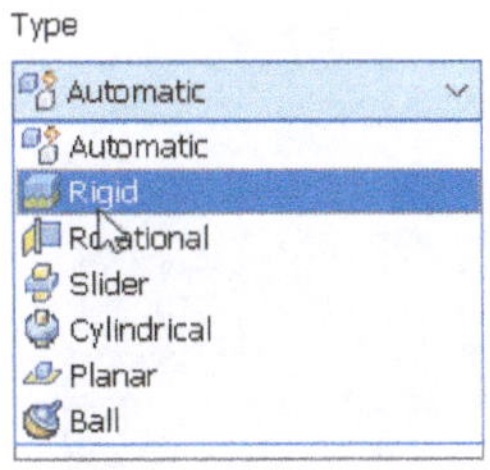

3. Select the top face on the pin.

4. Click on the corner point of the ViewCube, as shown.

5. Select the circular edge on the back face of the arm.

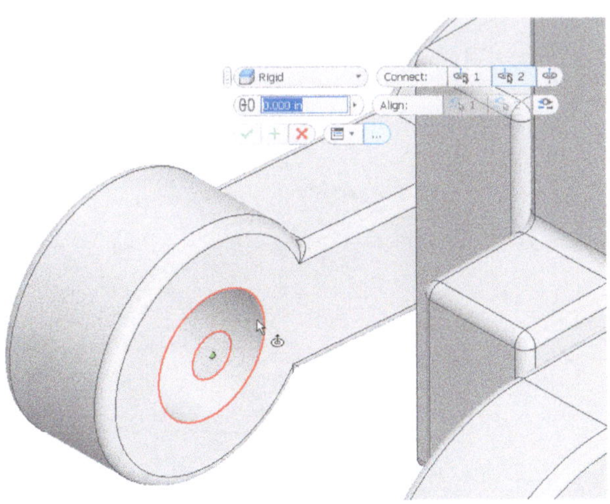

6. Click **OK**.

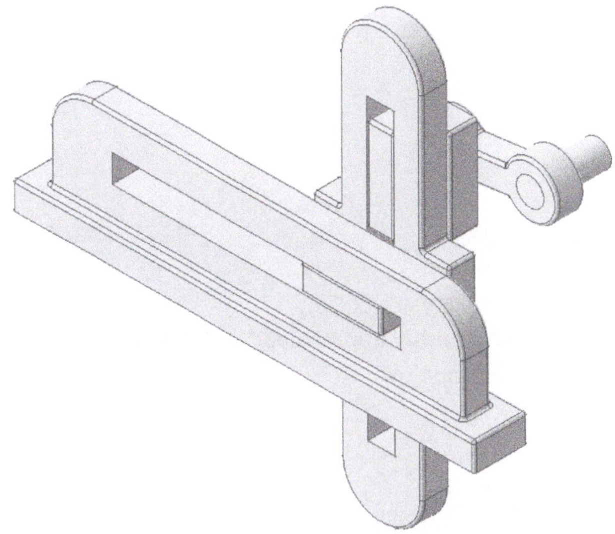

Adding more assembly joints

1. Create another rotational joint between the Pin and the Pivot.

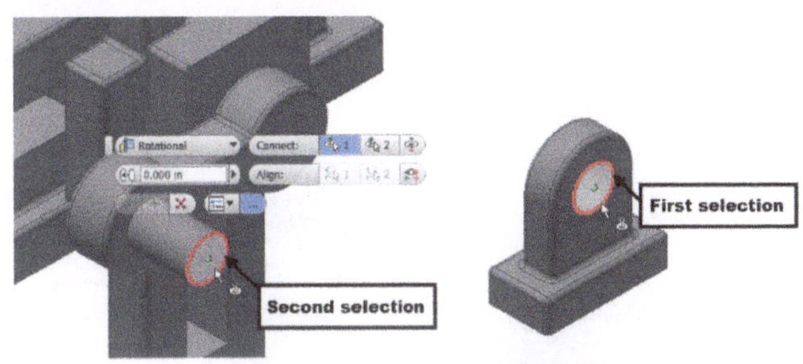

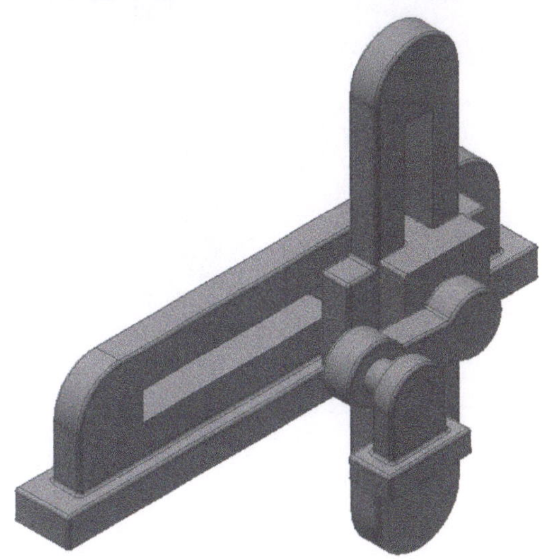

Next, you need to constrain the Pivot by applying constraints.

2. Click the **Assemble** button on the **Relationships**

panel.

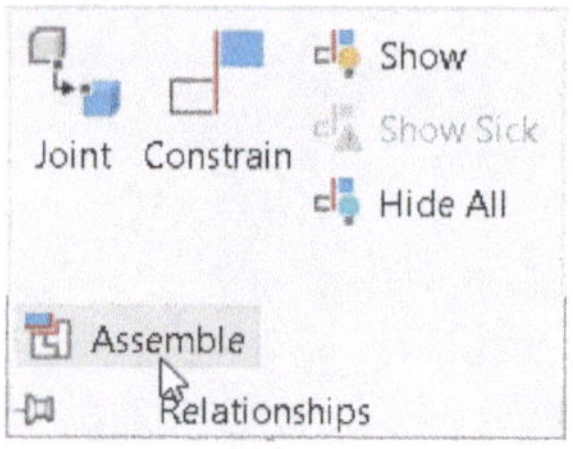

3. On the **Assembly** mini toolbar, select **Mate – Flush** from the drop-down.

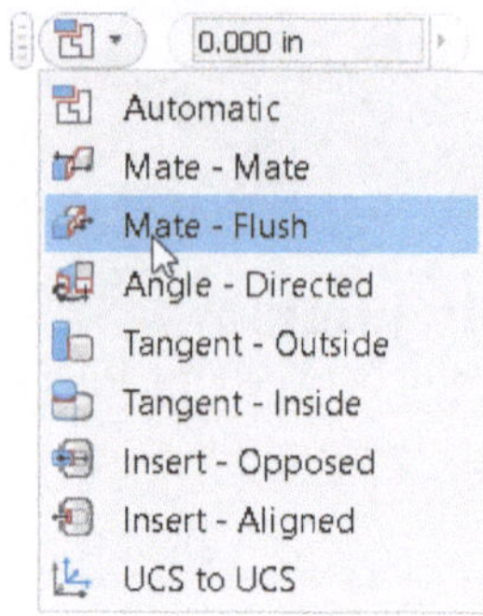

4. Select the bottom face of the Pivot, and then select the bottom face of the Base.

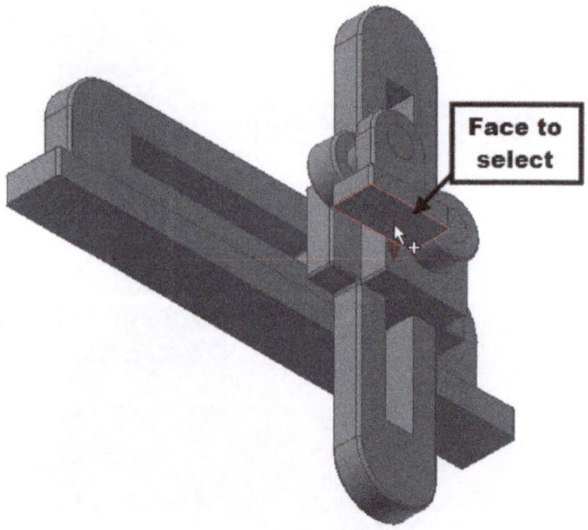

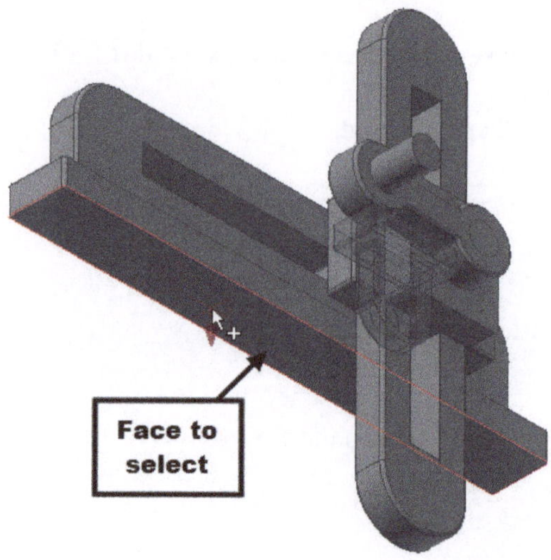

5. Click **Apply** (plus symbol on the mini toolbar).
6. Select the **XY Plane** of the Pivot and **XY Plane** of the Base from the **Browser window**.

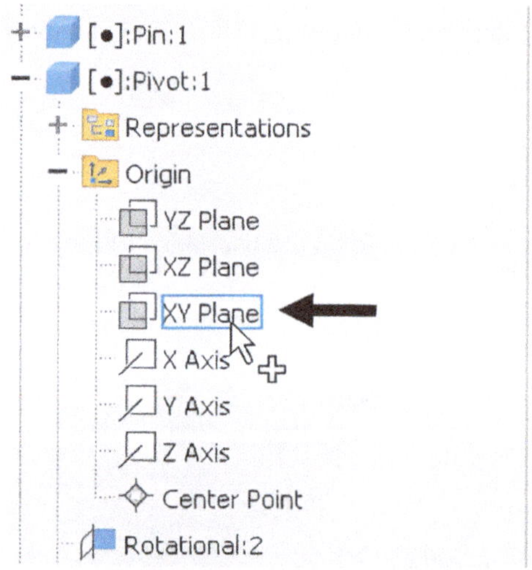

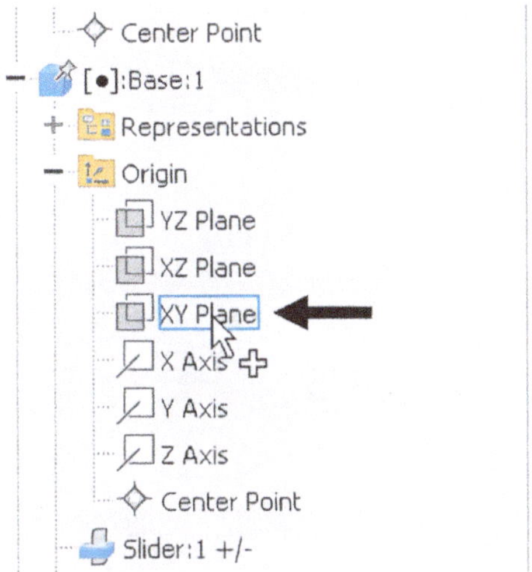

7. Click **OK** (checkmark on the mini toolbar).

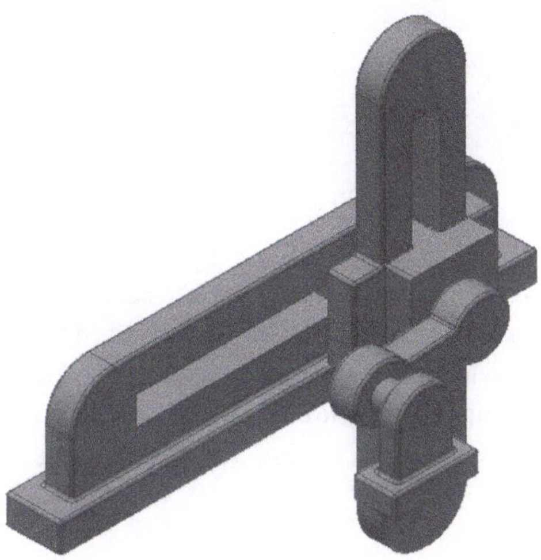

Driving the joints

1. In the Browser window, expand Pivot and click the right mouse button on the **Rotational** joint.
2. Select **Drive** from the shortcut menu.

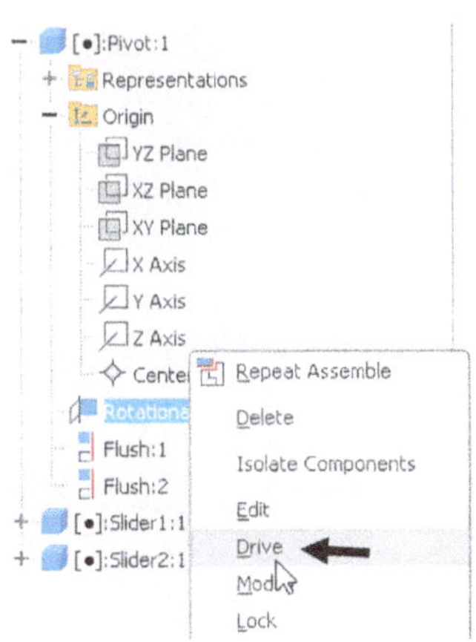

3. On the **Drive** dialog, type in 0 and 360 in the **Start** and **End** boxes, respectively.
4. Expand the dialog by clicking the double-arrow button located at the bottom. On the expanded dialog, you can define the settings such as drive adaptivity, collision detection, increment, and repetition.

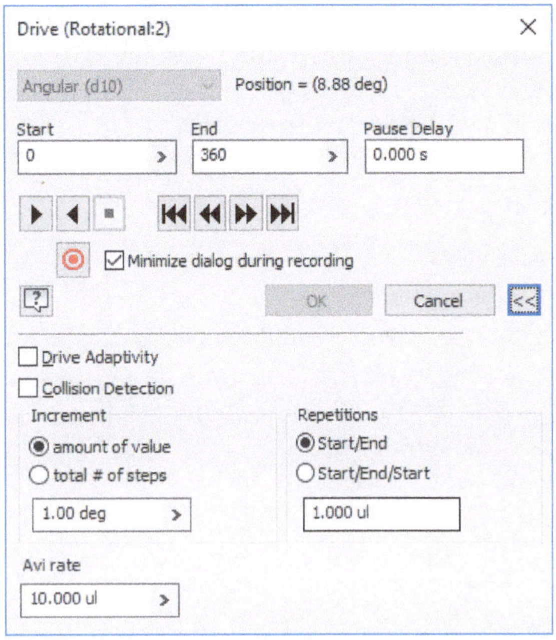

5. Click the **Record**  button on the dialog. Specify the name and location of the video file — Click **Save** and **OK**.
6. On the dialog, click the **Forward**  button to simulate the motion of the slider-crank assembly.
7. Click **OK** to close the dialog.

Creating Positions

1. In the Browser window, expand the **Representations > View** and notice that the **Master** representation is set as default.
2. Right click on the **Position** node, and then select **New**; a new position is created.

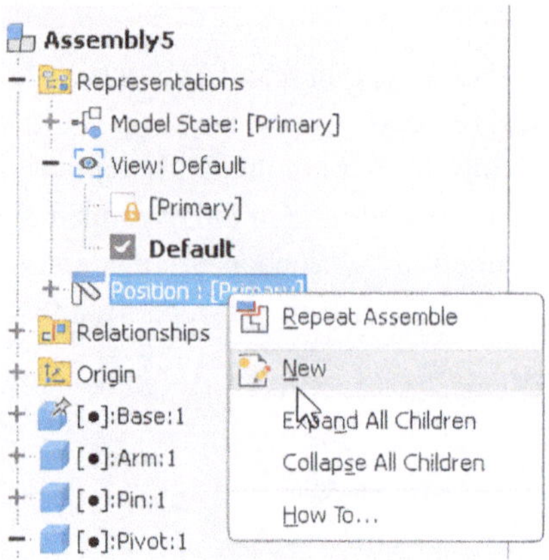

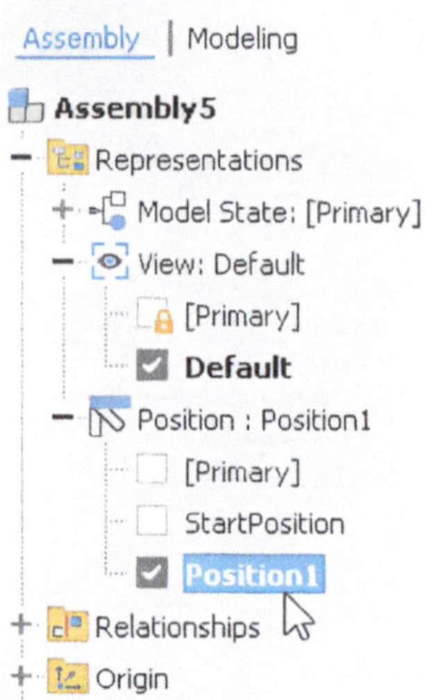

3. Double click on the **Position1** and type **StartPosition**; the view representation is renamed.
4. Click and drag the Slider1 to the left end, as shown.

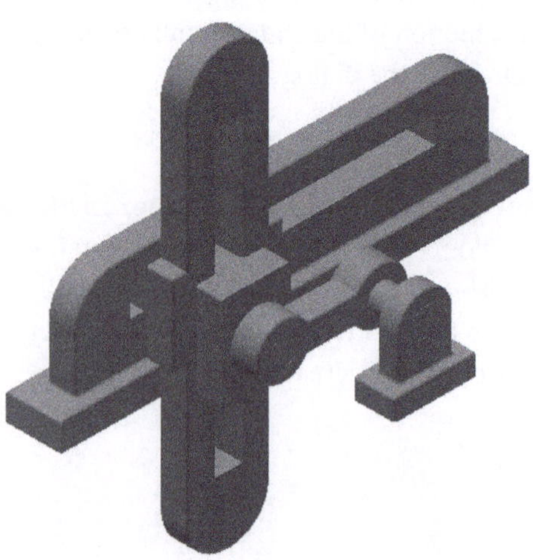

5. Double click on the **Primary** position to activate it.

Creating 3D PDF

Autodesk Inventor allows you to create a 3D PDF from the model. The 3D PDF file helps view the 3D model without any CAD application or viewer.

1. Click **File Menu > Export > 3D PDF**.

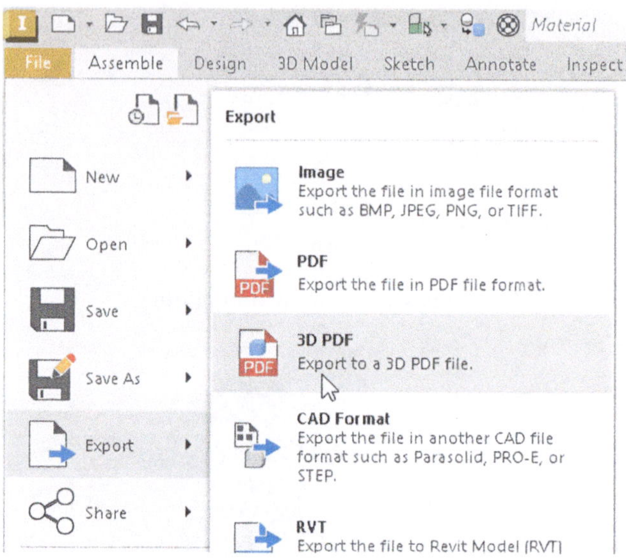

The **Publish 3D PDF** dialog appears on the screen. The **Anark Core** software powers it. On the Publish 3D PDF dialog, you can select the properties to be displayed on the PDF from the **Properties** section. You can also select the required design view representation, visualization quality, and export scope.

2. Leave the Template to the default setting.

If required, you can select another template by clicking the icon next to the Template path. You can also create a new 3D PDF template if you have Adobe Acrobat Pro. You can go through the Autodesk Inventor Help file to know the procedure to create a 3D PDF template.

3. Specify the **File Output Location**.
4. Check the **View PDF when finished** option.
5. Check the **Generate and attach STEP file** option.
6. Click the **Options** button next to the **Generate and attach STEP file** option; the **STEP file Save as Options** dialog appears on the screen.

On this dialog, select the required Application Protocol option and spline fit accuracy. You can also enter the authorization, author, organization, and description.

7. Click **OK** on the **STEP file save as Options** dialog.

Use the **Attachments** button, if you want to add any other attachments to the PDF file such as a spreadsheet, pdf, or text document.

8. Click **Publish** on the **Publish 3D PDF** dialog.

Inventor starts exporting the 3D model to the PDF file. After a few seconds, the 3D PDF file opens in the PDF viewer.

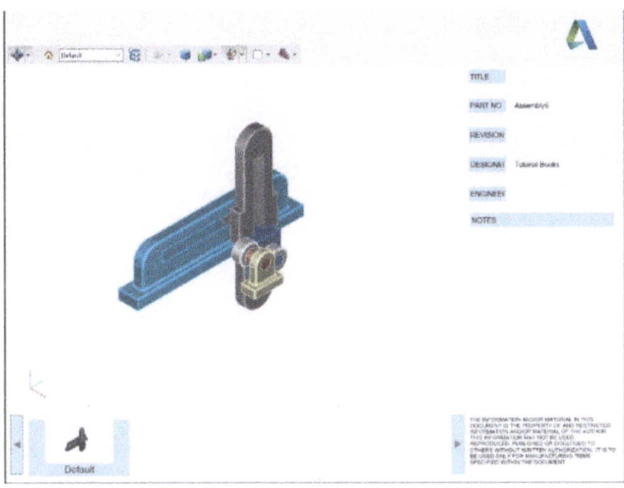

9. Click inside the graphics window of the PDF file, and then drag to rotate the model.
10. Click the drop-down located at the top left corner and notice the **View** options. These options are the same as that available on the Navigation Pane.

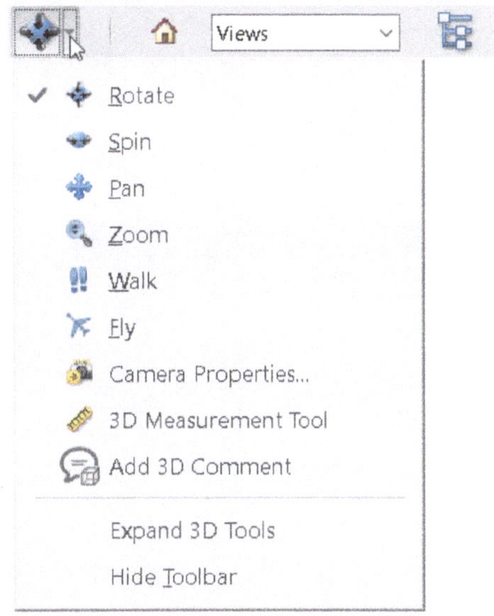

Likewise, examine the other options on the toolbar. These options are similar to that available on the View ribbon tab of the Autodesk Inventor application.

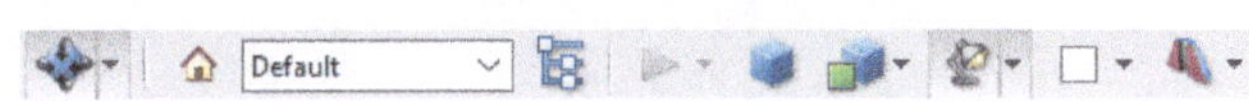

11. On the Sidebar, click the Attachments icon to view the STEP file.

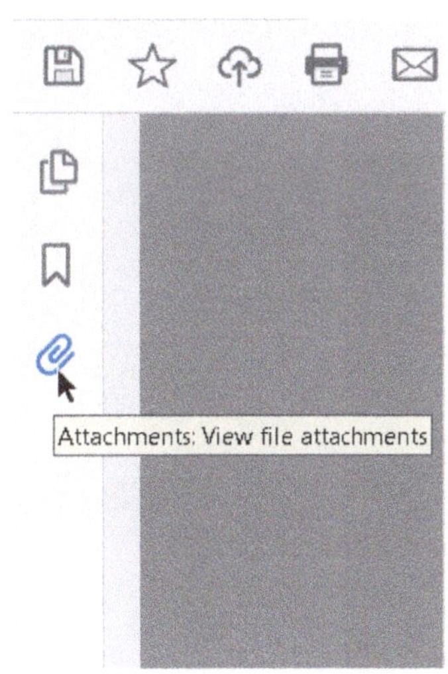

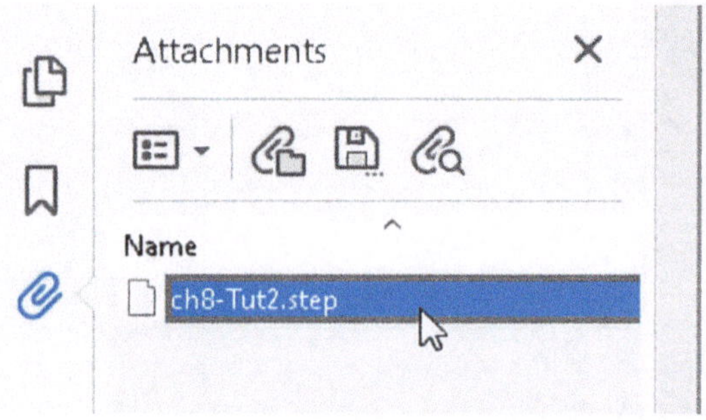

You can open or save the STEP file by right-clicking on it and select the corresponding option.

12. Close the 3D PDF file
13. Save and close the assembly and its parts.

Chapter 9: Dimensions and Annotations

In this chapter, you will learn to

- Create Centerlines and Centered Pattern
- Edit Hatch Pattern
- Apply Dimensions
- Place Hole callouts
- Place Leader Text
- Place Datum Feature
- Place Feature control frame
- Place Surface texture symbol
- Modify Title Block Information

TUTORIAL 1

In this tutorial, you create the drawing shown below.

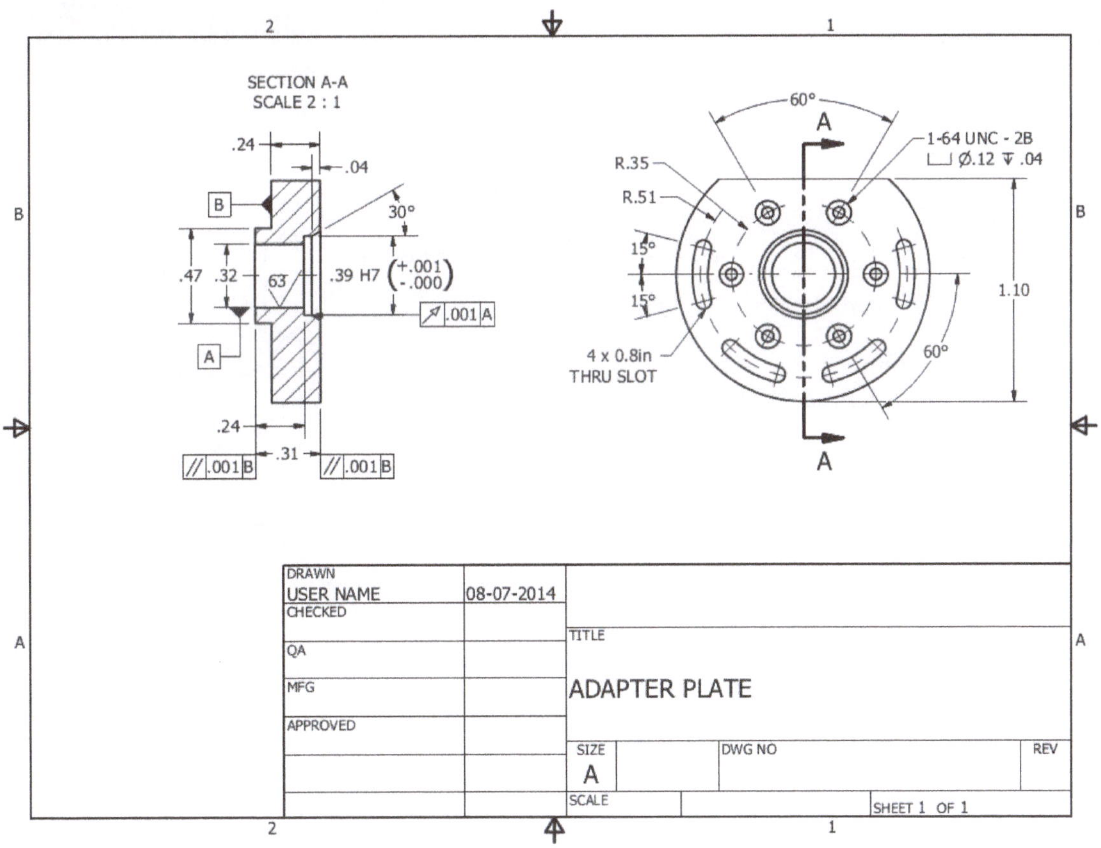

1. Open a new drawing file using the **Standard.idw** template.
2. In the Browser Window, click the right mouse on Sheet:1 and select **Edit Sheet**.
3. On the **Edit Sheet** dialog, select **Size > A**, and then click **OK**.
4. Click **Place Views > Create > Base** on the ribbon.
5. Click **Open an existing file**  button on the dialog.
6. Browse to the location of the Adapter Plate created in

Tutorial 1 of Chapter 6. You can also download this file from the companion website and use it.

7. Select the Adapter Plate file and click **Open**.
8. Set the **Scale** to 2:1.
9. Click the Front face on the ViewCube displayed in the drawing sheet.
10. Set the **Style** to **Hidden Line Removed**.
11. Click **OK** on the dialog.
12. Drag the view to the right side of the drawing sheet.
13. Click **Place Views > Create > Section** on the ribbon.
14. Select the front view.
15. Draw the section line on the front view.

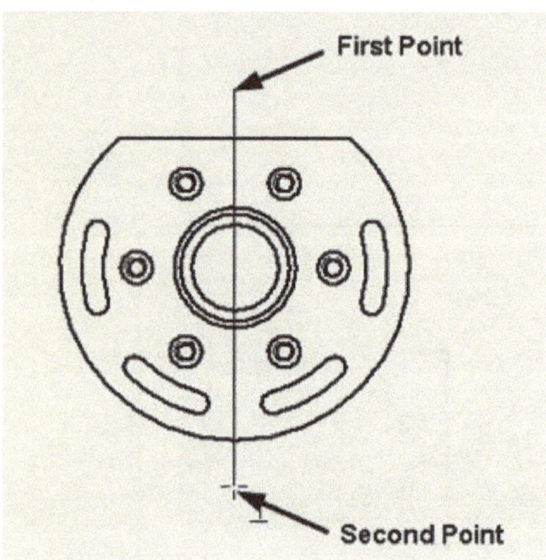

16. Right-click and select **Continue**.
17. Place the section view on the left side.

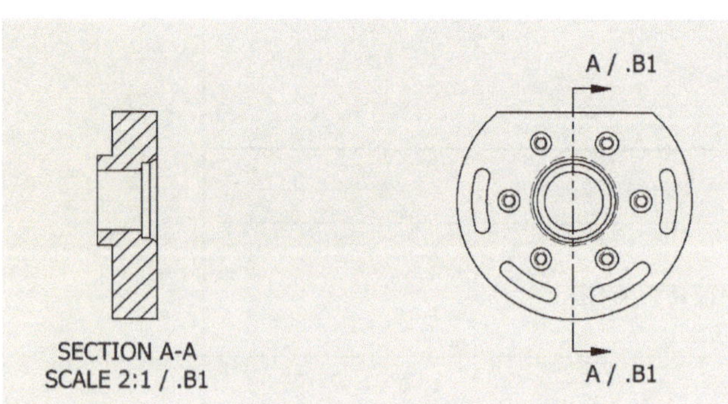

The **.B1** notation in your section view label (**A/.B1**) uses the standardized format:

B = View Sheet Index (indicates the drawing sheet where the view is located)

1 = View Sheet Zone (indicates the grid zone location on that sheet)

This matches the format defined in your **Format Text** dialog that appears when you double-click on the section view label:

<VIEW IDENTIFIER> / <VIEW SHEET NAME><VIEW SHEET INDEX>.<VIEW SHEET ZONE>

Creating Centerlines and Centered Patterns

1. Click **Annotate > Symbols > Centerline Bisector** on the ribbon.

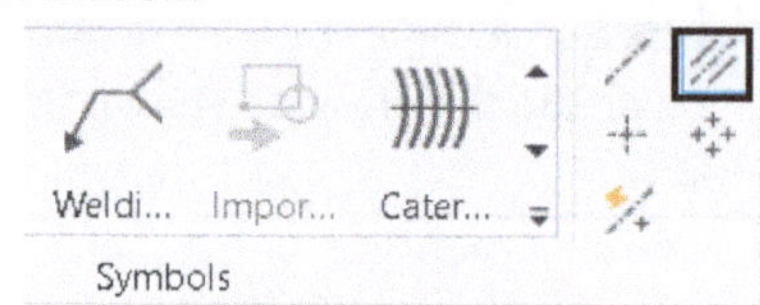

2. Select the parallel lines on the section view, as shown below; the centerline is created.

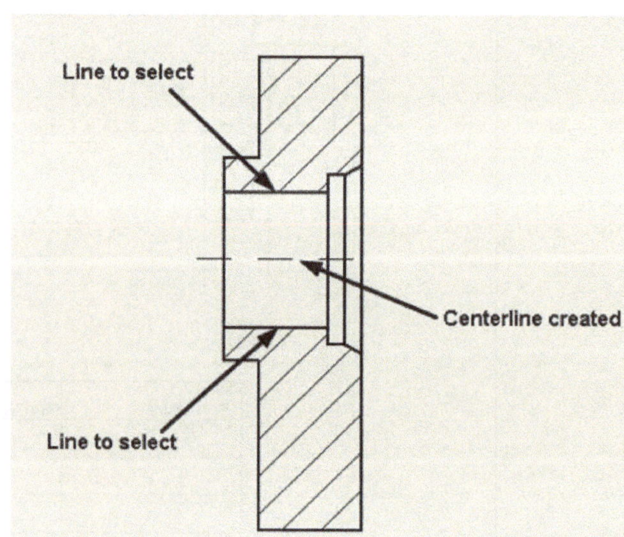

3. Click **Annotate > Symbols > Centered Pattern** on the ribbon.

4. Select the circle located at the center.

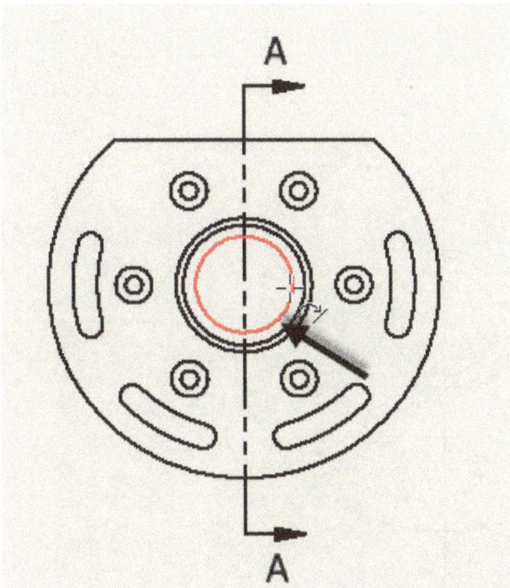

5. Select the center point of any one of the counterbored holes.

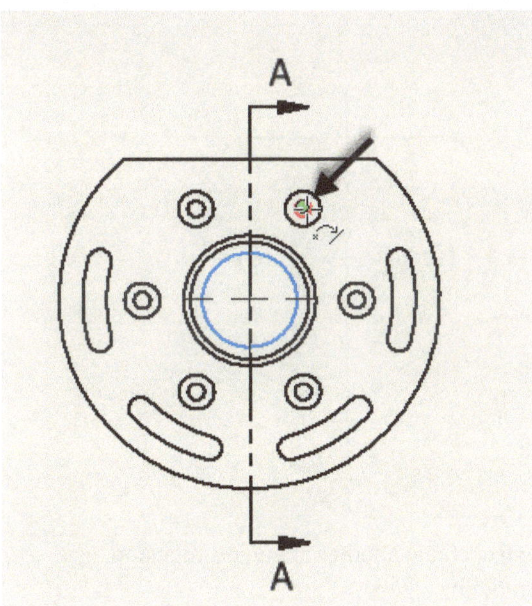

6. Select the center points of other counterbored holes.
7. Click the right mouse button and select **Create**.

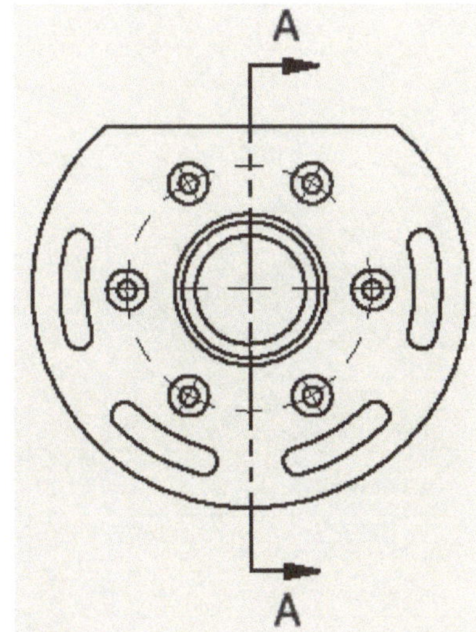

8. Likewise, create another centered pattern on the curved slots: Right-Click and select **Create**.

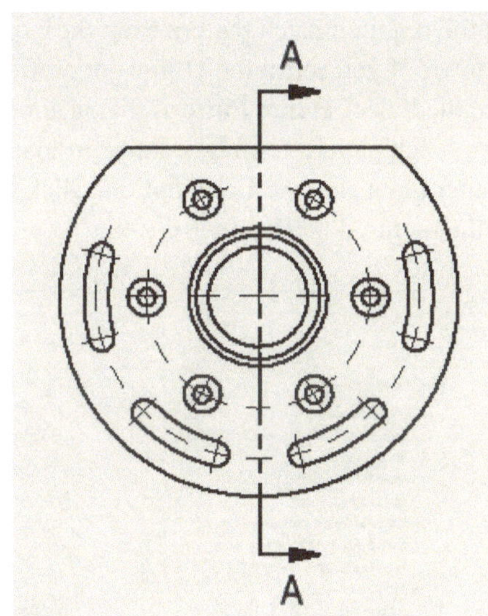

9. Press Esc to deactivate the tool.

Editing the Hatch Pattern

1. Double-click on the hatch pattern of the section view; the **Edit Hatch Pattern** dialog appears.

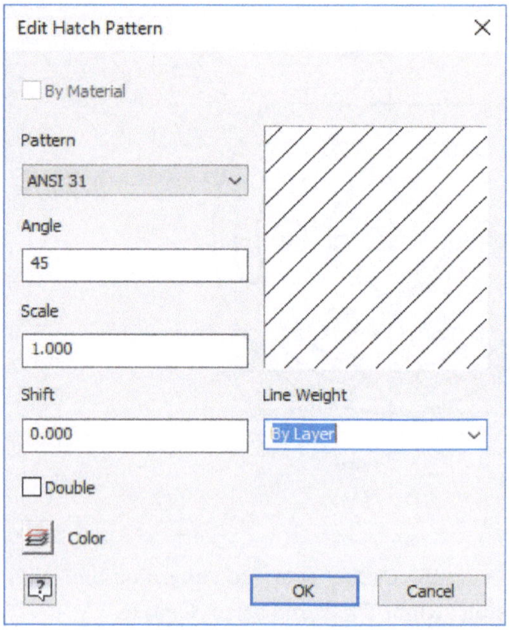

You can select the required hatch pattern from the **Pattern** drop-down. If you select the **Other** option from this drop-down, the **Select Hatch Pattern** dialog appears. You can select a hatch pattern from this dialog or load a user-defined pattern by using the **Load** option. Click **OK** after selecting the required hatch pattern.

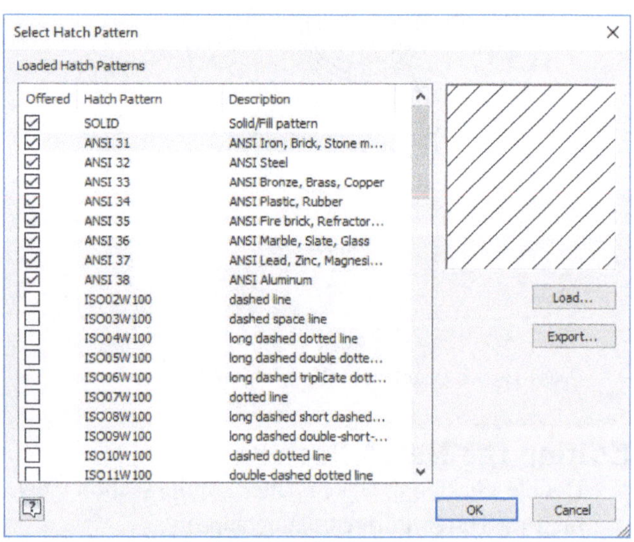

2. Click **OK**.

Applying Dimensions

1. Click **Annotate > Dimension > Dimension** on the ribbon.
2. Select the centerline on the slot located on the left.
3. Select the endpoint of the centerline of the hole located at the center.

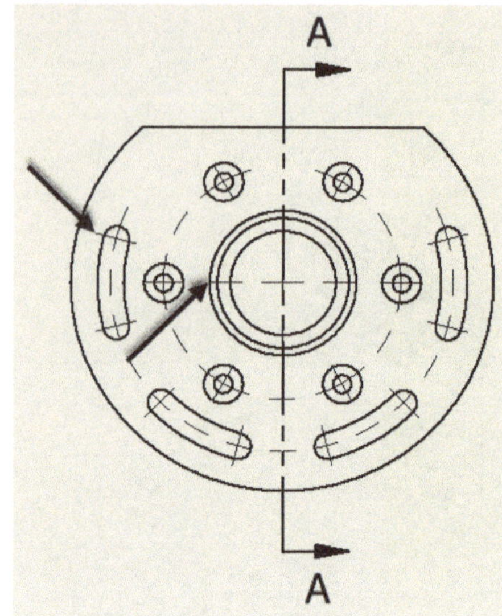

4. Move the pointer toward the left and click.
5. Click **OK**.

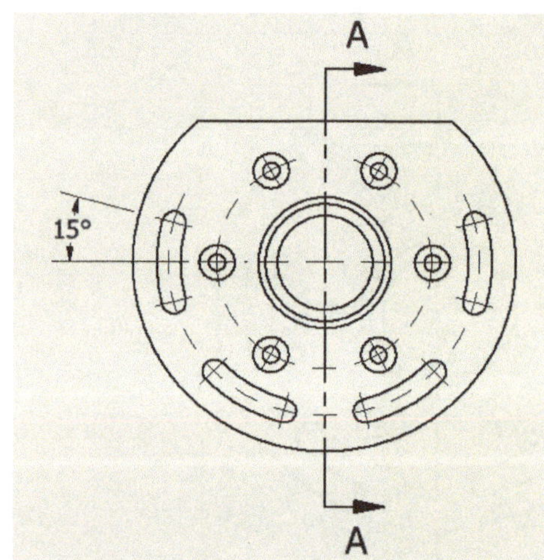

6. Likewise, create another angular dimension, as shown below.

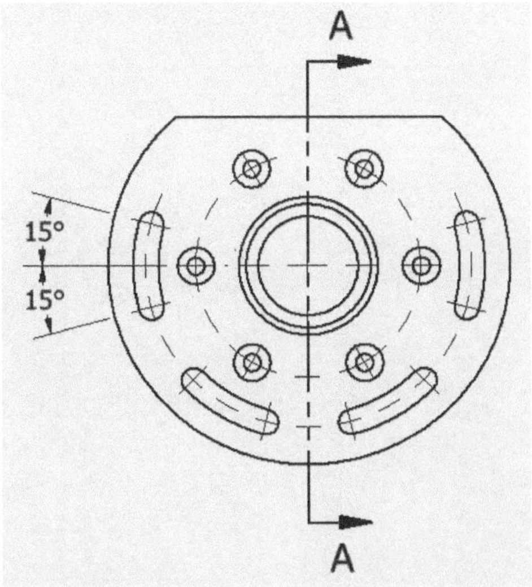

7. Create angular dimensions between the holes, and then between slots. To create the angular dimension between the slot, you need to create the angular dimension between the bolt circles.

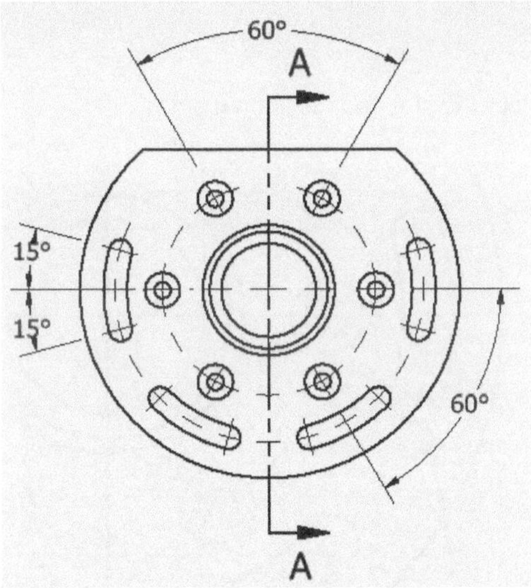

8. Dimension the pitch circle radius of the slots (activate the **Dimension** command and select the centreline passing through the slots. Next, right click and select **Dimension type > Radius**).

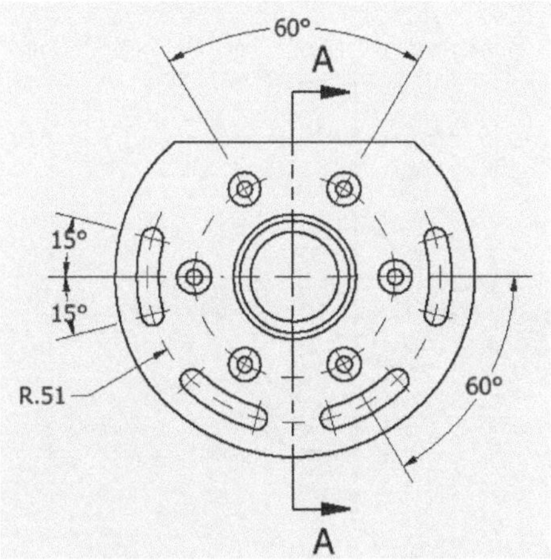

9. With the **Dimension** tool active, select the horizontal line of the front view and the lower quadrant point of view.

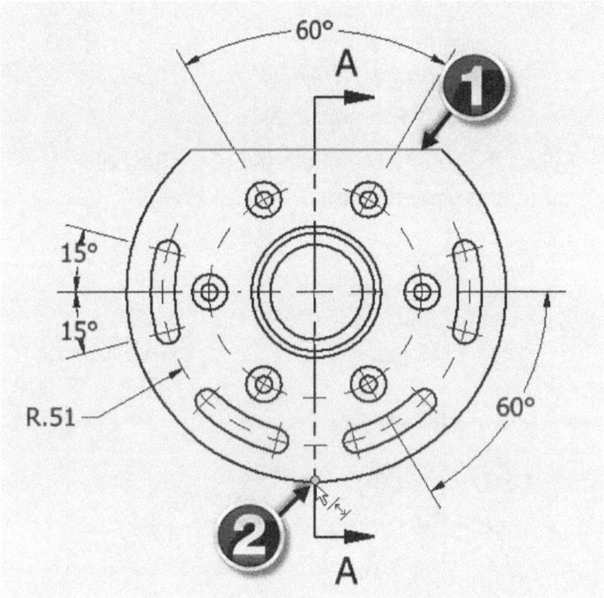

10. Place the dimension on the right side. Click **OK**.

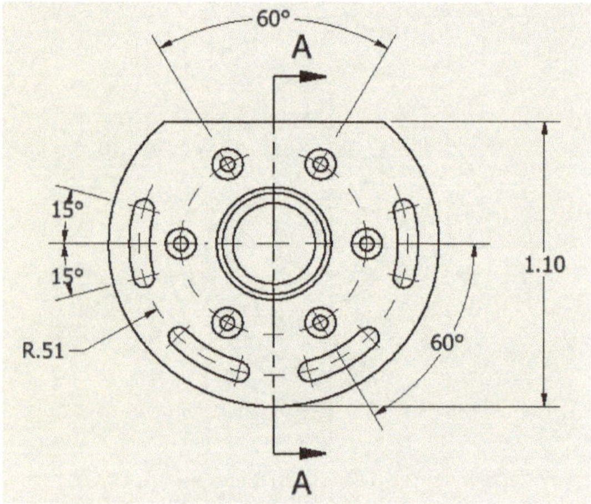

11. Click **Annotate > Feature Notes > Hole and Thread** on the ribbon.

12. Select the counterbore hole and place the hole callout, as shown below.

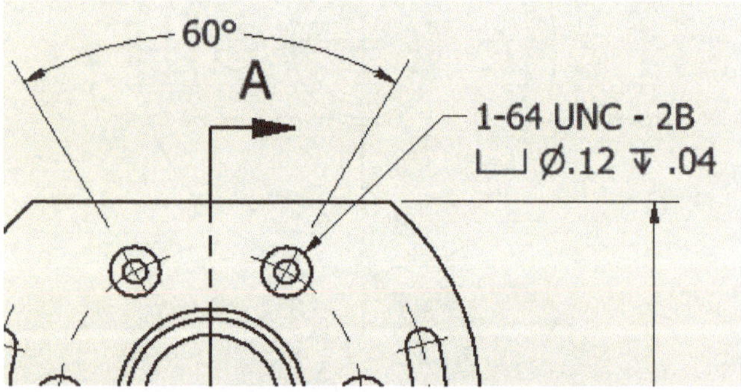

13. Add a pitch circle radius to counterbore holes.

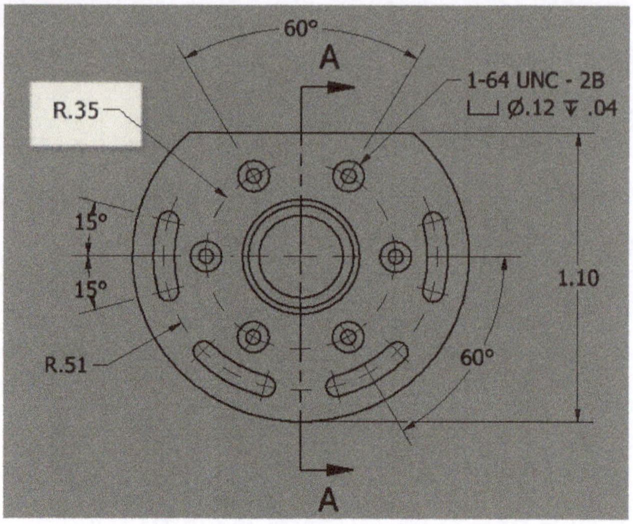

14. Click **Leader Text** on the **Text** panel.

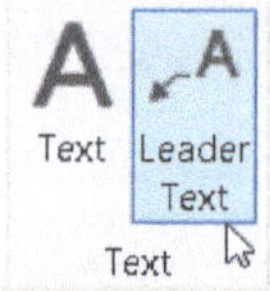

15. Select the slot end, as shown below.

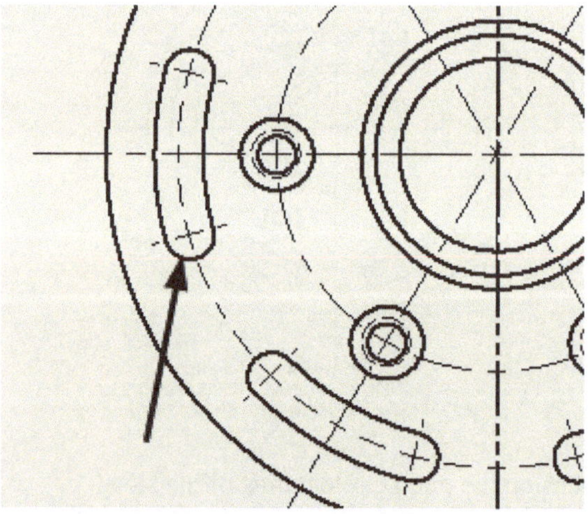

16. Move the cursor away and click.
17. Right-click and select **Continue**; the **Format Text** dialog appears.
18. Enter the text shown below.

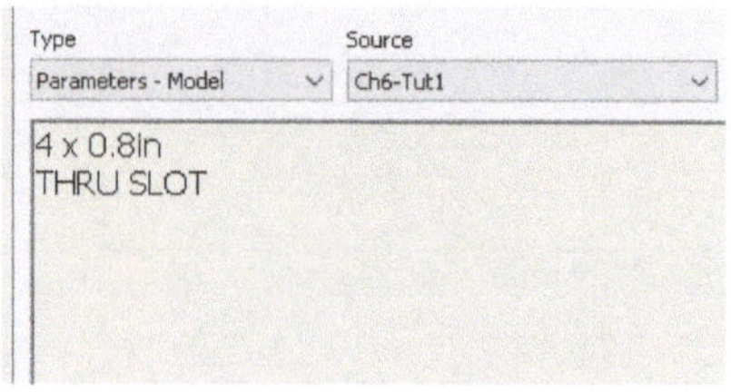

19. Click **OK** — Press the Esc key.

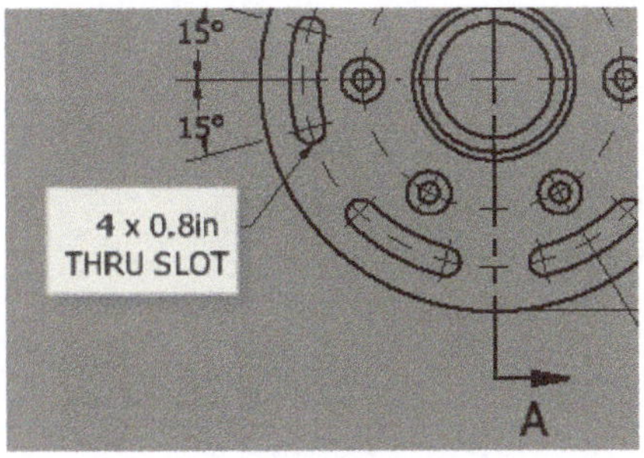

20. Double-click on the section label below the section view.
21. On the **Format Text** dialog, select all the text and set the **Size** to **0.120**. Click **OK**.

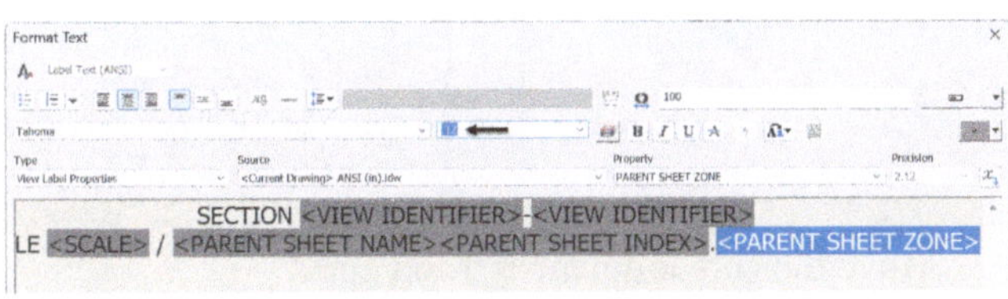

22. Drag and place the section label on the top.

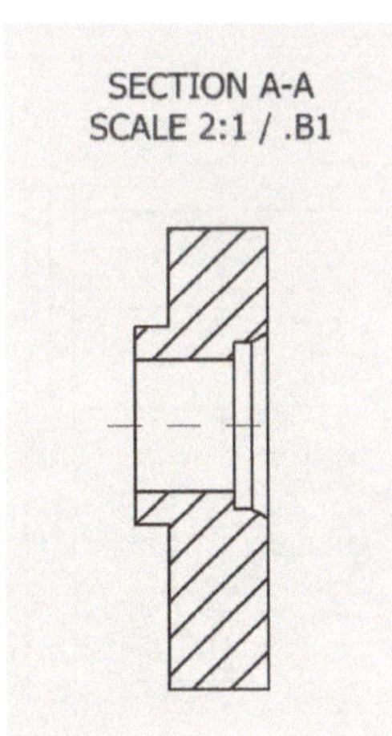

23. Click **Dimension** on the **Dimension** panel.
24. Select the lines, as shown below.

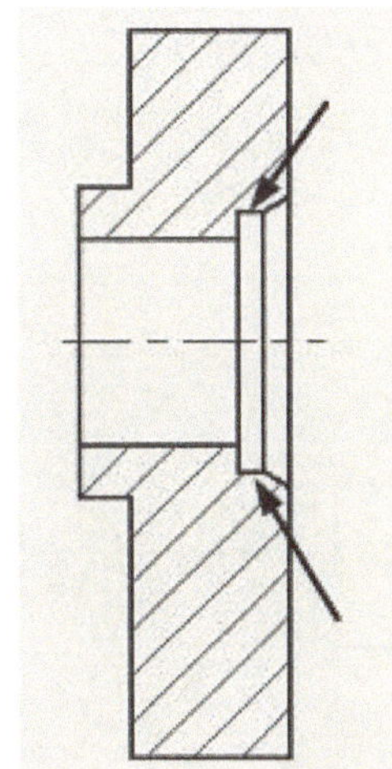

25. Move the pointer toward the right and click to place the dimension.
26. On the dialog, click the **Precision and Tolerance** tab.
27. Set the **Tolerance Method** to **Limits/Fits - Show tolerance**.
28. Select **Hole > H7**.
29. Set the **Primary Unit** value to **3.123**.
30. Set the **Primary Tolerance** value to **3.123**.

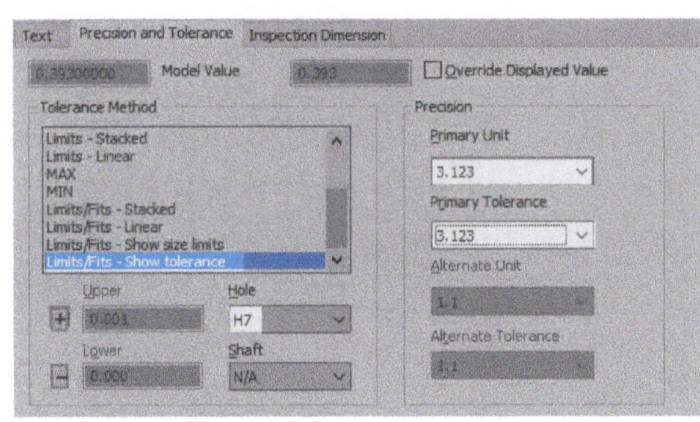

31. Click **OK**.

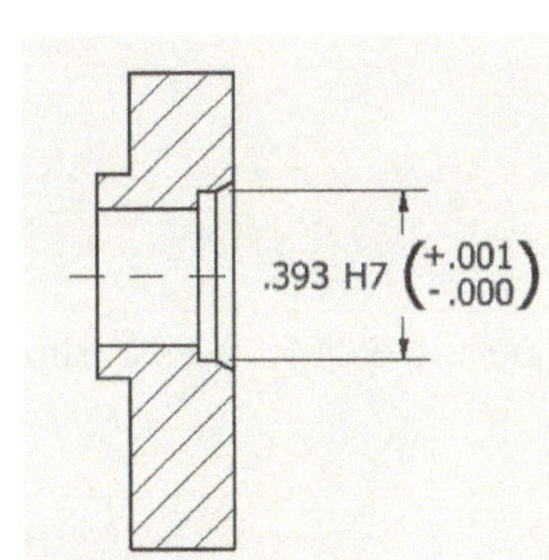

32. Likewise, apply the other dimensions, as shown below. You can also use the **Retrieve Dimensions**

tool to create the dimensions.

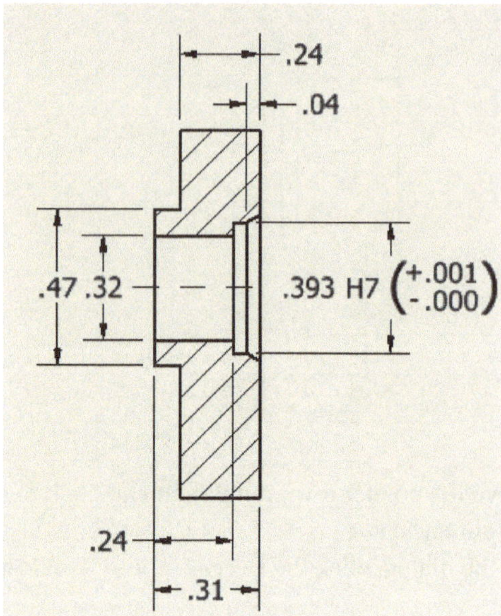

Placing the Datum Feature

1. Click **Annotate > Symbols > Datum Feature** on the ribbon.

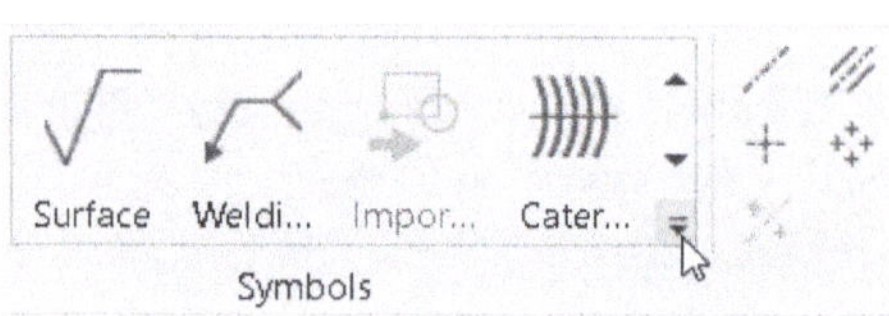

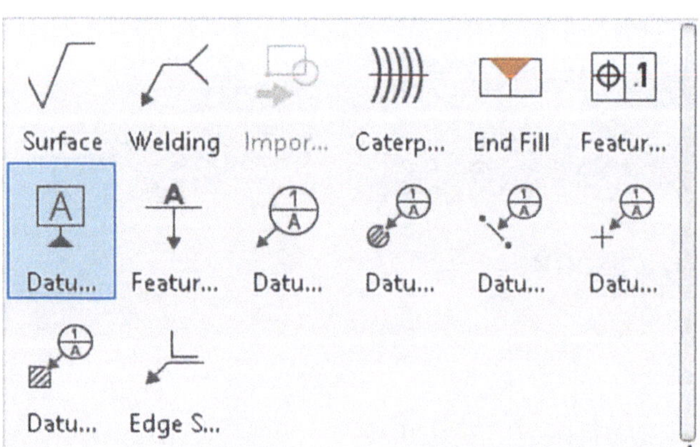

2. Select the extension line of the dimension, as shown below.

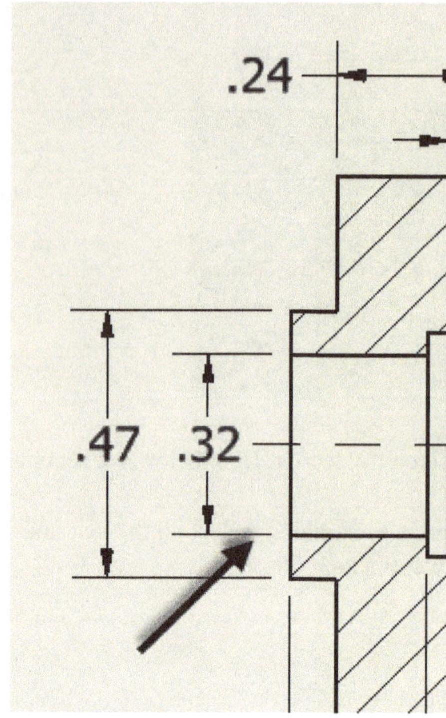

3. Move the cursor downward and click.
4. Move the cursor toward left and click; the **Format Text** dialog appears. Make sure that A is entered into the dialog.
5. Click **OK**.

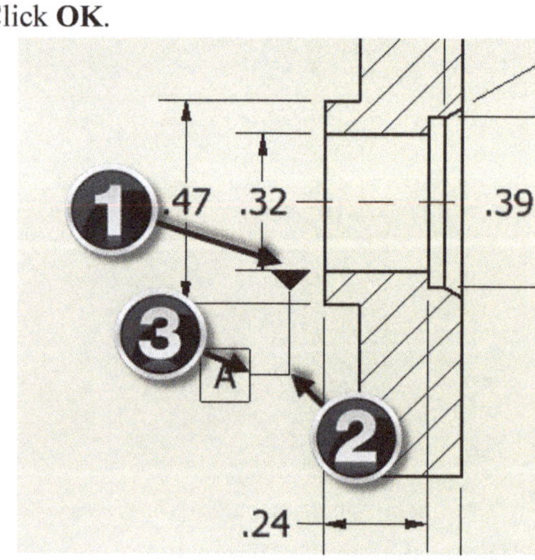

6. Likewise, place a datum feature B, as shown below. Press Esc.

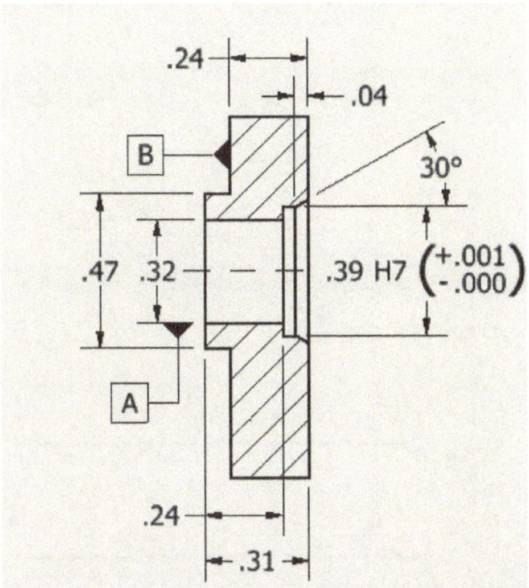

Placing the Feature Control Frame

1. Click **Annotate > Symbols > Feature Control Frame** on the ribbon.

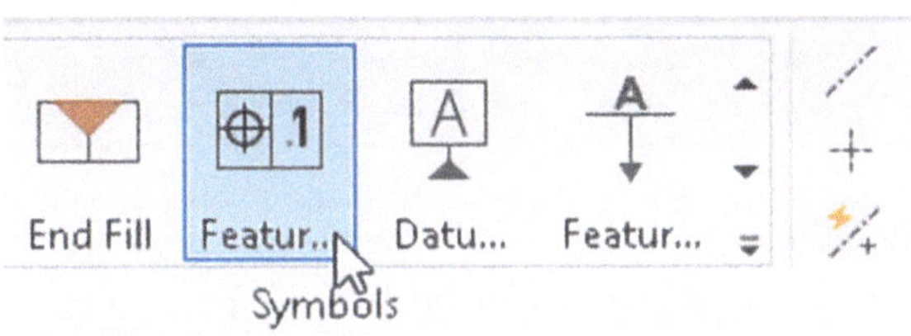

2. Select a point on the line, as shown below.
3. Move the cursor horizontally toward the right and click.

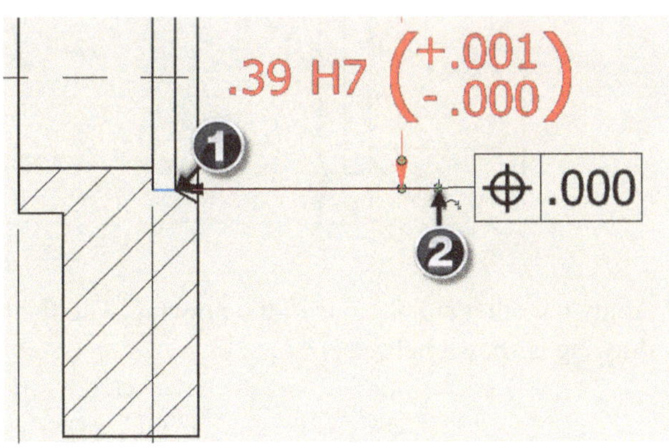

4. Right-click and select **Continue**; the **Feature Control Frame** dialog appears.

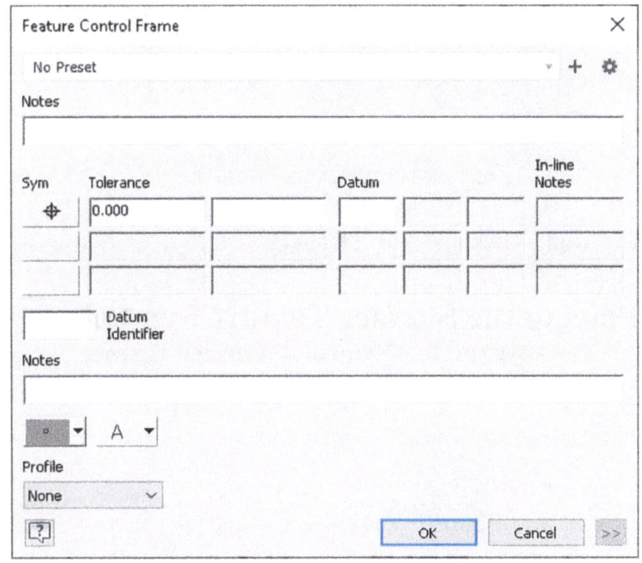

5. On the dialog, click the **Sym** button and select **Circular Run-out**.

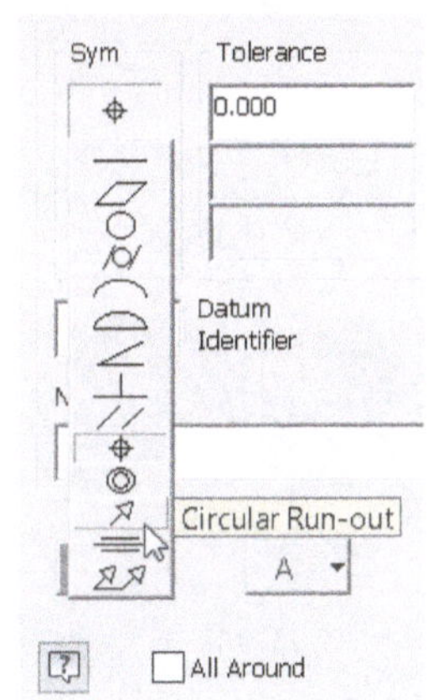

6. Enter 0.001 in the **Tolerance** box and **A** in the **Datum** box.

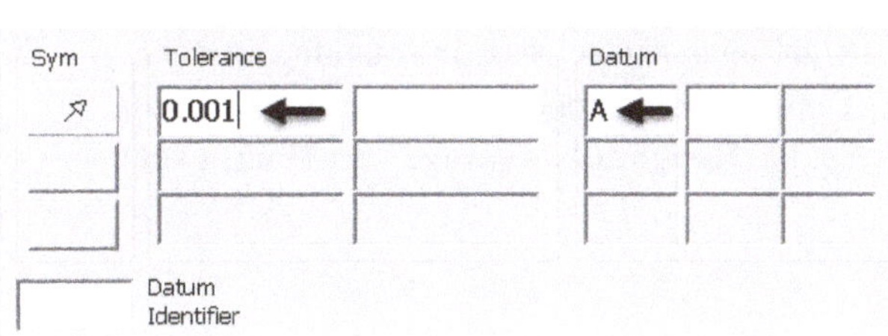

7. Click **OK**.

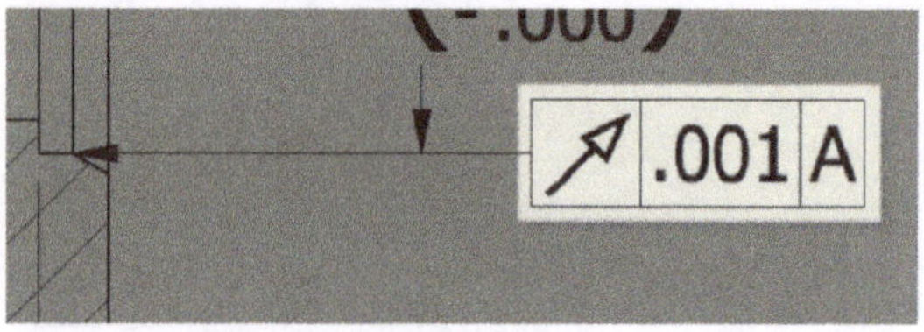

8. Right-click and select **Cancel**.

Placing the Surface Texture Symbols

1. Click **Annotate > Symbols > Surface Texture Symbol** on the ribbon.

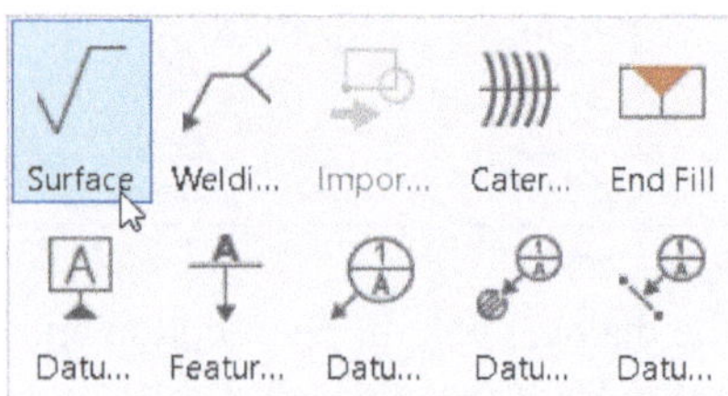

2. Click on the inner cylindrical face of the hole, as shown below.

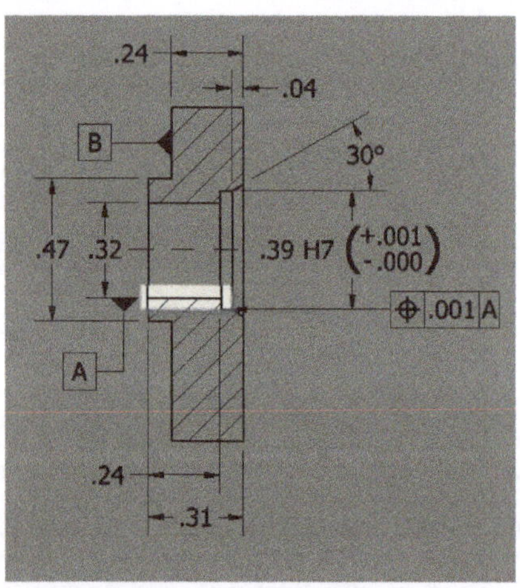

3. Right-click and select **Continue**; the **Surface Texture** dialog appears.
4. Set the **Roughness Average - maximum** value to 63.

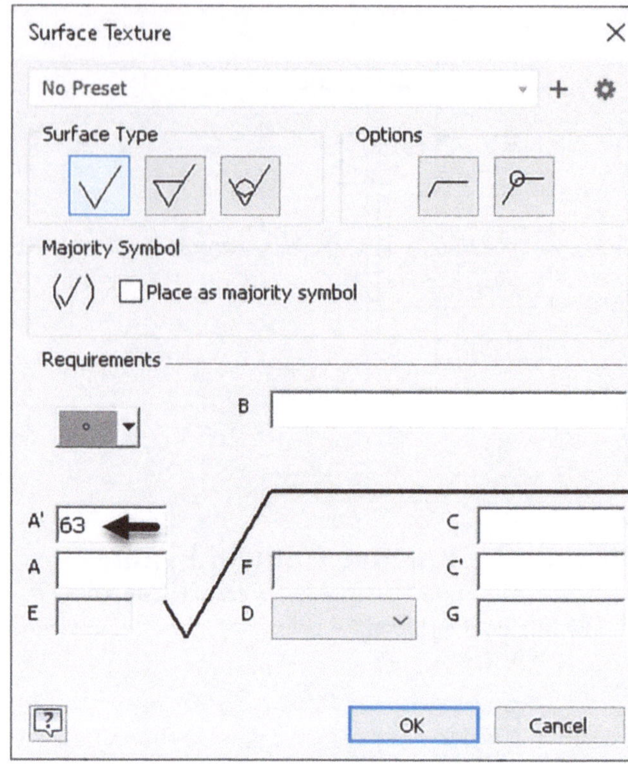

5. Click **OK**.
6. Right-click and select **Cancel**.

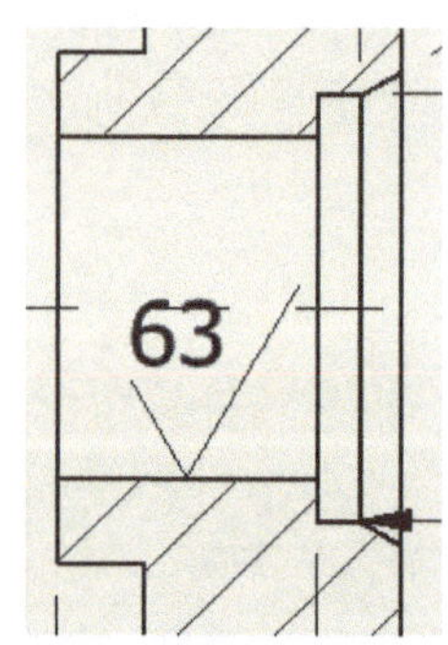

7. Apply the other annotations of the drawing. The final drawing is shown below.

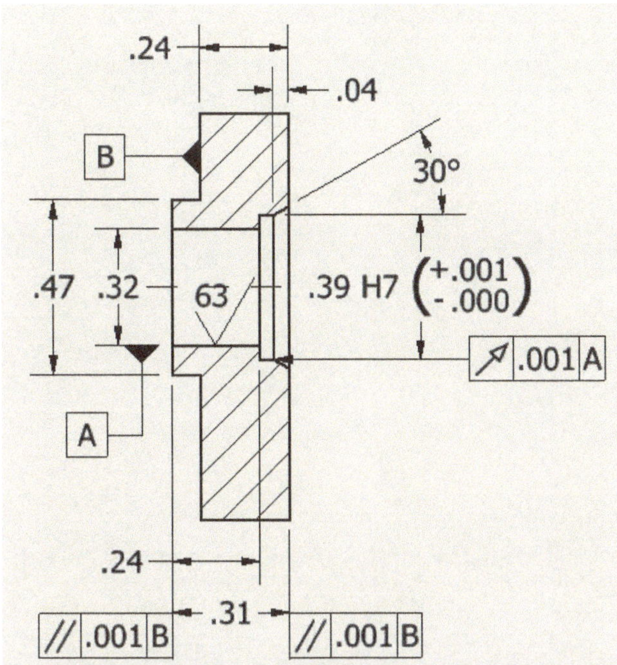

Modifying the Title Block Information

1. Right-click on the **Adapter Plate** in the **Browser window**. Select **iProperties** from the shortcut menu.

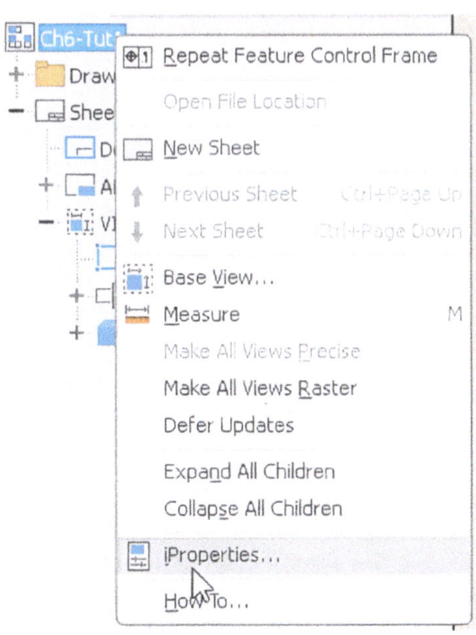

2. Click the **Summary** tab and enter the information, as shown next.

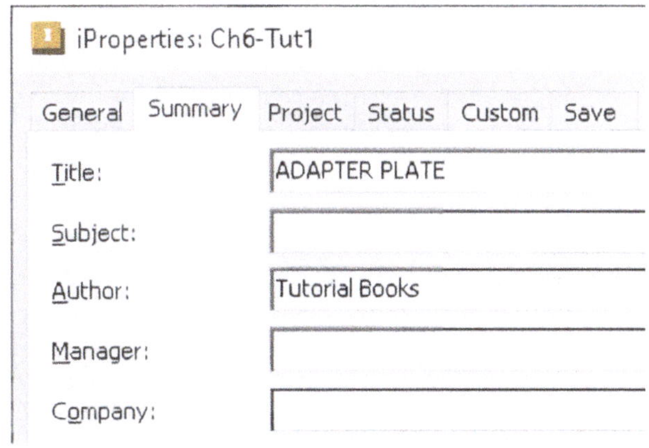

You can also update the Project information, drawing status, and other custom information in the respective tabs.

3. Click **OK**.
4. Save the file.
5. To export the file to AutoCAD format, click **File Menu > Export > Export to DWG**.
6. Click **Save**.
7. Close the file.

Chapter 10: Model-Based Dimensioning

Geometric Dimensioning and Tolerancing

During the manufacturing process, the accuracy of a part is an essential factor. However, it is impossible to manufacture a part with the exact dimensions. Therefore, while applying dimensions to a drawing, you need to provide some dimensional tolerances, which lie within acceptable limits. The following figure shows an example of dimensional tolerances applied to the drawing.

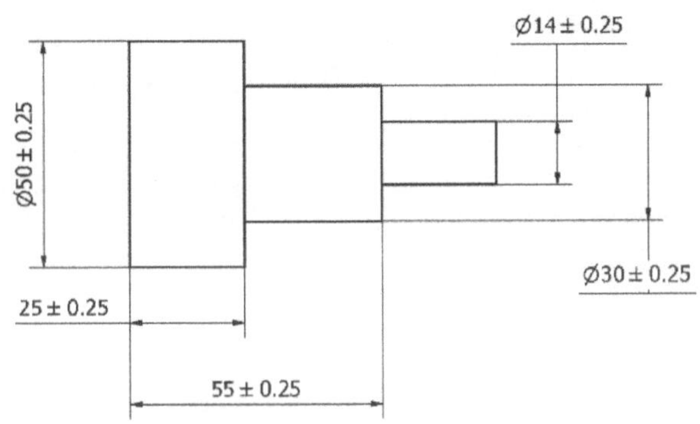

The dimensional tolerances help you to manufacture the component within a specific size range. However, the dimensional tolerances are not sufficient for manufacturing a component. You must give tolerance values to its shape, orientation, and position as well. The following figure shows a note, which is used to explain the tolerance value given to the shape of the object.

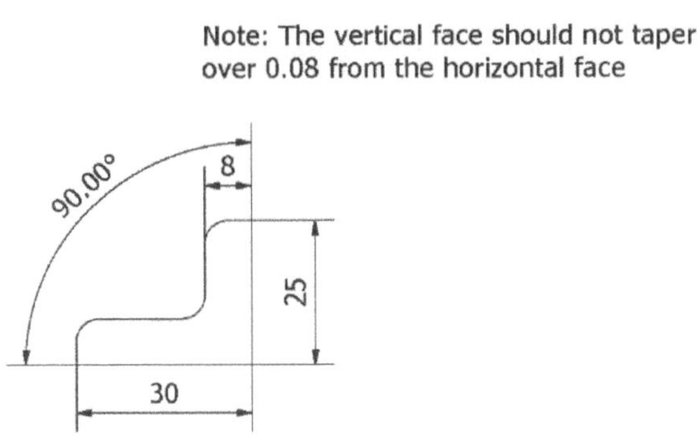

Providing a note in a drawing may be confusing. To avoid this, we use Geometric Dimensioning and Tolerancing (GD&T) symbols to specify the tolerance values to shape, orientation, and position of a component. The following figure shows the same example represented by using the GD&T symbols. In this figure, the vertical face to which the tolerance frame is connected must be within two parallel planes 0.08 apart and perpendicular to the datum reference (horizontal plane).

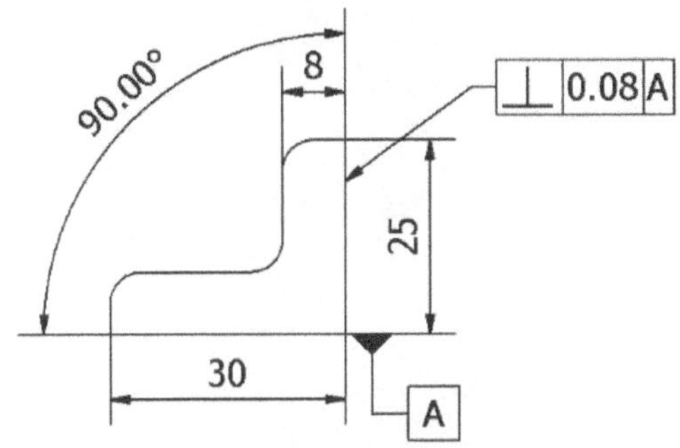

Providing GD&T in 2D drawings is a common and well-known method. However, you can provide GD&T information to 3D models as well. The tools available in the **Annotate** tab of the ribbon help you to add GD&T information to the 3D models based on the universal standards such as ASME Y14.41 – 2003 and ISO 16792: 2006. However, you can add GD&T information based on your custom standard as well.

In this chapter, you will learn to use **Annotate** tools to add GD&T information to the part models. There are many ways to add GD&T information and full-define the parts and assemblies. There are few methods explained in this chapter, but you need to use a method, which is most suitable for your design.

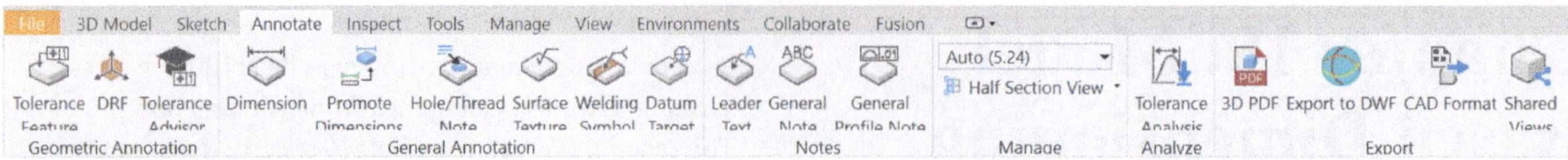

TUTORIAL 1

This tutorial teaches you to add tolerances to the 3D Model.

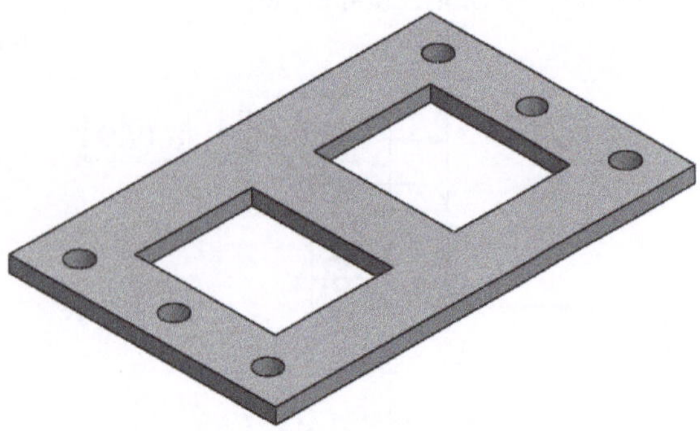

1. Download the Model-Based Dimensioning part files from the Companion website and open the Tutorial 1 file.
2. On the ribbon, click the **Tools** tab > **Options** panel > **Document Settings** to open the **Document Settings** dialog.
3. Click the **Standard** tab and select **ASME** from the **Active Standard** drop-down.
4. Click **OK**.
5. In the Browser Window, expand the **View** node, and then double click on the **Isometric** view.
6. Right click on the **Isometric** view, and then select **Annotation Scale > Auto**.

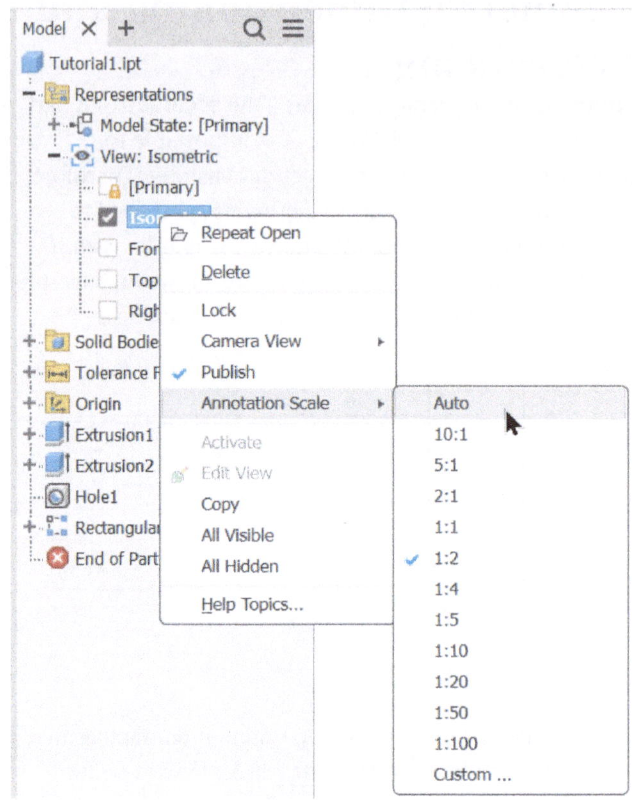

You can also change the **Annotation Scale** from the **Annotation Scale** drop-down available on the **Manage** panel of the **Annotate** ribbon tab.

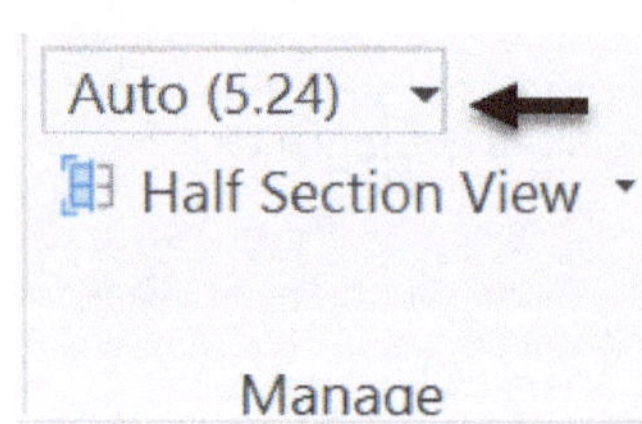

Adding Tolerances to the Model

1. On the ribbon, click **Annotate** tab > **Geometric Annotation** panel > **Tolerance Advisor** ; the **Tolerance Advisor** panel appears.
2. Click the **Face status Coloring** option located at the bottom on the **Tolerance Advisor** panel.

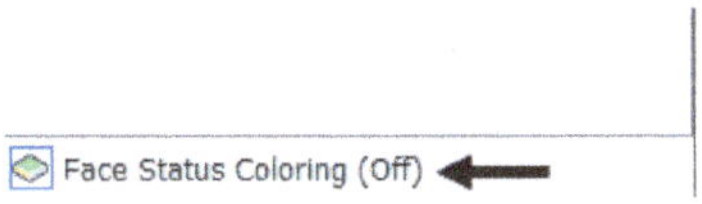

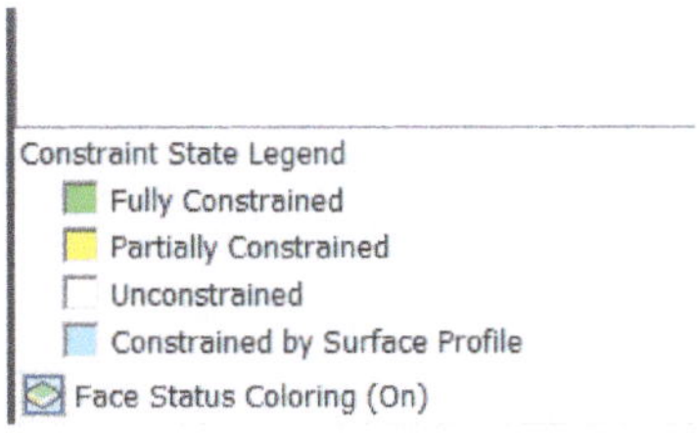

3. On the ribbon, click **Annotate** tab > **Geometric Annotation** panel > **Tolerance Feature**  .
4. Click on the top face of the model.
5. Click on the bottom face of the model.

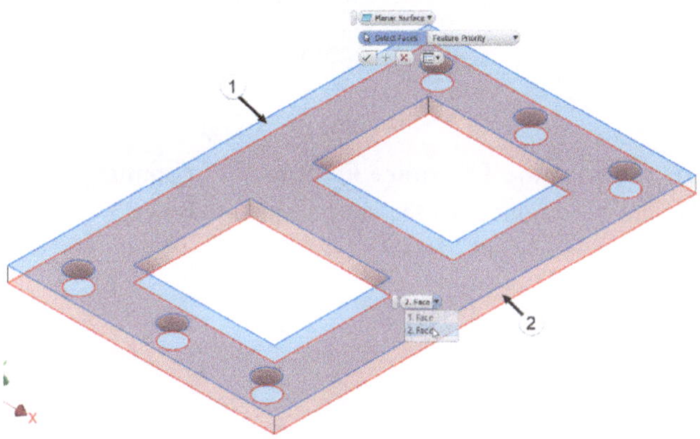

6. Select **Slab** from drop-down located on the Mini toolbar.

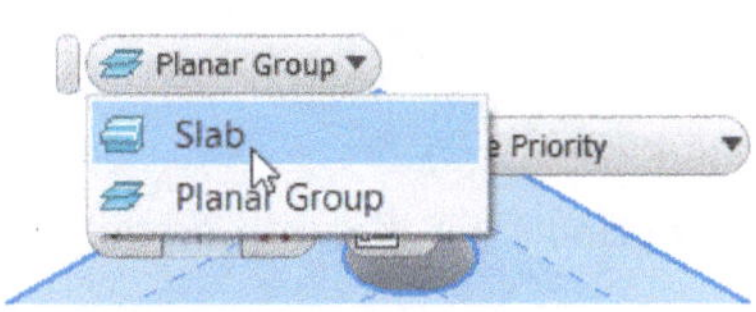

7. Click **OK**.
8. Right click and select the **Select Annotation Plane [Shift]** option.

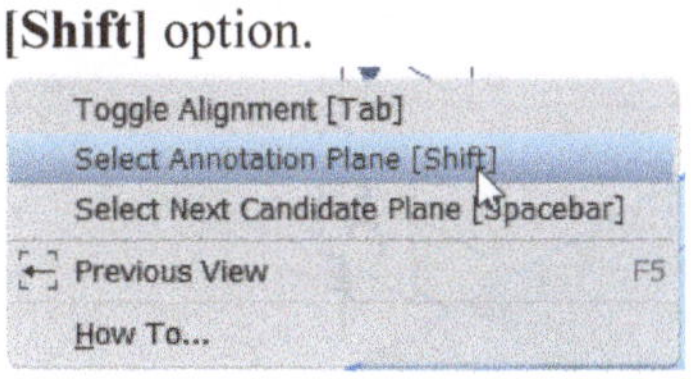

9. Select the face of the model, as shown.

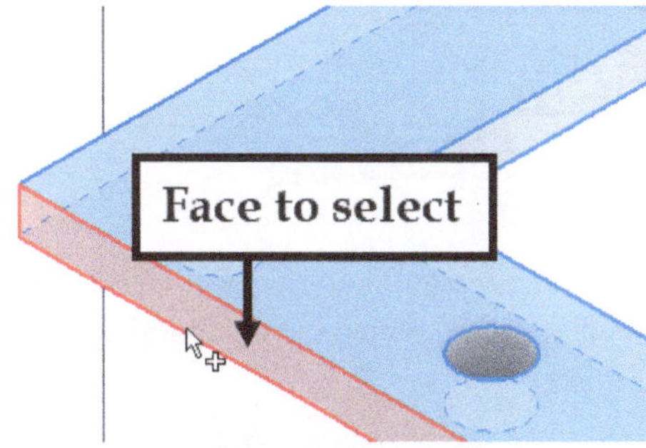

10. Move the pointer toward left, and then click.
11. Click on the dimension value.

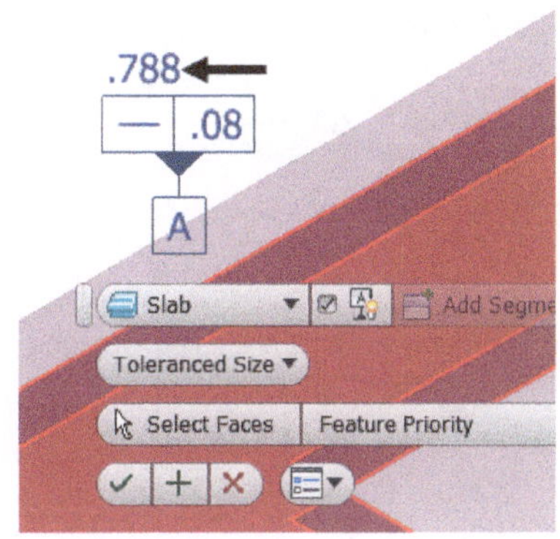

12. Select **Symmetric** from the **Tolerance Type** drop-down.

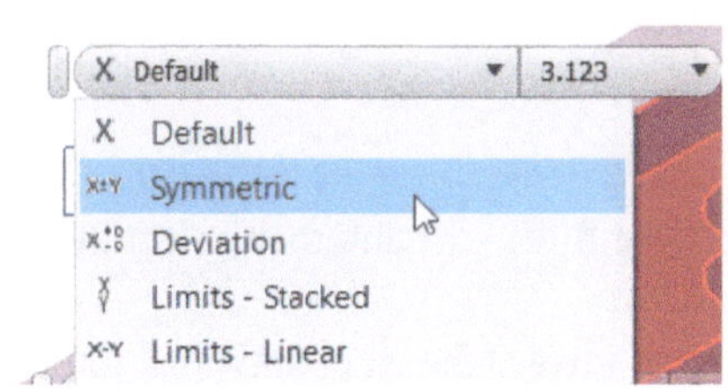

13. Click on the tolerance value displayed next to the dimension value.
14. Type .002 in the **Tolerance** box.

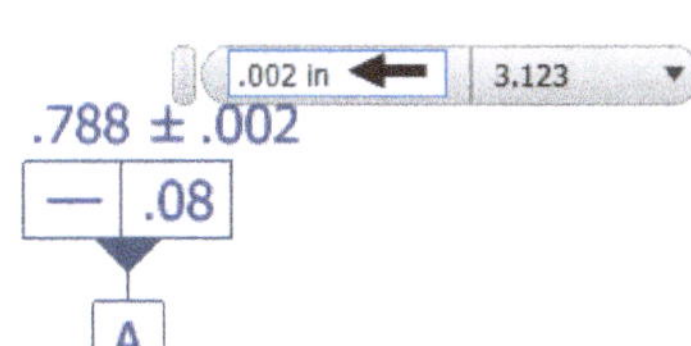

15. Click on the tolerance value in the feature control frame, and then type .002 in the **Tolerance** box.

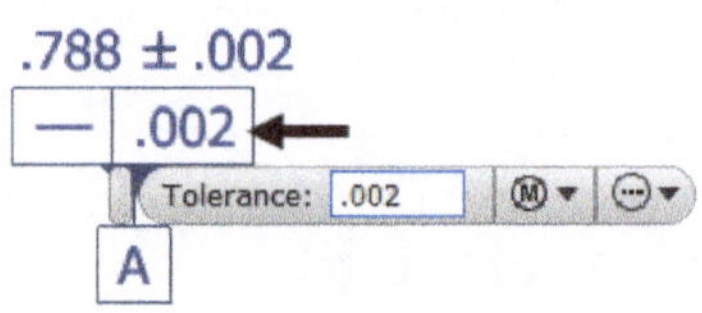

16. Click **OK**; the top and bottom faces of the model are displayed in green, which means that they are fully-constrained.

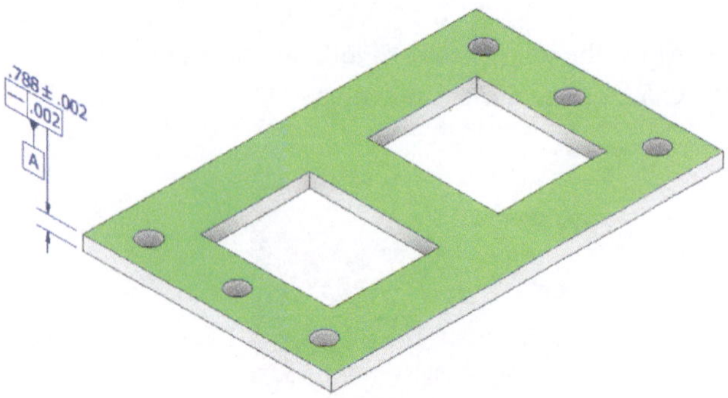

17. On the ribbon, click **Annotate** tab > **Geometric Annotation** panel > **Tolerance Feature**  .
18. Select the front and back faces of the model
19. Select the **Slab** option from the drop-down.

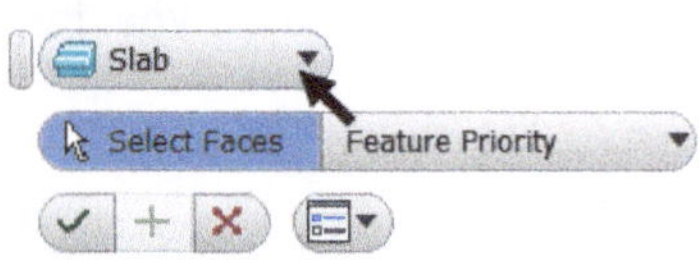

20. Click **OK**.
21. Press and hold the Shift key, and then select the top face of the model.
22. Move the pointer toward the right and click to place the tolerance feature.

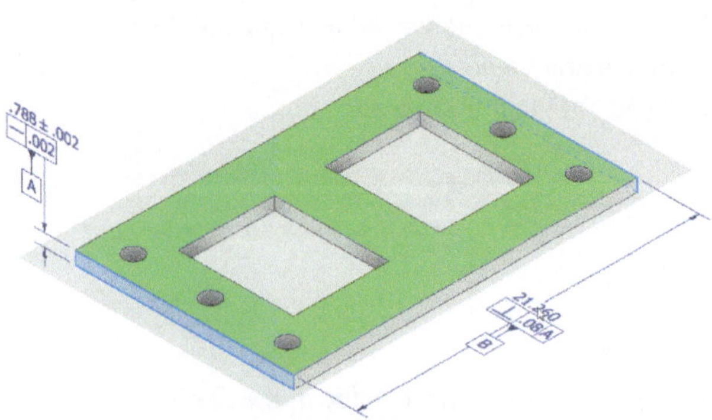

23. Specify the tolerance values, as shown.

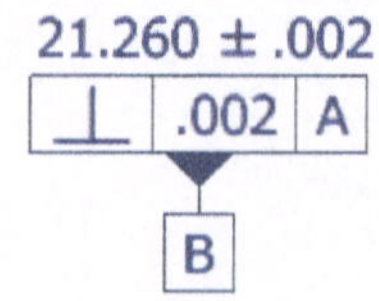

24. Click **OK** on the Mini toolbar.
25. Likewise, add the tolerance feature between the left and right-side faces, as shown.

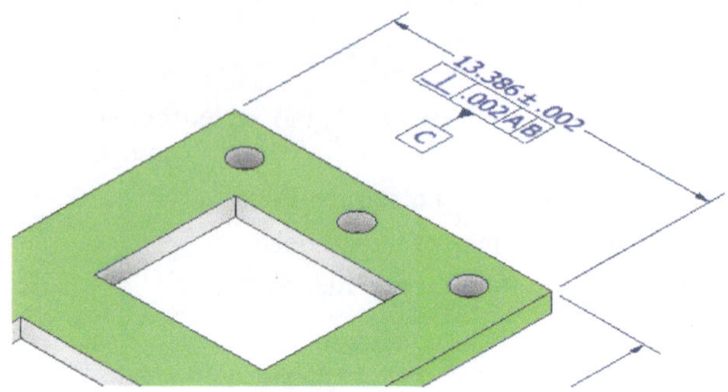

26. Activate the **Tolerance Feature**  command.
27. Select the faces of the cut feature, as shown.

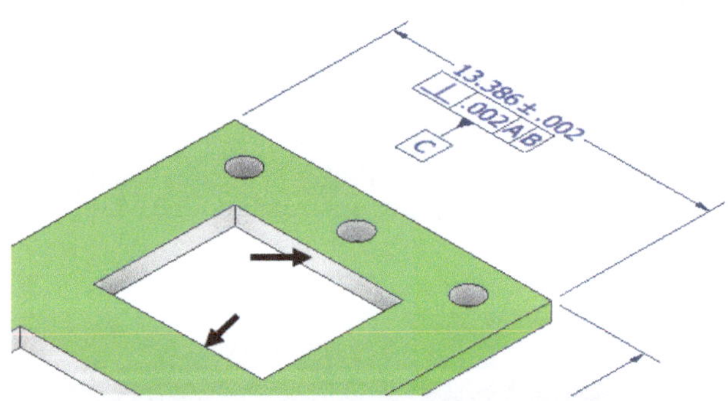

28. Select the **Slot** option from the drop-down from the Mini toolbar.

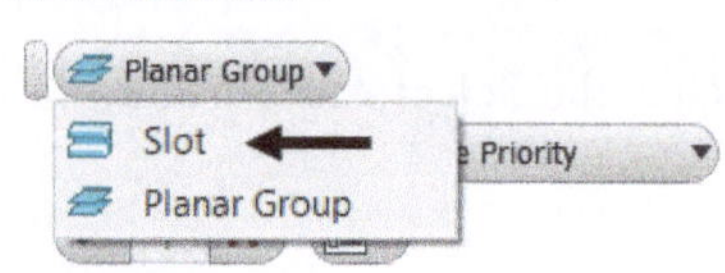

29. Click **OK**.
30. Press and hold the Shift key, and then select the top face of the model.
31. Move the pointer toward the left and click to place the tolerance feature.
32. Specify the tolerance values, as shown.

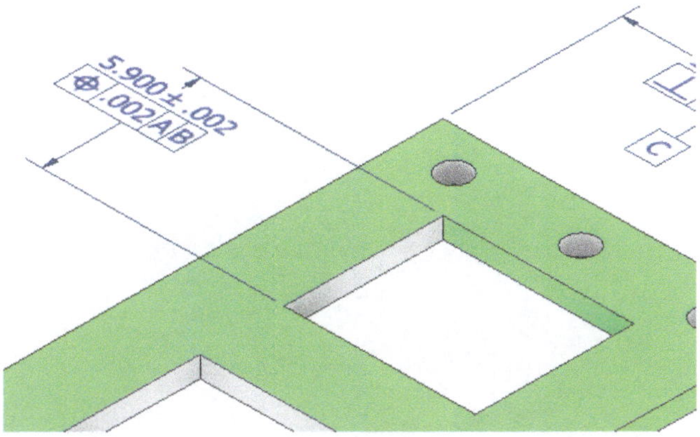

33. Likewise, add other tolerance features, as shown.

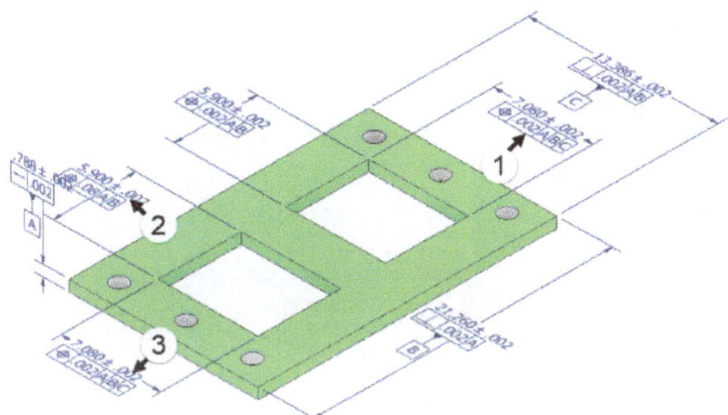

34. Activate the **Tolerance Feature** command.
35. Select any one of the holes.
36. Select the **Simple Hole Parallel Axes Pattern** option from the Mini toolbar.
37. Click **OK**.
38. Press and hold the Shift key, and then select the top face of the model.
39. Place the tolerance feature and add the tolerance values.

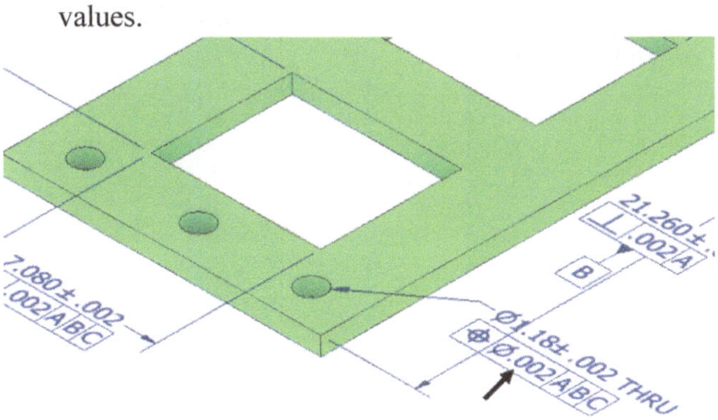

Notice that all the elements of the model are highlighted in green, which means that they are fully constrained.

40. On the **Model** tab of the Browser Window, expand the **Tolerance Features** folder and notice that all the model-based dimensions are listed.

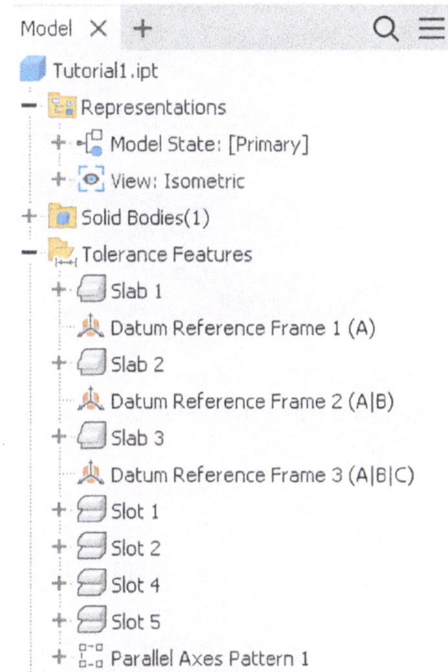

41. Right-click on the **Tolerance Features** folder and select **Hide All Annotations**; the model based dimensions are hidden.

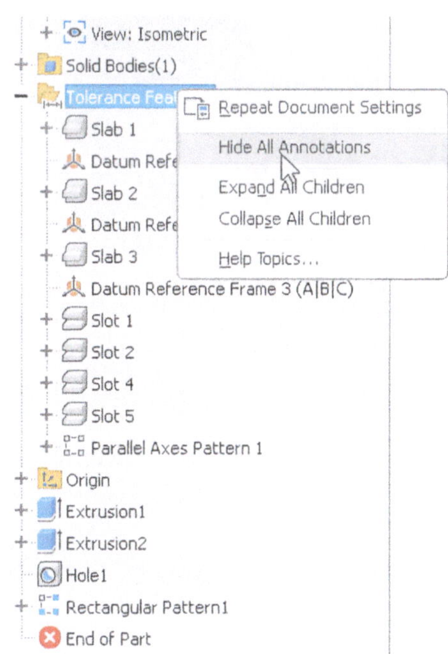

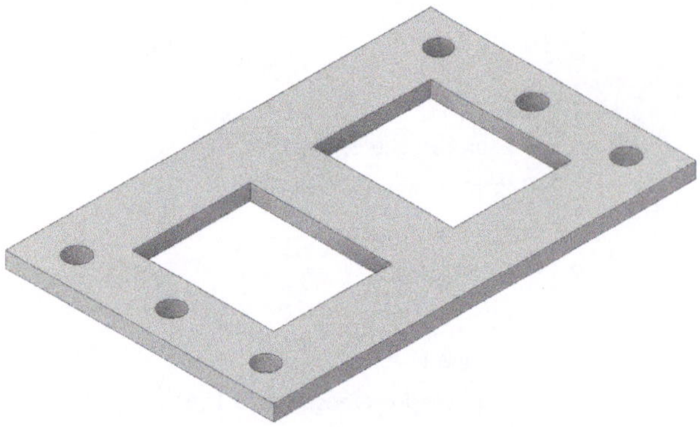

You can again display the hidden dimensions by right-clicking on the **Tolerance Features** folder and select **Show All Annotations**.

TUTORIAL 2

This tutorial teaches you to add weld symbol to the 3D Model.

1. Download the Model-Based Dimensioning part files from the Companion website and open the Tutorial 2 file.
2. On the ribbon, click **Annotate** tab > **General Annotation** panel > **Weld Symbol**  .
3. Select the bottom edge of the vertical plate, as shown.
4. Move the pointer toward right and click.

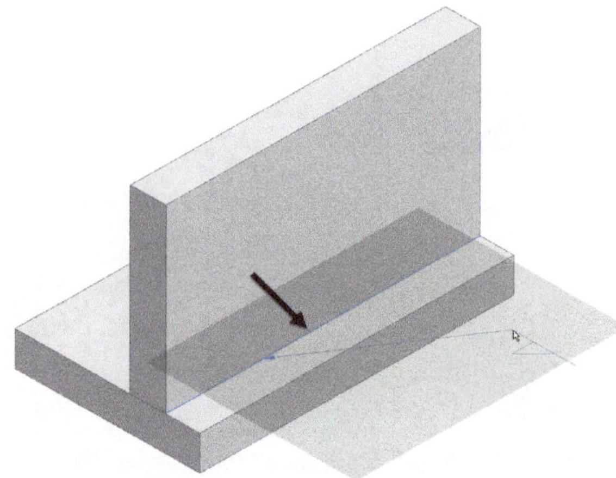

5. Right-click and select **Continue**.

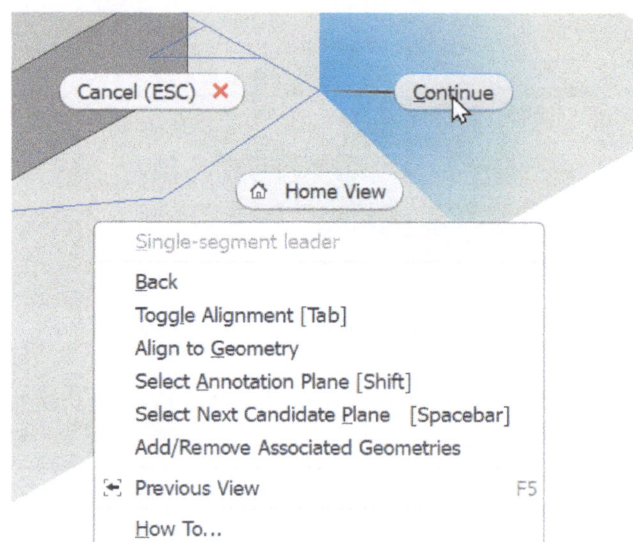

6. On the **Weld Symbol** dialog, type ¼ in the **Leg 2** box and click **OK**.

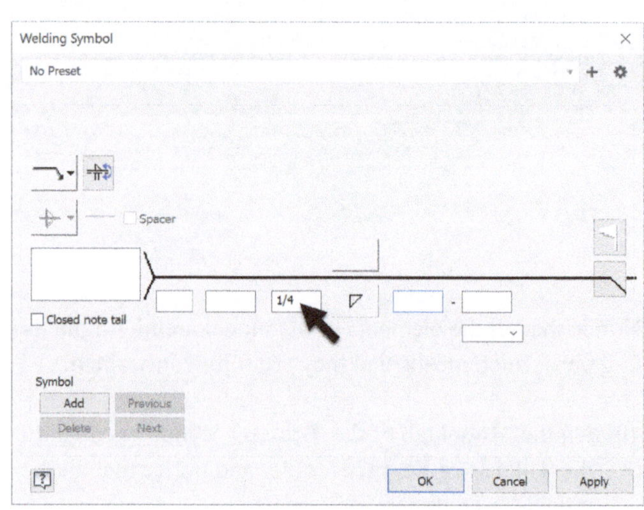

1/4

Chapter 11: Frame Generator

Autodesk Inventor provides a set of tools for creating frames. In addition to creating frames, you can use these tools for different applications. In this chapter, you will learn all of the tools used to create frames. You will also learn to create custom frame profiles and add them to your Library. The frame tools are located in the **Design** tab of the Ribbon.

TUTORIAL 1

In this tutorial, you create a simple weldment, as shown in the figure below.

1. Start a new part file using the **Standard (mm).ipt** template.
2. Create a skeleton sketch on the XZ plane, as shown.

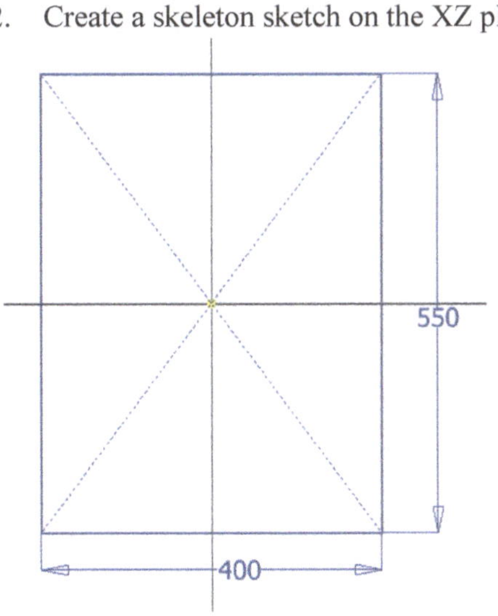

3. Click **Finish** on the ribbon.
4. On the ribbon, click **Tools > Options > Document Settings**.

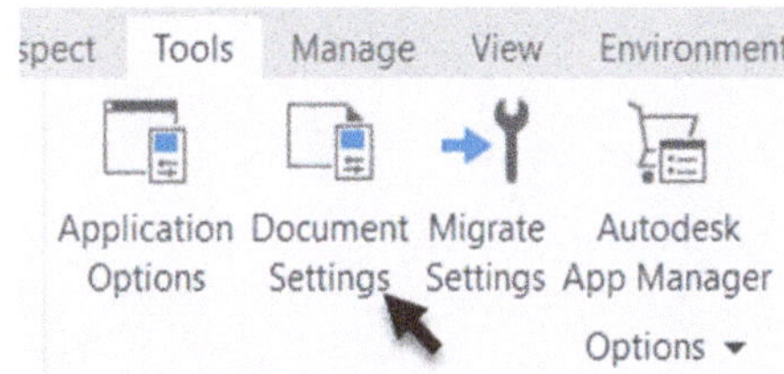

5. Click the **Bill of materials** tab on the **Document Settings** dialog.
6. Select the **Reference** option from the **Default BOM Structure** drop-down.

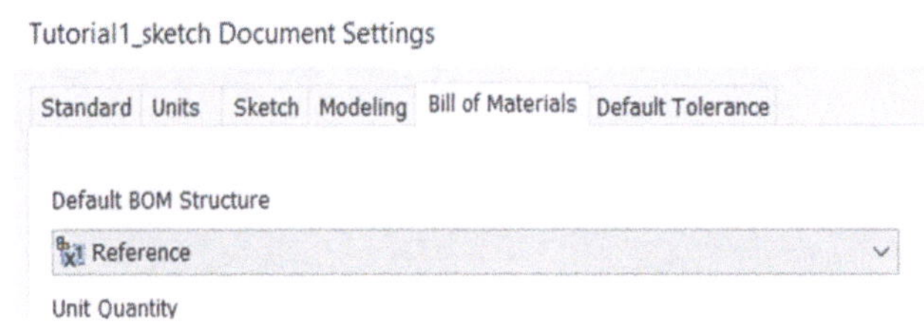

7. Click **OK**.
8. Click the **Save** icon on the Quick Access Toolbar.
9. Create a new folder and name it as **Frame Generator**.
10. Type **Tutorial1_Sketch** in the **File name** box.
11. Click the **Save** button.
12. Close the part file.
13. Click the **New** icon on the Quick Access Toolbar.
14. On the **Create New file** dialog, select **Template > en-US > Metric**.
15. Double-click on the **Standard(mm).iam** template.
16. Click the **Save** icon on the Quick Access Toolbar.
17. Type **Tutorial1_assembly** in the **File name** box.
18. Click the **Save** button.
19. Click **Assemble > Component > Place**  on the ribbon.
20. Browse to the **Frame Generator** folder and select the Tutorial1_Sketch part file.
21. Click **Open**.
22. Click in the graphics window to place the part consisting of the sketch.
23. Right click and select **OK**.

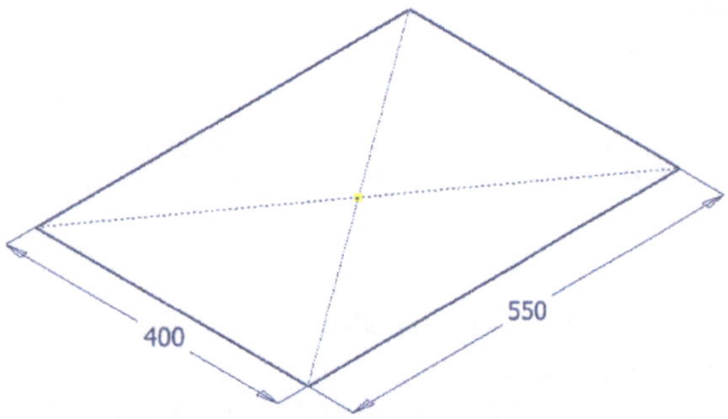

24. Click the **Design** tab on the Ribbon.
25. Click the **Insert Frame** button on the **Frame** panel.

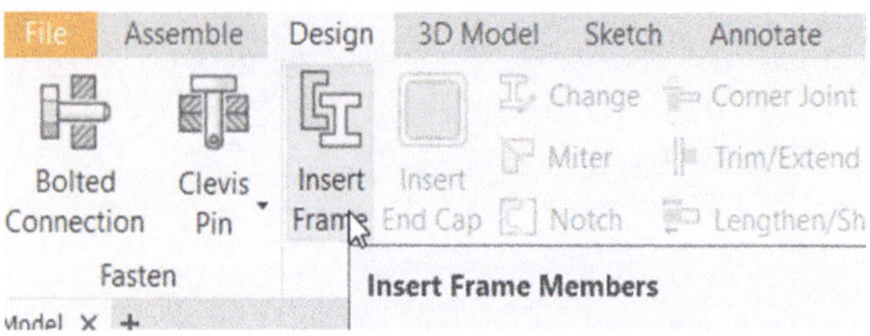

In this **Properties** panel, you need to define the parameters of the frame.

26. Select **I-Beams** from the **Category** drop-down.
27. Select **ANSI** from the **Standard** drop-down.
28. Select **ANSI S – S Shape - Sizes** from the **Family** drop-down.
29. Select **S3x5.7** from the **Size** drop-down.
30. Select **Steel, Mild** from the **Material** drop-down.

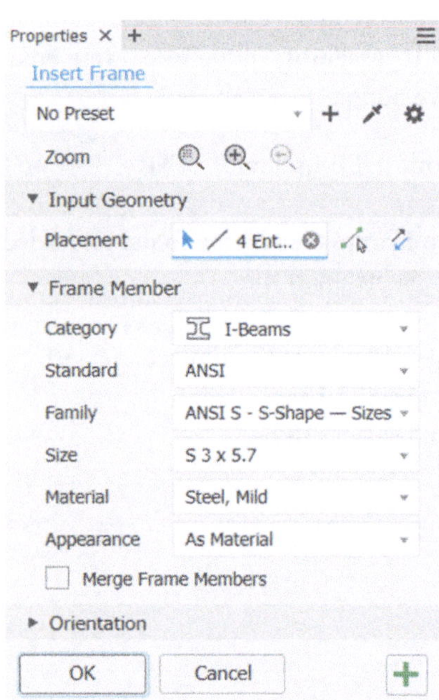

31. Select the vertical line and horizontal line of the skeleton sketch. The frames are created on the selected sketch segments.

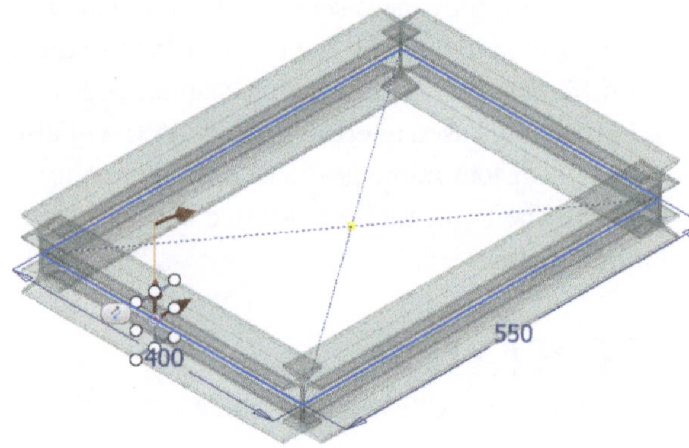

Next, you need to specify the orientation of the frames.

32. Expand the **Orientation** section on the **Properties** panel.
33. Type **45** in the **Rotate** box and notice that the frames are rotated by 45 degrees.

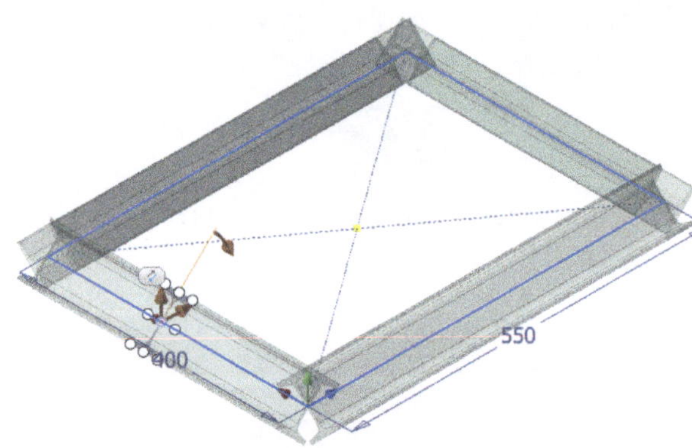

34. Change the **Rotate** value to 0.

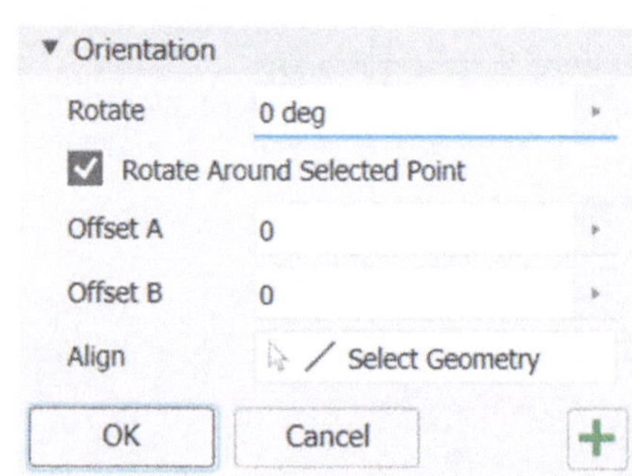

35. Zoom to the profile of the frame and notice the dots displayed on it. These dots help you to specify the

position of the profile on the selected line.

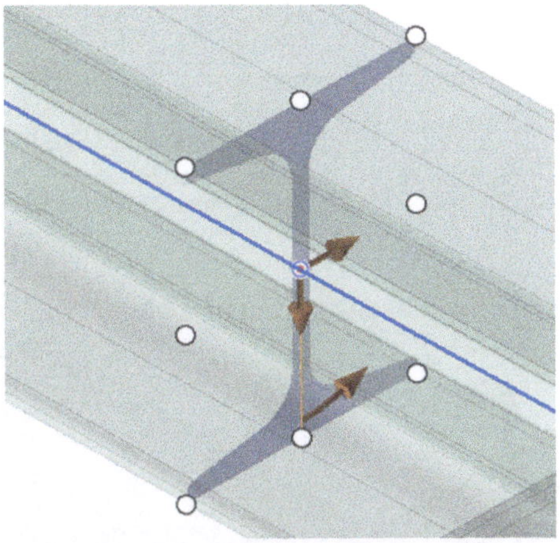

You can control the end condition of the frames by using the **Merge Frame Members** option in the **Frame Member** section. By default, this option is checked. As a result, the frames are merged at their ends. If you uncheck this option, the frames are not merged, and the corner treatment will not be applied.

36. Uncheck the **Merge Frame Members** option.
37. Click **OK**.
38. On the **Create New Frame** dialog, type **Tutorial1_frame.iam** in the **New Frame File Name** box.
39. Type **Tutorial1_skeleton.ipt** in the **New Skeleton File Name** box.
40. Click **OK**.

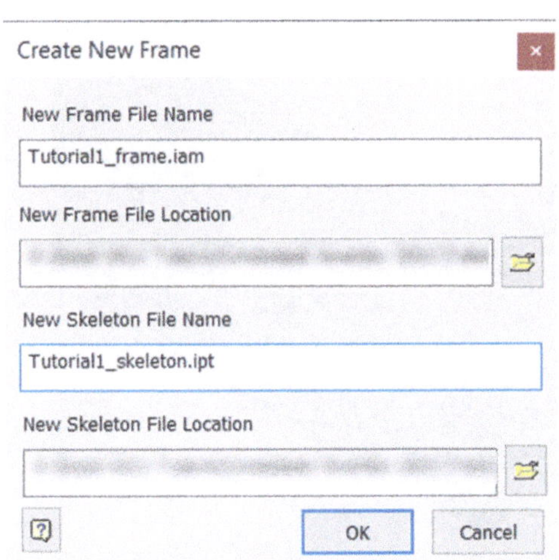

41. Click in the **Display Name** box of the first frame.
42. Type Tutorial1_frame1.

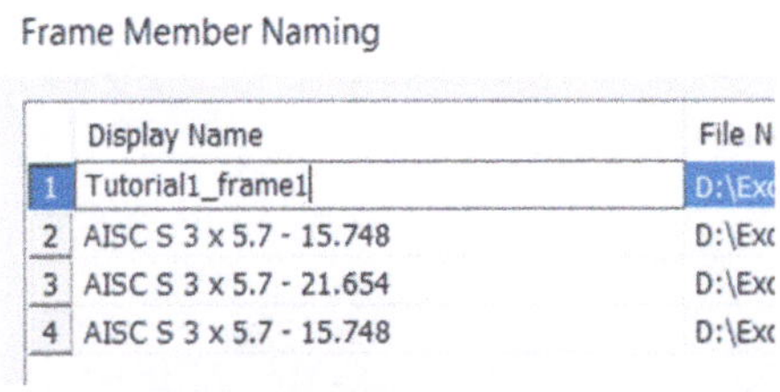

43. Likewise, change the display names of the other frames, as shown.

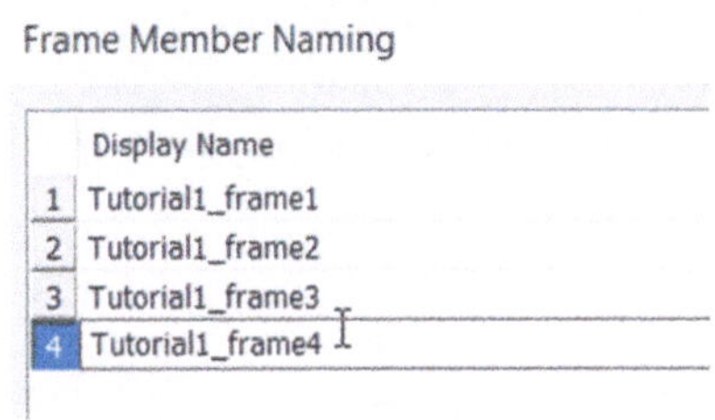

44. Click **OK**.

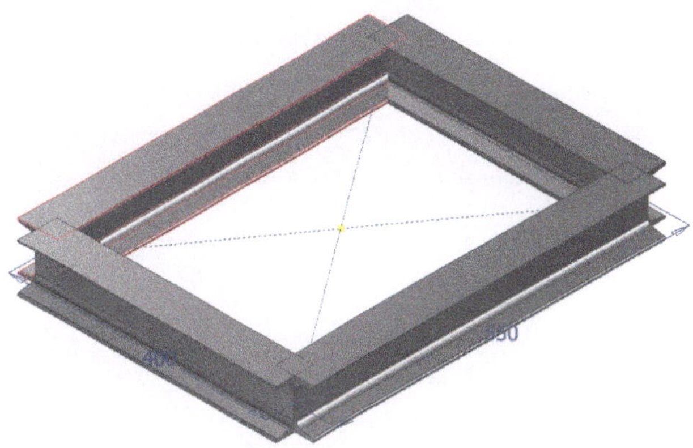

Applying the End treatments

You can apply the type of corner treatment by using the **Corner point**, **Miter**, **Trim/Extend**, and **Notch** commands.

1. On the ribbon, click **Design > Frame > Miter**.

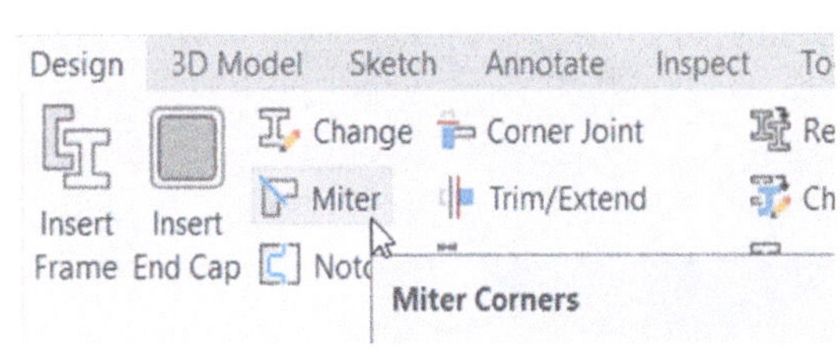

2. Select the two frames forming a corner, as shown.

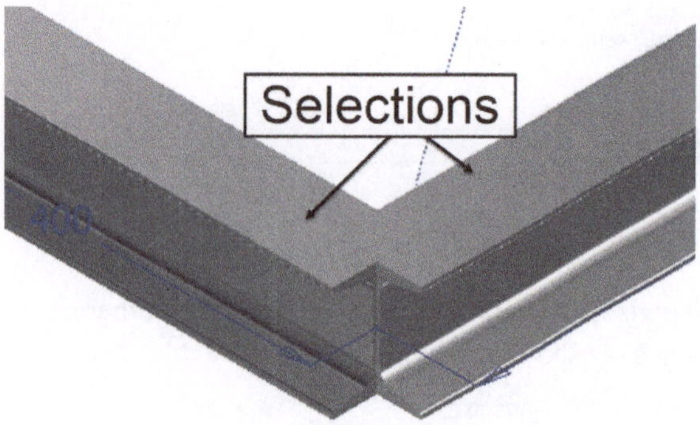

The **Miter Offset** box on the dialog helps you to specify a gap at the mitered corner.

3. Click **OK** to miter the corner.

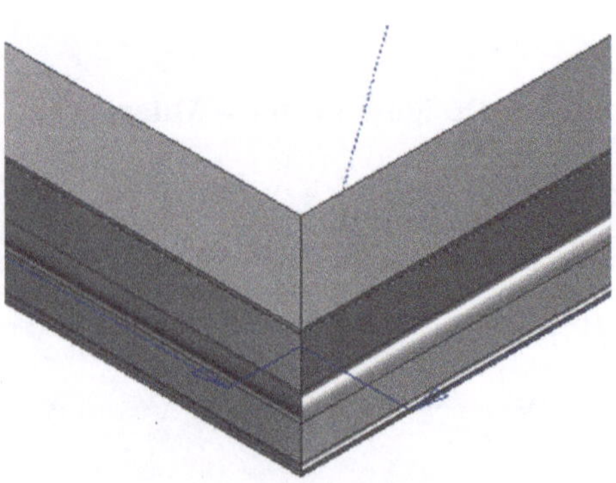

4. Click the **Undo** icon on the **Quick Access Toolbar**.

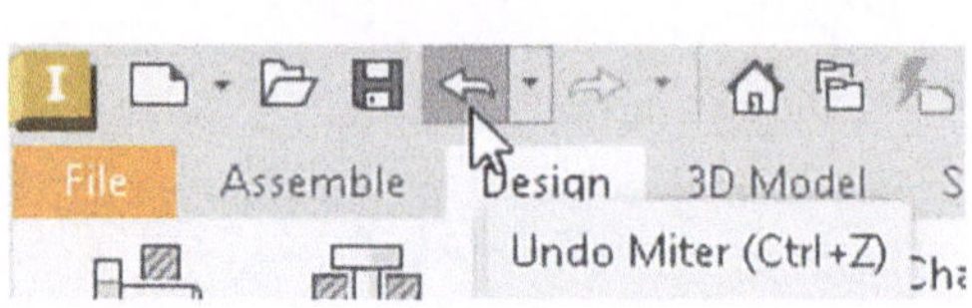

5. Click the **Corner Joint** icon on the **Frame** panel.

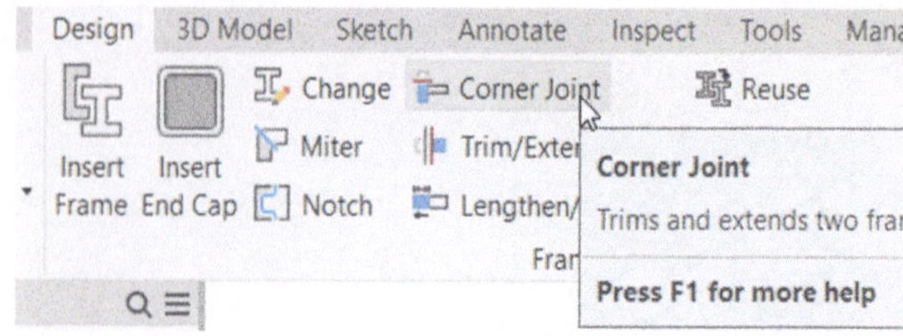

6. Select the horizontal and vertical frames, as shown.

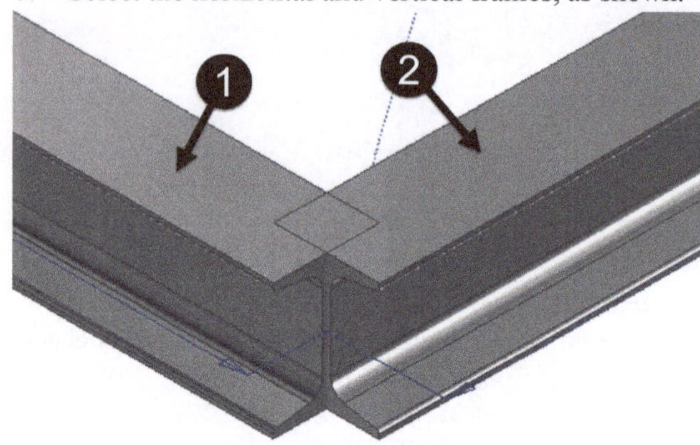

7. Click the **Apply and create new** trim icon on the bottom right corner of the **Properties** panel.

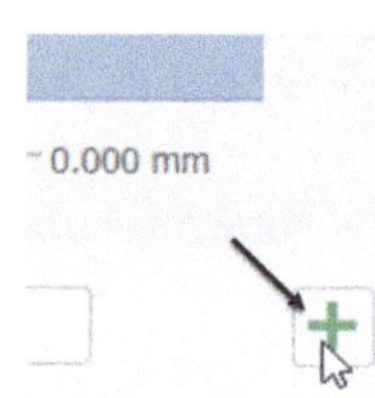

8. Select the vertical and horizontal frames on the other side.
9. Click the **Flip order of selected frame members** icon located next to the Frame Member selection box.

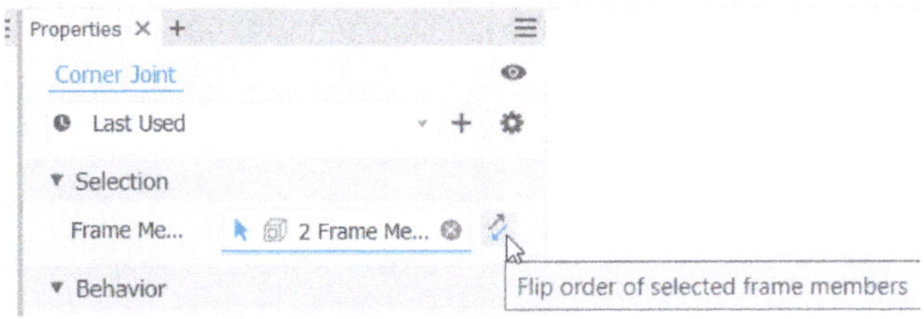

10. Click **OK**.

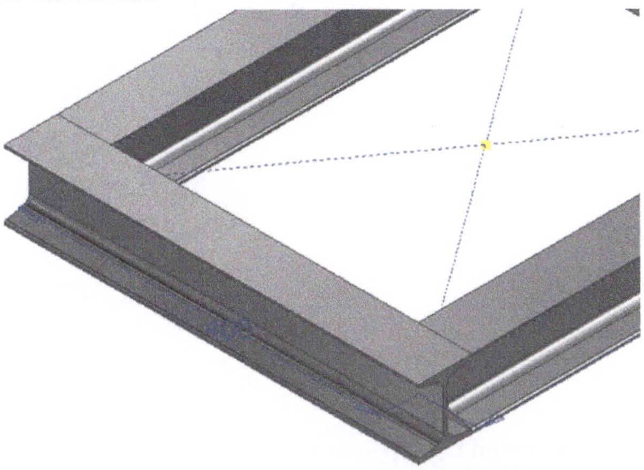

11. Click the **Undo** icon twice on the **Quick Access Toolbar**.
12. On the ribbon, click **Design > Frame > Trim/Extend**.

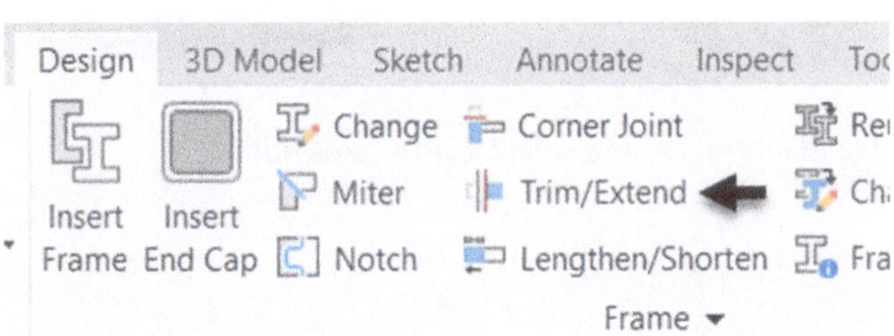

13. Select the side face of the frame, as shown. The tool is defined.

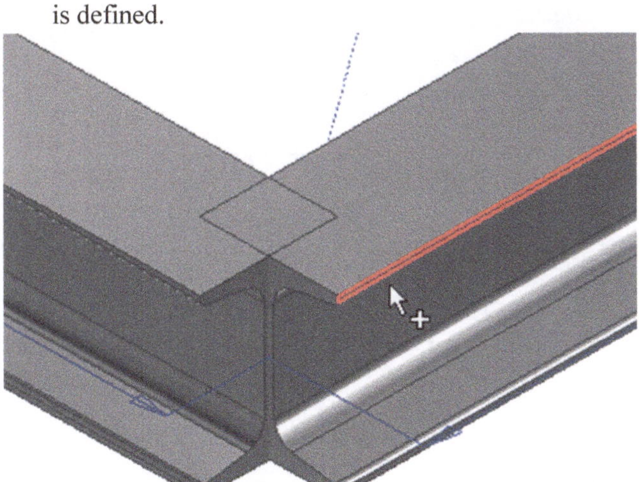

14. Select the frame, as shown.

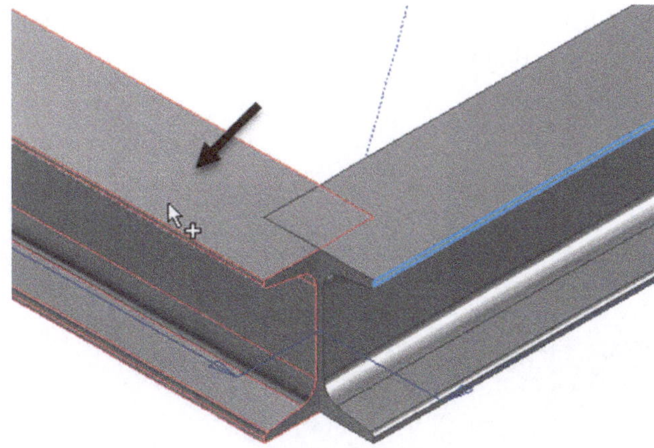

15. Click **OK**.

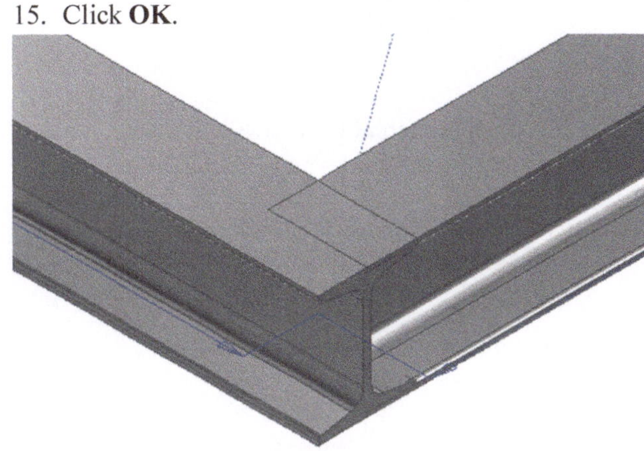

16. On the ribbon, click **Design > Frame > Notch**.

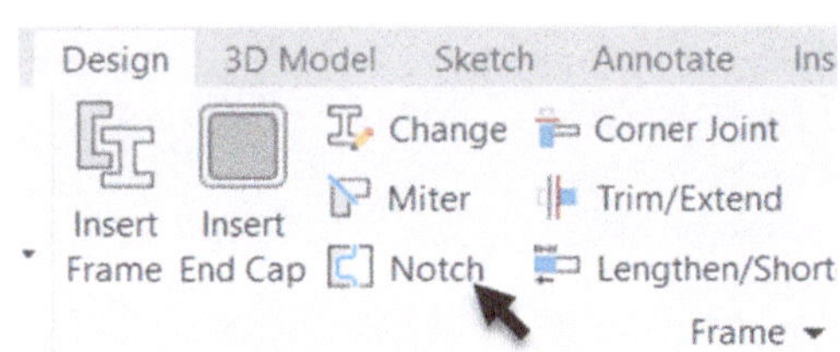

17. Select the frame member to notch cut, as shown.

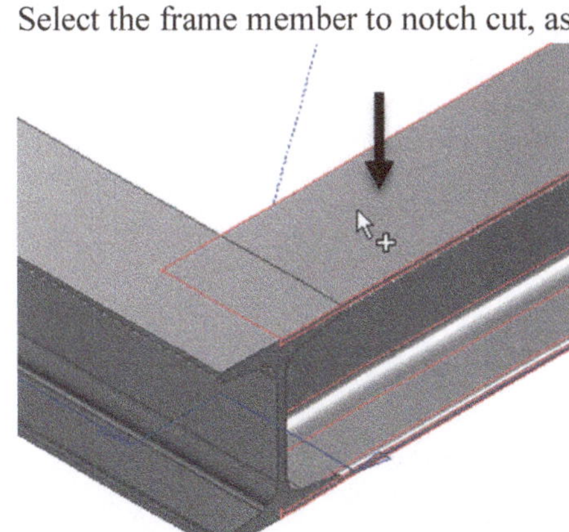

18. Click in the **Notch Tool** selection box and select the intersecting frame, as shown.

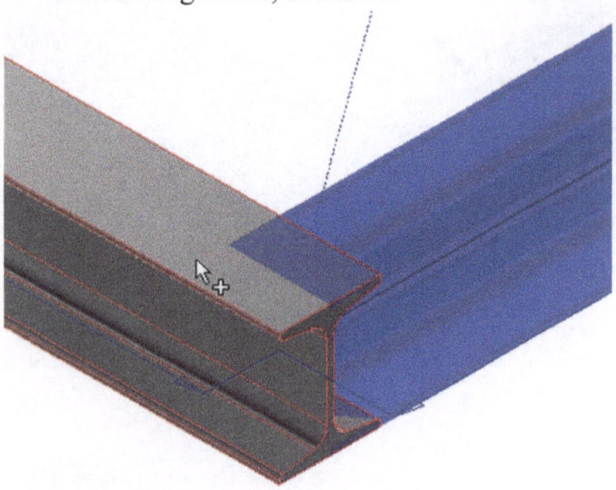

19. Click **OK**.
20. In the **Assembly** tab of the Browser Window, hover the cursor over the frames and select the notched frame.

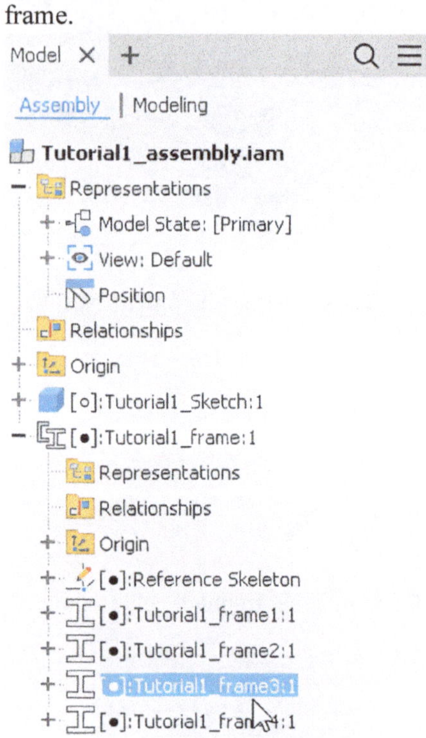

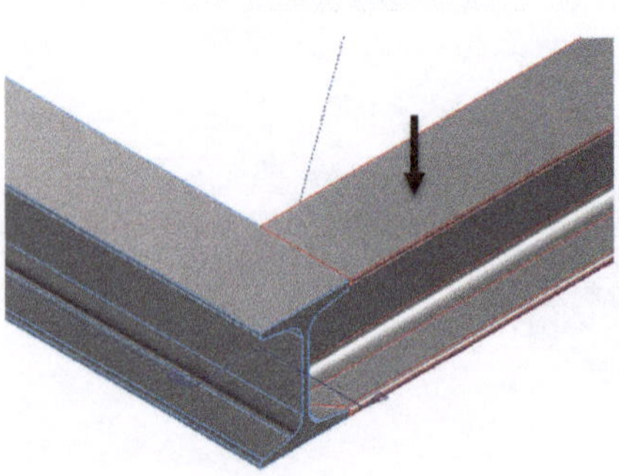

21. Right-click and select Isolate from the shortcut menu.

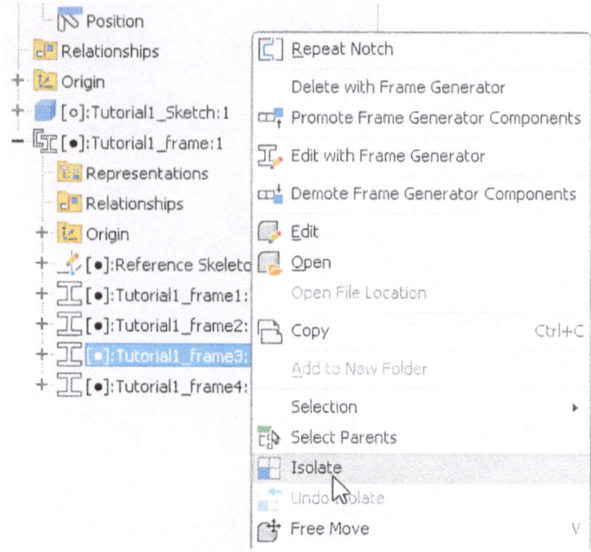

Notice the notch cut, as shown.

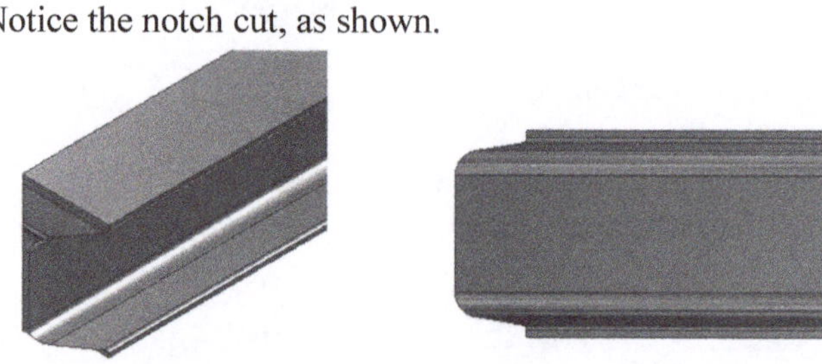

22. Right-click and select **Undo Isolation**.

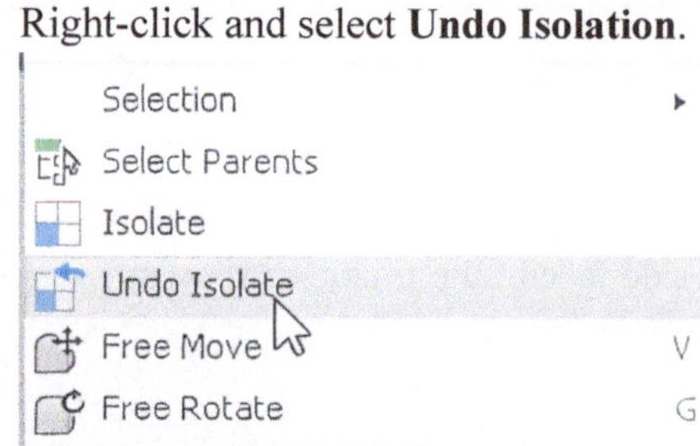

23. On the ribbon, click **Design > Frame > Lengthen/Shorten**.

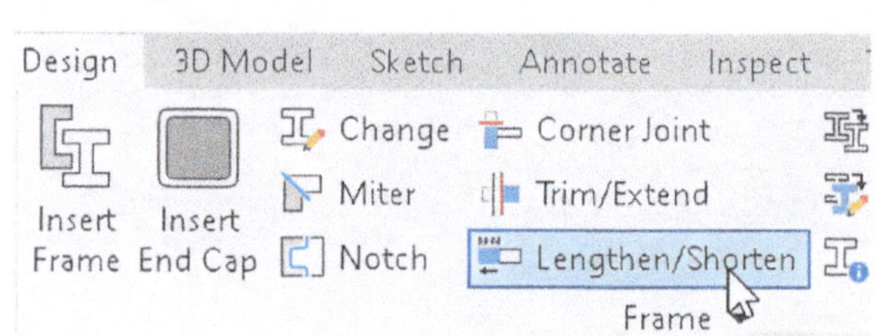

24. Select the frame member, as shown.

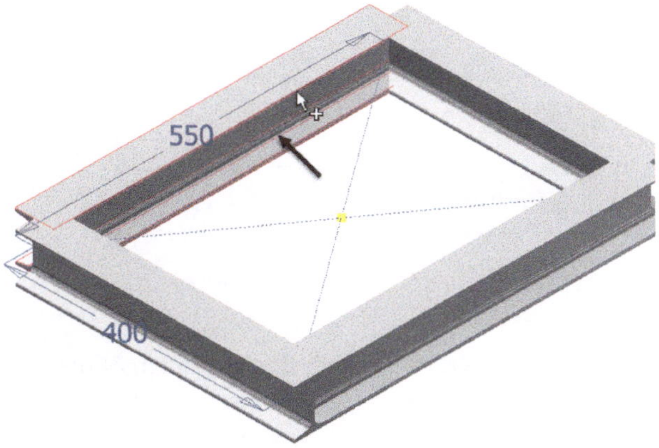

25. On the **Properties** panel, set the **Offset Direction** to **Symmetric** .
26. Click in the **Lengthen/Shorten** box and type **-30**.

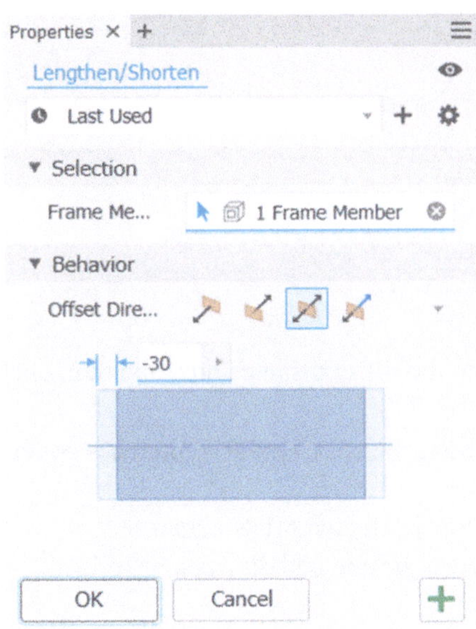

27. Click **OK**.

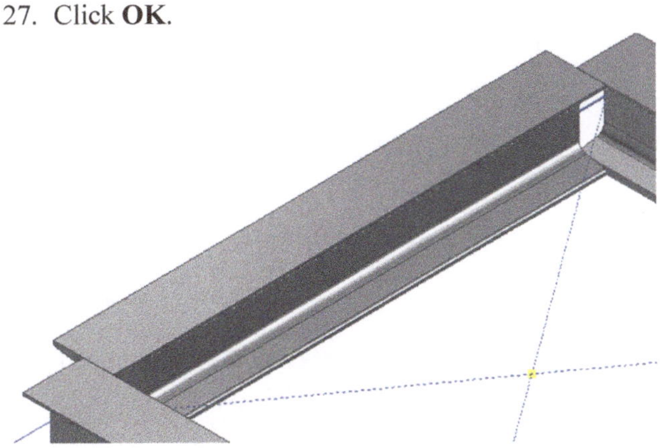

28. On the **Design** tab of the ribbon, expand the **Frame** panel and click the **Remove End Treatments** icon.

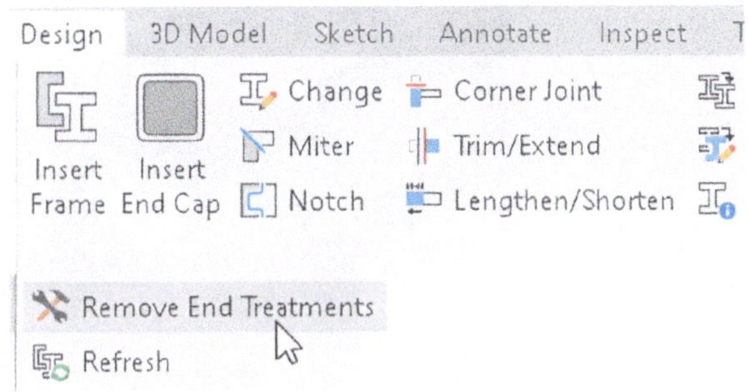

29. Select the two frame members with the end treatments, as shown.

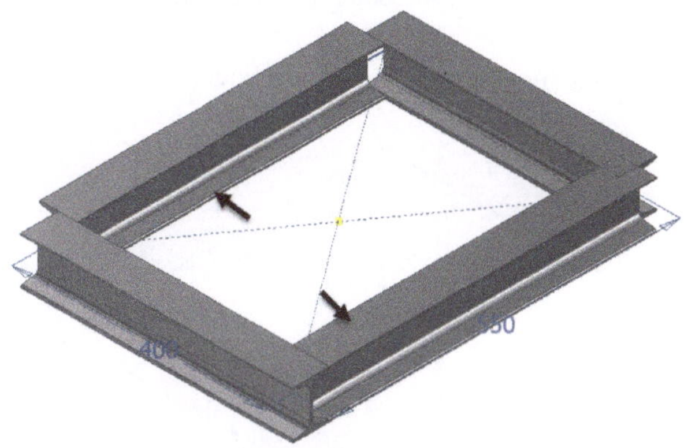

30. Click **OK**; the end treatments are removed.

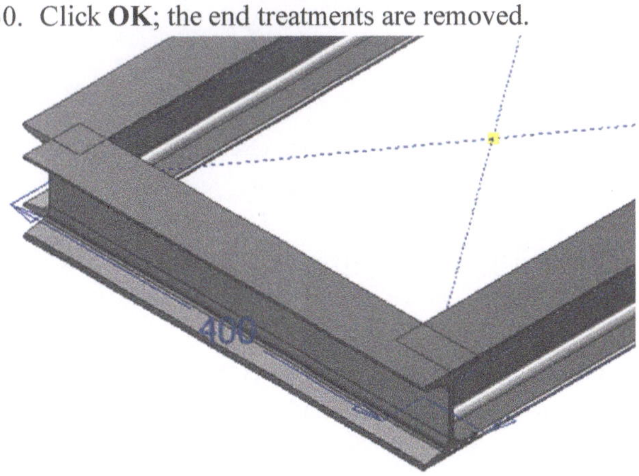

45. Save and close the document.

TUTORIAL 2

In this tutorial, you will create the weldment model, as shown.

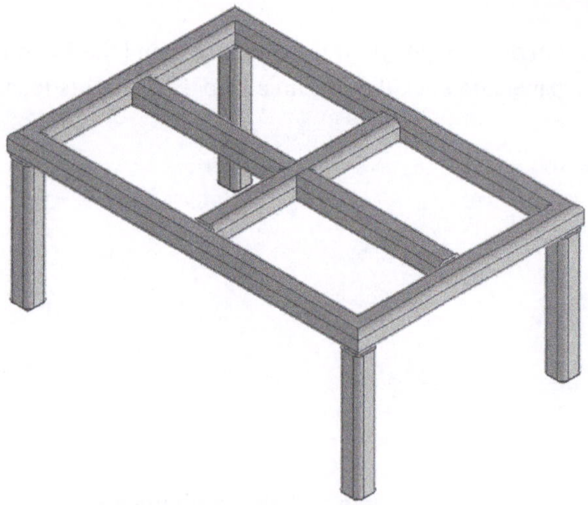

Creating the Skeleton sketch

1. Start a new part file using the Standard(mm).ipt template.
2. Create the skeleton sketch, as shown.

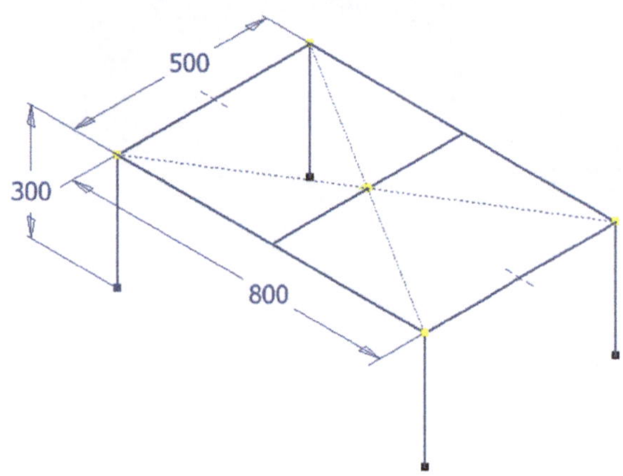

This skeleton sketch can be created as a 3D sketch or a combination of 2D and 3D sketches.

You can follow the steps given next to create the skeleton sketch.

3. On the Ribbon, click **3D Model > Work Features > Plane** drop-down **> Offset Plane**.

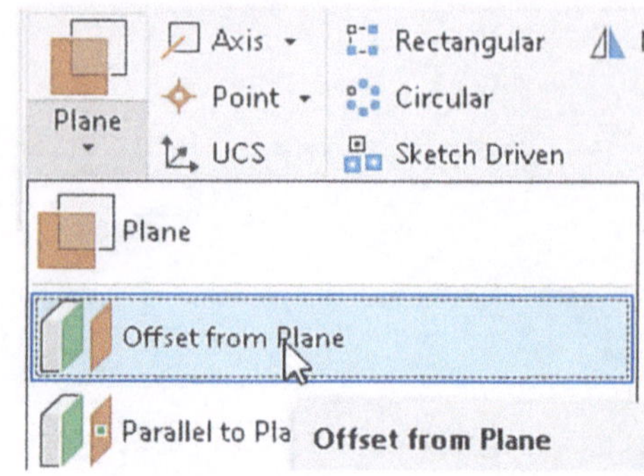

4. Select the XZ Plane from the Model tab of the Browser window.

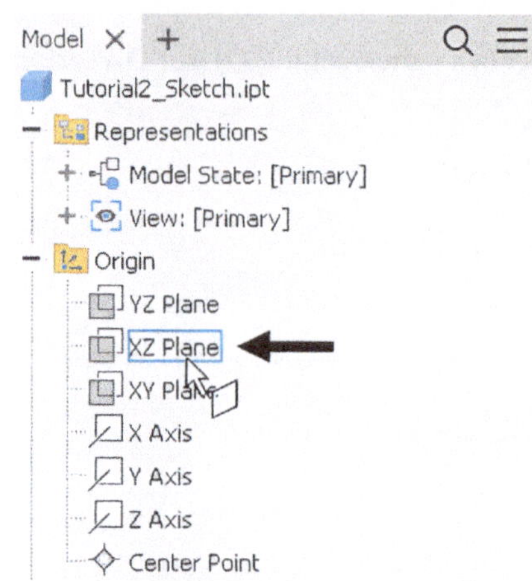

5. Type 300 in the offset distance box, and then click **OK**.
6. On the ribbon, click **3D Model > Sketch > Start 2D Sketch**.
7. Select the newly created offset plane.
8. Create a rectangle and add dimensions to it, as shown.

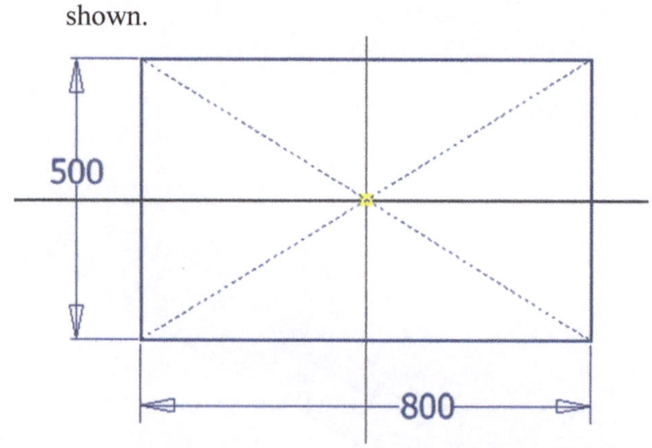

9. Create a vertical line connecting the midpoints of the horizontal lines, as shown.

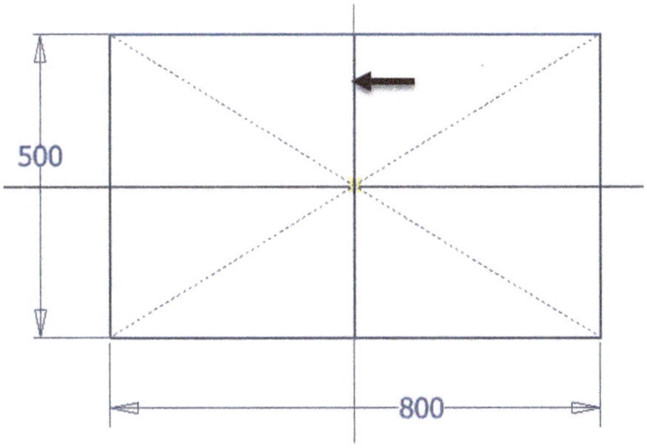

10. On the ribbon, click **Sketch** tab > **Create** panel > **Point**.

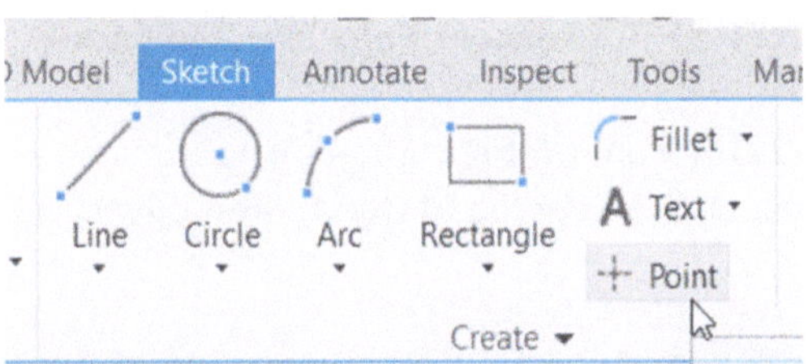

11. Select the midpoint of the left vertical line.

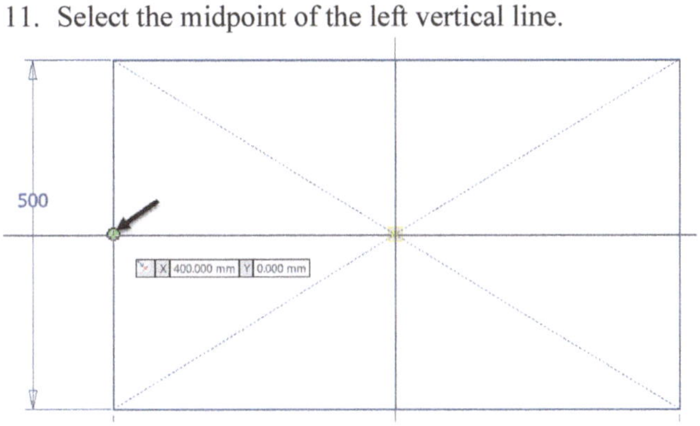

12. Select the midpoint of the right vertical line.

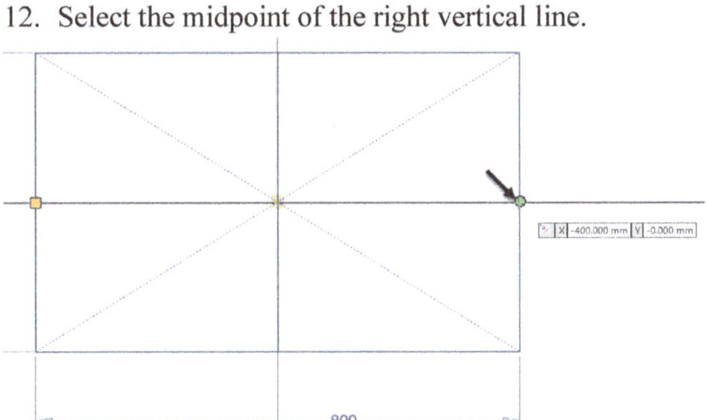

13. Click **Finish** on the ribbon.
14. On the ribbon, click **3D Model > Sketch > Start 3D Sketch**.

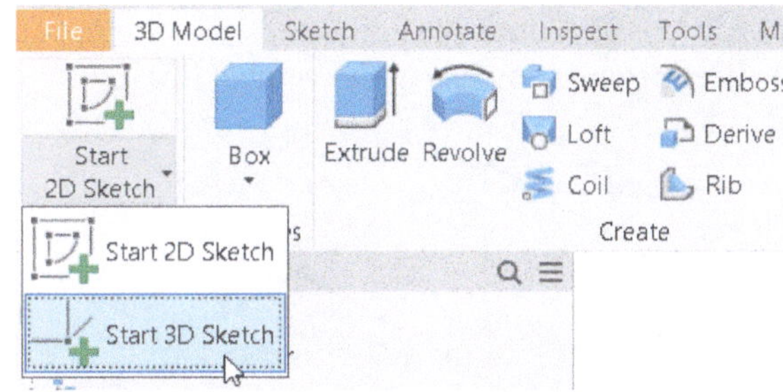

15. On the ribbon, click **3D Sketch > Draw > Line**.
16. Select the front left corner of the rectangle, as shown.
17. Move the pointer vertically downward, and then click.

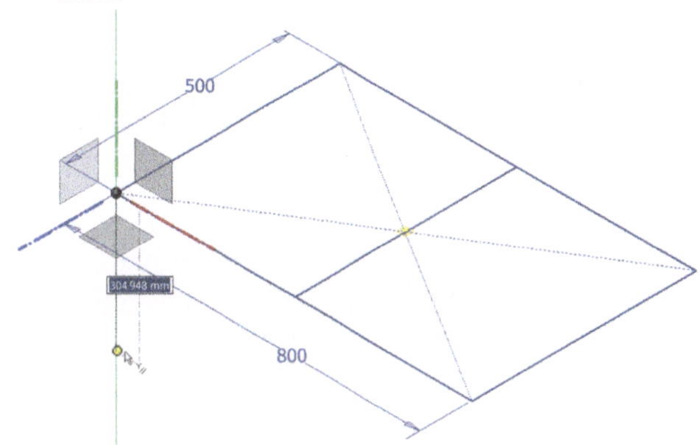

18. Press ENTER.
19. Likewise, create three more vertical lines at the corners, as shown.

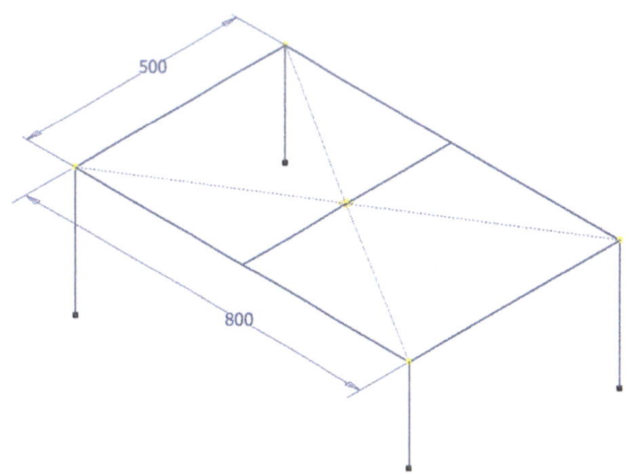

20. Click the **Equal** icon on the **Constrain** panel.

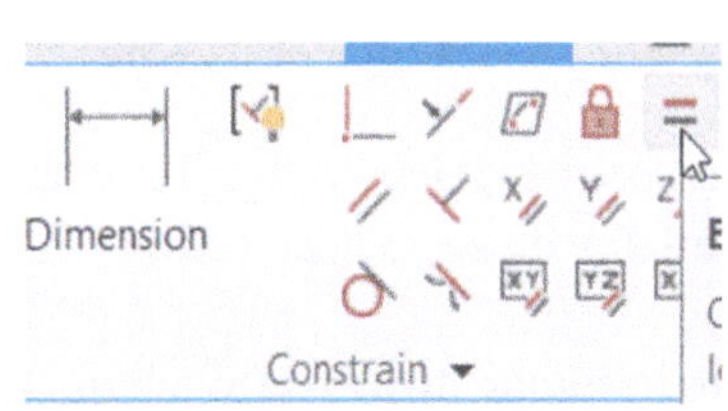

21. Make the vertical lines equal in length.
22. Add dimension to any one of the vertical lines.

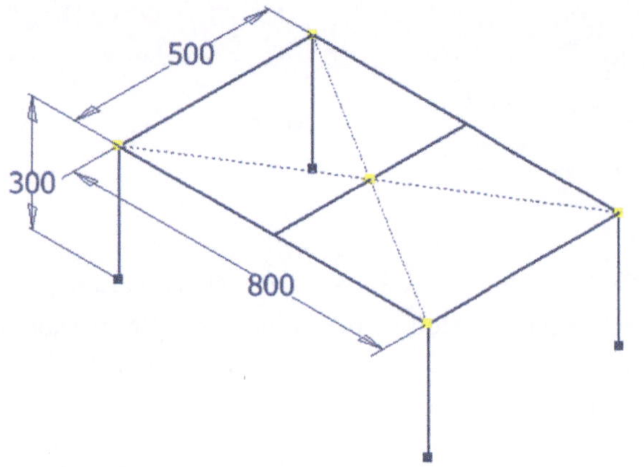

23. Click **Finish** on the ribbon.
24. On the ribbon, click **Tools > Options > Document Settings**.

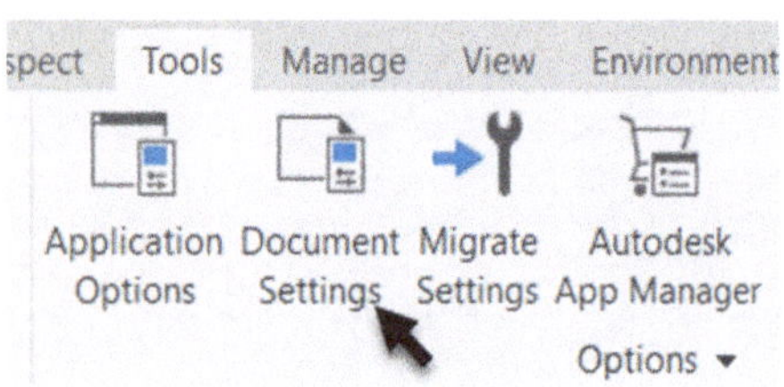

25. Click the **Bill of materials** tab on the **Document Settings** dialog.
26. Select the **Reference** option from the **Default BOM Structure** drop-down.

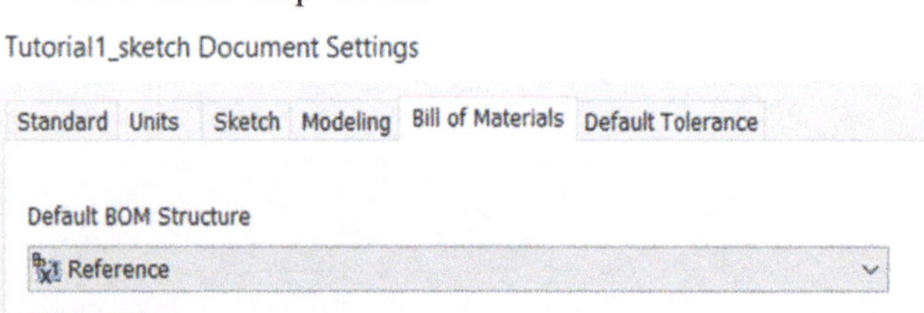

27. Click **OK**.
28. Click the **Save** icon on the Quick Access Toolbar.
29. Type **Tutorial2_Sketch** in the **File name** box.
30. Click the **Save** button.
31. Close the part file.

Adding Frames

1. Click the **New** icon on the Quick Access Toolbar.
2. On the **Create New file** dialog, select **Template > en-US > Metric**.
3. Double-click on the **Standard(mm).iam** template.
4. Click the **Save** icon on the Quick Access Toolbar.
5. Type **Tutorial2_assembly** in the **File name** box.
6. Click the **Save** button.
7. Click **Assemble > Component > Place**  on the ribbon.
8. Browse to the **Frame Generator** folder and select the Tutorial2_Sketch part file.
9. Click **Open**.
10. Click in the graphics window.
11. Click the **Insert Frame** button on the **Frame** panel on the **Design** tab.
12. Select **Square/Rectangular Tubes** from the **Category** drop-down.
13. Select **ANSI** from the **Standard** drop-down.
14. Select **ANSI AISC (Square) Tube** from the **Family** drop-down.
15. Select **2x2x1/4** from the **Size** drop-down.
16. Select **Steel, Mild** from the **Material** drop-down.

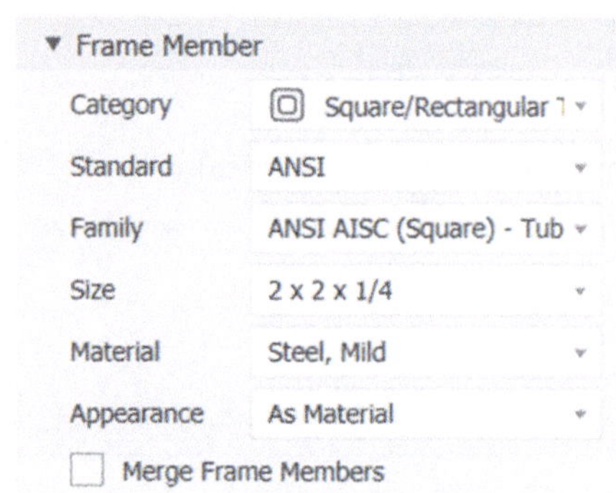

17. Click the **Specify frame location by two points** icon next to the **Placement** selection box.

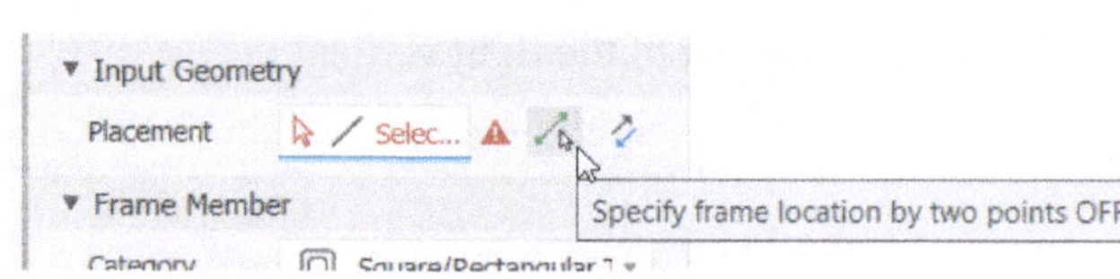

18. Select the points, as shown.

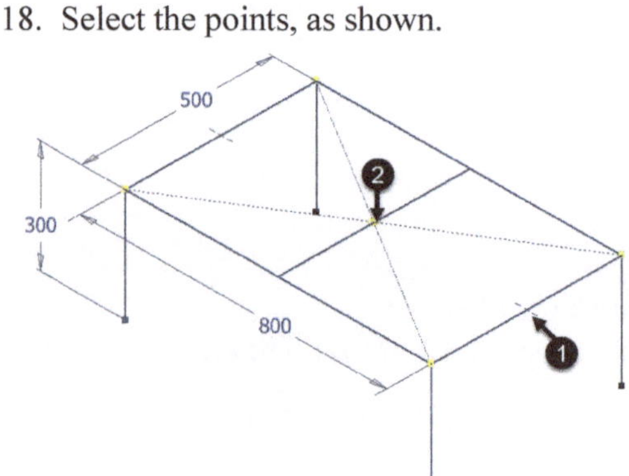

19. Click the **Zooms to frame manipulator** icon.

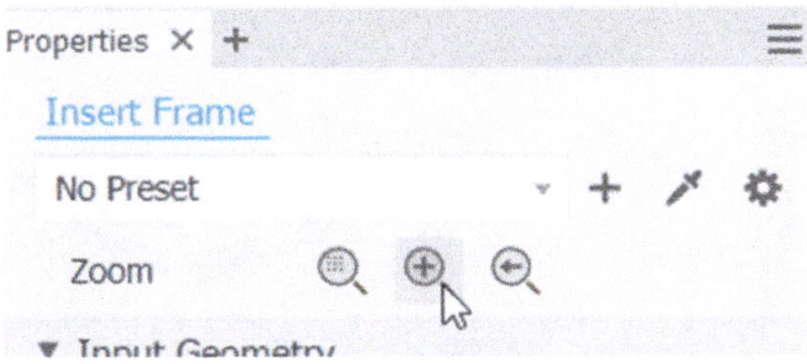

20. Select the lower alignment point of the frame, as shown.

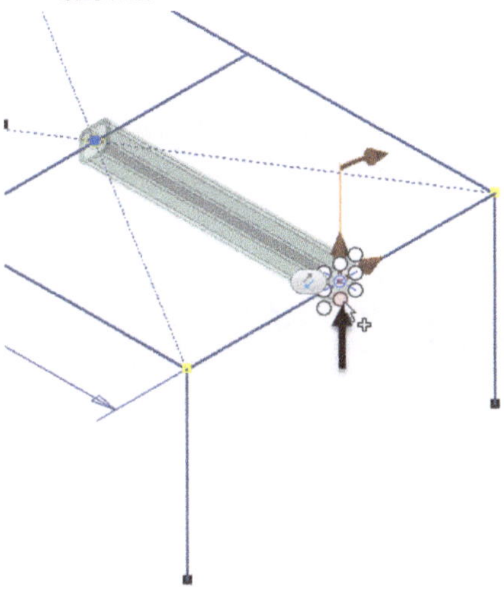

21. Click the **Apply and Create New Feature** icon.

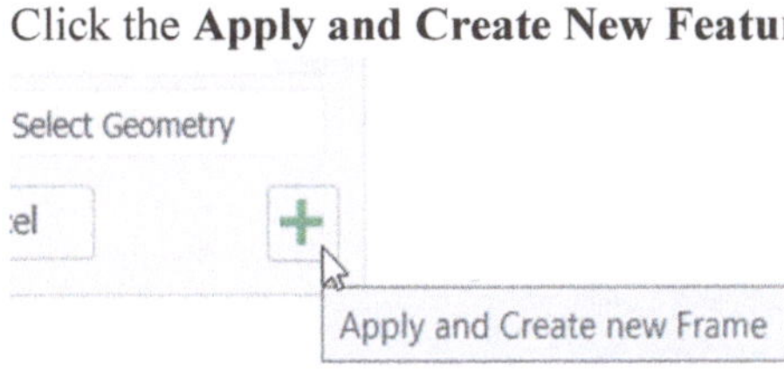

22. Click **OK** on the **Create New Frame** dialog.
23. Click **OK** on the **Frame Member Naming** dialog.
24. Select the points, as shown.
25. Click the **Apply and Create New Feature** icon.

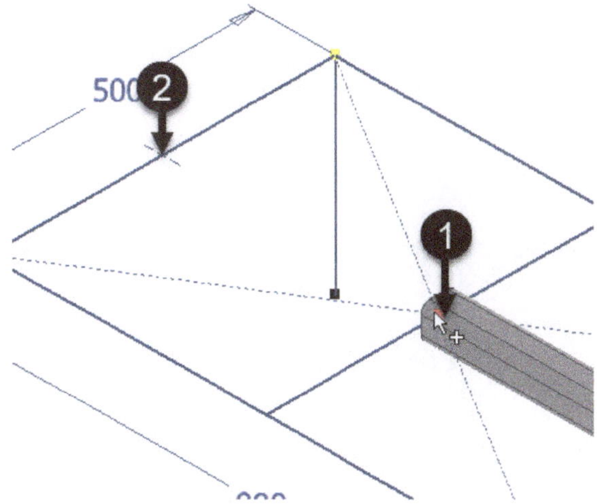

26. Click **OK** on the **Frame Member Naming** dialog.

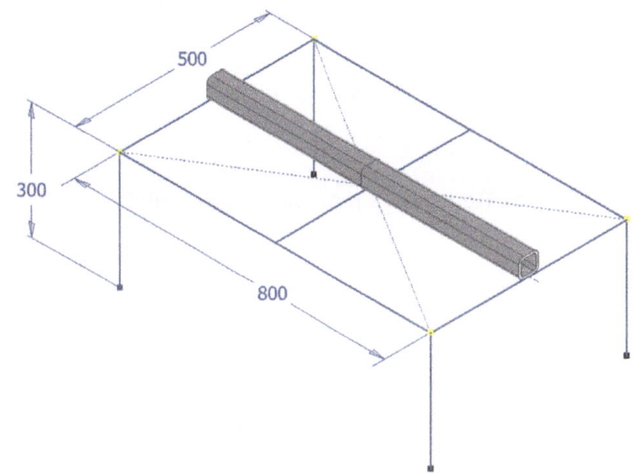

27. Click the **Insert Frame** button on the **Frame** panel.
28. Deactivate the **Specify frame location by two points** icon next to the **Placement** selection box.
29. Select the lower portion of the vertical line, as shown.

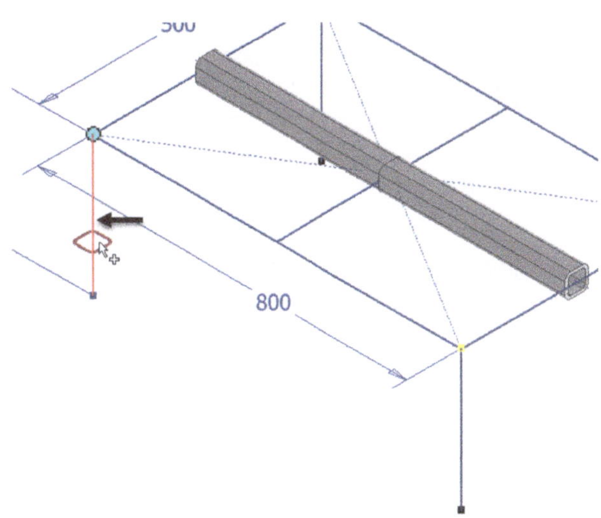

30. Select the center alignment point of the frame, as shown.

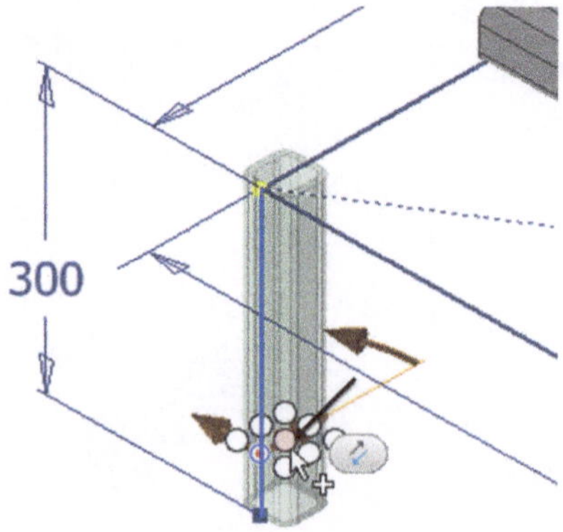

31. Click **OK**.
32. Click **OK** on the **Frame Member Naming** dialog.

Reuse the Frames

Autodesk Inventor allows you to reuse the existing frames to create the new frames.

1. Click the **Reuse** button on the **Frame** panel.

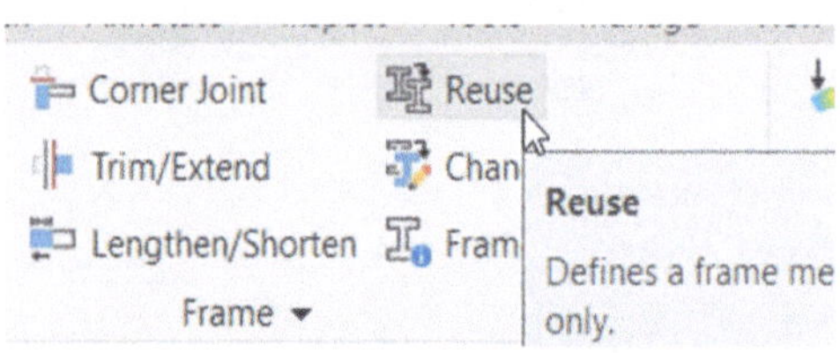

2. Select the vertical frame, as shown.

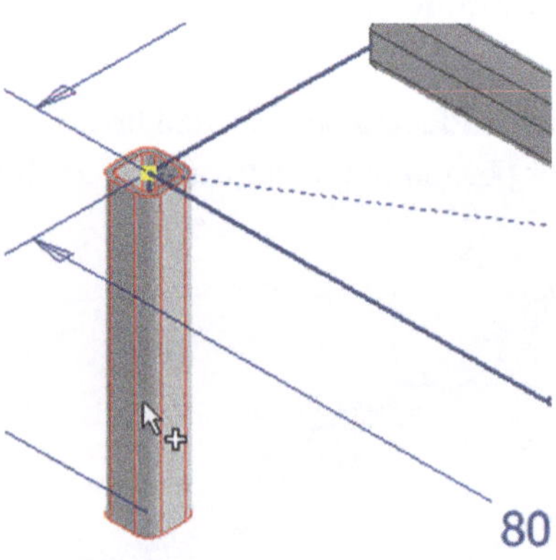

3. Click on the lower portions of the vertical lines of the skeleton sketch, as shown.

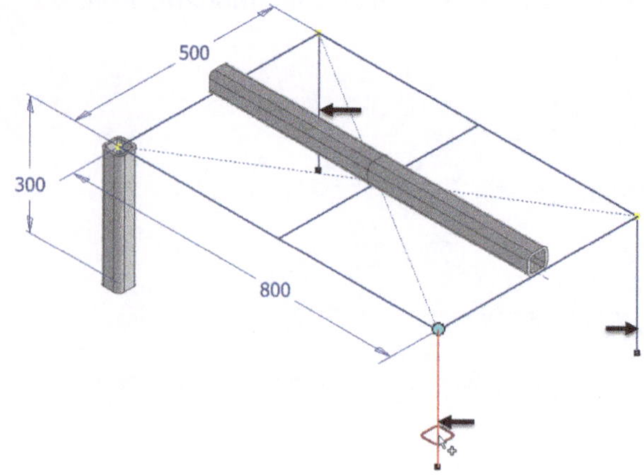

4. Click **OK**.
5. Click the **Insert Frame** button on the **Frame** panel.
6. Select the horizontal lines, as shown.

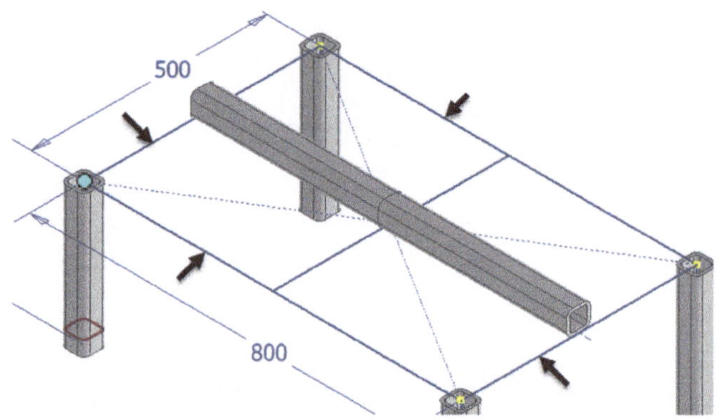

7. Select the lower alignment point of the frame, as shown.

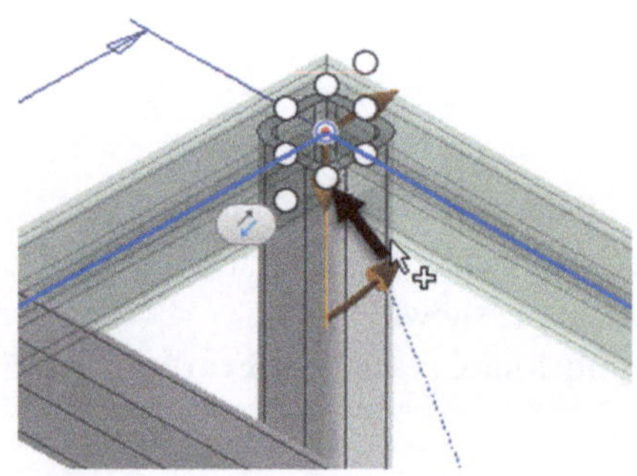

8. Check the **Merge Frame Members** option.
9. Click **OK**.
10. Click **OK** on the **Frame Member Naming** dialog.
11. Click the **Insert Frame** button on the **Frame** panel.
12. Select the horizontal line, as shown.

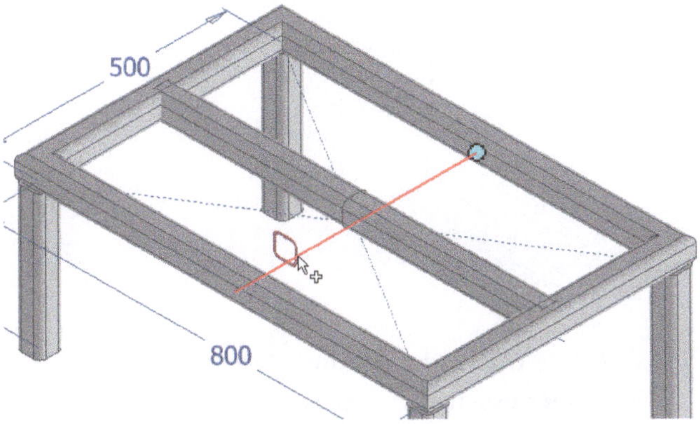

13. Select the lower alignment point of the frame.
14. Click **OK**.
15. Click **OK** on the **Frame Member Naming** dialog.

Trimming the Frames

The frames will be trimmed if you have created them as a single instance. However, if you have created the frames by activating the **Frame** tool several times, they will not be trimmed automatically. You need to trim those members by using the corner treatment commands.

1. Click the **Notch** button on the **Frame** panel.
2. Select the frames, as shown.
3. Click in the **Notch Tool** selection box and select the intersecting frame, as shown.

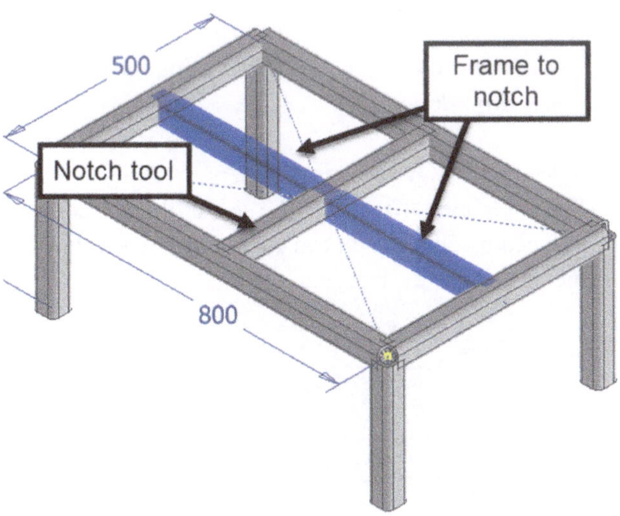

4. Click **OK**.
5. Click the **Trim/Extend** button on the **Frames** panel.
6. Select the flat face of the frame, as shown.
7. Click in the **Frame Member** selection box and select the intersecting frame, as shown.

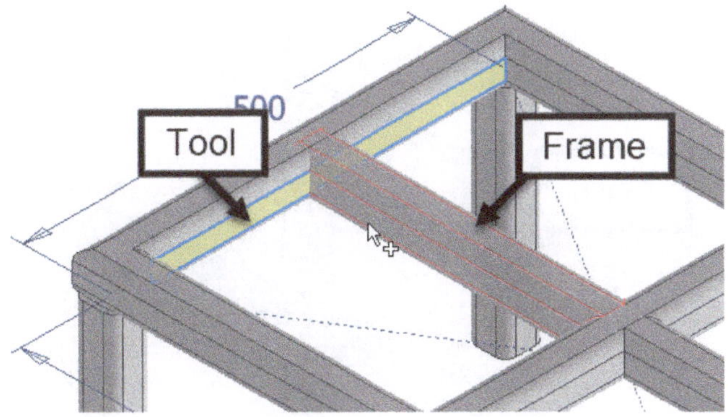

8. Likewise, trim the other frames, as shown.

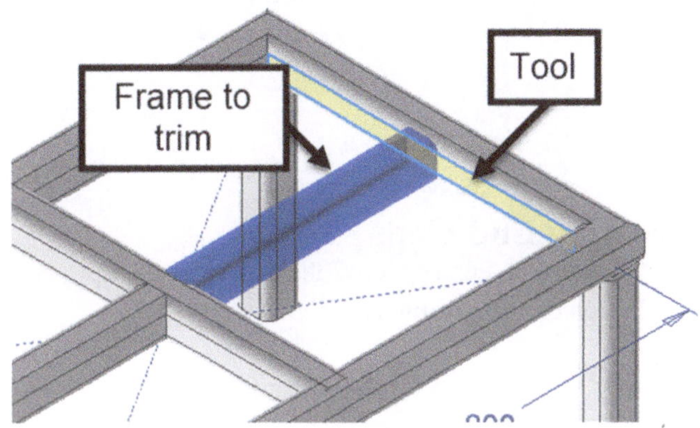

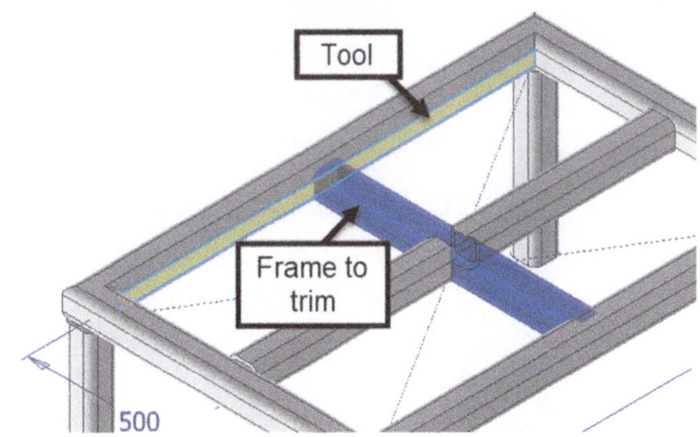

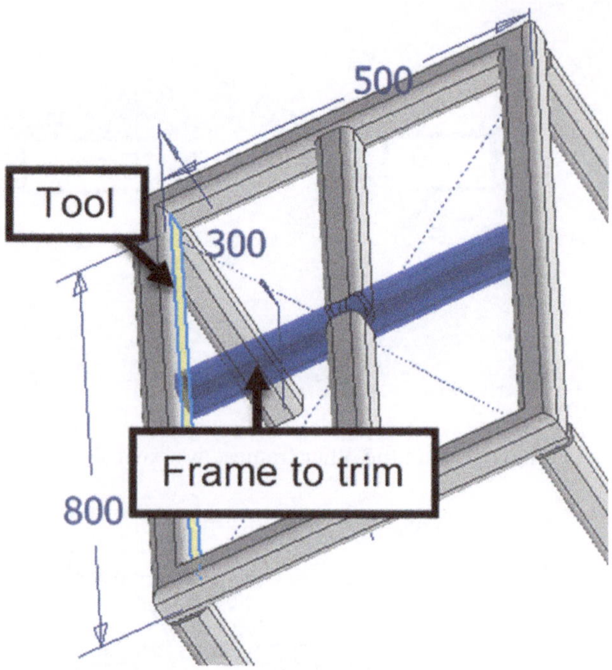

Creating End Caps

1. To create an end cap, click the **Insert End Cap** button on the **Frame** panel.

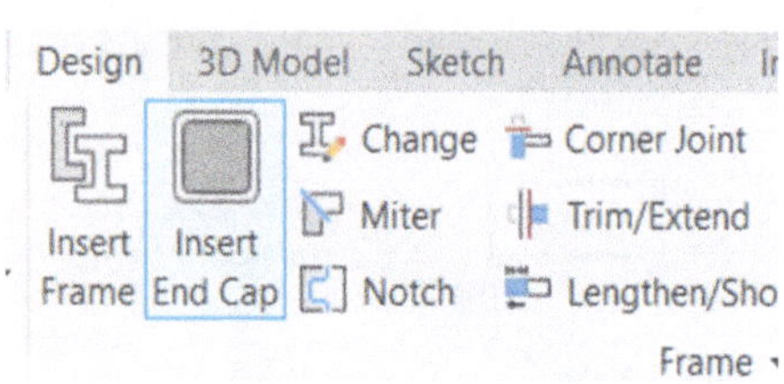

2. Orbit the model such that the bottom portion is displayed.
3. Select the end face of the frame, as shown.

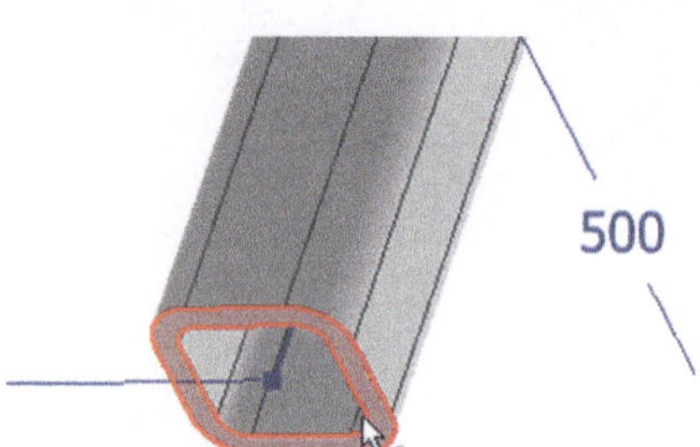

4. Click the **Outward Position** icon under the **Placement** section. The preview of the end cap appears on the outer face.

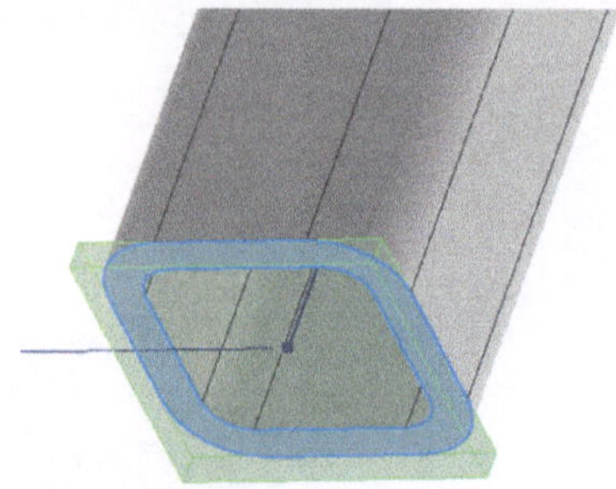

5. Click the **Internal Position** icon under the **Placement** section. The preview of the end cap appears inside the frame. The internal end cap means that it will be created inside the original length of the frame.

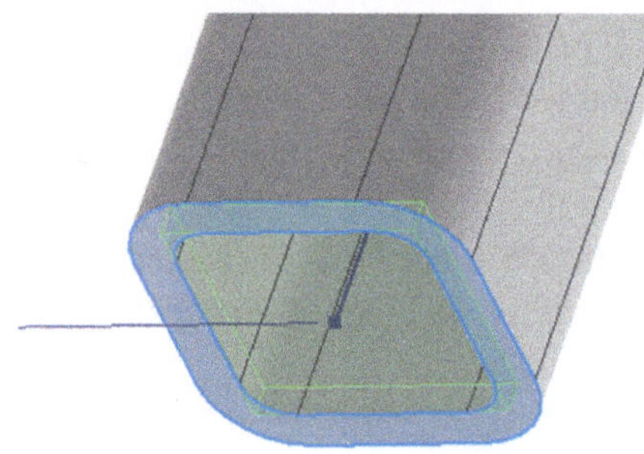

6. Click the **Outward Position** icon and specify the **Thickness** as **5**.

The size of the end cap can be defined using the options in the **Size** drop-down.

7. Select **Size > Offset – profile.**
8. Enter **5** in the **Offset** box. The size of the end cap is reduced by 5 mm. You can enter a negative value to increase the end cap size.

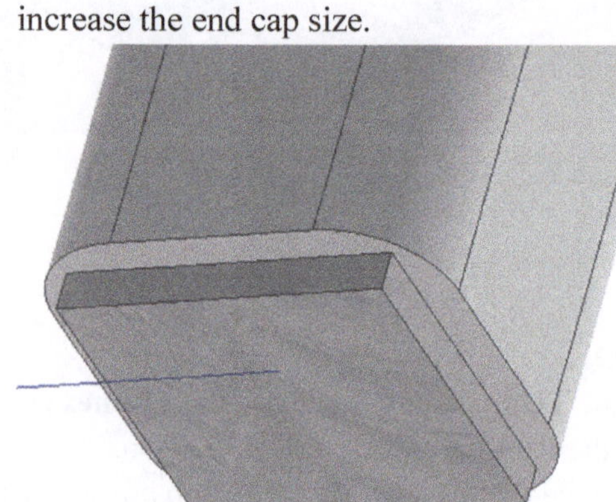

9. Select **Size > Offset – profile (ratio)**
10. Enter 50 in the **Offset** box. The size of the end cap is

reduced by 50 percent of the frame thickness.

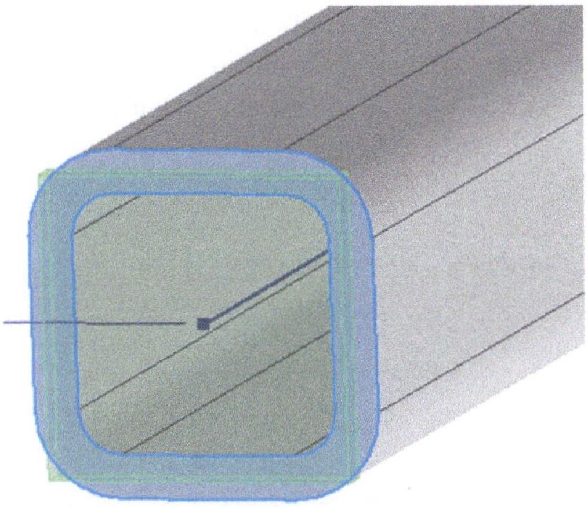

11. Select **Profile > Chamfered Corners (mm)**.
12. Type-in 5 in the **Chamfer** box.

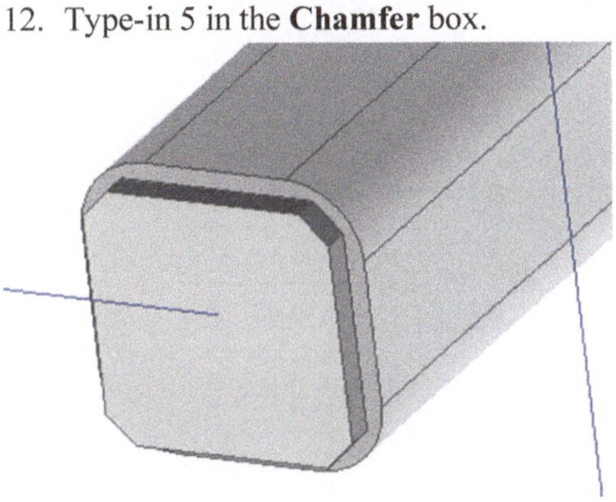

13. Select **Profile > Filletted Corners (mm)** and type-in 5 in the **Fillet** box.

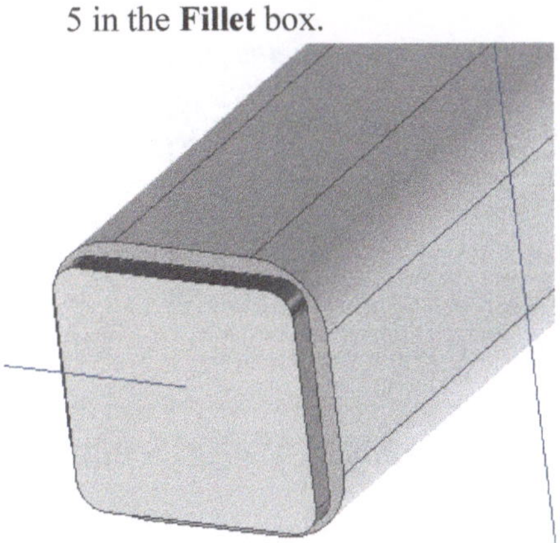

14. Select the end faces of the remaining vertical frames, as shown.
15. Click **OK** to create the end cap.
16. Click **OK** on the **Frame Member Naming** dialog.

TUTORIAL 3 (Creating Frame Drawings)

1. Open the Tutorial2_assembly.iam file.
2. Click the **File** tab, and then click **New**.
3. On the **Create New File** dialog, click **Templates > en-US > Metric**.
4. Go to the **Drawing – Create an annotated document** section, and then double-click on the **ANSI (mm).idw** template.
5. In the **Model** tab of the Browser window, right-click on **Sheet:1**, and then select **Edit Sheet**.
6. On the **Edit Sheet** dialog, select **A2** from the **Size** drop-down.
7. Click **OK**.
8. On the **Place Views** tab of the ribbon, click the **Base View** tool.
9. Create the views on the drawing sheet, as shown (refer to Chapter 4: Creating Drawings).

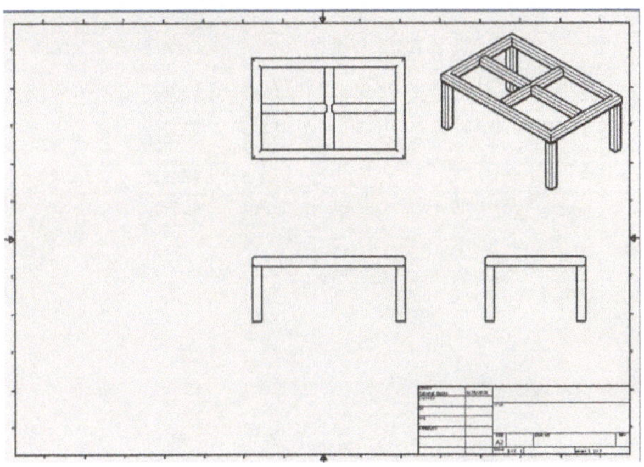

10. On the ribbon, click **Annotate > Table > Parts List**.

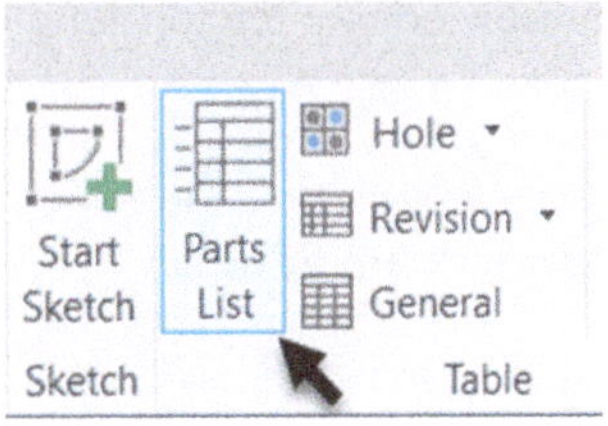

11. Select the Isometric view from the drawing sheet.
12. Select the **Structured** option from the **BOM View** drop-down.
13. Select the **All Levels** option from the **Level** drop-down.
14. Select **Direction to Wrap Table > Right**.
15. Click **OK**.

16. Click **OK** on the **BOM View Disabled** message box.
17. Select the top-left corner of the drawing sheet.

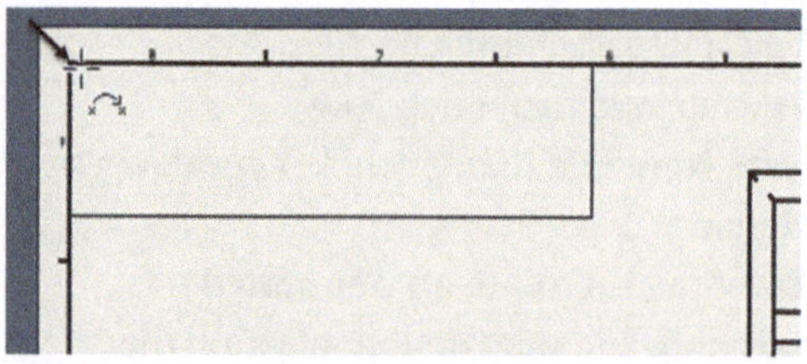

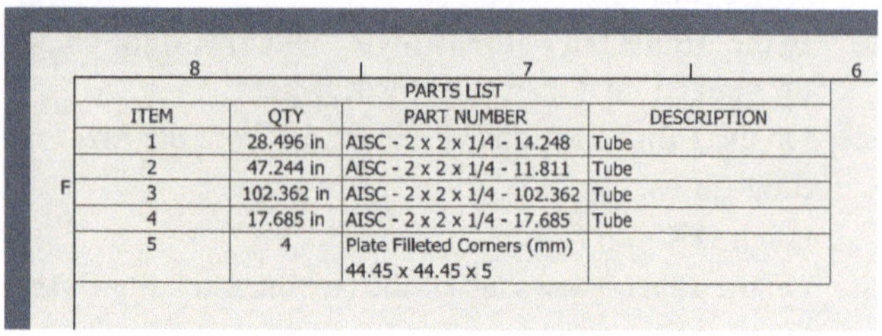

18. Right-click on the parts list and select **Edit Parts List**.

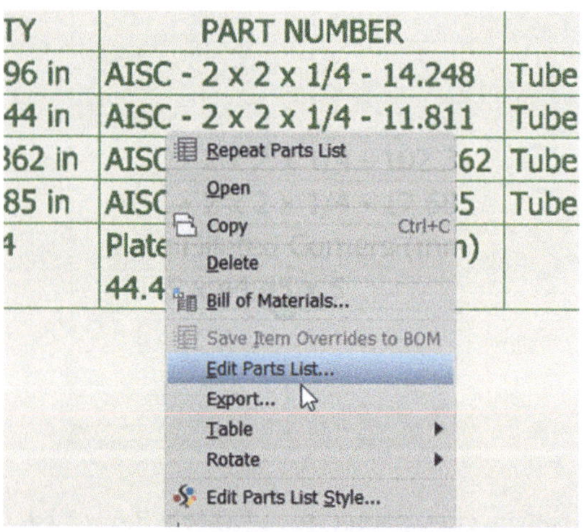

19. Click the **Column Chooser** icon on the top-left corner of the dialog.

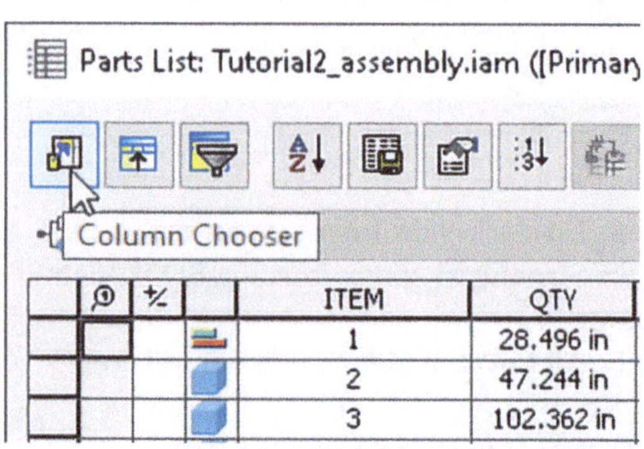

20. Select the **QTY** property from the **Selected Properties** list and click the **Remove** button.
21. Select the **BASE QTY** property from the **Available Properties** list, and then click the **Add** button.
22. Select the **ITEM QTY** property and click the **Add** button.
23. Click **OK**.

Notice the **BASE QTY** and **ITEM QTY** columns in the table.

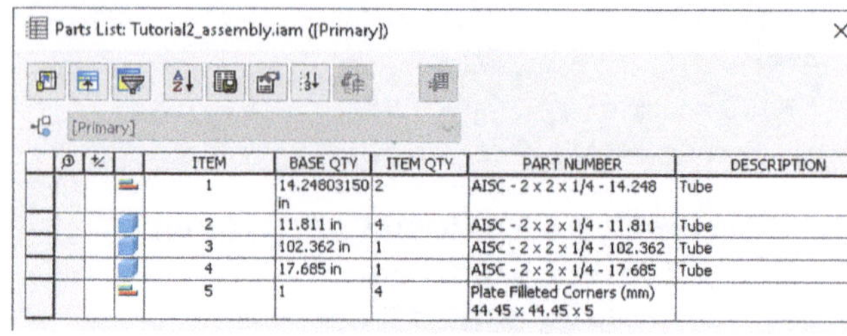

24. Click **OK**.
25. Adjust the column sizes by dragging them.

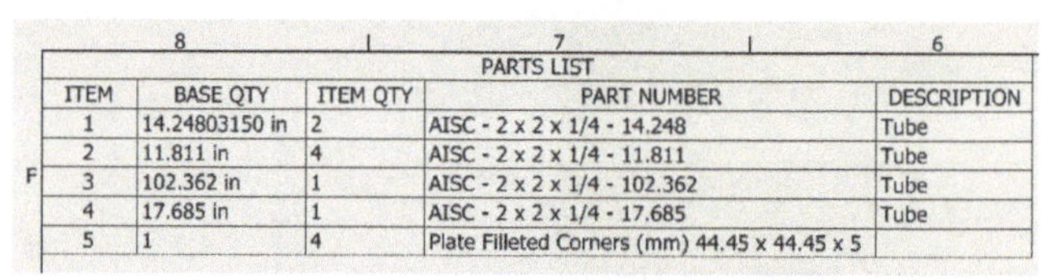

26. Click the **Tutorial2_assembly.iam** tab at the bottom.

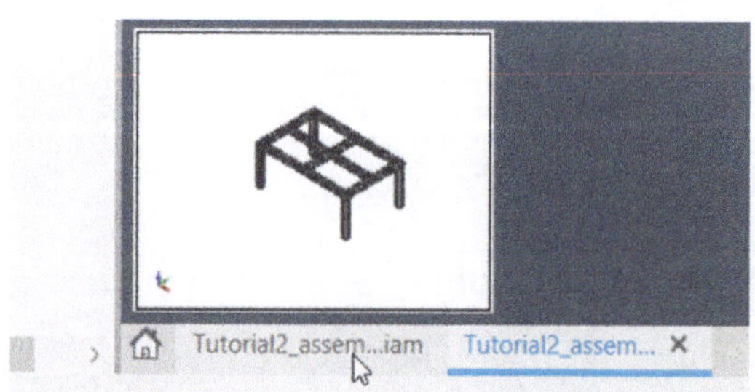

27. On the ribbon, click **Assemble > Manage > Bill of Materials**.

28. Click the **Add Custom iProperty Columns** icon on the dialog.

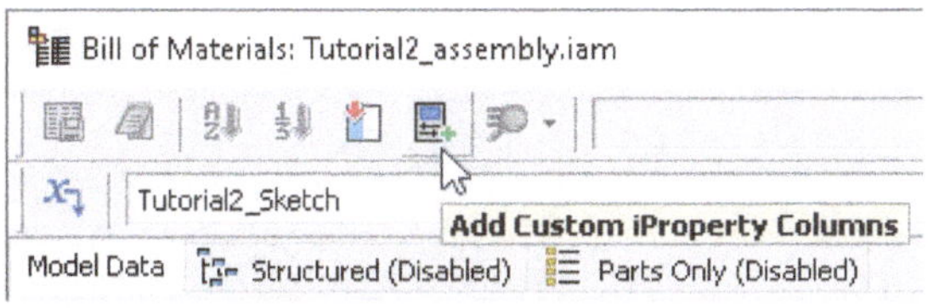

29. Click **<click to add iProperty column>** on the **Add Custom iProperty Columns** dialog.
30. Type CUTDETAIL1.
31. Click **<click to add iProperty column>**.
32. Type CUTDETAIL2.
33. Click **OK**.

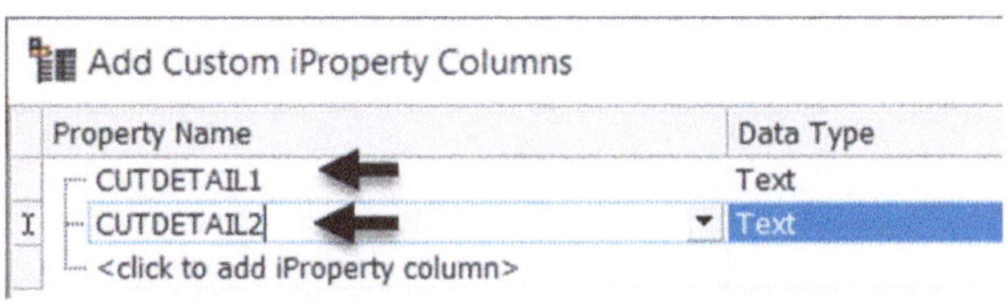

34. Click **Done**.
35. Click the **Tutorial2_assembly.idw** tab at the bottom of the window.

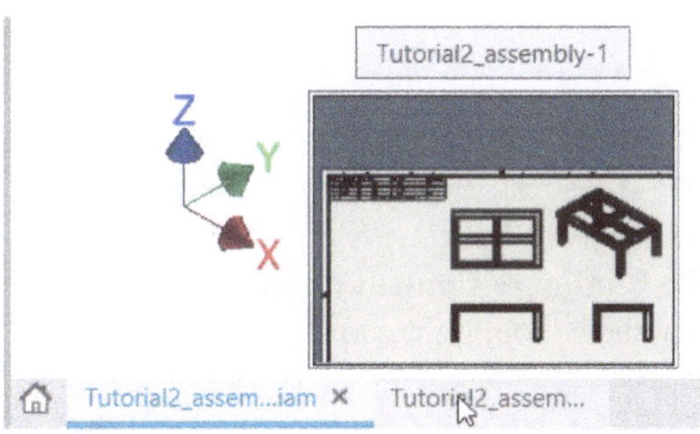

36. Right-click on the parts list and select **Edit Parts List**.
37. Click the **Column Chooser** icon on the top-left corner of the dialog.
38. Click the **New Property** button on the dialog.
39. Click **<click here to add new property>**.
40. Type CUTDETAIL1, and then press ENTER.
41. Click **<click here to add new property>**.
42. Type CUTDETAIL2, and then press ENTER.
43. Click **OK**.

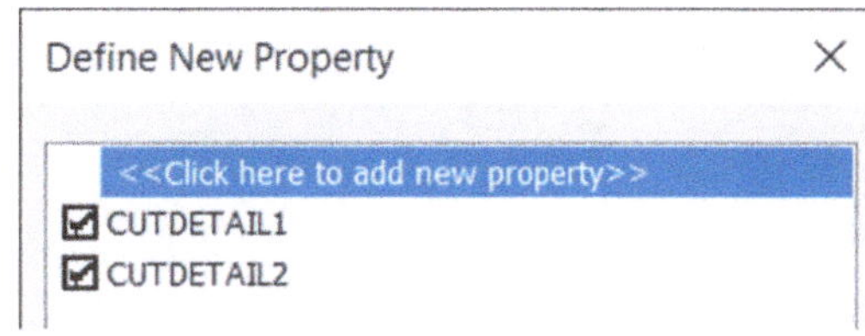

44. Click **OK**.
45. Right-click on the **CUTDETAIL1** column heading.
46. Select **Format Column**.

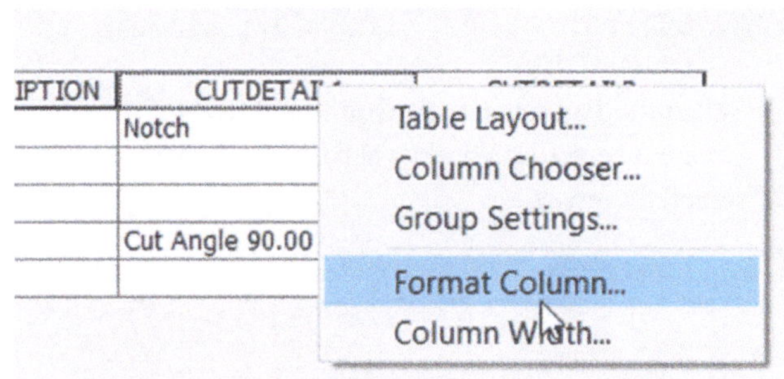

47. Type **END TREATMENT 1** in the **Heading** box, and then click **OK**.

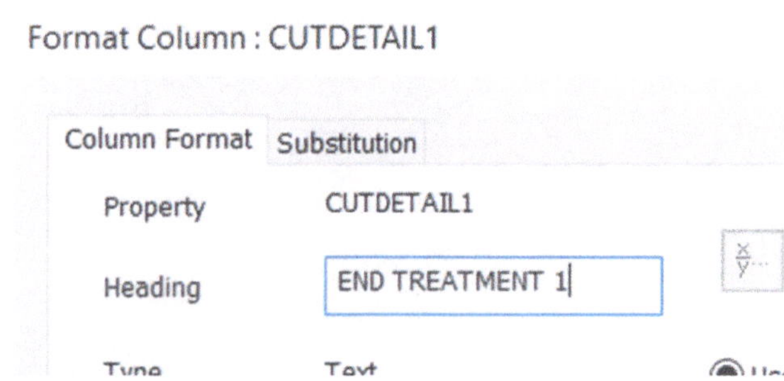

48. Likewise, change the Heading name of the **CUTDETAIL 2** column to **END TREATMENT 2**.
49. Click **OK** on the **Parts List** dialog.
50. Adjust the column sizes by dragging them.

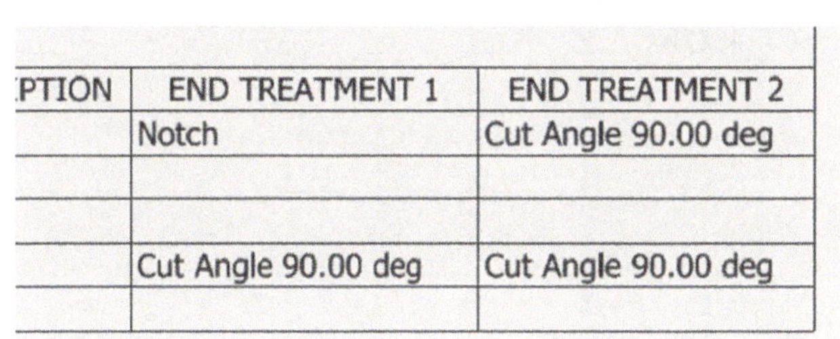

Adding Balloons

1. To add balloons, click **Annotate > Table > Balloon drop-down > Auto Balloon** on the ribbon.

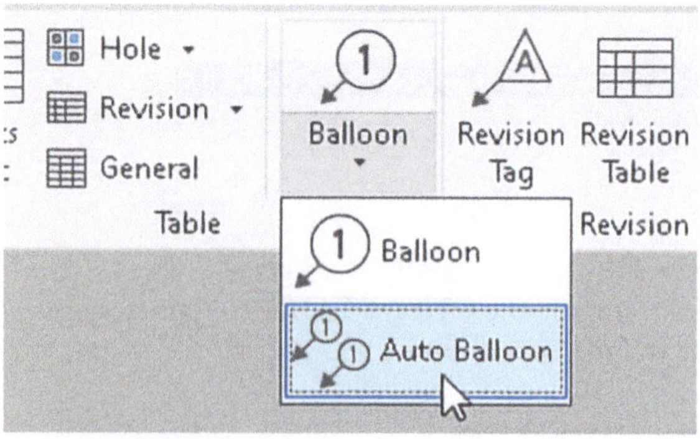

2. Select the Isometric view from the drawing.
3. Create a selection window across all the parts of the selected view.

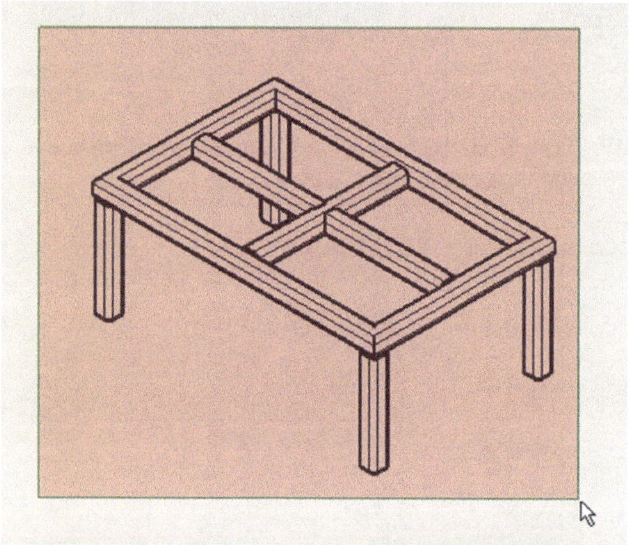

4. Select the **Around** option from the **Placement** section.
5. Click the **Select Placement** button, and then click in the drawing sheet.
6. Click **OK**.

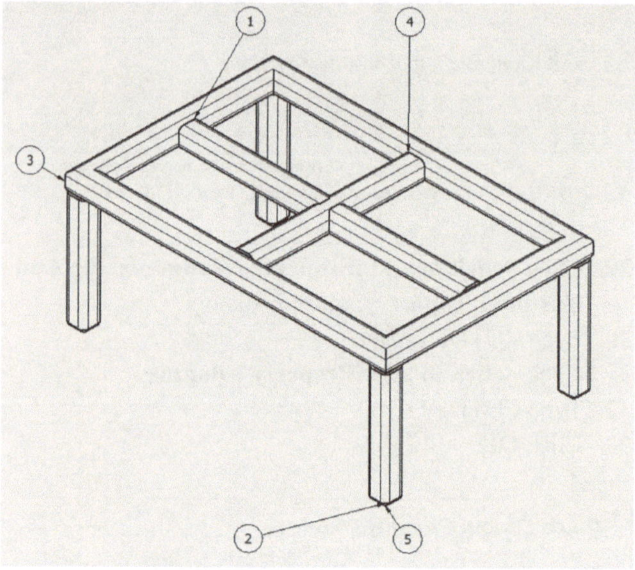

7. Save and close the drawing and assembly files.

TUTORIAL 4 (Creating Custom Profiles for frames)

If you want to create a frame using a profile that is not available in Autodesk Inventor, you can create a custom profile.

1. Click the **File** tab, and then click **Manage > Projects**.
2. Select the **Autodesk 2026 Basics Tutorial** project from the **Projects** dialog.
3. Click the **Configure Content Center Libraries** icon located at the bottom right corner.

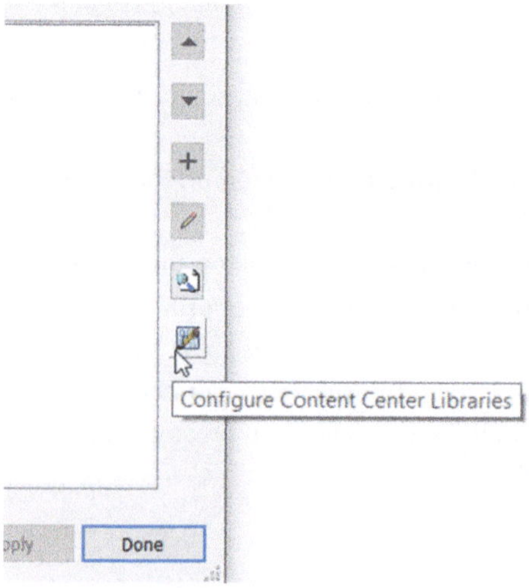

4. Click the **Create Library** icon on the **Configure Libraries** dialog.

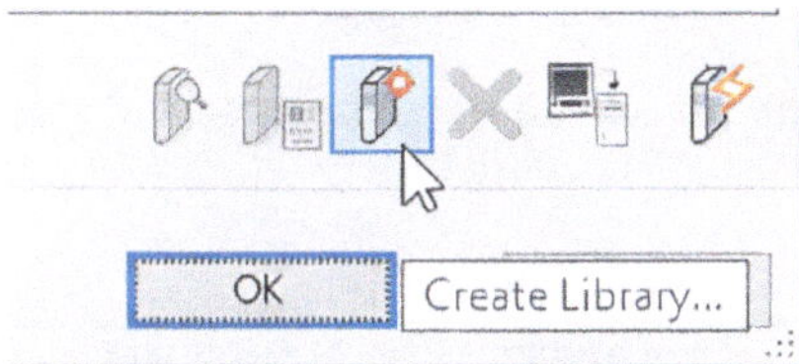

5. Type **Sample** in the **Display Name** box and click **OK**.
6. The **Sample** library is created with **Read/Write** access.

	Library	Access
☑	Inventor Parker	Read Only
☑	Inventor Routed Sys...	Read Only
☑	Inventor Sheet Metal	Read Only
☑	Sample	Read/Write
☐	My Library	Read Only

7. Click **OK**.
8. Make sure that **Autodesk Inventor 2026 Basics Tutorial** project is set as an active project.
9. Click **Save** and **Done**.
10. Open a new Part file using the **Standard (mm).ipt** template.
11. Create a sketch on any one of the planes, as shown in the figure.

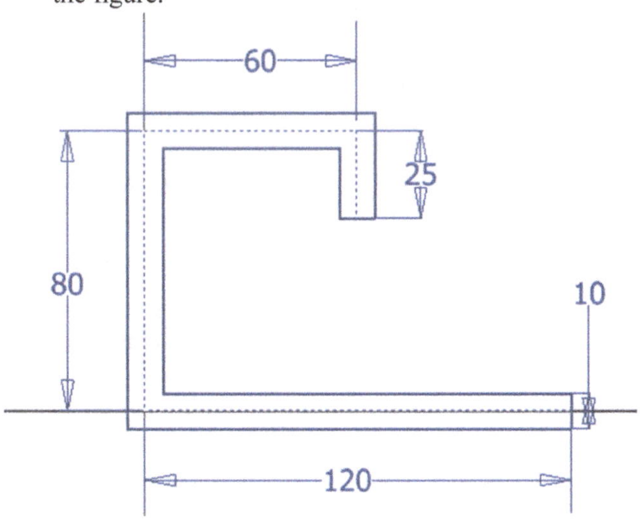

12. Finish the sketch.
13. Extrude the sketch symmetrically up to a distance of 1 mm.

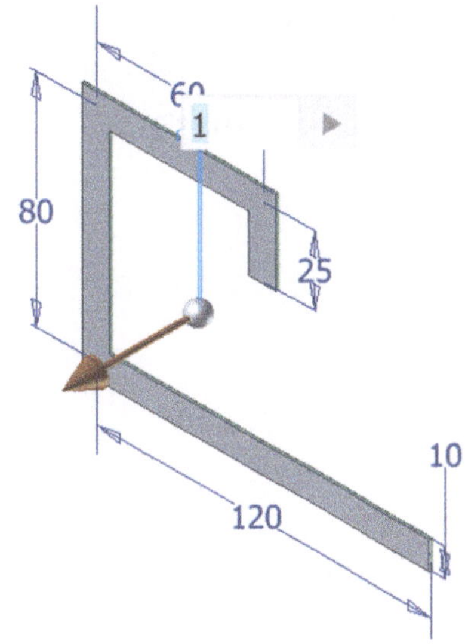

14. Save the file are Sample_profile.
15. On the ribbon, click **Manage > Parameters > Parameters**.

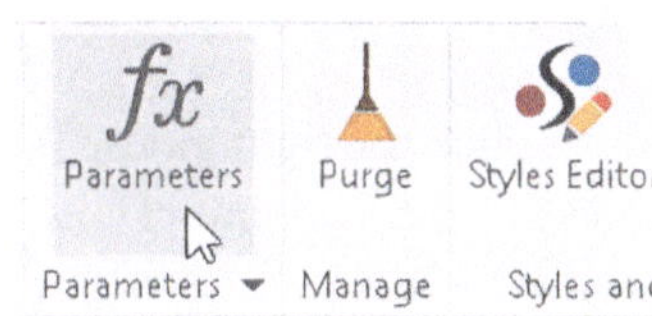

16. On the **Parameters** dialog, in the **Model Parameters** table, click in the **Parameter Name** cell of 80 mm Equation value.
17. Type-in **Height**.

Parameters

Parameter Name	Consumed by	Unit/Type	Equation	Nominal Value
Model Parameters				
d8	Sketch2	mm	120 mm	120.000000
Height	Sketch2	mm	80 mm	80.000000
d10	Sketch2	mm	60 mm	60.000000

18. Likewise, change the names of other parameters.

Parameters

Parameter Name	Consumed b	Unit/Typ	Equation
Model Paramet...			
Height	Sketch1	mm	80 mm
Halfwidth	Sketch1	mm	60 mm
Halfheight	Sketch1	mm	25 mm
Width	Sketch1	mm	120 mm
Thickness	Sketch1	mm	10 mm
Length	Extrusion1	mm	1 mm
d6	Extrusion1	deg	0.00 deg
User Parameters			

19. Click **Done** on the **Parameters** dialog.
20. Click the right mouse button in the graphics window and select **Dimension Display > Expression**.

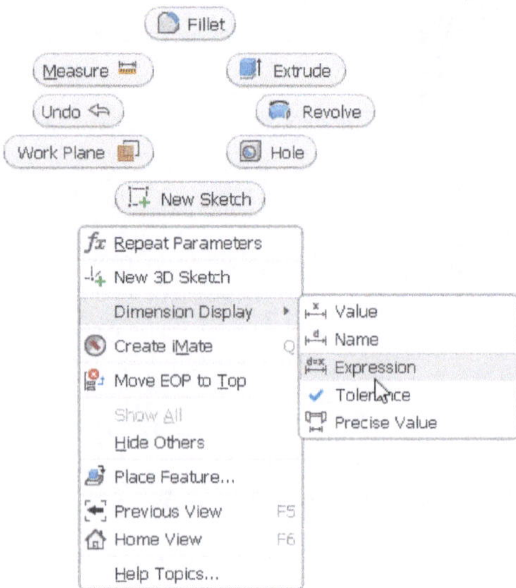

21. On the Browser window, click the right mouse button on the **Extrusion1** and select **Show Dimensions**. You will notice that the dimensions are shown along with the names.

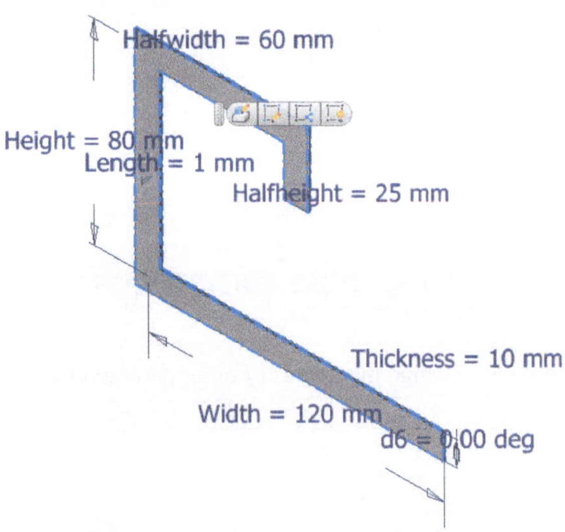

22. On the ribbon, click **Manage > Author > Create iPart**.

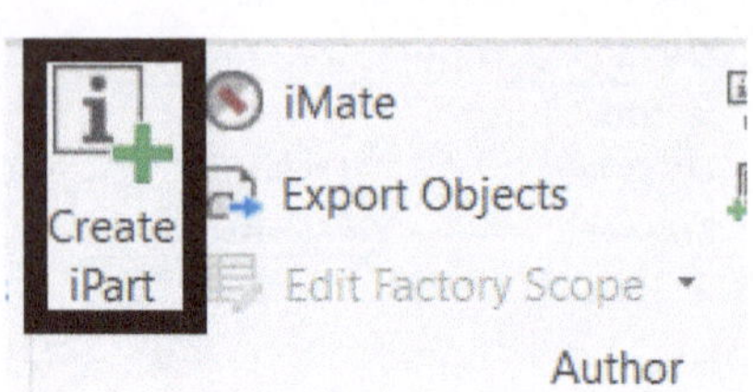

23. Click the right mouse button on the table and select **Insert Row**.

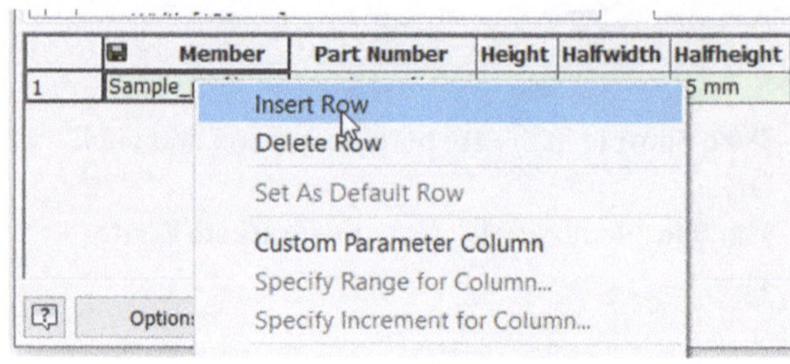

24. Likewise, insert another row.
25. Change the values in the table, as shown.

	Member	Part Number	Height	Halfwidth	Halfheigh	Width	Thickness	Length
1	Sample_profile-01	Sample_profile-80x120	80 mm	60 mm	25 mm	120 mm	10 mm	1 mm
2	Sample_profile-02	Sample_profile-60x100	60	60 mm	25 mm	100	10 mm	1 mm
3	Sample_profile-03	Sample_profile-40x60	40	40	25 mm	60	10 mm	1 mm

26. Click **OK** to close the dialog.
27. On the Quick Access Toolbar, click the **Save** icon.
28. Click **Manage > Author > Authoring** drop-down > **Structural Shape**.

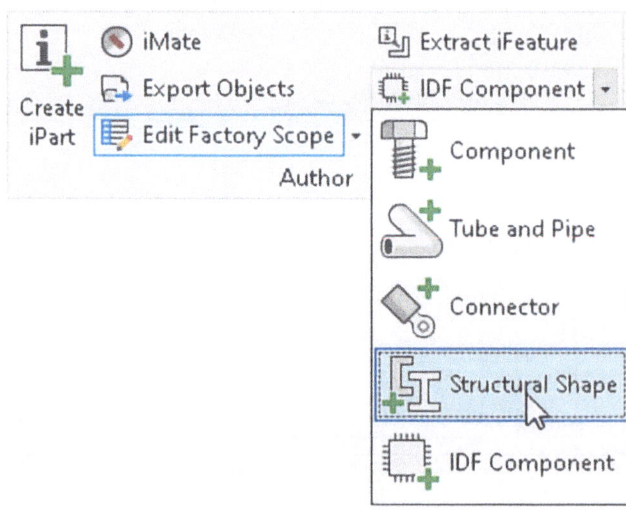

29. Select **Other** from the **Category** drop-down.
30. Select the **Notch Profile** option from the **Geometry Mapping** section.
31. Select the profile from the graphics window, as shown.

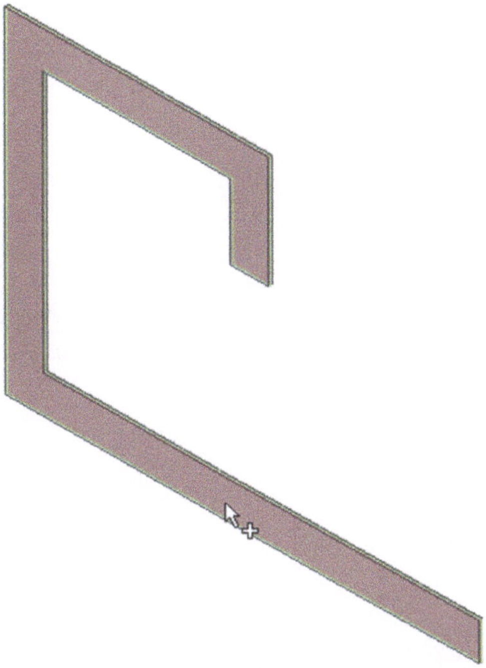

32. Click the **Parameter Mapping** tab and set the **Base Length** to **Length**.

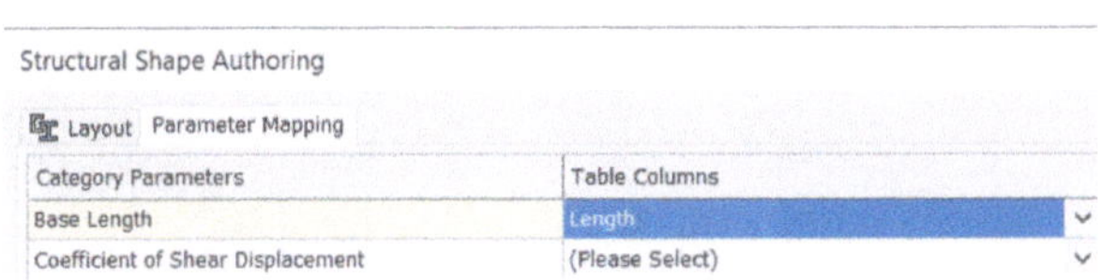

33. Click **OK** twice.
34. Click **Manage > Author > Authoring** drop-down > **Structural Shape**.
35. Click **Publish Now**.
36. Select **Sample** from the **Select Library to Publish to** drop-down.
37. Click **Next**.
38. Select the **Other** option and click **Next**.
39. Set the **Base Length** to **Length**, and click Next.
40. Select the **Member** option from the **Table Columns** section, and then click the **Arrow** button.
41. Click **Next**.
42. Specify the **Family Properties** and click **Next**.
43. Click **Publish** and **OK**.

Inserting the Custom Frame

1. Start a new Part document.
2. Create a sketch on the XY plane, as shown in the figure.

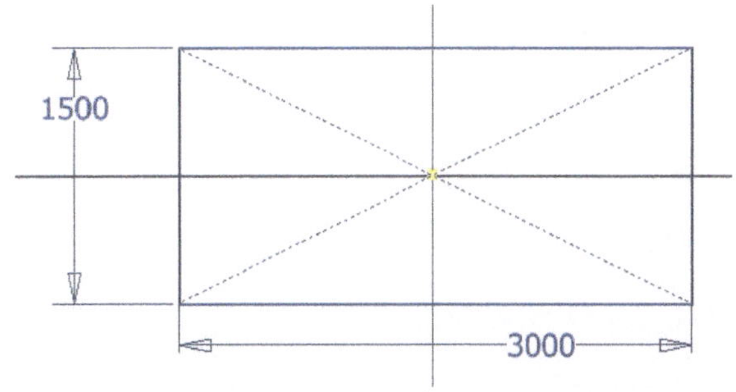

3. Finish the sketch.
4. Save the part file as Tutorial4_Skeleton.ipt.
5. Close the part file.
6. Click the **New** icon on the Quick Access Toolbar.
7. On the **Create New file** dialog, select **Template > en-US > Metric**.
8. Double-click on the **Standard(mm).iam** template.
9. Click the **Save** icon on the Quick Access Toolbar.
10. Type **Tutorial4_assembly** in the **File name** box.
11. Click the **Save** button.
12. Click **Assemble > Component > Place**  on the ribbon.
13. Browse to the **Frame Generator** folder and select the Tutorial4_Skeleton part file.
14. Click **Open**.
15. Click in the graphics window to place the sketch.
16. Click the **Insert Frame** button on the **Frame** panel of the **Design** ribbon tab.
17. Select the elements of the sketch.
18. Specify the settings on the **Properties** panel, as shown.

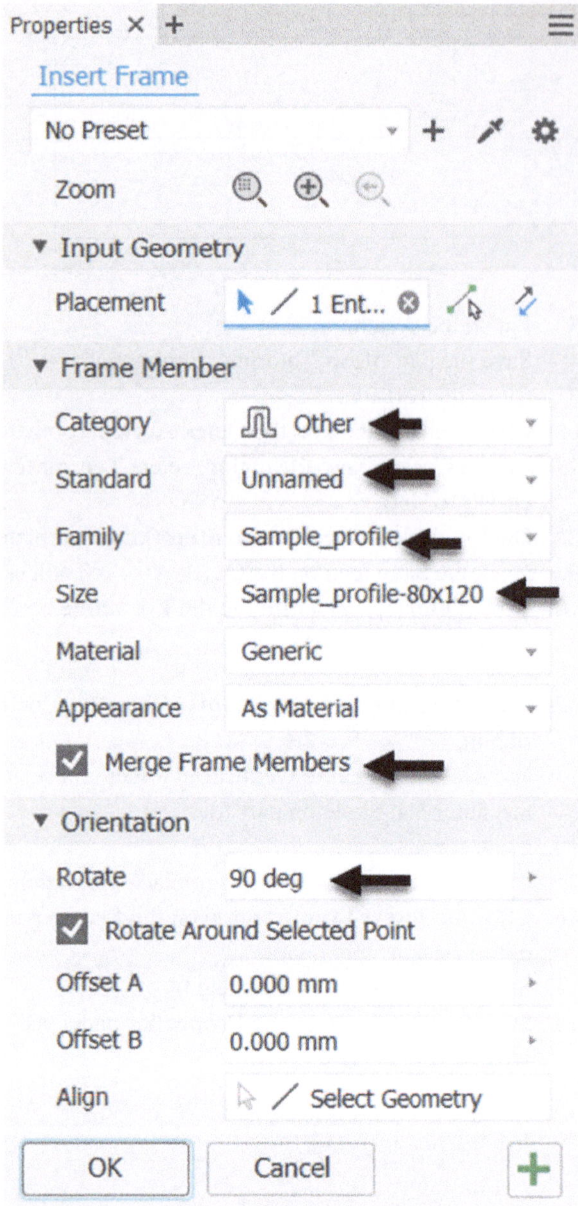

19. Click **OK**.
20. Click **OK** on the **Create New Frame** dialog.
21. Click **OK** on the **Frame Member Naming** dialog.

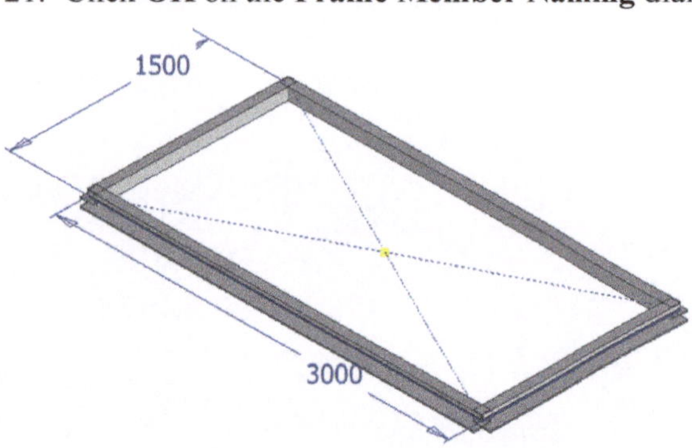

22. Save the file.

Printed at Repro India Ltd.